Peru

Other Travellers' Wildlife Guides

Belize and Northern Guatemala
Costa Rica
Ecuador and the Galápagos Islands

Peru

by David L. Pearson and Les Beletsky

Contributor:
Martha L. Crump

Illustrated by:
Priscilla Barrett, David Beadle, David Dennis, Daniel Lane,
John Myers, David Nurney, Fernanda Oyarzun, John O'Neill,
John Sill, and Andy Woodham

Interlink Books

An imprint of Interlink Publishing Group, Inc.
Northampton, Massachusetts

This edition first published 2005 by

INTERLINK BOOKS
An imprint of Interlink Publishing Group, Inc.
46 Crosby Street, Northampton, Massachusetts 01060
www.interlinkbooks.com

Library of Congress Cataloging-in-Publication Data
Pearson, David (David L.)
Perú / by David L. Pearson and Les Beletsky.—1st American ed.
p. cm.—(The traveller's wildlife guides)
Rev. ed. of: Perú. San Diego : Academic Press, 2001.
Includes bibliographical references and index.
ISBN 1-56656-545-6 (pbk.)
1. Animals--Perú. 2. Ecotourism—Perú--Guidebooks. 3. Perú—Guidebooks.
I. Beletsky, Les, 1956- II. Title. III. Series.
QL248.P43 2004
591.985—dc22
2004004611

Printed and bound in China

CONTENTS

PREFACE

This book and others in the series are aimed at environmentally conscious travellers for whom some of the best parts of any trip are glimpses of wildlife in natural settings; at people who, when speaking of a journey, often remember days and locations by the wildlife they saw: "That was where we watched the monkeys," and "That was the day we saw the hawk catch a snake." The purpose of this book is to heighten enjoyment of a trip and enrich wildlife sightings by providing you with information to identify several hundred of the most frequently encountered animals and plants of Perú, along with up-to-date information on their natural history, behavior, and conservation. Your skills at recognizing many of the species you see on your travels through Perú will be greatly enhanced with this book's color illustrations of 83 species of amphibians and reptiles, 71 mammals, more than 320 birds, 20 insects and arthropods, and with its drawings of common plants characteristic of each major habitat type.

The idea to write this book grew out of our own travel experiences and frustrations. First and foremost, we found that we could not find a single book to take along on a trip that would help identify all the types of animals and plants that interested us. There are bird and mammal field guides and plant identification handbooks, but their number and weight quickly accumulate until you need an extra suitcase just to carry them. Thus, the idea: create a single guide-book that travellers could carry to help them identify and learn about the different kinds of animals and plants they were most likely to see. Also, in our experience with guided tours, we've found that guides vary tremendously in their knowledge of nature and wildlife. Many, of course, are fantastic sources of information on the ecology and behavior of animals and plants. Some, however, know only about certain kinds of animals, birds, for instance. And many others, we found, knew precious little about animals or plants, and what information they did tell their groups was often incorrect.

Last, like most ecotravellers, we are concerned about the threats to many species as their natural habitats are damaged or destroyed by people; when we travelled, we wanted current information on the conservation statuses of species we encountered. This book provides the traveller with conservation information on many of the species pictured or discussed in the book.

A few administrative notes: because this book has an international audience, we present measurements in both metric and English system units. The scientific classification of common species by now, you might think, would be pretty much established and unchanging; but you would be wrong. These days, what with molecular methods to compare species, classifications of various species groups that were first worked out during the 1800s and early 1900s are undergoing radical changes. Many bird groups, for instance, are being reclassified after comparative studies of their DNA. The research is so new that many biologists are still arguing about the results. We cannot guarantee that all the classifications that we use in the book are absolutely the last word on the subject, or that we have been wholly consistent in the classifications we used. However, for most users of this book, such minor transgressions are probably too esoteric to be of much significance.

Finally, we have tried to make the style of writing interesting and readable, but at the same time challenging and precise. We have tried to avoid terse, dry, textbook prose, sometimes with narratives that include anthropomorphisms – providing plants and animals with human characteristics. We do this for fun; hopefully, in so doing, we have not offended our professional colleagues. Plants and animals do not, of course, reason and think like humans. If you do not appreciate our sense of humor, please ignore those sections; you should still have remaining a solid natural history guide to Perú.

We need to acknowledge the help of a large number of people in producing this book. First, much of the information we use is gleaned from published sources, and we owe the authors of these books and scientific papers a great deal of credit; their names and the titles of their publications are listed in the References and Additional Reading section, p. 249. We are especially indebted to Marty Crump (Northern Arizona University) for her writing of the amphibian chapter and for editing the reptile chapter. The amphibian and reptile chapters also benefitted much from contributions by William Lamar (University of Texas at Tyler), Lily Rodríguez (APECO, Lima), and Greg Vigle (Arizona State University, or ASU). In addition, sections or parts of sections were read and critiqued by several outside experts in that field, and their comments and corrections greatly increased the accuracy of the book. These experts included: Rose Ann Rowlett (Field Guides, Inc., Austin, Texas), birds; Andrew Smith (ASU), mammals; Phil DeVries (University of Oregon), Dave Nickle (Smithsonian Institution), Ian Kitching (British Museum), arthropods; and Les Landrum (ASU), plants. In Perú, Manuel Plenge and Gerardo Lamas (Museum of Natural History, Lima) helped with many details on local fauna and their distributions. Over the last 30 years Antonio Brack, Marc Dourojeanni, Terry Erwin, Max Gunther, Susana Müller, Carlos Ponce and Silvia Sánchez helped time and again with logistics, permits and friendly advice to make studies in Perú more effective. Nancy Pearson not only graciously suffered extended periods of neglect during the writing process of this book but she actually volunteered to read the entire manuscript. Her comments were numerous and enlightening. Stacey Combes helped edit the manuscript. Nancy Pearson and Pancho Enríquez provided the excellent habitat photos. D. Ahrenholz, J. Alcack, L. Avilés, E.M. Fisher, G.O. Krizek, D. Nunnallee, D. Paulson, R. Radtke, E.S. Ross, and S. Spector provided insect photos. We also wish to thank the artists who produced the marvelous illustrations: David Beadle (birds), Priscilla Barrett (mammals), David Dennis (amphibians and reptiles), Dan Lane (birds), John Myers (plants), Andy Woodham (fish), David Nurney (birds), John O'Neill (birds), John Sill (birds), and Fernanda Oyarzun (crab).

Please let us know of any errors, opinions on the book, and suggestions for future editions. We are interested in hearing of your wildlife travel experiences. Write care of the publisher or e-mail: ECOTRAVEL8@aol.com

Chapter 1

ECOTOURISM: TRAVEL FOR THE ENVIRONMENTALLY CONCERNED

- *What Ecotourism Is and Why It's Important*
- *How Ecotourism Helps; Ecotravel Ethics*
- *Perú: Environmental Threats and Conservation*

What Ecotourism Is and Why It's Important

Ecotourism or *ecotravel* is travel to (usually exotic) destinations specifically to admire and enjoy wildlife and undeveloped, relatively undisturbed natural areas, as well as indigenous cultures. The development and increasing popularity of ecotourism is a clear outgrowth of escalating concern for conservation of the world's natural resources and *biodiversity* (the different types of animals, plants, and other life forms found within a region). Owing mainly to peoples' actions, animal species and wild habitats are disappearing or deteriorating at an alarming rate. Because of the increasing emphasis on the importance of the natural environment by schools at all levels and the media's continuing exposure of environmental issues, people now have an enhanced appreciation of the natural world and an increased awareness of environmental problems globally. They also have the very human desire to want to see undisturbed habitats and wild animals before they are gone, and those with the time and resources increasingly are doing so.

But that is not the entire story. The purpose of ecotravel is actually twofold. Yes, people want to undertake exciting, challenging, educational trips to exotic locales – wet tropical forests, wind-blown deserts, high mountain passes, mid-ocean coral reefs – to enjoy the scenery, the animals, the nearby local cultures. But the second major goal of ecotourism is often as important: travellers want to help conserve the very places – habitats and wildlife – that they visit. That is, through a portion of their tour cost and spending into the local economy of destination countries – paying for park admissions, engaging local guides, staying at local hotels, eating at local restaurants, using local transportation services, etc. – ecotourists help to preserve natural areas. Ecotourism helps because local people benefit economically as much or more by preserving habitats and wildlife for continuing use by ecotravellers than they could by "harvesting" the habitats for short-term gain. Put another way, local people can sustain themselves better economically by participating in ecotourism than by, for instance, cutting down rainforests for lumber or hunting animals for meat or the pet trade.

Preservation of some of the Earth's remaining wild areas is important for a number of reasons. Aside from moral arguments – the acknowledgment that we share the planet with millions of other species and have some obligation not to be the continuing agent of their decline and extinction – increasingly we understand that conservation is in our own best interests. The example most often cited is that botanists and pharmaceutical researchers each year discover another wonder drug or two whose base chemicals come from plants that live, for instance, only in tropical rainforest. Fully one-fourth of all drugs sold in the USA come from natural sources – plants and animals. About 50 important drugs now manufactured come from flowering plants found in rainforests, and, based on the number of plants that have yet to be cataloged and screened for their drug potential, it is estimated that at least 300 more major drugs remain to be discovered. The implication is that if the globe's rainforests are soon destroyed, we will never discover these future wonder drugs, and so will never enjoy their benefits. Also, the developing concept of *biophilia*, if true, dictates that, for our own mental health, we had better preserve much of the wildness that remains in the world. Biophilia, the word coined by Harvard biologist E. O. Wilson, suggests that because people evolved amid rich and constant interactions with other species and in natural habitats, we have deeply ingrained, innate tendencies to affiliate with other species and actual physical need to experience, at some level, natural habitats. This instinctive, emotional attachment to wildness means that if we eliminate species and habitats, we will harm ourselves because we will lose things essential to our mental well-being.

If ecotourism contributes in a significant way to conservation, then it is an especially fitting reprieve for rainforests and other natural habitats, because it is the very characteristic of the habitats that conservationists want to save, wildness, that provides the incentive for travellers to visit and for local people to preserve.

How Ecotourism Helps; Ecotravel Ethics

To the traveller, the benefits of ecotourism are substantial (exciting, adventurous trips to stunning wild areas; viewing never-before-seen wildlife); the disadvantages are minor (sometimes, less-than-deluxe transportation and accommodations that, to many ecotravellers, are actually an essential part of the experience). But what are the actual benefits of ecotourism to local economies and to helping preserve habitats and wildlife?

The pluses of ecotourism, in theory, are considerable:

1   Ecotourism benefits visited sites in a number of ways. Most importantly from the visitor's point of view, through park admission fees, guide fees, etc., ecotourism generates money locally that can be used directly to manage and protect wild areas. Ecotourism allows local people to earn livings from areas they live in or near that have been set aside for ecological protection. Allowing local participation is important because people will not want to protect the sites, and may even be hostile toward them, if the people formerly used the

now-protected site (for farming or hunting, for instance) to support themselves, but are no longer allowed such use. Finally, most ecotour destinations are in rural areas, regions that ordinarily would not warrant much attention, much less development money, from central governments for services such as road building and maintenance. But all governments realize that a popular tourist site is a valuable commodity, one that it is smart to cater to and protect.

2   Ecotourism benefits education and research. As people, both local and foreign, visit wild areas, they learn more about the sites – from books, from guides, from exhibits, and from their own observations. They should come away with an enhanced appreciation of nature and ecology, an increased understanding of the need for preservation, and perhaps a greater likelihood of supporting conservation measures. Also, in many cases, a percentage of ecotourist dollars are funneled into research in ecology and conservation, work that will in the future lead to more and better conservation solutions.

3   Ecotourism can also be an attractive development option for developing countries. Investment costs to develop small, relatively rustic ecotourist facilities are minor compared with the costs involved in trying to develop traditional tourist facilities, such as beach resorts. Also, it has been estimated that, at least in some regions, ecotourists spend more per person in the destination countries than any other kind of tourists.

A conscientious ecotraveller can take several steps to maximize his or her positive impact on visited areas. First and foremost, if travelling with a tour group, is to select an ecologically committed tour company. Basic guidelines for ecotourism have been established by various international conservation organizations. These are a set of ethics that tour operators should follow if they are truly concerned with conservation. Travellers wishing to adhere to ecotour ethics should ascertain whether tour operators conform to the guidelines (or at least to some of them), and choose a company accordingly. Some tour operators conspicuously trumpet their ecotour credentials and commitments in their brochures and sales pitches. A large, glossy brochure that fails to mention how a company fulfills some of the ecotour ethics may indicate an operator that is not especially environmentally concerned. Resorts, lodges, and travel agencies that specialize in ecotourism likewise can be evaluated for their dedication to eco-ethics.

Basic ecotour guidelines, as put forth by the United Nations Environmental Programme (UNEP), the International Union for Conservation of Nature (IUCN), and the World Resources Institute (WRI), are that tours and tour operators should:

1   Provide significant benefits for local residents; involve local communities in tour planning and implementation.
2   Contribute to the sustainable management of natural resources.
3   Incorporate environmental education for tourists and residents.
4   Manage tours to minimize negative impacts on the environment and local culture.

For example, tour companies could:

1   Make contributions to the parks or areas visited; support or sponsor small, local environmental projects.
2   Provide employment to local residents as tour assistants, local guides, or local

naturalists.
3 Whenever possible, use local products, transportation, food, and locally owned lodging and other services.
4 Keep tour groups small to minimize negative impacts on visited sites; educate ecotourists about local cultures as well as habitats and wildlife.
5 When possible, cooperate with researchers; for instance, Costa Rican researchers are now making good use of the elevated canopy walkways in tropical forests that several ecotour facility operators erected on their properties for the enjoyment and education of their guests.

Committed ecotravellers can also adhere to the ecotourism ethic by disturbing habitats and wildlife as little as possible, by staying on trails, by being informed about the historical and present conservation concerns of destination countries, by respecting local cultures and rules, and even by actions as simple as picking up litter on trails.

Ecotourism, of course, is not a perfect remedy for threatened habitats and wildlife. Some negatives have been noticed, such as overuse of trails and the disruption of the natural behavior of wildlife when ecotourists intrude upon the animals' domains. On balance, however, most experts agree that in many situations, in most parts of the world, responsible ecotourism can have a positive role in conservation.

Perú: Environmental Threats and Conservation

As you might expect, Perú, with a population of almost 25 million and a poverty rate hovering between 30% and 40%, faces a host of environmental problems and disasters waiting to happen. The list includes overfishing of one of the greatest marine fisheries in the world, high rates of deforestation and overgrazing to accommodate hungry colonists in search of new agricultural fields and cattle pastures, logging companies interested in quick profits but not in conservation, introduction of domestic animals and plants that compete with native species, and misdirected government environmental policies. Mining currently dominates most political decisions; its economic power usually has its way. Pollution of rivers and coastal waters from mine tailings and chemical runoff is rampant. Perú is the second largest producer of cocaine in the world; during the 1980s and 1990s several violent revolutionary groups (brought under control in the late 1990s), that were often connected with drug-dealing, slowed economic development as well as conservation advances in many parts of the country. A recurring and nasty border war with Ecuador during the last 30 years (finally resolved with a treaty in 1998) channelled considerable development and conservation money into the defense budget. If these human-caused problems aren't bad enough, their impact on Perú is multiplied by what seems to be a constant parade of natural disasters – floods from heavy rains, droughts, tidal waves, earthquakes in which entire villages disappear, and volcanoes that erupt and destroy homes and lives. These uncontrollable forces often leave Perú staggering from one economic crisis to another – in a constant state of emergency. With these huge problems, it's easy to consider environmental protection a low priority and conservation measures a luxury.

Behind all this pessimism, however, there is hope. Numerous non-government organizations (NGOs), largely staffed by energetic, young Peruvians with a dream, are in many areas holding their own against environmental destruction. Environmental awareness is increasingly being taught in local schools and discussed on television and in newspapers. Large mining companies have discovered the advantages of positive public relations and are introducing better methods of discarding used chemicals and tailings. Politicians are slowly being pressured into at least proclaiming their advocacy for *green* (environment-enhancing) policies and programs. It is now less unusual to hear that they have taken a stand that benefits the environment. One of the strongest and most rapidly growing forces to benefit the environment in Perú is ecotourism. As its economic weight and effect on the country's GDP become more obvious, ecotourism's voice is being heard and its needs and desires heeded – sometimes even when they run counter to those of mining companies and plantation owners. Groups of NGOs, tourist agencies, and indigenous peoples are working together to solidify their power and convince the government that ecotourism is an important part of Perú's future. Your trip to Perú to experience its natural wonders can be a statement in itself that will benefit Perú's environment. If you want to be more than passively involved, however, use your influence to actively help Perú and its environment. If you see tour agencies, lodge operators, or officials following procedures or policies that run counter to the principle of ecotourism as a sustainable use of resources, say something to them. Also, seek out Peruvian and international non-profit NGOs that run on donations and make contributions.

In addition to local NGOs, a host of international environmental groups support or carry out conservation work in Perú. One important organization that focuses on animal preservation is the Wildlife Conservation Society (WCS, which officially endorses this series of books). Several projects supported by WCS funds are ongoing in the country, and three are briefly described here. One of the few acknowledged truths of ecotourism and of many other conservation measures is that, for local people and communities of modest means to accept and support conservation programs and nature reserves, they should be educated about the need for conservation and informed and consulted during the development process. In many cases, for their continued support, local people should benefit economically from a park, reserve, or ecotourism facility, or from other conservation programs. Note that local people are an important element of each of the conservation programs discussed below. It is also important to point out that in each of the projects, WCS works alongside local Peruvian conservation NGOs.

One WCS project involves the Vicuña (Plate 94), a wild relative of the domesticated Llama. Vicuña live only in the high Andes, in open grassland areas above 3500 m (11,500 ft) and, owing to historically heavy hunting for meat and for their hair (wool, or "fleece"), are an endangered species in parts of their range. Although Vicuña are endangered in some areas, they are fairly numerous in sections of Perú. Because there is a strong international market for Vicuña hair (considered one of the world's best fibers for making wool cloth), an opportunity exists to create, as conservationists say, a program of "sustainable resource utilization." (The word "sustainable" in a conservation context means using plants and animals in ways that are economically profitable for the local economy yet not ecologically harmful; use, in other words, that will not lead to significant ecosystem damage or to decline in biodiversity.) Local people can make a living by shearing free or captive Vicuña and selling the wool (the raw wool can sell for more than USD 500 per kg (USD 250 per lb). If done successfully, this could be a nice Vicuña conservation solution, because all sides benefit: people of high Andes villages benefit economically and Vicuña benefit because they are regarded locally as a precious resource to be protected.

The Peruvian government helped by declaring in 1995 that Vicuña and their hair are the property of the rural Andean communities on whose land they live, and by providing funds to begin maintaining some wild Vicuña in captivity (most Vicuña wool is collected now when wild, free Vicuña are herded together in annual round-ups and sheared). The local Andean communities of campesinos (country people) are now officially responsible for management, conservation, and sustainable use of Vicuña. WCS is helping with these responsibilities in a number of ways. Working in two communities near Arequipa in the Salinas and Aguada Blanca National Reserve (p. 41), WCS experts (led by biologist Catherine Sahley) and a local agency, Consejo Nacional de Camelidos Sud America, are helping the communities create sustainable Vicuña management plans by:

1 censusing Vicuña populations to determine if their numbers are stable or changing;
2 determining the effects of live-shearing on Vicuña (does it do the Vicuña harm? lead to increased mortality? decreased fertility?);
3 trying to determine whether the local communities actually benefit from Vicuña ownership in terms of increased income and/or better schooling and health-care.

Eventually, when all information is in, WCS wants to be able to recommend to the communities how best to capture and shear Vicuña and to determine whether it is better to hold some Vicuña in corrals or let them run free. If these programs are successful, survival of Vicuña may be assured for a long time to come, and many small Andean communities will be provided an important source of continuing income.

A second long-term WCS project seeks to protect seabirds and marine mammals at Punta San Juan, a remote 54-hectare (135-acre) peninsula and nature reserve that juts into the Pacific about 500 km (300 miles) south of Lima. Local industry is perhaps the main threat to the animals – guano mining that disturbs the nesting of seabirds such as Brown Pelicans, Peruvian Boobies, and Guanay Cormorants (Plates 20, 21; "guano," a valuable fertilizer, is produced from the long-accumulated, phosphate-laced droppings of seabirds) and fishermen who kill many Southern Fur Seals and South American Sea Lions (Plate 94) because they believe that the marine mammals deplete fish (mostly anchovies and sardines) in the local area, reducing the fishermen's own catch. Another major threat is El Niño climatic events, during which the usually cool Pacific currents that pass along coastal Perú are warmed, leading to reduced fish populations in the area and so to starvation (or migration) of animals that depend on these fish for food. The 1997–1998 El Niño was particularly intense; many "guano birds" starved or left Punta San Juan in search of other feeding areas, and fur seal and sea lion populations crashed. Fur seals declined, for instance, from a pre-El Niño population size in the area of about 6000, to fewer than 100 post-El Niño. Particularly threatened is the Humboldt Penguin (Plate 20), an endangered species now limited to a few small breeding colonies that live on cliffs of offshore islands and along a short bit of Pacific coast in Perú and Chile. The population of Humboldt Penguins at Punta San Juan fell to below 20 individuals during the

1997–1998 El Niño (some adults died, but many probably left the area), but has since rebounded to 1200+ individuals. Humboldt Penguins are threatened not only by El Niño events, but also by a lack of good nesting sites and by fishermen, who accidentally trap and kill these penguins in their fishing nets.

WCS projects at Punta San Juan, led by Peruvian biologist Patricia Majluf, in addition to population monitoring, include:

1   a veterinary program in which marine mammals and Humboldt Penguins are briefly captured and examined to obtain data on health; some animals are tagged, so their movements can be monitored.

2   a program in which fur seals are affixed with transmitters and tracked to their feeding areas, in an effort to determine if these seals and fishermen really compete for the same catch; early results show that the seals feed offshore, off the continental shelf, suggesting that they do not compete for fish with Punta San Juan's fishermen, who fish closer to the coast.

3   education programs in which local people are given information about ecology and conservation of the region's animal life.

4   a project to test whether Humboldt Penguins can breed successfully in artificial nests. Usually these penguins nest in guano burrows (or sometimes in protected areas under rocks). One reason for the penguin's small populations may be a lack of good nesting burrows. So WCS researchers are placing cement burrows in some areas and determining if the penguins will use them and if chicks can be reared successfully in them.

WCS was rewarded recently after 15 years of efforts at Punta San Juan; in 1998, the Peruvian government agreed that WCS could manage Punta San Juan for the next eight years. During this period, in addition to actively managing the site, WCS will establish a conservation, training, and research center at Punta San Juan, and will consult with the appropriate government agencies about ongoing guano mining in the area, with the objective of minimizing negative effects on seabird breeding. Conservation programs in the Punta San Juan reserve are essential because the area is one of the last major refuges in the southeastern Pacific for some marine mammals and seabirds, and its Humboldt Penguin colony is well-protected and the second largest in the world.

A third WCS project, one that is aimed at promoting sustainable ecotourism development, concerns the ecology of macaws (p. 128), which are the largest kinds of parrots. Perhaps you have seen television documentaries or glossy nature magazine coverage of the *geophagy* (earth-eating) behavior of these large and beautiful birds – giant red, blue, and green macaws and other parrot species in large groups, perched on river- or stream-banks, eating clay-containing soil from deposits exposed by a rushing waterway. The behavior itself is fascinating, and certainly an important question addressed by the WCS research team (led by biologist Charles Munn) is the obvious one – why do the parrots, fruit- and seed-eating birds, frequently eat clay? (Many individual macaws, identifiable by their idiosyncratic face markings, show up at these clay "licks" every two or three days. The team's research suggests that the main function of the parrots' soil-eating is to take advantage of the chemical compounds in the clay. Many of the fruit seeds that comprise the major part of the parrots' diet contain dangerous toxins that could kill the parrots; chemicals in the clay apparently counteract the toxins and perhaps protect the birds' gastro-intestinal tract from damage.) But much of the project's efforts are geared to conservation of the macaws and their habitats (particularly in and near Manu

National Park). And the macaws' "celebrity" may be a key to their conservation.

Why do the macaws and other parrots of the region need "saving"? Two reasons, one general, one specific. The Amazonian rainforest ecosystem that the parrots live in and are a part of is threatened by deforestation – by cutting of forests for industry (lumber, rubber extraction) and for increasing agriculture in the region – and by the inevitable encroachment of modern civilization. As habitat is destroyed, the parrots are increasingly threatened. Perhaps more insidious and immediate, however, is the capture of parrots for the illegal international trade in exotic pets. The capture and sale of these animals is considered to be one of the prime factors driving many of the species toward extinction. According to Traffic USA, an organization that monitors the wildlife trade, parrots probably make up the largest segment of the illicit trade in wild birds, comprising, during some periods, perhaps 25% of the industry. Parrots are in demand by collectors and pet-owners for obvious reasons – they are large and colorful and many can be trained to imitate human speech. Until recently, parrots from Central America and South America moved freely into the USA (the main market), meeting the demand for these birds. Starting in the mid-1970s, and continuing into the 1980s, first one, then a growing list of South and Central American countries banned parrot exports, cutting supplies and raising demand for parrots, thereby stimulating smuggling.

An ugly aspect of this illicit trade is the incredible waste it entails. Because animals must be hidden in boxes, crates, or more exotic contrivances, and smuggled across international borders, a huge proportion of the animals die in transit. For birds, which are in many ways delicate creatures, probably only about 10% survive capture and shipment. In addition to the loss/death of individual animals targeted by trappers, the parrot trade further harms parrot populations because young birds, often the most prized, are obtained by chopping down the trees containing nests, and the adult parents often will not attempt to breed again that year.

WCS has taken note that the clay-eating macaws of Manu and surrounding areas have become, in a sense, ecological "celebrities" – after repeated media exposure on television and in nature magazines – and believe that this very celebrity may provide a way to save them. At least 6000 tourists per year visit the traditional clay lick sites in and around Manu to watch the colorful parrots. To bring those ecotourists to the sites, and house, feed, and otherwise provision them, a local ecotourism industry has emerged. It employs perhaps a thousand or more local people and annually generates millions of dollars in foreign exchange for Perú. In fact, dividing the amount of money spent by ecotourists in the area by the number of parrots they watch at one popular lick, yields the very interesting formulation that each macaw that frequents that lick generates between USD 1000 and 5000 per year, and that, over its lifetime, a macaw may be responsible for up to USD 150,000 in tourist receipts. With this small but growing parrot-driven economy now at stake, local people and the Peruvian government have strong incentive to protect this obviously valuable resource – from parrot poachers and from local habitat destruction.

WCS, in addition to supporting long-term studies of the macaws' basic ecology and behavior (such as surveying and mapping nest sites and studying their breeding), is working closely with local indigenous groups to develop macaw-based ecotourism. This involves explaining to local communities the economic opportunities afforded by the parrots and helping to train indigenous people in the ecotourism market. Former parrot trappers are even trained as park guards. In addition, WCS's local nonprofit partner groups in Perú help with marketing the new ecotourism attractions to tour companies, and advise local communities on the establishment of ecolodges in the Manu area. The potential for conservation success of such programs may be considerable: at least one indigenous community that is embarking on ecotourism development recently banned all parrot hunting and capture in their 40,000 hectares (100,000 acres) of titled rainforest.

Selva Sur and Perú Verde are two local conservation groups that WCS works with to promote Peruvian ecotourism. These groups, which operate several ecotourism lodges in Perú (which are usually half-owned by local communities), also own 100% of an ecologically-aware travel agency known as InkaNatura, which can arrange trips to the ecolodges and to other spots as well. (www.inkanatura.com; in the USA: 888–278–7186).

Chapter 2

PERÚ: GEOGRAPHY
AND HABITATS

- *Geography and Climate*
- *Vegetation Patterns*
- *Major Habitats and Common Plant Species*
- *Environmental Close-up 1:* **Why is Farming So Difficult in the Tropics?**

Geography and Climate

Perú (Map 1, p. 11) is a medium-sized country (1,285,220 sq km, 496,224 sq miles) somewhat smaller than Alaska and a little more than twice the size of France. It is the third largest country in South America, after Brazil and Argentina. In terms of geographic variety, however, it takes a back seat to no one. There are three main geographic regions in Perú (Map 2, p. 37): the arid coast (*La Costa*), the high Andean region (*La Sierra*), and the verdant Amazonian lowlands (*La Selva*). With almost 25 million people, Perú has about 20 people per sq km (50 per sq mile), but the human population is not uniformly distributed. The coast has 48% of the country's inhabitants and is the site of Perú's largest city and capital, Lima, with a population of about 8 million. The Sierra has 43% of the population and features large cities such as Cuzco, Puno, Arequipa and Ayacucho. The remaining 9% live in the Amazonian Selva, which makes up more than half of the country's land area and includes major cities such as Iquitos in the north, Pucallpa in the central part, and Puerto Maldonado in the south. Nearly half of Perú's population is pure Native American, and many of them speak Quechua or Aymara as their first language.

The 3080 km (1925 miles) of coastline is made up of long, sandy beaches and a narrow strip of coastal lowlands that extends inland only 25 to 100 km (16 to 63 miles) before the Andes rise abruptly into the highlands. The coastal lowlands are interrupted in a few areas by medium or small estuaries, where rivers empty into the ocean. Here, freshwater carrying nutrients from the mountains produces mangrove forests in the far north and oases of vegetation in the deserts of the central and southern coasts. The mixture of freshwater and saltwater also produces fertile breeding areas for fish, birds and many marine invertebrates.

An ocean current 50 to 150 km (31 to 94 miles) wide and 40 m (130 ft) deep, called the Humboldt, or Peruvian, Current, moves north along the west coast of

Map 1 Perú, showing main cities and towns, rivers, and highland areas (those at or above 1200 m, 3900 ft, elevation).

South America. As this surface water moves, it causes an upwelling of dense, cold water from the ocean's bottom. In the winter (May to October), the temperature of the upwelling varies from 13 to 14°C (55 to 57°F), and in the summer (November to April) it varies from 15 to 17°C (59 to 63°F). The upwelling of cold water is laden with nutrients (from dead fish and other organisms) that previously had fallen to the bottom of the ocean. This great concentration of nutrients provides food for large numbers of tiny plants and animals called *plankton*. In turn, the plankton serve as food for fish, and the fish, in turn, make it possible for large populations of fish-eating birds and marine mammals to live here.

Even though the ocean is cold along Perú's coast, the land, baked by a tropical sun, is warm. As wind passes from the sea over the warm coastal plain, the air warms, expands, and sucks moisture out of the atmosphere like a sponge. Along the far northern coast, the cold ocean current has only a tentative hold on the climate, and from January to March, warmer tropical waters intrude far enough south to produce a short rainy season (annual totals range from less than 500 to

1300 mm, 20 to 50 in). This northern area, called *Tumbesiana*, has given rise to many unique plant and animal species that are shared only with extreme southern Ecuador. These species, which occur nowhere else on Earth, are known as *Tumbesian endemics*.

In the south, however, the cool Humboldt (Peruvian) Current just off shore is a more permanent fixture, and its hold is only relinquished during unusual years, when the Humboldt Current is forced far south by the warmer equatorial currents (El Niño). During these irregular periods, the temperature difference between the ocean and the land changes and rainfall on the northern and central coasts increases dramatically – sometimes by 5 to 10 times the normal amount. However, in the extreme south of coastal Perú and on into northern Chile, El Niño never extends its warming influence. Here the Atacama Desert dominates, and in some places no recorded rain has fallen since Europeans began keeping records more than 300 years ago. The only moisture that touches these land areas is in the form of dense fog called *garúa*. The upwelling of cool water from the bottom of the ocean together with its surfeit of accumulated nutrients creates a paradox of rich marine life adjacent to an almost lifeless land area. Except for bands of sparse fog vegetation on the tops of dunes and small hills, and narrow ribbons of vegetation along intermittent streams that cross the desert from the nearby Andes Mountains to the ocean, the landscape is stark sand, rocks and gravel.

Along the length of the Peruvian coast, a series of low, isolated hills called *lomas* rise from the narrow coastal plain. Because the tops of these hills are enshrouded for much of the year with thick fog, they have sufficient water to produce islands of low vegetation and provide refuge for many unique plants and animals (especially insects) adapted to these isolated habitats. Inland a short distance, the coastal plain rises abruptly into the heights of the west slope of the Andes Mountains. As moisture-laden air rises up these slopes, it cools and condenses as fog and occasionally as rain. This low level of rainfall produces a semi-desert area called the *vertiente andino* between 1000 and 2000 m (3300 and 6600 ft) elevation. It supports many unique desert-adapted plants and animals. Farther up the western slopes, with cooler temperatures and more reliable precipitation, small forests grow up to about 4000 m (13,200 ft), at which point (tree-line) this temperate forest disappears and gives way to the treeless, grassy *puna*. Because of poorer drainage, some parts of the puna are wetter than others, and these differences in moisture retention create great variety in high altitude habitats.

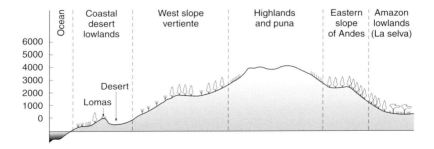

Figure 1 Cross-section of Perú showing how coastal desert, vertiente, puna, eastern slope, and Amazon region relate to elevation above sea level (in meters; 1 m = 3.3 ft).

The Sierra region runs north to south along the entire length of the country (Map 2, p. 37) and makes up the Peruvian section of the Andes Mountains. The highest parts of the range are the western (*Cordillera Occidental*) and eastern (*Cordillera Oriental*) ridges of mountains, which are separated by a plateau (*altiplano*) 3000 to 4000 m (9900 to 13,200 ft) high. The Peruvian altiplano begins in the north as an indistinct valley 10 to 20 km (6 to 13 miles) wide, but by the time it reaches southern Perú it is more than a 100 km (63 miles) across, a vast grassland puna that is home to the highest navigable lake in the world, Lago Titicaca. The two ridges are about 3000 to 5000 m (10,000 to 16,500 ft) high and are accented by towering, snow-covered volcanoes in the shape of near-symmetrical cones. Some of them are over 6000 m (19,800 ft) high, and the highest one (fourth highest mountain in South America), Huascarán, reaches 6768 m (22,204 ft).

The steep eastern slopes of the Andes fall off into the Amazon Basin. On these slopes, abundant moisture rises from the lowlands and condenses to produce rain and fog that support dense cloud forests. *La Selva*, the region below 300 m (990 ft) elevation in the Amazonian lowlands east of the Andes, covers more than half of Peruvian territory. The mighty Amazon River has its origin in the Andes of southern Perú. Together with thousands of tributaries, it drains all of eastern Perú but officially becomes the Amazon only where the Río Marañon meets the Río Ucayali near the city of Iquitos (Map 1) (The Brazilians, however, claim that the Amazon begins near Manaus, in Brazil, where the Río Negro joins the Río Solimões). From the base of the Andes, the terrain toward the east is flat and interrupted only by small hills (*colinas*) as far as the horizon. Seasonality is more distinct the farther south you go (dry season is July to September). Most precipitation is produced as water vapor rises above the forest canopy and cools to fall back down again as rainfall. Only 20% to 30% of the rainfall for this region comes via storm fronts, mainly from the Atlantic and Caribbean. During June and July, Antarctic cold fronts (*friajes*) occasionally make their way up to southern and central parts of Amazonian Perú. During a friaje period of two to four days, the temperature in lowland forests can fall to as low as 13°C (55°F), with wind and rain.

Visitors should keep in mind that, even during rainy parts of the year, it seldom rains all day. A typical pattern on the eastern Andean slopes and lowland forests, for instance, is sunny mornings and afternoon showers, but rainy nights and mornings with sunny afternoons are not unusual either. Some average annual rainfall values are as follows (see Map 1, p. 11, for locations): for the town of Arequipa, average annual rainfall = 137 mm (5.4 in) and driest months are May to October; for Cuzco, average annual rainfall = 589 mm (23.2 in) and driest months are May to August; for Iquitos, average rainfall = 3033 mm (119.4 in) and "driest" months are June to September; for Lima the average annual rainfall = 27 mm (1.1 in) and driest months are November to April. Also remember that, in contrast to temperate regions, where season largely determines temperature, in tropical Perú, elevation is the most important factor – the lower you are, the warmer you will be.

Vegetation Patterns

The most striking thing about tropical habitats is their high degree of species diversity. Temperate forests in Europe or North America often consist of only a few tree species. The norm in tropical forests is to find between 100 and 300 tree species within the area of a few hectares or acres. Sometimes after appreciating a specific tree and then looking around for another of the same species, you have to walk several kilometers before finding one. Ecologists say tropical areas have a much higher *species richness* than temperate regions – for plant life, as well as for some animals such as insects and birds. Perú has one of the richest floras in the world, with more than 35,000 species of plants. Some 5500, or 16%, of these plants are *endemic* to Perú (that is, they occur nowhere else in the world; see Close-up, p. 92).

During first visits to tropical forests, people from Europe, North America, and other temperate-zone areas are usually impressed with the richly varied plant forms, many of which are not found in temperate regions. Although not every kind of tropical forest includes all of them, you will usually see a number of highly typical plant forms and shapes.

Tree Shape and Forest Layering

Many tropical trees grow to great heights, with straight trunks rising 20 to 30 meters (65 to 100 ft) before branching. Tropical forests often appear layered, or *stratified,* and several more or less distinct layers of vegetation can sometimes be seen. A typical tropical forest has a surface herb layer (ground cover), a low layer of shrubs and immature trees, one or more lower levels of shorter trees, and a higher, or *canopy,* tree layer (Figure 2). In reality, there are no formal layers – just various species of trees that grow to different, characteristic, maximum heights. Lone, very tall trees that soar high above their neighbors are sometimes referred to as *emergents* and are characteristic of tropical forests. Trees whose *crowns,* or high leafy sections, are in the often continuous upper layer (below emergents) are part of the *canopy.* Many of the crowns of tropical trees in the canopy are characteristically shaped like umbrellas (Figure 2). Those in the next highest layers form the *subcanopy.* Shrubs, bushes and short or baby trees make up the *understory* (Figure 2). The *leaf litter* on the forest floor is a variable layer that during the dry season accumulates many dry leaves, uneaten fruits and fallen branches. However, it becomes very thin during the rainy season when warm temperatures and moist humidity permit fungi, insects and bacteria to quickly break down this organic material into chemicals and nutrients. These nutrients are taken up immediately by the shallow root systems of tropical trees and shrubs.

Large-leaved Understory Plants

Tropical forests often have dense concentrations of large-leaved understory herbs (Figures 2 and 3). Several plant families are usually represented: (1) Aroids, family Araceae, include plants such as *Dieffenbachia*, or Dumb Cane, and climbers such as *Monstera, Philodendron* (Figure 9), and *Syngonium*; (2) Marantas, family Marantaceae, including *Calantha insignis,* the Rattlesnake plant, which is a herb whose flattened yellow flowers resemble a snake's rattle; (3) *Heliconia* (Figure 11), family Heliconiaceae, which are large-leaved perennial herbs. The large leaves of these understory plants function (at least partially) to help gather the meager sunlight that makes its way though the canopy and subcanopy, so that adequate photosynthesis can take place to maintain the plants.

Figure 2 Exterior view of a typical tropical forest.

Figure 3 Interior view of a typical tropical forest.

Tree Bases and Roots

Any northerner visiting a tropical forest for the first time quickly stops in his or her tracks and stares at the bottoms of trees. The trunks of temperate zone trees may widen a bit at the base but they more or less descend straight into the ground. Not so in the tropics, where many trees are *buttressed* – side extensions of the base of the trunk emerge, descend, and spread out around the tree before entering the ground (Figure 3). The buttresses appear as narrow vertical ridges attached to the sides of a trunk. In older trees they are big and deep enough to hide a person (or a coiled snake!). The function of buttresses is believed to be tree support and, indeed, buttressed trees are highly wind resistant and difficult to blow down. But whether increased support is the primary reason that buttressing evolved is an open question, one that plant biologists study and argue over (the "hypotenuse theory" of shorter distances between the major roots and the crown is another hotly argued possible explanation). Another unusual root structure associated with the tropics is *stilt roots,* or *prop roots*. These are roots that seem to raise the trunk of a tree off the ground. They come off the tree some distance from the bottom of the trunk and grow out and down, entering the ground at various distances from the trunk (Figure 3). Stilt roots are characteristic of many palms and of trees, such as mangroves, that occur in habitats that are covered with water during parts of the year. Aside from anchoring a tree, functions of stilt roots are controversial.

Climbers and Vines

Tropical trees are often conspicuously loaded with climbing vines (Figures 2 and 3). Vines, also called *climbers, lianas,* and *bush-ropes,* are species from a number of plant families that spend their lives associated with trees. Some ascend or descend along a tree's trunk, perhaps loosely attached; others spread out within a tree's leafy canopy before descending toward the ground, free, from a branch. Vines are surprisingly strong and difficult to break; many older ones grow less flexible and more woody, sometime reaching the diameter of small trees. Common vines that climb trees from the ground up are Philodendrons and those of the genus *Monstera*.

Epiphytes

Epiphytes are plants that grow on other plants (usually trees) but do not harm their "hosts" (Figure 3). They are not parasites – they do not burrow into the trees to suck out nutrients; they simply take up space on trunks and branches. Ecologically, we would call the relationship between a tree and its epiphytes *commensal*: one party to the arrangement, the epiphyte, benefits – it gains growing space and access to more sunlight – and the other party, the tree, is unaffected. Epiphytes probably only harm trees when an epiphyte load becomes so heavy that the branch bearing it breaks off. How do epiphytes grow if they are not rooted in the host tree or the ground? Epiphyte roots that grow along the tree's surface capture nutrients from the air – bits of dust, soil, and plant parts that breeze by. Eventually, by collecting debris, each epiphyte develops its own bit of soil, into which it is rooted. Epiphytes are especially numerous and diverse in middle and higher-elevation rainforests, where persistent cloud cover and mist provide them with ideal growing conditions. *Orchids*, with their striking flowers that attract bees and wasps for pollination, are among the most famous kinds of epiphytes. *Bromeliads* (Figure 5), restricted to the Americas, are common epiphytes with sharply pointed leaves that grow in a circular pattern, creating a central tank, or *cistern*, in which collects rain water, dust, soil, and plant materials. Recent studies of bromeliads and other water-holding plants (called, in general, *phytotelmata*) show that these cisterns function as small aquatic eco-systems, with a number of different animals – insects, worms, snails, among others – making use of them. Several groups of amphibians are known to spend parts of their life cycles in these small pools (pp. 63, 66), and a number of species of tiny birds nest in bromeliads. Not all bromeliads are epiphytes; some grow on the ground as largish, spiny plants, such as *Puya* (Figure 4) in the puna, as well as pineapple (Figure 12). Other plants that grow as epiphytes are mosses and ferns.

Palms

The trees most closely associated with the tropics worldwide are *palms*. Being greeted by palm trees upon exiting a jet is a sure sign that you have arrived in a warm climate. In fact, it is probably temperature that limits palms mainly to tropical and subtropical regions. They grow from a single point at the top of their stems, and so are very sensitive to frost; if that part of the plant freezes, the plant dies. Almost everyone recognizes palms because, for trees, they have unusual forms: they have no branches, but all leaves (which are quite large and called *fronds*) emerge from the top of the single trunk; and their trunks are usually of the same diameter from base to top. Many taller palms have stilt roots propping them up. Some palms have no trunks, but grow as small understory plants. Coconut Palms, *Cocos nucifera* (Figure 8), found throughout the world's tropical beaches, were introduced along Perú's coast, and a number of other palm species are quite common.

Major Habitats and Common Plant Species

Using associations of particular plant species, several broad habitats can be distinguished in Perú. Each habitat consists of large numbers of unique plant species that characterize it and make it different from other habitats. Sometimes, particular animal species are also associated with individual habitats. Below are brief descriptions of Perú's major habitats and listings of some of the more abundant and recognizable types of vegetation that visitors are almost sure to see. Note that many plants occur in more than one habitat type, so although a tree like *Cecropia* (Figure 6), for instance, occurs throughout Perú's Amazon lowland forests, it and related species are also found up to middle elevations on the Eastern Andean slopes. Some common plants do not have English names. Forests that are pristine and have not been cut down by humans are called *primary* or *old growth forests*. Forests that have grown up in areas where humans earlier cut down the primary forest are called *secondary forests*.

Lowland Wet Forest

Perú's lowland wet forests in the Amazon are classic tropical rainforests with emergent trees and deciduous or evergreen canopy trees reaching 40 to 55 m

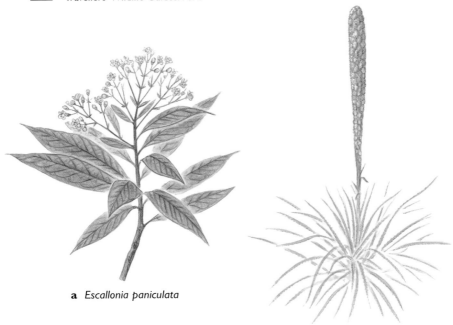

a *Escallonia paniculata*

b Puya,
Puya clava-hercules

c Polylepis Tree,
Polylepis incana

d *Espeletia hartwegiana*

Figure 4

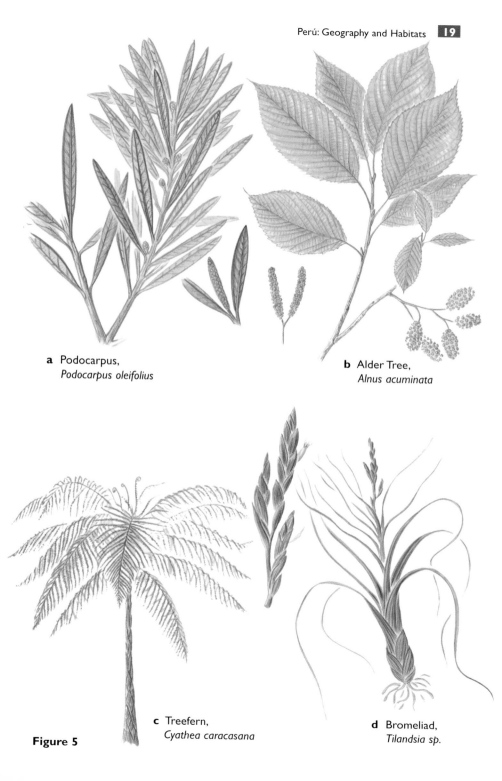

a Podocarpus,
Podocarpus oleifolius

b Alder Tree,
Alnus acuminata

c Treefern,
Cyathea caracasana

d Bromeliad,
Tilandsia sp.

Figure 5

a Bamboo,
Chusquea lehmannii

b Mauritia Palm,
Mauritia flexuosa

c Swamp Aroid,
Montrichardia arborescens

d Amazonian Cecropia,
Cecropia engleriana

Figure 6

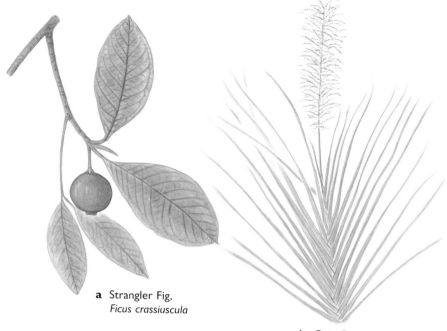

a Strangler Fig,
Ficus crassiuscula

b Caña Brava,
Gynerium sagittatum

Figure 7

c Willow,
Salix humboldtiana

d Ceiba, or Kapok, Tree,
Ceiba pentandra

a Bottle-trunk Ceiba,
Ceiba trichistandra

b Cordón Columnar Cactus,
Pilosocereus tweedyanus

c Acacia,
Acacia macracantha

d Coconut Palm,
Cocos nucifera

Figure 8

a Red Mangrove,
Rhizophora mangle

Figure 9

b Black Mangrove,
Avicennia germinans

c Philodendron,
Philodendron tripartitum

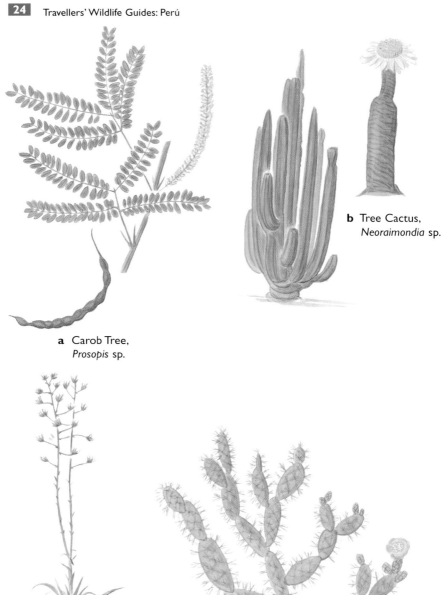

b Tree Cactus,
Neoraimondia sp.

a Carob Tree,
Prosopis sp.

d Tuna,
Opuntia sp.

c Century Plant, or Giant Agave,
Agave sp.

Figure 10

a Ginger,
Costus lima

b Ant-associated Melastome,
Maieta guianensis

c Piper,
Piper sp.

d Heliconia,
Heliconia sp.

e Banana Tree,
Musa x paradisiaca

Figure 11

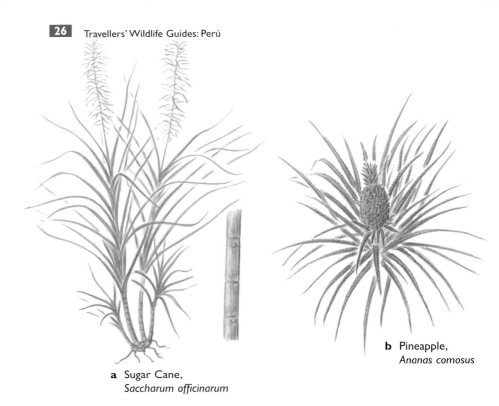

b Pineapple,
Ananas comosus

a Sugar Cane,
Saccharum officinarum

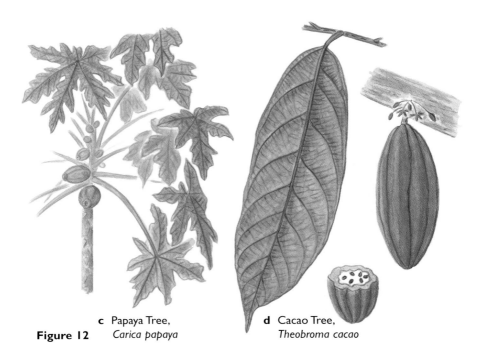

Figure 12

c Papaya Tree,
Carica papaya

d Cacao Tree,
Theobroma cacao

(130 to 180 ft) in height. Canopy trees have broad crowns and sub-canopy trees smaller and deeper crowns. Tree buttresses are very common and often extend high up on trunks. Palms are abundant, often with stilt roots. The ground in these forests is either mostly bare or sparsely covered with a herb layer. Vines and epiphytes are usually abundant. Biologically, these kinds of forests are probably the richest habitats on Earth – supporting the most species of both plants and animals per unit area (more plant species probably support greater animal richness).

In the *Selva*, the forest is made up of numerous patches of forest types, many types often occurring within a small area. Tall, cathedral-like tree species grow on higher ground that is never flooded by rising rivers, called *tierra firme*. Different types of trees grow in areas closer to rivers, areas that are more frequently flooded during the rainier season.

Some common, recognizable trees and shrubs of Perú's lowland wet forests are:

Ceiba pentandra: Ceiba, or Cotton Kapok, are massive, often epiphyte-laden, trees, large enough to be emergents, with broad, flat crowns (Figure 7). Frequently they are the only trees left standing when pastures are cleared. Fibrous kapok, from Ceiba pods, is used to stuff cushions and furniture. Canopy towers and canopy walkways constructed at some ecotravel lodges are usually built on massive Ceibas that rise above the rest of the canopy.

Strangler Fig (*Ficus crassiuscula*): The life cycle of a Strangler Fig (Figure 7) begins when seed remains of a strangler fig fruit are defecated by a bird or mammal high in the branches of another tree. Here a seed sprouts, and the fig tree starts out as an epiphyte. Its leaves grow out to capture the sun's energy and quickly produce its own canopy. Then it sends its roots down the trunk of the host until they form the scaffolding of a trunk and eventually reach the ground and burrow in. As it continues to grow, the fig eventually outcompetes the host tree for sunlight and nutrients, and kills the host, which it no longer needs for support.

Philodendron: The large, heart-shaped leaves of this semi-epiphytic climber/vine on trees are unmistakable (Figure 9).

Costus: Ginger is unique. Its stem grows as a spiral staircase, often a meter (3 ft) or more high (Figure 11). It is common on the forest floor in moister areas, and its flowers are bright and conspicuous, growing from a tiny pineapple-like base. Because its flowers bloom one at a time over several weeks, hummingbirds and insects can rely upon the presence of the nectar and pollen at the same place, so they can form daily routes of flower visitation, or "traplines" (see p. 141). The fruits that form from pollinated flowers also ripen sequentially so that tinamous and rodents, which eat the fruits, learn to return to the site every day for another prize.

Ant-associated Melastome (*Maieta* sp.): The species of the family of melastomes are among the most common in the undergrowth and easiest to recognize. The pattern on the leaves is unique – parallel cross veins running perpendicular to long veins. Species of the genus *Maieta* have distinctive hollow swellings at the base of each leaf that are covered with thick white hairs (Figure 11). Ants use these hollow areas as homes and apparently protect the leaves of the plant from being eaten by herbivorous insects.

Piper: This is a very common and widespread genus of tropical forest understory shrubs, with more than 120 species represented in Perú. The Spanish name is *Candela*, after the candle-like, erect, flowering structures (Figure 11). Bats, instead of insects or birds, act as pollinators on many of these shrubs. Usually 2 to 3 m (6 to 10 ft) high; occurs at elevations up to 2000 m (6500 ft). Black pepper is harvested from a species in the same family.

Heliconia: This genus of striking flowering plants is characteristic of tropical forests in the Americas; about 70 species occur in Perú. They grow within forests along streams and in sunny gaps, around clearings, and in disturbed areas such as roadsides and overgrown agricultural fields. *Heliconia* (*Platanillo*, in Spanish) have very large, banana-tree-like leaves; and their large, flat flowering structures are red, orange and yellow, resembling nothing so much as lobster claws (Figure 11). *Heliconia* are pollinated by hummingbirds and occur up to elevations of 2000 m (6500 ft).

Amazon River Edges and Cochas

Near the edges of rivers in Amazonian Perú grows a forest type (*riverine*, or flooded, forest) adapted to maturing quickly in clearings created by the water's scouring action. The fast-growing plants of these forests include the hollow *Cecropia*, five-meter high grasses (*caña brava*) and willows. These plants also predominate on islands in the larger rivers. Other types of forest vegetation are associated with the meandering river systems common in the eastern parts of Perú. As a meander forms, the momentum of the water slowly cuts out the banks on the outside of the curve. Eventually, the meander becomes U-shaped. Then, as the water continues to undercut the banks, the two tails of the "U" come closer and closer until, in a surge, the river cuts through the top of the "U". The meander is completely cut off from the river except at highest flood levels. In Perú, these cut-off meanders form oxbow lakes called *cochas*. A cocha no longer has a constant current to scour out accumulated tree trunks, sand, and floating vegetation. The cocha slowly fills in, and a series of forest types replace each other in an often predictable sequence. Floating lily pads and grasses die and accumulate to form soils that give more terrestrial plant species a toehold. *Cecropia* gives way to semi-terrestrial species such as Mauritia Palm and Chonta Palm, which in turn give way to flood forest species.

Some common, recognizable trees and shrubs of Perú's Amazonian river edges and cochas are:

Mauritia Palm (*Mauritia flexuosa*): These large palms (20 to 35 m, 66 to 115 ft) have fan-shaped leaves and grow in pure stands (*aguajales*) along the edges of cochas and in low, moist areas of the forest (Figure 6). They are home to several unique bird species such as the Point-tailed Palmcreeper and Zig-zag Heron.

Swamp aroid (*Montrichardia* sp.): Related to *Philodendron*, this tall, almost tree-like plant forms dense stands in swampy areas and along small rivers (Figure 6). It is a favorite food of the Hoatzin (p. 111), and apparently this bird gets its highly distasteful flesh from chemicals found in this plant.

Cecropia: These trees are conspicuous as *pioneer* species – they grow very quickly in disturbed areas of a forest, particularly in large, sunny gaps or clearings. Generally they are thinnish trees with very large, umbrella-like leaves. Most Cecropias harbor teeming colonies of stinging ants in their hollow trunks, and these ants end up protecting the tree from herbivores (or ecotravellers foolish enough to lean a hand on the Cecropia's trunk) while defending their nest site and food source. The Cecropias grow at low and middle elevations over much of Perú (Figure 6).

Caña Brava (*Gynerium* sp.): An early-succession cane-grass 5 to 6 m (to 20 ft) high, caña brava grows in dense stands along Amazonian river banks and low river islands recently scoured by floods (Figure 7). The caña brava on these river islands often forms the bulk of a unique habitat to which more than ten species of birds are restricted.

Willow (*Salix humboldtiana*): This small species of willow occurs along white-water rivers in the mid-elevations of the Andes, but also descends to the Amazon lowlands. Here it is common in pure stands on sand bars and low islands of larger rivers (Figure 7).

Tropical Dry Forest

The hills and low mountains east of the coastal plain from the Ecuadorean border south to the city of Trujillo are largely covered by tropical dry forest. Here, little or no rain falls for six months of the year, and the vegetation is adapted to a dry climate and short rainy season. Trees lose their leaves, roots go deep, cactus is common, and most of the tall trees grow along the rivers (called *gallery forest* or *riparian forest*). These tropical dry forests consist of relatively low, mostly deciduous, trees, usually in two layers: one 20 to 30 m (60 to 100 ft) high with large, broad crowns, and one 10 to 20 m (30 to 60 ft) high, more evergreen, with small crowns. Tree buttressing is relatively uncommon in dry forests. Vines are often present. Epiphytes are uncommon, but when present, bromeliads are the most conspicuous. The shrub layer is dense, and ground cover is sparse. These forests are not as species-rich as wet forests. Dry forest land is excellent for agriculture, and because of this, many of these forests throughout Latin America have been cleared. Because dry forests have a more open, less dense structure than wet forests, wildlife viewing in them is often far superior. These forests continue south in a narrow band of altitude between 1000 and 2000 m (3300 and 6600 ft) but give way eventually to shorter trees, bushes and cactus, a habitat called the semi-desert *vertiente andino*.

Some common, recognizable trees of tropical dry forests are:

Bottle-trunk Ceiba (*Ceiba trichistandra*): During the dry season, the bulging, green, and bottle-like trunk of these immense trees is leafless and obvious on hillsides sporting otherwise withered vegetation (Figure 8). During the rainy season, their leaves grow out quickly and the cotton-like pods attract parrots and other seed-eating birds, as well as monkeys.

Cordón Columnar Cactus (*Pilosocereus tweedyanus*): Looking much like the more familiar Saguaro cactus of Arizona, these tall cactus (Figure 8) rise above most of the short vegetation and bushes of the driest parts of coastal Perú.

Acacia sp.: These thorny desert trees are often the only leafy tree available during the dry season. They provide shade and cover for many animals, as well as nectar when their flowers are open (Figure 8).

Semi-desert Vertiente

On the lower western slopes of the Andes is a complex band of desert vegetation between 1000 and 1600 m (3300 and 5280 ft) elevation. This zone of vegetation is highly variable from north to south, but it includes many species of cactus and thorny bushes adapted to low levels of rainfall and fog.

Some common, recognizable trees of Perú's semi-desert vertiente are:

Tuna (*Opuntia* sp.): The familiar beaver-tail cactus of deserts, several species of this genus are abundant in the semi-desert vertiente (Figure 10); one species reaches up to the lower puna altitudes.

Tree cactus: These are large cactus with only a few ribbed branches; two species of the genus *Neoraimondia* are common on the lower coastal slopes of the Andes (Figure 10).

Century Plant (*Agave* sp.): The long, narrow leaves of this desert plant can be more than a meter (3.3 ft) long in some species (Figure 10). The leaves are crowded together at the base of the stem, and because of their stiff and sharply pointed shape, they form a rosette of protection (and thus are called *Spanish bayonet* by those unlucky enough to be stabbed by one). The name "century plant" comes from the single flowering and fruiting event that in some species occurs only after 30 or more years (evidently 30 years seems like a century to someone watching a plant grow). When a plant is ready to flower, it grows a giant flowering stalk 10 cm (4 in) or more in diameter and more than 5 m (16 ft) tall. This stalk can grow at an astonishing rate of 15 cm (6 in) per day. The long tubular flowers that grow at its tip are pollinated by a host of insects, bats and hummingbirds, including the largest hummingbird in the world, the Giant Hummingbird (Plate 47). In Perú this plant is grown together in rows to create fences. Its fibers are used to make rope, and leaves of some species are fermented to make alcoholic drinks (*mescal*).

Mangrove and Coastal Vegetation

Along the coast of extreme northern Perú, in areas where fresh or brackish water is predictable (such as along estuaries), mangroves are common and form another floral region with distinct plants and animals.

Some common, recognizable trees of Perú's coast are:

Mangroves: These are relatively short tree species of several unrelated plant families. They have in common the fact that they grow in areas exposed to salt water, usually around bays, lagoons, and other protected coastal infoldings. Common mangrove species are the Red Mangrove, *Rhizophora mangle* (Figure 9) and the Black Mangrove, *Avicennia germinans* (Figure 9).

Carob trees (*Prosopis* sp.): Dry savannahs with desert-adapted trees, such as Carob trees (Figure 10), often called *mesquites* or *algarrobales*, reach the coast in northern Perú. These trees have a central tap root that can extend 10 m (33 ft) or more down into underground sources of moisture.

Mid-elevation Cloud Forest

On the eastern slopes of the Andes, small changes in altitude can produce major changes in rainfall, cloudiness, and temperature. Many plant species adapted to a specific combination of rain, sunshine and temperature thus can only occur in a narrow range of elevations. Numerous distinct floral regions run in narrow altitudinal belts north to south along the length of the Andes. Rainfall is supplemented by dense clouds of fog that form regularly as the water vapor rising from the lowlands cools and condenses. *Cloud forest* is usually considered to occur where low-lying clouds bathe forests most days, rendering them dark, cool, and moist. The trees here are typically covered with thick layers of epiphytes – moss, orchids and bromeliads. Large patches of alders grow in areas disturbed by landslides. These rainforests are mixed deciduous and evergreen in their lower reaches and uniformly evergreen in higher areas. Canopy height generally declines as elevation increases, being at between 30 and 40 m (100 and 130 ft) at lower levels and between 20 and 30 m (60 and 100 ft) at higher elevations. These forests generally have two tree layers, canopy and subcanopy, and abundant vines. Tree buttressing is common in forest on mountains' lower slopes, but uncommon in higher-elevation areas.

Some common and recognizable plants of cloud forests are:

Podocarpus: This ancient relative of pine trees has remnant populations in the higher elevations of the Andean slopes. Some of the species grow to over 44 m (145 ft) tall and are found in pure stands. Other species are found as sparsely distributed individuals within montane forests and are not quite as tall (Figure 5).

Alnus acuminata: This alder is very similar to alder species from North America and Europe, but it is the only one found in South America. You will most likely see it on old land slides and clearings between 460 and 2600 m (1500 and 8600 ft) altitude on either slope of the Andes. Here it grows in large, pure stands until replaced by slower-growing but more shade-tolerant species (Figure 5).

Treeferns (*Cyathea* sp.): These plants are just what they sound like – very large ferns that attain the height of trees – some up to 20 m (65 ft) tall. They are common in many of Perú's forested habitats, from coastal areas to high elevations, being especially prevalent in some of the highest elevation rainforests (Figure 5).

Bromeliads: These pineapple relatives usually grow as epiphytes high up in the canopy, perched on top of the larger branches of trees. The bases of the long, narrow but thick leaves interconnect to form a tank which holds up to 5 liters (one gallon) of water. The beautiful flowers of bromeliads are often showy and bright red or pink (Figure 5).

Bamboo (*Chusquea* sp.): These tall, woody grasses grow in dense stands and are often 5 m (16 ft) tall (Figure 6). You are most likely to see them in moist protected gullies (*quebradas*) on the mid- to high slopes of the Andes, but they also grow in lowland forest areas with poor drainage. Bamboos produce their seed-like fruits at long intervals of 10 or more years. The entire population chooses the same year to flower, then dies. It is unknown how they synchronize their flowering over wide areas. Many species of insects, birds and mammals are tightly associated with these bamboo stands. When the stand dies, these animals must quickly disperse and find another stand in which to live – not an easy undertaking if all of the stands in a wide area have died at the same time.

High-altitude and Puna

Higher on the Andes' slopes, moisture levels drop off and the temperature falls considerably. Multitudes of low bushes form impenetrable fortresses for birds and mammals. In protected gullies (*quebradas*) temperate forests grow, the most intriguing inhabitant of which is a tree in the rose family called *Polylepis*. Above the Polylepis forests, shrubs and trees quickly disappear to form a wet or dry grassy area called *puna*. Here the cold, windy conditions drive the evolution of plants that hug the ground; in some ways, the puna landscape resembles an Alaskan tundra scene. Puna eventually gives way to glacial scree of bare gravel and rocks just below the permanent snow-line at about 5500 m (18,000 ft).

Some common, recognizable trees and shrubs of Perú's highlands and puna are:

Polylepis Tree (*Polylepis* sp.): Its shaggy red bark signals the presence of an entire community of plants and animals that are almost solely associated with groves of this high altitude tree species (Figure 4).

Puya (*Puya* sp.): This high altitude plant, typical of the puna, is a terrestrial bromeliad; that is, it grows on the ground, not as an epiphyte like most of its relatives. During the flowering season, the tall, white, and spike-like flower grows to more than 3 m (10 ft) above its thin, spiny leaves (Figure 4). Near inhabited areas, these spiky plants are burned so that livestock won't be impaled by the sharp leaves.

Escallonia sp.: This bush is evergreen, with clusters of small leaves. It is abundant and distinctive in moist puna areas. Its small, greenish flowers are formed together in long and slender racemes (elongated structures each with multiple flowers) that hang down (Figure 4).

Espeletia sp.: This high Andean puna herb is related to the sunflower and is a distinctive member of the habitat (Figure 4).

Pastures, Farms, and Plantations

Agriculture in Perú is split between traditional small family farms, usually of 5 to 10 hectares (12 to 25 acres), and large corporate plantations. Family farms, which are still plentiful, generally grow several crops, and plantations, single crops. The biggest export crops are coffee (*café*), cotton, sugar (Figure 12), and cocaine (*coca*), of which Perú produces much of the world's illicit product. Chocolate (*cacao*) (Figure 12), bananas (*plátanos*) (Figure 11), poultry, dairy products and llama wool are also important exports. Banana trees, with their large leaves and yellow fruit, originated in Asia. They occur in gardens, or *chacras,* mainly in the Amazon lowlands. Sugar Cane (*caña*), grown in several regions of Perú, but particularly in irrigated river valleys in the coastal lowlands, is a perennial grass that may have originated in the New Guinea region. Pineapple plants (Figure 12) are bromeliads, and are Neotropical in origin. They are grown mainly in the Amazon lowlands. Other common crops are corn (*maíz*), rice (*arroz*), and papaya (Figure 12). The potato most likely originated in the Andean highlands and more than a thousand varieties of this plant have been developed in Perú alone. In addition, crops such as tomatoes, tobacco, beans, cinchona (a member of the beet family), and many other lesser-known species, originated in Perú.

Environmental Close-up 1
Why is Farming so Difficult in the Tropics?

An experienced farmer from the temperate zone, such as one who worked in Iowa or France, gazing for the first time at a tropical rainforest, could be excused if he (or she) thought he saw a farming bonanza before him. It would be natural for him to exclaim: "Just cut down the forest and plant the cleared fields with a more useful crop, a cash crop. If those dense, tall trees can grow there so luxuriously, surely a field of alfalfa, corn, cotton, or soy beans should also grow wonderfully there! Why, with the perpetual warm weather and regular rain, you could probably have three or four harvests a year!" But it is not as easy as that; indeed, this type of thinking has led many hopeful farmers in the tropics into an economic and ecological disaster.

The main problem is that tropical soils, in contrast to most temperate soils, are often very nutrient-poor. In fact, tropical rainforests themselves, and the soil in which they are rooted, are of such different designs when compared with temperate forests and soils, that many of the agricultural rules a farmer would have learned in the temperate zones in North America and Europe don't even apply. For instance, in temperate zones, soils accumulate organic material in the form of dead leaves, fallen branches, dead animals and so on – they are essentially a natural compost heap. This accumulation of organic chemicals, including many of the basic nutrients that plants need to grow (such as nitrogen-containing compounds and phosphates), is possible because there is only a relatively short period each year when it is warm and moist enough for fallen plant and animal material to decompose completely. The bacteria, fungi and other soil organisms that make decomposition possible can't be active and break down dead tissues if it is too cold or dry. Thus, over time, organic materials build up in the soil and produce *humus* (rich black soil) and a large reservoir of nutrients sometimes 30 cm (a foot) or more deep. But this is not the case in tropical forests. Here the forest floor is generally so warm and humid throughout the year that any organic material falling to the forest floor is quickly broken down completely by the abundant *decomposer* termites, fungi and bacteria. There is little chance for a build-up of organic humus. The average depth of organic material below the floor of moist tropical forests is measured in millimeters (tenths of an inch) instead of centimeters (inches). In addition, most tropical soils are composed largely of old clay with a high content of aluminum and iron (thus the reddish soil visible in cleared areas); minerals in these soils useful to plants have long ago been weathered away.

How does the lush tropical vegetation of these forests exist if soils are so nutrient-poor? Actually, the plants do have access to nutrients, they just have to be ready to capture the nitrogen, phosphates and other nutrients almost as soon as they become available via the action of the soil decomposers. Instead of root systems that penetrate deep down into the soil, tropical trees tend to produce roots that grow sideways, close to the soil surface. Most roots in tropical forests are within 30 cm (1 ft) of the soil surface. Together with symbiotic fungi, called *mycorrhizae*, living in the roots, these trees (and other plants) with shallow roots are able to efficiently and quickly capture the nutrients as they become available – that is, the tree roots, being near the forest floor, are able to capture and absorb organic nutrients and minerals just as they are made available at the soil surface by the action of soil decomposers. Unlike temperate zone habitats, in which more than half of an area's nutrients are in the soil, tropical forest habitats often have only 1% of their nutrients in the soil at any one time. So where are the rest of the habitat's nutrients? They are stored in the cells of living plants. That means up to 99% of the nutrients in tropical forests are in the plants themselves. So if you cut tropical forest and burn off the dead vegetation, you lose almost all of the habitat's nutrients – they disappear by logging truck and/or into the air with the smoke. When the rains begin, the rest of the nutrients are eroded away.

The main consequence of tropical forest clearing and burning for agriculture is obvious. After one or two crops of corn are planted to replace the luxuriant tropical forest, the few nutrients left in the soil are used up. Because commercial fertilizer is too expensive for most farmers in the tropics, the sad alternative is to move to the next patch of forest, cut or burn it down, and squeeze out another couple of years of crops before the soil there is also exhausted. This wasteful, destructive procedure is known as *slash-and-burn agriculture* – moving every two or three years to a new patch of forest and cutting and/or burning it to provide temporarily productive fields.

Even selective timber removal from tropical forests is damaging, and so of limited economic use. This is because the shallow root systems, seeds in the soil, and decomposer communities are easily disrupted or killed by the compacting action of heavy tractors and equipment. Also, if too many trees are removed for timber, the total amount of nutrients in the system may fall below a critical minimum to maintain the rest of the uncut forest. In addition, large cleared areas (called *light gaps*) permit high levels of sunshine to strike the soil surface, baking the clay into a stone-like adobe called *laterite*. Seeds and roots cannot penetrate the laterite, and the forest can only regenerate itself in these areas with great difficulty. If that weren't bad enough, it turns out that trees with shallow root systems depend on dense stands of trees to protect themselves from high-wind storms. Large light gaps remove this protection and so the trees on the edge of a gap become easy victims of the next storm. When they fall, their neighbors become unprotected, and so on.

Beyond nutrient cycling problems for tropical farming, precipitation cycles also have different rules in tropical rainforests. Although rainfall is generally high compared with that in most temperate zone forests, cutting tropical forest to produce agricultural fields actually reduces rainfall that crops need. Through a process that moves water and nutrients up from the roots to the leaves (called *evapotranspiration*), water vapor escapes from leaf surfaces in tropical rainforests and builds up over the canopy. As this vapor rises it eventually cools and condenses. Tropical rainforests produce up to 70% of their own rainfall in this manner. Thus, if extensive areas of tropical forest are cleared and then burned off for crop farming or to create cattle pastures, most of the local nutrients and much rainfall are removed in one fell swoop.

What then are the alternatives for agriculture in rainforests? Theoretically, one plan would be to follow traditional agricultural practices. Indigenous peoples long ago developed a system that mimics natural processes, maintaining soil nutrients and so allowing for continual use of the same fields (that is, permits "sustainable" agriculture). They clear only small areas of the forest and then plant a mixed cultivation of fast-growing food crops, such as corn and beans, interplanted with slower-growing pepper and passion fruit, which are vines that grow up trees such as cacao, rubber, and fruit palms. They also plant crops with high numbers of mycorrhizae in their roots, which pump nutrients into the soil, enriching it and helping to recycle nutrients locally. Furthermore, rotation and succession of these crops help reduce the occurrence of plant pests and diseases. But this kind of sustainable agricultural system is obviously very labor intensive and involves careful, thoughtful planting. Tropical forestry agriculture can work, but only with great care and substantial training.

New farmers and new settlers who push into Neotropical rainforests to claim land and homestead, usually do not have such skillful knowledge. With high hopes they burn and plant, only to discover after a few years that the productivity of their fields has declined; they then move and start over again. Large-scale commercial ranching and farming operations prefer to continually grow single crops over large areas (that is, *monocultures*), which quickly deplete soil nutrients and require ever-increasing amounts of artificial fertilizers and pesticides to maintain. These agricultural forces – essentially mistreatments of tropical forests and soils for ill-informed farming – in combination have created what most consider to be an ecological disaster (disappearing tropical forests; increasingly poor soils for farming; increasing fertilizer and pesticide use and damage). Remedies, such as encouraging ecologically sustainable farming practices on large scales, are only beginning to be proposed. But until such practices are widely adopted, much farming in the tropics will continue to be difficult and ecologically damaging.

Chapter 3

PARKS AND RESERVES: BRIEF DESCRIPTIONS

- Perú's Parks and Reserves
- Tropical Dry Forest (TDF)
- Coastal Desert Lowlands (CDL)
- West Slope Vertiente and Lomas (WSV)
- Highlands and Puna (HAP)
- Eastern Slope of the Andes (ESA)
- Amazon Lowlands (AMA)

Perú's Parks and Reserves

One of Perú's first official conservation areas, part of what is now the Pacaya-Samiria National Reserve, was declared in 1940. It was set aside to manage populations of the Paiche fish (*Arapaima gigas*), which grows to be more than 80 kg (176 lb) of the most delicious and huge fillets you have ever eaten. Since then, nearly 5% of Perú's land area has been officially protected as national parks, national reserves, national forests, ecological reserves and national sanctuaries. Moreover, private ecotourism companies have purchased land or made arrangements with the government to manage additional areas specifically for ecotourism. Although Perú has some of the most sophisticated and well-educated conservation biologists in South America, their detailed management plans for development and long-term use of natural areas often have been derailed by major slumps in the economy, lack of long-term support from legislators and the executive branch of government, and the sad and violent acts of revolutionary groups (which are usually closely allied with illegal cocaine cultivation and marketing). The era of *Sendero Luminoso*, *Tupac Amaru* and other violent groups, however, is now on the wane, and hopefully it will soon be finished. Ecotravellers planning their visit to Perú need have less and less concern for revolutionary activity. Although Perú has problems, most of the parks and reserves detailed below are now wonderful places to visit.

We selected the parks and reserves described below for two reasons. Some of these areas are the ones most often visited by ecotravellers in Perú – by people who come on organized tours and also those who travel independently. Others are more remote, and to see them takes additional planning and effort. But because they are so remote, it is also less likely that illegal colonization, poaching and mining have altered or severely affected the quality of these habitats and their natural inhabitants. See Map 2 (below) for park locations. The animals profiled in the color plates are keyed to parks and reserves in the following way: the profiles list the Peruvian regions (TDF, Tropical Dry Forest; CDL, Coastal Desert

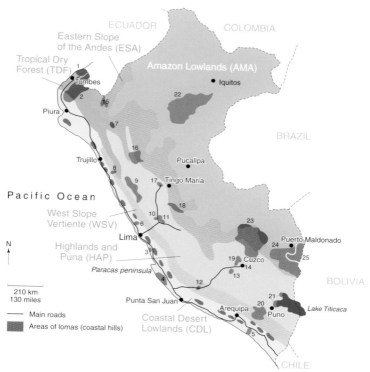

Tropical Dry Forest (TDF)
1 Manglares de Tumbes National Sanctuary
2 Noroeste Biosphere Reserve

Coastal Desert Lowlands (CDL)
3 Villa Swamps Reserve Zone
4 Paracas National Reserve
5 Mejía Lagoons National Sanctuary

West Slope Vertinentes and Lomas (WSV)
6 Lachay National Reserve

Highlands and Puna (HAP)
7 Cutervo National Sanctuary
8 Calipuy National Reserve
9 Callejón de Huaylas and Huascarán National Park
10 Huayllay National Sanctuary
11 Junín National Reserve
12 Pampas Galeras National Reserve

13 Ampay National Sanctuary
14 Cuzco area
20 Salinas and Aguada Blanca (Lake Salinas) National Reserve
21 Titicaca National Reserve

Eastern Slope of Andes (ESA)
15 Tabaconas Namballe National Sanctuary
16 Río Abiseo National Park
17 Tingo María National Park
18 Yanachanga-Chemillén National Park
19 Machu Picchu Historical Sanctuary and Natural Monument

Amazon Lowlands (AMA)
22 Pacaya Samiria National Reserve
23 Manu National Park
24 Tambopata-Candamo Reserve Zone
25 Bahuaja-Sonene National Park

Map 2 Perú, showing locations of parks and reserves, some main roads (the Pan American Highway runs along the coast), and the six regions used in the book to specify species ranges.

Lowlands; WSV, West Slope Vertiente; HAP, Highlands and Puna; ESA, Eastern Slope of the Andes; and AMA, Amazon Lowlands) in which each species is most likely to be found, and the parks listed below are arranged by these regions. Visitors who stay at lodges or resorts in the same regions as the parks listed below can expect to encounter similar types of habitats and wildlife as described for these parks and reserves. Tips on increasing the likelihood of seeing mammals, birds, reptiles, amphibians or flashy insects are given in the introductions to each of those chapters. For more particulars on planning your trip to Perú, choosing which areas to visit, places to stay, and transportation, we suggest you consult one of several ecotravel-friendly guides available at bookstores, such as *Perú: A Lonely Planet Travel Survival Kit*, by Rob Rachowiecki, or *Insight Guide: Perú*, edited by Pam Barrett.

Tropical Dry Forest (TDF)

Manglares de Tumbes National Sanctuary

In 1988, Perú declared 2972 hectares (7341 acres) of coastal mangroves near the Ecuadorean border as an ecological reserve. This area, at the deltas of the Río Tumbes and Río Zarumilla, is one of the most southern outposts of mangroves in South America and the main region of mangroves in Perú. It is also the only Peruvian home of the American Crocodile and several invertebrates and bird species peculiar to this habitat. In contrast to the massive destruction of mangroves along the entire coast of Ecuador, mainly for construction of artificial lagoons for commercial shrimp farming, the Peruvians apparently appreciate a habitat they have so little of. This attempt to save what little remains is encouraging. Access to much of the reserve is by motorized canoe from the city of Tumbes.

Noroeste Biosphere Reserve

This conservation area has 231,402 hectares (571,563 acres) and protects much of the remaining intact tropical lowland dry forest in Perú. It combines the Cerros de Amotape National Park, Tumbes Reserved Zone and the Angolo Hunting Reserve. This area protects many endemic plant and animal species unique to the Tumbesian area of southeastern Ecuador and northwestern Perú. It ranges in altitude from 200 to 1600 m (660 to 5280 ft), and, except for the short rainy season (January to March), is very hot and dry. Access is by road from Piura or Tumbes.

Coastal Desert Lowlands (CDL)

Villa Swamps Reserve Zone

Only 20 km (13 miles) south of Lima, this extensive marshy area (400 hectares, 1016 acres) near the town of Chorillos attracts many migrant birds as well as Peruvian school children on field outings. Trails, observation towers and an interpretive center make it an ideal morning trip out of Lima. Avoid weekends if you want to have the trails to yourself.

Paracas National Reserve

A spectacular reserve on the Paracas Peninsula (335,000 hectares, 827,450 acres), a trip here is a must to see wild coastal desert and concentrations of water birds that will leave you incredulous. A large part of the reserve protects inland marine waters where penguins (Plate 20), whales (Plate 95), fur seals (Plate 94) and Marine Otters (Plate 89) can be seen from high cliffs overlooking the ocean or from boats chartered in nearby towns. It is one of the few places left where Andean Condors (Plate 33) still glide over beaches. Interesting archaeological remains are another attraction. You can visit Paracas on a long day's trip from Lima (180 km, 113 miles south on the Pan American Highway), or you can stay in beach hotels at nearby Pisco or Paracas and explore the more remote parts of the reserve at your leisure.

Mejía Lagoons National Sanctuary

This small (690 hectares, 1704 acres) area of estuaries and brackish swamps serves as a major staging area for migratory shorebirds and wintering flamingos (Plate 21). In addition, 72 bird species nest here. It is located on the coast, 150 km (93 miles) southwest of Arequipa and 20 km (12 miles) south of the town of Mollendo.

West Slope Vertiente and Lomas (WSV)

Lachay National Reserve

This reserve (5070 hectares, 12,522 acres) in the Department of Lima protects a small part of the "Lomas" ecosystem, a series of 67 coastal hills jutting out of the stark coastal desert from Trujillo south to Chile. These hills receive virtually all their moisture in the form of heavy fog that covers their tops for much of the day in the winter (July to October). Many unique plant and animal species occur here, including several species of potatoes (*Solanum*). (Potato-based tourism, however, is not yet much developed.) The reserve is 105 km (65 miles) north of Lima and can be reached by road.

Highlands and Puna (HAP)

Cutervo National Sanctuary

This reserve consists of only 2500 hectares (6175 acres), but it protects some of Perú's last intact high elevation forest between 2200 and 3500 m (7260 and 11,550 ft). Such hard-to-see wildlife as Oilbirds (Plate 42), Cock-of-the-rock (Plate 62) and Spectacled Bear (Plate 88) all occur here. It is accessible by road from the coastal town of Chiclayo.

Calipuy National Reserve

Between 800 and 3600 m (2640 and 11,880 ft) in elevation, this large reserve (64,000 hectares, 158,080 acres) protects the largest population of Guanacos (wild cousin to the Llama) left in Perú as well as the densest stands of the giant bromeliad plant, *Puya raimondii* (similar to the Puya species shown on p. 18, but larger), remaining in the country. Access is from the Callejón de Huaylas (see below) and the tourist city of Huaraz.

Callejón de Huaylas and Huascarán National Park

The Callejón de Huaylas is a high Andean valley running north and south between the Cordillera Blanca and Cordillera Negra; the word spectacular is not enough to describe the natural beauty here. Snow-capped peaks rise on the east side of the valley, which at its bottom is 3000 m (10,000 ft) in elevation and semi-tropical. The Huascarán peak itself rises to 6768 m (22,204 ft), the highest point in Perú. It is the center of Huascarán National Park, which is a 340,000-hectare (839,800-acre) area of the Cordillera Blanca above 4000 m (13,200 ft). Nature watching, photography, hiking and mountain climbing are all popular pastimes here, based out of the tourist city of Huaraz, in the heart of the valley. The rainy season is from October to April.

Huayllay National Sanctuary

This small reserve of 6815 hectares (16,833 acres) protects a unique area of geological interest. Located south of the town of Cerro de Pasco and near the Junín National Reserve, its immense rock formations are striking and picturesque.

Junín National Reserve

This scenic reserve (21,460 hectares, 53,000 acres) includes prairie-like pampas and the beautiful Lake Junín (4100 m, 13,530 ft elevation) in the wet puna south of the town of Cerro de Pasco. Here it is easy to see many of the highland plant and animal species typical of the puna habitat. The Puna Grebe is a bird species that occurs nowhere else, and if you are persistent and lucky, you may see it among the reeds surrounding the lake. Many North American shorebirds use this area as a stopover in migration or winter here. Access to the reserve is relatively easy by car from the town of Junín on the main trans-Andean highway, between Lima and Tingo María. A boat and motor can be arranged to better see much of the aquatic flora and fauna.

Pampas Galeras National Reserve

The Peruvian center and administrative headquarters for the conservation program known as the Vicuña Project, this protected area (6500 hectares, 16,055 acres) has the largest Vicuña (small wild relative of the Alpaca; Plate 94) population in the world. This dry puna area is at 4000 m (13,200 ft) elevation, and it also protects many other highland species of plants and animals. You can get here by a three-hour car drive via the 64-km (40-mile) gravel road from the coastal town of Nazca.

Ampay National Sanctuary

Established in 1987, this reserve of 3635 hectares (8978 acres) protects large forests of the tall, primitive conifer tree, *Podocarpus* (page 19), and extensive stands of the bromeliad plant, *Puya raimondii* (similar to the Puya species shown on p. 18, but larger), in the puna highlands near the town of Abancay. This reserve is most easily approached from the city of Cuzco, 90 km (56 miles) to the east.

Cuzco Area

This large city at 3475 m (11,400 ft) elevation is a center of tourist activity. Although much of the attraction of the city is because of its cultural heritage as the ancient Incan capital, considerable natural wonders abound here as well. From the city center plaza, with hundreds of swifts flying over, to the tours of nearby Incan ruins of Sacsayhuamán, Puca Pucara and Ollantaytambo, the area sports many plants and animals that are typical of the dry puna.

Arequipa Area

The "White" city, Arequipa, at 2325 m (7630 ft), sits below an imposing volcano, El Misti (5822 m, 19,100 ft, high). Arequipa is an excellent base from which to visit several nearby sites for nature watching in the highlands as well as for descents into neighboring coastal habitats. Just east of Arequipa, on the road to Chiguata, is the Aguada Blanca Dam and its artificial lake. Farther west on this road is Lake Salinas, and together these two areas form the Salinas and Aguada Blanca National Reserve. This area, at 3900 m (12,800 ft) elevation, includes extensive puna habitat, where Vicuña (Plate 94) and small numbers of Guanaco graze, as well as an immense saline lake, where flamingos can be seen. East of this reserve, toward the Chilean border, are the only areas in the Peruvian puna where the ostrich-like Lesser Rhea (Plate 31) can be seen. About 180 km (112 miles) north of Arequipa is the awesome Colca Valley with mountain vistas, cultural interests and some wildlife.

Puno Area

A major city on the shores of Lake Titicaca, Puno is at 3827 m (12,629 ft) elevation. Several reserves protect the cultural traditions and natural habitats of the area. The Titicaca National Reserve has two sections that include most of the north end of the lake and adjacent puna habitat, much of which is best seen by boats chartered out of Puno. The Umayo Ecological Reserve protects an isolated lake south of Puno with extensive wet puna habitat as well as the archaeological ruins of Sillustani. You can see this area by car and a boat that ferries visitors out to an island in the middle of Lake Umayo.

Eastern Slope of the Andes (ESA)

Tabaconas Namballe National Sanctuary

One of Perú's newest national reserves, with an area of 29,500 hectares (72,865 acres), it is near the southern boundary of Ecuador and protects high altitude cloud forests and endangered animals such as the Spectacled Bear (Plate 88) and perhaps Mountain Tapir.

Río Abiseo National Park

Encompassing 274,520 hectares (678,064 acres), this park includes cloud forest throughout most of the Río Abiseo watershed. It is considered so critical for conservation's sake that in 1990 it was declared a World Heritage Site by UNESCO. It is home to the highly endemic and endangered Yellow-tailed Woolly Monkey (Plate 86) as well as to a pre-Incan archaeological center called the Great Pajatén. Access is very difficult and involves mounting an expedition from the coastal city of Trujillo.

Tingo María Area

A major city situated picturesquely in the Río Huallaga valley at 650 m (2145 ft) elevation, Tingo María is surrounded by cloud forest habitat. Tingo María National Park (18,000 hectares; 44,460 acres), near the city, contains areas representative of the east slope habitats of central Perú. The Cueva de las Lechuzas, or Oilbird Cave, is the most readily accessible nesting and roosting site for Oilbirds (Plate 42) in the country, and it is only 8 km (5 miles) from the city center. Disruption from violent revolutionary groups and an ideal cocaine-growing climate, however, made the area around the city of Tingo María off limits to tourists during much of the 1980s and 1990s. When this city again becomes safe for tourists, it will be a wonderful base from which to visit Tingo María National Park as well as other reserves on the main road east to Pucallpa, such as the Alexander von Humboldt National Forest, Cordillera Azul, Divisoria trail, and the narrow pass through an attractive canyon called El Boquerón del Padre Abad. On the central highway south and west toward Huánuco, the incredible Carpish Mountain pass enters bamboo stands and Andean temperate forest.

Yanachanga-Chemillén National Park

This large and remote park includes 122,000 hectares (301,340 acres) of mid-elevation cloud forest that reach down to the upper parts of the Amazonian lowlands, near Oxapampa, in the Department of Pasco.

Machu Picchu Historical Sanctuary and Natural Monument

Probably one of the best-known tourist sites in Perú, the idyllic Machu Picchu area of 32,592 hectares (80,502 acres) presents possibilities for so much cultural and natural sensory input that overload is a distinct possibility. From Andean Condors (Plate 33) and Cocks-of-the-rock (Plate 62) to mystical monuments of Incan divinity, Machu Picchu is a high priority for any tourist visiting Perú. At only 2300 m (7590 ft), it is a welcome relief from the higher altitude of Cuzco, the traditional access point for this sanctuary. The train ride from Cuzco takes in 112 km (70 miles) of mountain views. For the more adventurous, walking the old "Inca Trail" from Ollantaytambo is the only way to approach and appreciate Machu Picchu. This trail is 40 km (25 miles) long, and takes three or four days. Lodging is available at Machu Picchu for those on the train who want to stay more than a day.

Amazon Lowlands (AMA)

Iquitos Area

Iquitos, a large city in the northern Amazonian lowlands (at 106 m, 350 ft elevation) of Perú, can only be reached by air or boat, because no roads enter it from the outside world. South of Iquitos, the Marañon and Ucayali Rivers flow together to form the Amazon River. Iquitos is an important center of much of the country's ecotourism industry. Private lodges to the north and south provide comfortable access to extensive marsh, flooded forest, and tierra firme forest, and to what we consider the best canopy walkway in the Neotropics (at ACEER, the Amazon Center for Environmental Education and Research). The largest conservation unit in Perú, the Pacaya Samiria National Reserve (2,080,000 hectares; 5,137,600 acres), is 100 km (60 miles) southwest of Iquitos. It can be explored by chartered river boat out of Iquitos. With a mean annual rainfall of nearly 3 m (10 ft), the rainy season in this area runs from June through September and the rainier season is the rest of the year.

Manu National Park

Another immense park, Manu has 1,532,806 hectares (3,786,308 acres) of pristine habitat that ranges from puna on the Cordillera Oriental (4500 m, 14,850 ft) down to wet tropical forest in the Amazonian lowlands (240 m, 800 ft). In terms of biodiversity, this park has some of the highest numbers of plant and animal species in the world. Over 1000 species of birds, 15,000 species of plants, and 1000 species of butterflies have been recorded within the park's boundaries! Large areas have been so seldom hunted by people that monkeys and other large mammals are common and relatively unafraid. It is probably one of the best places in Perú to see Jaguar (Plate 90) – although even here it is not guaranteed. Several ecotourist lodges are located in special areas just outside the park, but access is difficult, with two-day motorized canoe trips necessary from access points below Cuzco or from the town of Puerto Maldonado.

Puerto Maldonado Area

The largest urban center in Perú's southern lowlands (256 m, 840 ft, elevation), with direct commercial flights from Lima, the frontier town of Puerto Maldonado is maturing both in its attitude and facilities for ecotravellers. It is the main access point for travel to several nearby natural areas – private and national. The Tambopata-Candamo Reserve Zone was established in 1990. This lowland reserve of 1,478,942 hectares (3,652,987 acres) is almost as large as Manu National Park and is almost as diverse in species of animals and plants. It includes most of the watershed of the Río Tambopata, with more than 900 species of birds, 20,000 species of plants and 1200 species of butterflies – and remember, unlike Manu, this reserve includes few highland habitats. In 1995, a third of the Tambopata-Candamo Reserve Zone was combined with The Pampas del Heath National Sanctuary, an area of unique grasslands habitat, to form the Bahuaja-Sonene National Park (537,053 hectares, 1,364,115 acres). Isolated patches of remnant marsh and grassland here are the home to species of plants and animals such as the Maned Wolf and Marsh Deer, otherwise known only from the extensive pampas of Bolivia and Brazil, more than 400 km (250 miles) to the south.

Chapter 4

HOW TO USE THIS BOOK: ECOLOGY AND NATURAL HISTORY

- *What is Natural History?*
- *What is Ecology and What Are Ecological Interactions?*
- *How to Use This Book*
  Information in the Family Profiles
  Information in the Color Plate Sections

What is Natural History?

The purpose of this book is to provide ecotravellers with sufficient information to identify many common plant and animal species and to learn about them and the families to which they belong. Information on the lives of plants and animals is known generally as *natural history*. More specifically, we can define it as the study of plants' and animals' natural habits, including especially their ecology, distribution, classification, and behavior. This kind of information is important to know for a variety of reasons: Researchers need to know natural history as background on the species they study, and wildlife managers and conservationists need natural history information because their decisions about managing animal populations must be partially based on it. More relevant for the ecotraveller, natural history is simply interesting. People who appreciate plants and animals typically like to watch them, touch them when appropriate, and know as much about them as they can.

What is Ecology and What Are Ecological Interactions?

Ecology is the branch of the biological sciences that studies the interactions between living things (animals and plants) and their physical environment and with each other. Broadly interpreted, these interactions take into account most everything we find fascinating about plants and animals – what nutrients they need and how they get them, how and when they breed, how they survive the rigors of extreme climates, why they are large or small, or dully or brightly colored, and many other facets of their lives.

A plant or animal's life, in some ways, is the sum of its interactions with other plants and animals – members of its own species and others – and with its environment. Of particular interest are the numerous and diverse ecological interactions that occur between different species. Most can be placed into one of several general categories, based on how two species affect each other when they interact; they can have positive, negative, or neutral (that is, no) effects on each other. The relationship terms below are used in the book to describe the natural history of various plants and animals.

Competition is an ecological relationship in which neither of the interacting species benefits. Competition occurs when individuals of the same or different species use the same resource – a certain type of food, nesting holes in trees, etc. – and that resource is in insufficient supply (*limiting resource*) to meet all their needs. As a result, both species are less successful than they could be in the absence of the interaction (that is, if the other were not present).

Predation is an ecological interaction in which one species, the *predator*, benefits, and the other species, the *prey*, is harmed. Most people think of predation as something like a mountain lion eating a deer, and they are correct; but predation also includes such things as a wasp killing a caterpillar or an insect eating a seed.

Parasitism, like predation, is a relationship between two species in which one benefits and one is harmed. The difference is that in a predatory relationship, one animal kills and eats the other, but in a parasitic one, the parasite feeds slowly on the *host* species and usually does not kill it. There are internal parasites, like protozoans and many kinds of worms, and external parasites, such as leeches, ticks, and mites. Even a deer munching on the leaves of a bush can be considered a type of parasitism.

Some of the most intriguing ecological relationships are *mutualisms* – interactions in which both participants benefit. Plants and their pollinators engage in mutualistic interactions. A bee species, for instance, obtains a food resource, nectar or pollen, from a plant's flower; the plant it visits benefits because it is able to complete its reproductive cycle when the bee transports pollen to another plant. In Perú, numerous plants, such as the undergrowth bush *Maieta* (p.25), exhibit mutualism with the ants that live in them: the ants obtain food (the plants produce nectar for them) and shelter from the plant and in return, the ants defend the plants from plant-eating insects. Sometimes the species have interacted so long that they now cannot live without each other; theirs is an *obligate* mutualism. For instance, termites (Plate 96) cannot by themselves digest wood. Rather, it is the single-celled animals, protozoans, that live in their gut that produce the digestive enzymes that digest wood. At this point in their evolutionary histories, neither the termites nor their internal helpers can live alone.

Commensalism is a relationship in which one species benefits but the other is not affected in any obvious way. For example, epiphytes (p. 16), such as orchids and bromeliads, that grow on tree trunks and branches obtain from trees some shelf space to grow on, but, as far as anyone knows, neither hurt nor help the trees. A classic example of a commensal animal is the Remora, a fish that attaches itself with a suction cup on its head to a shark, then feeds on scraps of food the shark leaves behind. Remora are *commensals*, not parasites – they neither harm nor help sharks, but they benefit greatly by associating with sharks. Cattle Egrets (Plate 24) are commensals – these birds follow cattle, eating insects and other small animals that flush from cover as the cattle move about their pastures; the cattle, as far as we know, couldn't care one way or the other (unless they are concerned about that certain loss of dignity that occurs when the egrets perch not only near them, but on them as well).

A term many people know that covers some of these ecological interactions is *symbiosis*, which means living together. Usually this term suggests that the two interacting species do not harm one another; therefore, mutualisms and commensalisms are the symbiotic relationships discussed here.

How to Use This Book

The information here on animals is divided into two sections: the *plates*, which include artists' color renderings of various species together with brief identifying and location information; and the *family profiles*, with natural history information on the families to which the pictured animals belong. The best way to identify and learn about Peruvian animals may be to scan the illustrations before a trip to become familiar with the kinds of animals you are likely to encounter. Then when you spot an animal, you may recognize its general type or family, and can find the appropriate pictures and profiles quickly. In other words, it is more efficient, upon spotting a bird, to be thinking, "Gee, that looks like a flycatcher," and be able to flip to that part of the book, than to be thinking, "Gee, that bird is partly yellow" and then, to identify it, flipping through all the animal pictures, searching for yellow birds.

Information in the Family Profiles

Classification, Distribution, Morphology

The first paragraphs of each profile generally provide information on the family's classification (or *taxonomy*), geographic distribution, and *morphology* (shape, size, and coloring). Classification information is provided because it is how scientists separate plants and animals into related groups, and often it enhances our appreciation of various species to know these relationships. You may have been exposed to classification levels sometime during your education, but if you are a bit rusty, a quick review may help: *Kingdom* Animalia: all the animal species detailed in the book are members of the animal kingdom. *Phylum* Chordata, *Subphylum* Vertebrata: all the species in the book with backbones and an internal skeleton are vertebrates. The arthropods, including insects, spiders, and crabs, lack a backbone or internal skeleton, and they are placed in the broad category of Invertebrata. *Class*: the book covers several vertebrate classes: Amphibia (amphibians), Reptilia (reptiles), Aves (birds), and Mammalia (mammals); and invertebrate classes: Insecta (insects), Arachnida (spiders), Decapoda (crabs). *Order*: each class is divided into several orders, the members of each order sharing many characteristics. For example, one of the mammal orders is Carnivora, the carnivores, which includes mammals with teeth specialized for meat-eating – dogs, cats, bears, raccoons, weasels. *Family*: Families of animals are subdivisions of each order that contain closely-related species that are very similar in form, ecology, and behavior. The family Canidae, for instance, contains all the dog-like mammals – coyote, wolf, fox, dog. Animal family names end in *-dae*; subfamilies, subdivisions of families, end in *-nae*. *Genus*: Further subdivisions; within each genus are grouped species that are very closely related – they are all considered to have evolved from a common ancestor. *Species*: the lowest classification level; all members of a species are similar enough to be able to breed and produce living, fertile offspring.

Example:	Classification of the Gray-breasted Mountain-Toucan (Plate 54):
Kingdom:	Animalia, with more than 2 million species
Phylum:	Chordata, Subphylum Vertebrata, with about 47,000 species
Class:	Aves (birds), with about 9000 species
Order:	Piciformes, with about 400 species; includes honeyguides, woodpeckers, barbets, and toucans
Family:	Ramphastidae, with about 40 species; all the toucans
Genus:	*Andigena*, with 4 species; one group of toucans
Species:	*Andigena hypoglauca*, known to its friends as Gray-breasted Mountain-Toucan

Some of the family profiles in the book cover animal orders, while others describe families or subfamilies.

Species' distributions vary tremendously. Some species are found only in very limited areas, whereas others range over several continents. Distributions can be described in a number of ways. An animal can be said to be *Old World* or *New World*; the former refers to the regions of the globe that Europeans knew of before Columbus – Europe, Asia, Africa; and the latter refers to the Western Hemisphere – North, Central, and South America. Perú falls within the part of the world called the *Neotropics* by biogeographers – scientists who study the geographic distributions of living things. A Neotropical species is one that occurs within southern Mexico, Central America, South America, and/or the Caribbean Islands. The terms *tropical*, *temperate*, and *arctic* refer to climate regions of the Earth; the boundaries of these zones are determined by lines of latitude (and ultimately, by the position of the sun with respect to the Earth's surface). The tropics, always warm, are the regions of the world that fall within the belt from 23.5 degrees North latitude (the Tropic of Cancer) to 23.5 degrees South latitude (the Tropic of Capricorn). The world's temperate zones, with more seasonal climates, extend from 23.5 degrees North and South latitude to the Arctic and Antarctic Circles, at 66.5 degrees North and South. Arctic regions, more or less always cold, extend from 66.5 degrees North and South to the poles. The position of Perú with respect to these zones is shown in Map 3.

Several terms help define a species' distribution and describe how it attained its distribution: *Range*. The particular geographic area occupied by a species. *Native or Indigenous*. Occurring naturally in a particular place. *Introduced*. Occurring in a particular place owing to peoples' intentional or unintentional assistance with transportation, usually from one continent to another; the opposite of native. For instance, pheasants were initially brought to North America from Europe/Asia for hunting, Europeans brought rabbits and foxes to Australia for

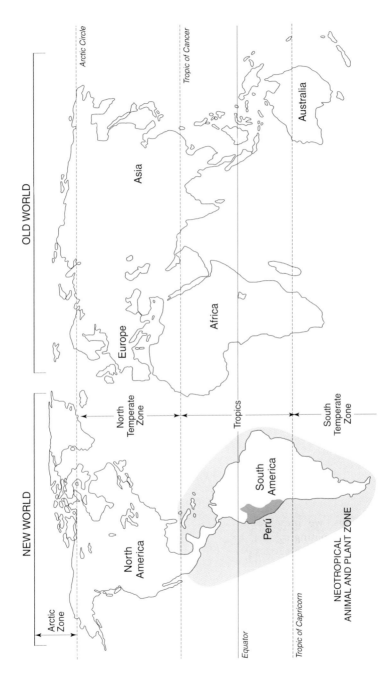

Map 3 Map of the Earth showing the position of Perú; Old World and New World zones; tropical, temperate, and arctic regions; and the Neotropical animal life zone.

sport, and the British brought European Starlings and House Sparrows to North America. *Endemic.* A species, a genus, an entire family, etc., that is found in a particular place and nowhere else. The White-winged Guan is endemic to dry wooded valleys of northwestern Perú. Galápagos Finches are endemic to the Galápagos Islands; nearly all the reptile and mammal species of Madagascar are endemics; all species are endemic to Earth (as far as we know). *Cosmopolitan.* A species that is widely distributed throughout the world.

Ecology and Behavior

In these sections, we describe some of what is known about the basic activities pursued by each group. Much of the information relates to when and where animals are usually active, what they eat, and how they forage.

Activity Location – *Terrestrial* animals pursue life and food on the ground. *Arboreal* animals pursue life and food in trees or shrubs. Many arboreal animals have *prehensile* tails, long and muscular, which they can wrap around tree branches to support themselves as they hang to feed or to move about more efficiently. *Cursorial* refers to animals that are adapted for running along the ground. *Fossorial* means living and moving underground.

Activity Time – *Nocturnal* means active at night. *Diurnal* means active during the day. *Crepuscular* refers to animals that are active at dusk and/or dawn.

Food Preferences – Although animal species can usually be assigned to one of the feeding categories below, most eat more than one type of food. Most frugivorous birds, for instance, also nibble on the occasional insect, and carnivorous mammals occasionally eat plant materials.

> *Herbivores* are predators that prey on plants.
> *Carnivores* are predators that prey on animals.
> *Insectivores* eat insects.
> *Granivores* eat seeds.
> *Frugivores* eat fruit.
> *Nectarivores* eat nectar.
> *Piscivores* eat fish.
> *Omnivores* eat a variety of things.
> *Detritivores*, such as vultures, eat dead stuff.

Breeding

In these sections, we present basics on each group's breeding particulars, including type of mating system, special breeding behaviors, durations of egg incubation or *gestation* (pregnancy), as well as information on nests, eggs, and young.

Mating Systems – A *monogamous* mating system is one in which one male and one female establish a pair-bond and contribute fairly evenly to each breeding effort. In *polygamous* systems, individuals of one of the sexes have more than one mate (that is, they have harems): in *polygynous* systems, one male mates with several females, and in *polyandrous* systems, one female mates with several males.

Condition of young at birth – *Altricial* young are born in a relatively undeveloped state, usually naked of fur or feathers, eyes closed, and unable to feed themselves, walk, or run from predators. *Precocial* young are born in a more developed state, eyes open, and soon able to walk and perhaps feed themselves.

Notes

These sections provide interesting bits and pieces of information that do not fit elsewhere in the account, including associated folklore.

Status

These sections comment on the conservation status of each group, including information on relative rarity or abundance, factors contributing to population declines, and special conservation measures that have been implemented. Because this book concentrates on animals that ecotravellers are most likely to see – that is, on more common ones – few of the profiled species are immediately threatened with extinction. The definitions of the terms that we use to describe degrees of threat to various species are these: *Endangered* species are known to be in imminent danger of extinction throughout their range, and are highly unlikely to survive unless strong conservation measures are taken; populations of endangered species generally are very small, so they are rarely seen. *Threatened* species are known to be undergoing rapid declines in the sizes of their populations; unless conservation measures are enacted, and the causes of the population declines identified and halted, these species are likely to move to endangered status in the near future. *Vulnerable to threat*, or *near-threatened,* are species that, owing to their habitat requirements or limited distributions, and based on known patterns of habitat destruction, are highly likely to be threatened in the near future. Several organizations publish lists of threatened and endangered species, but agreement among the lists is not absolute.

Where appropriate, we also include threat classifications from the Convention on International Trade in Endangered Species (CITES) and the United States Endangered Species Act (ESA) classifications. CITES is a global cooperative agreement to protect threatened species on a worldwide scale by regulating international trade in wild animals and plants among the 130 or so participating countries. Regulated species are listed in CITES Appendices, with trade in those species being strictly regulated by required licenses and documents. CITES Appendix I lists endangered species; all trade in them is prohibited. Appendix II lists threatened/vulnerable species, those that are not yet endangered but may soon be; trade in them is strictly regulated. Appendix III lists species that are protected by laws of individual countries that have signed the CITES agreements. The USA's Endangered Species Act works in a similar way – by listing endangered and threatened species, and, among other provisions, strictly regulating trade in those animals. The International Union for Conservation of Nature (IUCN) maintains a "Red List" of threatened and endangered species that often is more broad-based and inclusive than these other lists, and we refer to the Red List in some of the accounts.

Information in the Color Plate Sections

Pictures

Among amphibians, reptiles, and mammals, males and females of a species usually look alike, although often there are size differences. For many species of birds, however, the sexes differ in color pattern and even anatomical features. If only one individual is pictured, you may assume that male and female of that species look exactly or almost alike; when there are major sex differences, both male and female are depicted. The animals shown on an individual plate, in most cases, have been drawn to the correct scale relative to each other. A note about amphibian and reptile illustrations: many of Perú's amphibians and reptiles are very variable in their coloring and color patterns, making illustrating them particularly difficult. Also, for some species, very few good photographs exist from which an artist can work. The practical result of this is that some of the amphibians and reptiles you find in the wild may not look exactly like their pictures in this book.

Name

We provide the common English name for each profiled species and the scientific, or Latin, name. Often, in Perú, the local name for a given species varies regionally. For some species, there is no agreed-upon Spanish name; for a few, there is no English name.

ID

Here we provide brief descriptive information that, together with the pictures, will enable you to identify most of the animals you see. The length given for an amphibian is the distance from the tip of its snout to its vent (the opening at the rear of the animal through which wastes, and eggs or sperm, exit); therefore, frogs' long legs are not included in their reported lengths. For reptiles, we give total lengths, including tails, unless we mention that the tail is not included. For mammals, size measures given are generally the lengths of the head and body, but do not include tails. Birds are measured from tip of bill to end of tail. For birds commonly seen flying, such as seabirds and hawks, we provide wingspan (wing tip to wing tip) measurements, if known. For most birds, we use to describe their sizes the terms: *very large* (more than 1 m, 3.3 ft); *large* (49 cm to 1 m, 1.6 to 3.3 ft); *mid-sized* (20 to 48 cm, 8 in to 1.5 ft); *small* (10 to 19 cm, 3.5 to 7 in); and *tiny* (less than 10 cm, 3.5 in).

Habitat/Region

In these sections we list the regions and habitat types in which each species occurs and provide symbols for the habitat types each species prefers. A species said to occur on the *Andean slopes* occurs in the area between the higher mountains and the coastal lowlands to the west or the Amazon region to the east (see Map 2, p. 37). In general, *low elevation* refers to between 0 and 500 m (0 and 1600 ft) above sea level; *middle elevation* means between 500 and 1200 m (1600 and 4000 ft); and *higher elevation* means greater than 1200 m (4000 ft).

Explanation of habitat symbols:

= Lowland wet forest.

= Lowland dry forest.

= Highland forest and cloud forest. Includes middle elevation and higher elevation wet forests and cloud forests.

= Highland puna (grassy areas above tree-line).

= Forest edge and streamside. Some species typically are found along forest edges or near or along streams; these species prefer semi-open areas rather than dense, closed, interior parts of forests.

Also included here: open woodlands, tree plantations, and shady gardens.

= Pastureland, non-tree plantations, savannah (grassland with scattered trees and shrubs), gardens without shade trees, roadside. Species found in these habitats prefer very open areas.

= Desert. A few hardy species occur in the open sandy flats and bare dunes of the coastal desert between the ocean and the first hills rising into the western slope of the Andes.

= Coastal hills (lomas) and mid-elevation semi-desert habitats (vertiente) of the western slopes above 1000 m (3300 ft).

= Freshwater. For species typically found in or near lakes, streams, rivers, marshes, swamps.

= Saltwater/marine. For species usually found in or near the ocean, rocky intertidal area, or ocean beaches.

REGIONS (see Map 2, p. 37):

TDF   Tropical Dry Forest
CDL   Coastal Desert Lowlands (*La Costa*)
WSV   West Slope Vertiente and Lomas (semi-desert fog vegetation)
HAP   Highlands and Puna (*La Sierra*)
ESA   Eastern Slope of the Andes (cloud forest)
AMA   Amazon Lowlands (*La Selva*)

Example

Plate 54d

Gray-breasted Mountain-Toucan
Andigena hypoglauca
ID: Large (41 cm, 1.3 ft); blue-gray breast; large orange bill with yellow square at base and remainder of lower mandible black.

HABITAT: Cloud forest canopy and forest edge between 2700 and 3400 m (9000 and 11,200 ft).

REGION: ESA

Chapter 5

AMPHIBIANS

by Martha L. Crump

Introduction

We know from the fossil record that during the middle of the Paleozoic Era (the Devonian period, about 380 million years ago), fish with lungs that could breathe air were common in freshwater lakes. These lunged fish had fins in the shape of stubby lobes. They probably used these fins to support themselves on the bottoms of their ponds while waiting for prey to swim by, and to waddle about on land during times when their ponds dried. Both of these characteristics, lungs and lobed fins, allowed the fish to survive for brief periods on land. About 365 million years ago, these fish evolved into the first *tetrapods* (terrestrial vertebrates) – the *amphibians*. As you would expect, this evolution involved drastic changes in support and locomotor systems, feeding mechanisms, and breathing organs, to name but a few modifications.

The word amphibian comes from the Greek *amphibios,* meaning "living a double life," in reference to the fact that most amphibians spend part of their lives in water and part on land. Approximately 4700 species of living amphibians are known today. Biologists separate amphibians into three main groups. The largest group, with about 4100 species, is the *frogs* (Order Anura, "without tails", which includes *toads*), followed by the *salamanders* (Order Caudata, the "tailed" amphibians) with about 430 species, and a little-known group, the *caecilians* (suh-SEAL-ians, Order Gymnophiona), with approximately 170 species. Three hundred and fifteen species of amphibians have been reported from Perú: 297 frogs and toads, 3 salamanders, and 15 caecilians.

General Characteristics and Classification of Amphibians

Most amphibians retain the reproductive pattern of their fish ancestors and return to water to breed because their eggs dry out easily. Most frogs and toads have *external fertilization*; that is, as the female releases her eggs, the male releases sperm onto them – outside the body. Only a few species have internal fertilization. In contrast, most salamanders and all caecilians have *internal fertilization*. Most amphibians pass through the aquatic phase of their "two-world" lifestyle only as eggs and free-swimming larvae (larval frogs and toads are called *tadpoles;* larval salamanders and caecilians are just called *larvae*). Some amphibians, however, are fully aquatic as adults. Still other species lay their eggs in moist areas on land and never enter standing water. Water is essential for all amphibians because, in addition to lungs, they breathe through their skin. In order to do this, their skin must be kept moist. Thus, even species that are fully terrestrial in all phases of their lives require a humid environment.

Most *salamanders* look like lizards, with four limbs and a long tail. They are easily distinguished from lizards, however, by their skin. Salamanders have skin that is kept moist by mucus, whereas lizards have scales. A few aquatic species of salamanders have four tiny legs, and several have only the two front legs. Salamanders range in size from among the smallest known terrestrial vertebrates, with body lengths of less than 1.5 cm (0.6 in), to a giant Asian species that grows to 2 m (6.5 ft). Because their skin is susceptible to drying out, salamanders inhabit moist environments. Familiar salamanders of North America and Europe typically live on the ground, hidden under logs when they're not active. They forage for invertebrate prey such as insects, worms, and spiders in the leaf litter and under rocks or decaying logs. Many live near streams in moist forests. Some species, however, are completely aquatic, spending their entire lives in swamps, ponds, lakes, and rivers. Others live in trees (*arboreal*) or underground (*fossorial*). Most salamanders secrete poisons from glands in the skin as a defense against predators. Some of the most toxic species are brightly colored to warn potential predators of their toxicity. About 90% of all salamanders have internal fertilization. In these species, males produce packets of sperm called *spermatophores*. In most species, during courtship males deposit spermatophores onto the substrate, then lead the females over them, at which point they are picked up into the females' bodies.

Salamanders are found mostly in North America and in northern Europe and Asia. One family, however, the Plethodontidae, is common and diverse in Central America, and a few species of this family occur in South America. Salamanders are not known from tropical regions of the Old World. The three species known from Perú are all *lungless salamanders* (Family Plethodontidae). Plethodontidae is the largest salamander family, with nearly 270 species in North, Central and South America; oddly, one genus also occurs in southern

Europe and Sardinia. In the absence of lungs, all respiration in plethodontid salamanders takes place through the skin. Two of the species in Perú live in lowland rainforest; the third is found at elevations of about 1000 m (3300 ft). The two lowland salamanders have heavily webbed front and hind feet; they are active at night, moving around on leaves up to 2 m (6.5 ft) above the ground, where they forage for insects and other small, moving prey. During the day they sleep in moist leaf litter on the ground. The higher elevation species is very unusual for *Bolitoglossa* salamanders in having small feet and very small toes; the species is thought to be mainly terrestrial. Although little is known about reproduction in Peruvian salamanders, they probably do it like others in the subfamily. If so, they have internal fertilization via spermatophores, their eggs are deposited on land, and the females guard the eggs, which develop directly into tiny salamanders. The AMAZONIAN SALAMANDER (Plate 1), ranging in color from dark gray to reddish brown, is the largest of the three P e r u v i a n salamanders and is found in lowland rainforests. Individuals reach lengths of 9 cm (3.6 in), though most are smaller.

Most people have never heard of *caecilians*, and fewer still have ever seen a live one. Caecilians resemble large earthworms with rings around their bodies. They lack limbs throughout their lives, and they either have short tails or none at all. Their bodies feel slimy because they are covered with mucus. In fact, it is very difficult to hold onto one! Caecilians are poorly known because they are found exclusively in tropical regions (in Africa, Asia, and Central and South America) and because they are difficult to find. Caecilians live either underground or in water. The only time you are likely to see the underground ones is following heavy rain, when the soil becomes saturated and they rise to the surface. Because their eyes are covered with skin or bone, caecilians are essentially blind. Caecilians have sensory organs called *tentacles*, small fleshy projections located between the eyes and the nostrils. The tentacles function in picking up chemical stimuli and thus help in locating insects, worms, and other ground-dwelling prey. Of the species for which the mode of reproduction is known, about 75% have internal fertilization of eggs that undergo development inside the mother's body; the young are born as tiny but fully formed baby caecilians. Although the other 25% of the species for which reproductive patterns are known also have internal fertilization, they have aquatic larvae. The SOUTH AMERICAN CAECILIAN (Plate 1), a terrestrial burrower, reaches 50 cm (20 in) in length and about 1.5 cm (0.6 in) in diameter; the body is blue with lighter blue rings. The eyes are visible through the thin skin, and are slightly raised at the surface.

Frogs and *toads* are found just about everywhere in the world except in some extremely dry deserts, on some islands, and near the North and South poles. All frogs and toads have four limbs as adults; their rear limbs are much larger than their front limbs. Most of them are strong jumpers and can cover long distances. Some brightly colored species have poisonous skin secretions that protect them from predators. Others have toxins, but are dull in color. Males use mating calls to attract females during the breeding season; each species has its own particular call, and females respond only to that one type of call. Almost all adult frogs and toads eat insects, spiders, and other invertebrates; a few species eat other frogs and even small lizards, snakes, birds, and mammals. Presumably all Peruvian species breed via external fertilization. During mating, the male mounts the back of the female and holds on to her tightly with his front legs (*amplexus*). As she releases her eggs, he releases sperm over them. Although most species abandon their eggs, some have elaborate forms of parental care. Most species have aquatic tadpoles; in some species the eggs develop directly into tiny froglets. The 297 species of frogs and toads known from Perú are diverse in body shape, size, color, and habits (see Family Profiles).

Seeing Amphibians in Perú

With 315 of the Earth's 4700 living amphibians, Perú has nearly 7% of the world's species. With luck and perseverance, you could see 30 or more species in a few weeks. The specific examples discussed and profiled in this chapter should allow you to identify any amphibian you find, at least to its family or genus. One of the reasons ecotourists enjoy learning about amphibians is that, unlike with birds and mammals, it is often possible to watch and photograph the animals up close. In fact, because many species are small, you need to get close to be able to identify them. For more information on Peruvian amphibians, a great source is *Guide to the Reptiles and Amphibians of the Peruvian Lower Amazon* by W. W. Lamar.

Finding amphibians is relatively easy. One way is simply to search the ground in the forest during the day, especially near streams, ponds, or other moist areas, and look for frogs and toads hopping about. A second way is potentially more rewarding and a lot of fun: with a flashlight, carefully search the tops of leaves at night up to 2 m (6.5 ft) above the ground. With some patience, you are likely to encounter at least a few nocturnal, arboreal frogs and salamanders. You'll also find some bizarre-looking insects! Good places to try this include road edges, along forest trails, or in any forest edge area. By far the best way to see a high diversity of frogs at night is to locate small temporary ponds along forest edges, in swampy areas, along the edges of roads, or near rivers. Up to a dozen species might be calling at one time at some temporary ponds. Many species call from leaves or branches over the water, others while floating in the water, others from the ground next to the pond. When large numbers of frogs are calling, such *breeding aggregations* make a loud racket that can be heard from some distance away. If you find a shallow pond during the day, the frogs will be sleeping – some on leaves over the water, others on the ground. Search for eggs and tadpoles in the water, and then return with a flashlight after dark to look for adults. Look carefully, for even at a pond crawling with frogs, many will blend in with their surroundings and be difficult to locate.

Family Profiles

1. Toads

Although many people think of frogs and *toads* as two distinct groups, all toads are frogs just as all poodles are dogs. The common name "toad" is used for species in several families of frogs, but the main family of toads is the Bufonidae, a worldwide group of about 380 species. Most *bufonid* toads, especially those in the genus *Bufo*, have thick, dry skin that enables them to live in dry habitats. Toads typically have short, squat, heavy bodies with relatively short limbs, and broad rounded snouts. Many species have distinct bony crests between the eyes. Bufonids lack teeth, an unusual condition among frogs. The majority are colored dull olive to dark brown, although there are exceptions, such as the Day-Glo orange GOLDEN TOAD, *Bufo periglenes*. Most toads have scattered wart-like bumps on the skin of the upper surface of the body. Most also have a pair of prominent, large *parotoid glands* on the shoulder area, one behind each eye. Toads range from tiny species less than 2 cm (0.8 in) in length as adults, to the COLOMBIAN GIANT TOAD, *Bufo blombergi*, which grows to 25 cm (10 in).

Thirty-two species of toads occur in Perú, distributed from the coastal desert lowlands (e.g., PERÚ COAST TOAD, Plate 1) to the dry highlands (e.g., WARTY TOAD, Plate 1) to the Amazonian lowlands on the other side of the Andes Mountains (e.g., MARINE TOAD, Plate 1). Most Peruvian toads resemble the familiar species found in the United States and Europe, but there is one group that bears little resemblance to their more ordinary cousins. These are the *stubfoot toads* of the genus *Atelopus*, with seven species in the country. They are mostly found at higher elevations on the Andean slopes in cloud forest. Four of the Peruvian species of stubfoot toads have long slender bodies and limbs (such as PEBAS STUBFOOT TOAD, Plate 1); the other three have heavy-set bodies with short limbs. All have pointed snouts, and feet formed into roughly triangular-shaped paddles, often with extensive thick webbing of the toes. Many are brightly colored, with patterns of black and yellow or green. Peruvian stubfoot toads are small, ranging from 2 to 5 cm (0.8 to 2.0 in).

Natural History
Ecology and Behavior
Most toads of the genus *Bufo* are nocturnal (although some are primarily active by day) and terrestrial, spending much of their time foraging for invertebrate prey on the ground. Because of their thick dry skin, many species of toads are able to live away from water and often in very dry places. Their parotoid glands secrete a noxious, milky poison that serves as a defense against would-be predators. The dark tan or brown colors typical of most toads allow them to blend in with the soil and dead leaves on the forest floor. The MARINE TOAD inhabits open areas such as clearings, forest edges, and around human habitation, although juveniles are also found in forests. You will most likely encounter this species as it sits near lights at night, attracted by the insects flying into the light.

Most stubfoot toads have a distinctly different way of life from their more drab *Bufo* relatives. They live around mountain streams, and although they spend time on the ground they also move about or sleep on leaves or branches. The bright yellow, orange, and red colors of some species warn potential predators of potent toxins secreted by glands in the skin. Species found at high elevations are usually day-active, and many of these are darkly colored. Some of the low elevation stubfoot toads are day-active as well.

Breeding
Most bufonid toads lay their eggs in water; the eggs hatch into tadpoles. Males call from in or near the water to attract females. The male grasps the female (*amplexus*) and deposits sperm over the eggs she releases into the water. Bufonids are unique in their habit of laying eggs in two long strings, one from each ovary, as opposed to the clumps of eggs produced by most frogs. Each egg is connected

to the one before and after it, like beads in a necklace. Sometimes the strings of eggs sink to the bottom of the pond, but usually they get entwined around vegetation. The MARINE TOAD breeds in a wide variety of temporary and permanent bodies of water, each female producing 8000 to 20,000 eggs and then abandoning them. Needless to say, there is considerable predation on the tadpoles ... otherwise Perú would be overrun with toads in no time!

The breeding habits of many South American toads are poorly known, and this is especially true for stubfoot toads. These toads usually lay their strings of eggs attached to rocks or boulders in streams. Their tadpoles have a large suction-cup-like structure on the belly with which they attach themselves to rocks in swiftly flowing streams.

Notes

People from many different cultures in the world use toads as medicines. For example, 18th-century physicians used powder made from dried toads to lower a patient's fever. The Chinese make a powder from *Bufo* parotoid secretion. Called Ch'an Su, this powder is used in treating heart ailments, for drying boils and abscesses, and for healing ulcers. It seems odd that *Bufo* secretion is so widely used as medicine – until you learn that the secretion contains epinephrine (adrenaline) and norepinephrine, chemicals known to stimulate the human heart and to help the human body deal with stress.

Other uses for parotoid secretions have been invented as well. The parotoid secretions of the MARINE TOAD are often one of the ingredients of a complex soup concocted by Haitian witch doctors to induce near-death comas and to create "zombies." The secretions of COLORADO RIVER TOADS, *Bufo alvarius*, contain powerful hallucinogenic chemicals. Smoking dried parotoid secretions has become a popular pastime among some foolhardy people in Arizona and California! Anthropologists have speculated that the ancient cultures of Mesoamerica may have used toad parotoid secretions as hallucinogens during religious ceremonies, as abundant images of toads with prominent parotoid glands have been found on sculptures and engravings at archaeological sites.

Status

Unfortunately, we know little about the population status of most toads in Perú. Although no bufonid is officially listed as being endangered, anecdotal reports suggest that many populations of stubfoot toads are declining. Several species of *Bufo* from Chile, Mexico, Puerto Rico, Costa Rica, and the US mainland are considered threatened or endangered. On the other hand, the MARINE TOAD has become a pest when it has been introduced into areas where it is not native. For example, the toad has been widely introduced into sugarcane-growing areas around the world to control insect pests (thus its alternate common name, Cane Toad). But the toads don't just feed on sugarcane pests. They eat beneficial insects and other frogs. Among other places, it has become established in parts of Australia, New Guinea, Hawaii, and southern Florida (USA), where it is abundant and threatens native amphibians due both to competition and direct predation. In addition, these large toads cause the death of pet dogs and cats, which, when they attack the toads, can receive a fatal mouthful of parotoid secretion.

Profiles

Perú Coast Toad, *Bufo limensis*, Plate 1c
Marine Toad, *Bufo marinus*, Plate 1d
Warty Toad, *Bufo spinulosus*, Plate 1e
Pebas Stubfoot Toad, *Atelopus spumarius*, Plate 1f

2. Rainfrogs

The common name for frogs in the Family Leptodactylidae is *rainfrogs*. The common name stems from the fact that breeding activity is most intense following heavy rains. (This points out how relatively useless many common names are, because *most* frogs are more reproductively active following heavy rains!) Leptodactylids occur in Mexico, Central and South America, and the Caribbean; a few species are found as far north as the southern United States. With about 900 species, and new ones being discovered each year, rainfrogs make up the largest family of frogs. As a group, they have almost exactly the same wide range of body sizes that bufonid toads have. Species range from 1.2 cm to 25 cm (0.5–10 in). Perú is home to about 108 species, most of which live in restricted habitats and have small ranges within the country. Peruvian rainfrogs belong to three main groups, or subfamilies, distinguished by body size, shape, and lifestyle.

One subfamily is represented by only two species in Perú, of which one is the AMAZON HORNED FROG (Plate 2). This frog resembles a hopping mouth, with a huge head relative to its body. The large head and wide mouth allow this frog to eat other frogs, lizards, and even baby birds and small rodents when they get the chance. These robust, tan or green frogs reach lengths of nearly 12 cm (4.8 in).

A second subfamily is represented by 25 species in Perú, all of which have the unusual form of reproduction of constructing foam nests (see Breeding, below). One example is the BASIN WHITE-LIPPED FROG (Plate 2), often found calling from shallow water in clearings and in swampy areas in the forest. These terrestrial frogs are medium in size, reaching lengths of about 6 cm (2.4 in). The robust SMOKY JUNGLE FROG (Plate 2) can reach 17 cm (6.8 in) in length. Both of these species are members of the genus *Leptodactylus*, frogs that superficially resemble common North American frogs such as *bullfrogs* or *leopard frogs*. Most *Leptodactylus* frogs are tan or brown, with varying patterns of large spots or bands on a stout body. Their limbs are relatively short, the head is broad and rounded, and most species have prominent folds of skin on each side of the upper part of the body. The tips of the toes lack expanded discs; the front feet lack webbing, and the hind feet are only slightly webbed.

The third subfamily is represented by 81 species in Perú. The ones you are most likely to see belong to the genus *Eleutherodactylus*, for example the PERÚ ROBBER FROG (Plate 3). *Eleutherodactylus* frogs are generally small (2 to 7 cm, 0.8 to 2.8 in), and most are arboreal. Many species are patterned with various shades of yellow, tan, gray, brown, or black. Some have contrasting yellow, cream, orange, or red spots on the thighs or in the groin; often you can only see the spots when the frog extends its legs. Many species have color patterns that vary greatly among individuals, making identification difficult. Most *Eleutherodactylus* have distinctly expanded discs on toes of both the front and hind feet; these discs provide a firm grip on leaves and branches. The toes generally lack webbing and are slender and delicate. The genus *Eleutherodactylus* contains well over 550 of the 900 species of rainfrogs. It is the most species-rich genus of vertebrates in the world. Frogs in the genus *Telmatobius*, belonging to the same subgroup as *Eleutherodactylus*, live in a strikingly different habitat – cold water streams. The MARBLED WATER FROG (Plate 3), for example, is almost completely aquatic and lives at high elevations in puna habitat. Another *Telmatobius*, the TITICACA WATER FROG, *Telmatobius culeus*, lives at nearly 4000 m (13,000 ft) in Lake Titicaca, on the border between Perú and Bolivia.

Natural History
Ecology and Behavior
Amazon Horned Frogs spend much of the time partially buried in leaf litter. They are classic sit-and-wait predators (that is, they sit and wait for something to move rather than actively searching for prey). Hunkered in the leaf litter, they remain still until an unsuspecting prey moves nearby, at which point they lunge for the catch.

The 13 species of *Leptodactylus* rainfrogs in Perú occur mainly in lowland rainforests, where they frequent low-lying marshy areas and temporary ponds. Five species are also found in cloud forests on the eastern slope of the Andes. One species lives in tropical dry forest. All species are nocturnal and terrestrial. They are opportunistic feeders that eat just about any animal that they can catch and swallow, including many types of invertebrates and small amphibians and reptiles. Many *Leptodactylus* have noxious skin secretions (for defense), which they exude when handled. If you pick up one of these frogs, be sure to wash your hands afterwards. And don't rub your eyes! SMOKY JUNGLE FROGS often sleep by day in large holes in the ground. They emerge at night and, sitting next to their cavities for a quick retreat if needed, give their loud "whooop" calls.

Of the 47 species of *Eleutherodactylus* rainfrogs found in Perú, 19 are found in the Amazonian lowlands, 18 in the cloud forests of the eastern slopes of the Andes, and seven species are found in both of these habitats. One species is found only in puna, and another occurs in both cloud forest and puna. Many species have fairly restricted distributions. One of the exceptions is the PACHITEA ROBBER FROG (Plate 3), which is widespread in the lowland rainforests of central and southern Perú. Although some species are active in the leaf litter by day, most species are nocturnal. They perch on leaves between 1 and 3 m (3 to 10 ft) above the ground, where they feed on insects and spiders. These small frogs are themselves preyed upon by birds, bats and other small mammals, as well as by a variety of tree snakes, and even by large invertebrates such as tarantulas.

Breeding
Amazon Horned Frogs lay their eggs scattered about on the bottom of shallow ponds. This unusual pattern of egg-laying probably improves survivorship of the young, as the tadpoles readily eat eggs and hatchlings of their own species. If the eggs are spread out, there's less chance that they will all be eaten. Some of the other groups within the family, for example the genus *Telmatobius*, also lay their eggs directly in the water.

Many leptodactylids, including several genera (plural of genus) profiled here – *Edalorhina*, *Leptodactylus*, *Physalaemus*, and *Pleurodema* – suspend their eggs in a foam nest made by the male while the pair is mating. While the male holds on to the female tightly with his front legs, he kicks his feet and stirs a mixture of water and air with the eggs, mucus, and sperm. This white froth (the consistency of whipped-up egg whites), in which the eggs are suspended, floats on the surface of the water and helps protect the developing eggs from predators and from drying out. After hatching, the tadpoles swim out of the foam and complete their development in the water. Each female produces hundreds or thousands of eggs per clutch.

In contrast, *Eleutherodactylus* rainfrogs typically produce only a few large eggs (usually 5 to 60), but each has a high energy investment. These frogs breed on land in the absence of standing water. Males of most species call from low vegetation to attract the larger females. At least two species of *Eleutherodactylus* have internal fertilization (extremely rare for frogs), but as far as we know, all Peruvian species have external fertilization. The fertilized eggs are deposited in a moist, secluded place such as in a cavity of a decaying log, beneath leaf litter, or tucked between the leaves of a bromeliad plant. The eggs require about 30 to 60 days to develop, depending on the species. Eventually they hatch as tiny but fully formed froglets. This type of development is called *direct*, because there is no free-swimming larval stage.

Notes

Several species of frogs that are closely related to the MARBLED FOUR-EYED FROG (Plate 2) have two large, brightly colored glands in the groin region of the body. When frightened, these frogs often assume a defensive posture in which they lower the head and raise the back end up in the air, exposing the glands to the predator. At least to a human, these glands resemble large eyes – the eyes of a much larger animal – thus the name "four-eyed frog" for members of this genus, *Pleurodema*.

Rainfrogs, like most amphibians, have glands in their skin that secrete milky substances of varying degrees of toxicity and offensive smell. When the frog is molested by a predator, it secretes the noxious fluid and in many cases the predator backs off, allowing the amphibian to escape. SMOKY JUNGLE FROGS secrete a potent substance called "leptodactylin," named after its genus *Leptodactylus*. The effects of leptodactylin on a predator are drastic, including blocking neuro-muscular activity and over-stimulating parts of the nervous system. Interestingly, in some parts of the species' range, native peoples eat these frogs after removing the skin under running water. Purportedly the meat tastes like (what else?) chicken.

A favorite field biologist's trick to play on the uninitiated is to say that he or she will shine a flashlight in a Smoky Jungle Frog's eyes and that the other person should circle around behind and grab the large frog with both hands. When the other person grabs the unsuspecting frog, it gives out a loud yelp reminiscent of a cat whose tail has been stepped on. Shocked, the other person will drop the frog and be left with slime all over his or her hands – two ways Smoky Jungle Frogs have of defending themselves.

Status

We don't know what constitutes normal, healthy population sizes and distributions for most species of rainfrogs. Some species are known from only a few specimens collected from one place. Many have been discovered recently, so we have no historical records for comparison of population sizes. Although no Peruvian rainfrog is officially classified as threatened or endangered, given the extensive deforestation that has occurred in some areas of the country and the very limited ranges of some species, it is likely that declines are occurring.

Profiles

Amazon Horned Frog, *Ceratophrys cornuta*, Plate 2a
Basin White-lipped Frog, *Leptodactylus mystaceus*, Plate 2b
Smoky Jungle Frog, *Leptodactylus pentadactylus*, Plate 2c
Eyelash Frog, *Edalorhina perezi*, Plate 2d
Marbled Four-eyed Frog, *Pleurodema marmorata*, Plate 2e
Río Mamore Robber Frog, *Eleutherodactylus fenestratus*, Plate 3a
Perú Robber Frog, *Eleutherodactylus peruvianus*, Plate 3b
Pachitea Robber Frog, *Eleutherodactylus toftae* Plate 3c
Perú Andes Frog, *Phrynopus peruvianus*, Plate 3d
Marbled Water Frog, *Telmatobius marmoratus*, Plate 3e

3. Treefrogs

The *treefrogs*, family Hylidae, are a large group of about 740 species, with a nearly worldwide distribution. More than 500 species occur in the New World, where they are most abundant and diverse in the tropics. Because many species have bright colors and large eyes, they have joined animals such as parrots, monkeys, and the jaguar, as popular icons associated with rainforests. Relatively stable moisture and temperature conditions prevalent in tropical forests allow treefrogs to inhabit at least the lower levels of the forest. Eighty-four species occur in Perú.

Most treefrogs are small and have long, slender limbs relative to their body size and large feet with varying amounts of webbing. The toes usually end in expanded "discs" that have pads on the bottom; these toe pads provide a firm grip as the frogs move about on leaves and branches. Treefrogs typically have a slender waist and a large, broad head and snout. Although most of the species you are likely to encounter in Perú are between 2.5 and 5 cm (1 and 2 in) long, adults of various species range in length from 1.7 cm (0.7 in) to 15 cm (6 in). Some species are green or brown, with or without patterns of darker green or dark brown. Other species are brightly colored, often in shades of yellow or orange. One group of treefrogs, the *leaf frogs* (genus *Phyllomedusa*), have exceedingly long limbs and opposed thumbs and first toes (usually without webbing); they often walk slowly and deliberately instead of jumping.

Natural History
Ecology and Behavior

As their name suggests, most treefrogs spend much of their time among leaves and branches of shrubs and trees. Most live in lower vegetation 1 to 3 m (3 to 10 ft) above the ground. They forage at night for invertebrate prey, and they sleep during the day in the vegetation. There are exceptions, however. Some species are terrestrial, some are fossorial (burrowing), and others are semi-aquatic. One group of treefrogs, of which the CASQUE-HEADED TREEFROG (Plate 4) is a member, feeds almost exclusively on other small frogs. Many treefrogs can change colors with respect to time of day; they are often lighter when they are sleeping and darker at night when they are active. These changes are generally associated with light and moisture conditions.

Breeding

One of the more fascinating aspects of treefrogs is the diversity in the ways they reproduce. In fact, treefrogs have the widest array of reproductive patterns of any single family of frogs. These patterns range from the "standard" mode of laying eggs directly in water (eggs that hatch into tadpoles) to remarkable species that brood their eggs in a protective pouch on the mother's back. Most of the unusual modes of reproduction are restricted to the tropics. The COMMON MARSUPIAL FROG (Plate 4) has a pouch-brooding type of reproduction. Eggs are pushed into the pouch, and after they hatch the female releases the tadpoles into a pond where development continues. In some of the other species within the genus, the eggs develop directly into froglets inside the pouch. Another fascinating mode of reproduction is exhibited by the CASQUE-HEADED TREEFROG. In this species, the female broods a small clutch of large eggs exposed on her back, not inside a pouch. Mucous glands from the female's skin secrete a sticky substance that allows the eggs to adhere to her back. All development takes place within the egg capsules (*direct development*), and eventually froglets pop out. Many treefrogs lay their eggs on leaves above standing water. For example, in the WHITE-LINED LEAF FROG (Plate 4), males call (a harsh "cluck") from perches over temporary ponds. The female deposits a clutch of about 600 to 1000 eggs on a leaf over-hanging the water. The eggs hatch into tadpoles within 10 days or so and drop into the water below (if they're lucky and there still is water below), where they complete their development until metamorphosis into frogs. Other treefrogs, such as the COMMON CLOWN TREEFROG (Plate 5), deposit smaller clutches of smaller eggs on leaves over water.

Although many species of treefrogs in the wet tropics have evolved repro-ductive independence of standing water, there are still many species that lay their eggs directly in water. Most of these avoid permanent bodies of water, presumably because of the danger of predation on eggs and tadpoles by fish. Many treefrog species, such as the POLKADOT TREEFROG (Plate 6), RED-SKIRTED TREEFROG (Plate 6), and COMMON FLAT TREEFROG (Plate 5) breed only in temporary ponds. These ponds are formed when low-lying areas fill with rainwater. Because these ponds dry out quickly, fish cannot survive in them. The frogs still must con-tend with abundant aquatic insect predators, however, which exact a large toll on their numbers. A few species of treefrogs lay their eggs in small pools of water that accumulate in the central parts, or *cisterns*, of bromeliad plants, or in depressions and cavities of tree limbs and trunks. Another unusual mode of reproduction is exhibited by the GIANT GLADIATOR FROG (Plate 4), which breeds along the edges of rivers. The male uses his feet to scoop out a depression up to 40 cm (16 in) in diameter in the mud or sand. After water seeps in and fills his depression, he calls and, if lucky, attracts a female to lay up to several thousand eggs in his nest.

Clutch size (the number of eggs produced during a breeding bout) is highly variable among species. Some, particularly those that lay their eggs directly in water, produce large numbers (up to 2000 or more per clutch). Generally the fewest eggs per clutch are found in species that have parental care (often fewer than 50 eggs). Intermediate numbers are typical of species that lay their eggs on leaves over water. In areas with distinct wet and dry seasons, most treefrogs breed during the wet season when ponds are available. In less seasonal environments, such as in the eastern lowlands of Perú, treefrogs breed sporadically year-round; most breeding activity occurs after heavy rains, again when aquatic sites are most numerous. In contrast, the Giant Gladiator Frog breeds during the dry season, when the level of the rivers is lower.

The fact that each species has its own preferred time and place for breeding helps to reduce competition for breeding sites. Furthermore, because some species deposit their eggs directly in water, some above water, and others are independent of water for reproduction, there is less demand on the available sites than there would be without this reproductive diversity. If all the frogs bred only in temporary ponds, all at the same time, food would likely be severely limited for the tadpoles.

Notes

Adult treefrogs avoid or escape predators by rapid jumping, *cryptic coloring* that allows them to blend into their environment, loud, startling screams or squawks given when grabbed by predators, curling up and playing dead, and poisons in their skin. Many treefrogs (and other types of frogs) have contrasting color patterns (such as bands of dark purple on an orange background) on surfaces of the limbs and the body that are usually hidden. These colors are only visible when the limbs are extended. When a frog jumps to escape danger, these contrasting color patches, called *flash coloration*, attract the predator's attention. Then when the frog assumes a sitting position the predator has lost the image because the frog is now cryptic once again. Leaf frogs have especially pronounced flash coloration. The flanks of the WHITE-LINED LEAF FROG are green above and red below a row of cream spots.

One of the leaf frogs that occurs in Perú is the GIANT MONKEY FROG, *Phyllomedusa bicolor*. Men from the Mayoruna indigenous tribe along the Brazil/Perú border use this frog's skin secretion as a drug for "hunting magic". Captive frogs are harassed until they release their defensive secretions. The secretions are collected and dried into a powder. Prior to a hunting expedition, the men inflict burns on their arms or chest and introduce the powder into these open wounds. The chemicals rapidly enter the bloodstream and cause intense vomiting, elevated pulse rate, and incontinence for the next hour. The person lapses into a state of listlessness that lasts up to several days. Eventually the person wakes and feels "godlike" in strength and confident of a successful hunt because his senses are sharpened.

Status

We have so little information on populations of Peruvian treefrogs that it is impossible to determine the status of most species. Given the present high rate of forest clearing and disturbance, some species undoubtedly are declining, particularly those with restricted ranges, specialized habitat requirements, or small population sizes.

Profiles

Casque-headed Treefrog, *Hemiphractus scutatus*, Plate 4a
Common Marsupial Frog, *Gastrotheca marsupiata*, Plate 4b
White-lined Leaf Frog, *Phyllomedusa vaillanti*, Plate 4c
Giant Gladiator Frog, *Hyla boans*, Plate 4d
Quacking Treefrog, *Hyla lanciformis*, Plate 5a
Common Laughing Frog, *Osteocephalus taurinus*, Plate 5b
Blotched Milk Frog, *Phrynohyas coriacea*, Plate 5c
Common Flat Treefrog, *Scinax rubra*, Plate 5d
Common Clown Treefrog, *Hyla leucophyllata*, Plate 5e
Sarayacu Treefrog, *Hyla parviceps*, Plate 6a
Red-skirted Treefrog, *Hyla rhodopepla*, Plate 6b
Polkadot Treefrog, *Hyla punctata*, Plate 6c

Jade Treefrog, *Hyla granosa*, Plate 6d
Koechlin's Treefrog, *Hyla koechlini*, Plate 6e
Short-legged Treefrog, *Hyla leali*, Plate 7a
Lesser Treefrog, *Hyla minuta*, Plate 7b

4. Poison-dart Frogs

Poison-dart frogs, family Dendrobatidae, are popular as rainforest poster animals. They are also commonly pictured on note cards, T-shirts, and even ties and boxer shorts. Much of the charm of these frogs is that many species have bright colors that warn predators of their extraordinary toxicity. The 175 species in the family are restricted to the warm tropical climates of Central and South America. Perú is home to about 38 species, some of them endemic (found nowhere else). Poison-dart frogs, in fact, typically have very restricted ranges. New species are still being discovered as previously unexplored areas of rainforest and cloud forest are being surveyed.

Poison-dart frogs are small; adults range from little more than 1.5 cm (0.6 in) to about 5 cm (2 in). Most species have large eyes and a short head and snout. The body and limbs are fairly short and stout, and the toes end with expanded tips that are usually rectangular. Toes of the front feet lack webbing; although most species have no webbing on the back feet, some are partially webbed.

The most striking characteristic of many poison-dart frogs is their spectacularly bright coloration, often with a metallic shine. Colors range from red, orange, and yellow to blue, purple, and green. Often these bright colors are combined with black, in contrasting patterns of stripes, spots, or mottling. Some species have only one color on the upper surface of the body, but some, such as the RUBY POISON-DART FROG (Plate 7), have two or more colors. Some species, such as the SPOT-LEGGED POISON-DART FROG (Plate 7) have bright colors restricted to their limbs or in the armpits or groin. The bellies of some species are mottled blue and black or blue and white.

Fully half the species in the family, however, are not brightly colored. These are frogs in the genus *Colostethus*, such as the AMAZON ROCKET FROG (Plate 7). Their colors range from dull tan to dark brown, allowing the frogs to blend in with their surroundings. Frogs of this genus often have pale cream to yellowish stripes along the upper and/or lower sides of the head and body. The undersides are often cream, pale yellow, or tan; some have a spotted pattern on a darker background. *Colostethus*, although similar in habits to others in the family, do not produce highly toxic skin secretions. One Peruvian species of *Colostethus* is found in the coastal desert lowlands. Five species are found only in the cloud forests of the eastern slope of the Andes, and another five are found only in the Amazonian lowlands; two species are found both in the cloud forests and Amazonian lowlands. Most of the 25 colorful, toxic species likewise are restricted to one type of habitat: 11 are found only in Amazonian lowlands and nine only in cloud forest; four are found in both habitats. The remaining species is found both in cloud forest and in a small patch of Pacific tropical forest located in the extreme northwest of the country. Generally, *Colostethus* are found at higher elevations than are the brightly colored, toxic members of the family.

Natural History
Ecology and Behavior

Poison-dart frogs are terrestrial. By day they hop about in the leaf litter foraging for invertebrates such as insects and spiders. Although they eat a wide variety of prey, ants and termites make up at least two-thirds of their diet. Some species sleep at night on leaves, usually less than 1 m (3 ft) above the ground. Some of the drab species are also active at night, although to a lesser extent. One characteristic of poison-dart frogs is that they move rapidly, taking short jumps and often darting about in irregular paths. They can be extremely difficult to catch! Some of the brightly colored species are abundant in primary forest near small streams; others prefer secondary forest or swampy areas. Many of the drab species are poorly known, partially because they are wary and secretive (not surprising considering their lack of potent skin toxins and warning colors). Nearly all poison-dart frogs live near streams or bromeliad plants, sites where their tadpoles develop (see Breeding, below).

The bright colors of the toxic species of poison-dart frogs send a warning to potential predators: Danger! Don't eat me! Poison-dart frogs have some of the most toxic poisons of any frogs. The poisons, secreted by glands in the skin, are fat-soluble alkaloids that affect nerves and muscles, causing paralysis. Biologists speculate that the source of the poisons may come from the frogs' food because when poison-dart frogs are removed from their native habitat and fed on fruit flies and baby crickets instead of their natural diet of ants, they lose their toxicity. Something in their natural diet of ants may be necessary for the frogs to be able to produce their own poisons.

Breeding

Reproduction in poison-dart frogs is unlike that of most other frogs. Eggs are deposited on land, and then a parent transports the tadpoles to water for further development. Each species has its own particular set of courtship behaviors. In general, the behavior involves the male calling from his territory to attract a female. When a receptive female appears, he leads her to an appropriate egg-laying spot. After mating, one or the other of the parents (depending on the species) stays with the eggs, and in some species the parent empties fluid from its bladder onto the eggs to keep them moist. After the eggs hatch into tadpoles, the guarding parent straddles the tadpoles. They climb onto the parent's back and are then transported to a nearby stream or water-filled plant. Most poison-dart frogs care for their young only until they deposit the tadpoles in water. A few species that deposit their tadpoles in water-filled bromeliads, however, go one step further. The female lays infertile eggs into the water for the tadpoles to eat. Based on observations of a few well-studied species, poison-dart frogs produce small numbers (usually 6 to 20) of relatively large eggs. Some species in fairly constant environments (with little seasonal change) may breed throughout the year.

Notes

The name "poison-dart frog" refers to the fact that some species are used by indigenous people in South America to poison blowgun darts for hunting. Only three species, all in the genus *Phyllobates*, are known to be used to poison blowgun darts. For this reason, some herpetologists argue that only *Phyllobates* should be called poison-dart frogs and that species of the other toxic genera in the family are more appropriately called poison frogs; many refer to *Colostethus* as *rocket frogs*.

In the northern Chocó of Colombia, hunters poison their darts with secretions of two different species of *Phyllobates* by impaling hapless frogs on sharp sticks, and then slowly roasting them over a flame to gather the secretions.

The poison, spread on the sharp ends of the darts, is strong enough to rapidly debilitate even large prey such as monkeys. The most poisonous species of dart-frog was discovered only about 20 years ago in Colombia, and was named *Phyllobates terribilis* (the TERRIBLE YELLOW POISON-DART FROG) in reference to the extraordinary toxicity of its poison. In the southern Chocó, the Indians use *P. terribilis* to poison darts, but unlike the two species to the north, the bright yellow or orange frog is spared death. This species is so toxic that the person only needs to rub his dart tip briefly on the back of a frog. The frogs are then released unharmed. The poison from this frog is in fact one of the most potent natural toxins found on Earth. Indirect estimations suggest that each frog has enough poison to kill ten people or about 20,000 mice! The hunters handle these frogs with leaves, avoiding direct contact with their skin. There is no effective antidote known for the toxin.

Status

Very little is known about the populations of most species of poison-dart frogs. Since many species have restricted ranges, poison-dart frogs are especially susceptible to habitat destruction and over-collecting. For this reason, and because of their beauty and popular appeal in the pet trade, all poison-dart frogs are listed on CITES Appendix II.

Profiles

Amazon Rocket Frog, *Colostethus marchesianus*, Plate 7c
Ruby Poison-dart Frog, *Epipedobates parvulus*, Plate 7d
Spot-Legged Poison-dart Frog, *Epipedobates pictus*, Plate 7e

5. Other Frogs

Although the family Ranidae, or *true frogs*, has a nearly worldwide distribution (and over 700 species), the family's only representative in Perú is the AMAZON RIVER FROG (Plate 8). These frogs, which resemble North American bullfrogs and can grow to 13 cm (5 in) in length, are medium to dark green, with fully webbed hind feet, no webbing on the front feet, prominent external ear discs, and distinct folds of skin on the upper sides of the body. The largest frog in the world belongs to the family Ranidae, the GIANT SLIPPERY FROG, *Conraua goliath*, from west Africa, at 30 cm (12 in).

The Family Centrolenidae, *glass frogs*, consists of about 120 species found only in Central and South America. Twenty-two species (for example, TRUEB'S COCHRAN FROG, Plate 8) are known from Perú. These tiny frogs are usually less than 3 cm (1.2 in) long. Some species have translucent skin on the undersides of the body and limbs, which in many species reveals the internal organs (including liver and beating heart) and bones, thus the name glass frogs. The upper surface of the body is usually pale green, often with distinct spots and flecks of white, yellow, green, blue, or brown. Glass frogs resemble small treefrogs in appearance, with large eyes and long limbs and large feet that are usually at least partially webbed. The toes have expanded discs.

Narrowmouthed toads, Family Microhylidae, contrary to what the family name suggests, are neither tiny treefrogs nor toads. There are about 315 species in the family, distributed nearly worldwide. Most narrowmouthed toads look ridiculous with their rotund bodies, short stubby limbs, and tiny pointed heads. Lifestyles are highly variable, including terrestrial, fossorial (burrowing), and arboreal.

Microhylids live in arid deserts, in wet rainforests, and in just about all habitats between these extremes. They range in size from tiny (1 cm, 0.4 in) to medium-sized frogs (10 cm, 4 in). Only eight species are known from Perú. If you spot a small (usually less than 5 cm, 2 in), dull gray to dark brown, smooth-skinned frog that resembles a mud-covered golf ball with legs and a pointed head, hopping about on the ground, you probably have found a narrowmouthed toad. In some places, the BOLIVIAN BLEATING FROG (Plate 8), a narrowmouthed toad, is the most abundant terrestrial frog active at night.

Another frog family represented by only two species in Perú is one of the most bizarre on Earth. The SURINAM TOAD (Plate 8), Family Pipidae, looks like it has been run over by a truck and its head smashed into a triangular mass. Small, beady eyes and nostrils are perched on top of this unusual-looking head. This completely aquatic frog (about 17 cm, 6.8 in, body length) has an extremely flattened, tan body with flattened limbs. The hind feet are completely webbed, but the long fingers of the front feet are not. These frogs live in permanent ponds and swamps in the Amazonian lowlands. They are virtually helpless on land. There are 30 species in the family, most of which occur in sub-Saharan Africa.

Natural History
Ecology, Behavior, and Breeding

The AMAZON RIVER FROG is found in lowland forest, and is active mostly at night in or near ponds, lakes, streams, and swamps. These frogs are often found in association with treefrogs and rainfrogs at temporary ponds. They are more aquatic than are most forest frogs, usually seen within 5 m (16 ft) of water. Amazon River Frogs lay 5000 to 7000 eggs directly in the water. Like other frogs in the genus *Rana*, Amazon River Frogs are strong jumpers with powerful hind limbs.

In Perú, glass frogs are found mainly in cloud forest habitat on the eastern slopes of the Andes. Two species are found in the Amazonian lowlands. Most species live near small streams in primary (old growth) forest. Especially at high elevations, many species seem to prefer spray zones at the edges of small cascading waterfalls. Glass frogs are nocturnal and arboreal. They feed on a wide variety of small invertebrates. Many species of glass frogs are apparently rare, and many have restricted ranges, with some species known only from a few individuals collected within very small areas. Males call for females from leaves overhanging streams or from rocks. Females deposit clutches of 15 to 50 eggs on the surfaces of leaves or on rocks above the water. Males of some species guard the eggs from predators until they hatch. In some areas, parasitic flies lay their eggs in glass frog egg clutches; after hatching, the maggots feed on the frog eggs. Thus, in some species, the guarding male protects his offspring from these flies. The tadpoles drop into the stream below and burrow into the mud or sand, where they complete their development into frogs.

Narrowmouthed toads are usually nocturnal, and most are terrestrial. Many are burrowers. All eight species in Perú occur in the Amazonian lowlands; one species also occurs in the cloud forests of the eastern slope of the Andes. Most prefer primary forest, but some are also found in secondary forest and along forest edges. Although many species feed almost exclusively on ants and/or termites, other invertebrate prey, such as beetles, are also eaten. Narrowmouthed toads congregate to breed at small forest ponds, especially during or immediately following heavy rain. Males call from the edge or the surface of the water. If you hear what sounds like a sheep "baaaahing" from the edge of a pond, you're probably hearing a BOLIVIAN BLEATING FROG. Mating occurs in the water and females deposit 100 to 600 eggs, which hatch into tadpoles. One group of narrowmouthed toads deposits a small number of eggs (5 to 10) in water-filled bromeliad plants. Instead of feeding on an external source of food, the tadpoles develop into frogs by metabolizing their large supplies of yolk. Worldwide, narrowmouthed toads exhibit a wide variety of breeding strategies, including terrestrial eggs with direct development and parental care.

The SURINAM TOAD is found in Perú only in the Amazonian lowlands. These frogs do not have tongues, so they capture their food differently than do most frogs. Surinam Toads rest motionless in the water with their arms outstretched. As soon as they sense any food-sized moving creature within range, they bring their arms together and scoop the object into their mouths. Surinam Toads feed mainly on fish and invertebrates. The reproductive behavior of this genus is unique. The pair somersaults through the water, in a series of elaborate acrobatics, with the female releasing eggs, the male fertilizing those eggs, and then the fertilized eggs falling onto the back of the female. Pressure of the male during amplexus ensures that the eggs (about 80 per clutch) are pressed into the soft skin on the back of the female, after which the skin swells rapidly around the eggs. Safely embedded in the mother's back, the eggs travel with her until they pop out of her skin as fully formed froglets a few months later.

Status

Although no species of these four frog families is considered to be threatened or endangered in Perú, most of the species are too poorly known to make informed recommendations concerning population status. Glass frogs are the most likely to be threatened because of their restricted ranges, specialized habitats, and preference for undisturbed forests and clean water.

Profiles

Amazon River Frog, *Rana palmipes*, Plate 8a
Trueb's Cochran Frog, *Cochranella truebae*, Plate 8b
Bolivian Bleating Frog, *Hamptophryne boliviana*, Plate 8c
Surinam Toad, *Pipa pipa*, Plate 8d

Environmental Close-up 2
Frog Population Declines

The Problem

Since the late 1980s, scientists have reported that many populations of frogs, toads, and salamanders are declining in numbers. Some populations, and in fact entire species, have disappeared entirely. Several major questions are being asked:

1   How widespread is the problem?
2   Are amphibian population declines a special case, happening for reasons unrelated to the general loss of biodiversity? and
3   If there is a generalized worldwide amphibian decline, what are the causes?

The available data indicate a widespread pattern of amphibian declines. There are reports from low elevations and high elevations, from the United States, Central America, the Amazon Basin, the Andes, Europe, and Australia. Habitat loss almost certainly contributes to general declines in population sizes of amphibians, and in this sense, amphibian declines are part of the worldwide loss of biodiversity. But what is going on with amphibians seems to be more extreme than the declines seen in other animals. Why would amphibians be more vulnerable? One reason is that because amphibians have thin, moist skin that they use for breathing, chemical pollutants found in the water, soil, and air are able to enter their bodies. Secondly, many amphibians are exposed to double jeopardy because they live both on land (usually in the adult stage) and in the water (usually the egg and larval stages).

So what could be causing the observed declines of amphibians? One possible cause is environmental pollution, for example acid rain – rain that is acidified by various atmospheric pollutants, leading to lake and river water being more acidic. Acidic water is known to decrease fertilization success because sperm become less active and often disintegrate. The eggs that are fertilized often develop abnormally. Another suggestion is that the increased level of ultraviolet (UV) radiation, due to the thinning of the protective atmospheric ozone layer, might be damaging. Frogs often lay their eggs in shallow water directly exposed to the sun's rays, tadpoles often seek shallow water where the temperatures are warmer, and some juvenile and adult frogs bask for warmth. Studies have shown that increased levels of UV light kill some species of frog eggs and can interact chemically with diseases and acid rain to increase amphibian mortality rates. Another possible cause is global warming. Some species of amphibians may not be able to adapt to the warmer, drier climate the world is currently experiencing. For example, drought during a severe El Niño year in 1986–1987 has been implicated in the declines and disappearances of 40% (20 of 50 species) of the frog species (including the Golden Toad) that used to live in the vicinity of Monteverde, Costa Rica. The frogs may have died directly from desiccation (drying out), or they may have been so stressed that they became more vulnerable to disease, fungus, or windborne environmental contaminants. Another cause of some population declines is a parasitic chytrid fungus that has been identified from Central America, the United States, and from Australia. The fungus seems to infest especially the victims' bellies – the area where frogs take up water. Thus, one speculation is that the frogs may be suffocating and drying out. Another possibility is that the fungus may release toxins that are lethal to the frogs when they are resorbed into the skin. Scientists are wondering where the killer fungus will show up next, and what is stressing amphibians to make them more vulnerable to pathogens such as fungus. They're also wondering if people (including researchers and ecotourists) could inadvertently be spreading the fungus on their shoes and boots. Perhaps non-human animals are spreading the fungus.

The Controversy

Not all biologists agree that amphibian declines are a phenomenon over and above the worldwide decline in biodiversity. Scientists who study natural fluctuations in size of animal populations point out that populations of many animals cycle between scarcity and abundance. Many insects are known for their wildly fluctuating population sizes. Population levels of vertebrates also fluctuate with environmental conditions such as food availability and density of prey. For example, voles and lemmings, small rodents of the arctic tundra, are well known for one year being at low population densities (a few per acre or hectare) but several years later, being at very high densities (thousands per acre or hectare). Skeptics point out that, unless those sounding the alarm of amphibian declines can show that the declines are not part of natural cycles, it is too early to panic. They emphasize that the only way to document natural population cycles is to monitor amphibian populations during long-term field studies. Unfortunately, few such studies have been done.

Those scientists who believe that widespread amphibian declines are real and suspect that people are the direct or indirect cause argue that we need to act *now*. Although they agree that we need to initiate long-term studies, they believe we can't wait for the conclusions of such studies 10 or 20 years down the road before we try to reverse the situation. At that point, they argue, it will be too late to do anything but record extinctions.

The Future

The controversy will continue. The important consequence of the debate is that many investigators are working on the problem, considering many different possible causes, from climatic change to a parasitic fungus. A major problem is that even if the scientific consensus right now were that disease, fungi, pollution, climate change, increased level of UV radiation, or some combination, were causing worldwide amphibian declines, the interest and resources are currently lacking to do anything about it on the massive scale required. Because amphibians and reptiles are not uniformly liked and respected, preservation efforts for these animals, except for special cases like sea turtles, will always lag behind conservation efforts made on behalf of birds and mammals. Fortunately, however, because the current conservation emphasis is on preserving entire ecosystems, rather than particular species, amphibians will benefit even if they don't have feathers or fur.

Chapter 6

REPTILES

Edited by Martha L. Crump

Introduction

The fascinating colors, shapes and behaviors of *reptiles* pique the interest of biologists and non-biologists alike. To see many species of reptiles in the wild, however, you need to walk slowly and quietly and look closely. The reason is that, to avoid predation, most reptiles are inconspicuous and often flee from the approach of humans. There are some exceptions. For example, crocodilians and iguanas are *not* inconspicuous and do *not readily* flee from humans. Small lizards can be quite common along forest trails. And geckos are often common in the lodges where ecotourists stay.

General Characteristics and Classification of Reptiles

Reptiles have been around for a long time, arising during the late Paleozoic Era, some 300 million years ago. Today more than 7000 species live in almost all regions of the Earth, with a healthy contingent in the American tropics. Perú has 364 species, of which 185 are snakes, 158 are lizards, 16 are turtles, and five are crocodilians. Reptile skin is covered with tough scales, which cuts down significantly on water loss from reptile body surfaces. The development of this trait permitted vertebrates to remain for extended periods on dry land. Most of today's reptiles are completely terrestrial. In contrast, most amphibians lack a tough skin and must remain in or near water or moist places, lest they dry out. Reptiles have much more efficient heart and blood systems than those of amphibians. This increased efficiency allows for a high blood pressure and the sustained muscular activity required for living on land. The crocodilians even have a completely four-chambered heart that is otherwise found only in birds and mammals. A reptile egg is covered with a shell that provides mechanical protection, but at the same time allows movement through the shell of respiratory gases and water vapor. One of the major differences between a reptile egg and an amphibian egg is that the reptile embryo is surrounded by a membrane called the *amnion*. This membrane provides the developing embryo with a fluid environment, and thus, unlike most amphibians, reptiles do not have to return to the water to deposit their eggs.

Reptile biologists recognize four major living groups. The *turtles* and *tortoises* (land turtles) constitute one group, with about 260 species worldwide. Some turtles live on land throughout their lives. The *sea turtles* live in the oceans, coming ashore only to lay eggs. Most turtles live in lakes and ponds. Some eat plants, some are carnivorous, and others eat both plants and animals. Turtles are easily distinguished by their unique body armor – tough plates that cover their back and belly, creating wrap-around shells into which head and limbs are retracted when a turtle is faced with danger. The *crocodiles* and their relatives, large predatory carnivores that live along the shores of swamps, rivers, and estuaries, constitute a small second group of 22 species. The third group is represented by two lizard-like species of *tuataras*, found only on small islands off the coast of New Zealand. The fourth group consists of the *squamates,* which are the 3300 *lizard* species and 3500 *snakes*. Lizards and snakes have very similar skeletal traits, indicating that they are closely related.

Except for a few species that are legless, lizards walk on all four limbs. Many are ground-dwelling animals, but a fair number spend much of their lives in trees. Almost all are capable of moving quite rapidly. Most lizards are insectivorous, but some, especially larger ones, eat plants, and several prey on amphibians, other lizards, mammals, birds, and even fish. The ecological success of lizards is likely due primarily to a combination of their efficient predation on insects and other small animals as well as their low daily energy requirements. Lizards rely primarily on external sources of heat such as the sun to raise their internal temperature enough to be active. When it gets too hot they use behavior such as seeking shade to lower their internal temperature so they can again be active. However, when the external temperature falls too much, instead of burning up stored energy to maintain their body temperature (like birds and mammals), they just let their internal temperature drop and become inactive. Their cooled bodies go into a resting state that needs little energy. In some ways, this can be considered an advantage over birds and mammals, which must continually seek food to maintain constant body temperatures.

Most Peruvian lizards eat insects, spiders, and mites. Lizards employ two main foraging strategies. Some, such as the small microteid lizards, are *active searchers*. They move continually while looking for prey, nosing about in the leaf litter of the forest floor. *Sit-and-wait* predators, highly camouflaged, remain motionless on the ground or on tree trunks or branches, waiting for prey to happen by. When they see a likely meal, they snatch it if it is close enough or dart out to chase it down. Many lizards are territorial, defending territories from other members of their species with displays, such as bobbing up and down on their front legs, spreading out their colorful *dewlaps* (throat fans), and raising their head crests. Lizards are especially common in deserts and semi-deserts, but they are numerous in other habitats as well. They are active primarily during the day, except for many of the gecko species, which are nocturnal.

Snakes probably evolved from burrowing lizards, and all are limbless. Although all snakes are carnivores, their methods of capturing prey differ. Several groups of species have evolved glands that manufacture toxic venom that is injected into prey through the teeth. The venom immobilizes and kills the prey, which is then swallowed whole. Other snakes strike out at and then wrap themselves around their prey, constricting the prey until it suffocates. Most snakes are nonvenomous; they seize prey with their mouths and rely on their size and strong jaws to subdue it. Snakes have no eardrums for hearing, but they can detect ground vibrations through their bodies. They generally rely most on vision and smell to locate prey, although members of two families have thermal sensor organs on their heads that detect the heat of prey animals.

The success of snakes is at least partially attributable to their ability to devour prey that is larger than their heads (their jaw bones are highly mobile and can be moved easily out of their socket joints on the cranium to accommodate large prey as it is swallowed). Because they eat large items, they need to search for and capture prey only infrequently. For this reason, they can spend long periods hidden and secluded, safe from predators. Like lizards, snakes use either active searching or sit-and-wait foraging strategies.

As is true for lizards, temperature regulates a snake's life, and is the key to understanding their ecology. Unlike birds and mammals, snakes' body temperatures are determined primarily by how much heat they obtain from the physical environment. Many can only be active when they gather sufficient warmth from the sun. They have some control over their body temperature, but it is behavioral rather than physiological. Snakes can lie in the sun or retreat to shade to raise or lower their internal temperatures to within a good operating range, but only up to a point. They must "sit out" hours or days in which the air temperature is either too high or too low. This dependence on air temperature affects most aspects of snakes' lives, from date of birth, to food requirements, to the rapidity with which they can strike at prey.

Snakes are themselves prey for hawks and other predatory birds, other snakes, as well as for some mammals. Many snakes are quite conspicuous against a solid color, with their bold and colorful skin patterns. Against their normal backdrops, however, such as a leaf-strewn forest floor, they are highly camouflaged. They rely on their *cryptic coloration*, and sometimes on speed, to evade predators. Within a species male and female snakes usually look alike, although in some there are minor differences between the sexes in color patterns or the sizes of their scales.

Seeing Reptiles in Perú

Most species of reptiles in Perú are shy and often difficult to observe. They spend most of their time concealed or still. Few vocalize like birds or frogs, so you cannot use sound to find them. The superb cryptic coloration of many snakes means that snakes probably will see more of you than you will of them. Because of the difficulty people have seeing snakes before getting very close to them, the rule for exploring any area known to have venomous snakes or any area for which you are unsure, is NEVER to place your hand or foot anywhere that you cannot see first. Do not climb rocks or trees; do not clamber over rocks where your hands or feet sink into holes or crevices; do not reach into bushes or trees. Walk carefully along trails and try to watch your feet and where you are going. Don't be frightened, but be respectful.

If you want to see reptiles, there are a few ways to increase the chances. Knowing about activity periods helps. Lizards and many snakes are active during the day, but some snakes are active at night (often on low vegetation). Thus, a night walk with flashlights that is organized to find amphibians will surely also yield some reptile sightings. For instance, many small lizards and some snakes sleep on leaves and branches above the ground, in the same places where treefrogs are active. In lowland rainforest, many lizards are active by day on tree trunks, and also in sunny areas near forest edges. Weather is also important. Snakes and lizards are often more active in sunny, warm weather. If all else fails, look for small snakes and lizards by CAREFULLY moving aside rocks and logs with a robust stick or with your boots. Because there are some venomous snakes that are difficult to identify correctly, all snakes are best observed from a safe distance unless you are accompanied by someone who is very familiar with the animals. For more detailed information on reptiles in Perú, see *Guide to the Reptiles and Amphibians of the Peruvian Lower Amazon* by W. W. Lamar.

Unfortunately, common names of reptiles are not standardized, as they are for birds. Common names for many South American reptiles are especially troublesome. For example, some people call *Ameiva ameiva* the Amazon Racerunner; others call it the Giant Ameiva. How is the uninitiated supposed to know it's the same species? Many other species have no generally accepted common names. For the sake of consistency, where possible we use here the common names adopted by Lamar (1997; see p. 250) and some of those that appear in previous books in the Ecotravellers' Wildlife Guide series. Unless otherwise indicated, body lengths are given as total lengths (tail included).

Family Profiles

1. Crocodilians

Remnants of the age when reptiles ruled the world, today's 22 species of crocodilians (*alligators, caimans*, and *crocodiles*), generally inspire awe, respect, a bit of fear, and a great deal of curiosity. Crocodilians are distributed over most tropical and sub-tropical areas of the world. Five species are found in Perú, but the one most likely to be seen is the SPECTACLED CAIMAN (Plate 9), probably the most abundant crocodilian in the New World. This species is mid-sized, occasionally reaching a length of about 2.5 m (8 ft). The much larger BLACK CAIMAN (Plate 9) can reach a length of 6 m (18+ ft). In contrast to these larger caimans, the SMOOTH-FRONTED CAIMAN (Plate 9) is a forest-dwelling species that only grows to about 1 m (3 ft) in length. The AMERICAN CROCODILE, *Crocodylus acutus*, is also found in the northwest of Perú. Perú's caimans occupy inland creeks, ponds, lakes, and rivers.

Natural History
Ecology and Behavior
Although crocodilians usually move slowly over land, they can cover ground rapidly in short bursts. They are easiest to see as they bask in the sunshine along banks of rivers, streams, and ponds. Most of their time is spent in the water, however. Crocodilians in the water are largely hidden, resembling floating logs. This unassuming appearance allows them to move close to shore and seize animals that come to the water to drink. Crocodilians are meat-eaters, but they also eat carrion. Juvenile caiman eat primarily aquatic insects; adults prey on fish and amphibians. Large adult BLACK CAIMAN eat mammals. Crocodilians often forage at night, when they can be seen on the surface of the water; their eyes reflect red when you shine a flashlight on them.

Caiman sometimes excavate burrows along waterways, into which they retreat to escape predators and, when water levels fall too low, to *aestivate* (sleep until water conditions improve). Crocodilians may use vocal signals extensively in their behavior, but their sounds have been little-studied. Juveniles give alarm calls when threatened, and parents respond by coming quickly to their rescue.

Crocodilians have some of the most developed parental care behaviors of any reptile. Nests are guarded, and one or both parents often help hatchlings free themselves from the nest. In some species, parents carry hatchlings to water. Females may remain with and protect the young for up to two years. This complex parental care in crocodilians is sometimes used by scientists who study dinosaurs to support the idea that dinosaurs may have exhibited complex social and parental behaviors. Crocodilians are long-lived animals, many surviving 60+ years in the wild.

Young, very small caiman are eaten by a number of predators, including larger caiman, birds such as herons, storks, egrets and Anhingas, and a variety of mammals such as Jaguars. Large adults apparently have only two enemies: people and large anacondas.

Breeding
During courtship, male crocodilians often defend aquatic territories, giving displays with their tails – up-and-down and side-to-side movements – that probably serve both to defend the territory from other males and to court females. Typically the female makes the nest by scraping together grass, leaves, twigs, and sand or soil, into a pile near the water's edge. She then buries 20 to 30 eggs in the pile that she, and sometimes the male, guard for about 70 days until hatching. Nests of the SMOOTH-FRONTED CAIMAN are sometimes located near termite mounds in the forest. As in the turtles and some lizards, the sex of developing crocodilians is determined largely by the temperature of the ground around the eggs (see p. 79); males develop at relatively high temperatures, females at lower ones.

Caiman young from a single brood may remain together in the nest area for up to 18 months. Caiman breed during both wet and dry parts of the year.

Notes

Although larger caiman are potentially dangerous to people, they are not particularly aggressive. Caiman are usually inoffensive, most being below a size where they try to eat land mammals. Local people sometimes swim near SPECTACLED CAIMAN and SMOOTH-FRONTED CAIMAN without concern; but the same is most assuredly NOT true of the larger BLACK CAIMAN!

Because of their predatory nature and large size, crocodilians play important roles in the history and folklore of many cultures, going back at least to ancient Egypt, where a crocodile-headed god was known as Sebek. The Egyptians even built and named a holy city, Crocodilopolis, in honor of crocodiles. These ancient people apparently welcomed crocodiles into their canals, possibly as a defense from invaders. It may have been believed by Egyptians and other African peoples that crocodiles caused blindness, probably because the disease called river blindness results from infestation with a river-borne parasitic roundworm. To appease the crocodiles during canal construction, a virgin was sacrificed to the reptiles. Indeed, providing crocodiles with virgins seems to have been a fairly common practice among several cultures, showing a preoccupation with these animals (and with virgins). Even today, carvings of crocodiles are found among many relatively primitive peoples, from South America to Africa to Papua New Guinea. The ancient Olmecs of eastern Mexico also had a crocodile deity.

Status

Most crocodilian species worldwide were severely reduced in numbers during the 20th century. Several were hunted almost to extinction for their skins. In the USA, hunting almost caused AMERICAN ALLIGATORS to go extinct. In 1961 hunting alligators was made illegal, but poaching continued. Thanks to the 1973 Endangered Species Act, which gave protection to alligators, they have returned to most of the areas from which they were eliminated. Crocodile and alligator farms (with captive-bred stock) and ranches (wild-caught stock) in many areas of the world now provide skins, leaving wild populations relatively unmolested. Many of the Latin American crocodilians were hunted heavily during the first half of the 20th century. Today, only the Spectacled Caiman is hunted in large numbers, particularly in the Pantanal region of Brazil. All crocodilians are listed by the international CITES agreements, preventing or highly regulating trade, and their numbers have been steadily rising during the past 20 years. Nevertheless, most of the 22 crocodilian species are still threatened or endangered.

Profiles

Spectacled Caiman, *Caiman crocodilus*, Plate 9a
Black Caiman, *Caiman niger*, Plate 9b
Smooth-fronted Caiman, *Paleosuchus trigonatus*, Plate 9c

2. Turtles

It is a shame that *turtles* are rarely encountered in the wild (at least at close range) because they are intriguing to watch, and they are generally innocuous and inoffensive. It is always a pleasant surprise stumbling across a turtle on land, perhaps laying eggs, or discovering a group of them basking in the sunshine on rocks or logs along a river's edge or in the middle of a pond. The 260 living turtle species are grouped into 12 families that can be divided into three types by their typical habits and body forms. Two families comprise the *sea turtles*, ocean-going animals whose females come to shore only to lay eggs. The members of nine families, containing most of the species, live in freshwater habitats – lakes and ponds – except for the *box turtles*, which live on land (*terrestrial*). Finally, one family contains the *land tortoises*, which, as their name suggests, are all terrestrial.

Turtles all have the same basic body plan: bodies encased in tough shells (made up of two layers – an inner layer of bone and an outer layer of scale-like plates); four limbs, sometimes modified into flippers; highly mobile necks; toothless jaws; and small tails. This body plan must be among nature's best, because it has survived unchanged for a long time; turtles have looked more or less the same for at least 200 million years. Enclosing the body in heavy armor above and below apparently was an early solution to the problems vertebrates faced when they moved onto land, providing rigid support in the absence of the buoyancy of water and protection from predators and desiccation (drying out).

Turtles range in color from brown to black to green, with many being olive-green. They range in size from tiny *terrapins* 11.5 cm (4.5 in) long to giant LEATHERBACK SEA TURTLES (Plate 10) that can grow to more than 2 m (6.5 ft) long, 3.6 m (12 ft) across (flipper to flipper), and that weigh 600+ kg (1300+ lb). Leatherbacks are the heaviest turtles. In many turtle species, females are larger than males. Two sea turtle and three freshwater families are represented in Perú. The single family of land tortoises is represented in Perú by the YELLOWFOOT TORTOISE (Plate 9).

Natural History
Ecology and Behavior

The diet of freshwater turtles changes as they develop. Early in life they are carnivorous, eating almost anything they can get their jaws on – snails, insects, fish, frogs, salamanders, reptiles. As they grow the diet of many species changes to herbivory. Turtles are slow-moving on land, but they can retract their heads, tails, and limbs into their shells, rendering them almost impregnable to predators – unless they are swallowed whole, such as by crocodilians. Long-lived animals, individuals of many turtle species typically live 25 to 60 years in the wild. As is typical of most, if not all, reptiles, a turtle grows throughout its life.

The turtles of Perú occupy a variety of habitats. Sea turtles (Plate 10) live in the open oceans, except when females come onto land to lay their eggs. Some of the aquatic freshwater species spend most of their time in lakes and ponds, but a few leave the water to forage on land. The YELLOW-SPOTTED RIVER TURTLE (Plate 9) is most often seen sunning itself on logs in the water or on muddy beaches of rivers in remote and undisturbed parts of the Amazonian lowlands. One of nature's most bizarre turtles is the MATAMATA (Plate 11) – bizarre because of the fleshy proboscis that extends from its snout and because its mouth seemingly is in a perpetual grin. Matamatas live in rivers, where they spend much of their time resting in one position on the bottom, waiting for an unsuspecting meal to come by, at which point they lunge at the fish or invertebrate. The freshwater TWIST-NECKED TURTLE (Plate 11) is a type of *sideneck turtle*, so-called because when one withdraws its head, it bends its neck to one side of the body between the gap in its upper and lower shells; they are unable to fully retract the neck and head within the shell as can many other turtles and tortoises. The

YELLOWFOOT TORTOISE is found on moist ground in lowland forests in the Perú departments of Loreto, Huanuco, Madre de Dios, and Ucayali. A very similar tortoise occurs in the department of San Martin, also in the wet Amazonian lowlands.

If turtles can make it through the dangerous juvenile stage, when they are small and soft enough for a variety of predators to eat them, they enjoy very high year-to-year survival – up to 80% or more of an adult population usually survives from one year to the next. However, there is very high mortality in the egg and juvenile stages. Nests are not guarded, and many kinds of predators, such as crocodiles, lizards, and, especially, armadillos, dig up turtle eggs or eat the hatchlings.

Breeding

Courtship in turtles can be quite complex. In some, the male swims backwards in front of the female, stroking her face with his clawed feet. In the tortoises, courtship often involves between-the-sexes butting and nipping. All turtles lay their leathery eggs on land. The female digs a hole in the earth or sand, deposits the eggs into the hole, then covers them and departs. It is up to the hatchlings to dig their way out of the nest and navigate to water. Many tropical turtles breed at any time of year.

Although the numbers of eggs laid per nest varies extensively among the Peruvian freshwater turtles (from one to about 100), in general, these turtles lay small clutches. The reason seems to be that, because of the continuous warm weather, they need not breed in haste like their northern cousins, putting all their eggs in one nest. The danger with a single nest is that if a predator finds it, a year's breeding is lost. Tropical turtles, by placing only one or a few eggs in each of several nests spread throughout the year, are less likely to have predators destroy their total annual breeding production. Also, it may pay to lay a few big eggs rather than many small ones because bigger hatchlings may be less vulnerable to predators.

Notes

There is an intriguing relationship between turtle reproduction and temperature that nicely illustrates the intimate connection between animals and the physical environment. For many vertebrates, the sex of an individual is determined by the kinds of sex chromosomes it has. In people, if each cell has an X and a Y chromosome, the person is male, and if two Xs, female. In birds, it is the opposite. But in most turtles, it is not the chromosomes that matter, but the temperature at which an egg develops. In most turtles studied to date, eggs incubated at constant temperatures above 30°C (86°F) all develop as females, whereas those incubated at 24 to 28°C (75 to 82°F) become males. At 28 to 30°C (82 to 86°F), both males and females are produced. In some species, a second temperature threshold exists – eggs that develop below 24°C (75°F) again become females. (In the crocodiles and lizards, the situation reverses, with males developing at relatively high temperatures and females at low temperatures.) The exact way that temperature determines sex is not clear although it is suspected that temperature directly influences a turtle's developing brain. Scientists haven't yet figured out *why* these temperature effects exist. Is there some advantage of this system to the animals that we as yet fail to appreciate? Or is it simply a consequence of reptile structure and function, some fundamental constraint of their biology?

Status

The ecology and status of populations of most freshwater and land turtles are poorly known, making it difficult to determine whether population numbers are stable or changing. Several species of large river turtles have virtually disappeared from all but the most remote streams and lakes. This rapid decline is due largely to over-harvesting of their eggs, which are buried in sandy river bars. These nests are easily found by local people, who then sell them to food markets in regional cities. The YELLOW-SPOTTED RIVER TURTLE and the YELLOWFOOT TORTOISE are considered threatened in Perú by the IUCN Red List. Worldwide, sea turtles are heavily exploited by people, and almost all of them are threatened. Sea turtle eggs are harvested illegally for food in many parts of the world, including Perú, and adults of some species are taken for meat and for their shells. Many adults also die accidentally in fishing nets and collisions with boats. All sea turtles profiled here are listed as endangered by CITES Appendix I.

Profiles

Yellowfoot Tortoise, *Geochelone denticulata*, Plate 9d
Yellow-spotted River Turtle, *Podocnemis unifilis*, Plate 9e
Green Sea Turtle, *Chelonia mydas*, Plate 10a
Hawksbill Sea Turtle, *Eretmochelys imbricata*, Plate 10b
Leatherback Sea Turtle, *Dermochelys coriacea*, Plate 10c
Olive Ridley Sea Turtle, *Lepidochelys olivacea*, Plate 10d
Twist-necked Turtle, *Platemys platycephala*, Plate 11a
Matamata, *Chelus fimbriatus*, Plate 11b

3. Colubrids: Your Regular, Everyday Snakes

Many people think that all *snakes*, particularly tropical species, are venomous, and hence, must be avoided at all cost. Unfortunately, this "reptile anxiety" prevents some people from enjoying tropical forests. In Perú, the vast majority of snakes are NOT venomous. Of the 186 species of snakes in the country, only 32 are venomous enough to be dangerous to humans. Venomous snakes in the American tropics tend to be nocturnal, secretive, and hard to find, even if you are looking for them. Therefore, with caution, you can enjoy your days in Perú without worrying unduly about venomous snakes. If you do find one, you will likely discover that it is a beautiful animal and worth a look.

The largest group of snakes are those of the Family Colubridae – the *colubrid* snakes. Most of these are nonvenomous or, if venomous, dangerous only to small prey, such as lizards and rodents. This is a worldwide group comprising over 1700 species, including about three-quarters of the New World snakes. About 130 species occur in Perú. Most of the snakes with which people are familiar, such as *water, brown, garter, whip, green, rat,* and *king snakes,* are colubrids, a family that has a wide variety of habits and lifestyles. It is not possible to provide a general physical description of all colubrid snakes because of the great variety of shapes and colors associated with their respective lifestyles. Most people will not get close enough to notice, but an expert could identify colubrids by their anatomy. Colubrids have rows of teeth on the upper and lower jaws but they do not have hollow, venom-injecting fangs in front on the upper jaw.

Natural History
Ecology and Behavior

Because colubrids vary so much in their natural history, we will concentrate on the habits of the species illustrated (Plates 11, 12, 13), which are representative of several general types. Typical lifestyles of various colubrids are terrestrial, burrowing, arboreal, and aquatic. Arboreal snakes spend most of their time in trees and shrubs. *Sharpnose snakes* (STRIPED SHARPNOSE SNAKE and SOUTH-ERN SHARPNOSE SNAKE, Plate 12), for instance, are slender arboreal snakes that inhabit lowland forests in Perú and feed on lizards and frogs. Their thin, long bodies resemble vines and if not moving, these snakes are very difficult to see. They rely on camouflage for both hunting and protection: they freeze in place when alerted to danger. BLUNT-HEADED TREESNAKES (Plate 11) are also arboreal. They have broad and squarish heads, long, thin bodies, and large, bulging eyes. They forage at night for small frogs and lizards. Another group of slender nocturnal-arboreal tree snakes are the *thirst snakes* (Plate 11c), or *snail-eaters*, which, as you might expect, feed on snails (and slugs but apparently little else). Both blunt-headed snakes and thirst snakes are lightweight tree snakes that are slightly flattened sideways, and can move from branch to branch over open gaps that are half the length of their bodies. COMMON CAT-EYED SNAKES (Plate 11) cruise through the vegetation around ponds at night, look-ing for frogs or leaf frog eggs to eat. (Leaf frogs lay their eggs on leaves above the water; p. 63.)

A common terrestrial snake is the COMMON MUSSURANA (Plate 12). It has a broad range in the Neotropics in wet and semi-dry lowland areas. Hunting by day or night, mussuranas have a varied diet, including other snakes. In fact, they even capture and eat the deadly FER-DE-LANCE (Plate 15) and are appreciated for this habit by knowledgeable local people. Mussuranas subdue their prey with a combination of slow-acting venom and physical constriction.

There are many species of small snakes, such as the GIANT EARTHSNAKE (Plate 13), which live much like worms, inhabiting the thick layer of leaf litter on the forest floor; some also burrow into the soil. However, unlike worms, these snakes sometimes climb into low vegetation at night to sleep. Not surprisingly, they eat mostly worms – the most abundant food in their habitat. The many varieties of *false coral snakes* (for example the BLACK-HEADED CALICO SNAKE, Plate 13) are also terrestrial forest dwellers that inhabit the leaf litter and rotting logs. They are brightly colored to fool predators, as these snakes visually mimic venomous *coral snakes* (p. 83). Many people assume that false coral snakes have no fangs or venom, but in fact many species have fangs in the rear of the mouth associated with venom glands.

Breeding

Relatively little is known of the breeding patterns of Peruvian colubrids. The typical number of eggs per clutch varies from species to species, but some, such as the BLUNT-HEADED TREESNAKE, lay small clutches of one to three eggs. Most snakes that lay eggs deposit them in a suitable location and depart; the parents provide no care of the eggs or young.

Notes

Snakes' limbless condition, their manner of movement, and the venomous nature of some of them, have engendered for these intriguing reptiles fear from people, stretching back thousands of years. Myths about the evil power and intentions of snakes are ubiquitous. But one need go no farther than the Old Testament, where the snake plays the pivotal role as Eve's corrupt enticer, responsible for people's expulsion from the Garden of Eden. Because these myths cross so many cultures around the world, sociobiologists have hypothesized that this fear may be instinctive. Some studies of monkey behavior seem to support this possibility. Whether or not this fear is instinctive behavior or learned is controversial. We lean toward the learned behavior argument, based primarily on our visits to grade schools with live snakes in hand. Most grade school kids seem to lack the fear often exhibited by their parents.

Status

The only one of Perú's colubrid snakes that is regulated for conservation purposes is the COMMON MUSSURANA (CITES Appendix II listed). On the other hand, little is known about the biology and population sizes of most colubrids. Long-term studies are necessary to determine if population sizes are stable or changing. Because individual species normally are not found in great numbers, for many species it will always be difficult to tell if and when they are threatened. World-wide, about 30 colubrids are listed as vulnerable, threatened, or endangered. The leading threats are habitat destruction and the introduction by people of exotic animals that prey on snakes at some point in their life cycles, such as Marine Toads, Cattle Egrets, armadillos, and fire ants.

Profiles

Ornate Thirst Snake, *Dipsas catesbyi*, Plate 11c
Blunt-headed Treesnake, *Imantodes cenchoa*, Plate 11d
Common Cat-eyed Snake, *Leptodeira annulata*, Plate 11e
Striped Sharpnose Snake, *Xenoxybelis argenteus*, Plate 12a
Southern Sharpnose Snake, *Xenoxybelis boulengeri*, Plate 12b
Black-skinned Parrot Snake, *Leptophis ahaetulla nigromarginatus*, Plate 12c
Olive Whipsnake, *Chironius fuscus*, Plate 12d
Common Mussurana, *Clelia clelia*, Plate 12e
South American Water Snake, *Helicops angulatus*, Plate 13a
Giant Earthsnake, *Atractus major*, Plate 13b
Common False Viper, *Xenodon rabdocephalus*, Plate 13c
Black-headed Calico Snake, *Oxyrhopus melanogenys*, Plate 13d

4. Dangerous Snakes and Boas

For convenience, we group together in this section what are usually considered the more dangerous snakes, those that are highly venomous and large ones that kill by squeezing their prey – *anacondas* and *boas*. Anacondas are a kind of boa, and of the entire group, only the anacondas are considered potentially dangerous to adult humans (and then only if you were very much in the wrong place at the wrong time). Most of the venomous snakes and constrictors are well camouflaged, secretive in their habits, and/or nocturnal. (For more information on venomous snakes in Latin America, see *The Venomous Reptiles of Latin America*, by J. A. Campbell and W. W. Lamar 1989.)

Vipers, of the Family Viperidae, comprise most of the New World's venomous snakes. If you are trying to capture and eat a large animal without the benefit of legs and feet, any way of quickly stopping the prey from wriggling free of your grasp would be advantageous. These snakes have evolved just such a method – a venom-injection mechanism: long, hollow fangs that introduce poison into the prey. Snake venoms are complex substances that contain a variety of proteins designed to destroy specific targets, such as nerves or blood. Therefore generalities about the effects from a certain type of snake's venom are often misleading. From a practical standpoint, what is important is that, if at all possible, the snake involved in a bite incident should be correctly identified; appropriate treatment can then be given. Typically, vipers coil prior to striking. They vary considerably in size, shape, color pattern, and lifestyle. Many of the vipers are referred to as *pit-vipers* because they have thermal-sensitive "pits," or depressions, between their nostrils and eyes that are sensory organs. Pit-vipers occur from southern Canada to Argentina, as well as in the Old World. The familiar venomous snakes of North America are pit vipers – *rattlesnakes, copperheads, water moccasins*, as are about half of Perú's venomous snakes.

Fifteen *viperid* species occur in Perú. The deadly FER-DE-LANCE (Plate 15) is abundant in lowland wet forest areas and along watercourses in drier areas. Most are shorter than the maximum length of 2 m (6.5 ft). They are slender snakes with lance- or spear-shaped heads (hence the name, which means "iron spear"). AMAZON BUSHMASTERS (Plate 15), the largest venomous snakes of the Western Hemisphere, inhabit lowland wet forest areas. They are the large-headed giants of the pit-vipers, reaching lengths of 2.5 to 3.6 m (8 to 12 ft).

The Family Elapidae contains what are regarded as the world's deadliest snakes, the Old World *cobras* and *mambas*. In the Western Hemisphere, the group is represented by the *coral snakes* – slender snakes that are usually quite gaily attired in rings of red, yellow and black. They have a very powerful venom. Sixteen species, one of which is LANGSDORFF'S CORAL SNAKE (Plate 15), occur in Perú. Coral snakes rarely grow longer than 1 m (3 ft). In addition to the coral snakes, *elapids* are also represented in Perú by a single species of *sea snake*. The yellow and black PELAGIC SEA SNAKE, *Pelamis platurus*, which occurs only in the extreme northwest of the country, is the only New World species of a group of highly venomous marine snakes, most of which inhabit coastal waters around Australia and Southeast Asia. Fortunately, all elapids in Perú, although having highly toxic venom, have small fangs, making it difficult for them to bite humans effectively.

Members of the Family Boidae kill their prey by constriction. This family encompasses 63 species that are distributed throughout the world's tropical and sub-tropical regions. They include the Old World *pythons* and the New World boas and anacondas. The pythons and anacondas are the world's largest snakes. Six boa species are found in Perú. One of them, the RED-TAILED BOA (Plate 14), occurs over a wide range of habitat types, wet and dry, from sea level up to about 1000 m (3300 ft). This boa reaches lengths of about 4 m (13 ft), but typical specimens are only 1.5 to 2.5 m (5 to 8 ft) long. They have shiny, smooth scales and a back pattern of dark, squarish shapes that provides good camouflage against an array of backgrounds. In general body form, the COMMON ANACONDA (Plate 14) is similar to the Red-tailed Boa, but the anaconda is a more massive snake. The other boas in Perú, such as the AMAZON TREE BOA (Plate 14) and RAINBOW BOA (Plate 14) are more slender and much smaller, reaching about 2 m (6.5 ft) in length.

Natural History
Ecology and Behavior

FER-DE-LANCE are primarily terrestrial, although both adults and, more commonly, juveniles, sometimes sleep and rest in vegetation. They inhabit moist forests but also some drier areas. They eat birds and mammals such as opossums. Like other pit-vipers (and some other snakes), they can sense the heat radiated by prey animals, which assists their foraging. Searching by heat detection probably works for both warm-blooded prey (birds, mammals) as well as cold-blooded (lizards, frogs), as long as the prey is at a higher temperature than its surroundings. BUSHMASTERS are terrestrial snakes that feed chiefly on mammals. They are mainly nocturnal and therefore, even where fairly common, are infrequently seen. In a recent Costa Rican study during which these snakes could be followed closely because they were outfitted with radio transmitters, biologists learned that the Bushmaster diet consisted almost entirely of rather large forest rats. Typically, a Bushmaster would lie in wait for days or even weeks at the same spot on the ground, usually beneath a tree; after capturing a rat, the snake moved to a new site. This lazy, low-energy lifestyle has its advantages; the same study calculated that a single snake would need to eat only about six rats per year to survive!

Coral snakes are usually secretive and difficult to study; consequently relatively little is known about their ecology and behavior in the wild. They apparently forage by crawling along slowly on the ground, intermittently poking their heads into the leaf litter. They eat lizards, caecilians (Plate 1), and small snakes, which they kill with their powerful venom. They are often found under rocks and logs, and many probably burrow into the soil for protection, and while foraging. They can be day- or night-active.

A number of nonvenomous or mildly venomous colubrid snakes (p. 80), as well as at least one caterpillar species, mimic the bright, striking coral snake color scheme: alternating rings of red, yellow (or white), and black. In Perú alone, at least ten species of colubrids imitate, to varying degrees, the color patterns of coral snakes (for example, the BLACK-HEADED CALICO SNAKE, Plate 13). The function of the *mimicry* apparently is to take advantage of the avoidance behavior many predatory animals show toward the lethal coral snakes. Ever since this idea was first proposed more than a hundred years ago, the main argument against it has been that it implied either that the predators had to be first bitten by a coral snake to learn of their toxicity and then survive to generalize the experience to all snakes that look like coral snakes, or that the predators were born with an innate fear of the coral snake color pattern. It has now been demonstrated experimentally that several bird predators on snakes (motmots, kiskadees, herons, and egrets) need not learn that a coral snake is dangerous by being bitten. They avoid these snakes instinctively from birth. Thus, many snakes have evolved as defensive mechanisms color schemes that mimic that of coral snakes.

All Peruvian boas are mainly nocturnal. Some are terrestrial, but do sometimes climb into the vegetation; others are primarily arboreal. The COMMON ANACONDA, however, is mostly aquatic, foraging in or very near large bodies of water such as in the backwaters of rivers or swamps. Boa diets include reptiles, birds, and mammals. Prey, recognized by visual, chemical (smell), or heat senses, is seized with the teeth after a rapid, open-mouth lunge. As it strikes, a boa or anaconda also coils around the prey, lifting it from the ground, and then constricts, squeezing the prey. The prey cannot breathe and suffocates. When the prey stops moving, the snake swallows it whole, usually starting with the head.

Breeding

Details of the breeding in the wild of most tropical vipers are not well known. Many may follow the general system of North American rattlesnakes, which have been much studied. Females attract males when they are ready to mate by releasing *pheromones* (odor chemicals) into the air and also, through the skin of their sides and back, onto the ground. Males search for females. When one is located, the male accompanies and courts her for several days before mating occurs. North American rattlers have distinct breeding periods, but many tropical vipers may breed at almost any time of year.

Unlike the colubrids, most of the vipers give birth to live young. The FER-DE-LANCE has a reputation as a prolific breeder, females giving birth to between 20 and 70 young at a time. Each is about 20 cm (8 in) long at birth, fully fanged with active poison glands, and dangerous. The BUSHMASTER, the only egg-laying viperid of the New World, usually produces small clutches of 10 or fewer eggs. Coral snakes lay eggs, up to 10 per clutch. All boas in Perú, including the ANACONDA, give birth to live young. Litters vary between 12 and 60.

Notes

All of the venomous snakes discussed in this section, if encountered, should be given a wide berth. Watch them only from a distance. Very few visitors to the tropics, even those that spend their days tramping through forests, are bitten by venomous snakes. Remember that this venom-delivery system is a highly evolved prey-capture strategy, and only secondarily a defensive mechanism. Venom is energetically costly to produce, and venomous snakes can bite without injecting any venom. They can also vary the amount of venom injected. Even if venom is injected, one does not necessarily receive a fatal dose. Within the same species, the toxicity of a snake's venom can vary geographically, seasonally, and from individual to individual.

The brightly colored coral snakes are rarely seen by people because of their secretive habits. Most are usually quite docile. However, if threatened, some give a frightening defensive display: they erratically snap their body back and forth, swing their head from side to side with the mouth open, and bite any object that is contacted. Although their mouth and fangs are small, their venom is very powerful. Be advised not to adhere to rules learned for hiking or camping in North America about how to distinguish, based on coloring, coral snakes from nonvenomous mimic snakes. The snakes in South America don't follow the rules.

Boa personalities vary; some are docile, others are very willing to defend themselves. Boas may hiss loudly at people, draw their head back with mouth open in a threat posture, and bite. They have large sharp teeth that can cause deep puncture wounds. Therefore, even though boas present no threat to people, keeping a respectful distance is advised.

To the Arakmbut forest people of Amazonian Perú, "toto" are harmful spirits that live mainly in the forest. Venomous snakes are considered to be toto who come from far away to seek victims in the local community. Venomous snakes are also thought to be weapons (living arrows) used by armadillos to kill enemies. The reason for this belief perhaps stems from the fact that snakes are sometimes seen entering and exiting armadillo burrows.

Status

None of Perú's vipers or coral snakes is officially considered threatened or endangered. Both the RED-TAILED BOA and RAINBOW BOA are regulated for conservation purposes; they are both listed in CITES Appendix II. Some of the other boas may be threatened in some areas of the country by habitat destruction and by capture for the pet trade; otherwise boas seem to do well living near people and are still common in many parts of Perú and the rest of the New World tropics.

Profiles

Red-tailed Boa, *Boa constrictor*, Plate 14a
Amazon Tree Boa, *Corallus hortulanus*, Plate 14b
Rainbow Boa, *Epicrates cenchria*, Plate 14c
Common Anaconda, *Eunectes murinus murinus*, Plate 14d
Langsdorff's Coral Snake, *Micrurus langsdorffi*, Plate 15a
Fer-de-lance, *Bothrops atrox*, Plate 15b
Amazon Bushmaster, *Lachesis muta*, Plate 15c

5. Geckos

Geckos are fascinating organisms because, of their own volition, they have become "house lizards." The family, Gekkonidae, is spread throughout tropical and subtropical areas of the world, with about 870 species. In many regions, geckos have invaded houses and buildings, becoming ubiquitous adornments of walls and ceilings. Ignored by residents, they move around dwellings chiefly at night, munching insects. Twenty-one species occur in Perú.

Peruvian geckos are fairly small lizards, usually gray or brown, with large eyes. They have thin, soft skin, covered usually with small, granular scales that produce a slightly lumpy appearance. Many have large fingers and toes with well-developed claws and broad specialized pads that allow them to cling to vertical surfaces and even upside-down on ceilings. The way geckos manage these feats has engendered a fair amount of scientific detective work. Various forces have been implicated in explaining the gecko's anti-gravity performance, from the ability of their claws to dig into tiny irregularities on man-made surfaces, to their large toes acting as suction cups, to an adhesive quality of friction. The real explanation appears to lie in the series of minuscule hair-like structures on the bottoms of the finger and toe pads, which provide attachment to walls and ceilings by something akin to surface tension – the same property that allows some insects to walk on water. Not all Peruvian geckos have these toe pads, however; for example, the toes of the AMAZON STREAK LIZARD (Plate 15) lack expanded disks. Most adult geckos are only 5 to 10 cm (2 to 4 in) in length, tail excluded; tails can double the length. Because lizard tails frequently break off and regenerate (p. 91), their length varies tremendously; gecko tails are particularly fragile.

Natural History
Ecology and Behavior

Although most lizards are active during the day and inactive at night, many gecko species, such as the COMMON HOUSE GECKO (Plate 15) are nocturnal. In natural settings, they are primarily ground dwellers but, as their behavior in buildings suggests, they are also excellent climbers. Geckos feed chiefly on insects. In fact, it is their ravenous appetite for cockroaches and other insect undesirables that render them welcome house guests in many parts of the world. Unlike the great majority of lizards, which do not vocalize, geckos at night are avid little chirpers and squeakers. They communicate with each other with loud calls – surprisingly loud for such small animals. Various species sound differently. The word "gecko" approximates the sound of calls from some of the Asian species.

Geckos are *sit-and-wait* predators. Instead of wasting energy actively searching for prey that is usually highly alert and able to flee, they sit still for long periods, waiting for unsuspecting insects that venture a bit too near, then lunge, grab, and swallow. Geckos rely chiefly on their *cryptic coloration* and their ability to flee rapidly for escape from predators, which include snakes and birds during the day and snakes, owls, and bats at night. When cornered, geckos give threat displays; when seized, they give loud calls to distract predators, and they bite. Should the gecko be seized by its tail, it breaks off as a last resort, allowing the gecko time to escape, albeit tail-less. Although it causes considerable stress to the animal, the tail usually regenerates. Some geckos when seized also secrete thick, noxious fluids from their tails, which presumably discourages predators.

Breeding

Almost all geckos are egg-layers. Mating occurs after courtship, which involves a male displaying to a female by waving his tail around, followed by some mutual nosing and nibbling. Clutches usually contain only one to a few eggs, but a female may lay several clutches per year. There is no parental care; after eggs are deposited, they and the tiny geckos that hatch from them are on their own.

Status

More than 25 gecko species are listed as rare, vulnerable, threatened, or endangered, but they are almost all restricted to the Old World. The MONITO GECKO, found only on Monito Island, off Puerto Rico, is endangered. None of Perú's geckos is officially considered threatened, but most are very poorly known.

Profiles

Amazon Streak Lizard, *Gonatodes humeralis*, Plate 15d
Common House Gecko, *Hemidactylus mabouia*, Plate 15e

6. Iguanas and Relatives

The Iguanidae is a large group of lizards that is considered a single family by some experts but divided into several separate families by others. For convenience's sake, we will consider all of the 750 species in this group as *iguanoids*. They are found only in the New World, with 81 species in Perú. Most of the lizards commonly encountered by ecotravellers, or that are on their viewing wish-lists, are members of this group. It includes the very abundant *anolis lizards* (for example, the SLENDER ANOLE and the COMMON FOREST ANOLE, Plate 16) and the spectacular GREEN IGUANA (Plate 16).

The iguanoids are a rich and varied group exhibiting diverse habits. Many in the family are brightly colored and have adornments such as crests, spines, or throat fans. They range in size from tiny anolis lizards, or *anoles*, only a few centimeters in total length and a few grams in weight, to Green Iguanas, which are up to 2 m (6.5 ft) long. The AMAZON WOOD LIZARD (Plate 16) attains total lengths up to 32 cm (13 in); a distinct row of large, spiny scales on their backs yields a bristly appearance. Some species of small iguanoids (especially anoles) are very common in natural areas in Perú and also around human habitations.

Natural History
Ecology and Behavior

You can't mistake the GREEN IGUANA; it's the large lizard resembling a dragon sitting in the tree near the river. Iguanas are common inhabitants of many Neotropical rainforests, in moist areas at low to middle elevations. They are often common in town squares and city parks along the coast. Considered semi-arboreal, they spend most of their time in trees, usually along waterways. They don't move much, and when they do it's often in slow-motion (but they can move very quickly when surprised or threatened). They are herbivores as adults, eating mainly leaves and twigs and, more occasionally, fruit; insects are eaten by juveniles. When threatened, an iguana sitting on a branch out over a river will drop from its perch into the water, making its escape underwater; they are good swimmers. During their breeding season, males establish and defend mating territories on which live one to four females.

Anoles are small, diurnal, often arboreal lizards with streamlined bodies. Many species are represented in Perú and many are frequently encountered; others, such as those that live in the high canopy, are rarely seen. Some are ground dwellers, and others spend most of their time on tree trunks perched head toward the ground, visually searching for insect prey. Many sleep at night on leaves. Anoles are well-known for their territorial behavior. Males defend territories on which one to three females may live. In some species males with territories spend up to half of each day defending their territories from males looking to establish new territories. The defender will roam his territory, perhaps 30 sq m (325 sq ft), occasionally giving territorial advertisements – repeatedly displaying his extended throat fan, or *dewlap*, and performing *push-ups*, bobbing his head and body up and down. Trespassers that do not leave the territory are chased and even bitten. Anoles are chiefly *sit-and-wait* predators on insects and other small invertebrates. Anoles themselves are frequent prey for many birds (motmots, trogons, and others) and snakes.

The AMAZON THORNYTAIL (Plate 18) apparently lives only in high treetops, in lowland rainforest. This spectacular lizard (males in breeding condition have an orange head and black body) has a short, spiky tail and looks unlike any of the other arboreal iguanoids in Perú. Although you probably won't see any up close, you may be able to watch them through binoculars.

Some of the iguanoids in Perú live on the ground. PERÚ PACIFIC LIZARDS (Plate 17) are diurnal and terrestrial; they are often found on riverbanks. These lizards are very agile, and they often run bipedally, using their tails for balance. Males are strongly territorial, and they aggressively defend their home sites from other males. These lizards usually seek shelter in burrows either that they excavate themselves or that birds or mammals have abandoned. Another diurnal, terrestrial iguanoid that seeks shelter in holes in the ground or in logs is the PINK-BELLIED LEAF LIZARD (Plate 17). On warm days, SPINY WHORLTAIL LIZARDS (Plate 17) can be seen all over the ruins at Machu Pichu. If the weather is not sunny, these lizards will be hidden in deep crevices. TSCHUDI'S PACIFIC LIZARDS (Plate 17) live in sandy areas in the coastal desert lowlands. Active by day, they sometimes dive into the sand head-first and "swim" through the sand.

Breeding

Breeding in GREEN IGUANAS usually occurs during the early part of the dry season. These large lizards lay clutches that average about 40 eggs. They are laid in sandy soil, in burrows that are 1 to 2 m (3 to 6.5 ft) long, dug by the females. After laying her clutch, a female iguana fills the burrow with dirt, giving the site a final packing down with her nose. After the young hatch, they eat the feces of adult Green Iguanas. The most plausible explanation for this odd behavior is that by eating feces, they inoculate their guts with bacteria that help in digesting cellulose from the plants they eat. Anoles are also egg-layers. Most species lay a single egg at a time, although some of the larger species lay up to three eggs. Anoles may produce eggs every few weeks and breed throughout the year. The three species of Pacific lizards profiled here usually lay from one to six eggs per clutch.

Notes

Iguanoids are not poisonous, and they will not bite unless given no other choice. Large iguanas are hunted by local people for food. Many people say iguanas are delicious; supposedly they taste just like chicken. The AMAZON THORNYTAIL is thought to be poisonous by some indigenous peoples, who believe that its spiny tail can inflict a fatal sting; the tail is actually harmless.

Via interactions between the external environment and their nervous and hormonal systems, many iguanoids have the ability to change their body color. Such color changes may be adaptations that allow them to be more *cryptic*, to blend into their surroundings, and hence, to be less detectable to predators. Alterations in color throughout the day may also aid in temperature regulation; lizards must obtain their body heat from the sun, and darker colors absorb more heat. The feat is accomplished by moving pigment granules within individual skin cells either to a central clump (causing that color to diminish) or spreading them evenly about the cell (enhancing the color). It is now thought that the stimulus to change colors arises with the physiology of the animal rather than with the color of its surroundings.

Status

GREEN IGUANAS are regulated for conservation purposes; they are listed on CITES Appendix II. Because they are hunted for meat, they are scarce in some localities. None of Perú's other iguanoids is currently considered threatened or endangered.

Profiles

Green Iguana, *Iguana iguana*, Plate 16a
Slender Anole, *Norops fuscoauratus*, Plate 16b
Common Forest Anole, *Norops trachyderma*, Plate 16c
Amazon Wood Lizard, *Enyalioides laticeps*, Plate 16d
Pink-bellied Leaf Lizard, *Stenocercus roseiventris*, Plate 17a
Spiny Whorltail Lizard, *Stenocercus crassicaudatus*, Plate 17b
Perú Pacific Lizard, *Microlophus peruvianus*, Plate 17c
Tschudi's Pacific Lizard, *Microlophus thoracicus*, Plate 17d
Tiger Pacific Lizard, *Microlophus tigris*, Plate 18a
Blue-lipped Tree Lizard, *Tropidurus umbra ochrocollaris*, Plate 18b
Amazon Thornytail, *Uracentron flaviceps*, Plate 18c

7. Other Lizards

The *skinks* are a large family (Scincidae, with nearly 1100 species) of small and medium-sized lizards with a worldwide distribution. Skinks are easily recognized because they look different from other lizards, being slim-bodied with relatively short limbs, and having smooth, shiny scales that produce a satiny look. Many skinks are in the 5 to 9 cm (2 to 4 in) long range, not including the tail, which can easily double an adult's length. The BLACK-SPOTTED SKINK (Plate 18) is one of only two species of skinks found in Perú.

Teids, Family Teiidae, are a New World group of about 105 species, distributed throughout the Americas. Most are tropical residents, inhabiting most areas below 1500 m (5000 ft) in elevation. Twelve species occur in Perú. Many species, such as the GOLDEN TEGU (Plate 19), and the AMAZON RACERUNNER (Plate 19) are diurnal sun-baskers, and are often quite abundant and conspicuous along trails, roads, beaches, and in forest clearings. Known for their alert behavior and fast movements, they are often easily spotted but difficult to approach closely. The Golden Tegu, found in the eastern lowlands, can reach a length of almost 1 m (3 ft). If you surprise one along a trail, it can startle you by making a lot of noise as it crashes through the vegetation to escape. *Teids* have slender bodies, angular, pointed heads and long, slender, whip-like tails (usually much longer than the body). The scales of the larger conspicuous species are very small, giving them a velvety or shiny appearance. Some teids are striped, others are striped and spotted, or irregularly blotched.

The family Gymnophthalmidae, often called *microteids*, is composed of about 140 species, 35 of which occur in Perú. Many of these are 10 to 15 cm (4 to 6 in) in length, including tail. You find them mostly in rainforest leaf litter, but they can be secretive and hard to see. Of this group, the PUNA LIZARD (Plate 19) is profiled here; many other small, dull gray to brown species are very similar.

Natural History
Ecology and Behavior

Many skinks are found in moist ground habitats such as near streams and springs or under wet leaf litter. A few species are arboreal, and some are burrowers. Skinks use their limbs to walk but when the need arises for speed, they move by making rapid wriggling movements with their bodies, snake-fashion, with little leg assistance. Through evolutionary change, in fact, some species have lost limbs entirely, all movement being handled snake-fashion. Skinks are day-active lizards, and in the tropics they are most active in the morning hours; they spend the heat of midday in sheltered, insulated hiding places, such as deep beneath the leaf litter. Some skinks are sit-and-wait foragers, whereas others actively seek their food. They consume many kinds of insects, which they grab, crush with their jaws or beat against the ground, then swallow whole. Predators on Peruvian skinks include snakes, larger lizards, birds, and mammals such as coati, armadillo, and opossum. Skinks generally are not seen unless searched for. Most species are quite secretive, spending most of their time hidden under rocks, vegetation, or leaf litter. The two species found in Perú are diurnal and terrestrial. They are most common in semi-open forests.

The sun-basking teids actively search for their food, which can include just about any animal small enough to eat. Typically they forage by moving slowly along the ground, poking their nose into the leaf litter and under sticks and rocks. Although most are terrestrial, many also climb into lower vegetation to hunt. Teids have a characteristic gait, moving jerkily forward while rapidly turning their head from side to side. The small microteiids inhabit leaf litter in more shaded areas and forage for invertebrate prey such as insects; most prefer old growth forest and shun more disturbed areas.

Breeding

Skinks are either egg-layers or live-bearers. The BLACK-SPOTTED SKINK gives birth to three to five live young; the eggs are protected within the mother's body throughout development. They breed sporadically all year. Peruvian teids are egg-layers; females produce small clutches that average three to five eggs. Individuals produce two or more clutches per year. The AMAZON RACERUNNER lays two to six eggs, buried in the sand or loose soil. Among the teids and microteids, some species exhibit what for vertebrates is an odd method of reproduction. All individuals in these species are female. They breed by *parthenogenesis*. Females lay unfertilized eggs, which all develop as females that, barring mutations, are all genetically identical to mom. (A few species of fish and many insects also reproduce this way.) Some argue that this *asexual* breeding indicates that the males in the population are a drain on resources and thus a luxury. It is likely that parthenogenetic species arise when individuals of two different but closely related, sexually reproducing, "parent" species mate and, instead of having hybrid young that are sterile (a usual result, as when horses and donkeys mate to produce sterile mules), have young whose eggs result in viable females.

Notes

Many lizards, including the skinks, teids, microteids, and geckos, have a drastic predator escape mechanism: they leave their tails behind for the predator to attack and eat while they make their escape. The process is known as *tail autotomy* – "self removal." Owing to unusual anatomical features of the tail vertebrae, the tail is only tenuously attached to the rest of the body; when the animal is grasped forcefully by its tail, the tail breaks off. The shed tail then wriggles vigorously for a while, diverting a predator's attention for the instant it takes the lizard to find shelter. A new tail can grow to replace the lost one, but this loss of a major body part is evidently stressful for the lizard. Tail-deprived individuals often become inactive and sometimes die.

Is autotomy successful as a lifesaving tactic? Some snakes that have been dissected have had nothing but skinks in their stomachs – not whole bodies, just tails! Also, a very common finding when a field biologist surveys any population of small lizards (catching as many as possible in a given area to count and examine) is that often 50% or more have regenerating tails. This indicates that tail autotomy is common and successful in preventing predation.

Status

The GOLDEN TEGU is regulated for conservation purposes; it is listed on CITES Appendix II. No other of Perú's skinks, teids, or microteids is known to be threatened or endangered. As is the case for many reptiles and amphibians, however, many species have not been sufficiently monitored to ascertain the true status of populations.

Profiles

Black-spotted Skink, *Mabuya nigropunctata*, Plate 18d
Amazon Racerunner, *Ameiva ameiva*, Plate 19a
Forest Whiptail, *Kentropyx pelviceps*, Plate 19b
Golden Tegu, *Tupinambis teguixin*, Plate 19c
Puna Lizard, *Proctoporus bolivianus*, Plate 19d

Environmental Close-up 3
Endemism and High Species Diversity: Why Perú?

An organism is *endemic* to a place when it is found only in that place. But the size or type of place referred to is variable: a given species of frog, say, may be endemic to the Western Hemisphere, to a single continent such as South America, to a small mountainous region of Perú, or to a speck of an island off Perú's coast.

A species' history dictates its present distribution. When it's confined to a certain or small area, the reason is that: (1) there are one or more barriers to stop further spread (an ocean, a mountain range, a thousand km of tropical rainforest in the way), (2) the species evolved only recently and has not yet had time to spread, or (3) the species evolved long ago, spread long ago, and now has become extinct over all but a remnant part of its prior range. A history of isolation also matters: the longer a group of animals and plants is isolated from their close relatives, the more time they have to evolve by themselves and to change into new, different, and unique groups. The best examples are on islands. Some islands once were attached to mainland areas but continental drift and/or changing sea levels led to their isolation in the middle of the ocean; other islands arose suddenly via volcanic activity beneath the seas. Take the island of Madagascar. Once attached to Africa and India, the organisms stranded on its shores when it became an island had probably 100 million years in isolation to develop into the highly endemic fauna and flora we see today. It's thought that about 80% of the island's plants and animals are endemic – half the bird species, about 800 butterflies, 8000 flowering plants, and essentially all the mammals and reptiles. Most of the species of lemurs of the world – small, primitive but cute primates – occur only on Madagascar, and an entire nature tourism industry has been built there around the idea of endemism: if you want to see wild lemurs, you must go there. Other examples of islands with high concentrations of endemic animals abound: Indonesia, where about 15% of the world's bird species occur, a quarter of them endemic; Papua New Guinea, where half the birds are endemic; the Philippines, where half the mammals are endemic; and the Galápagos Islands, where 42% of the resident bird species occur nowhere else in the world.

Recent biological surveys of mainland Perú show that it supports a surprising number of species (some of which are endemic but most of which are not). Perú is, in fact, considered one of 10 or so "mega-diversity" countries in the world. It has more species of animals and plants than some countries that are 20 times larger (Table 1, p. 93).

Perú's high biodiversity is due to several factors:

1   Virtually all groups of animals and plants, such as lizards, insects, birds, and trees, show a pattern of species number related to latitude. The higher latitudes (the north and south poles are at 90°E latitude and the equator is at 0°E latitude) have few species and as you sample at lower and lower latitudes toward the equator the number of species increases. This pattern is called a *latitudinal gradient in species diversity* and is likely caused by an increasing availability of sunlight energy, photosynthetic rates and, therefore, increasing food availability, as you move toward the equator. Perú is near the equator, where the world's greatest species diversity occurs.

2   Owing to Perú's varied topography, there is a multitude of habitat types, and

Table 1. Number of species of selected animal groups in Perú (1,285,220 sq km, 496,224 sq miles, in area) and in the USA (9.4 million sq km, 3.6 million sq miles), the number of those that are endemic to Perú, and a comparison to the worldwide number of species.

Group	Total no. of species in USA	Total no. of species in Perú	Number of species endemic to Perú (% endemic)	Approximate no. of species worldwide (% in Perú)
Mammals	428	431	46 (11)	4630 (9)
Birds	768	1703	109 (6)	9040 (19)
Reptiles	261	364	98 (27)	7000 (5)
Amphibians	194	315	128 (41)	4700 (7)
Butterflies	678	4250	430 (10)	24,000 (18)
Tiger Beetles	111	96	20 (21)	2250 (4)

some highly isolated habitats that act as "biological islands" (for example, inland highland areas surrounded by lower-lying regions – such as forest habitats around the isolated upper Río Marañon valley or separated mountain ranges near Tingo María). These isolated areas support large numbers of endemic species, and the wide range of habitat types, especially at different altitudes, makes room for lots of species, endemic and non-endemic, to exist in a relatively small area.

3   The Amazon area of Perú is part of the most species-rich area in the world. To understand this area's current diversity, we have to look at its geological history. Over the last 100,000 years or so there have been ten-thousand-year cycles of drought and heavy rainfall. These cycles changed large parts of this immense forest region into grassland-savannah and back to forest over and over again. Because of the Andes Mountains and the shape of the continental coastline, rainfall across that Amazon Basin is not, and probably never has been, uniform. Even today, in the middle of a high rainfall part of the cycle, small pockets of forest with 3 to 4 m (10 to 13 ft) of annual rainfall can be surrounded by forest areas with less than 1.5 m (5 ft) of annual rainfall. During the most severe drought epochs, annual rainfall totals were probably cut by a third or more. Only the high rainfall forest pockets were able to maintain themselves against the inroads of fire that changed the drier forest areas to grasslands and savannah. The patches of cool, moist tree areas within a great sea of open grasslands became islands, or forest *refugia*, for the plants and animals adapted to forests. Isolated for tens of thousands of years, many of these populations of plants and animals changed (evolved) into different species and no longer were capable of breeding with members of their former species in other forest refuges. When the drought cycle shifted back to high rainfall, the plants in the forest islands began to expand out and reclaim the grassland habitat. Eventually the expansion of these forests brought them into contact with each other again. At the zones of contact where the forests met, they once more formed a continuous forest habitat. The species formed during the period of isolation could now spread and mix into a newly connected forest, thus greatly enriching the diversity of species. Scientists have been able to discern 15 to 20 Amazonian forest refuges formed various times

throughout the Pliocene and Pleistocene geological periods. The most persistent and largest of these historical forest islands includes the area covering most of present-day northeastern Perú – the "Napo Refuge." Because it has been intact forest for hundreds of thousands of years, it has been a productive area in which new species could evolve and a stable area in which older and now endemic species could persist – an accumulation of species that helps explain the high diversity in the region.

Chapter 7

BIRDS

- *Introduction*
- *General Characteristics and Classification of Birds*
- *Features of Tropical Birds*
- *Seeing Birds in Perú*
- *Family Profiles*

Introduction

By far the most common vertebrate animals you will see on a visit to Perú are birds. Unlike many other terrestrial vertebrates, birds are most often active during the day, visually conspicuous and usually quite vocal as they pursue their daily activities. But why are birds so much more conspicuous than other vertebrates? The reason lies in the essential nature of birds: they fly. The ability to fly is one of nature's premier anti-predator escape mechanisms, and animals that can fly well are released from the danger of being stalked by a large proportion of the predators in an area. Most mortality from predators among tropical birds happens while they are eggs or helpless young in the nest. Once they reach adulthood, their mortality rate by predation falls to very low levels. By being able to escape most predation, they are released from much of the tyranny of natural selection that places a premium on camouflage, unobtrusiveness and shyness. Thus they can be both reasonably conspicuous in their behavior and also reasonably certain of daily survival. Most flightless land vertebrates, tied by gravity to moving in or over the ground or on plants, are easy prey unless they are quiet, concealed, and careful or, alternatively, very large or fierce; many smaller ones, in fact, have evolved special defense mechanisms, such as poisons or nocturnal behavior.

Not only are birds among the easiest animals to watch, but they are among the most beautiful. Experiences with Perú's birds will almost certainly provide some of your trip's most memorable naturalistic moments. Your first view of a flock of huge and noisy Blue-and-yellow Macaws flying over the forest in the Amazon or a flock of thousands of Guanay Cormorants swimming and diving close to shore at Paracas Peninsula will be highlights you will want to share with everyone.

General Characteristics and Classification of Birds

Birds have one trait that they share with no other vertebrates – they have *feathers*. Feathers evidently evolved from reptilian scales, and they, together with most everything else in and on the bird body, serve to lighten the load and provide the power to make flight possible. The feathers provide an ultralight but durable protective covering. The hollow bones of the skeleton provide a light but sturdy framework to attach powerful flight muscles, especially on the breast. The teeth are replaced by an expanded part of the digestive tract, the *gizzard*, which along with the reduction and rearrangement of many internal organs makes the center of gravity more aerodynamically positioned. A four-chambered heart together with warm-bloodedness and a super-efficient lung system make possible an accelerated use of energy to sustain the physiologically expensive costs of flight. Finally, the forelimbs have evolved to become sublime wings, with spoilers to overcome wing-tip air turbulence, ailerons for maneuvering, and such a host of detailed adaptations for flight control that engineers at the Boeing Company can only marvel with envy.

Birds began evolving from reptiles during the Jurassic Period of the Mesozoic Era, perhaps 150 million years ago, and then there was an explosive development of new species during the last 50 million years or so. The development of flight is the key factor behind birds' evolution, their historical spread throughout the globe, and their current ecological success. Flight, as mentioned above, is a fantastic predator evasion technique, but it also permits birds to move over long distances in search of particular foods or habitats, and its development opened up for vertebrate exploration and exploitation an entirely new and vast theater of operations – the atmosphere.

At first glance, birds appear to be highly variable beasts, ranging in size from 135-kg (300-lb) ostriches to 4-kg (10-lb) eagles to 3-g (a tenth of an ounce) hummingbirds. However, when compared with other types of vertebrates, birds are remarkably standardized physically. The reason is that, whereas mammals or reptiles can be quite diverse in form and still function as mammals or reptiles (think how different in form are lizards, snakes, and turtles), if birds are going to fly, the physics of aerodynamics narrowly dictate which shape and form will most efficiently stay in the air. (The flying mammals, bats, also follow these dictates.) Thus all flying birds have a similar gestalt, or body plan. Only birds like ostriches, which lost their ability to fly, developed very unbird-like body shapes.

Bird classification is one of those areas of science that continually undergoes revision. Currently more than 9000 separate species are recognized worldwide, and they are placed in 2040 genera (plural of genus). These genera are grouped into 170 families, which in turn are grouped into 28 to 30 orders, depending on whose classification scheme you want to follow. The orders are roughly divided into two major groups, the perching (dickie bird) species such as robins, sparrows and jays (known technically as the *passerine* birds, of Order Passeriformes) and all the rest (Non-passerines), which includes everything from penguins, ducks and herons to parrots, kingfishers and hawks. For purposes in this book we divide birds into various groups: those that are unrelated but occur together in broad habitat types; those that are similar in appearance and might be easily confused; and finally, those that are closely related (and thus often found in similar habitats and also often similar in appearance).

Features of Tropical Birds

The first thing to know about tropical birds is that they are exceedingly diverse. There are many more species of birds in the tropics than in temperate or arctic regions (see Close-up, p. 92). For instance, somewhat fewer than 700 bird species occur regularly in North America north of Mexico, and about 3300 species occur in the Neotropics (Central and South America). But nearly 1700 species are found in Perú – more than half of the species of the Neotropics and nearly 19% of all the species in the world!

Tropical birds, like their temperate zone brethren, eat insects, seeds, nectar, fruits and, for the predaceous species, meat. A big difference, however, is the degree of specialization in tropical species. In temperate areas fruit is such a temporary resource that few species can afford to make their living as confirmed *frugivores*, but in many tropical areas fruit is available throughout much of the year, so bird species have evolved bills, digestive systems and behavior that make them experts on finding and eating fruits. Similarly, species that eat insects (*insectivores*), seeds (*granivores*), flower nectar (*nectarivores*) and, to some degree, even the meat-eaters (*carnivores*), have high degrees of specialization.

Mating systems of birds show a pattern of inequality between the sexes. Females generally have the most power to choose mates. Each male is thus left with the task of convincing these picky females that he and he alone is the most appropriate one to father her young. A male can scream this message with louder or prettier songs, longer and more colorful tail feathers, or a combination of sounds, colors and behavioral antics that increase his chances of convincing the female of his gene superiority.

Mating systems range from single territorial males with one female (*monogamy*) to one male having numerous female mates (*polygyny*) and even some cases of a female having numerous male mates (*polyandry*). Among tropical birds, monogamy apparently is the most common form of mating, although we now know that a lot of extracurricular sneaking around goes on. Monogamous mating is perhaps made most obvious when the males sing on the boundaries of their territories to declare to all the world, but especially to other males of the same species, "Stay out. This is my home and you are not welcome to tarry here." Polygyny is less common but often made obvious by the many bizarre behaviors associated with this mating system. Among polygynous species, males often have to congregate together, each strutting his gene superiority so that a female can compare them side by side and make her choice – a kind of beauty contest. This type of congregated male courting is called a *lec* (often spelled *lek*, the original Swedish form). Females in this type of society are usually single working mothers because the father, after mating, has no further contact with his mate or his eventual offspring. Polyandry is the rarest type of mating system, and it is practiced primarily by only three groups of birds in Perú, the rheas, tinamous and the jacanas. In these cases males guard nests and females dump eggs in each of several males' nests after mating with them.

Breeding seasons in the tropics tend to be longer than in temperate areas but are usually closely tied to the wet season and the abundance of food associated with it, especially heavy concentrations of insect life and ripening fruit. In Perú, birds in the coastal areas breed primarily from January to March. In the mountains they breed from June to September. In the Amazon the breeding season is more ambiguous, with some species breeding almost every month of the year, but the majority of species nest during the early rainy season, in November to January. One notable aspect of bird breeding in the tropics that has long puzzled biologists is that clutches of the small land birds (passerines) are usually small, most species typically laying only two eggs per nest. Similar birds that breed in temperate zone areas usually have clutches of three to five eggs. Possible explanations are:

1   small broods attract fewer nest predators;
2   because such a high percentage of nests in the tropics are destroyed by predators, it is not worth putting too much energy and effort into any one nest; and
3   with the increased hours of daylight during the summer breeding season in northern areas, temperate zone birds have more time each day to gather enough food for extra nestlings.

Finally, tropical birds include some of the most gorgeously attired birds in the world. Many have bright, flashy colors and vivid plumage patterns, with some of Perú's parrots, toucans, trogons, cotingas, and tanagers, claiming top honors. Why so many tropical birds possess highly colored plumages is unknown, but it may be at least partially explained by the presence of a large number of species in which males are under natural selection pressures by female mating choices to have gaudy plumage. Also, although people take more notice of birds with bright, striking plumage colors and patterns, we should point out that, actually, most species in the tropics are dull-colored and visually unremarkable.

Seeing Birds in Perú

We chose for illustration and profiling below 322 species that are among Perú's most frequently seen birds. The best way to spot these birds is to follow three easy steps: (1) Look for them at the correct time. You can see birds at any time of the day, but your best chance of seeing them is when they are most active and singing frequently, during early morning and late afternoon. Some species of owls, potoos and nightjars are strictly nocturnal, and the best way to see them is to follow their calls at night and find them in the beam of your flashlight. (2) Be quiet as you walk along trails or roads, and stop periodically to look around carefully. Not all birds are noisy, and some, even brightly colored ones, can be quite inconspicuous when they are directly above you in the forest canopy. Trogons, for instance, beautiful medium-sized birds with green backs and bright red or yellow bellies, are notoriously difficult to see among branches and leaves. Sometimes sitting or standing quietly, especially along a stream, is the best way to see otherwise shy denizens. (3) BRING BINOCULARS on your trip. You would be surprised at the number of people who visit tropical areas with the purpose of viewing wildlife and don't bother to bring binoculars. They need not be an expensive pair, but binoculars are essential to bird viewing. If you become excited about wildlife in the middle of your trip and have no binoculars, many eco-lodges rent them out by the day.

A surprise to many people during their first trip to a habitat like rainforest or high elevation puna is that they do not immediately see or hear hordes of birds upon entering a trail. During large portions of the day, in fact, these habitats are mainly quiet, with few birds noticeably active. The birds are there, but many are inconspicuous – small brownish birds near to the ground, and greenish, brownish, or grayish birds in the tops of the vegetation. A frequent, at first discombobulating experience, is that you will be walking along a trail, seeing few birds, and then, suddenly, a *mixed species foraging flock* with many species swooshes into view, filling the bushes and trees around you at all levels with birds – some hopping along the ground, some moving through the brush, some clinging to tree trunks, others in the canopy – more birds than you can easily count or identify – and then, just as suddenly, the flock is gone, moved on in its meandering path through the forest. If the trail system is extensive, sometimes you can move quietly ahead of the flock and let it pass by you again and again. This works especially well for low-moving flocks of antbirds, ovenbirds, woodcreepers and flycatchers. High-moving flocks, with birds such as tanagers and cotingas, are much harder to follow and are often best seen from canopy towers built at several jungle lodges throughout the country.

It would be a shame to leave Perú without seeing at least some of its spectacular birds, such as condors, macaws, toucans, trogons, and tanagers. If you have trouble locating such birds, be sure and let people around you know of your interest – tourguides, resort employees, park personnel. Everyone involved in Perú's tourist industry wants to share the country's richness of natural beauty, and they can either tell you the best places to go for particular birds or send you to someone who knows.

Family Profiles

1. Penguin

The 17 species of the *penguin* family (Spheniscidae) are all restricted to the southern hemisphere, with one species on the equator in the Galápagos Islands. The largest species stands 1 m (3 ft) tall and the smallest stands only 30 cm (1 ft) tall. All are flightless and use their highly modified wings for propulsion underwater. These wings are unique in that, unlike in other birds, the bones are fused together and the wings cannot be folded. The feathers that cover the penguins' bodies and wings are small and dense, looking more like large scales than proper feathers. Their feet are placed far back on the body, and they have webbing between the toes and long sharp nails. The feet are used for steering and braking underwater and for clambering up steep and slippery slopes when going ashore. Most species are highly social, great numbers of individuals foraging together at sea and breeding in colonies.

The HUMBOLDT PENGUIN (Plate 20) is the only species of penguin found in Perú. Standing 72 cm (28 in) tall, it is one of the medium-sized species of penguins. On land, their black and white form and upright stance make them easy to recognize. In the water they lie low on the surface, looking like short-necked ducks. Sometimes they swim with only their heads exposed above the surface. Older chicks can be nearly the size of adults but are gray in color. This species nests on off-shore islands and is found only along the west coast of South America, from Perú to central Chile.

Natural History
Ecology and Behavior
The HUMBOLDT PENGUIN is not as social as other penguins and during the non-breeding season normally occurs only in pairs or small groups of five to six. However, during times when the water is colder, 10 to 15 or more individuals gather together, perhaps because food is more concentrated. Their food includes fish, crustaceans and squid, all of which are captured in their strong, sharp bills during underwater pursuit. Their mouths are lined with rear-facing spines that help them hold onto and swallow slippery and wiggling prey. Although some large penguin species in the Antarctic can dive to depths of nearly 275 m (900 ft) and stay under for almost 20 minutes, the Humboldt Penguin seldom stays under for more than two minutes and although it occasionally dives to a maximum depth of 30 m (100 ft), it usually remains within a meter (3 ft) of the surface. Parents feed young on shore by regurgitating food caught at sea.

Breeding
Breeding on small islands off the coast of Perú, the HUMBOLDT PENGUIN is monogamous and may mate for life. It can be found breeding almost any time of year, but usually only if there is an extended period of abundant prey. They lay one or two eggs in burrows in the ground or in protected areas under rocks, but usually only a single young survives. Both parents incubate the eggs and feed the young for nearly two months, after which it begins to care for itself.

Notes
Fossil evidence and comparison of skull bones show that penguins likely evolved from flying albatross-like ancestors. Even today, the most primitive penguin species actually have tubular nostrils, a character otherwise restricted to albatrosses and petrels. The HUMBOLDT PENGUIN is closely related to the GALÁPAGOS PENGUIN, and it is likely that some Humboldt Penguins that strayed to the Galápagos on the cold Humboldt Current were the ancestors of the Galápagos species.

Status

El Niño-induced changes in water temperature can drastically affect fish and squid populations, which in turn directly affect penguin survival and chances for reproduction. Major changes in the habitat, whether natural, caused by humans, or a deadly combination of both, create a potential for drastically affecting populations of this penguin species. In addition, some individuals are still taken for human consumption and for the illicit pet trade, and many are thought to be killed each year in fishing nets. As a result, the present population in the wild is thought to be fewer than 10,000 birds, and the Humboldt Penguin is considered endangered by some authorities; it is CITES Appendix I listed.

Profile

Humboldt Penguin, *Spheniscus humboldti*, Plate 20c

2. Tubenose Birds

The *tubenose seabirds* (Order Procellariiformes; 115 species worldwide, 30 in Perú) includes the *shearwaters, storm-petrels, diving-petrels* and *albatrosses*. All of them are found only in *marine* (sea water) habitats, and they spend their entire lives at sea except for short periods of nesting on islands. They have peculiar tube-shaped nostrils and distinctly hooked upper bills. Like many seabirds, they have a large gland between and above their eyes that permits them to drink seawater; it filters salt from the water and concentrates it. This highly concentrated salt solution is excreted in drops from the base of the bill and the nostril tubes direct the salt to the end of the bill, where they can be easily discharged. Off the coast of Perú, species of the families of storm-petrels (Hydrobatidae), diving-petrels (Pelecanoididae) and shearwaters (Procellariidae) are the tubenoses most frequently seen by ecotravellers. Albatross species seldom come near enough the coast to be seen from land or from small boats around the coastal islands. These sea-going behemoths have wingspans of up to 3.6 m (12 ft) and weigh up to 9 kg (20 lb). At the other end of the size spectrum of tubenoses, the WHITE-VENTED STORM-PETREL (Plate 20) is only 15 cm (6 in) long. It is commonly seen near the coast, especially at sites where sewage or fish products are being discarded directly into the ocean. Shearwaters, especially the SOOTY SHEARWATER (Plate 23), can often be seen streaming by just offshore in huge flocks as they skim over the surface on their stiff wings. The PERUVIAN DIVING-PETREL (Plate 20) looks like a tiny penguin as it swims on the surface and dives underwater. To escape danger, however, unlike any penguin, it flies quickly away.

Natural History
Ecology and Behavior

Members of the tubenoses have perhaps the best developed sense of smell of any birds, and they use this ability to locate their young and nest sites when returning from extended foraging trips. Tubenoses produce a vile-smelling stomach oil that they regurgitate and squirt at enemies. This oil makes an excellent sun-tan lotion but wreaks havoc on your clothes and social life. Albatrosses use a type of flight, known as *dynamic soaring*, that takes advantage of strong winds blowing across the ocean's surface. Their efficient but peculiar soaring flight takes them in huge loops from high above the ocean surface, where the wind is fastest, down toward the surface, where friction slows the wind, and then up into the faster wind again to give them lift for the next loop – a kind of roller-coaster flight that requires virtually no wing flapping. Shearwaters, with their smaller bodies and shorter wings, use dynamic soaring only during the windiest times. More often they alternate quick flaps of their stiff wings with long glides. The storm-petrels, on the other hand, have a fluttering flight low over the water's surface that sometimes brings their long hanging legs in contact with the water, making it look like they are walking on water. Albatrosses feed on squid, fish and invertebrates near the surface. Shearwaters dive underwater from the surface and, using their wings for propulsion, pursue fish. Storm-petrels delicately pluck invertebrates and other prey items from the surface of the sea, using their wings to flutter and hover just above the water. Most species feed during the day far out at sea and return to their nesting islands at night. Albatrosses, shearwaters and storm-petrels are not above eating garbage thrown overboard from ships, as well as floating carrion such as dead whales and seals. Diving-petrels use their wings like paddles to feed on *plankton* (small floating plants and animals) underwater. They have a pouch under their tongues in which they can store the plankton to eat later or bring back to their young at the nest.

Breeding
Tubenoses are monogamous and most breed in colonies on islands. On the breeding islands, they have elaborate courtship dances and display flights. These behaviors help strengthen pair-bonds, but they also coordinate hormone releases and synchronize mating readiness. A female albatross lays one large egg in a scraping on the bare ground. The other tubenoses all lay their single egg in a burrow dug by the adults or in rocky crevices. Incubation and brooding of the young is alternated with the male, each shift lasting several days to weeks. The other adult flies out to sea and searches for food. When it returns, it feeds the chick regurgitated food and stomach oil and takes its turn at brooding. When the chick's demand for food becomes overwhelming, both adults leave it alone for long periods as they search great distances over the ocean for enough food. After about 6 to 8 weeks (7 months for albatross), the chick is large enough to fledge and fly. Albatrosses take 5 to 7 years to mature and stay at sea this whole time before finally returning to their birth place to breed.

Notes
Storm-petrels get their name from the Greek word *"petros,"* which refers to the biblical disciple Peter, who tried to walk on water, just like storm-petrels appear to be doing when feeding. Shearwaters, especially the plump young, have been a source of food for centuries. In Australia, shearwaters are called "mutton birds," and the half-grown young are harvested in some areas for their stomach oil and feather down.

Status
Because of their often highly restricted nesting sites on small islands and vulnerability during the nesting period, many species of tubenoses are at risk. Albatrosses cannot become airborne readily from land and are easy victims for humans and introduced predators. Cats and rats, if carelessly released by humans, can wreak havoc on an entire island's population of storm-petrels. The PERUVIAN DIVING-PETREL is listed as threatened (IUCN Red List), and three other species of tubenoses that use Peruvian coastal waters for migration or wintering are also considered threatened: BLACK PETREL, COOK'S PETREL and GALÁPAGOS PETREL.

Profiles

White-vented Storm-petrel, *Oceanites gracilis*, Plate 20a
Wedge-rumped Storm-petrel, *Oceanodroma tethys*, Plate 20b
Peruvian Diving-Petrel, *Pelecanoides garnotii*, Plate 20d
Sooty Shearwater, *Puffinus griseus*, Plate 23e

3. Pelican Allies and Flamingos

Along Perú's rich coasts, the pelicans and their relatives are the most conspicuous of the seabirds. Some also penetrate inland into the Amazon region. Many of these Peruvian seabirds commonly seen by visitors from northern temperate areas are the same species or very similar to species found back home. Some, however, are members of groups restricted to the tropics. As a group, pelicans and their relatives are incredibly successful animals, present often at breeding and roosting colonies in enormous numbers. Their success is largely owed to incredibly rich food resources – the fish and invertebrate animals (crabs, mollusks, insects, jellyfish) produced in the sea and on beaches and mudflats. The dark side of this abundance of food is that during El Niño years, when the warm but nutrient-poor tropical currents displace the cold nutrient-rich currents, severely depleting food supplies, it is seabirds that suffer most drastically; some species, in fact, suffer up to 80% mortality rates during these periods.

All of the birds treated here (except the flamingo) are members of Order Pelecaniformes: *Boobies*, in the Family Sulidae (9 species worldwide, 5 in Perú), are large seabirds known for their sprawling breeding colonies on offshore islands and for plunging into the ocean from heights to pursue fish. The islands on which they nest accumulate phosphate-rich *guano* (bird dropping) that is meters thick and mined by Peruvian fertilizer companies. Boobies have tapered bodies, long, pointed wings, long tails, long, pointed bills, and often, brightly colored feet. The PERUVIAN BOOBY (Plate 20) is the most common species of booby seen from the coast. *Pelicans*, Family Pelecanidae (8 species worldwide, 2 in Perú), are large-headed and heavy-bodied seabirds, and, with their big, saggy throat pouches, are among the most recognizable of coastal seabirds. The most common species is the huge PERUVIAN PELICAN (Plate 21). Although usually you will see flocks of pelicans flying low over the water in a long line just off the beach, they often soar to great heights on updrafts at bluffs along the beach or even over buildings in downtown Lima. The GUANAY CORMORANT (Plate 21) is a medium-sized bird, mostly black, with short legs, long tail, and longish bill with a hooked tip. It is Perú's most abundant coastal seabird and is in the family Phalacrocoracidae (28 species worldwide, 3 in Perú). The ANHINGA (Plate 21), of the family Anhingidae (4 species worldwide, 1 in Perú), is similar to cormorants, with males all blackish and females and immatures with buffy heads and necks. Anhinga bills, however, are long and thin with a sharp point. They have long tails and very long, thin necks, and when they occasionally soar to great heights with tail and wings spread, they resemble soaring hawks or eagles with long necks. Anhingas occur both in coastal mangroves and along rivers and lakes in the Amazonian selva.

The other group covered in this section, the *flamingos*, Family Phoenicopteridae (5 species worldwide, 3 in Perú), is represented here by the CHILEAN FLAMINGO (Plate 21). Flamingos are variously placed in their own order, Phoenicopteriformes, or placed in with the ducks and geese in the order Anseriformes. All three Peruvian species nest on saline lakes of the Andes above 4000 m (13,000 ft).

During the Austral (southern hemisphere) winter, June through September, some individuals migrate to the coast, and several hundred spend this time in the lagoons of the Paracas and Mejiia reserves (see pp. 38–39).

Natural History
Ecology and Behavior

All of these seabirds except the flamingo feed mainly on fish, and they have developed a variety of ways to catch them. Boobies, which also eat squid, plunge dive from 15 m (50 ft) or more above the ocean surface to catch fish in their serrate-edged bills. Unlike almost all other birds, boobies do not have holes or nostrils at the base of the upper bill for breathing. The holes are closed over to keep seawater from rushing into their lungs as they dive deep into the ocean. They have to breathe through their mouths. Pelicans eat fish almost exclusively. Unlike all the other pelicans in the world, the PERUVIAN PELICAN, and its much smaller but closely related cousin that occasionally reaches the northern coast of Perú, the BROWN PELICAN, plunge-dive to catch fish. While underwater the throat sac expands when the pelican opens its bill and is used like a net to scoop up fish up to 30 cm (1 ft) long. Rising to the surface, the pelican then drains out the water from its bill pouch and swallows the fish before flying up to plunge-dive again. Pelicans appear ungainly as they sit on rocks or on beaches along the coast, but they are excellent fliers. They can use updrafts to soar for hours high above the coastline. At other times a flight of them will pass by just skimming the ocean's surface in a long line or "V" formation. Unlike the other members of their order, which often make distinctive squawks and screeches, particularly on their breeding islands, pelicans are generally silent. Diving from the surface of lakes, rivers, lagoons, and coastal saltwater areas, NEOTROPIC CORMORANTS (Plate 21) and ANHINGAS pursue fish underwater, using their large webbed feet for propulsion. Cormorants, which eat crustaceans as well as fish, catch the fish in their hooked bills. They often feed in large groups, especially when fish are concentrated in a small area. They roost and nest together in large colonies, usually on island peaks or in the tops of tall trees, and they move between roosting and feeding areas in large "V"-shaped flocks. Anhingas are solitary and spear prey underwater on the tips of their sharp bills.

Flamingos are *filter-feeders*. They use their tongue and open bill to first suck in water laden with microscopic crustaceans and then to expel the water through the sieve-like filters on the edges of the closed bill. They usually concentrate in brackish waters that tend to have high densities of these tiny swimming crustaceans.

Breeding

Except for the ANHINGA, all these species nest in large colonies either on isolated islands or, as in the case of the flamingos, on isolated salt flats, both of which are relatively predator-free. Some breed on ledges, slopes or cliffs (boobies and cormorants), some in trees (cormorants and Anhinga), and some on tops of shrubs or bare ground if no vegetation is available (pelicans). The flamingos construct mud-sided dikes around their nests in shallow salt lakes. All of these species are monogamous, and both mates share in nest-building, incubation and feeding young. In some groups like the pelicans, the male gathers sticks and stones for the nest, but the female actually constructs the nest. Individuals keep the same mate for several seasons and tend to return to the same site on the same island to nest. PERUVIAN PELICANS lay 2 or 3 eggs, which are incubated for 30 to 37 days, but usually only one young is raised successfully. PERUVIAN BOOBY females lay 1 or 2 eggs, which are incubated for about 45 days. Only one chick normally survives, often pecking its nest mate to death. NEOTROPIC CORMORANTS begin breeding when they are 3 or 4 years old. Two to 4 eggs are incubated for about 4 weeks, and the young fledge 5 to 8 weeks after hatching.

Notes

Boobies are sometimes called *gannets*, particularly by Europeans. The term booby apparently arose because the nesting and roosting birds seemed so bold and fearless toward people, which was considered stupid. Actually, the lack of predators on their nesting islands and cliffs meant they had never developed, or alternatively had lost, fear responses to large mammals like humans. Anhingas are also known as *darters*, the name derived from the way the birds underwater swiftly thrust their necks forward to spear fish on the points of their bills. Because they often swim with bodies submerged and only long necks and heads above water, they are also often called *snake-birds*. Cormorants have been used for centuries by people in China, Japan and Central Europe as fishing birds. A ring is placed around the cormorant's neck so that it cannot swallow its catch. Then, usually on a long leash, it is permitted to swim underwater to pursue fish. When the bird returns to the surface, it is reeled in, usually with an unswallowable fish clenched in its bill.

Status

None of the *pelecanid* seabirds that occur along the shores of mainland Perú is considered threatened or endangered. However, years of El Niño can devastate them so that their populations are reduced to tiny remnant populations within 18 months, the normal length of an El Niño event. In the past, these remnant populations have always eventually recovered. However, with the recent technological advances in fishing techniques and equipment, people have been able to so efficiently depress the fisheries in even these hardest of times that the post-El Niño recovery of fish as well as seabird populations could be threatened in the near future. In the highlands, however, two of the three species of flamingos, ANDEAN FLAMINGO and PUNA FLAMINGO, are considered threatened.

Profiles

Peruvian Booby, *Sula variegata*, Plate 20e
Peruvian Pelican, *Pelecanus thagus*, Plate 21a
Neotropic Cormorant, *Phalacrocorax brasilianus*, Plate 21b
Guanay Cormorant, *Phalacrocorax bougainvillii*, Plate 21c
Red-legged Cormorant, *Phalacrocorax gaimardi*, Plate 21d
Anhinga, *Anhinga anhinga*, Plate 21e
Chilean Flamingo, *Phoenicopterus chilensis*, Plate 21f

4. Gulls and Terns

On the open ocean, over coastal estuaries, on Andean lakes and along Amazonian rivers, the closely related *gulls* and *terns* are often present in large numbers; they are among the most obvious birds seen by travellers to Perú. They feed on fish and other aquatic and marine invertebrates, and they are often mesmerizing as they dive, swoop and soar in search of their food or in noisy encounters with each other. At rest, gulls and terns perch on sandy beaches and mudflats almost always in flocks of single or mixed species.

Gulls and terns are members of the Order Charadriiformes, which also includes the shorebirds (Plates 29 and 30). The gulls and terns are in the family Laridae (85 species worldwide, 26 in Perú). Terns are smaller, more streamlined forms of gulls. On the coast of Perú, several species of terns winter or are transient in migration. The LARGE-BILLED TERN (Plate 23) and the tiny YELLOW-BILLED TERN (Plate 23) are restricted to the large rivers of the Amazon, where they are permanent residents. They are noisy and obvious as they fly along a river or roost on isolated sand islands. The BLACK SKIMMER (Plate 23) is closely related to the gulls and terns but is placed in its own family, the Rynchopidae (3 species worldwide, one in Perú). It is the most bizarre and memorable of all these gull-like species, with its all-black body and huge red bill, the lower part of which extends beyond the tip of the upper part. The skimmer is usually seen roosting on sand bars in the rivers of the Amazonian lowlands but is also found in migration along coastal estuaries. In flight its long, arched wings are distinctive.

Natural History
Ecology and Behavior
These seabirds eat mainly fish and invertebrates. The terns feed primarily on fish, which they catch by hovering high over the water and then diving into the water to grab an unlucky fish that has tarried too long near the surface. Flocks of terns will often concentrate, repeatedly diving on a school of fish forced to the surface by larger, predatory fish. Terns on rivers of the Amazonian lowlands are more sparsely encountered, probably because the fish are generally not as concentrated or common as on the coast. Gulls are less elegant and less choosy in their pursuit of food. They wade in shallow water to catch opportunistically a wide variety of organisms. They are also not above scavenging on dead animals or even in garbage and sewage effluent. *Skimmers* use their peculiar flight and even more peculiar bill to pluck fish and large invertebrates from the water's surface. They fly low over the water with their blade-like bills open and the lower mandible skimming the surface. When they strike a small crustacean or fish, they quickly close the bill and catch it. Frequently they skim a line in the water and then turn to skim back along the same line.

Breeding
As with most seabirds, these gulls and their allies all breed in noisy colonies, usually on an isolated island or remote sand spit. Generally these species are monogamous, male and female sharing brooding and feeding the young. Males often present food to prospective mates in a ritual feeding that apparently provides clues to a female of the male's ability to catch quality prey and as a provider for their offspring. Because they nest on the ground, they have little protection from predators, although they will vigorously dive-bomb, peck and defecate on intruders into their nesting colony, human or otherwise. They lay up to 4 eggs, which are incubated for about 30 days. Young are fed when they push their bills down into their parents' throats, in effect forcing the parents to regurgitate food stored in their *crops* – enlargements of the top part of the esophagus. The low river islands on which the skimmer and the two Amazonian tern species nest are frequently flooded, and a large proportion of the young drown.

Notes
Skimmers on the coast do not nest there and are apparently migrants from inland. No one knows the route they use, but it probably involves some high altitude flights over the Andes.

Status

None of these mainland species are threatened, but habitat destruction, pollution and human interference on nesting areas make some populations vulnerable. The more limited ranges and specialized habitats for the ANDEAN GULL, LARGE-BILLED TERN and YELLOW-BILLED TERN, however, make these species more sensitive to increasing water contamination and inroads from growing human populations along puna lakes and Amazonian rivers.

Profiles

Gray Gull, *Larus modestus*, Plate 22a
Band-tailed Gull, *Larus belcheri*, Plate 22b
Franklin's Gull, *Larus pipixcan*, Plate 22c
Gray-headed Gull, *Larus cirrocephalus*, Plate 22d
Andean Gull, *Larus serranus*, Plate 22e
Inca Tern, *Larosterna inca*, Plate 23a
Large-billed Tern, *Phaetusa simplex*, Plate 23b
Yellow-billed Tern, *Sterna superciliaris*, Plate 23c
Black Skimmer, *Rynchops niger*, Plate 23d

5. Herons and Egrets

Herons and *egrets* are beautiful medium to large-sized wading birds that enjoy broad distributions throughout temperate and tropical regions around the world. Herons, egrets, and the more elusive *bitterns* constitute the heron family, Ardeidae, which includes about 60 species. Seventeen species occur in Perú, most of which breed there. Herons frequent all sorts of aquatic habitats: along rivers and streams, in marshes and swamps, and along lake and ocean shorelines. The difference between what is called an egret and what is called a heron is arbitrary and inconsistent. Generally, however, the term egret is reserved for species that are all white. Most herons and egrets are easy to identify. They are the tallish birds standing upright and still in shallow water or along the shore, staring intently into the water. They have slender bodies, long necks (always folded back in a flattened "S" in flight and sometimes when perched or resting, producing a short-necked, hunched appearance), long, pointed bills, and long legs with long toes. Peruvian species range in height from 0.3 to 1.3 m (1 to 4 ft). Most are attired in soft shades of gray, brown, blue, or green, and black or all white. Close up, many are exquisitely marked with small colored patches of facial skin or broad areas of spots or streaks; the *tiger-herons*, in particular, are strongly barred or streaked. During the breeding season both sexes of some species acquire long back and head plumes, and leg and bill color become brighter. The bizarre and poorly known BOAT-BILLED HERON (Plate 24) is sometimes placed as a single species in its own family, Cochleariidae; it occurs from western Mexico south, throughout the Amazon, to northern Argentina.

Natural History

Ecology and Behavior

Until recently, the CATTLE EGRET (Plate 24) was confined to the Old World, where it made its living following herds of large mammals such as elephant and buffalo. How it got to the New World is intriguing. Whereas many of the animals that have recently crossed oceans and spread rapidly into new continents have done so as a result of people's intentional or unintentional machinations, these egrets did it on their own. Apparently the first ones to reach the New World were from Africa. Perhaps blown off-course by a storm, they first landed in northern South America in about 1877. Finding the New World to its liking, during the next decades the species spread far and wide, finding abundant food where tropical forests were cleared for cattle grazing. Cattle Egrets have now colonized much of northern South America, Central America, all the major Caribbean islands, and much of the United States. The Cattle Egret first arrived on the coast of Perú in 1961 and is now also common in cleared areas of the Amazonian lowlands. Unlike all the other herons and egrets, it rarely enters the water but, instead, in upland areas, eats insects flushed by the feet of large grazing mammals such as cows. The other herons are mainly sit-and-wait hunters along water edges. Some species wait with infinite patience for prey to move and then strike out in a flash with their bill to grab the fish, frog or crab. The SNOWY EGRET (Plate 24), however, often staggers around in the shallows like a drunken sailor trying to scare up prey that are then easy targets for its bill. The North American GREEN HERON, a close relative of the STRIATED HERON (Plate 25), is known to swish bait (like bread stolen from a picnic area) in the water and attract fish to within striking range of its bill. The CAPPED HERON (Plate 25), RUFESCENT TIGER-HERON (Plate 24) and the BOAT-BILLED HERON, with its grotesquely large bill, are denizens of small forest streams. These herons are often so well camouflaged that you can pass close by them in your canoe without noticing them. At day break and again just before sunset they are more likely to be out in the open. The Boat-billed Heron, however, is nocturnal, and your best chance of seeing it is by shining a flashlight in the tangled foliage along waterways at night or finding a small group in a protected roost within dense thickets during the day. It uses its huge bill to grope in the water for frogs, fish and shrimp.

Breeding

Most herons are social birds, roosting and breeding in colonies, often several species together. Some, however, like the tiger-herons, are predominantly solitary. Herons are known for their often elaborate courtship displays and ceremonies, which continue through pair-formation and nest-building. Generally the female constructs the nest from sticks presented to her by the male. The nests are in trees, reeds or occasionally on the ground. Both sexes incubate the 3 to 7 eggs for 16 to 30 days, and both feed the young for another 35 to 50 days until they fledge.

Herons and egrets often lay more eggs than the number of chicks they can successfully feed. This seems contrary to our usual view of nature, which we regard as finely tuned through natural selection so that behaviors avoid waste. The likely answer to this puzzle is that this behavior allows a pair to raise the maximum number of offspring every year even if food levels are unpredictable from year to year. Females lay eggs one or two days apart, and start incubating with the first egg. Chicks hatch out at the same intervals, and so the young in a single nest are of different ages and quite different sizes. The largest chick in each nest receives the most food, probably because it can more easily attract the adults and get to the food they regurgitate. These larger chicks on occasion will also kill their smaller siblings (*siblicide*), especially if food is scarce. If there is sufficient food, the next biggest chicks will also be able to eat often enough to survive. In years of super-abundant food, even the smallest chicks will be able to eat enough. Thus, laying more eggs than can be reared as chicks most years may be to insure that many chicks are raised in the years of abundance.

Notes

All herons have a distinctive comb on the flattened middle toe of each foot. They use it to groom themselves and spread bits of specialized feathers, called *powder down*, throughout their body surface. Powder down is found in only a very few other birds in the world; its function appears to be to help clean the large body feathers when they become full of fish scales and grime.

Status

Some of Perú's herons and egrets are fairly rare, but they are not considered threatened species because they are more common in other parts of their ranges, outside the country.

Profiles

Boat-billed Heron, *Cochlearius cochlearius*, Plate 24a
Snowy Egret, *Egretta thula*, Plate 24b
Cattle Egret, *Bubulcus ibis*, Plate 24c
Great Egret, *Ardea alba*, Plate 24d
Rufescent Tiger-Heron, *Tigrisoma lineatum*, Plate 24e
Cocoi Heron, *Ardea cocoi*, Plate 25a
Striated Heron, *Butorides striatus*, Plate 25b
Capped Heron, *Pilherodius pileatus*, Plate 25c

6. Marsh and Stream Birds

Marsh and stream birds are a collection of unrelated species that share habitats of standing and running water surrounded by grasses, bushes, trees and other relatively thick vegetation. They do not rely heavily on flight but rather swim in the water or walk on and through vegetation near the water. They tend to be shy and retiring, and they often slink away from danger before a predator (or an approaching canoe with tourists) has a chance to see them.

Ibises are related to storks, and their curved bills, long necks and long legs make them easy to identify. Ibises fly with the head and neck stretched forward and with a slow, flapping flight that is alternated with short glides. Together with the spoonbills, they form the family Threskiornithidae (32 species worldwide, 6 in Perú). The PUNA IBIS (Plate 25) of marshy grasslands at elevations above 3000 m (9900 ft) is probably the easiest species of this family to see in Perú. The *jacanas* (jha-SAH-nahs) form a worldwide family, Jacanidae (8 species worldwide). Only one species, the WATTLED JACANA (Plate 26), is found in Perú, and it is common in lowland marshes of the Amazon. It has incredibly long toes for walking on floating vegetation without sinking. Female jacanas are larger than males, and immatures are lighter and streaked. The *rails*, family Rallidae (140 species worldwide, 26 in Perú), are often shy and difficult-to-see inhabitants of swampy areas. The large GRAY-NECKED WOOD-RAIL (Plate 25) is common in marshy forested areas throughout the Amazonian lowlands and is the rail you are most likely to encounter. In the highlands, many lakes have duck-like relatives of rails called *coots*, such as the GIANT COOT (Plate 28). The SUNBITTERN (Plate 26) belongs to the family Eurypigidae, which is represented in the New World by only this one species; it occurs from southern Mexico to southern Bolivia. In Perú, it is found in the lowlands throughout the Amazon. When a Sunbittern's wings are spread, the bars and spots on its wings create a striking "sunburst" pattern. The SUNGREBE (Plate 26) is in the family Heliornithidae, and it is not related to grebes but rather is a close cousin to the Sunbittern. It is a small duck-like species that swims under the vegetation hanging low over forested streams. There are two other similar species in the family, one each in tropical Africa and Asia, where they are called *finfoots*. The HOATZIN (Plate 26) is one of the most intriguing and unusual species you will see in the flooded forests and marshes of Amazonian Perú. There is only one species in its family, Opisthocomidae (closely related to cuckoos). It is restricted to the upper Amazon and its tributaries. This turkey-sized bird looks for all the world like some prehistoric dinosaur with feathers. The HORNED SCREAMER (Plate 26) belongs to a uniquely South American family, Anhimidae, which is related to ducks and which has two other species in it. This immense bird looks like a plump black and white heron on the ground but like an eagle with long legs when it flies. It has a deep liquid call that carries for miles. It is found throughout the Amazon. The SILVERY GREBE (Plate 28), in the Family Podicipedidae (20 species worldwide, 7 in Perú), is a small duck-like species found in Perú only in open and marshy lakes of the high altitude puna. Its small size and thin bill immediately separate it from any of the true ducks that also occur on these high lakes.

Natural History
Ecology and Behavior

Ibises use their long, curved bills to probe for food in shallow water, grass and mud. They eat small mammals, frogs, and insects. Rails and coots feed on a wide variety of animal and plant material. The GRAY-NECKED WOOD-RAIL is more often heard than seen in flooded forest and thick river-edge vegetation. At dawn and dusk several pairs will sing in a chorus together. Their raucous, almost maniacal laughing call, "to-tooky, to-tooky," gradually tapers off until only one individual is left singing. Occasionally this rail emerges briefly into open areas in the early morning or late afternoon. The WATTLED JACANA is common and easy to see in flooded grasslands and open marshy areas. It uses its immensely long toes to walk on floating vegetation and lily pads. Sharp spurs on its wing are used for fighting other jacanas and against predators. The SUNBITTERN lives along forested streams and flooded forest where they walk along searching for insects, crabs, frogs, crayfish and small fish. The SUNGREBE swims in among the roots and overhanging leaves of thick vegetation along lakes and streams, where it feeds on frogs, worms, crustaceans, and insects. It runs across the surface of the water and flies low to escape predation, and your best view will probably be as it skitters away from your canoe into the dense vegetation.

HOATZINS are usually in loose flocks of 5 to 10 birds in bushes along the edges of slow-moving streams or forested lakes. They announce their displeasure at your presence with hisses and croaks just before they weakly flap their wings to fly to the next branch over the water. They eat only leaves and have a digestive system, similar to a cow's, that uses fermentation to digest otherwise undigestible plant parts. You will most likely see the HORNED SCREAMER in grassy marshes as it flies up noisily. Screamers graze on marsh vegetation, and also perch frequently in the tops of trees to make their loud calls. They are strong fliers and can soar to great heights. The SILVERY GREBE feeds in puna lakes by diving after fish and invertebrates. It can adjust its buoyancy and simply sink out of sight, or it can leap forward out of the water for a more athletic dive.

Breeding

Ibises are monogamous and nest colonially in trees or in reeds near the water. Nests are made of sticks and contain up to 5 eggs. Chicks take food regurgitated from the adults' mouth and throat. Rails build their nests in moist areas either in reeds or grass. Coots construct large nests on small islands of floating vegetation. Egg numbers per nest are often high and range from 2 to 16. Jacanas are unusual in that they are often *polyandrous* (one female mates with numerous males). Males each defend small territories from other males, but each female has a larger territory that encompasses 2 to 4 male territories. Males build nests of floating, compacted aquatic vegetation, into which the female deposits 3 or 4 eggs. The male incubates the nest for 21 to 24 days and then cares for the chicks by himself. Jacanas also are able to move their young chicks in case of flooding or danger by holding them under their closed wings and running to safety. The SUNBITTERN is well-known for its spectacular courtship and threat display in which the tail and wings are spread to reveal a sunburst pattern of yellows, blacks and rust colors. It makes a rounded cup-like nest in a tree or bush, and apparently both mates incubate and feed the 2 to 3 young. The SUNGREBE makes a flat nest of sticks and reeds, often on branches of dead trees low over the water. The 2 to 5 eggs are incubated by both parents. The male has a unique adaptation to protect the fledged young. In case of danger, the small chicks climb into pouches in the skin under the wings and the male dives underwater to escape.

The HOATZIN's 2 to 4 eggs are incubated for 28 days by both parents in a stick nest placed several meters out over the water in a tree branch. Some observations suggest that groups of up to 6 adults may be involved cooperatively in incubating and feeding the young. When in danger, the young jump from the nest into the water and swim underwater to clamber up another bush. To facilitate their tree-climbing ability, they have an extra, opposable, digit on the naked wing that they use like a hand. This extra digit is lost as the chick matures and its feathers and wings develop so it can fly. Grebes are monogamous and build a floating nest of aquatic material. This way a rise or fall in the water level of the marshy lake will not affect the safety of the 2 to 6 eggs or young. When both adults are away from the nest at the same time, they cover the eggs or chicks with vegetation to keep them warm and camouflaged from potential enemies. Both mates are equally involved in incubation and guarding the striped chicks, which soon leave the nest. The young continue to be dependent on the adults for 3 to 4 weeks as they swim around the pond and hide in vegetation at night. HORNED SCREAMERS, like their relatives, geese and swans, mate for life. Their nests are in shallow water and made of sticks and vegetation. The 5 eggs are incubated for 40 days and screamers are full-grown in about 4 months.

Notes

The term "skinny as a rail" referred originally not to a railroad track but to the bird. Rails are extremely flattened from side to side so they can fit into narrow spaces – thus the saying. Hoatzins are large birds with few chances to escape hunters, yet virtually no indigenous peoples use hoatzins for food (although their eggs are often eaten). The reason is that among the plants and leaves they eat is one common aroid plant (*Montrichardia*) (p. 20) that grows along the edges of Amazonian-region lakes. It has a thick woody stem and heart-shaped leaves. The leaves contain chemicals that when eaten are absorbed by the muscles and convey a smell and taste not unlike a sewer. Even a starving person would likely turn down a serving of Hoatzin.

Status

The endemic PUNA, or JUNÍN, GREBE and JUNÍN RAIL are listed as threatened. Cattle grazing, pollution and increasing human contact in the puna are likely causes. The BROWN WOOD-RAIL, which inhabits the coastal tropical dry forest area of extreme northern Perú, is also listed as threatened. HORNED SCREAMER populations in Amazonia have fallen dramatically in the last two decades, probably owing to hunting pressure.

Profiles

Puna Ibis, *Plegadis ridgwayi*, Plate 25d
Gray-necked Wood-rail, *Aramides cajanea*, Plate 25e
Wattled Jacana, *Jacana jacana* Plate 26a
Sunbittern, *Eurypyga helias*, Plate 26b
Sungrebe, *Heliornis fulica*, Plate 26c
Hoatzin, *Opisthocomus hoazin*, Plate 26d
Horned Screamer, *Anhima cornuta*, Plate 26e
Silvery Grebe, *Podiceps occipitalis*, Plate 28c
White-tufted Grebe, *Rollandia rolland*, Plate 28d
Giant Coot, *Fulica gigantea*, Plate 28e

7. Ducks

Members of the Family Anatidae, which includes about 150 species of *ducks, geese* and *swans*, are all associated with water. They are distributed throughout the world in habitats ranging from open sea to high mountain lakes. Although abundant and diverse in temperate regions, only a relatively few species migrate to or reside in the tropics. Ducks vary quite a bit in size and coloring, but most share the same major traits: duck bills, webbed toes, short-tails, and long, slim necks. Plumage color and patterning vary, but there is a preponderance within the group of grays and browns, and black and white, although many species have at least small patches of brighter colors. In some species male and female look alike, but in others there is a high degree of difference between the sexes. About 21 species occur in Perú, from tidal marshes on the coast to the cold puna lakes at high elevations, to the Amazon lowlands. The TORRENT DUCK (Plate 27), living in white-water streams on the eastern slopes of the Andes, is the most unusual of the ducks in Perú – the male and female are so differently colored that they are often mistaken for separate species.

Natural History
Ecology and Behavior

Ducks eat aquatic plants, small fish and invertebrates, but some, such as the MUSCOVY DUCK (Plate 27) and the ORINOCO GOOSE (Plate 28), regularly graze on grasses, moist upland vegetation and terrestrial insects. More typical is the dabbling feeding behavior of WHITE-CHEEKED PINTAILS (Plate 27) and YELLOW-BILLED PINTAILS (Plate 27), which dip their bills into the water while swimming. Sometimes they will tip their rear ends into the air while trying to reach a bit deeper into the water for a morsel, but they do not dive underwater. As their name suggests, TORRENT DUCKS pursue their food of fish underwater in fast-flowing mountain streams. They propel themselves with their feet, dodging large boulders and mastering the powerful currents with ease. They often sit for long periods resting on the top of large mid-stream boulders.

Breeding

All these ducks except one nest on the ground in protective vegetation near their feeding areas. The MUSCOVY DUCK nests in tree cavities often more than 15 m

(50 ft) above the ground. Typically duck nests are lined with downy feathers that the female plucks from her breast. In most species of ducks the female alone performs the duties dealing with nesting and caring for the young. In larger species, such as geese and swans, the pair typically mates for life, and both parents are more equally involved in raising the young. The young hatch feathered and able to run within a few minutes (*precocial*); they can swim and feed themselves soon after. The parents' main role is to guard them against predators and teach them how to find food.

Notes

Ducks, geese and swans have been objects of people's attention since ancient times, chiefly as a food source. These birds typically have tasty flesh, are fairly large and thus economical to hunt, and usually easier and less dangerous to catch than many other animals, particularly large mammals. Owing to their frequent use as food, several wild ducks and geese have been domesticated for thousands of years; Perú's native MUSCOVY DUCK, in fact, in its domesticated form is a common farmyard inhabitant in several parts of the world. Wild ducks also adjust well to the proximity of people, to the point of taking food from them – a practice that surviving artworks show has been occurring for at least 2000 years. Hunting ducks and geese for sport is also a long-practiced tradition. As a consequence of these long interactions between ducks and people, and the research on these animals stimulated by their use in agriculture and sport, a large amount of scientific information has been collected on the group; many of the ducks and geese are among the most well-known of birds. The close association between ducks and people has even led to a long contractual agreement between certain individual ducks and the Walt Disney Company.

Status

The populations of all the species profiled here have been affected to some degree by hunting pressures. The ORINOCO GOOSE is especially susceptible to people's presence and has disappeared from all but the most isolated rivers in Perú. The MUSCOVY DUCK has suffered a similar but not so extreme fate throughout its range in the Neotropics. When these ducks were more common, local hunters would tether a female to a tree and then kill males that came a-courting; with this method, up to 50 males could be lured to their deaths in a single day. The other species are still relatively common in their appropriate habitats.

Profiles

Muscovy Duck, *Cairina moschata*, Plate 27a
White-cheeked Pintail, *Anas bahamensis*, Plate 27b
Yellow-billed Pintail, *Anas georgica*, Plate 27c
Puna Teal, *Anas puna*, Plate 27d
Torrent Duck, *Merganetta armata*, Plate 27e
Orinoco Goose, *Neochen jubata*, Plate 28a
Andean Goose, *Chloephaga melanoptera*, Plate 28b

8. Shorebirds

Spotting *shorebirds* is usually a priority only for visitors to the Neotropics who are rabid birdwatchers. The reason for the lack of interest is that many shorebirds in Perú are visitors from their nesting grounds in North America. Of course, being mostly brown and lacking in reasonably distinguishing characteristics may have something to do with it as well. Nevertheless, it can be a treat watching these fellow travellers in their tropical wintering areas as they forage in meadows, along streams, on mudflats and on sandy ocean beaches. When a large flock, often of several species, rises from a sand bar, it is fun to follow its progress until out of sight. The resident (year-round) species of shorebirds in Perú are intriguing for their combination of similarities to and frequently jarring differences from their migratory cousins. Shorebirds are traditionally placed along with the gulls in the avian Order Charadriiformes. They are global in distribution, and we profile species from four families found in Perú. Most shorebirds, regardless of size, have a characteristic "look." They are usually drably colored birds (especially during the nonbreeding months), darker above, lighter below, with long, thin legs for wading through wet meadows, mud, sand, or surf. Depending on feeding habits, bill length varies from short to very long.

The *sandpipers*, Family Scolopacidae, are a worldwide group of approximately 85 species. About 30 species occur in Perú, some being quite abundant during much of the year, yet all but a few high altitude species are migrants that nest in the Arctic of North America. However, some nonbreeding individuals of these migrants can be present in Perú any month of the year. Most of the Peruvian sandpipers range from 15 to 48 cm (6 to 19 in) long. They are generally slender birds with straight or curved bills of various lengths and live on sandy beaches or mudflats along the coast or in the Amazon. The ANDEAN SNIPE (Plate 30), however, is a resident of the high altitude Andes. It usually occurs around moist areas with grass, but sometimes in drier areas as well. This is a "heart attack" bird – the only time you are likely to see it is as it rises up from almost under your feet, startling you while you are hiking through grassy puna.

Plovers, in the Family Charadriidae, are small to medium-sized (15 to 30 cm, 6 to 12 in) shorebirds with short tails and straight, relatively stout, dove-like bills. They are mostly shades of gray and brown but some have bold color patterns such as a broad white or dark band on the head or chest. Worldwide, there are more than 60 species. Thirteen species occur regularly in Perú, five of which are resident non-migratory species.

The family of the *stilts*, Recurvirostridae, has 10 species worldwide but only two species in Perú. The BLACK-NECKED STILT (Plate 28) congregates in flocks of 5 to 100 in estuarine ponds and tidal flats along the coast. The flocks are so noisy you often hear them before you can see them. In the Amazonian lowlands, this stilt is much less common. The most bizarre and unusual of all the families in the shorebird order, the *seedsnipes* (Thinocoridae, 4 species in western and southern South America) has three species in Perú. Looking more like crosses between doves and quails, species such as the RUFOUS-BELLIED SEEDSNIPE (Plate 30) occur high in the Andes between 4500 m (14,750 ft) and just below snow-line. Other species, like the LEAST SEEDSNIPE (Plate 30), are found on the dry coastal plain. Seedsnipes are so camouflaged that they are often hard to see, even when you are right on top of them. Listen for their low whistling calls. They feed on the ground among low vegetation, mainly on seeds.

Natural History
Ecology and Behavior
Even though shorebirds are all excellent fliers, they spend a lot of time on the ground foraging and resting. When pursued, they often prefer running to flying away. Sandpipers tend to use their bills to probe into the soil or mud for small

invertebrates, and different shapes and lengths of bills help the various sandpiper species find different prey even when they are feeding side by side. The plovers use their bills to take prey or even seeds off the soil surface and never probe. Stilts take advantage of their long legs and bill to probe mud in deeper water, sometimes feeding with their heads entirely underwater. The short-legged and short-billed seedsnipes, of course, eat seeds. They apparently do not drink free-standing water but instead get the water they need from vegetation they eat. Many shorebirds, especially among the sandpipers, establish winter feeding territories along stretches of beach; they use the area for feeding for a few hours or for the day, defending it aggressively from other members of their species. Many of the sandpipers and plovers are gregarious birds, often seen in large groups, especially when they are travelling. Several species make long migrations over large expanses of open ocean.

Breeding
Most shorebird nests are simply small depressions in the ground in which eggs are placed; some of these are in sand, on gravel or on a grass hummock. Seldom do the adults prepare the nest with more than a few pebbles. In almost all these shorebird families monogamy is the rule, and both parents incubate the eggs. In the seedsnipe, however, the female incubates the eggs while the male stands guard some distance from the nest. Shorebird young are precocial, able to run and feed themselves soon after hatching. Parents usually stay with the young to guard them until they can fly, 3 to 5 weeks after hatching. Adults of many ground-nesting species, such as these shorebirds, protect their nests and young by performing a "broken wing" display. At the approach of a predator, the adult runs in front of the danger, calling, and dragging one of its wings on the ground as if it is severely injured. The predator sees an easy meal and follows after the adult, which is able to keep just out of the striking range of the predator and leads it away from the young that are hidden in the nest or in the grass. If this fails, species like stilts fly close to the predator and hassle it until it leaves.

Notes
The manner in which flocks of thousands of birds, particularly shorebirds, fly in such closely regimented order, executing abrupt maneuvers with precise coordination, such as when all individuals turn together in a split second in the same direction, has puzzled biologists and engendered some research. The questions include: What is the stimulus for the flock to turn – is it one individual within the flock, a "leader," from which all the others take their "orders" and follow into turns? Or is it some stimulus from outside the flock that all members respond to in the same way? And how are the turns coordinated? Everything from "thought transference" to electromagnetic communication among the flock members has been advanced as an explanation. After studying films of DUNLIN, a North American and Eurasian sandpiper, flying and turning in large flocks, one biologist has suggested that the method birds within these flocks use to coordinate their turns is similar to how the people in a chorus-line know the precise moment to raise their legs in sequence or how "the wave" in a sports stadium is coordinated. That is, one bird, perhaps one that has detected some danger, like a predatory falcon, starts a turn, and the other birds, seeing the start of the flock's turning, can then anticipate when it is their turn to make the turn – the result being a quick wave of turning coursing through the flock.

Status

None of the shorebirds of Perú is threatened or endangered. However, a major goal for conservation of shorebirds is the need to preserve critical migratory stopover points – pieces of coastal habitat, sometimes fairly small, that hundreds of thousands of shorebirds settle into to stock up on food mid-way during their long migrations. These *staging areas* are vital for shorebird populations, and several such areas likely exist in Perú. These very sites, however, are also heavily threatened from construction of shrimp farms and pollution from herbicide and pesticide runoff from nearby banana plantations.

Profiles

Black-necked Stilt, *Himantopus mexicanus*, Plate 28f

Whimbrel, *Numenius phaeopus*, Plate 29a
Pied Lapwing, *Vanellus cayanus*, Plate 29b
Andean Lapwing, *Vanellus resplendens*, Plate 29c
Diademed Sandpiper-Plover, *Phegornis mitchelli*, Plate 29d
Killdeer, *Charadrius vociferus*, Plate 29e
American Oystercatcher, *Haematopus palliatus*, Plate 29f

Black-bellied Plover, *Pluvialis squatarola*, Plate 30a
Andean Snipe, *Gallinago jamesoni*, Plate 30b
Spotted Sandpiper, *Actitis macularia*, Plate 30c
Sanderling, *Calidris alba*, Plate 30d
Rufous-bellied Seedsnipe, *Attagis gayi*, Plate 30e
Least Seedsnipe, *Thinocorus rumicivorous*, Plate 30f

9. Tinamous and Rhea

The *tinamous* are an interesting group of secretive but very vocal chicken-like birds that are occasionally seen walking on forest trails. However, they represent an ancient group of birds more closely related to ostriches and rheas than chickens. The family, Tinamidae, with about 45 species, is confined in its distribution to the Neotropics, from Mexico to southern Chile and Argentina; 27 species occur in Perú, from coastal dry forest and high altitude puna to Amazon rainforest, where most of the species live.

Tinamous are medium-sized birds, 23 to 45 cm (9 to 18 in) long, chunky-bodied, with fairly long necks, small heads, and slender bills. They have short legs and very short tails. The back part of a tinamou's body sometimes appears higher than it should be, a consequence of a dense concentration of rump feathers. Tinamous are attired in understated, protective colors – browns, grays, and olives; often the plumage is marked with dark spots or bars. Male and female look alike, with females being a little larger than males. One of the four species you are most likely to encounter in Perú, the ANDEAN TINAMOU (Plate 31), is restricted to grassy puna areas. The other three are found in lowland primary and secondary forests of the Amazon, and your encounter is most likely to be by ear rather than by eye. The UNDULATED TINAMOU (Plate 31) makes one of the most common sounds of secondary forest in the Amazon. The call, two low whistles followed by a longer note slurred upwards, is ubiquitous all day long. If you have patience and can stand still for ten to twenty minutes, you can mimic the whistle and sometimes call in an individual close enough to see it. The slightest movement, however, will send it scurrying away. During the drier seasons, when dry leaves accumulate on the forest floor, you can often detect these birds by the crackling sounds of their feet disturbing the leaves.

A surprise to many ecotravellers is that they can see an ostrich-like bird in South America. Only two species of *rheas* exist (Family Rheidae), and they are both limited to southern South America. These ostrich equivalents are open-country species. In Perú, the LESSER RHEA (Plate 31), which ranges also from Patagonia in Argentina to Bolivia and northern Chile, still exists, but only in remnant populations in more isolated puna areas of the southern part of the country. Large, long-legged, long-necked and flightless, they are very shy and run quickly from danger. The Lesser Rhea, at a meter long (3.3 ft) and weighing up to 25+ kg (55 lb), is surpassed in size in Perú only by the Andean Condor.

Natural History
Ecology and Behavior
Except for the GREAT TINAMOU (Plate 31), which sleeps in trees, tinamous are among the most terrestrial of birds, foraging, sleeping and breeding on the ground. They are very poor at flying, doing so only when alarmed by a predator, and then merely for a short distance. They are better at running along the ground, the mode of location called *cursorial*. The tinamou diet consists chiefly of fruit and seeds, but they will also eat insects and other invertebrates. Some species use their feet to scratch and dig at the soil to feed on roots and termites. Tinamous often avoid predators by standing still or squatting, easily blending in with the surrounding vegetation. Sometimes they will slowly and quietly, almost ghost-like, walk away from danger. If you get too close to a tinamou, it will fly upwards in a sudden burst of loud wing-beating and fly to a new hiding spot in the undergrowth. In the early evening, one of the most delightful parts of the Neotropical forest is the serenade of melodious whistles that makes tinamous such a characteristic part of Amazon habitats.

Rheas occur up to 5000 m (16,500 ft) elevation and are usually found in small groups of 5 to 15. They feed mainly on grass, roots and seeds, but they will also eat lizards and small rodents. They regularly graze among deer or cattle.

Breeding
Tinamous are *polyandrous* (one female mates with several males), like their Ostrich relatives. Each male has a nest on the ground that he guards and broods. Females wander around choosing a series of males to mate with and dumping a few eggs in each nest. Perhaps this is a way females have of not putting all their eggs in one basket. One nest can have up to 12 eggs deposited by numerous females. Of course each male also mates with numerous females as they make their rounds, so this mating system is *polygynous* as well as polyandrous. The nest itself is seldom more than an indentation in the forest floor, often hidden in a thicket or at the base of a tree.

Each rhea male defends a large territory, and he tries to attract a harem of females to mate with him. As a nest, he makes a hollow in the ground, and he alone is in charge of incubating the eggs. Each of the females can lay up to 15 eggs, and a male with a harem of 6 to 8 females can have a nest full of 90 or more eggs. Incubation lasts six weeks, and the young stay with the father, who guards them for an additional five months.

Notes
Outside of protected areas, all tinamous are hunted extensively for food. Tinamou meat is considered tender and tasty, albeit a bit strange-looking; it has been

described variously as greenish and transparent. Many species of tinamous have eggs that are large, with an extremely glossy surface. Their colors are also bright, from purple, green and greenish yellow to rusty. Actually seeing them, you have to wonder how these bright eggs can ever escape the attention of the many nest predators that prowl the forest floor. One hypothesis is that in the nest these shiny eggs act like mirrors, reflecting the surrounding vegetation so that they become virtually invisible. Rheas are hunted often and are considered a source of delicious meat.

Status

The tinamous' camouflage coloring and secretive behavior must serve the birds well because, although hunted for food, many species of tinamous apparently maintain healthy populations even in populated countryside. However, in Perú, two species are listed as threatened or endangered (IUCN Red List) – KALINOWSKI'S TINAMOU and TACZANOWSKI'S TINAMOU. Both are very large species of the open puna and subject to intensive hunting pressure. Similarly, the LESSER RHEA population in Perú has been severely reduced through hunting and habitat destruction. Although this species is still common in some lowland areas of southern Argentina, it is officially considered endangered (CITES Appendix I and USA ESA listed); the other rhea species, the GREATER RHEA, which ranges from northeastern Brazil to central Argentina, is CITES Appendix II listed.

Profiles

Great Tinamou, *Tinamus major*, Plate 31a
Little Tinamou, *Crypturellus soui*, Plate 31b
Undulated Tinamou, *Crypturellus undulatus*, Plate 31c
Andean Tinamou, *Nothoprocta pentlandii*, Plate 31d
Lesser Rhea, *Pterocnemia pennata*, Plate 31e

10. Guans and Trumpeter

Large, pheasant-like birds strutting about the tropical forest floor or fluttering about in trees and running along high branches, are bound to be members of the *guan* family, Cracidae. This family, related to pheasants and chickens and distributed from southern Texas to Argentina, contains more than 40 species of guans, *chachalacas* and *curassows*. Fifteen species are found in Perú.

Peruvian guans as a group range in length from 56 to 91 cm (20 to 36 in) – as large as small turkeys – and weigh up to 4 kg (9 lb). They have long legs and long, heavy toes. Many have conspicuous crests. The colors of their bodies are generally drab – gray, brown, olive, or black and white; some appear glossy in the right light. They typically have small patches of bright coloring such as yellow, red, or orange on parts of their bills, cheeks, or on a hanging throat sac called a *dewlap*. The SPECKLED CHACHALACA (Plate 32) is by far the most common species of this family in Perú. At dawn in the Amazon, a flock of these pheasant-sized birds will give a chorus of their loud and raucous calls, that, with some imagination, can be rendered as a rapid "chachalaca" repeated over and over. Then another flock will answer from across the river and the signaling will go back and forth for a half-hour or until it's time to start feeding. If you have the great fortune to see a RAZOR-BILLED CURASSOW (Plate 32), count yourself among the lucky. It will be an indication that you are in pristine Amazon forest, as these large, and unfortunately delicious, birds are easily hunted and thus rare in many areas. The female is similar to the black and white male but somewhat smaller. Listen for the series of very low-pitched humming or "booming" noises of the males early in the morning and on moonlit nights.

The PALE-WINGED TRUMPETER (Plate 32) is similar in appearance to the guans, but it is related instead to the rails and cranes. It is placed in its own small family of three species, Psophiidae; two of the family's species are found in Perú. True to its name, the Pale-winged Trumpeter has a loud deep call that is not unlike an untuned trumpet. When disturbed, trumpeters growl like dogs and thump their bodies with closed wings. Where they are hunted, trumpeters are very shy, and you will be lucky to see this tall bird slinking away into the undergrowth of primary forest. As it is commonly kept as a pet by local people, you are most likely to see it running around a village bullying chickens. Trumpeter sexes are similar, and both weigh about 1 kg (2.2 lb).

Natural History
Ecology and Behavior
Guans are birds of the forest, and the larger the species, the more it is limited to denser forest. All of the guans roost in trees at night, and some, such as the chachalacas and *piping-guans*, rarely ever descend to the ground. They prefer to eat fruits, seeds and insects from the tree tops. The larger guans spend more time on the forest floor, eating fallen fruits and insects, but they often feed in the tree tops as well. The curassows spend all but their roosting time at night on the ground. The smaller species are often in flocks, but the larger species are more solitary. Trumpeters also feed on the forest floor, scratching with their feet to stir up large insects and looking for fallen fruits. They are almost always in flocks of 5 to 20 or more individuals that usually move along the forest floor, but they do fly to the tree-tops to escape danger and roost at night.

Breeding
Guans are all monogamous breeders in which the sexes share reproductive duties. The nest is a simple open construction of twigs and leaves placed in a tree or shrub several meters from the ground. Two to 4 eggs are incubated for 22 to 34 days. The young leave the nest soon after hatching to hide in surrounding vegetation, where, unlike most species with precocial young, they are fed by the parents. Within a few days the young can fly short distances. The breeding biology of trumpeters is very poorly known. Nests have been reported from large holes in trees and the top of a palm tree. The female apparently incubates the 6 to 8 eggs alone. The young are black with streaks and bars of rusty and cinnamon; they follow one or both parents away from the nest soon after hatching.

Notes
Curassows are frequently kept as pets in local villages, but they are shy birds in captivity. Trumpeters kept as pets, however, quickly become attached to the owner's home and poultry. They take on the mantle of dominant boss and protector. They readily chase dogs and wild predators from chickens, and even unfamiliar humans can expect to be challenged with a growl from these birds, which apparently think they are German Shepherds. They are surprisingly affectionate pets, and if you can get close enough to one to scratch it gently on the back of the head, it will follow you for the rest of the day.

Status
A variety of factors converge to assure that the guans will remain a problem group into the foreseeable future. They are chiefly birds of the forests at a time when

Neotropical forests are increasingly being cleared. They are desirable game birds, hunted by local people for food. In fact, as soon as new roads penetrate virgin forests in Central and South America, one of the first chores of settlers is to shoot curassows for their dinners. Unfortunately, curassows reproduce slowly, raising only small broods each year. Exacerbating the problem, their nests are often placed low enough in trees and vegetation to make them vulnerable to a variety of predators, including people. In the face of these unrelenting pressures on their populations, guans are among the birds thought most likely to survive in the future only in protected areas, such as national parks. Almost a third of Perú's guan species are listed as threatened or endangered: WATTLED CURASSOW, RUFOUS-HEADED CHACHALACA, SOUTHERN HELMETED CURASSOW, WHITE-WINGED GUAN and BEARDED GUAN.

Profiles

Speckled Chachalaca, *Ortalis guttata*, Plate 32a
Spix's Guan, *Penelope jacquacu*, Plate 32b
Blue-throated Piping-guan, *Pipile cumanensis*, Plate 32c
Razor-billed Curassow, *Mitu mitu*, Plate 32d
Pale-winged Trumpeter, *Psophia leucoptera*, Plate 32e

11. Vultures

Birds at the very pinnacle of their profession, eating dead animals, *vultures* are highly conspicuous and among the most frequently seen birds both in rural areas and in towns and cities. That they feast on rotting flesh does not reduce the majesty of these large, soaring birds as they circle for hours over fields and forest. They are large birds, generally black or brown, with hooked bills and curious, unfeathered heads whose bare skin is often richly colored in red, yellow, or orange. Male and female vultures look alike, but males are slightly larger than females.

The family of American vultures, Cathartidae, has only seven species, with representatives from Canada to southern Argentina. Six species occur regularly in Perú. The ANDEAN CONDOR (Plate 33), with a 3 m (10 ft) wingspan and distinctive wing pattern, in Perú is most likely to be encountered in the high altitude puna. A few individuals, however, can also be found along the coast, especially at Paracas Peninsula.

Natural History
Ecology and Behavior

Vultures are carrion eaters of the first order. Most soar during the day in groups looking for and, in the case of some species, smelling for food. They can cover many miles daily in their search for dead and rotting bodies and garbage. With their super eyesight, fine-tuned sense of smell, and ability to cover so much ground each day searching, vultures are nature's most efficient garbage collectors. Apparently their bills and feet are not strong enough to dismember fresh meat. The bare skin of their heads and large nostrils on the bill aid them in avoiding problems of gore accumulating on their heads and interfering with seeing, hearing and breathing.

KING VULTURES (Plate 33), GREATER YELLOW-HEADED VULTURES (Plate 33), and ANDEAN CONDORS are usually seen in pairs or solitarily, but the other two species are more social, roosting and foraging in groups of various sizes.

BLACK VULTURES (Plate 33), in particular, often congregate in large numbers at feeding places, and it is common to find a flock of them at any village dump. At small to medium-sized carcasses, there is a definite pecking order among the vultures: Black Vultures are dominant to TURKEY VULTURES (Plate 33), and can chase them away; several Black Vultures can even chase away a King Vulture, which is the bigger bird. However, in an area with plenty of food, all three species may feed together in temporary harmony. When threatened, vultures may spit up partially digested carrion, a strong defense against harassment if ever there was one.

Black and Turkey Vultures roost communally, the two species often together. A common observation has been that once an individual finds a food source, other vultures arrive very rapidly to share the carcass. Biologists strongly suspect that the group roosting and feeding behavior of these birds are related, and that the former increases each individual's food-finding efficiency. In other words, a communal roost serves as an information center for finding food.

Breeding
Vultures are monogamous breeders. Both sexes incubate the 1 to 3 eggs, which are placed on the ground in protected places or on the floor of a cave or tree cavity. Eggs are incubated for 32 to 58 days. Both sexes feed the young regurgitated carrion for 2 to 5 months until they can fly. Nest predation is very rare, and given the long length of time the apparently helpless nestlings are exposed to danger, the best explanation is that the stench of the carrion and decaying animal flesh around the nest and chicks keep potential predators away.

Notes
Being such large and conspicuous birds, and being carrion-eaters associated with death, guaranteed that vultures would figure prominently in the art and culture of most civilizations. The vultures of Egypt and Old World mythology, however, are actually feather-challenged eagles and only distantly related to the superficially similar New World vultures. Recent comparative studies of DNA suggest that the New World Vultures are more closely related to storks than to hawks and eagles.

Status
The only Peruvian vulture in trouble is the ANDEAN CONDOR. The northern populations have declined considerably, and the coastal population no longer breeds on the coast. In Ecuador this species has become extremely rare. In Colombia and Venezuela it is virtually extinct. Only in the southern part of its range, from central Perú to Argentina and Chile, does it seem to be holding its own. The main causes of condor declines in the 20th century were hunting (they were persecuted especially because ranchers believed they ate newborn cattle and other domesticated animals), their ingestion of poisonous lead shot from the carcasses they fed on, and the thinning of their eggshells owing to the accumulation of organochlorine pesticides (DDT) in their bodies.

Profiles
Turkey Vulture, *Cathartes aura*, Plate 33a
Black Vulture, *Coragyps atratus*, Plate 33b
Greater Yellow-headed Vulture, *Cathartes melambrotus*, Plate 33c
King Vulture, *Sarcoramphus papa*, Plate 33d
Andean Condor, *Vultur gryphus*, Plate 33e

12. Hawks, Eagles, and Kites

The raptor family, Accipitridae, is an immense group that worldwide includes about 200 species of *hawks, eagles* and *kites* (47 in Perú). Species in this family vary considerably in size and in patterns of their generally subdued color schemes, but all are similar in overall form. They are fierce-looking birds with strong feet, hooked, sharp claws, or *talons*, and strongly hooked bills. The plumages of the two sexes are usually similar, but females are larger than males, in some species extremely so. Juvenile raptors often spend several years in subadult plumages that differ in pattern and brightness from the adults.

Natural History
Ecology and Behavior

Although many raptors are common birds, typically they spread themselves out thinly over large areas, as is the case for all *top predators* (predators at the pinnacle of the food chain; such predators have too few prey available to support large populations). Some large eagles that feed on monkeys or sloths, such as the HARPY EAGLE (Plate 35), may need a territory of a 1000 sq km (385 sq miles) or more to ensure sufficient food for itself and its nestlings. Most species have developed unique hunting techniques to increase efficiency of prey capture. Among the kites, for instance, the AMERICAN SWALLOW-TAILED KITE (Plate 34) soars over forest canopies and open areas searching for reptiles, especially snakes sunning themselves in the open. The kite swoops down on a reptile and carries it off to a perch to devour. The SLENDER-BILLED KITE has a peculiarly long, narrow, curved bill that enables it to specialize on eating giant snails that inhabit the Amazonian forests. With this bill the kite can easily slip past the otherwise protective door (operculum) that the snail closes across the opening of its shell to protect itself. The bill then extracts the juicy body of the snail like some specialized escargot fork. The DOUBLE-TOOTHED KITE (Plate 34) has an unusual association with monkey troops, and you are most likely to see this kite near active primates. As the monkeys jump from branch to branch they often scare large insects out of hiding. Before these panicked insects can reach refuge, the kite quickly grabs them. Large grasshoppers and katydids are among the most common prey items taken by kites in this way.

Among the hawks, the ROADSIDE HAWK (Plate 34) is a generalist, eating everything from small birds and mammals to insects and even an occasional lizard or snake. Forest clearings and scrub edges are actually beneficial for this hawk because it has little competition in these places and these human-altered habitats make the type of prey it prefers more common.

Breeding

Many raptors are territorial, a solitary individual or a breeding pair defending an area for feeding and, during the breeding season, for reproduction. Displays that advertise a territory and that also may be used in courtship consist of spectacular aerial twists, loops, and other acrobatic maneuvers. Hawk, eagle and kite nests in general are constructed of sticks that both sexes place in a tree or on a rocky ledge. Some nests are lined with leaves. Usually only the female incubates the 1 to 6 eggs, for about a month. The male hunts prey for the female while she sits on the eggs, and after the first chicks hatch out, he continues to give prey to the female, which then tears it up to give in turn to the chicks. When the chicks are a little bigger and the demand for food rises, both mates hunt and feed the chicks directly. The young can fly at 28 to 120 days, bigger species taking longer to fledge than the smaller species.

Notes

Large, predatory raptors have doubtless always attracted people's attention, respect, and awe. Wherever eagles occur, they are chronicled in the history of civilizations. Early Anglo-Saxons were known to hang an eagle on the gate of any city they conquered. Some North American Indian tribes and also Australian Aboriginal peoples deified large hawks or eagles. Several states have used likenesses of eagles as nation symbols, among them Turkey, Austria, Germany, Poland, Russia and Mexico. Eagles are popular symbols on regal coats of arms and one of their kind, a fish-eater, was chosen as the emblem of the USA (although, as most USA schoolchildren know, Benjamin Franklin would have preferred that symbol to be the Wild Turkey.)

Status

Several of Perú's hawks and eagles are considered threatened or endangered, such as the HARPY EAGLE (CITES Appendix I listed) and CRESTED EAGLE (CITES Appendix II), both of which were formerly much more common in Perú. However, many of these large raptors enjoy extensive distributions external to the country, often ranging from Mexico to northern or central South America, and are more numerous in other regions. The GRAY-BACKED HAWK of Perú's north coastal forests is considered threatened. A few hawks adapt well to peoples' habitat alterations. A case in point is the common ROADSIDE HAWK. It prefers open habitats and, especially, roadsides. It has expanded its range and numbers in Perú in areas with deforestation and road-building that previously were large tracts of inaccessible closed forest. Conservation measures aimed at raptors are bound to be difficult to formulate and enforce because the birds are often persecuted for a number of reasons (hunting, pet and feather trade, ranchers protecting livestock) and they roam very large areas. Also, some breed and winter on different continents, and thus need to be protected in all parts of their ranges, including along migration routes. Further complicating population assessments and conservation proposals, there are still plenty of Neotropical raptor species about which very little is known. For example, the approximately 80 species of raptor that breed primarily in Central and South America (excluding the vultures), breeding behavior has not been described for 27 species and nests are unknown for 19 species. The typical prey taken by 6 species is unknown.

Profiles

American Swallow-tailed Kite, *Elanoides forficatus*, Plate 34a
Double-toothed Kite, *Harpagus bidentatus*, Plate 34b
Plumbeous Kite, *Ictinia plumbea*, Plate 34c
Black-chested Buzzard-Eagle, *Geranoaetus melanoleucus*, Plate 34d
Roadside Hawk, *Buteo magnirostris*, Plate 34e
Harpy Eagle, *Harpia harpyja*, Plate 35a
Ornate Hawk-Eagle, *Spizaetus ornatus*, Plate 35b
Variable Hawk, *Buteo polysoma*, Plate 35d

13. Falcons and Osprey

Closely related to the hawks, eagles and kites, the *falcons* and their allies, the *forest-falcons* and *caracaras*, are placed in their own family, Falconidae. The family has about 60 species worldwide, 17 in Perú. Externally, they look like kites and other hawks. The main differences are found in subtle but consistent divergences in internal structures of the skeleton that indicate separate evolutionary branches.

The OSPREY (Plate 35), or Fishing Eagle, occurs worldwide and is the only species in its family, Pandionidae. Its large size, white and black color pattern, peculiarly bowed wing profile in flight, and its obligatory association with water – coastal estuaries to Amazonian rivers – make it easy to recognize. Its loud whistles are frequent, especially when a neighboring Osprey invades its home space. Although it is common throughout lowland and even, occasionally, highland Perú, it has never been recorded breeding in South America. The population is a migratory and nonbreeding one, even though many individuals are present all months of the year.

Natural History
Ecology and Behavior

Typical falcons are best known for their remarkable eyesight and fast, aerial pursuit and capture of moving prey such as flying birds. The PEREGRINE FALCON, which occurs in highland and coastal Perú, is considered to be the fastest bird in the world, achieving speeds of more than 192 kph (120 mph) in a steep stoop on prey. For a prey item to be able to avoid or escape this speed of attack seems impossible, yet many if not most potential prey do escape. The falcon's rate of successful attacks is low, and it must often try numerous times before finally catching something to eat or feed to its young. The hunting behavior of falcons has, over evolutionary time, shaped the behavior of their prey animals. Falcons hit perched or flying birds with their talons, stunning the prey and sometimes killing it outright. An individual bird caught unawares has little chance of escaping the rapid, acrobatic falcons. But birds in groups have two defenses. First, each individual in a group benefits because the group, with so many eyes and ears, is more likely to spot a falcon at a distance than is a lone individual, thus providing all in the group opportunities to watch the predator as it approaches and so evade it. This sort of anti-predation advantage may be why some animals stay in groups. Second, some flocks of small birds, such as starlings, which usually fly in loose formations, immediately tighten their formation upon detecting a flying falcon. The effect is to decrease the distance between birds, so much so that a falcon flying into the group at a fast speed and trying to take an individual risks injuring itself – the "block" of starlings is almost a solid wall of bird; the close formation also makes a single victim more difficult to target. Biologists believe that the flock tightens when a falcon is detected because the behavior reduces the likelihood of an attack.

As suggested by its name, the most typical of the falcons profiled here, the BAT FALCON (Plate 36), hunts at dusk for early flying bats. During the day it goes after swallows and other birds, but often it also takes large flying insects. The caracaras are all scavengers and nest robbers. The BLACK CARACARA (Plate 36) is especially fond of raiding dense nesting colonies of Yellow-rumped Caciques (Plate 77) for eggs and nestlings. The amount of bare skin on the side of the face of a species is often a reflection of how much scavenging it does. As with the vultures, fewer face feathers on caracaras makes accumulation of gore and blood less likely and the head easier to clean. The LAUGHING FALCON (Plate 36) is a snake specialist and the forest-falcons are almost entirely bird predators. One of the easiest ways to see the elusive forest falcons is to attract them by squeaking or kissing the back of your hand loudly when you hear one calling nearby. This sound mimics the distress calls of small birds – a call to supper for the forest-falcon.

The OSPREY is the quintessential fisherman. It hovers over the water until a fish rises close enough to the surface. Then the Osprey plunges, sometimes all but the upstretched wings underwater, to grab the fish in its extremely long, sharp talons. The soles of its feet are rough to better hold slippery fish. After emerging from the water and violently shaking itself to rid the feathers of water, it turns the fish head-forward and flies to a nearby dead tree to feast on its bounty.

Breeding

Falcons nest in vegetation, in a tree or rock cavity, or on a ledge. Some make stick nests, but others make no obvious nest preparation. Incubation of the eggs takes 25 to 35 days and in most species is performed only by the female. (In caracaras both sexes participate in incubation.) The male feeds the female until the chicks hatch, and then both sexes feed the chicks. The nestlings fledge after 25 to 49 days in the nest, but the parents continue to feed the youngsters for several weeks after they fledge, until they are proficient hunters.

Notes

People have had a close relationship with falcons for thousands of years. Falconry, in which captive falcons are trained to hunt and kill game at a person's command, may be the oldest sport, with evidence of it being practiced in China 4000 years ago and in Iran 3700 years ago. One of the oldest known books on a sport is *The Art of Falconry*, written by the King of Sicily in 1248. Although falconry is not as widely practiced today, many countries have aficionados who continue the tradition.

Status

At least two of Perú's falcons are considered threatened. The ORANGE-BREASTED FALCON (CITES Appendix II) was never common in Perú, but now it can be looked for in only a few sites on the east slopes of the Andes and in the Amazonian lowlands. The PLUMBEOUS FOREST-FALCON is a rare and highly localized species on the west slope of the Andes from southwestern Colombia to northwestern Perú. Little is known of its biology. The RED-THROATED CARACARA formerly was a fairly common Peruvian resident but evidently is now declining in the Amazon region. This species feeds mainly on wasp and bee larvae, and insecticide spraying may be affecting both the bird itself as well as the availability of its specialized prey. By contrast, the YELLOW-HEADED CARACARA has expanded recently into the Amazon of Perú, probably due to forest felling and the creation of vast open areas – its preferred habitat.

Profiles

Osprey, *Pandion haliaetus*, Plate 35c
Black Caracara, *Daptrius ater*, Plate 36a
Mountain Caracara, *Phalcoboenus megalopterus*, Plate 36b
Laughing Falcon, *Herpetotheres cachinnans*, Plate 36c
Collared Forest-Falcon, *Micrastur semitorquatus*, Plate 36d
Aplomado Falcon, *Falco femoralis*, Plate 36e
Bat Falcon, *Falco rufigularis*, Plate 36f

14. Pigeons and Doves

The *pigeon* family, Columbidae, includes about 255 species worldwide, 27 in Perú. It is a diverse group with representatives on every continent except Antarctica. In

Perú, pigeons and *doves* inhabit environments from desert scrub to lowland rainforest, cloud forest, and puna. In general, the smaller species are called doves and the larger species pigeons, but there is considerable inconsistency.

All pigeons are generally recognized as such by almost everyone, a legacy of people's familiarity with domestic and feral pigeons. Pigeons worldwide vary in size from the dimensions of a sparrow to those of a small turkey; Perú's species range in body length from 15 to 35 cm (6 to 14 in). Doves and pigeons are plump-looking birds with compact bodies, short necks, and small heads. Legs are usually fairly short. Bills are small, straight, and slender. Typically there is a swollen bulge (*cere*) at the base of the bill. Body colors are generally soft and understated grays and browns with an occasional splash of bolder black or white. Some have subtle patches of iridescence, usually on the neck or wings. The female tends to have similar, if somewhat duller, plumage to the male.

Natural History
Ecology and Behavior

Most pigeons and doves are at least partially arboreal, but several spend most of their time on the ground. They eat seeds, ripe and unripe fruits, berries and, very rarely, insects. They do not have hard bills for seed cracking and thus swallow their food whole. Their chewing is accomplished in the *gizzard*, a muscular portion of the stomach in which food is smashed against small pebbles and other grit eaten from the soil. As they walk on the ground, all species characteristically bob their heads. Camouflage and rapid flight are the two most important anti-predator tactics used by doves. Many species are gregarious to some degree, and some form large flocks during the nonbreeding season.

Breeding

Doves and pigeons are monogamous breeders. Nests are shallow, open affairs of loose twigs, plant stems and roots placed on the ground, rock ledges or in shrubs and trees. Reproductive duties shared by male and female include nest-building, incubating the 1 or 2 eggs, and feeding the young. All doves and pigeons feed their young regurgitated *pigeon's milk*, a protein-rich fluid produced by sloughing off cells lining the *crop*, an enlarged portion of the esophagus otherwise used for food storage. As the chicks grow older, the proportion of solid food fed to them grows greater until no more pigeon's milk is supplied. Incubation time ranges from 11 to 28 days, depending on species size.

Notes

Although many pigeons today are very common, some species met extinction within the recent past. There are two particularly famous cases. The DODO was a large, flightless pigeon, the size of a turkey, with a large head and strong, robust bill and feet. Dodos lived, until the 17th century, on the island of Mauritius, in the Indian Ocean, east of Madagascar. Reported to be clumsy and stupid (hence the expression, "dumb as a dodo"), but probably just unfamiliar with and unafraid of predatory animals, such as people, they were killed by the thousands by sailors who stopped at the island to stock their ships with food. This caused population numbers to plunge; the birds were then finished off by the pigs, monkeys, and cats introduced by people to the previously predator-free island – animals that ate the Dodos' eggs and young. The only stuffed Dodo in existence was destroyed by fire in Oxford, England, in 1755.

North America's PASSENGER PIGEON, a medium-sized, long-tailed member of the family, suffered extinction because of overhunting and because of its habits of roosting, breeding, and migrating in huge flocks. People were able to kill many thousands of them at a time on the Great Plains in the central part of the USA, shipping the bodies to markets and restaurants in large cities through the mid-1800s. It is estimated that when Europeans first settled in the New World, there were three billion Passenger Pigeons, a population size perhaps never equaled by any other bird, and that they may have accounted for up to 25% or more of the birds in what is now the USA. It took only a little more than 100 years to kill them all; the last one died in the Cincinnati Zoo in 1914. The common ROCK DOVE, the urban pigeon with which everyone who has visited a city or town is familiar, is a native of the Old World. Domesticated for thousands of years and transported around the world by people, feral populations have colonized all settled and many unsettled areas of the Earth. In the wild, they breed and roost in cliffs and caves.

Status
In Perú, only two species of the pigeon family are considered threatened: the OCHRE-BELLIED DOVE, a Tumbesian endemic restricted to the coast of southwestern Ecuador and northwestern Perú, and the PERUVIAN PIGEON, restricted to the tropical dry forests of northern Perú.

Profiles
Band-tailed Pigeon, *Columba fasciata*, Plate 37a
Pale-vented Pigeon, *Columba cayennensis*, Plate 37b
Ruddy Pigeon, *Columba subvinacea*, Plate 37c
White-tipped Dove, *Leptotila verreauxi*, Plate 37d
Ruddy Quail-Dove, *Geotrygon montana*, Plate 37e
Croaking Ground-Dove, *Columbina cruziana*, Plate 38a
Black-winged Ground-Dove, *Metriopelia melanoptera*, Plate 38b
Bare-faced Ground-Dove, *Metriopelia ceciliae*, Plate 38c
Eared Dove, *Zenaida auriculata*, Plate 38d
Pacific Dove, *Zenaida meloda*, Plate 38e

15. Parrots

Everyone knows *parrots* as caged pets, so discovering them for the first time in their natural surroundings is often a strange but somehow familiar experience (like a dog-owner's first sighting of a wild coyote). One has knowledge and expectations of the birds' behavior and antics in captivity, but how do they act in the wild? Along with toucans, parrots are probably the birds most commonly symbolic of the tropics. The 300+ parrot species that comprise the Family Psittacidae (the "P" is silent; try referring to parrots as *psittacids* to impress your friends and tour guide!) are globally distributed across the tropics with a few species spilling over into the temperate zones. In Perú, 49 different species are found, and they occupy habitats from coastal desert to high altitude forest to the Amazon lowlands. Parrot fanciers have their own lexicon of common names that often bear no resemblance to the common names used by ornithologists. In Perú the common names most widely used divide this family mainly by size: smallest of all are the sparrow-sized *parrotlets*, about 10 cm (4 in) long; the *parakeets* are long-tailed or short-tailed but small (20 to 30 cm, 8 to 12 in); the *parrots* are larger (30 to 45 cm, 12 to 18 in); and the *macaws* are the largest (60 to 100 cm, 24 to 40 in).

Parrots, regardless of size, share a set of distinctive traits that set them apart from all other birds. They are short-necked with a compact and stocky body. All have a short, hooked bill with a hinge on the upper half that provides great mobility for handling food and for clambering around branches and vegetation. Legs are short, and feet, with toes that are very dexterous, are highly adapted for grasping. Although most species are green, many depart from this scheme, often in a spectacular fashion, with gaudy blues, reds and yellows. Parrots' raucous calls in flight, with the birds usually in flocks, make them easy to detect, but when they land in a tree overhead, they can virtually disappear instantaneously. Only the steady rain of discarded fruit parts gives away their presence. Your best view will probably be when a flock suddenly departs a feeding tree, or when a flock is located loafing and squabbling the afternoon away in an isolated, open tree. To distinguish the various species: listen for differences in their voices, look for the length of the tail, and watch for the way they flap their wings – deep and full strokes or twittering, shallow strokes. In all of the Peruvian parrots, the sexes are very similar or identical in appearance.

The star attractions of the parrot world in Perú are the *macaws*. There are two sizes of macaws; some species, like the CHESTNUT-FRONTED MACAW (Plate 39), are only a bit larger (at 46 cm, 18 in) than the largest parrots, while others, such as the SCARLET MACAW (Plate 39) and the BLUE-AND-YELLOW MACAW (Plate 39), are enormous (90 cm, 35 in). The macaws have the loudest voices of all the parrots in Perú, and you will inevitably hear them long before you see them appear from a line of trees. Their slow but steady wingbeats together with their long tails make them unmistakable.

Natural History
Ecology and Behavior

Parrots are incredibly noisy, highly social seed- and fruit-eaters. Some species give their assortment of harsh, often screeching vocalizations throughout the day, others only in flight, and others call from communal roosts mainly before leaving and when arriving. Many species roost in groups for the night, sometimes in the thousands, in more protected parts of the forest or on islands. Often several species roost together. During early morning, flocks of parrots leave the roost, moving out to cover the forest in search of fruiting trees. They may travel up to 75 km (45 miles) or more in a day. In the afternoon the flocks begin to head back from all directions to the same roosting site. At certain times of the year, parrots of many species concentrate in huge wheeling flocks around high river banks to eat clay from the soil (p. 7). A possible explanation for this behavior is that the clay, or the chemicals in it, aids in digestion. Another hypothesis is that clay helps counteract some of the potent toxins present in many fruits. If you can find such a parrot "salt lick," be sure to spend some time there; early morning is usually best.

Parrots use their special locomotory talent to clamber methodically through trees in search of fruits and flowers, using their powerful feet to grasp branches and their bills as, essentially, a third foot. Just as caged parrots, they will hang at odd angles and even upside down, the better to reach some delicious morsel. Parrot feet also function as hands, delicately manipulating food and bringing it to the bill. Parrots feed mostly on fruits and nuts, buds of leaves and flowers, and on flower parts and nectar. They are usually considered frugivores, but careful study reveals that when they attack fruit, it is usually to get at the seeds within. The powerful bill slices open fruit and crushes seeds. As one bird book colorfully put it, "adapted for opening hard nuts, biting chunks out of fruit, and grinding small seeds into meal, the short, thick, hooked parrot bill combines the destructive powers of an ice pick (the sharp-pointed upper mandible), a chisel (the sharp-edged lower mandible), a file (ridged inner surface of the upper mandible), and a vise." Thick, muscular parrot tongues are also specialized for feeding, used to scoop out pulp from fruit and nectar from flowers. Parrots, unlike most frugivorous birds, are not ingesting seeds and then eventually dispersing them when they defecate. They are, more technically, seed predators. However, some studies suggest that because of the large amount of uneaten fruit that they drop to the ground, they make available fruits and their seeds to be dispersed by ground frugivores such as tinamous and rodents. These ground-dwelling species are more properly seed dispersers because they eat the pulp but do not regularly destroy the seeds contained within.

Breeding

Parrot breeding is monogamous and pairing is often for life. Nesting is carried out during the dry season and, for some, into the early wet season. Most species breed in cavities in dead trees, although a few build nests. Macaw nests are almost always placed 30 m (100 ft) or more above the ground. A female parrot lays 2 to 8 eggs, which she incubates alone for 17 to 35 days while being periodically fed regurgitated food by her mate. The helpless young of small parrots are nest-bound for 3 to 4 weeks, those of the huge macaws, 3 to 4 months. Both parents feed nestlings and fledglings.

Notes

Parrots have been captured for people's pleasure as pets for thousands of years; Greek records exist from 400 BC describing parrot pets. The fascination stems from the birds' bright coloring, their ability to imitate human speech and other sounds (strangely enough, they do not appear to mimic sounds in the wild), their individualistic personalities (captive parrots definitely like some people while disliking others), and their long life spans (up to 80 years in captivity). Likewise, parrots have been hunted and killed for food and to protect crops for thousands of years. Some Peruvian Incan pottery shows scenes of parrots eating corn and being scared away from crops. Historically, people have killed parrots to protect crops – Charles Darwin noted that in Uruguay in the early 1800s, thousands of parakeets were killed to prevent crop damage.

Macaws, the largest parrots, are thought to have been raised in the past for food in the West Indies, and macaw feathers were used as ornaments and had ceremonial functions. One of the Incan legends about the origin of the Incan people concerned macaws: Two brothers, who lived on a mountain, to discover who had been making use of their kitchen to cook meals while they were out at work, pretended one day to leave the house in the early morning, but hid instead. To their surprise, two macaws soon entered the house and began preparing a meal. The brothers jumped out of their hiding place and shut the door, trapping the large birds inside. The birds, furious, tried to escape, but only the larger one was successful. The brothers captured the smaller macaw, a female, and it became their wife. The three of them lived for many years on the mountain. Eventually the wife-macaw had six sons and daughters. All of the Incas, it was said, were descended from the macaw's six children.

Status

Seventy or more parrot species are threatened or endangered worldwide, and at least 8 species that occur in Perú are currently threatened. The GOLDEN-PLUMED PARROT is associated with cloud forests and a rare coniferous tree, *Podocarpus* (page 19). Its highly spotty distribution is shrinking owing mainly to habitat destruction. The MILITARY MACAW has been reduced by habitat destruction throughout its range from Mexico to northern Argentina. The YELLOW-FACED PARROTLET, SPOT-WINGED PARROTLET and RED-FACED PARROT are all smaller species with limited ranges that are considered threatened in Perú. The ranges and abundances of some other species, such as the RED-AND-GREEN MACAW (Plate 39), have been severely reduced during the past 100 years, primarily due to destruction of forests. Whereas during the early years of the 20th century this macaw was common throughout Amazonian lowland areas, now it is absent from much of the area.

Many Peruvian parrot species still enjoy healthy populations and are frequently seen. Unfortunately, however, parrots are subject to three powerful forces that, in combination, take heavy tolls on their numbers: Parrots are primarily forest birds, and forests are increasingly under attack by farmers and developers; parrots are considered agricultural pests by farmers and orchardists owing to their seed- and fruit-eating, and are persecuted for this reason; and parrots are among the world's most popular cage birds. Several Peruvian species, especially the larger macaws, are prized as pets, and nests of these parrots are often robbed of young for local sale as pets or to international dealers. To get to the young birds, the nest tree, often a dead palm, is cut down. Few of the chicks survive the tree fall, and one of the few cavity nest sites around has been eliminated for renesting. For every macaw that reaches the market place, perhaps 20 to 50 die in the process. Without fast, additional protection, many more Peruvian parrots soon will be threatened.

Profiles

White-eyed Parakeet, *Aratinga leucopthalmus*, Plate 38f
Blue-and-yellow Macaw, *Ara ararauna*, Plate 39a
Scarlet Macaw, *Ara macao*, Plate 39b
Red-and-green Macaw, *Ara chloroptera*, Plate 39c
Chestnut-fronted Macaw, *Ara severa*, Plate 39d
Mealy Parrot, *Amazona farinosa*, Plate 39e
Red-bellied Macaw, *Ara manilata*, Plate 39f

Yellow-headed Parrot, *Amazona ochrocephala*, Plate 40a
Cobalt-winged Parakeet, *Brotogeris cyanoptera*, Plate 40b
Blue-headed Parrot, *Pionus menstruus*, Plate 40c
Black-headed Parrot, *Pionites melanocephalus*, Plate 40d
Canary-winged Parakeet, *Brotogeris versicolurus*, Plate 40e
Dusky-headed Parakeet, *Aratinga weddellii*, Plate 40f

16. Cuckoos and Anis

Many of the *cuckoos* and *anis* (AH-neez) are physically rather plain but behaviorally rather extraordinary. As a group they employ some of the most bizarre breeding practices known among birds. Cuckoos and anis are considered by some to be in the same family, Cuculidae, which, with a total of 130 species, enjoys a worldwide distribution including both temperate and tropical areas; 16 species occur in Perú. While the cuckoos are shy and solitary birds of woodlands, forests and dense thickets, anis are bold, obvious and gregarious birds of savannahs, brushy scrub and river edges. Anis make you wonder where they perched before the advent of fences.

Most cuckoos are medium-sized, slender, long-tailed birds. Male and female mostly look alike, attired in plain browns, tans, and grays, often with streaked or spotted patches. Several have alternating white and black bands on their tail undersides. (Many cuckoos of the Old World are more colorful.) They have short legs and bills that curve downwards at the end. The STRIPED CUCKOO (Plate 41) is found commonly in open and cut-over brushlands on the east side of the Andes. Occasionally it will fly up from the ground or low vegetation and sit motionless on a fence post for many minutes. More often, however, you will be made aware of its presence by what must be the most persistent, and sometimes most irritating, song of these open areas – two short whistles, the second note higher, and given over and over every two or three seconds throughout the middle of the day. The SQUIRREL CUCKOO (Plate 41) is a large red-brown species of secondary and primary forest throughout the lowlands on both sides of the Andes. Its long tail, with a little imagination resembling a squirrel's tail, is often all you see of it as it runs down a branch.

Anis are conspicuous medium-sized birds, glossy black all over, with iridescent sheens particularly on the head, neck and breast. Their bills are exceptionally large, with humped or crested upper ridges. The SMOOTH-BILLED ANI (Plate 41) is an abundant and obvious bird throughout cleared areas of Amazonian Perú and on the marshy margins of lakes and rivers. Its all-black color, loose and floppy flight, and large bill make it easy to recognize. The GREATER ANI (Plate 41) is a much larger edition with a distinct bluish tinge to the all-black body and a white eye. It occurs along forested streams and lakes of the Amazon lowlands. When the members of a flock start their loud and discordant vocalizations, it sounds like a boiler factory.

Natural History
Ecology and Behavior
Most of the cuckoos are arboreal. They eat insects, apparently having a special affinity for caterpillars. They even safely consume hairy caterpillars, which are avoided by most other predators because they have painful stinging hairs or even toxic poisons. Cuckoos have been seen snipping off one end of a hairy caterpillar, squeezing the body with the bill and beating it against a branch until the toxic entrails fall out. They then can swallow the remains safely. How they get around the hairs is still a mystery, however. A few cuckoos, such as the GROUND CUCKOO, are ground-dwellers, eating small birds, snakes and lizards as well as insects. They are most often seen around army ant swarms, where they eat large insects as well as small antbirds attracted to the swarm.

The highly social anis forage in groups, usually on the ground. Frequently they feed around cattle, grabbing the insects that are flushed out of hiding places by the grazing mammals. They eat mostly bugs, but also a bit of fruit. Anis live in groups of 8 to 25 individuals, each group containing 2 to 8 adults and several juveniles. Each group defends a territory from other groups throughout the year. The flock both feeds and breeds within its territory.

Breeding
Cuckoos in the Old World are highly evolved *brood parasites*. They build no nests of their own, and the females lay their eggs in the nests of other species (the

hosts). Immediately after hatching, the young cuckoo nestlings push the rightful heirs out of the nest, and the host adults then raise the young cuckoos as their own offspring. In the New World, only a few cuckoo species, such as the STRIPED CUCKOO and the PHEASANT CUCKOO, are brood parasites. The rest are typical monogamous breeders. The male feeds the female in courtship, especially during her egg-laying period. Both sexes build the plain platform nest that is made of twigs and leaves and placed in a tree or shrub. Both sexes incubate the 2 to 6 eggs for about 10 days, and both parents feed the young.

Anis, consistent with their highly social ways, are *communal breeders*. In the most extreme form, all individuals within the group contribute to a single nest, several females laying eggs in it – up to 29 eggs have been found in one nest. Many individuals help build the stick nest and feed the young. Although this behavior would seem to benefit all the individuals involved, actually it is the dominant male and female that gain the most. Their eggs go in the communal nest last, on top of all the others, which often get buried. Also some females roll eggs out of the nest before depositing their own; thus it pays to be last.

Notes

The name cuckoo comes from the calls made by a common species in Europe, which is also the source of the sounds for cuckoo clocks.

Status

The STRIPED CUCKOO has been expanding its range within Perú, it being a species that does well in the forest edge, thicket, and open areas that increasingly are created through deforestation.

Profiles

Striped Cuckoo, *Tapera naevia*, Plate 41a
Squirrel Cuckoo, *Piaya cayana*, Plate 41b
Groove-billed Ani, *Crotophaga sulcirostris*, Plate 41c
Smooth-billed Ani, *Crotophaga ani*, Plate 41d
Greater Ani, *Crotophaga major*, Plate 41e

17. Owls and Oilbird

Most *owls* are members of the Family Strigidae, which has about 120 species worldwide, 25 in Perú. Most species are nocturnal, and they share distinctive features such as large heads with forward-facing eyes, hooked bills, plumpish bodies and sharp claws (talons). They tend to be camouflaged in colors of gray, brown and black. The group includes species that range in size from 15 to 75 cm (6 to 30 in). The sexes are similar, but females tend to be considerably larger. Because it is frequently active during the day, the FERRUGINOUS PYGMY-OWL (Plate 42) is one owl species that you are likely to see. It is the size of a large sparrow, and its high-pitched, staccato whistles are common in scrub areas and forest edges of the lowlands. On the coast and in the mountains, other, similar-looking, species are also active during the day and likely to make themselves fairly obvious by perching out in the open or calling. For owls active at night, try locating them by their call notes and songs. When you locate an owl this way, shine a flashlight on it to see it well. Often owls will sit for a long time on the same perch calling and looking around, even in the bright beam of your flashlight. Note the body size and facial patterns to identify them. Also, watch for the "ear" tufts, which are usually evident on species that have them; but they can also be flattened and difficult to see.

The OILBIRD (Plate 42) is the only species in the Family Steatornithidae. This strange species is 46 cm (18 in) long and has a wingspan of about 90 cm (3 ft). Its beak is powerful and hooked with long hair-like feathers at either side. Apparently the Oilbird is related to both the owls and the nightjars. It is found only in localized areas in northwestern South America, from Venezuela to northern Bolivia, usually in immense colonies associated with large caves. There are but a few such caves known in Perú, from the highlands near Quito to the lower slopes on both sides of the Andes. Occasionally, dispersing individuals show up in different areas, usually found roosting during the day in a bush or other vegetation. The warm brown color and silver-white spots are distinctive.

Natural History
Ecology and Behavior
In general, owls occupy a variety of habitats: forests, clearings, fields, grasslands, mountains and marshes. They are considered the nocturnal replacements of the day-active birds of prey, the hawks, eagles and falcons. Although most owls hunt at night, some hunt at twilight (*crepuscular* activity) and some during the day. Owls eat a broad range of animals, from small mammals, birds and reptiles to insects and earthworms. Larger owls often develop a taste for smaller owls. Owl vision is good in low light (mainly in black and white, as they are considered to be largely colorblind). In the absence of moonlight and under the cloak of a forest canopy, however, owls hunt using their ears to locate prey. Not only are the ears themselves extremely sensitive, but the two ears have different-sized openings. The effect of this asymmetry is comparable to the way you turn your head back and forth to better locate a sound. The owl can locate sounds without turning its head, especially important in flight. In addition, owls have soft flight feathers and a sound baffle of fringed feathers on the leading edge of the wings that provide a cloak of silence during flight; few prey can hear them coming. They swallow small prey whole, but instead of digesting or defecating the hard bones, fur and feathers, they regurgitate these parts in compact *owl pellets*. These gray oblong pellets often accumulate beneath an owl's favorite perch. If you come across some of these pellets, pull them apart to see what the owl has been dining on.

The OILBIRD is one of the few bird species in the world to use bat-like *echolocation*, a type of sonar, to help it navigate, especially through the pitch-black caves it inhabits. It utters clicking noises that echo off the cave walls, ceiling and rocks, and hearing the echoes, an oilbird can avoid the obstacles in its path. Hundreds of birds emerge from their cave entrance every evening to spend the night searching for high-fat-content fruits, like palm fruits. Each night, they fly long distances of up to 50 km (30 miles) from their cave. When they find suitable fruits, they fly up to the fruits and pull them off the tree often without landing. Before the light of dawn they return to the cave to spend the day.

Breeding
Most owls are monogamous breeders. They do not build nests themselves, but either take over nests abandoned by other birds or nest in cavities such as tree or rock holes. Incubation of the 1 to 10 eggs is usually conducted by the female alone for 4 to 5 weeks, but she is fed regularly by her mate. Upon hatching, the female broods the young while the male continues to hunt for her and the young. The chicks fledge after 4 to 6 weeks in the nest.

OILBIRDS live permanently in pairs and roost year-round at their nest sites on ledges within their cave. The nest itself, little more than a mound with a slight depression in it, is made of droppings and partially-digested fruit pulp. The 4 eggs are laid over a two-week period, but incubation begins with the first egg and lasts about 34 days. The young hatch at the same intervals at which they were laid as eggs, and being fed only fruits (low in proteins), they develop very slowly. After about 70 days the young are very chubby – often weighing much more than the adults. At the end of three or four months they lose weight, develop adult plumage and leave the nest – nearly six months after being laid as an egg.

Notes

The forward-facing eyes of owls are a trait shared with only a few other animals: humans, most other primates, and to a degree, the cats. Eyes arranged in this way allow for almost complete binocular vision (both eyes can see the same object but from a slightly different angle), a prerequisite for good depth perception, which, in turn, is important for quickly judging distances when catching prey. However, owl eyes cannot move much, so owls swivel their heads to look left or right. Owls in many parts of the world, including Perú, are considered an omen of bad luck, or even worse, death. Many indigenous people kill owls when they encounter them to avoid any future visits and bad news brought by owls. Young oilbirds have long been harvested from their caves by people for their fat deposits. Historically, their carcasses were boiled down to provide oil for lamps and cooking.

Status

Owls in Perú are threatened primarily by forest clearing, but no species is considered endangered. The OILBIRD has such highly localized colonies, that a single fire or hunter can quickly kill all the birds in an entire cave. In Perú, the best defense has been to not publicize the location of newly discovered colony sites. Many of the known caves are officially protected.

Profiles

Tropical Screech-Owl, *Otus choliba*, Plate 42a
Spectacled Owl, *Pulsatrix perspicillata*, Plate 42b
Ferruginous Pygmy-Owl, *Glaucidium brasilianum*, Plate 42c
Burrowing Owl, *Speotyto cunicularia*, Plate 42d
Oilbird, *Steatornis caripensis*, Plate 42e

18. Nightjars and Potoo

Species of birds known as *nightjars* are in the Family Caprimulgidae, which has about 70 species worldwide, 18 species in Perú. Like their closest relatives, the owls, nightjars are primarily nocturnal. They have a very characteristic appearance. In the New World, most range in size from 16 to 32 cm (6 to 12 in) long. They have long wings, medium or long tails, and big eyes. Their small, stubby bills enclose big, wide mouths that they open in flight to scoop up flying insects. Many species have bristles around the mouth area, which act as a food funnel. With their short legs and weak feet, they are poor walkers – flying is their usual mode of locomotion. The plumage of these birds is uniformly cryptic: mottled, spotted and barred mixtures of browns, grays, tans and black. They often have white patches on their wings or tails that can be seen only in flight. The PAURAQUE (Plate 43) is the most common nightjar in Perú.

The closely related *potoos*, a small group that occurs only from Mexico south into Argentina, are placed in their own family, the Nyctibiidae. There are 7 potoo species, 5 of which occurr in Perú, but you are likely to find only two of them, the COMMON POTOO (Plate 43) and the GREAT POTOO (Plate 43). At night, when it is active, the Common Potoo gives a mournful series of long, slow and low descending whistles. The locals often call it *madre de la luna* (mother of the moon) or *alma perdida* (lost soul) because of its tendency to sing on full-moon nights and the seeming tragedy emoted by its song. During the day potoos sit on branches, usually out in the open, and with their camouflaged coloring and their bills pointed into the air, they look like dead branches.

Natural History
Ecology and Behavior
Most nightjars are night-active birds, with some becoming active at twilight (*crepuscular* activity). They feed on flying insects, which they catch on the wing, either by forays out from a perched location on the ground or from tree branches, or with continuous circling flight. You can see some species feeding on insects drawn to lights at night. Others you will see only as you flush them from their day-time roost on the ground or in low vegetation. Their camouflage coloring makes them difficult to see, even when you are close to them. The potoos are solitary species that hunt at night for large insects and small birds, lizards and occasionally mammals. A potoo's immense mouth opens like a cavern to catch prey in flight.

Breeding
Nightjars breed monogamously. No nest is built, but instead the female lays her one or two eggs on the ground in a small depression, usually under a bush or a rock. Either the female alone or both sexes incubate the eggs for 18 to 20 days, and both parents feed the young once they hatch. As is typical of many ground-nesting species, regardless of family, nightjars engage in *broken-wing displays* to distract predators away from the nest and young. When a predator approaches their nest, they flop around on the ground, often with one or both wings held down as if injured, making gargling or hissing sounds, all the while moving away from the nest. Potoos build no nest but lay a single egg in a crevice of a large branch or stump, usually high up in a tree. The breeding biology is poorly known, but apparently both sexes are involved with incubation.

Notes
Other names for nightjars are *goatsuckers* and *nighthawks*, both of which are mis-leading nicknames. At twilight some species fly low over the ground near grazing animals, such as goats. The birds often fly right next to the mammals to catch insects being scared up as they walk through the grass. Evidently the assumption was that these birds were after the goats' milk, and a legend was born. These often pointed-winged species of birds were also mistaken for hawks flying around at dusk and at night, when accurate identification was difficult, and the name "nighthawk" has stuck ever since. One of the nightjars, North America's COMMON POORWILL, may be the only bird known actually to hibernate, as some mammals do, during very cold weather. During their dormant state, poor-wills save energy by reducing their metabolic rate and their body temperature, the latter by about 22°C (40°F).

Status
None of the Peruvian nightjars are threatened. In the New World, the WHITE-WINGED NIGHTJAR of Brazil and Paraguay and the PUERTO RICAN NIGHTJAR occur in very limited areas and are endangered.

Profiles

Sand-colored Nighthawk, *Chordeiles rupestris*, Plate 43a
Pauraque, *Nyctidromus albicollis*, Plate 43b
Ladder-tailed Nightjar, *Hydropsalis climacocerca*, Plate 43c
Common Potoo, *Nyctibius griseus*, Plate 43d
Great Potoo, *Nyctibius grandis*, Plate 43e

19. Swifts and Swallows

Swifts and *swallows* are remarkably similar in appearance and behavior, but they are not closely related. They both rely on the same feeding technique, catching insects on the wing during long periods of sustained flight. Swifts, although superficially resembling swallows, are instead closely related to hummingbirds. There are 80 or so species of swifts (Family Apodidae) worldwide in temperate and tropical areas; 13 species are found in Perú, some albeit rarely. Swifts, like swallows, are slender, streamlined birds, with long, pointed wings. They are 9 to 25 cm (3.5 to 10 in) long and have very short legs, short tails or long, forked tails, and very short but broad bills. Swifts' tails are stiffened to support the birds as they cling to vertical surfaces. The sexes look alike: sooty-gray or brown, with white or grayish rumps or flanks. Many are glossily iridescent. The most widespread and among the largest species in Perú is the WHITE-COLLARED SWIFT (Plate 44). Although they nest behind waterfalls high in the mountains, they can be expected anywhere in the lowlands, often in immense and noisy flocks high in the air, where they seek insect concentrations. The SHORT-TAILED SWIFT (Plate 44) is a lowland species in the Amazon region; its tailless appearance and light gray rump are the best characters to use to distinguish it from several similar species found in the same area. It, however, is usually the most common of these "tailless" swift species.

The swallow family, Hirundinidae, is related to perching birds such as flycatchers, warblers and sparrows. There are 80 species of swallows worldwide, and 19 species in Perú, 4 of which winter here or pass through on their way to or from North American breeding grounds. Swallows are small, streamlined birds, 11.5 to 21.5 cm (4.5 to 8.5 in) long, with short necks, bills and legs. They have long, pointed wings and, often, forked tails, wonderfully adapted for fast and sustained flight; they have amazing ability to maneuver in the air as they pursue flying insects or chase each other for competitive or amorous intentions. Some are colored in shades of blue, green or black, but many are gray or brown. The sexes look alike, at least to us.

Natural History
Ecology and Behavior

Among the birds, swifts and swallows represent the pinnacle of flying prowess and aerial pursuit of insects. It seems as if they fly effortlessly all day, circling low over water and land, or flying in seemingly erratic patterns high overhead. Swifts especially are perpetual fliers, rarely roosting except at night, when they come together in large groups to spend the non-flying hours gathered on a vertical cliff face behind a waterfall, inside a hollow tree, or among the fronds of a palm tree. They roost on these vertical surfaces clinging with their tiny but sharply clawed feet and bracing themselves against the sides of the roost with their stiff tail feathers. A swift spends more time airborne than any other type of bird, even copulating in the air in a death-defying tail-spin that gives meaning to the concept of sexual thrills. The name "swift" is apt, as these are the fastest flying birds in level flight, moving along at up to 160 kph (100 mph). Swifts can be told from swallows by their faster, more twittering wingbeats, made possible by an exceptionally short arm bone (the humerus). Some species of swift hunt every day for insects hundreds of miles from their nesting area. The chicks of swifts have the ability to go into short-term physiological inactivity (*torpor*) during extended periods of inclement weather, when no insects are flying. They can endure the lack of food for up to a week by lowering their body temperatures and energetic requirements (and thus their need for food).

Swallows also take insects on the wing as they fly back and forth over water and open areas. Some also eat berries. Swallows perch more frequently than swifts, often resting during the hottest parts of the day on tree branches over water or open areas. Directly after dawn, however, and at dusk, swallows are always airborne. Because swallows depend each day on capturing enough insects, their daily habits are largely tied to the prevailing weather. Flying insects are thick in the atmosphere on warm, sunny days, but relatively scarce on cold, wet ones. Therefore, on good days, swallows, can catch their fill of bugs in only a few hours of flying, virtually anywhere. But on cool, wet days, they may need to forage all day to find enough food, and they tend to do so over water or low to the ground, where under such conditions bugs are more available.

Breeding
Swifts are monogamous, and most are colonial breeders, but some nest solitarily. The sexes share nesting chores. Nests are usually attached to vertical surfaces of rocks, tree cavities or palm fronds, depending on the species of swift. The nests consist of plant pieces, twigs and feathers glued together with the birds' saliva. One to 6 eggs are incubated for 16 to 28 days, with young fledging at 25 to 65 days of age. Swallows are also monogamous; many species breed in dense colonies of hundreds to thousands of pairs. They make nests of mud and some plant material, which they attach to vertical surfaces, or they nest in cavities of trees, or tunnel into vertical banks. Both sexes or the female alone incubates the 3 to 7 eggs for 13 to 16 days. Both parents help feed the young for 18 to 28 days, until the young fledge.

Notes
Nests of swifts in some parts of the Old World are almost totally made of saliva, and these nests are harvested to make birds' nest soup. Swallows have a long history of beneficial association with people. In the New World, owing to their insect-eating habits, they have been popular with people going back to the time of the ancient Mayan civilization. Mayans, it is believed, respected and welcomed swallows because they reduced insect damage to crops. In fact, Cozumel (the word refers to swallows), off Mexico's Yucatán Peninsula, is the Island of Swallows. People's alterations of natural habitats, harmful to so many species, are often helpful to swallows, which adopt buildings, bridges, road culverts, road banks, and quarry walls as nesting areas. BARN SWALLOWS in some areas of North America have for the most part given up nesting in anything other than human-crafted structures. The result of this close association is that, going back as far as ancient Rome, swallows have been considered good luck. Superstitions attached to the relationship abound; for example, it is said that the cows of a

farmer who destroys a swallow's nest will give bloody milk. Arrival of the first migratory Barn Swallows in Europe is considered a welcoming sign of approaching spring, as is the arrival of CLIFF SWALLOWS at some of California's old Spanish missions.

Status

So little is known of many species of swifts that we are uncertain of their populations' sizes or vulnerabilities. None of the swallows that breeds or winters in Perú is threatened, but the PALE-FOOTED SWALLOW of the eastern slope of the Andes is so local in Perú that habitat or nesting site destruction could quickly threaten its status.

Profiles

White-collared Swift, *Streptoprocne zonaris*, Plate 44a
Short-tailed Swift, *Chaetura brachyura*, Plate 44b
Fork-tailed Palm-Swift, *Tachornis squamata*, Plate 44c
White-winged Swallow, *Tachycineta albiventer*, Plate 44d
White-banded Swallow, *Atticora fasciata*, Plate 44e
Blue-and-white Swallow, *Notiocheilidon cyanoleuca*, Plate 44f
Southern Rough-winged Swallow, *Stelgidopteryx ruficollis*, Plate 45c

20. Hummingbirds

Hummingbirds are birds of extremes. They are among the most recognized kinds of birds, the smallest of birds, and arguably the most beautiful, albeit on a small scale. Fittingly, much of their biology is nothing short of amazing. Found only in the New World, the hummingbird family, Trochilidae, contains about 330 species, 116 of which call Perú home! The variety of forms encompassed by the family, not to mention the brilliant iridescence of most of its members, is indicated by the diversity and inventiveness needed by biologists to give descriptive names to these species: emeralds, sunangels, sunbeams, comets, metaltails, fairies, woodstars, woodnymphs, pufflegs, sabrewings, thorntails, thornbills, sicklebills and lancebills. Hummingbirds live in a broad spectrum of habitats from Alaska to southern Argentina. Various species are resident at snow-line in the Andes (4000 m, 13,000 ft) down to deserts and mangrove areas along the coast. All they seem to require to live in a region is a reliable supply of flower nectar and a few insects for protein.

Almost everyone can identify hummingbirds (call them hummers to sound like an expert). They are mostly tiny birds, usually clad in iridescent metallic greens, reds, violets and blues, that whiz by us at high speeds, the smallest of them more resembling big insects than respectable birds. Most hummers are in the range of only 6 to 13 cm (2.5 to 5 in) long, although a few of the larger kinds reach 20 cm (8 in), and they tip the scales at an almost imperceptibly low 2 to 9 g (most being 3 to 6 g) – the weight of a large paper-clip! Bill length and shape vary extensively among species. Many of them have distinctively formed bills to fit precisely into a species or genus of flowers from which that hummingbird species delicately draws its liquid food. Males are usually more colorful than females, and many males have *gorgets*, bright, glittering throat patches that in the right light are red, violet, green or blue. A little turn of the head will change the reflection to black. Not all hummers are so vividly outfitted, however. One group, called the *hermits* (supposedly because of their solitary ways), has dull greenish brown and gray plumages. Hummers have tiny legs and feet; in fact, they are included by most ornithologists with the swifts (p. 137) in the avian Order Apodiformes, which means "without feet." With more than 100 species to be seen in Perú, we can only begin to introduce you to some of its hummingbirds. The 20 species we have chosen to profile include a cross-section of the ranges of sizes, colors and adaptations you can see in various habitats throughout the country. These species are also the ones you are most likely to see and be able to identify by their habitats and distinctive traits.

Natural History
Ecology and Behavior

Because of their many anatomical, behavioral and ecological specializations, hummingbirds have long attracted the research attention of biologists. The outcome is that we know quite a lot about these tiny birds:

1   Hummers are capable of very rapid, finely controlled, acrobatic flight, more so than any other type of bird. The bones of their wings have been modified to allow for stationary hovering flight as well as the unique ability to fly backwards. Their wings beat in a figure-eight-shaped wingstroke and at a speed beyond our ability to distinguish the individual beats – up to 80 times per second. Because most people see hummers only during the birds' foraging trips, they often appear to be flying continuously, as they zip from flower to flower. They do, however, perch every now and again, providing the best chance to see them well.

2   Hummingbirds have very fast metabolisms, a necessary condition for small, warm-blooded animals. To pump enough oxygen and nutrient-delivering blood around their little bodies, their hearts beat up to 10 times faster than human hearts – 600 to 1000 times per minute. To obtain sufficient energy to fuel their high metabolism, hummingbirds must eat many times each day. They can starve quickly without almost constant feeding. At night, when they are inactive, they burn much of their available energy reserves and on cold nights, if not for special mechanisms, they would surely starve to death. The chief method to avoid energy depletion on cold nights is to enter into a sleep-like state of *torpor*, during which the body's temperature is lowered to just above that of the outside world, from 17 to 28°C (30 to 50°F) below their normal daytime operating body temperature. This torpor means they virtually stop using and needing energy; in effect, they hibernate each night. If you ever find a hummingbird perched as if in a daze early on a cool morning, it is not sick – just not yet warmed up and ready for its active life in the daytime.

3   All hummingbirds are *nectarivores* – they get most of their nourishment from consuming nectar from flowers (thus the name "chupaflor" in Spanish, which means flower-sucker). They have long, thin bills and specialized tongues, which they can extend amazing distances into the long thin flowers and the nectar, or sugar water, reward that awaits them at the bottom. This is done while the hummingbird hovers, but a few species must land on the flower and even turn their heads upside down to get access to the nectar. The advantage for the flower to provide this nectar reward is that the hummingbird's head must pass by the male parts of the flower, which have pollen on their surfaces. This pollen sticks to the feathers of the hummingbird, and then some of it is jostled to drop off on the female parts of the

next flower – thus achieving *pollination*, or sex via an intermediary. Because nectar is primarily a sugar and water solution, hummingbirds need to obtain additional nutrients, such as proteins, from other sources, especially when feeding growing chicks. Thus, they also eat insects and spiders, which they catch in the air or pluck from leaf surfaces or even from spider webs. Some recent studies suggest that these insects make up a much larger proportion of a hummingbird's diet than is generally believed, some going so far as to suggest that some hummingbird species visit flowers more often to catch insects there than to gather nectar.

4   Hummingbird-pollinated flowers are often shaped to permit only a single or a few species of hummingbirds with the matching shape and length of bill to be able to reach the nectar source. The advantage to the hummingbirds is that insects and other species of hummingbirds cannot compete for the nectar in that species of flower. The advantage to the flower is that these specialized hummingbirds won't be wandering around visiting lots of other species of flowers and dropping their valuable pollen in all the wrong places. The specialization ensures that the next flower visited is highly likely to be of the same species, and thus these flowers don't have to produce much extra pollen. They can use that energy instead to make better roots, more leaves and other useful parts that otherwise might have been sacrificed. Interlopers in this *mutualistic* interaction are a group of pollen-eating mite species. Mites are minuscule arthropods, allied with the spiders and ticks. Some mites may spend their lives on a single plant, feeding and reproducing, but others, perhaps searching for mates or new sites to colonize, try to reach other plants. Walking to another plant for such a small animal is almost out of the question. What to do? The mites jump onto the bills of hummingbirds when the birds visit flowers and become hitchhikers on the bird, usually hiding in their nostrils. The passengers leap off the bird's bill during a subsequent visit to a plant of the same species that they left, necessary because the mites are specialized for certain plants. Recent research suggests that the passenger mites monitor the scents of flowers to identify the correct type, to know when to get off the bus.

5   Many hummers are highly aggressive birds, energetically defending individual flowers or feeding territories from all other hummingbirds, regardless of species, as well as from large insects. Not all are territorial, however. Some are *trapline feeders*, repeatedly following a regular route around a large undefended section of the habitat and checking the same series of widely spaced flowering plants for their nectar. Unlike many plants that put out all their flowers at the same time, and then only for a short period, these trapline types of plants put out only one or a few flowers each day, but they continue doing so for several weeks, so the hummingbirds can learn about and depend on this nectar source. Some traplines can be more than 1 km (0.6 mile) long. Whether a bird defends a territory or not depends on the balance of the costs of energy used and the benefits of energy (in terms of resources) gained. If the flowers in an area are super-abundant, providing sufficient food for all, or if the flowers are so spread out that no one hummingbird could possibly defend them all (as in trapline flowers), then owning and defending a territory is not cost-effective. If the opposite is the case, and by keeping away interlopers from a defendable area with limited nectar, a hummingbird can keep more of the nectar for itself, then a territory is worthwhile.

Predators on hummingbirds include small agile hawks and falcons, large frogs, and insects such as preying mantises, which ambush the small birds as they feed at flowers. Another hazard is large spider webs, from which sometimes a poor hummingbird cannot extricate itself.

Breeding

Hummingbirds are polygamous breeders in which females do almost all the work. In some species a male in his territory advertises for females by singing squeaky songs. A female enters the territory and, following often spectacular aerial courtship displays, mates. She then leaves the male's territory to nest on her own. Other species are lec breeders, especially some of the hermits. Three to 25 males gather in a cleared area of the forest undergrowth, each with a tiny mating territory in that area in which he sings his squeaky little song in the hope of impressing and attracting a passing female to mate with him. The males spend hours there each day during the breeding season, singing their little hearts out. When a female enters a lec area, she chooses a lucky stud from among the males and mates with him. A male might spend months at a lec but have only one 15-minute mating interaction with a female, or, if his song is pitiful and unimpressive, mate with no females at all. Other males, presumably the Placido Domingos and Garth Brooks of the hummingbird-world, attract more females with their songs and mate with many of them in a season. (This is not to imply that Placido and Garth are promiscuous.) The females construct their tiny nests from plant parts, mosses, lichens, feathers, animal hairs and spider webbing. The nests are placed on the top of small branches, often attached with spider webbing. Hermits use this spider webbing to weave together the sides of the tip of a large-leafed plant. They then add plant material to construct a nest that hangs on the underside of the leaf, protected from rain and predators. Female hummers lay 2 eggs, incubate them for 15 to 19 days, and feed the chicks regurgitated nectar and insects for 20 to 26 days until they fledge.

Notes

Intriguingly, some hummingbirds are as curious about us as we are of them. A common occurrence while following a trail is to be closely approached by a passing hummingbird, which stops in mid-air to size up the large primate, darts this way and that to view the intruder from all angles, then, its curiosity apparently satisfied, zips off into the forest. You can increase your chances of this type of encounter by wearing a bright red bandanna, or tying one to your pack as you hike. Hummers always seem eager to investigate a new source of nectar, and the red color is usually their cue to a freshly opened flower. Several eco-lodges in the higher elevations and on the coast have hummingbird feeders on their porches. Dozens of flashy large hummingbirds chase each other to gain access to the sugar water while you sit only a meter or two away. For some reason, these hummingbird feeders do not work well in the lowlands, probably because they attract so many wasps and bees.

Several groups of Indians used colorful, iridescent hummingbird feathers in their wedding ornaments. Hummingbird bodies have a long mythical history in Latin America of being imbued with potent powers as love charms. Having a dead hummer in the hand or pocket is thought by some even today to be a sure way to appear irresistible to a member of the opposite sex. Even powdered hummingbird is sold for this purpose. The Arakmbut forest people of Amazonian Perú believe that a hummingbird seen in the forest is a sure sign of a Jaguar being nearby; when spotting such a bird while in the forest, they become more cautious and often return home quickly.

Status

At least 30 species of hummers are currently threatened or considered vulnerable to threat. In Perú, at least six are threatened, including the LITTLE WOODSTAR (considered endangered by some), PURPLE-BACKED SUNBEAM, CHILEAN WOOD-STAR, ROYAL SUNANGEL, MARVELOUS SPATULETAIL and GRAY-BELLIED COMET. Several other Peruvian species are very uncommon in the country, but are more abundant in other parts of their ranges.

Profiles

Rufous-breasted Hermit, *Glaucis hirsuta*, Plate 45a
White-necked Jacobin, *Florisuga mellivora*, Plate 45b
White-bearded Hermit, *Phaethornis hispidus*, Plate 45d
Little Hermit, *Phaethornis longuemareus*, Plate 45e
Long-tailed Hermit, *Phaethornis superciliosus*, Plate 45f
Black-throated Mango, *Anthracothorax nigricollis*, Plate 46a
Fork-tailed Woodnymph, *Thalurania furcata*, Plate 46b
Sparkling Violet-ear, *Colibri coruscans*, Plate 46c
Amazilia Hummingbird, *Amazilia amazilia*, Plate 46d
Speckled Hummingbird, *Adelomyia melanogenys*, Plate 46e

Tyrian Metaltail, *Metallura tyrianthina*, Plate 47a
Giant Hummingbird, *Patagona gigas*, Plate 47b
Collared Inca, *Coeligena torquata*, Plate 47c
Black-breasted Hillstar, *Oreotrochilus melanogaster*, Plate 47d
Bronze-tailed Comet, *Polyonymus caroli*, Plate 47e
Oasis Hummingbird, *Rhodopis vesper*, Plate 48a
Long-tailed Sylph, *Aglaiocercus kingi*, Plate 48b
Black-eared Fairy, *Heliothryx aurita*, Plate 48c
Peruvian Sheartail, *Thaumastura cora*, Plate 48d
Sword-billed Hummingbird, *Ensifera ensifera*, Plate 48e

21. Trogons

Although not as familiar to most people as other gaudy birds such as toucans and parrots, *trogons* are generally regarded by wildlife enthusiasts as among the globe's most visually impressive and glamorous birds. The Family Trogonidae inhabits tropical and semi-tropical regions throughout the Neotropics, Africa and south-eastern Asia. It consists of about 40 species (10 in Perú), all of them colorful, medium-sized birds with compact bodies, short necks and short, almost parrot-like bills. The largest of these species, the *quetzals*, are the most dazzling. Considering the broad and widely separated geographic areas over which the species of this family are spread, the uniformity of the family's body plan and plumage pattern is striking. Males are consistently more colorful than the females and have metallic or glittering green, blue or violet heads, backs and chests. Their breasts and undersides are contrasting bright red, yellow or orange. The duller females usually have the bright back and head colors replaced with brown or gray, but they share the males' brightly colored breasts and bellies. The characteristic tail is long and squared off, with horizontal black and white stripes on the underside. Trogons usually sit erect with their distinctive tails pointing straight down to the ground.

Natural History
Ecology and Behavior

You usually see trogons by themselves or occasionally in pairs. In spite of their persistent calls, they are often difficult to locate and see. Their bright colors meld into the colors of the foliage, and except during their fast and darting flight, they tend to sit still for long periods. At a fruiting tree they will fly up to a fruit and grab it in the bill without landing. They take big insects and occasionally small lizards in much the same way. They are probably most easily seen as part of a *mixed-species feeding flock* in the canopy. At these times they move around more and tend to sit out in the open for short periods.

Breeding

Trogons are monogamous, nesting in tree cavities and occasionally in excavations in arboreal ant or termite nests. Generally the female incubates the 2 or 3 eggs overnight, and the male takes over during the day. Incubation is 17 to 19 days. Young are tended by both parents, and fledge at 14 to 30 days old.

Notes

The RESPLENDENT QUETZAL of Central America, a large trogon with extremely long tail feathers, is revered and held sacred by several indigenous groups. The skin of trogons and quetzals is so thin that it has been described as being like wet toilet paper. Why is a question no one yet has been able to answer satisfactorily, but it does mean that you are unlikely to ever see trogons fighting with each other; the slightest cut would be severe.

Status

The trogons and quetzals of Perú are fairly common, and apparently none is threatened. However, the RESPLENDENT QUETZAL of Central America is considered endangered (CITES Appendix I listed) because of hunting and continuing destruction of its cloud forest habitat.

Profiles

Golden-headed Quetzal, *Pharomachrus auriceps*, Plate 49a
White-tailed Trogon, *Trogon viridis*, Plate 49b
Collared Trogon, *Trogon collaris*, Plate 49c
Violaceous Trogon, *Trogon violaceus*, Plate 49d
Masked Trogon, *Trogon personatus*, Plate 49e

22. Kingfishers

Kingfishers are handsome, bright birds, and most of Perú's are easy to see. Most often found along forest streams, large rivers and lowland lakes, they are included in the worldwide Family Alcedinidae (but the New World species are sometimes split into their own family, Cerylidae). Nearly 100 species occur throughout the world in temperate and tropical areas, and 5 of the 6 New World species are found in Perú. They range in size from 12 to 46 cm (5 to 16 in), but all are similar in form: large heads with very long, robust, straight bills, short necks, and short legs. Their colors are blue-gray or oily green above with white and chestnut breasts. The largest species in Perú, the RINGED KINGFISHER (Plate 50), is loud and obvious on large rivers and lakes of lowlands on both sides of the Andes. Its blue-gray back and head, along with its large size, separate it from the other local kingfishers. It often flies high overhead as it moves from one water area to another, giving its far-carrying "check" call. An oily green back and head is characteristic of the other four Peruvian species.

Natural History
Ecology and Behavior
New World kingfishers, as the name suggests, are all mainly *piscivores*, or fish-eaters. Usually seen hunting alone, a kingfisher sits quietly on a low branch over water, attentively scanning the water below. When it sees a fish, it swoops down and dives head first into the water, sometimes as deep as 60 cm (2 ft) to catch the unwary fish in its bill. If successful, the kingfisher returns to its perch, beats the hapless fish several times on the branch and then swallows it head first. The RINGED KINGFISHER will also hover over the water several seconds before making the plunge. Occasionally kingfishers will go after tadpoles and large aquatic insects. Kingfishers have a buzzy and fast flight when moving low over the water's surface.

Kingfishers are highly territorial, noisily defending their territory from other members of the same species with noisy chattering, chasing and fighting. They inhabit lowland forests and waterways, but occasionally the Ringed Kingfisher is found at ponds in cloud forests at 2500 m (8000 ft) (see Close-up, p. 227).

Breeding
Kingfishers are monogamous breeders that nest in tunnels excavated from vertical or near-vertical banks over water. Both mates help defend their territory, and both also help dig the nest tunnel, which can be 0.75 to 1.5 m (2 to 5 ft) deep. Both parents incubate the 3 to 8 eggs for a total of 19 to 26 days. They feed their young increasingly large fish until they fledge at 25 to 38 days old. Fledglings continue to be fed outside the nest by the parents for up to 10 weeks. Eventually the parents expel the young from the territory, and the young must then establish their own. The kingfishers are notoriously bad housekeepers, and the stench of decaying fish and droppings is often your first clue that a nest tunnel is nearby. This very stench, however, may be so overpowering that it overwhelms the delicate olfactory senses of predators and discourages them from entering to eat what would otherwise be easy prey.

Notes
Kingfishers are the subject of a particularly rich mythology, a sign of the bird's conspicuousness and its association throughout history with oceans, lakes, and rivers. The power over wind and waves that was attributed by sailors to the god Halcyon was passed on to the Halcyon bird, or the kingfisher, which became credited with protecting sailors and calming storms. The seven days before and after the winter solstice were thought to be the days when this kingfisher nested and were thus days of peace and calm, the "halcyon" days.

Status
All the New World kingfisher species are moderately common to abundant and none is considered threatened.

Profiles
Ringed Kingfisher, *Ceryle torquata*, Plate 50a
Green Kingfisher, *Chloroceryle americana*, Plate 50b
Green-and-rufous Kingfisher, *Chloroceryle inda*, Plate 50c

Amazon Kingfisher, *Chloroceryle amazona*, Plate 50d
American Pygmy Kingfisher, *Chloroceryle aenea*, Plate 50e

23. Jacamars and Puffbirds

Two interesting and closely related Neotropical families distantly related to king-fishers are the *jacamars* and *puffbirds*. The jacamar family (Galbulidae) includes 18 species, with 9 in Perú, and the puffbird family (Bucconidae) includes about 30 species, with 21 in Perú. Species of both families are generally forest dwellers, mostly in warm lowlands. Jacamars are by far the flashier members of the two families, with most having glittering green and blue backs and heads, and noisy vocalizations. Some have described them as resembling over-sized hummingbirds because of their colors and long, sharp bills. They are, however, much larger than hummingbirds (15 to 31 cm, 6 to 12 in, long) and have distinctly different behavior. Puffbirds are, in contrast, much duller in color – mainly subdued browns and grays or black and white. Their size range is somewhat smaller than that for jaca-mars, 15 to 28 cm (6 to 11 in). Their bills are moderately long but most are very thick and often end in a small hook.

Natural History
Ecology and Behavior
You are most likely to see jacamars along small forest streams and at forest clear-ings. Here they sit, usually in pairs or family groups, chattering away, moving their heads back and forth and waiting for a large butterfly, dragonfly, or other tasty insect to fly by. One of them then darts out and deftly snatches the insect out of the air with the tip of its long bill and then returns to a perch, often the same one from which it launched the aerial attack. After slamming the insect against the perch a couple of times, it removes the wings and swallows the body. If you find a pile of discarded butterfly and other insect wings on a path, this is a good sign for you to look up and search for a jacamar roosting overhead. They often have a series of favorite perches they use through the day, so if it's not there when you first look, check again later.

Most puffbirds are less gaudy and noticeable than jacamars. However, a few species are show-offs, and you have a good chance of seeing them. The WHITE-NECKED PUFFBIRD (Plate 51) is striking with its black and white colors, but you will see it only if you look for it in the canopy, where it often sits on an open branch by itself for an hour or more without moving. If you are visiting one of the canopy towers built in Amazonian Perú, you will have a better possibility of seeing one without straining your neck looking up to the tops of trees. It and most other puffbirds hunt by waiting patiently for a lizard, small snake or large insect to walk or run on a nearby trunk or on the ground. Then the puffbird swoops from its perch and snatches the luckless prey in its bill. The BLACK-FRONTED NUNBIRD (Plate 52) makes itself so obvious, vocally and visually, that you will have a hard time not noticing it. Usually 2 to 6 individuals will sit on a branch together high up in a tree and sing their rollicking and raucous song for several minutes, each one trying to sing louder than its neighbor. Apparently the name "nunbird" was applied by some scientist unappreciative of the local chorus of nuns in black and white habit he had to endure in his childhood church. This species hunts for lizards and large insects running on tree trunks and branches in the mid-levels of lowland primary forests of the Amazon region, and is usually associated with mixed-species foraging flocks in the canopy. Occasionally a family group of nunbirds will follow a troop of monkeys and catch the large insects scared into flight by movements of the monkeys. The most commonly seen puffbird in Perú, and the most bizarre in appearance, is the SWALLOW-WINGED PUFFBIRD (Plate 51). This black, white, and rufous species appears to have no tail. It sits, usually in pairs or small groups, in isolated tree tops in the middle of cleared fields or along large rivers of the Amazonian lowlands. All of a sudden one or all of the group will fly out a long distance, swoop to catch a small insect in the air and then return to the same perch. Their wings are long and tapered, and misidentifications as swallows are common. Even at rest they resemble husky swallows, or as one wag put it, "like swallows on steroids."

Breeding

Jacamars nest in short, horizontal burrows they dig in steep hillsides or in river banks. Both parents incubate the 2 to 4 eggs for a total of 20 to 22 days. They feed insects to the young for 19 to 26 days until fledging. Little is known about breeding in puffbirds, but some nest in burrows on the forest floor and some in burrows excavated from arboreal termite nests. The WHITE-FRONTED NUNBIRD surrounds its tunnel entrance with sticks to hide the hole. Numerous adults appear to feed the young in a helpers-at-the-nest behavior also known from several other families such as jays. Both mates share in tunnel excavation, incubation and feeding the young. The SWALLOW-WINGED PUFFBIRD digs vertical nesting tunnels in sandy soil that are up to 2 m (6.5 ft) deep.

Notes

Puffbirds of several species have been called stupid ("bobo") because they often sit still, depending on camouflage, and permit close approach. But these birds actually can be quite stealthy in their behavior and movements; many pass by near forest trails without our noticing – even on popular tourist trails.

Status

Among the puffbirds, populations of the LANCEOLATED MONKLET, a small brown and white bird that ranges from Costa Rica south to the Amazon regions of Perú and Brazil, appear to be declining, and this species may be near-threatened.

Profiles

White-eared Jacamar, *Galbalcyrhynchus leucotis*, Plate 51a
Bluish-fronted Jacamar, *Galbula cyanescens*, Plate 51b
White-necked Puffbird, *Notharchus macrorhynchus*, Plate 51c
Swallow-winged Puffbird, *Chelidoptera tenebrosa*, Plate 51d
White-chested Puffbird, *Malacoptila fusca*, Plate 51e
Black-fronted Nunbird, *Monasa nigrifrons*, Plate 52a

24. Motmots

With beautiful coloring but a ridiculous name, *motmots*, related to the kingfishers, have several distinctive features. The nine species in the family, Momotidae, are all Neotropical; four occur in Perú. Three are found in the lowlands, and one in mid-elevation cloud forests. They occur in all types of forest, from primary to flooded, secondary to open orchards, suburban parks and even tropical dry forest areas of the northwestern coast. Motmots are colorful, long, slender, medium-sized birds (32 to 48 cm, 16 to 19 in, long). They all have long, broad bills somewhat curved down at the ends and with serrate edges, adapted to grab and hold their animal prey. The most peculiar feature, however, is their tail. In many motmots, two central feather shafts grow much longer than the others. With preening, feather barbs just above the ends of the shafts drop off, producing a short length of naked shaft and an isolated feather patch on the end called a *racquet*. General motmot colors are soft hues of cinnamon, and the BLUE-CROWNED MOTMOT (Plate 52) adds a black face and blue-green to turquoise head. Its deep, hollow call of "BOO-boop," probably the source of the common name of motmots, is given at 3- to 5-second intervals for long periods. The Blue-crowned is the motmot you will most likely encounter either in primary forests or in cut-over areas almost anywhere in eastern and northwestern Perú below 500 m (1600 ft) elevation.

Natural History
Ecology and Behavior
Motmots are predators on large insects, spiders, and small frogs, lizards and snakes, which they snatch off leaves or from the ground while they are in flight. Typically they perch quietly on tree branches, regularly swinging their long tails from side to side, until they spot a suitable meal moving. They then dart out quickly and seize the prey in their bill, carry it back to their perch and eat it. If the prey is large and struggling, the motmot will thwack it against the branch several times to dispatch it before swallowing it. Motmots are also frugivores, eating small fruits up to the size of plums, which they collect from trees while hovering. You will find motmots almost always by themselves, even though they may pair for the entire year. Pairs tend to separate during the day to feed. They start their daily activities before dawn and continue to well past twilight, after most day-active birds have gone to bed.

Breeding
Male and female motmots are similar in size and color. Some of their low-key courtship activities include calling back and forth high up in the trees, and holding bits of green leaves in their bills. Motmots are burrow nesters, like their kingfisher cousins. Both male and female help dig the burrow, often placed in the vertical bank of a riverside or road cut. Tunnels can be up to 4 m (13 ft) long, but most are on the order of 1.5 m (4 ft). Both parents incubate the 2 to 4 eggs. Young are fed and brooded by male and female for 24 to 30 days, at the end of which the juvenile motmots are able to fly from the burrow entrance.

Notes
Because of the characteristic swinging of the tail from side to side, one common name for motmots in South America is *relojero*, or clock-maker, evidently referring to the pendulum-like ticking of the tail. This group is one of the few in which there are more species in Central America than in South America; this is likely the result of a different and probably unique historical origin and subsequent historical movements of this group.

Status
None of Perú's motmots are considered endangered or threatened. Several motmot species are rare over parts of their ranges in the Neotropics, but are not considered threatened owing to their greater abundance in other parts of their ranges.

Profiles

Rufous Motmot, *Baryphthengus martii*, Plate 52b
Broad-billed Motmot, *Electron platyrhynchum*, Plate 52c
Blue-crowned Motmot, *Momotus momota*, Plate 52d

25. Toucans and Barbets

The *toucans* and *barbets* are two closely related groups considered as separate families by some experts and as part of the same family by others; both groups are cousins to the woodpeckers. The barbets have a broad distribution in the tropics of Africa, southern Asia and the Neotropics (Subfamily Capitoninae), with a global total of about 75 species, 6 of which are found in Perú. Barbets are colorful, with patches of red, orange, yellow, black and white. Males are generally brighter than females. Several species are known for duet singing between mates. Often one mate sings every other note (an *antiphonal* duet) and the other mate fills in the missing notes in such a perfect, coordinated manner that it sounds like one seamless composition. Ranging in size from 15 to 20 cm (6 to 8 in), barbets are stocky birds with stout but not long bills; they are considerably smaller than toucans. The BLACK-SPOTTED BARBET (Plate 53) is common in the lowland primary and secondary forests of the Amazonian selva. It is frequently in mixed-species feeding flocks in the canopy.

Toucans are stunning, and no other word suits them better. Their shape, brilliant color patterns, and tropical quintessence make them one of the most popular "poster animals" for the tropical forests of the Americas. Most ecotravellers want to see toucans, and with a little luck, they will. The toucan family, Ramphastidae, has about 40 species, all restricted to the Neotropics. Perú has 17 species, including some of the smaller types called *aracaris* (AH-rah-SAH-rees) and *toucanets*. Your first sighting of a toucan in the wild will be exciting – the large size of the bird, the bright colors, the enormous almost cartoonish bill all combine to match or surpass the toucan of your imagination. If you see it in flight, it will somewhat resemble a flying banana, as it alternately flaps and sails in its undulating flight (smaller species fly more directly with a buzzy flight). The toucans' most distinctive mark, their bill, looks so ungainly and heavy you might wonder how they can maintain their balance while perched on a branch or in flight. Actually, the bill is mostly hollow and lightweight.

The large toucans (Plate 54) in Perú are all most common in primary forest, but a fruiting tree in secondary (recently cut) forest nearby can easily tempt them. Up high in the cloud forest, the GRAY-BREASTED MOUNTAIN-TOUCAN (Plate 54), with its brilliant blue-gray and black plumage, is the largest toucan you will see on the east slopes of the Andes. Also here high in the mountain forests, you can see the small green EMERALD TOUCANET (Plate 53). The greatest variety of toucans, however, is among the aracaris, with their numerous variations on the theme of yellow breast, dark back and squealing vocalizations. You will usually see aracaris as a flock flying by one at a time in a long procession (moving from tree to tree in "strings"). The most solitary of the species is the GOLDEN-COLLARED TOUCANET (Plate 53). Even though it is common in the primary forests of the Amazonian selva, it is shy and hard to see. Only by its persistent call, which sounds like the tooting of a toy train, does it signal its abundance.

Natural History
Ecology and Behavior

Barbets and toucans live in moist forests from sea level to 3000 m (10,000 ft). You often see barbets in mated pairs among large *mixed-species foraging flocks* in the sub-canopy. They commonly eat fruits and seeds, but they also take insects and even small lizards. Almost all toucans are social and gregarious. When they forage at a fruiting tree, they reach with their long bills to the outermost fruits, grasp one with the tip of the bill, toss it in the air and swallow it. Toucans also raid other birds' nests to eat eggs and nestlings. Toucans have a mean reputation among smaller birds, and not just because of their nest-robbing proclivities. Apparently toucans take umbrage at other bird species feeding in the same fruiting tree and may at times eat adult birds of small sizes. When a flock of toucans lands in a tree, most of the other birds, even large parrots such as macaws, will quickly abandon the site.

Breeding

Both barbets and toucans nest in tree cavities, either natural cavities or those built originally by woodpeckers. Barbets occasionally use their bills to enlarge holes in softer or dead wood. Nests can be any height above ground up to 30 m (100 ft) or more. Both sexes incubate and feed the 2 to 4 young. Both toucans and barbets are apparently monogamous. Some species of toucans, like the COLLARED ARACARI, seem to breed cooperatively, with numerous helpers at the nest in addition to the mother and the father bringing food to the young. Frugivorous birds such as toucans are critical for dispersing seeds from parent trees and helping to maintain the healthy plant diversity of Neotropical forests (see Close-up, p. 177).

Notes

The colorful rump and tail feathers of toucans are commonly used to construct the feathered crowns of the native people in the Amazonian region of Perú. If someone tries to sell or even give you one of these crowns, however, you must decline; it is against both Peruvian and international law to export or even possess them.

Status

Habitat clearing and hunting are the main factors explaining declines of toucan populations in some parts of Perú, but none of the species is considered threatened at this time. Several toucans are CITES Appendix II listed, as species that are vulnerable to threat.

Profiles

Scarlet-crowned Barbet, *Capito aurovirens*, Plate 53a
Black-spotted Barbet, *Capito niger*, Plate 53b
Lemon-throated Barbet, *Eubucco richardsoni*, Plate 53c
Emerald Toucanet, *Aulacorhynchus prasinus*, Plate 53d
Golden-collared Toucanet, *Selenidera reinwardtii*, Plate 53e
Chestnut-eared Aracari, *Pteroglossus castanotis*, Plate 54a
Curl-crested Aracari, *Pteroglossus beauharnaesii*, Plate 54b
Lettered Aracari, *Pteroglossus inscriptus*, Plate 54c
Gray-breasted Mountain-Toucan, *Andigena hypoglauca*, Plate 54d
Cuvier's Toucan, *Ramphastos cuvieri*, Plate 54e

26. Woodpeckers

Everyone knows what a *woodpecker* is, at least by name and perhaps by their cartoon incarnations. They are highly specialized forest birds that occur almost everywhere in the world (even in some places without trees) except Australia, New Zealand and Antarctica. The family, Picidae, includes more than 200 species that range in size from the tiny *piculets* (9 cm, 3.5 in long) to the largest woodpeckers (50 cm, 20 in). Thirty-six species of various sizes occur throughout Perú's diverse habitats. They all share strong, straight and chisel-like bills, very long and barbed tongues, and sharp toes that spread widely for clinging to tree trunks. All but the small piculets also have stiffly reinforced tail feathers that support them as they climb on vertical surfaces. To accommodate their constant banging and drumming with their bills on wood surfaces, they have extra-spongy bone at the base of the bill to absorb shock waves. They come mostly in subdued shades of gray, green, black and white, frequently with bars and streaks. Most, however, have bright patches of crimson, especially males.

Natural History
Ecology and Behavior
Woodpeckers are adapted to cling to a tree's bark and move lightly over its surface, listening and looking for insects. They drill holes into bark where they hear insects chewing on the wood and then use their long, often sticky tongues to extract the juicy morsels, which include both adult insects and grubs (insect larvae). Some species, such as the YELLOW-TUFTED WOODPECKER (Plate 56), commonly act like flycatchers as they sally out from perches high in trees to catch flying insects in the air. Many species also eat fruit, nuts and nectar from flowers. The piculets use the smallest branches of trees and bushes, usually low in the forest, and, lacking a long stiff tail like the other woodpeckers, clamber about pecking on horizontal branches. In flight, woodpeckers typically undulate up and down with an alternating short burst of rapid wing beating; this causes a rise in altitude that is followed by a short period of folded-wing gliding in which altitude is lost. They sleep and rest in cavities they excavate from trees. Woodpeckers use their bills and their pecking ability in three ways: for drilling holes to get insect food; for excavating holes for roosting and nesting; and for *drumming*, that is, extra rapid beats usually on a hollow surface that amplifies the sound for communication to other woodpeckers.

The holes that woodpeckers excavate for their own nests are used over and over again by a plethora of birds and mammals that cannot excavate their own cavities. Some of these interlopers use abandoned woodpecker holes, but others, such as some aracaris, will at times evict woodpeckers from their active cavity. These cavities are vital for protection from nest predators and are thus at a premium; their availability may affect the population sizes of many species dependent on them. A species or group of species whose presence or absence directly affects the ability of many other species to persist in a habitat is called a *keystone* species. In this case, the protection of woodpeckers, which can be considered keystone species, is important because their absence would harm a large number of other bird species.

Breeding
Woodpeckers are monogamous, and some live in large social or family groups. Tropical woodpeckers usually remain paired throughout the year. Both mates are involved with the nest excavation, the interior of which they line with wood chips. Both sexes incubate the 2 to 4 eggs for 11 to 18 days, males typically taking the night shift. They feed the young for 20 to 35 days until fledging. Juveniles remain with the parents outside the nest for several months.

Notes

Woodpeckers often damage trees and buildings in their quest for food and nest sites. They also eat fruits from orchards and gardens and so are considered to be pests in some parts of the tropics. The ANDEAN FLICKER (Plate 55), which occurs in the treeless puna of highland Perú, makes its nest and roosting hole in clay banks. The adobe mud huts built by people in this region are perfect for the flicker's tunnel-building behavior, but the flickers' work is unappreciated by those living in these dwellings. Often the local people shoot four of these pesky woodpeckers and tie their bodies so that they dangle from each corner of the house – to warn other flickers of the punishment for trespassing.

Status

None of Perú's woodpecker species is considered threatened, but several of the larger species in coastal primary forest are declining with continued forest clearing.

Profiles

Plain-breasted Piculet, *Picumnus castelnau*, Plate 55a
Spot-breasted Woodpecker, *Colaptes punctigula*, Plate 55b
Andean Flicker, *Colaptes rupicola*, Plate 55c
Crimson-mantled Woodpecker, *Piculus rivollii*, Plate 55d
Cream-colored Woodpecker, *Celeus flavus*, Plate 55e
Lineated Woodpecker, *Dryocopus lineatus*, Plate 56a
Yellow-tufted Woodpecker, *Melanerpes cruentatus*, Plate 56b
Crimson-crested Woodpecker, *Campephilus melanoleucos*, Plate 56c
Red-necked Woodpecker, *Campephilus rubricollis*, Plate 56d

All of the bird families considered below are *passerine*, or *perching birds*, members of Order Passeriformes (see p. 98).

---

27. Woodcreepers

Woodcreepers, Family Dendrocolaptidae, are small to medium-sized brown birds that pursue a mostly arboreal existence. About 50 species are distributed from Mexico to Argentina, 26 in Perú. They occur in moist lowland forest, tropical dry and thorn forest, and all the way up in altitude to cloud forests. Although their long stout bills, stiff tail feathers and tree trunk climbing recall woodpeckers, these birds are more closely related to flycatchers; the similarities to woodpeckers are superficial and coincidental – what biologists term *evolutionary convergence*. Most are slender birds that range in size from 20 to 36 cm (8 to 14 in). The sexes look alike, with plumages of various shades of brown, chestnut and tan. Most have spotting, streaking or banding, but different species are confusingly similar and their identification to species is frustrating at best.

Natural History
Ecology and Behavior

Woodcreepers feed by hitching upwards on tree trunks and also horizontally along branches, peering under bark and into moss clumps and epiphytes, using their stout bills to probe and catch prey in tight nooks and crannies. Unlike woodpeckers, they do not drill holes in search of prey or drum with their bills. The foraging procedure among the various species follows a standard theme but with many variations. An individual flies to the base of a tree and then spirals up the trunk, using its stiff tail for support and sharp toenails for purchase on the bark's surface. Near the top of the tree the bird flies down to the base of the next tree and repeats the process. Some species, however, use smaller trees or even bamboo, others tend to stay higher in the canopy, and some frequently follow army ant swarms to catch large insects flying up to escape the horde. In these cases, the woodcreepers will hunt from the base of a tree near the ground or sometimes right on the ground. They will also fly out to catch insects on the wing. Usually woodcreepers are solitary but occasionally a pair will forage together. Some species, however, commonly forage in *mixed-species foraging flocks* of the forest undergrowth or the canopy.

Breeding
Most woodcreeper species practice standard monogamy, with the sexes equally sharing nesting chores and care of the young. In some, however, no real pair-bonds are formed, and after mating, females nest alone. Nests are usually in tree crevices or holes and occasionally in arboreal termite nests. Parents line nests with wood chips. The 2 or 3 eggs are incubated for 17 to 21 days and young fledge 18 to 24 days after hatching.

Notes
Some woodcreepers have reputations for being extremely aggressive toward other species, for example, harassing and evicting roosting or nesting woodpeckers from tree cavities.

Status
Most woodcreepers in Perú are common to abundant. Species in northwestern forests that are threatened by habitat destruction have large ranges that extend into Central America, with many healthy populations outside of Perú.

Profiles
Olivaceous Woodcreeper, *Sittasomus griseicapillus*, Plate 57a
Wedge-billed Woodcreeper, *Glyphorynchus spirurus*, Plate 57b
Long-billed Woodcreeper, *Nasica longirostris*, Plate 57c
Buff-throated Woodcreeper, *Xiphorhynchus guttatus*, Plate 57d

28. Ovenbirds

Ovenbirds are small, often brown, often inconspicuous birds that are sometimes extremely difficult to tell apart. They are also known for occupying a wide range of habitats. There are a mind-numbing 240+ species of this family (Furnariidae), which occurs from Mexico to Argentina. Perú has 112 species, many of which are differentiated by no more than subtle shades of brown. We profile six species that are easy to identify and that you are most likely to see in various Peruvian habitats, from open puna grasslands and cloud forests of the Andean slopes, to the drier lowlands of coastal Perú, and the moist forests of the Amazonian lowlands.

Natural History
Ecology and Behavior
Ovenbirds are all insectivores that mainly glean their resting prey from undersides of leaves and branches. Most ovenbirds live low in their habitats or even on the ground, but a few are regular in the canopy of tall forests. Although dully colored and unobtrusive in behavior, they are interesting because of the diversity of ecological niches they occupy. They have invaded almost every habitat in South

America. In this remarkable "radiation," the various species have developed such a breadth of adaptations that they have become similar to and behave like unrelated families that occupy those respective niches in other parts of the world. Thus, there are ovenbird "replacements" of thrushes, wheatears, pipits, dippers, larks, wagtails, nuthatches and chickadees (tits). One special bird is the PERUVIAN SEASIDE CINCLODES (Plate 58), which is virtually the only passerine bird in the world that lives exclusively in a salt water habitat.

Breeding
Many ovenbirds appear to mate for life. Virtually all species of ovenbirds use closed nests. Some, such as *xenops,* make tunnels in vertical banks; others use tree cavities or construct elaborate structures of twigs or mud. The nests of the family's namesake, the several species called *horneros* (genus *Furnarius*), are mind-boggling. They build large domed nests out of clay, sometimes 30 cm (12 in) in diameter. The shape is much like a small-scale replica of the old bread ovens also made of clay and used by early European colonists in the New World. Usually these nests are placed in exposed areas 1 or 2 m (3 to 6 ft) off the ground. The sun bakes the clay brick hard and few predators can break down its walls. More clever predators, however, try to use the entrance of the nest to gain access to eggs or chicks, but are usually foiled by the large but false tunnel that leads down into the clay mass and then ends abruptly. The actual nest entrance leads up unobtrusively from the fake tunnel.

Notes
The oven-shaped nests of the PALE-LEGGED HORNERO (Plate 58) are a common part of the scenery in lowland Perú. They are so durable that each one lasts for years. Often, other species of birds use these cavities for their own nests after the ovenbirds have abandoned them.

Status
Most ovenbirds in Perú are common and have extensive ranges, but nine species, including the PALE-TAILED CANASTERO, WHITE-BELLIED CINCLODES, HENNA-HOODED FOLIAGE-GLEANER, and APURIMAC SPINETAIL, are considered vulnerable because of their extremely small ranges and specialized habitats. Habitat destruction and brush fires could easily push such species to very low populations and even to extinction. The ROYAL CINCLODES is on the IUCN Red List as critically endangered.

Profiles
Coastal Miner, *Geositta peruviana*, Plate 58a
Bar-winged Cinclodes, *Cinclodes fuscus*, Plate 58b
Pale-legged Hornero, *Furnarius leucopus*, Plate 58c
Pearled Treerunner, *Margarornis squamiger*, Plate 58d
Andean Tit-Spinetail, *Leptasthenura andicola,* Plate 58e
Peruvian Seaside Cinclodes, *Cinclodes taczanowskii*, Plate 58f

29. Antbirds

Antbirds are small and medium-sized, often drab inhabitants of the lower parts of forests. Many are difficult to see, but often they are loud and vocal. The family of antbirds, Formicariidae, has about 200 species, all restricted to the Neotropics, with 126 in Perú. The name comes not from their eating ants but from the behavior of some of these species to use army ants to scare up insect prey for them.

Antbirds range in size from 8 to 36 cm (3 to 14 in). The smaller ones are called *antwrens* and *antvireos*. The mid-sized ones are the *antbirds*, and larger species are called *antshrikes, antthrushes* and *antpittas*. In detail these species are quite varied in appearance and body shape. Males are generally colored with understated shades of brown, gray, black and white. Females are generally duller than the males, with olive-brown or chestnut predominating. Some species have bright red eyes or patches of bright bare skin around the eye. Some, like the GREAT ANTSHRIKE (Plate 59), are bold and often emerge from the scrubby bushes to sing and scold. Others, like the RUFOUS ANTPITTA (Plate 59), are shy and incredibly difficult to see as they run through undergrowth.

Natural History
Ecology and Behavior
Antbirds generally occur in thick vegetation in secondary and primary forests. A few species run on the forest floor, but most are in low to middle parts of the forest. A very few are up in the canopy. Most species are insectivorous, but some of the larger species also eat fruit, lizards, snakes and frogs. Most species glean for their prey by searching the undersides of leaves and branches. A few hawk for flying insects, and a number always follow army ant swarms (that is, they are *obligate* ant followers). These species wait at the advancing line of army ants as they raid the forest floor (see p. 244). Panicked insects run or fly up from the ant onslaught into the waiting bills of the antbirds. Often several species of antbirds, along with woodcreepers and many other bird species, jostle each other for the best positions to catch the escaping insects.

Breeding
Many antbirds appear to mate for life. Courtship feeding occurs in some of these birds, males passing food to females prior to mating. Many antbirds build cup nests out of pieces of plants that they weave together. Nests are usually placed in a fork of branches low in a tree or shrub. Some nest in tree cavities. Male and female share nest-building duty, as well as incubation of the 2 or 3 eggs and eventually feeding insects to the young. Incubation is 14 to 20 days, and young remain in the nest for 9 to 18 days. Some of the obligate ant-following species have abbreviated courtship and nesting behavior, apparently to facilitate their following the army ants when these mobile insect colonies move on from their temporary bivouacs in the forest. In some antbird species, family groups remain together, male offspring staying with the parents, even after acquiring mates.

Notes
The strange compound names of these birds, such as antwrens and antshrikes, arose partially because, to the naturalists who first named them, there were obvious parallels in size and, at least superficially, appearance, of these various species to North American, European and Asian wrens and shrikes. These common names are only confusing because some birds similarly named, such as the ant-tanagers, really are tanagers (p. 170) that follow army ants and are not members of the antbird family. Some ornithologists prefer to consider the ground-dwelling antpittas and antthrushes as their own separate family, Formicariidae, and the "typical" antbirds as the Family Thamnophilidae.

Status
Five Peruvian antbirds are presently considered threatened or endangered: RUFOUS-FRONTED ANTTHRUSH, ASH-THROATED ANTWREN, GRAY-HEADED

ANTBIRD, BLACK-TAILED ANTBIRD, and YELLOW-RUMPED ANTWREN. They all have small geographic ranges and thus are extremely vulnerable to forest clearing and habitat destruction.

Profiles

Great Antshrike, *Taraba major*, Plate 59a
Barred Antshrike, *Thamnophilus doliatus*, Plate 59b
Black-Spotted Bare-eye, *Phlegopsis nigromaculata*, Plate 59c
White-flanked Antwren, *Myrmotherula axillaris*, Plate 59d
Black-faced Antthrush, *Formicarius analis*, Plate 59e
Rufous Antpitta, *Grallaria rufula*, Plate 59f

30. Manakins

The *manakins*, Family Pipridae, are a Neotropical group of about 60 species, with 25 in Perú. They are small, compact, stocky passerine birds, 9 to 19 cm (3.5 to 7.5 in) long, with short tails and bills, and two attention-grabbing features: brightly colored plumages and some of the most elaborate courtship displays among birds. Some male manakins are outstandingly beautiful, predominantly glossy black but with brilliant patches of bright orange-red, yellow, or blue on their heads and/or throats. Some have deep blue on their undersides and/or backs. The exotic appearance of male manakins is sometimes enhanced by long, streamer-like tails, up to twice the length of the body, produced by the elongation of two of the central tail feathers. Females, in contrast, are duller and less ornate, usually shades of yellowish olive-green or gray. To accompany the bird's courtship displays, the wing feathers of some species, when moved in certain ways, make whirring or snapping sounds.

The BLUE-CROWNED MANAKIN (Plate 60) is one of the most common species of manakins in the lowland forests of the Amazon region and northwestern Perú. The males of this species, however, are relatively solitary and rarely form organized mating lecs (see below). The males of the BAND-TAILED MANAKIN (Plate 60), in contrast, form noisy and active lecs in the lowlands of the Amazon. Listen for their explosive, nasal calls from the understory. Unlike its colorful cousins, both sexes of the relatively large THRUSH-LIKE MANAKIN (Plate 60) are dull. Common in the low undergrowth of primary and secondary humid lowland forests, this species is solitary and does not form lecs. It is most often found by its distinctive whistled song. Some ornithologists think this species is so different that it is better placed in the cotinga family.

Natural History
Ecology and Behavior

Manakins are highly active forest birds, chiefly of warmer, lowland areas, although some range up into cloud forests. Residents of the forest understory, they eat mostly small fruits, which they pluck from bushes and trees while in flight, and they also take insects from the foliage. Largely *frugivorous*, manakins are important seed dispersers of the fruit tree species from which they feed. (The cozy relationships between fruit trees and the birds that feed on them are explored in the Close-Up on p. 177.) Manakins are fairly social animals when it comes to feeding and other daily activities, but males and females do not pair. They employ a non-monogamous mating system and, in fact, most of our knowledge about manakin behavior concerns their breeding behavior – how females choose males with which to mate and, in particular, male courting techniques. To use the ornithological jargon, manakins are *promiscuous* breeders. No pair-bonds are formed between males and females. Males mate with more than one female and females probably do the same. After mating, females build nests and rear young by themselves. Males, singly or in pairs, during the breeding season stake out display sites on tree branches, in bushes, or on cleared patches of the forest floor, and then spend considerable amounts of time giving lively vocal and visual displays, trying to attract females. An area that contains several of these performance sites is called a *lec*, and thus manakins, along with other birds such as some grouse, some cotingas, and some hummingbirds, are *lecking* breeders.

At the lec, male manakins *dance*, performing elaborate, repetitive, amazingly rapid and acrobatic movements, sometimes making short up and down flights, sometimes rapid slides, twists, and turn-arounds, sometimes hanging upside down on a tree branch while turning rapidly from side to side and making snapping sounds with their wings. The details of a male's dance are *species specific*, that is, different species dance in different ways. Females, attracted to lecs by the sounds of male displays and by their memories of lec locations – the same traditional forest sites are used from one year to the next – examine the energetically performing males with a critical eye and then choose the ones they want to mate with, sometimes making the rounds several times before deciding. In a few species, two and sometimes three males (*duos* and *trios*) join together in a coordinated dance on the same perch. In their dance the males alternate *leapfrog hops* with bouts of slow, *butterfly flight*. In these curious cases, one male is dominant, one subordinate, and only the dominant of the pair eventually gets to mate with interested females. Why the subordinate male appears to help the dominant one obtain matings (are they closely related? Do subordinate males stand to inherit display sites when the dominants die? Do subordinates achieve "stolen" matings with females when the dominants are temporarily distracted?), why the manakins dance at all, and on what basis females choose particular males to become the fathers of their young, are all areas of continuing scientific inquiry.

Breeding

Males take no part in nesting. The female builds a shallow cup nest that she weaves into a fork of tree branches, 1 to 15 m (3 to 50 ft) from the ground. She incubates the 1 or 2 eggs for 17 to 20 days, and rears the nestlings herself, bringing them fruit and insects, for 13 to 20 days. Manakins, like most birds that use open, cup-like, nests, often suffer very high rates of nest destruction. In one small study, only about 7% of eggs survived the incubation stage and hatched. Most nests were lost to predators, for which the suspect list is quite lengthy: ground-dwelling as well as arboreal snakes, birds such as motmots, puffbirds, toucans and jays, large arboreal lizards, and mammals such as opossums, capuchin monkeys, kinkajous and coatis.

Notes

Colorful manakin feathers were often used by the indigenous peoples of Central and South America for ornamental purposes, especially for clothing and masks used during dances and solemn festivals.

Status

None of the Peruvian manakins is currently considered to be threatened.

Profiles

Blue-crowned Manakin, *Pipra coronata*, Plate 60a
Band-tailed Manakin, *Pipra fasciicauda*, Plate 60b
White-crowned Manakin, *Pipra pipra*, Plate 60c
Round-tailed Manakin, *Pipra chloromeros*, Plate 60d
Thrush-like Manakin, *Schiffornis turdinus*, Plate 60e

31. Cotingas

Owing to their variety of shapes, sizes, ecologies, and breeding systems, as well as to their flashy coloring, *cotingas* are usually considered to be among the Neotropic's glamour birds. Family Cotingidae is closely allied with the manakins and flycatchers and contains about 70 species, with 40 in Perú. The cotingas include species from tiny, warbler-sized birds to large, crow-sized birds. Primarily fruit- and insect-eaters, some eat only fruit (which among birds is uncommon). In some species the sexes look alike, but in many the males are stunningly attired in bright spectral colors while the females are plain. There are territorial species that breed *monogamously* and *lecking* species that breed *promiscuously* (see below); all in all a very eclectic family.

Among the Peruvian cotingas are *pihas*, *"typical" cotingas*, *Cock-of-the-rocks*, *umbrellabirds* and *fruitcrows*, the last two being quite large. Perhaps the only generalizations that apply to these birds is that all have short legs and relatively short, rather wide bills, the better to swallow fruits. Males of some of the group are quite ornate, with patches of gaudy plumage in unusual colors. For instance, some of the typical cotingas are lustrous blue and deep purple, and some are all white; others are wholly black, or green and yellow, or largely red or orange or gray. The ANDEAN COCK-OF-THE-ROCK (Plate 62) is one of the most dramatic species of cotingas in Perú, and it is also a lecking species. Three to 80 large, bright red, crested males gather to attract rather dull-colored females at historical lec sites often used for decades. Males of the almost equally handsome BLACK-NECKED RED-COTINGA (Plate 61) also lec, in the extreme northeastern lowlands. They are noisy and sometimes easy to see at historical courting sites. PURPLE-THROATED FRUITCROWS (Plate 62) live in highly social flocks of 5 to 10 individuals. They seldom leave the canopy of primary lowland forest in the Amazon. Listen for their distinctive calls, which are loud and slurred whistles interspersed by rude hacking noises, like someone getting ready to spit. If you try mimicking their whistles, you can often attract them in close to you as they investigate this intruder into their territory. One Peruvian cotinga that you will hear repeatedly in the forest of the Amazonian lowlands, but probably never see, is the SCREAMING PIHA (Plate 61). Its ear-splitting shrill whistles are given by numerous males from the tops of widely separated, tall trees in primary forest. Their plain gray plumage makes them almost impossible to see, but females are more interested in how individual males sing in their lecs than in how colorful they are.

Natural History
Ecology and Behavior

Cotingas primarily inhabit the high canopy of the forest. They are fruit specialists, a feature of their natural history that has engendered much study. They eat small and medium-sized fruits that they take off trees, often while hovering. Some cotingas, such as fruitcrows and pihas, supplement the heavily frugivorous diet with insects taken from the treetop foliage, but others, particularly the species called *fruiteaters*, feed exclusively on fruit. This dependence creates both problems and benefits (as detailed in the Close-up, p. 177); one consequence is that when young are fed only fruit, the nestling period can be unusually long because rapidly growing nestlings require protein that an all-fruit diet provides only at a low rate. Because of the cotingas' feeding specialization on fruit, they are vital as dispersers of tree seeds. Owing to their high-canopy habits, the precise fruits cotingas go after often are difficult to determine. They feed heavily at palms, laurels, and incense trees, and also at, among others, members of the blackberry/raspberry family.

Breeding

Some cotingas pair up, defend territories from *conspecifics* (individuals of the same species), and breed conventionally in apparent monogamy. But others, such as umbrellabirds, cock-of-the-rocks and pihas, are lecking species, in which several males individually stake out display trees in the same area and repeatedly perform vocal and visual displays to attract females. Females enter display areas, called *lecs*, assess the jumping and calling males, and choose the ones they wish to mate with. With this type of breeding, females leave after mating and then nest and rear young alone.

Several species of cotingas are *altitudinal migrants*, breeding in higher-elevation forests but spending the "off" season in lowland forests. Nests, usually placed in trees or bushes, are generally small, open, and inconspicuous, some nest cups being made of loosely arranged twigs, some of mud, and some of pieces of plants. Many species lay only a single egg, some 1 or 2 eggs. Incubation is 17 to 28 days and the nestling period is 21 to 44 days, both stages quite long for passerine birds.

Notes

Because they are often dubbed onto the soundtrack of movies and TV programs with "jungle" settings, calls of the SCREAMING PIHA likely will be a strangely familiar part of your first hike into Amazonian lowland forest. The sound is now so widely used by the entertainment industry that it could be considered trite – until you stand in the midst of a small group of these males each calling from the top of a different tree. Even from a kilometer (half-mile) away, the sound penetrates the vegetation; if you are directly beneath a calling male, you may well have to hold your hands over your ears to stop the ringing.

Status

Of the Peruvian cotingas, only two are considered threatened. The recently discovered CHESTNUT-BELLIED COTINGA (first described by researchers in 1994) is known only from a few high altitude forest sites in southern Ecuador and adjacent northern Perú. The WHITE-CHEEKED COTINGA inhabits a few high elevation patches of *Podocarpus* forest above Lima. The tiny geographic ranges of these two cotingas make them vulnerable.

Profiles

Black-necked Red-Cotinga, *Phoenicircus nigricollis*, Plate 61a
Plum-throated Cotinga, *Cotinga maynana*, Plate 61b
Red-crested Cotinga, *Ampelion rubrocristatus*, Plate 61c
Green-and-black Fruiteater, *Pipreola riefferii*, Plate 61d
Screaming Piha, *Lipaugus vociferans*, Plate 61e
Amazonian Umbrellabird, *Cephalopterus ornatus*, Plate 62a

Purple-throated Fruitcrow, *Querula purpurata*, Plate 62b
Bare-necked Fruitcrow, *Gymnoderus foetidus*, Plate 62c
Masked Tityra, *Tityra semifasciata*, Plate 62d
Andean Cock-of-the-rock, *Rupicola peruviana*, Plate 62e

32. American Flycatchers

The *American flycatchers* comprise a huge group of passerine birds that is broadly distributed over most habitats from Alaska and northern Canada to the southern tip of South America. The flycatcher family, Tyrannidae, is considered among the most diverse of avian groups. Some experts even combine American flycatchers, manakins (Pipridae) and cotingas (Cotingidae) into one megafamily, but we will follow the narrower definition of what constitutes the flycatcher family. With more than 380 species, the flycatchers usually contribute a hefty percentage of the avian biodiversity in every locale. For instance, it has been calculated that flycatchers make up fully one tenth of the land bird species in South America, and perhaps one-quarter of Argentinean species. In Perú, the group is represented by a healthy contingent of about 235 species.

Flycatchers range in length from 6.5 to 30 cm (2.5 to 12 in). At the smallest extreme are some of the world's tiniest birds, weighing, it is difficult to believe, only some 7 g (1/4 ounce). Their bills are usually broad and flat, the better to snatch flying bugs from the air. Tail length is variable, and some species even have long, forked tails, which probably aid the birds in their rapid, acrobatic, insect-catching maneuvers. Most flycatchers are dully turned out in shades of gray, brown and olive-green, and the sexes are generally similar in appearance. Many species have some yellow in their plumage, and a relatively few are quite flashily attired in, for example, bright expanses of red or vermilion. A great many of the smaller, drabber flycatchers, clad in olives and browns, are extremely difficult to tell apart in the field, even for experienced birdwatchers. One set of frequently seen flycatchers that are easy to see and identify all share bright yellow breasts and some variation on a theme of white eyelines and dark heads. The most likely species of this group of flycatchers you will see in Perú include the GREAT KISKADEE (Plate 64), the LESSER KISKADEE (Plate 64), the SOCIAL FLYCATCHER (Plate 64) and the TROPICAL KINGBIRD (Plate 64). These are all widespread species found in open areas and can be distinguished by presence or absence of rufous coloring in the wings and tail, size of the bill, and habitat. High up in the puna a group of flycatchers called *ground-tyrants* practices very un-flycatcher-like behavior. They run on long legs in open grassland and rocky areas, looking more like thrushes than self-respecting flycatchers. One of the most common species of this group in highland Perú is the PLAIN-CAPPED GROUND-TYRANT (Plate 63).

Natural History
Ecology and Behavior
Flycatchers are common over a large array of different habitat types, from snow-line in the puna to lowland moist forests, treeless plains and grasslands, marshes and mangrove swamps. As their name implies, flycatchers are primarily insectivores, obtaining most of their food by employing the classic flycatching technique. They perch motionless on tree or shrub branches or on fences or telephone wires, then dart out in short, swift flights to snatch from the air insects foolhardy enough to enter their field of vision; they then return time and again to the same perch to repeat the process. Many flycatchers also snatch insects from foliage, and

many also supplement their diets with berries and seeds. Some of the larger fly-catchers will also take small frogs and lizards, and some, such as the GREAT KISKADEE, consider small fish and tadpoles delicacies to be plucked from shallow water at the edges of lakes and rivers. A few species, like the PIRATIC FLYCATCHER (Plate 64), have ceded flycatching to their relatives and are now, as adults, almost completely *frugivorous*.

Many flycatchers show marked alterations in their lifestyles as seasons, loca-tions and feeding opportunities change. Such ongoing capacity for versatile behavior in response to changing environments is considered a chief underly-ing cause of the group's great ecological success. An excellent example is the EASTERN KINGBIRD'S drastic changes in behavior between summer and winter. Breeding during summer in North America, these black and white flycatchers are extremely aggressive in defending their territories from birds and other animals, and they feed exclusively at that time on insects. But a change comes over the birds during the winter, as they idle away the months in South America's Amazon Basin. There, Eastern Kingbirds congregate in large, nonterritorial flocks with apparently nomadic existences, and they eat mostly fruit.

Breeding

Almost all of the relatively few tropical flycatchers that have been studied inhabit exclusive territories that mated, monogamous pairs defend for all or part of the year. Some forest-dwelling species, however, breed *promiscuously*: groups of males call and display repeatedly at traditional courting sites called *lecs*, attracting females that approach for mating but then depart to nest and raise young by themselves. Many flycatchers are known for amazing courtship displays, males showing-off to females by engaging in aerial acrobatics, including flips and som-ersaults. In monogamous species, males may help females build nests. Some build cup nests, roofed nests, or globular hanging nests placed in trees or shrubs, oth-ers construct mud nests that they attach to vertical surfaces such as rock walls, and some nest in holes in trees or rocks. Tropical flycatchers generally lay 2 eggs that are incubated only by the female for 12 to 23 days; nestlings fledge when 14 to 28 days old.

The *tody flycatchers* construct large, hanging, woven, or "felted," nests that take up to a month or more to build. These nests tend to hang from slender vines or weak tree branches, which provides a degree of safety from climbing nest predators such as snakes and small mammals. Often, however, such efforts are ineffective – nest predation rates are quite high. In response, some of the tody fly-catchers purposefully build their nests near to colonies of stinging bees, appar-ently seeking additional protection from predators. The PIRATIC FLYCATCHER lives up to its name. This scoundrel species drives hard-working caciques, oropen-dolas and even other flycatchers from their nests and usurps them for its own.

Notes

Flycatchers in Perú are notorious because of the difficulty of distinguishing the many similar species in the field. Some can only be readily distinguished by their voices, so if you have feelings of frustration trying to figure this group out, you are not alone.

Status

Five species of flycatchers in Perú are listed as threatened or endangered. Three of them, PACIFIC ROYAL FLYCATCHER, GRAY-BREASTED FLYCATCHER, and

OCHRACEOUS ATTILA, have small and declining populations in the Tumbesian tropical dry forest. The other two are in the highlands. The ASH-BREASTED TIT-TYRANT is restricted to small patches of quickly disappearing *Polylepis* forest. The WHITE-TAILED SHRIKE-TYRANT has become extremely rare and local throughout its range in the high Andes puna from Ecuador to Argentina; no one understands why its populations seem to be declining so precipitously.

Profiles

Black-billed Shrike-Tyrant, *Agriornis montana*, Plate 63a
Vermilion Flycatcher, *Pyrocephalus rubinus*, Plate 63b
Common Tody-Flycatcher, *Todirostrum cinereum*, Plate 63c
Torrent Tyrannulet, *Serpophaga cinerea*, Plate 63d
Plain-capped Ground-Tyrant, *Muscisaxicola alpina*, Plate 63e
Black Phoebe, *Sayornis nigricans*, Plate 63f

Tropical Kingbird, *Tyrannus melancholicus*, Plate 64a
Great Kiskadee, *Pitangus sulphuratus*, Plate 64b
Lesser Kiskadee, *Pitangus lictor*, Plate 64c
Social Flycatcher, *Myiozetetes similis*, Plate 64d
Piratic Flycatcher, *Legatus leucophaius*, Plate 64e

Long-tailed Tyrant, *Colonia colonus*, Plate 65a
White-browed Chat-Tyrant, *Ochthoeca leucophrys*, Plate 65b
Short-tailed Field-Tyrant, *Muscigralla brevicauda*, Plate 65c
Many-colored Rush-Tyrant, *Tachuris rubrigastra*, Plate 65d
Andean Negrito, *Lessonia oreas*, Plate 65e

33. Jays

Jays are members of the Corvidae, a passerine family of 115 species that occurs just about everywhere in the world – or, as ecologists would say, corvid distribution is *cosmopolitan*. The group also includes the *crows, ravens* and *magpies*. Although on many continents birds of open habitats, jays of the Neotropics are primarily woodland or forest birds. Jays, aside from being strikingly handsome birds, are known for their versatility, adaptability, and for their seeming intelligence. In several ways, the group is considered by ornithologists to be one of the most highly developed of birds. They are also usually quite noisy.

Members of the family range in length from 18 to 77 cm (7 to 30 in), many near the higher end – large for passerine birds. *Corvids* have robust, fairly long bills and strong legs and feet. Many of them (crows, ravens, rooks, jackdaws) are all or mostly black, but the jays are different, being attired in bright blues, purples, greens, yellows and white. In corvids, the sexes generally look alike. The COMMON RAVEN is the largest passerine bird in the world, but although its range encompasses several continents, it does not extend to Perú. The only representatives of this family in Perú are 6 species of jays, most of which you will see in small family groups (theirs, not yours).

Natural History
Ecology and Behavior

Jays eat a large variety of foods (and try to eat many others) and so are considered *omnivores*. They feed on the ground, but also in trees, eating carrion, insects (including some flying ones), fruits and nuts, and also robbing bird eggs and nestlings. They are considered to be responsible for a significant percentage of the nest predation on many songbird species, particularly those with open-cup nests. Bright and versatile, they are quick to take advantage of new food sources and to find food in agricultural and other human-altered environments. Jays use their feet to hold food down while tearing it with their bills. Hiding food for later consumption, *caching*, is practiced widely by the group.

Most corvids are quite social, Peruvian jays being no exception. Most of these species remain all year in small groups of relatives, 5 to 10 individuals strong. They forage together within a restricted area, or *home range*, and at the appropriate time, breed together on a group-defended territory. Jays are usually raucous and noisy, giving varieties of harsh, grating, loud calls as the foraging flock straggles from tree to tree, but at times they can be amazingly quiet and unobtrusive, especially during the breeding season.

Breeding

Several species of jays raise young cooperatively. Generally the oldest pair in the group breeds and the other members serve only as *helpers*, assisting in nest construction and feeding the young. Courtship feeding is common, the male feeding the female before and during incubation, which she performs alone. Bulky, open nests, constructed primarily of twigs, are placed in trees or rock crevices. Two to 7 eggs are incubated for 16 to 21 days, the young then being fed in the nest by parents and helpers for 20 to 24 days.

Notes

Although members of the crow family are considered by many to be among the most intelligent of birds, and by ornithologists as among the most highly evolved, corvid folklore is rife with tales of crows, ravens and magpies as symbols of ill-omen. This undoubtedly traces to the group's frequently all-black plumage and habit of eating carrion, both sinister traits. COMMON RAVENS, in particular, have long been associated in many Northern cultures with evil or death, although these large, powerful birds also figure more benignly in Nordic and Middle Eastern mythology. Several groups of indigenous peoples of Northwestern North America consider the Raven sacred and sometimes, indeed, as a god.

Status

Some of the 6 species of jay that occur in Perú are fairly rare, but none is considered threatened. Many corvids adjust well to people's activities, often expanding their ranges when they can feed on agricultural crops.

Profiles

White-tailed Jay, *Cyanocorax mystacalis*, Plate 66a
Violaceous Jay, *Cyanocorax violaceus*, Plate 66b
Green Jay, *Cyanocorax yncas*, Plate 66c
White-collared Jay, *Cyanolyca viridicyana*, Plate 66d

34. Wrens and Dipper

Wrens are small, brownish species with an active, snappish manner and, characteristically, erect, upraised tails. Most skulk in thick undergrowth, but a few are *arboreal*, staying in trees in more open areas. Approximately 75 wren species comprise the family Troglodytidae, a group that except for one Eurasian species is confined to the Western Hemisphere; 23 species occur in Perú. Among other traits, wrens are renowned for their singing ability, vocal duets, and nesting behavior. They range in length from 10 to 22 cm (4 to 9 in) and usually appear mainly in shades of brown or reddish brown, with smaller bits of tan, gray, black and white. Some of these birds are tiny, weighing in at less than 15 g (half an ounce). Wings and tails are frequently embellished with finely barred patterns. Wrens have rather broad, short wings and owing to this, are considered poor flyers. The sexes look alike. The marsh-inhabiting DONACOBIUS (Plate 68) of the Amazonian lowlands, a species that occurs in small colonies, is so large and unusually colored that for years ornithologists considered it a type of mockingbird. Only with recent DNA studies has it found a more comfortable home in the wren family.

Dippers are similar to wrens in coloring and chunky shape, but they are specialized for living along fast-flowing streams in mountainous areas, the only truly aquatic family of passerines. The family, Cinclidae, has 5 species worldwide, but only the WHITE-CAPPED DIPPER (Plate 66) occurs in Perú. Unmistakable in their habitat, dippers are usually seen bouncing up and down on their legs (thus the name dipper) on large boulders in white-water streams on either slope of the Andes. They fly low over the water in a buzzy flight, but most distinctive is their ability to walk into the water of these rapidly moving streams and forage among underwater rocks and on stream beds. The sexes are indistinguishable by color or size.

Natural History
Ecology and Behavior

Most wrens are *cryptically colored* and fairly secretive in their habits as they sneak, hop and poke around the low levels of the forest, and through thickets, grasslands, and marshes, searching for insects. They are completely *insectivorous* or nearly so. Often spending the year living in pairs, they defend territories in which during the breeding season they will nest. The HOUSE WREN (Plate 67) is the same species as in North America and familiar to many. It is ubiquitous throughout Perú up to 4000 m (13,000 ft) elevation, except for in undisturbed forested areas. Some of the larger wrens, such as the THRUSH-LIKE WREN (Plate 67) of the Amazon lowlands and the FASCIATED WREN of the tropical dry forest of coastal southern Perú, spend their days higher in the trees in small family flocks, and, owing to their size, are a bit bolder in their movements. Their loud songs also make them obvious. After breeding, wrens will use their nests as roosting places – or "dormitories," as one researcher puts it. Some species actually build specific nests for roosting that are of a different structure than nests for raising young. The vocalizations of wrens have been studied extensively. Especially talented, a pair of DONACOBIUS will call back and forth as they lose sight of each other while foraging in dense marsh grasses of the Amazonian lowlands, keeping in contact. The mated pairs sing some of the bird world's most complex duets, male and female rapidly alternating in giving parts of one song (as we think of it), so rapidly and expertly that it actually sounds as if one individual utters the entire sequence. Such duets probably function as "keep-out" signals, warning away from the pair's territory other members of the species, and in maintaining the pair-bond between mated birds. The MUSICIAN WREN (Plate 67) has to be heard to be believed. If you hear what sounds like a child learning to whistle in the undergrowth of the Amazonian forest, it is probably this species. It is most easily seen as it participates in undergrowth *mixed-species foraging flocks* that move low through denser parts of the forest.

Dippers forage primarily for larvae of aquatic insects, but they also take small clams, crayfish and fish. They plunge from a rock or stream bank into the rushing water and use their wings to swim underwater. Their song is a loud trill, used to mark territorial boundaries along the stream.

Breeding

The wrens of Perú are mainly monogamous, but some like the DONACOBIUS breed *cooperatively*, with members of the small family group helping out at the single nest of the parents. Nests, generally of woven grass, are placed in vegetation or in tree cavities. They are small but elaborate nests, roofed, with inconspicuous side entrances. Intriguingly, in some species the male builds many more nests on his territory than his mate (or mates, in *polygynous* species) can use, apparently as a courtship signal, perhaps as an inducement for a female to stay and mate. Only the female incubates the 2 to 5 eggs, for 13 to 19 days. Sometimes she is fed by the male during this period. Nestlings are fed by both parents for 14 to 19 days, until fledging.

The single species of dipper in Perú constructs a large, domed nest usually on a vertical cliff but sometimes on the underside of a bridge. Apparently monogamous, both sexes participate in nest construction. The nest is primarily of moss and lined with dry leaves and vegetation. The 4 or 5 eggs hatch in 16 days and the young are fed by both parents. Each pair is highly territorial and defends a stretch of the stream year-round.

Notes

The HOUSE WREN has one of the most extensive ranges of any bird species in the Western Hemisphere. It nests from North America to throughout South America. One of the reasons for its extensive range is that it often nests in association with people and their structures. These birds root about near and in human settlements, looking for insects. Nests are often placed in crannies and crevices within buildings or other structures. (Many wrens nest in naturally occurring cavities, hence the family name, Troglodytidae, or "cave dweller.")

Underwater swimming of the dipper is made possible by a series of adaptations that include a third eye-lid (*nictitating membrane*), which protects the eye surface underwater, extra dense plumage to protect against buffeting against rocks by the strong currents, and an extra large oil gland at the base of the tail to keep the feathers moisture-proof.

Status

Most of the wren species that occur in Perú are fairly or very abundant. Although none is threatened, the INCA WREN (Plate 67), with its tiny range near the Machu Picchu ruins, is vulnerable. The dipper is also fairly common, although with its restricted habitat, water pollution could drastically affect its food supply locally and so threaten it in certain areas – especially below mining operations.

Profiles

White-capped Dipper, *Cinclus leucocephalus*, Plate 66e
Inca Wren, *Thryothorus eisenmanni*, Plate 67a
Thrush-like Wren, *Campylorhynchus turdinus*, Plate 67b
Southern Nightingale-Wren, *Microcerculus marginatus*, Plate 67c
Gray-breasted Wood-wren, *Henicorhina leucophrys*, Plate 67d
House Wren, *Troglodytes aedon*, Plate 67e
Musician Wren, *Cyphorhinus aradus*, Plate 67f
Donacobius, *Donacobius atricapillus*, Plate 68b

35. Thrushes and Mockingbirds

The more than 300 species of *thrushes* inhabit most terrestrial regions of the world and include some of the most familiar park and garden birds. The family, Turdidae, has few defining, common features that set its members apart from other groups, as perhaps could be expected; so large an assemblage of species is sure to include a significant amount of variation in appearance, ecology, and behavior. *Thrushes, robins, nightingale thrushes* and *solitaires* of the Western Hemisphere are slender-billed birds that range from 12.5 to 31 cm (5 to 12 in) in length. In Perú there are 23 species of this family, some of which are migrants from nesting grounds in North America. Generally they are not brightly colored; instead, they come in drab browns, grays, brown-reds, olive, and black and white. The sexes are very similar in appearance. During their first months of life, young thrushes are clad in distinctively spotted plumages.

Many species of thrushes have adapted to living near humans and benefitting from their environmental modifications. On five continents, a thrush is among the most common and recognizable of garden birds, including North America's AMERICAN ROBIN, Europe's REDWING and BLACKBIRD, and Perú's GREAT THRUSH (Plate 68), which is common throughout the highlands, even in the middle of large towns. Thrushes in general are famous for their rich and musical sounds, and one of the champion songsters of the world is the LAWRENCE'S THRUSH (Plate 68). It is easily overlooked in the primary forests of the Amazon, but it is one of the most remarkable mimics in South America. It sings high in the forest all day long, and the song of a single individual may include song phrases of up to 35 other species; with some patience, this songster supreme can usually be found on its favorite perch day after day.

Although superficially similar to the thrushes, the family of *mockingbirds*, Mimidae, is now thought to be most closely related to the starlings. The *mimids*, which also include *thrashers* and *catbirds*, are found only in the New World. These medium-sized birds (20 to 30 cm, 8 to 12 in) have long tails and rather short and rounded wings. Most species have strong, moderately long bills, often downcurved. The species tend toward gray, brown or rufous, often with flashes of white in the tail and wings. There is no distinct difference in the plumages of the sexes. Only a few species actually mimic calls and songs of other species. Of the 30+ species in the family, only the LONG-TAILED MOCKINGBIRD (Plate 68) is found in Perú. Here it is common and obvious in dry forest and scrub areas of the coastal lowlands and vertiente andino south to Arequipa.

Natural History
Ecology and Behavior

Many thrushes eat fruits, some are primarily *insectivorous*, and most are at least moderately *omnivorous*. Although generally arboreal birds, many thrushes frequently forage on the ground for insects, other arthropods and, a particular favorite, delicious earthworms. Some of the thrushes in Perú associated with gardens and lawns forage like the familiar thrushes from North America or Europe – they hop and walk along the ground, stopping at intervals, cocking their heads to peer downwards. These birds are residents of many kinds of habitats – deep forest, forest edge, clearings, and other open areas such as shrub areas and grasslands, gardens, parks, suburban lawns, and agricultural areas. Many thrushes are quite social, spending their time during the nonbreeding season in flocks of the same species, feeding and roosting together. Some of the tropical thrushes, like the BLACK-BILLED THRUSH (Plate 68), evidently make seasonal migrations within the Amazon, following changing food supplies.

The mockingbirds feed on fruits, seeds and insects. Many feed on the ground using their curved bills to dig and probe for prey in soft soils and leaf litter. With their long tails and the open habitats they prefer, they are often one of the most conspicuous bird species present. They tend to be highly territorial and often solitary throughout the year.

Breeding

Thrushes breed monogamously, male and female together defending exclusive territories during the breeding season; pairs may associate year round. Nests, usually built by the female and placed in tree branches, shrubs, or crevices, are open and cup-shaped, made of grass, moss, and like materials, and often lined with mud. Two to 6 eggs (usually 2 or 3) are incubated by the female only for 12 to 14 days. Young are fed by both parents for 12 to 16 days prior to their fledging. The mockingbirds are monogamous, and both sexes participate in building the bulky, open cup-shaped nest of twigs and lining it with hair or grass. It is placed low in a bush or occasionally on the ground. The 2 to 4 eggs are generally incubated by the female alone for about two weeks. The chicks are then fed by both parents for another 13 to 19 days until they fledge.

Notes

English colonists in the New World gave the AMERICAN ROBIN, a thrush, its name because it resembled England's common ROBIN, an Old World flycatcher – both birds have reddish breasts. The New World bird, however, is more closely related to Europe's BLACKBIRD, also a common garden bird and a true thrush; and you wonder why common names of birds can be so confusing.

Status

Although several thrushes in many different parts of the world are vulnerable to threat or are now considered threatened, none of the species that breed in Perú are in imminent danger. Some of the species known as solitaires have suffered recent population declines in accessible areas, probably owing to poaching for the pet trade: these birds are famous in Perú for their grand, flute-like songs. The LONG-TAILED MOCKINGBIRD in Perú appears to have adapted well to cultivation and forest clearing and is thriving.

Profiles

Long-tailed Mockingbird, *Mimus longicaudatus*, Plate 68a
Great Thrush, *Turdus fuscater*, Plate 68c
Lawrence's Thrush, *Turdus lawrencii*, Plate 68d
Black-billed Thrush, *Turdus ignobilis*, Plate 68e

36. Wood Warblers

More than 110 species of the spritely and often beautiful family of New World *wood warblers* (Parulidae) are found from Alaska to Argentina. In Perú, 22 species occur: 8 species that are migrants from nesting grounds in North America, and 14 species that are non-migratory. Most of the migratory species are easy to see as they forage high in trees of secondary and primary forests, but they do little singing on their wintering grounds and for most of their stay in Perú are clad in subdued colors that make them difficult to identify. The non-migratory species, in contrast, sing loudly and wear the same plumage all year round. Unfortunately, they tend to skulk in the dense undergrowth, and many of them at their brightest plumage are as dull as the winter plumages of the migratory species. The plumages of both sexes of non-migratory species tend to be similar, but in migratory species, only the males acquire a brilliant summer plumage. Warblers all have thin, narrow bills and both migratory and non-migratory species regularly participate in mixed-species foraging flocks.

The BLACKBURNIAN WARBLER (Plate 69) is a common migrant that spends its winter (September to April) in the higher-elevation forests of both slopes. The CANADA WARBLER (Plate 69) is another common winter visitor to Perú (October to April) and also spends most of its time in higher-elevation forests, but during migration it can be common in the undergrowth of primary forest in the Amazonian lowlands. Found only along forested streams of the lower slopes of the Andes and in the lowlands of the coast and the Amazon, the BUFF-RUMPED WARBLER (Plate 69), resident year-round, is largely terrestrial. Its loud ringing song, buff rump seen in flight, and association with forested streams on the east slope of the Andes make it easy to find and identify.

Natural History
Ecology and Behavior
Wood warblers are largely insect eaters. Some species, such as the *redstarts*, sally out like flycatchers to snatch flying insects in the air. Some species probe flowers and buds with their thin bills for insects hiding there. Most species, however, glean insects from undersides of leaves and twigs. The quality of songs among these warblers ranges from loud and clear notes to insect-like trills and buzzes.

The migratory distances for species nesting in North America involve thousands of kilometers. The BLACKPOLL WARBLER, for instance, winters as far south as Bolivia and nests as far north as northern Canada. For many years, North American scientists interested in warblers and many other songbirds concentrated their research on the birds' ecology and behavior during breeding, essentially ignoring the fact that the birds spent more than half of each year wintering in the tropics, many of them in South America. Now, with the realization that the birds' biology during the nonbreeding season is also important for understanding their lives, their ecology and behavior during the winter have become areas of intense interest. Being addressed in research studies are such questions as: Are species that are territorial during breeding also territorial on their wintering grounds, and if so, in what way? Do individual birds return to the same spot in the tropics each year in winter as they do for nesting during the North American spring? Do migratory birds compete for food on their wintering grounds with those species that remain all year in the tropics? Why do the migratory species of warblers have dull plumages on the wintering grounds, and why do the non-migratory species have the same plumage all year around?

Breeding
Most warbler species place their nests in trees or shrubs, but some nest on the ground or in tree cavities. The nest shape is usually an open cup-like structure, but in the tropics many species build a domed nest with an entrance at the side. Warblers are primarily monogamous, but the females do most if not all the nest construction. The 2 to 4 eggs are incubated by the female for about 12 days. After

hatching, the chicks are fed by both parents for 8 to 12 days in the nest, and continue to be fed by the parents for a few weeks after leaving the nest.

Status

No warblers that occur in Perú are known to be threatened. Two other warblers, however, are now endangered – KIRTLAND'S WARBLER, which breeds in the USA (Michigan) and winters in the Bahamas, and SEMPER'S WARBLER, which occurs only on the Caribbean island of St. Lucia. Kirtland's Warbler, which nests only in stands of young Jack-pine trees, has been victimized by its own specialization on one type of breeding habitat combined with a shrinking availability of that habitat, by destruction of its wintering habitat, and by BROWN-HEADED COWBIRDS, which lay their eggs in the nests of warblers and other species, reducing their reproductive success (see p. 174). It is suspected that mongooses, which were introduced to St. Lucia by people and which are predators on bird nests, play a major role in endangering Semper's Warbler, which nests on or near the ground. Ten to 12 additional wood warbler species are probably now at risk, but there is at present insufficient information about their populations to judge their statuses with any certainty. The BACHMAN'S WARBLER, which nested throughout the southeastern USA and wintered in Cuba, apparently became extinct in the 1960s.

Profiles

Slate-throated Redstart, *Myioborus miniatus*, Plate 69a
Spectacled Redstart, *Myioborus melanocephalus*, Plate 69b
Blackburnian Warbler, *Dendroica fusca*, Plate 69c
Canada Warbler, *Wilsonia canadensis*, Plate 69d
Three-striped Warbler, *Basileuterus tristriatus*, Plate 69e
Buff-rumped Warbler, *Basileuterus fulvicauda*, Plate 69f
Tropical Parula, *Parula pitiayumi*, Plate 70f

37. Flower-piercers, Conebills, and Honeycreepers

This group of species does not fit obviously into any single family, and no two ornithologists seem to agree on who their closest relatives are. Some experts place the *flower-piercers, conebills* and *honeycreepers* in the tanager family, Thraupidae. Others have them related to the finches and placed as a subfamily within the Emberizidae (sparrows and seedeaters). Yet others place some of them with the wood warblers, Parulidae. All these species are associated with flowers, and many of them are very colorful. In all, 29 species of this group occur in Perú. The flower-piercers occur mainly at higher altitudes on both slopes of the Andes, and they have a peculiar bill that is upturned and hooked at the end. The conebills are also primarily in the higher altitudes, but honeycreepers and *dacnis* are most common in the lowlands. The GIANT CONEBILL (Plate 70) is limited to *Polylepis* forests in the highlands of the Andes. It crawls up and down the reddish trunks of these trees like a nuthatch searching for insects. You will most likely see the dacnis and honeycreepers in high canopy flocks of the lowland forests. An easy way to see them well is from one of the canopy towers constructed by lodges in the Amazonian lowlands. The BANANAQUIT (Plate 70), which is either lumped into the warbler group or is the only member of its own family, Coerebidae (its classification is controversial), is a tiny yellow and olive/grayish bird with a broad Neotropical distribution: from southern Mexico and the Caribbean to northern Argentina. It is a common species in lowland urban areas and disturbed habitats

– so people have been a boon to its spread. In Amazonia, its presence indicates that the primary forest has been largely disturbed in the area.

Natural History
Ecology and Behavior
Flower-piercers use their peculiar bills to bore holes into the base of a flower and rob nectar. Unlike more gracious species, such as hummingbirds, which enter a flower properly to reap a reward of nectar, and often obtain a deposit of pollen on the head, flower-piercers bypass the pollination system and cheat the flower by not paying for the nectar reward by spreading pollen. Most large flowers at mid to high altitudes in Perú will have small holes in their bottoms, indicating how ubiquitous these cheaters are. Flower-piercers also glean insects from vegetation and eat fruits. Conebills, bananaquits, dacnis and honeycreepers also probe flowers, but only occasionally for nectar. More frequently they are searching for insects. They also commonly eat fruits, and are most easily seen in *mixed-species foraging flocks* moving through the upper parts of the forest.

Breeding
Most species in this group build open, cup-shaped nests of moss and grass. They are presumably monogamous, but little is known about their breeding biology. Unusual among birds, BANANAQUITS build not only breeding nests, but also lighter, domed dormitory nests, where they sleep individually. Both Bananaquit sexes build the round, domed, breeding nest. Only the female incubates the 2 or 3 eggs, for 12 to 13 days. Both parents feed the chicks in the nest for 17 to 19 days by regurgitating food to them.

Status
Some of the species in this group have extremely small geographical ranges, which makes them vulnerable; extensive habitat destruction in these areas could easily threaten these birds. At the present time, however, only the TAMARUGO CONEBILL, an endemic of extreme southern Perú and northern Chile, is considered threatened.

Profiles
Cinereous Conebill, *Conirostrum cinereum*, Plate 70a
Giant Conebill, *Oreomanes fraseri*, Plate 70b
Black-throated Flower-piercer, *Diglossa brunneiventris*, Plate 70c
Masked Flower-piercer, *Diglossopis cyanea*, Plate 70d
Bananaquit, *Coereba flaveola*, Plate 70e

Yellow-bellied Dacnis, *Dacnis flaviventer*, Plate 71b
Purple Honeycreeper, *Cyanerpes caeruleus*, Plate 71c
Blue Dacnis, *Dacnis cayana*, Plate 71e
Green Honeycreeper, *Chlorophanes spiza*, Plate 71f

38. Tanagers
Tanagers comprise a large New World group of beautifully colored, small passerine birds, most of which are limited to tropical areas. They are among the tropics' most common and visible birds, primarily owing to their habit of associating in *mixed-species foraging flocks* that gather in the open, often near human habitation, to feed in fruit trees, and they are a treat to watch. All told, there are some 230 species of tanagers (Family Thraupidae), the group including the *typical tanagers*

and the *euphonias*. Some of the tanagers, such as the SUMMER TANAGER (male all red, female yellow-olive), breed in North America and migrate to winter in Perú and other parts of South America. Tanagers inhabit all forested and shrubby areas of the American tropics, over a wide range of elevations, and are particularly numerous in wet forests and forest edge areas. Not devotees of the dark forest interior, most prefer the lighter, upper levels of the forest canopy and more open areas; some prefer low, brushy habitat. More than 105 species of tanagers call Perú home.

Tanagers vary from 9 to 28 cm (3.5 to 11 in) in length, with most concentrated near the smaller end of the range. They are compact birds with fairly short, thick bills and short to medium-long tails. Tanagers' outstanding physical attribute is their bright coloring – they are strikingly marked with patches of color that traverse the entire spectrum, rendering the group among the most fabulously attired of birds. It has been said of the typical tanagers (genus *Tangara*) that they must "exhaust the color patterns possible on sparrow-sized birds." Yellows, reds, blues and greens predominate, although a relatively few species buck the trend and appear in plain blacks, browns, or grays. The sexes usually look alike. Euphonias are small, stout tanagers, whose appearances revolve around a common theme: males blue-black above, with yellow foreheads, breasts and bellies; and females all dull olive. We profile typical species found commonly in each of the mainland habitats of Perú. They all tend to be relatively easy to distinguish by their color patterns and habitat preference.

Natural History
Ecology and Behavior

Most tanager species associate in mixed-species tanager flocks, usually together with other types of birds. Finding eight or more tanager species in a single group is common. A mixed flock will settle in a tree full of ripe fruit such as berries and enjoy a meal. These flocks move through forests or more open areas, searching for fruit-laden trees and also gleaning for insects. Although most species are arboreal, a few are specialized ground foragers, taking seeds and bugs. Tanagers usually go after small fruits that can be swallowed whole, such as berries, plucking the fruit while perched. After plucking it, a tanager rotates the fruit a bit in its bill, then mashes it and swallows. (Ecologists divide frugivorous birds into *mashers*, such as tanagers, and *gulpers*, such as trogons and toucans, which swallow fruit whole and intact.) One explanation is that mashing permits the bird to enjoy the sweet juice prior to swallowing the rest of the fruit. This fits with the idea that mashers select fruit based partially on taste, whereas gulpers, which swallow intact fruit, do not. Tanagers, as mashing frugivores, sometimes drop the largest seeds from the fruits they consume before swallowing but, nonetheless, many seeds are ingested; consequently, these birds are active seed dispersers (see Close-Up, p. 177). Some ecologists believe tanagers to be among the most common dispersers of tropical trees and shrubs, that is, they are responsible for dropping the seeds that grow into the trees and shrubs that populate the areas they inhabit. Euphonias, for example, are crucial for the mistletoe life cycle because, after eating the berries, they deposit their seed-bearing droppings on tree branches, where the seeds germinate, the mistletoe plants starting out there as parasites.

Some tanagers, such as the *ant-tanagers*, are frequent members of mixed-species flocks of the undergrowth (along with antbirds, woodcreepers and others) that spend their days following army ant swarms, feeding on insects that rush from cover at the approach of the devastating ants. Euphonias specialize on mistletoe berries, but eat other fruits and some insects as well. Some tanagers are *altitudinal migrants*, seasonally moving to higher or lower elevation habitats.

Breeding

Most tanagers appear to breed monogamously, although a number of bigamists have been noted (BLUE-GRAY TANAGER, Plate 74, among them). Breeding is concentrated during the transition from dry to wet season, when fruit and insects are most plentiful. In many species, male and female stay paired throughout the year. Males of many species give food to females in nuptial feeding, and during courtship displays make sure that potential mates see their brightly colored patches. Either the female alone or the pair builds a cup nest in a tree or shrub. Two eggs are incubated by the female only for 12 to 18 days and young are fed by both parents for 12 to 18 days prior to their fledging. A pair of tiny euphonias build a nest with a roof and a side entrance, often within a bromeliad plant.

Notes

The word tanager comes from the Brazilian Tupi Indian word "tangara," which is also used as the genus name for a group of tanagers.

Status

Four Peruvian tanagers are currently considered threatened or endangered, GOLDEN-BACKED MOUNTAIN-TANAGER, MASKED MOUNTAIN-TANAGER, GREEN-CAPPED TANAGER, and ORANGE-THROATED TANAGER. All four have highly restricted or disjunct ranges at higher elevations in the Andes. In addition, several of the euphonias are increasingly scarce and the reason may be that, although they are not hunted for the international pet trade, they are prized as cage birds within South American countries.

Profiles

Golden Tanager, *Tangara arthus*, Plate 71a
Blue-and-black Tanager, *Tangara vassorii*, Plate 71d

Green-and-gold Tanager, *Tangara schrankii*, Plate 72a
Paradise Tanager, *Tangara chilensis*, Plate 72b
Turquoise Tanager, *Tangara mexicana*, Plate 72c
Beryl-spangled Tanager, *Tangara nigroviridis*, Plate 72d
Bay-headed Tanager, *Tangara gyrola*, Plate 72e
Orange-eared Tanager, *Chlorochrysa calliparaea*, Plate 72f

Grass-green Tanager, *Chlorornis riefferii*, Plate 73a
Thick-billed Euphonia, *Euphonia laniirostris*, Plate 73b
White-vented Euphonia, *Euphonia minuta*, Plate 73c
Opal-rumped Tanager, *Tangara velia*, Plate 73d
Common Bush-Tanager, *Chlorospingus ophthalmicus*, Plate 73e
Swallow Tanager, *Tersina viridis*, Plate 73f

Scarlet-bellied Mountain-Tanager, *Anisognathus igniventris*, Plate 74a
Blue-winged Mountain-Tanager, *Anisognathus somptuosus*, Plate 74b
Hooded Mountain-Tanager, *Buthraupis montana*, Plate 74c
Palm Tanager, *Thraupis palmarum*, Plate 74d
Blue-gray Tanager, *Thraupis episcopus*, Plate 74e
Blue-and-yellow Tanager, *Thraupis bonariensis*, Plate 74f

White-shouldered Tanager, *Tachyphonus luctuosus*, Plate 75a

Magpie Tanager, *Cissopis leveriana*, Plate 75b
Masked Crimson Tanager, *Ramphocelus nigrogularis*, Plate 75c
Blue-capped Tanager, *Thraupis cyanocephala*, Plate 75d
Silver-beaked Tanager, *Ramphocelus carbo*, Plate 75e

39. American Orioles and Blackbirds

Diversity is the key to comprehending the *American orioles* and *blackbirds*. The passerine family Icteridae includes about 95 species, 35 of which occur in Perú. They vary extensively in size, coloring, ecology and behavior, but they also partition neatly into very different groups called *blackbirds, caciques (kah-SEE-kays), cowbirds, grackles, meadowlarks, oropendolas* and *orioles* (distinct from the unrelated family of birds called orioles in Eurasia and Africa). These *icterids* range over most of North, Central, and South America. Distinguishing this varied assemblage from most other birds is a method for feeding known as *gaping* – a bird places its closed bill into crevices or under leaves, rocks or other objects, then forces the bill open, exposing the previously hidden space to its prying eyes and hunger. The icterid group inhabits marshes and almost all types of terrestrial habitats, and occupies warm lowland areas, middle elevations, as well as colder, mountainous regions. Many of these birds have adapted well to human settlements and are common denizens of gardens, parks, and urban and agricultural areas.

Icterids range in length from 15 to 56 cm (6 to 22 in) – medium to fairly large-sized birds. Bills are usually sharply pointed and conical. Black is the predominant plumage color in the group, but many combine black with bright reds, yellows, or oranges. In some species, the sexes are alike (particularly in the tropical species), but in others, females look very different from males, often more cryptically outfitted in browns, grays, or streaked plumage. Pronounced size differences between the sexes, females being smaller, are common; male oropendolas, for instance, may weigh twice as much as females. Bills and eyes are sometimes brightly colored. The wide ranges of sizes, shapes, colors, mating systems and breeding behaviors of these birds have attracted considerable interest from avian researchers.

Natural History
Ecology and Behavior
Icterids occur in all sorts of habitat types – woodlands, thickets, grassland, marshes, forest edges, and the higher levels of closed forests – but they are especially prevalent in more open areas. Their regular occupation of marshes has always been viewed as interesting, as they are not otherwise obviously adapted for living in aquatic environments – they do not have webbed feet, for example, nor are they able to float or dive. They are *omnivorous,* eating a wide variety of foods including insects and other small animals, fruit and seeds. A common feature of the group is that although they are primarily seed-eaters (*granivores*) during the nonbreeding periods, they become *insectivorous* during breeding, and feed insects to the young. Gaping for food is frequent and will be seen repeatedly if you observe these birds for any length of time. Oropendolas and caciques join in mixed-species foraging flocks in the canopy; in a single fruit tree you may see two or more species feeding with several species of tanagers, honeycreepers, and others. Outside of the breeding season, icterids, particularly the blackbirds and grackles, typically gather in large, sometimes enormous, flocks that can cause damage to roosting areas and agricultural crops.

Breeding

Icterid species pursue a variety of breeding strategies. Some, such as the orioles, breed in classically monogamous pairs, male and female defending a large territory in which the hanging pouch nest is situated. The TROUPIAL (Plate 77), however, has the peculiar habit of using recently abandoned colonies of cacique nests and laying its eggs in one of them instead of building its own nest. The caciques and the oropendolas nest in colonies. The members of an oropendola colony weave large, bag-like or pouch-like nests that hang from the ends of tree branches, many on the same tree. In Costa Rica, researchers documented a rare form of non-monogamous breeding. Three to 10 male MONTEZUMA'S OROPENDOLAS establish a colony in a tree (often an isolated one) and defend a group of 10 to 30 females that will mate and nest in the colony. The males engage in fighting and aggressive displays, competing among themselves to mate with the females. The most dominant males (the *alpha* birds) in each colony, usually heavier males, obtain up to 90% of all matings, and therefore, are the fathers of most of the colony's young. Caciques, also with pouch-like nests, breed either solitarily in the forest or in colonies. In one study it was noted that each cacique in a colony tries to locate its nest toward the center of the colony, presumably because there is less of a chance of suffering nest predation at the colony's center.

Breeding colonies of caciques and oropendolas are often located in trees that contain or are near large bee or wasp nests. The wasps or bees swarm in large numbers around the birds' nests. Apparently the birds benefit from this close association because the aggressiveness the stinging insects show toward animals that try to raid the birds' hanging nests offers a measure of protection. Icterid nests range from hanging pouches woven from grasses and other plant materials, to open cups lined with mud, to roofed nests built on the ground, hidden in meadow grass. Nests are almost always built by females. The female also incubates the 2 to 3 eggs, for 11 to 14 days, while the male guards the nest. Nestlings are fed for 10 to 30 days either by both parents (monogamous species) or primarily by the female (polygamous species).

Most of the cowbirds, like some cuckoo species, are *brood parasites*, building no nests themselves. Rather, females, after mating with one or more males, lay their eggs, one in each nest and up to 14 or more per season, in the nests of other species – other icterids as well as species in other families. The *host* species then incubate and raise these foster young. Some of the cowbirds specialize on icterid hosts – the GIANT COWBIRD (Plate 76) parasitizes only caciques and oropendolas. Its occurrence is apparently restricted only by the presence of colonies of its hosts, various cacique and oropendola species. Some host species have evolved the abilities to recognize cowbird eggs and eject them from their nests, but others have not. The cowbirds benefit from this selfish behavior by being freed from nest-building and tending chores – what must amount to significant savings of energy and also decreased exposure to predators. The host species suffer reproductive harm because a female cowbird often ejects a host egg when she lays her own (when the nest is left unguarded). Also, more often than not, the cowbird's young are larger than the host's own, and are thus able to out-compete them for food brought to the nest by the adult birds. The host's own young often starve or are significantly weakened.

How can brood parasitic behavior arise? Evolutionary biologists posit that one way would be if, long ago, some female cowbirds that built nests had their nests destroyed mid-way through their laying period. With an egg to lay but no nest in which to place it, females in this situation may have deposited the eggs in the nests of other species, which subsequently raised the cowbird young. Alternatively, the nesting behavior of the Troupial, which uses old cacique nests, suggests another possible evolutionary road to brood parasitism: if a female Troupial didn't bother to wait for the caciques to finish using their nests before she laid her egg, she could quickly develop a brood parasitic lifestyle.

Notes

"Cacique" is an interesting name for a bird: in Spanish it means "chief" or "boss;" in Mexico, it also has the suggestion of "tyrant;" in Chile and some other parts of South America, it means "one who leads an easy life."

Status

One of the icterids of Perú is presently considered threatened, the highly endemic and poorly known SELVA CACIQUE. In addition, the PALE-EYED BLACKBIRD is known from only forested lake sites in the western Amazon, four sites in Amazonian Perú and three in Ecuador. Recent oil exploration, dynamite fishing and habitat destruction on these lakes could easily bring the Peruvian population of this species to the brink of extinction. In North America, the BROWN-HEADED COWBIRD, an open country species like all other cowbirds, has been able to expand its range with deforestation. Because it does not regularly penetrate into extensive forests, many forest-dwelling songbird species, especially migrants from South America, were long-protected from this brood parasite. Now, with only small forest remnants (which are readily entered by cowbirds) left throughout much of eastern North America, these other small songbirds have been overwhelmed not only by loss of habitat but also by increased rates of cowbird parasitism. This combination of factors together with habitat destruction in Perú may help explain the precipitous decline of some North American species that winter in Perú.

Profiles

Peruvian Meadowlark, *Sturnella bellicosa*, Plate 76a
Scrub Blackbird, *Dives warszewiczi*, Plate 76b
Giant Cowbird, *Scaphidura oryzivora*, Plate 76c
Yellow-hooded Blackbird, *Agelaius icterocephalus*, Plate 76d
Oriole Blackbird, *Gymnomystax mexicanus*, Plate 76e

Olive Oropendola, *Psaracolius bifasciatus*, Plate 77a
Crested Oropendola, *Psarocolius decumanus*, Plate 77b
Russet-backed Oropendola, *Psarocolius angustifrons*, Plate 77c
Yellow-rumped Cacique, *Cacicus cela*, Plate 77d
Troupial, *Icterus icterus*, Plate 77e

40. Sparrows and Finches

The New World *sparrows* and *finches* are a large, diverse group, totaling about 320 species, that includes some of South America's most common and visible passerine birds. The group's classification is continually being revised, but here we can consider them to be separate families: the sparrows, *seedeaters*, *grassquits*, and some types of finches in Family Emberizidae, and the *grosbeaks* and *saltators* in Family Cardinalidae. The *siskins* are in the closely related family Fringillidae. These groups are almost *cosmopolitan* in distribution, meaning representatives occur just about everywhere, in all kinds of habitats and climates, from Alaska and northern Canada south to Tierra del Fuego.

Sparrows and finches are generally small birds, 9 to 22 cm (3.5 to 9 in) in length, with relatively short, thick, conical bills, that are specialized to crush and open seeds. In some species, the upper and lower halves of the bill can be moved from side-to-side, the better to manipulate small seeds. Sparrows have relatively large feet that they use in scratching the ground to find seeds. Coloring varies greatly within the group but the plumage of most is dull brown or grayish, with many sporting streaked backs. The sexes generally look alike. We profile 17 species of these birds that are common and easily seen in various habitats throughout Perú.

Natural History
Ecology and Behavior

Sparrows and finches are mostly seed-eaters (*granivores*), although many are considered almost *omnivorous*, and even those that specialize on seeds for much of the year often feed insects to their young. Some species also eat fruit. Sparrows in Perú mainly inhabit open areas such as grassland, parkland, brushy areas, and forest edge. They are birds of thickets, bushes, and grasses, foraging mostly on the ground or at low levels in bushes or trees. Because many species spend large amounts of time in thickets and brushy areas, they can be quite inconspicuous. Whereas in North America sparrows constitute perhaps the most important group of seed-eating birds, they are less dominant in the Neotropics. Other groups of birds, such as pigeons (p. 126), occupy more of the seed-eating niche in South American countries than do sparrows and, as a consequence, one encounters sparrows much more often in North than in South America.

Most species are strongly territorial, a mated pair aggressively excluding other members of the species from sharply defined areas. In the *typical sparrows*, pairs often stay together all year; other species within the group often travel in small family groups. Sometimes, territories are defended year round and almost all available habitat in a region is divided into territories. The result is that those individuals that do not own territories must live furtively on defended territories, always trying to avoid the dominant territory owner, retreating when chased, and waiting for the day when the owner is injured or dies and the territory can be taken over. Only when one of these *floaters* ascends in the hierarchy to territorial ownership status can he begin to breed. In species that have this kind of territorial system, such as the RUFOUS-COLLARED SPARROW (Plate 80), the "floater" individuals who live secretly on other individual's territories, waiting and watching, were termed by their discoverer an *avian underworld*, and the name has stuck.

Breeding

Most sparrows and finches are monogamous breeders. The female of the pair usually builds a cup-shaped or, more often in the tropics, a domed nest, from grasses, fine roots and perhaps mosses and lichens. Nests are concealed on the ground or low in a shrub or tree. The female alone incubates 2 to 3 eggs, for 12 to 14 days. Both male and female feed nestlings, which fledge after 10 to 15 days. Most breeding is accomplished from March through August. Some species, such as the abundant and conspicuous RUFOUS-COLLARED SPARROW, breed almost continually through the year.

Notes

The New World sparrows and finches have been especially well-studied by scientists, and thus they have contributed substantially to our general knowledge of birds. For instance, studies of North America's SONG SPARROW and the Neotropic's RUFOUS-COLLARED SPARROW provided the basis for much of the information we have about avian territoriality and many other kinds of behavior.

Status

The PLAIN-TAILED WARBLING-FINCH and RUFOUS-BREASTED WARBLING-FINCH occupy narrow ranges of highland forest and are listed as threatened or endangered. The SLENDER-BILLED FINCH of the southern coastal lowlands of Perú is vulnerable to cutting of the river-associated forests and shrubs that it inhabits. The BLACK MASKED FINCH occurs in pampas grasslands and in Perú is restricted to the Pampas del Heath Reserve.

Profiles

Streaked Saltator, *Saltator albicollis*, Plate 78a
Red-capped Cardinal, *Paroaria gularis*, Plate 78b
Blue-black Grassquit, *Volatinia jacarina*, Plate 78c
Chestnut-bellied Seed-Finch, *Oryzoborus angolensis*, Plate 78d
Buff-throated Saltator, *Saltator maximus*, Plate 78e
Golden-billed Saltator, *Saltator aurantiirostris*, Plate 78f

Chestnut-bellied Seedeater, *Sporophila castaneiventris*, Plate 79a
Yellow-bellied Seedeater, *Sporophila nigricollis*, Plate 79b
Black-and-white Seedeater, *Sporophila luctuosa*, Plate 79c
Plumbeous Sierra-Finch, *Phrygilus unicolor*, Plate 79d
Peruvian Sierra-Finch, *Phrygilus punensis*, Plate 79e
White-winged Diuca-Finch, *Diuca speculifera*, Plate 79f

Band-tailed Seedeater, *Catamenia analis*, Plate 80a
Collared Warbling-Finch, *Poospiza hispaniolensis*, Plate 80b
Rufous-collared Sparrow, *Zonotrichia capensis*, Plate 80c
Hooded Siskin, *Carduelis magellanica*, Plate 80d
Southern Yellow Grosbeak, *Pheucticus chrysogaster*, Plate 80e
Greenish Yellow-Finch, *Sicalis olivascens*, Plate 80f

Environmental Close-up 4
Frugivory: Animals That Eat Fruit and the Trees That Want Them To

Frugivory from the Animal's Point of View

A key feature of tropical forests, and of the animal communities that inhabit them, is the large number of birds (cotingas, finches, manakins, parrots, orioles, tanagers, toucans and trogons make up a partial list), mammals, and even some fish that rely on fruit as a diet staple. Fruit-eating, or *frugivory*, represents a trade-off, each participant – the fruit-bearing tree and the fruit-eating animal – offering the other something of great value (and therefore it is a kind of mutualism; see p. 45). The complex web of relationships between fruit-eaters and fruit-producing trees is particularly interesting because it nicely demonstrates ecological interactions between plant and animal, between food producer and food consumer, between predator and prey, and the mutual dependence sometimes engendered by such relationships.

Benefits of Frugivory for Animals

Most small and medium-sized tropical forest birds, many mammals, and some fish eat either fruits or small animals such as insects, or they eat both. But it is the fruit-eating habit that accounts for much of the incredible ecological success of animals in the tropics. For birds, many more species occupy the Earth's tropical areas than temperate zones and, ecologists believe, about 20% of the difference is directly attributable to the tropical birds' superior abilities to exploit fruit resources. In fact, probably 50% of tropical bird biomass (the summed weight of all tropical birds alive at one time) is supported by fruit-eating. You would think, therefore, that fruit must be tremendously profitable "prey" for birds, and in several ways it is:

1   Fruit is conspicuous. First consider insects as food. Palatable insects are often small and/or inconspicuous; they hide or blend in extremely well with their surroundings. Finding such insects is a chore that takes a lot of time. Ripe fruit, on the other hand, usually attracts attention to itself, being sweet-smelling, brightly colored, and displayed out in the open.

2   Fruit is easy to stalk, run down, catch, kill, and devour. Insects, as far as we can tell, are absolutely loath to be eaten – they run, hide, and resist to the end; some even spray noxious chemicals at their attackers. Fruit, however, never attempts escape and, in fact, when it is ripe and so most attractive to frugivores, it is most easily separated from the tree that bears it.

The underlying reason for points (1) and (2), which becomes more clear when considering frugivory from the trees' point of view (see below), is that fruits are made to be consumed by animals. It is their *raison d'etre*. Owing to this, trees could hardly be expected to make their fruit difficult to locate or pluck. Thus we have a major ecological insight: insects benefit by not being eaten, but unless its fruit is eaten, a plant gains nothing from the effort to produce it.

3   Fruit is abundant. When a bird locates a tree with fruit, there is often a large amount available for consumption. Thus, meeting a day's nutritional requirements means finding one or, at most, a few, fruit-bearing trees.

4   Fruit in the tropics is usually available year-round. There are wide-ranging consequences of points (3) and (4) for avian frugivores. That fruit is always available and abundant means that birds can safely specialize on it – evolve special ways to pluck, eat, and digest it – without encountering times of the year when no fruit is available, forcing the birds to search for food that they are ill-equipped to handle. Owing to fruit's abundance, species that concentrate on fruit often are quite successful, meaning that within a given area the numbers of individuals of these species can be quite large. But the greatest influence of frugivory on the lives of birds is that, because fruit is abundant and easy to locate and eat, birds can fulfill nutritional needs in only a few hours, leaving many hours each day available to pursue other activities. In contrast, an avian insectivore or piscivore (specializing on insects or fish, respectively), to survive may have to hunt most of each day.

The abundance of fruit, in fact, probably permitted the evolution of polygamous and promiscuous breeding in tropical birds. Take the manakins and cotingas that breed promiscuously. Males establish display sites on tree branches or on ground courts. Several of these display sites near each other constitute a lec. Females visit lecs, attracted by the males' vocalizations and dancing display antics, compare the males displaying, and choose one or more to mate with. Afterwards, the females go off by themselves to nest and raise their young. At their lecs, male manakins, for instance, spend up to 80% to 90% of daylight hours during the breeding season displaying and trying to attract females (the more they are able to convince to mate with them, the more offspring the males will have in the next generation). The free time frugivory affords permits both the prolonged display time in these breeding systems as well as the requisite ability of females to raise young themselves.

Also, when food is fairly scarce or difficult to locate or catch, to insure adequate supplies for themselves and their young, birds may need to defend individual territories and struggle to keep out other members of their species. Furthermore, male and female may need to continue their pairing past actual mating because one parent foraging alone cannot provide sufficient food for the young. But establishing a territory to defend the fruit it holds is unnecessary because there is usually fruit enough for all that want it. (In fact, usually birds cannot eat all the fruit that ripens on a tree.) It is far more efficient to forage in groups, to be social feeders, as are toucans and parrots, and so to each day have help in finding trees bearing ripe fruit (sometimes easier said than done because trees within a small area usually do not ripen simultaneously).

Problems of Frugivory

Have birds encountered difficulties in the process of specializing on fruit? Yes, there are some associated problems:

1   Fruits, although providing plentiful carbohydrates and fats, are relatively low in protein, so these birds, although easily meeting their daily calorie needs, sometimes have "protein deficits" that they must ease by feeding occasionally on insects or other animals (the occasional snail or frog, the odd lizard). Few bird species eat fruit exclusively. The ones that do, such as many cotingas, need make special provision for their all-fruit diet. For instance, because rapidly growing young need good amounts of protein, cotinga nestlings, fed only fruit by their parents, grow relatively slowly, and so spend perhaps 50% more time in the nest than non-frugivorous birds of the same size. Many of these birds nest in tree cavities where their slow-developing young are better-protected from the many nest predators roaming tropical habitats. Also, some of these birds seek out unusual fruits that are high in proteins and fats, such as avocados.

2   Eating liquidy fruit pulp means that frugivores consume a lot of water, which is both bulky and heavy, and which must be transported for a time (which uses up energy) and disposed of regularly.

3   The birds' nutrition comes from the fleshy fruit pulp. The seeds that are eaten incidentally are usually indigestible or even poisonous and must be, like water, carried for a while and then disposed of – either by regurgitation or after being passed through the digestive tract.

4   When a species specializes on a particular type of fruit, it becomes vulnerable to any temporary or permanent decline in the fruit's availability. (It appears that most avian frugivores avoid such vulnerability by not being overly specialized: in a study that followed the feeding habits of 70 fruit-eating species in the tropics, researchers discovered that each bird species consumed, on average, 10 species of fruits.)

Frugivory from the Tree's Point of View

It is clear what birds get from frugivory, but what of the trees, which are picked clean of the fruit that they spend so much time and energy producing? The answer is that the trees, by having birds eat, transport, and then drop their seeds, achieve efficient reproduction – something well worth their investment in fruit. The trees make use of birds as winged, animate, seed dispersal agents.

Why don't trees just let their seeds drop to the ground? It turns out that seeds dropped near the parent most often do not survive. They die because they must compete with the much larger parent for sun and other nutrients. Also, specialized insects that eat seeds can more easily find and destroy seeds that are in large accumulations, like under the mother tree. Seeds carried some distance from the parent tree have a better chance of germination and survival, and they will not compete with the parent tree (also, because in the tropics trees of the same species often do not grow near each other, seeds dropped by birds are unlikely to be regularly competing with any trees of the same species). Furthermore, because they are more spread out, seed predators are less likely to find them. Thus, seed dispersal by birds enhances a parent tree's prospects for successful reproduction, and also allows the tree to colonize new sites.

The tree's use of animal power for seed dispersal is exquisitely fine-tuned. As seeds are being readied, fruit is green, hard, and bitter-tasting – unappealing fare to birds (and to people!). When the seeds mature and are ready for dispersal and germination, the surrounding fruit brightens in color, becomes softer and easier to pluck from the tree, and in a *coup de grâce*, trees inject sugars into fruits, making them sweet and very attractive.

Not all animals attracted to fruits are good seed dispersers. Some, notably the parrots, eat and digest seeds, acting as predators rather than dispersers. These seed destroyers, however, in the course of their movements from branch to branch often knock many fruits out of the canopy that fall to the forest floor. Here, frugivorous animals that can't climb trees well, such as tinamous and agoutis, await this largesse. They eat the fruit, dispersing seeds later when they defecate, or cache it in the ground for later consumption, where seeds may later germinate.

Ecological Consequences of Frugivory for Birds, Trees, and Ecosystems

As tropical birds have benefitted in several ways by specialization on fruit, so too have trees. In fact, ecologists now suspect that together with pollination by insects, bats and birds, seed dispersal by birds and other vertebrate animals was and is responsible for the initial spread and current domination of the Earth by flowering plants. They estimate that upwards of 80% of trees and shrubs in tropical wet forests have their seeds dispersed by animals. These plants provide the nutrients to support large, healthy populations of frugivorous birds and bats. Moreover, the great species diversity of plants in the tropics may be largely linked to frugivorous animals continually eating fruits and spreading seeds into new areas. Such constant dispersal, which also allows continual, healthy genetic mixing, is beneficial for plant populations, always working to decrease the chances that individual species will go extinct. In fact, the more successful a tree species is at being "preyed upon" by birds, the more its seeds will be dropped over a wide area, and the more abundant it will become.

One potential problem for trees, though, is that if their fruit is eaten by only one or two bird species, that strict dependence for seed dispersal brings vulnerability. If the bird that disperses such a specialist tree for some reason declines in abundance and becomes extinct, so too, in short order, will the tree species. Most tree species, however, enjoy the seed dispersal services of at least several bird species.

The trade-offs that the birds and trees make, the conflicting strategies to survive and complete their life cycles, are fascinating. Think about it from one evolutionary perspective: the beneficial aspect of the interaction for the tree – having a bird transport its seeds – is the negative aspect for the animal, which has no "desire" to carry seeds from which its gets no benefit. The beneficial aspect for the bird – the fruit pulp that the plant manufactures to attract animals – is the negative part of the interaction for the plant, which loses the energy and nutrients required to make the fruit. Frugivory is one of the tropic's most important and compelling ecological interactions, and one that currently attracts strong interest from ecological researchers. Frugivory may even have been a causative factor in the early evolution of color vision, as the first fruit-eaters that could easily distinguish ripe and unripe fruit plainly would have had advantages over those that could not.

A Fruitful Connection Between Land and Water

The PIRANHA, thanks to cartoons and horror movies, is etched into our minds as a blood-thirsty fish of the Amazon. Here it supposedly reduces large animals, unlucky enough to fall into the water, to nothing but bones within minutes. Although some do eat flesh, their reputations are greatly exaggerated. They do occasionally bite swimmers, but this behavior is very rare in Perú. We regularly swim near these intriguing fish, and in 30 years have never had so much as a nibble – except on a fishing line. The biggest threat these fish pose to people may be when freshly caught piranha are flopping around on the bottom of a fisherman's canoe, with bare toes exposed to their sharp teeth.

There are 25 piranha species in the Amazon Basin – some black and others white; a few are red-bellied. Regardless of their reputation, piranhas also eat a lot of fruits floating in the water. All species are primarily frugivores when young, and, even as adults, fruits are a major to occasional part of their diets, depending on the species. Only six species of piranhas (red-bellied species in the genus *Pygocentrus*), however, are primarily flesheaters as adults. Even then the flesh they eat is usually in the form of fins and scales of other fish. In Perú, apparently two or three extremely similar species of this red-bellied genus occur. *Pygocentrus ternetzi* (Figure 13; adult body length 20 to 30 cm, 8 to 12 in) is representative of them all.

During the rainier season in Perú's Amazon lowlands, rivers flood and low forest, dry for most of the year, has up to 1 m (3 ft) or more of water standing at the bases of the trees. Many of these trees time their flowering and fruiting to coincide with this flooding, their specialized fruits dropping to float in the water below. Fish, including piranhas, swim in among the bases of the trees to devour the fruits or chew at their outer coverings. Many seeds are dropped or pass through the fish digestive system to be defecated somewhere else in the flooded forest. The seeds fall to the forest floor, and if lucky, germinate when the floods recede. Not only does this story dispel the undeserved super-carnivore

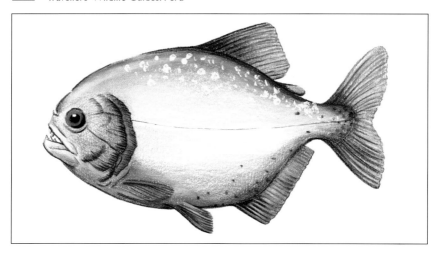

Figure 13 Piranha, *Pygocentrus ternetzi.*

reputation of piranhas, it also dispels the idea that aquatic and terrestrial systems are very separate. That a fish serves as a major seed disperser for a terrestrial tree is just one of many examples of how differently we must look at and study this diverse area.

Chapter 8

MAMMALS

- *Introduction*
- *General Characteristics and Classification of Mammals*
- *Features of Tropical Mammals*
- *Seeing Mammals in Perú*
- *Family Profiles*
  1. *Opossums*
  2. *Anteaters, Sloths, and Armadillos*
  3. *Bats*
  4. *Primates*
  5. *Carnivores*
  6. *Peccaries, Deer, and Llama Relatives*
  7. *Rodents and Rabbit*
  8. *Manatee and Tapirs*
  9. *Seals*
  10. *Whales and Dolphins*
- *Environmental Close-up 5: Of Kingfishers and Competition: Big Bills and Little Bills and How They Got That Way.*

Introduction

Leafing through this book, you may have noticed that there are many more profiles of birds than mammals. At first glance you might see this as discriminatory, especially because people themselves are mammals and, owing to that direct kinship, are often keenly interested and motivated to see and learn about mammals. What's going on? Aren't mammals as good as birds? Why not include more of them? There are several reasons for the discrepancy – good biological reasons. One is that, even though the tropics generally have more species of mammals than temperate or Arctic regions, the total number of mammal species worldwide, and the number in any region, is almost always much less than the number of birds. In fact, there are only about 4630 mammal species in the world, as compared with 9040 birds, and that relative difference is reflected in Perú's fauna. Another compelling reason not to include more mammals in a book on commonly sighted wildlife, is that, even in regions of South America sporting high levels of mammalian diversity, you will rarely see mammals – especially if you are a short-term visitor. Mammals are delicious fare for any number of predatory beasts (eaten in good numbers by reptiles, birds, other mammals, and even the odd amphibian), but most mammals lack a basic protection from predators that birds possess, the power of flight. Consequently, most have been forced into being active nocturnally, or, if active during daylight hours, they are highly secretive. Birds often show themselves with abandon, mammals do not. An exception is monkeys. They are fairly large and primarily arboreal, which keeps them safe from a number of kinds of predators, and thus permits them to be noisy and relatively conspicuous. A final reason for not including more mammals in the book is that about 170 (40%) of the 431 mammal species that occur in Perú are bats. They are for the most part nocturnal animals that, even if you are lucky enough to get good looks at them, are very difficult for anyone other than an expert to identify to species.

General Characteristics and Classification of Mammals

Mammals as a group first arose, so fossils tell us, approximately 245 million years ago, splitting off from the primitive reptiles during the late Triassic Period of the Mesozoic Era, somewhat before the birds did the same thing. Four main traits distinguish mammals from other vertebrates, and each of these traits helped mammals spread into most of the habitats around the world. Hair on their bodies insulates and helps maintain constant internal temperatures as well as protecting the skin from injuries; milk production for the young frees mothers from having to search for specific foods for their offspring; the bearing of live young instead of eggs allows breeding females to be mobile and hence safer than if they had to guard eggs for several weeks; and advanced brains, together with highly integrated sensory systems, contribute to mammals' breadth of survival mechanisms.

Mammals are quite variable in size and form, many being highly adapted – changed through evolution – to specialized habitats and lifestyles: bats specialized to fly, marine mammals specialized for their aquatic world, deer specialized to run swiftly, etc. The smallest mammals are the *shrews*, tiny insect eaters that weigh as little as 2.5 g (a tenth of an ounce). The largest are the whales, weighing in at up to 160,000 kg (350,000 lb, half the weight of a loaded Boeing 747) – as far as anyone knows, the largest animals that have ever lived.

Mammals are divided into three major groups, primarily according to reproductive methods. The *monotremes* are an ancient group that actually lays eggs and still retains some other reptile-like characteristics. Only four species of them survive, 1 platypus and 3 spiny anteaters, and they are found only in Australia and New Guinea. The *marsupials* give birth to live young that are relatively undeveloped. When born, the young crawl along mom's fur to attach themselves to her nipples, usually inside her pouch, where they find milk supplies and finish their development. There are about 240 marsupial species, including kangaroos, koalas, wombats and opossum, and they are limited in distribution to Australia and the Neotropics (the industrious but road-accident-prone VIRGINIA OPOSSUM also inhabits much of Mexico and the USA). The majority of mammal species are *eutherians*. These animals are distinguished from the other groups by having a well-developed placenta, which efficiently connects a mother to her developing babies, allowing for long internal development. This trait, which allows embryos to develop to a fairly mature form in safety, and for the female to be mobile until birth, has allowed these mammals to colonize successfully and prosper in many habitats. These mammals include those with which most people are intimately familiar: rodents, rabbits, cats, dogs, bats, primates, elephants, horses, whales – everything from house mice to ecotravellers. The 4600 species of living mammals are grouped into about 115 families, which are in turn categorized into about 20 orders.

Features of Tropical Mammals

There are several important features of tropical mammals and their habitats that differentiate them from temperate zone mammals. First, tropical mammals face different environmental stresses than do temperate zone mammals, and they respond to stresses in different ways. Many temperate zone mammals, of course, must endure extreme variation within a year; from cold winters with snow and low winter food supplies to hot summers with dry weather and abundant food. Many of them respond with *hibernation*, staying more or less dormant for several months until conditions improve. Tropical mammals, except in the high altitude puna, do not encounter such extreme annual changes, but they do face dry seasons, up to 5 months long, that sometimes severely reduce food supplies. For some surprising reasons, they cannot alleviate this stress by hibernating, waiting for the rainy season to arrive with its increased food supplies. When a mammal in Canada or Alaska hibernates, many of its predators leave the area. This is not the case in the tropics. A mammal sleeping away the dry season in a burrow would be easy prey to snakes and other predators. Moreover, a big danger to sleeping mammals would be … army ants! These voracious insects (p. 244) are very common in the tropics and would quickly eat a sleeping mouse or squirrel. Also, external parasites, such as ticks and mites, which are inactive in extreme cold, would continue to be very active on sleeping tropical mammals, sucking blood and doing considerable damage. Last, the great energy reserves needed to be able to sleep for an extended period through warm weather may be more than any mammal can physically accumulate. Therefore, tropical mammals need to stay active throughout the year. One way they counter the dry season's reduction in their normal foods is to switch food types seasonally. For instance, some rodents that eat mostly insects during the rainy season switch to seeds during the dry; some bats that feed on insects switch to dry-season fruits.

The abundance of tropical fruit brings up another interesting difference between temperate and tropical mammals: A surprising number of tropical mammals eat a lot of fruit, even among the carnivore group, which, as its name implies, should be eating meat. All the carnivores in Perú, save the Puma, Jaguar and otters, are known to eat fruit. Some, such as the Spectacled Bear, seem to prefer fruit. Upon reflection, that these mammals consume fruit makes sense. Fruit is very abundant in the tropics, available all year, and, at least when it is ripe, easily digested by mammalian digestive systems. A consequence of such *frugivory* (fruit-eating) is that many mammals have become, together with frugivorous birds, major dispersal agents of fruit seeds, which they spit out or which travel unharmed through their digestive tracts to be deposited in feces far from the mother tree (see Close-Up, p. 177). Some biologists believe that, even though the carnivores plainly are specialized for hunting down, killing, and eating animal prey, it is likely that fruit has always been a major part of their diet.

Finally, there are some differences in the kinds of mammals inhabiting tropical and temperate regions. For instance there is only a single Neotropical bear species, distributed sparsely from the highlands of Venezuela to southern Bolivia. There are few social rodents like beavers and prairie dogs and very few rabbit species. On the other hand, some groups occur solely in the tropics or do fabulously there. There are about 50 species of New World monkeys, all of which occur in tropical areas (20 occur in Perú). Arboreal mammals such as monkeys and sloths are plentiful in tropical forests, probably because there is a rich, resource-filled, dense canopy to occupy and feed in. Also, the closed canopy blocks light to the ground, which only allows an undergrowth that is sparse and poor in resources, and consequently permits few opportunities for mammals to live and feed there. Bats thrive in the tropics, being very successful both in terms of number of species and in their abundances. Seven families of bats occur in Perú, including more than 170 species; only 4 families and 40 species occur in the entire USA, an area more than 100 times larger than Perú's. While most of the North American bats are insect eaters, the Peruvian bats are quite varied in lifestyle, among them being fruit-eaters, nectar-eaters, fish-eaters and even a few that consume other animals or their blood.

The social and breeding behaviors of various mammals are quite diverse. Some are predominantly solitary animals, males and females coming together occasionally only to mate. Others live in family groups. Like birds, female mammals have most of the say in choosing a mate, but unlike most bird species, where both mates are necessary to raise the young and monogamy (one male mates with one female) is thus common, milk production among female mammals usually frees the male from caring for the young. He is better off and more likely to get more of his genes into the next generation by convincing additional females to mate with him. This leads to polygyny (one male mates with a harem of several females) or promiscuity (a sexual free-for-all where dominant males tend to mate with a mind-numbing array of females) as the most common mating systems among mammals. Monogamy is uncommon but polyandry (one female mates with several males) is even rarer among mammals than birds. Depending on resources like food availability and access to mates, some mammal species are rigorously territorial, others are not.

Seeing Mammals in Perú

No doubt about it, mammals are tough to see. You could go for two weeks and, if in the wrong places at the wrong times, see very few of them. A lot of luck is involved – a tapir, a small herd of peccaries, or a porcupine happens to cross the trail just a bit ahead of you, or by chance someone in your group spots a sloth in a tree. We can offer three pieces of mammal-spotting advice: first, if you have time and are a patient sort, stake out a likely looking spot near a stream or watering hole, be quiet, and wait to see what approaches. Second, try taking quiet strolls along paths and trails very early in the morning. At this time, many nocturnal mammals are quickly scurrying to their day shelters. Third, although only for the stout-hearted, try searching with a flashlight at night around field stations or campgrounds. After scanning the ground (for safety's sake as well as for mammals), shine the light toward the middle regions of trees and look for bright, shiny eyes reflecting the light. You will certainly stumble across some kind of mammal or another; then it is simply a matter of whether you scare them more than they scare you. Doing the same thing at night from a canoe can also be a good way to spot eye-shine of mammals in the vegetation along the edge of a stream or forested lake.

Some mammals, of course, you can see more reliably. Monkeys, for instance, are often easy to see in many of Perú's national parks, and squirrels and peccaries are frequently sighted in lowland areas of the Amazon. Banish all thoughts right now of ever encountering "Otorongo," the Jaguar, which, in Perú is found regularly now only in isolated regions of the Amazonian lowlands. Even there, however, your chances of encountering one are slim, although their tracks on beaches are a regular sight in Manu National Park.

Family Profiles

1. Opossums

Marsupials are an ancient group, preceding in evolution the development of the *true*, or *placental*, mammals, which eventually replaced the marsupials over most parts of the terrestrial world. Marsupials alive today in the Australian and Neotropical regions therefore are remnants of an earlier time when the group's distribution spanned the Earth. Of the eight living families of marsupials, only three occur in the New World, and only one, the *opossums*, occurs in Perú. This family, Didelphidae, is distributed widely over the northern Neotropics (with one member, the VIRGINIA OPOSSUM, reaching far northwards into the USA). Twenty-five species represent the family in Perú. They are a diverse group, occupying essentially all of the country's habitats up to about 3300 m (11,000 ft) elevation. Some, such as the COMMON OPOSSUM (also called SOUTHERN OPOSSUM; Plate 81), are abundant and frequently sighted, while others are rarer or shier.

All opossums are basically alike in body plan, although species vary considerably in size. Their general appearance probably has not changed much during the past 40 to 65 million years. Basically, these mammals look like rats, albeit in the case of some, such as the Common Opossum, like large rats. Their distinguishing features are pointed snouts, short legs, a long, often hairless tail, which is usually *prehensile* (that is, opossums can wrap it around a tree branch and hang from it), and large, hairless ears. Opossums come in a narrow range of colors – shades of gray, brown, and black. Male and female opossums generally look alike, but males are usually larger than females of the same age. Females in about half of the species have pouches for their young on their abdomens. Opossum hind feet have five digits each, one digit acting as an opposable thumb.

Natural History
Ecology and Behavior

Most opossums are night-active omnivores, although some also can be seen during the day. Their reputation is that they will eat, or at least try to eat, almost anything they stumble across or can catch; mostly they take fruit, eggs, invertebrates and small vertebrate animals. The COMMON OPOSSUM forages mainly at night, often along ponds and streams, sometimes covering more than a kilometer (half-mile) per night within its home range, the area within which it lives and seeks food. Opossums that have been studied are not territorial – they do not defend part or all of their home ranges from others of their species. Some opossums forage mainly on the ground, but most are good climbers and are able to forage also in trees and shrubs; and some species are chiefly arboreal. The WATER OPOSSUM (Plate 81) is semi-aquatic and feeds primarily on fish, crustaceans and large insects it catches in the clear water of streams and lakes at the base of the Andes. Water Opossums are not shy, and if you see a pair of mammalian eyes reflecting light as they move quickly across the water's surface, it is likely to be this species. The female's pouch can be sealed to protect the young from drowning while in the water. The terrestrial BROWN FOUR-EYED OPOSSUM (Plate 81) and the arboreal LONG-FURRED WOOLLY MOUSE OPOSSUM (Plate 81) are both much shier and warier. They concentrate on insects for food, but during times of the year when there are lots of fruit, your best chance to see them is at a fruiting tree. After a night's foraging, an opossum spends the daylight hours in a cave, a rock crevice, or a cavity in a tree or log.

Predators on opossums include owls, snakes, and carnivorous mammals. Some opossums apparently are somewhat immune to the venom of many poisonous snakes. The response of the Common Opossum to threat by a predator is to hiss, growl, snap its mouth, move its body from side to side, and finally, to lunge and bite. They often try to climb to escape. The VIRGINIA OPOSSUM, a common North and Central American species, is famous for faking death ("playing possum") when threatened, but that behavior is rare or absent in the outwardly very similiar Common Opossum.

The Common Opossum has what can be considered a commensal relationship with people. Throughout its range in northern South America, populations of these opossums are concentrated around human settlements, particularly near garbage dumps, where they feed. They also partake of fruit crops and attack farmyard birds. Consequently, this species of opossum is more likely to be seen near towns or villages than in uninhabited areas. Of course, these opossums pay a price for the easy food – their picture commonly is found in the dictionary under "road kill."

Breeding

Opossums are unsociable animals and usually observed singly. The exception is during the breeding season, when males seek and court females, and two or more may be seen together. Female opossums give birth only 12 to 14 days after mating. The young that leave the reproductive tract are only about 1 cm (a half inch) long and weigh less than half a gram (one-hundreth ounce). These tiny opossums, barely embryos, climb unassisted along the mother's fur toward her nipples.

They then grasp a nipple in their mouth, either within the pouch, or, if a species without a pouch (like the BROWN FOUR-EYED OPOSSUM or the mouse opossums), directly on her chest. The nipple swells to completely fill the young's mouth, essentially attaching it to the mother for about 2 months. Usually more young are born (up to 20) than make it to the nipples to attach correctly. In studies, 6 young, on average, are found on the females' nipples (they have up to 13 nipples). Following this attached phase, the female continues to nurse her young for another month or more, often in a nest she constructs of leaves and grass in a tree cavity or burrow.

Notes

COMMON OPOSSUMS are known as foul-smelling beasts. Their reputation probably stems from the fact that they apparently enjoy rolling about in fresh animal droppings. Also, when handled, they employ some unattractive defense mechanisms – tending to squirt urine and defecate.

Status

Five of Perú's opossum species are considered threatened, primarily by habitat destruction: BUSHY-TAILED OPOSSUM, one species of mouse opossum, and three species of short-tailed opossum. Opossum meat is not regarded as tasty, so these mammals are rarely hunted for food. Opossums, chiefly COMMON OPOSSUMS, are killed intentionally near human settlements to protect fruit crops and poultry, and unintentionally but frequently by cars.

Profiles

Brown Four-eyed Opossum, *Metachirus nudicaudatus*, Plate 81b
Common Opossum, *Didelphis marsupialis*, Plate 81c
Long-furred Woolly Mouse Opossum, *Micoureus demerarae*, Plate 81d
Water Opossum, *Chironectes minimus*, Plate 81e

2. Anteaters, Sloths, and Armadillos

Anteaters, *sloths*, and *armadillos* are three types of very different-looking mammals that, somewhat surprisingly, are closely related. The group they belong to is the Order Edentata, meaning, literally, without teeth. However, because all but the anteaters have some teeth, the name is a misnomer. The *edentates* are New World mammals specialized to eat ants and termites, or to eat leaves high in the forest canopy. Although the *edentates* might look and behave differently, they are grouped together because they share certain skeletal features and aspects of their circulatory and reproductive systems that indicate close relationships. Because anteaters and sloths are so unique and found only in the tropical and semi-tropical forests of Central and South America, they are perhaps the quintessential mammals of the region, the way that toucans and parrots are the quintessential Neotropical birds. If given a choice of mammals, most visitors to Perú would probably prefer to see a Jaguar, but it is far more likely that the characteristic Neotropical mammal they spot will be a sloth.

The anteater family, Myrmecophagidae, has four species, all restricted to Neotropical forests, and three of which are found in Amazonian Perú: the very rare, 2 meter-long (6.5 ft) GIANT ANTEATER (Plate 82), the SOUTHERN TAMANDUA (Plate 82), and the small PYGMY, or SILKY, ANTEATER (Plate 81). Because the last species is a nocturnal tree-dweller, the anteater you are most likely to see during your trip is a tamandua.

There is nothing else like a sloth. They vaguely resemble monkeys ("deformed monkeys," according to one chronicler), but their slow-motion lifestyle is the very antithesis of most primates' hyperkinetic lives. There are two families of sloths, the two-toed and three-toed varieties, distinguished by the number of claws per foot. There are five sloth species, three of which occur in Perú. The two-toed sloths (Family Megalonychidae) weigh about 5 to 8 kg (11 to 17.5 lb) and are active only at night. The much smaller three-toed sloths (Family Bradypodidae, meaning slow-footed) weigh, on average, about 4 kg (9 lb), are pale yellowish or brown with a round, white face with dark side stripes, and are active both during day and night. Their hair is long and stiff, producing a shaggy look. Long limbs end in feet with three curved claws that they use as hooks to hang from tree branches.

Armadillos are strange ground-dwelling mammals that, probably owing to the armor plating on their backs, are protected from many predators. The family, Dasypodidae, contains about 20 species that are distributed from the southern tip of South America to the central USA, with four species in Perú. The endangered GIANT ARMADILLO (Plate 82) (up to 1.5 m, 5 ft, in length, including the tail, and weighing about 30 kg, 65 lb) is rare in the lowland forests of the Amazon, but where present, huge holes it makes in the forest floor advertise the fact. The uncommon GREAT LONG-NOSED ARMADILLO of the lowland forests and the abundant NINE-BANDED ARMADILLO (Plate 82) are very similar in appearance (70 cm, 27.5 in, in length, including the tail). Because all the other species are entirely nocturnal, you are most likely to see only the Nine-banded Armadillo, which is often also active during the day. It is also the species that extends into the USA. All these armadillos are grayish or yellowish, with many crosswise plates of hard, horn-like material on their backs (bony plates underlie the outer horny covering).

Natural History
Ecology and Behavior

Anteaters are mammals highly specialized to feed on ants and termites; some also dabble in bees. From an anteater's point of view, the main thing about these social insects is that they live in large colonies, so that finding one often means finding thousands. The anteaters' strong, sharp, front claws are put to use digging into ant colonies in or on the ground, and into termite nests in trees (the very abundant, dark, globular, often basket-ball sized *termitarium* attached to the trunks and branches of tropical trees). Their long, thin snouts are used to get down into the excavation, and their extremely long tongues, coated with a special sticky saliva, are used to extract the juicy insects. The SOUTHERN TAMANDUA and SILKY ANTEATER are largely arboreal. They have prehensile tails for hanging about and moving in trees, allowing them to get to hard-to-reach termite nests. Particular about their food, anteaters don't generally go after army ants or large, stinging ants that might do them harm. Tamanduas rest in hollow trees or other holes during midday, but are otherwise active, including nocturnally. They forage both on the ground and in trees, usually solitarily. Each individual's home range, the area in which it lives and seeks food, averages about 70 hectares (170 acres). Anteaters are fairly slow-moving animals and their metabolic rates low because, although ants and termites are plentiful and easy to find, they don't provide a high nutrition, high energy diet. Deceptively placid and shy, anteaters, especially the GIANT ANTEATER, if attacked, can rear back and slash with deadly accuracy and force, using their powerful front legs and sharp claws to disembowel or severely injure enemies.

Sloths are active almost exclusively in trees, feeding on leaves as they hang upside down. "Active" is probably the wrong word to describe their behavior. Sloths, particularly the three-toed ones, move incredibly slowly – so much so that at one time it was mistakenly thought that a sloth spent its entire life moving about slowly in a single tree. Detailed observations have shown that sloths do indeed switch trees, but, on average, only once every two days. When switching, they do not cross open ground, but move between the trees' overlapping branches. This is smart, both because slowly descending to the ground and then climbing another tree would be a waste of time and energy and because a slow-moving sloth on the ground would be easy, defenseless prey for a variety of predators – snakes, large cats, and eagles. (One person clocked a female sloth on the ground as moving only 4.5 m, 14 ft, in a minute – and that was in rapid response to the call of her offspring!) Sloths can swim, however, and you should look for them crossing small rivers.

Besides their slow movements that probably help sloths escape notice from predators searching the canopy, the surface of their hair has many grooves and pits in which algae and fungi readily grow to turn the animal greenish and camouflaged. Not only do sloths support plants on their bodies, they support insects as well. A number of different beetle and moth species spend at least parts of their life cycles living on sloths. One moth species, a "sloth moth," lives as an adult moth in the hair of a sloth, reproducing by laying its eggs in sloth droppings. While the three-toed sloths are docile and non-aggressive, the two-toed sloths are dangerous and can do considerable damage, even in slow motion, with their front claws. All species of sloths apparently come down from their elevated perches only about once per week, to urinate and defecate at the base of a tree. Why they do so, instead of just defecating from the heights, remains a mystery. The three-toed sloths, but not the two-toed sloths, take extra time to dig a small hole, void themselves, and cover the droppings. During this 30–minute period, the animals are dangerously vulnerable to predators.

Leaves are notoriously difficult to digest, so a diet of pure leaves provides little nutrition. That means the sloths must eat a lot of them to survive. Sloths have very low metabolic rates and relatively low body temperatures; in fact, at night, sloths save energy by lowering their body temperatures to almost match that of the environment. Sloths are solitary and apparently territorial – only one per tree is permitted (or a female together with her young). Look for sloths in large, leafy trees (particularly Cecropias), as they hang upside down, their hook-like claws grasping the branches. Two-toed sloths will often eat fruits in addition to leaves, so also look for them at night in fruiting trees.

Some armadillos, such as the GIANT ARMADILLO, specialize on ants and termites. This species uses its immense bulk and large claws on its front feet to quickly dig out these insects from their nests in the ground. The NINE-BANDED ARMADILLO, however, is more omnivorous, eating many kinds of insects, small vertebrates, and also some plant parts. Usually they spend the day foraging alone, but several family members may share the same sleeping burrow they have dug out with their sharp claws. They are generally slow-moving creatures that, save for their armor plating, would be easy prey for predators. When attacked, they curl up into a ball so that their armor faces the attacker, their soft abdomens protected at the center of the ball. Few natural predators can harm them. However, like opossums, they are frequently hit on roads by automobiles.

Breeding

Female anteaters bear one offspring at a time, and lavish attention on it. At first the newborn is placed in a secure location, such as in a tree cavity, and the mother returns to it at intervals to nurse. Later, when it is old enough, the young-ster rides on the mother's back. After several months, when the young is about half the mother's size, the two part ways. Breeding may be at any time of year. Sloths also produce one young at a time. Following 6 months of pregnancy, the offspring is born. It is then carried about and fed by the mother for about 4 months, at which point it is put down and must forage for itself. Until it is a year old or so, the juvenile forages within its mother's home range; then it moves out on its own. Sloths not only move slowly, they grow slowly. Apparently they do not reach sexual maturity until they are three years old, and they may live for 20 to 30 years. Female armadillos, after 70-day pregnancies, produce several young at a time, usually four. For some unknown reason, each litter of armadillo young arises from a single fertilized egg, so that if a female has four young, they are always identical quadruplets.

Notes

GIANT ANTEATERS are also known as Ant Bears, for obvious reasons. Frequently, three-toed sloths are captured and released into city parks and plazas, where they survive amazingly well.

Status

Overall, the edentate mammals are not doing badly, but all suffer population declines from habitat destruction. One problem in trying to determine the status of their populations is that many are nocturnal, and some of the armadillos spend most of their time in burrows. The result is that nobody really knows the real health of some populations. However, two species of armadillos (ANDEAN HAIRY ARMADILLO and LONG-NOSED ARMADILLO) are considered threatened. The GIANT ARMADILLO, because of over-hunting, is considered endangered (CITES Appendix I listed). The GIANT ANTEATER has been exterminated from much of its range in South and Central America, and is considered threatened (CITES Appendix II listed). Tamanduas are found throughout lowland Perú but, outside of protected areas, they are sometimes killed as pests by locals. The SILKY ANTEATER is thought to be fairly common, but because their populations naturally are sparse and also because they are so difficult to spot, good information on them is lacking. Perú's three sloth species apparently are fairly common, although, again, there is no good infor-mation on their populations. Some biologists suspect that three-toed sloths are one of the most abundant larger mammals of Neotropical forests. One sloth, Brazil's MANED THREE-TOED SLOTH, is endangered (CITES Appendix I and USA ESA listed).

Profiles

Silky Anteater, *Cyclopes didactylus*, Plate 81a
Southern Two-toed Sloth, *Choloepus didactylus*, Plate 82a
Brown-throated Three-toed Sloth, *Bradypus variegatus*, Plate 82b
Nine-banded Armadillo, *Dasypus novemcinctus*, Plate 82c
Giant Armadillo, *Priodontes maximus*, Plate 82d

Giant Anteater, *Myrmecophaga tridactyla*, Plate 82e
Southern Tamandua, *Tamandua tetradactyla*, Plate 82f

3. Bats

Because they are so hard to see or hear, *bats* have always been considered foreign, exotic, and mysterious, even in our own backyards. Unlike any other mammals, they engage in sustained, powered flight ("rats with wings," in the memorable phrasing of an unappreciative acquaintance). Bats are active at night and navigate the dark skies chiefly by "sonar," or *echolocation*: by broadcasting ultrasonic sounds – extremely high-pitched chirps and clicks – and then gaining information about their environment by "reading" the echoes. They also use this sonar to locate prey such as flying insects and surfacing fish. Although foreign to people's primate sensibilities, bats, precisely because their lives are so very different from our own, are increasingly of interest to us. In the past, of course, bats' exotic behavior, particularly their nocturnal habits, engendered in most societies not ecological curiosity but fear and superstition.

Bats are widely distributed, inhabiting most of the world's tropical and temperate regions, except for some oceanic islands. With a worldwide total of about 980 species, the bats are second in diversity among mammals only to the rodents. Ecologically, they can be thought of as night-time replacements for birds, which dominate the daytime skies. Bats of the Neotropics, although often hard to see and, in most cases, difficult for anyone other than experts to identify (because of their great diversity), are tremendously important mammals. Their numbers tell the story: 39% of all Neotropical mammal species are bats, and there are often more species of bats in some Neotropical forests than of all other mammal species combined. Researchers estimate that bats make up most of the mammalian biomass (the total amount of living tissue, by weight) in any given Neotropical region. Of the 431 species of mammals that occur in Perú, almost 170 are bats. We profile 10 species that represent a spectrum of the types of bats you are most likely to encounter.

Bats have true wings that are made of thin, strong, highly elastic membranes that extend from the sides of the body and legs to cover and be supported by the elongated fingers of the arms. (The name of the order of bats, Chiroptera, refers to the wings: *chiro*, meaning hand, and *ptera*, wing.) Other distinctive anatomical features include bodies covered with silky, longish hair; toes with sharp, curved claws that allow the bats to hang upside down and are used by some to catch food; scent glands that produce strong, musky odors; and, in many, very odd-shaped folds of skin on their noses (*noseleaves*) and prominent ears that aid in echolocation. Like birds, bats' bodies have been modified through evolution to conform to the needs of energy-demanding flight: they have relatively large hearts, low body weights, and high metabolisms.

Bats, although they come in a variety of sizes, are sufficiently standardized in form such that all species are easily recognized by everyone as bats. Females in most species are larger than males, presumably so they can fly when pregnant. Bat species in Perú weigh 5 to 200 g (0.2 to 7 oz) and have wingspans of 5 to 80 cm (2 to 31 in). Bats tend not to occur above 500 m (1600 ft) elevation, but at night in almost any lowland habitat this group of mammals takes over. At dusk, when it is not yet too dark to see them, some species are already flying over streams and forests. During the night as you walk along a closed forested path, bats frequently will fly past the beam of your flashlight. They may even brush your body with their wings as they swiftly fly by in hot pursuit of a scrumptious insect. Don't panic. They are harmless, unless you act like an insect. Contrary to folk-stories, bats absolutely do NOT make nests in your hair.

Natural History
Ecology and Behavior

Most Neotropical bat species specialize in eating insects (a single individual has been estimated to eat up to 1200 insects per hour!). They use their sonar not just to navigate the night but to detect insects, which they catch on the wing, pick off leaves, or scoop off the ground. Bats use several methods to catch flying insects. Small insects may be captured directly in the mouth; some bats use their wings as nets and spoons to trap insects and pull them to their mouth; and others scoop bugs into the fold of skin membrane that connects their tail and legs, then somersault in midair to move the catch to their mouth. Small bugs are eaten immediately on the wing, while larger ones, such as big beetles, are taken to a perch and dismembered. However, not all species are insectivores. Neotropical bats have also expanded ecologically into a variety of other feeding niches: some specialize in eating fruit, feeding on nectar and pollen at flowers, preying on vertebrates such as frogs or birds, eating fish, or drinking blood.

Bats are highly social animals, roosting and often foraging in groups. They spend the daylight hours in *day roosts*, usually tree cavities, shady sides of trees, caves, rock crevices, or, these days, in buildings or under bridges. Some bats make their own individual roosting sites in trees by biting leaves so that they fold over, making small tents that shelter them from predators as well as from the elements. More than one species of bat may inhabit the same roost, although some species will associate only with their own kind. For most species, the normal resting position in a roost is hanging by their feet, head down, which makes taking flight as easy as letting go and spreading their wings. Many bats leave roosts around dusk and then move to foraging sites at various distances from the roost. Night activity patterns vary, perhaps serving to reduce food competition among species. Some tend to fly and forage intensely in the early evening, become less active in the middle of the night, then resume intense foraging near dawn; others are relatively inactive early in the evening, but more active later on. Bats do not fly continuously after leaving their day roosts, but group together at a *night roost*, a tree for instance, where they rest and bring food. Fruit-eaters do not rest in the tree at which they have discovered ripe fruit, where predators might find them, but instead make several trips per night from the fruit tree to their night roost.

If you see any bats on your trip to Amazonian Perú, they likely will be LONG-NOSED BATS (Plate 84). They roost in groups up to 30 or more on the underside of logs and along banks of rivers and lakes. They hang in a line, evenly spaced but so well camouflaged that you will have to look carefully to see them. They readily take flight in the daytime if you come too close, and fly ahead of your canoe like a flock of large, whitish butterflies. At dusk they begin to feed on tiny insects low over the water. The WHITE-LINED SAC-WINGED BAT (Plate 83) is one of the most frequently encountered bats of Perú's lowland forests. By day they roost in groups of 5 to 50 in hollow trees or caves, rocks, or buildings; they are often seen under overhangs at ecotourist facilities. They leave roosts just before dark to commence their insect foraging, which they do under the forest canopy, usually within 300 m (1000 ft) of their roosts. Individual males defend territories in the day roosts, and they have harems of up to 9 females each. After birth, a mother carries her pup each night from the day roost and leaves it in a hiding place while she forages. Pups can fly at about 2 weeks old, but continue to nurse for several months. The GREATER FISHING BAT (Plate 83) is relatively large and orange-colored. Fishing bats (sometimes called *bulldog bats*) roost in hollow trees and buildings near fresh or salt water. They have very large hind feet and claws that they use to pull fish, crustaceans, and insects from the water's surface. These bats fly low over still water, using their sonar to detect the ripples of a fish just beneath or breaking the water's surface. Grabbing the fish with their claws, they then move it to their mouth, land, hang upside down, and feast. The FALSE VAMPIRE BAT (Plate 83) is the New World's largest bat, with a wingspan of up to 80 cm (2.5 ft). They feed on vertebrates such as birds, rodents, and other bats. (The name originates with the mistaken belief of early European explorers that the largest, meanest-looking bat in the region must be the blood-sucker of which they had heard so many tales.) Some of the animals they prey on weigh as much as they do, but these bats are fierce, with large canine teeth, shearing molars, and powerful jaw muscles. They roost in small groups, usually a pair of adults and their recent offspring. Apparently, False Vampires, although they forage alone, are good family bats: young pups at night are left in the day roost to be guarded by an adult or subadult family member; the returning foragers are greeted with mutual "kissing" when they return (one observer compared it to the mutual muzzle licking and nosing practiced by wolves when they greet one another). Adult "babysitter" bats may be fed by the returning foragers. The COMMON LONG-TONGUED BAT or NECTAR BAT (Plate 84) is a small bat with a misleading name. Although it can hover for a few seconds at flowers to take pollen or nectar, most of its omnivorous diet consists of fruit and insects. It roosts in large groups in both dry and wet forest habitats. Young use their teeth to cling to their mothers' fur after birth, being carried along during foraging trips; pups can fly on their own at about a month old. The SHORT-TAILED FRUIT BAT (Plate 84) is another small and very common species that lives in large groups, up to several hundred, usually in caves or tree cavities. They are primarily fruit-eaters, but also seasonally visit flowers for nectar. Usually they pick fruit from a tree, then return to a night roost to consume it. After giving birth, females carry their young for a week or two during their nightly foraging; older young are left in the day roost. Because of their abundance and frugivory, these bats are critical dispersers of tree seeds in Neotropical forests. A medium-sized fruit-eater in wet and dry forests, the JAMAICAN FRUIT-EATING BAT (Plate 83) also takes insects and pollen from flowers. It plucks fruit and carries it to a night roost 25 to 200 m (80 to 650 ft) away to eat it. Observers estimate that nightly each bat carries away from trees more than its own weight in fruit. Jamaican Fruit-eating Bats roost in caves, hollow trees, or in foliage. Breeding is apparently polygynous (a single male mates with more than one female), because small roosts are always found to contain one male plus several females (up to 11) and their dependent young.

Vampire bats are the only mammals that feed exclusively on blood, the only true mammalian parasites. Only three living species of these notorious blood-eating vampires are known, and they range from northern Mexico south to Argentina. All three are found in Perú, and two of them eat blood only from birds (including poultry if available). The COMMON VAMPIRE BAT (Plate 83), however, specializes on mammalian blood. Day roosts are in hollow trees and caves, and they can be instantly recognized by the accumulation of their tar-like droppings. At night, vampires fly out, using both vision (they have larger eyes and better vision than most bats) and sonar to find victims. They not only fly well and quietly, they use the extra long thumb on their wing like a front foot to allow agile walking, running, and hopping – of great assistance in perching on, feeding on, and avoiding swats by their prey. They use their sharp incisor and canine teeth to bite the awake or sleeping animal, often on the neck, and remove a tiny piece of flesh. An anti-clotting agent in the bat's saliva keeps the small wound oozing blood. The vampire laps up the oozing blood – they do not suck it out. The feeding is reported to be painless (we won't ask how researchers know this, but, with a shudder, we can guess). Because blood is mostly water and proteins, which, unlike fats and carbohydrates, cannot be stored easily, each bat must consume a blood meal (of about half its body weight) at least every 60 hours or starve to death. Vampires breed at any time of the year; older young are fed blood from the mother's mouth for several months until they can get their own. Although they rarely feed on humans, when they do, they prefer biting people at sleep on the nose or toes. If you see local people sleeping with a basket over their heads and their feet, or if your host insists you sleep under mosquito netting even when there are no mosquitos around, consider taking appropriate protection. If you don't, those scabs on the end of your nose or fingers in the morning will give you great bragging rights back home.

The SUCKER-FOOTED BAT (Plate 84) is a tiny bat with peculiar, circular adhesive cups on its thumbs and feet. It roosts most commonly in small family groups (2 to 9) in rolled up banana or *Heliconia* leaves or fronds. The "sucker" cups adhere to the leaves. When in a few days the leaf matures and unfurls, the family must seek a new home. Interestingly, unlike most bats, the Sucker-foots in their roosts adhere head upwards. They are common in lowland rain forests and gardens and can be a startling surprise as they fly suddenly out of the young rolled leaf you have just disturbed along the trail. During the night they feed on insects in openings of the forest and along rivers. The BLACK MYOTIS (Plate 84) is a common representative of a group of tiny bats that are distributed widely over the Neotropics. They roost in large groups in hollow trees and buildings; males usually roost separately from females and their young. At sunset they leave the roost in search of flying insects, and return just before dawn. Young are carried by the mother for a few days after birth, but are then left behind with other young in the roost when the female leaves to forage. Pups can fly at about 3 weeks of age, are weaned at 5 to 6 weeks, and are reproductively mature at only 4 months.

Bats are beneficial to forests and to people in a number of ways. Many Neotropical plants have bats, instead of bees or birds, as their main pollinators. These species generally have flowers that open at night and are white, making them easy for bats to find. They also give off a pungent aroma that bats can home in on. Nectar-feeding bats use long tongues to poke into flowers to feed on nectar – a sugary solution – and pollen. As a bat brushes against a flower, pollen adheres to its body, and is then carried to other plants, where it falls and leads to cross-pollination. Fruit-eating bats, owing to their high numbers, are important seed dispersers (see Close-Up, p. 177), helping to regenerate forests by transporting and dropping fruit seeds onto the forest floor. Also, particularly helpful to humans, bats each night consume enormous numbers of annoying insects.

Bats eat a variety of vertebrate animals; unfortunately for some of them, they play right into the bat's hands … uh, feet. Some bats that specialize on eating frogs, it has been discovered, can home in on the calls that male frogs give to attract mates. These frogs are truly in a bind: if they call, they may attract a deadly predator; if they do not, they will lack for female company. Some types of bat prey, on the other hand, have developed anti-bat tactics. Several groups of moth species, for instance, can sense the ultrasonic chirps of some echolocating insectivorous bats; when they do, they react immediately by flying erratically or diving down into vegetation, decreasing the success of the foraging bats. Some moths even make their own clicking sounds, which apparently confuse the bats, causing them to break off approaches.

Relatively little is known about which predators prey on bats. The list however, includes birds-of-prey (owls, hawks), snakes, other mammals such as opossums, cats, and (yes) people, and even other bats, such as the carnivorous False Vampire Bat. Squirrel Monkeys actually hunt tent-roosting bats that they find in tree leaves. Tiny bats, such as the 3 to 5 g (0.1 to 0.2 oz) Black Myotis, are even captured and eaten by large spiders and cockroaches. Bats, logically, are usually captured in or near their roosts, where predators can reliably find and corner them. One strong indication that predation is a real problem for bats is that many species reduce their flying in bright moonlight. Bats showing this "lunar phobia" include the Jamaican Fruit-eating Bat and Short-tailed Fruit Bat. On the other hand, others, like the very small White-lined Sac-winged Bat, do not decrease their activity levels under a full moon, perhaps because they hunt mostly in the darker understory of forests.

Breeding

Bat mating systems are diverse. The males of some species have harems of 2 to 10 females, but various species employ monogamy, polygyny, and/or promiscuity; the breeding behavior of many species has yet to be studied in detail. Some Peruvian species breed at particular times of the year, but others have no regular breeding seasons. Most bats produce a single pup at a time.

Notes

Bats have frightened people for a long time. The result, of course, is that there is a large body of folklore that portrays bats as evil, associated with or incarnations of death, devils, witches, or vampires. Undeniably, it was the bats' alien lives – their activity in the darkness, flying ability, and strange form – and people's ignorance of bats, that were the sources of these myriad superstitions. Many cultures, worldwide, have evil bat legends, from Japan and the Philippines, to Europe, the Middle East, Australia, and Central and South America. Many ancient legends tell of how bats came to be creatures of the night. But the association of bats with vampires – blood-sucking monsters – may have originated in recent times with Bram Stoker, the English author who in 1897 published *Dracula* (the title character, a vampire, could metamorphose into a bat). Vampire bats are native only to the Neotropics. Stoker may have heard stories of their blood-lapping ways from travellers, and for his book, melded the behavior of these bats with legends of vampires from India and from Slavic Gypsy culture. Although not all New World cultures imparted evil reputations to bats, it is not surprising, given the presence of vampire bats, that some did. The Mayans, for instance, associated bats with darkness and death; there was a "bat world," a part of the underworld ruled by a bat god, through which dead people had to pass.

Speaking of vampire bats, they presumably are much more numerous today than in the distant past because they now have domesticated animals as prey. Before the introduction of domesticated animals to the Neotropics, vampires would have had to seek blood meals exclusively from wild animals such as deer and peccaries (two species, however, are specialists on bird blood); now they have, over large parts of their range, herds or flocks of large domesticated animals to feed on. In fact, examinations of blood meals reveal that vampire bats in settled areas feed almost exclusively on ranch and farm animals – cattle, horses, poultry, etc. Vampire bats rarely attack people, although it is not unheard of. Out of fear and ignorance, there is a tendency for local people to kill any large bat. Most of these large bats, however, are fruit and insect-eating bats that are critical for pollination, seed dispersal and insect control. Vampire bat eradication can only be justified in agricultural areas, but it must discriminate and leave unharmed all the other bat species in the area as well as vampire bats living away from settled areas. In some regions, bats, especially vampire bats, may transmit rabies. As most of them will bite in self-defense, it's best to avoid handling any bat bare-handed. If you must handle bats, make sure you have your rabies prophylactic shots and wear gloves.

Status

Determining the statuses of bat populations is difficult because of their nocturnal behavior and habit of roosting in places that are hard to census. With some exceptions, all that is known for most Neotropical species is that they are common or not common, widely or narrowly distributed. Some species are known from only a few museum specimens, or from their discovery in a single cave, but that does not mean that there are not healthy but largely hidden wild populations. Because many forest bats roost in hollow trees, deforestation is obviously a primary threat. Twelve species of Peruvian bats are on the IUCN Red List of Threatened Animals. All the bats profiled here are common or, in the case of the FALSE VAMPIRE BAT, naturally fairly rare. Many bat populations in temperate regions in Europe and the USA are known to be declining and under continued threat by a number of agricultural, forestry and architectural practices. Traditional roost sites have been lost on large scales by mining and quarrying, by the destruction of old buildings, and by changing architectural styles that eliminate many building overhangs, church belfries, etc. Many forestry practices advocate the removal of hollow, dead trees, which frequently provide bats with roosting space. Additionally, farm pesticides are ingested by insects, which are then eaten by bats, leading to death or reduced reproductive success.

Profiles

Greater Fishing Bat, *Noctilio leporinus*, Plate 83a
Jamaican Fruit-eating Bat, *Artibeus jamaicensis*, Plate 83b
Common Vampire Bat, *Desmodus rotundus*, Plate 83c
White-lined Sac-winged Bat, *Saccopteryx bilineata*, Plate 83d
False Vampire Bat, *Vampyrum spectrum*, Plate 83e

Short-tailed Fruit Bat, *Carollia perspicillata*, Plate 84a
Sucker-footed Bat, *Thyroptera tricolor*, Plate 84b
Common Long-tongued Bat, *Glossophaga soricina*, Plate 84c
Long-nosed Bat, *Rhynchonycteris naso*, Plate 84d
Black Myotis, *Myotis nigricans*, Plate 84e

4. Primates

Most people, it seems, find *monkeys* (in Spanish, *monos*) striking, even transfixing, when first encountered, but then responses diverge. Some people adore the little primates and can watch them for hours, whether it be in the wild or at zoos. Others, however, find them a bit, for want of a better word, unalluring – even to the point of making people slightly uncomfortable. It is probably the same characteristic of monkeys that both so attracts people and turns them off, and that is their quasi-humanness. Whether or not we acknowledge it consciously, it is this trait that is the source of all the attention and importance attached to monkeys and apes. They look like us, and, truth be told, they act like us, in a startlingly large number of ways. Aristotle, 2300 years ago, noted similarities between human and nonhuman primates, and Linnaeus, the Swedish originator of our current system for classifying plants and animals, working more than 100 years pre-Darwin, classed people together in the same group with monkeys. Therefore, even before Darwin's ideas provided a possible mechanism for people and monkeys to be distantly related, we strongly suspected there was a link; the resemblance was too close to be accidental. Given this bond between people and other primates, it is not surprising that visitors to parts of the world that support nonhuman primates are eager to see them and very curious about their lives. Fortunately, Perú provides homes for many monkey species, some of them still sufficiently abundant in protected areas to be readily located and observed.

Primates are distinguished by several anatomical and ecological traits. They are primarily arboreal animals. Most are fairly large, very smart, and highly social – they live in permanent social groups. Most have five very flexible fingers and toes per limb. Primates' eyes are in the front of the skull, facing forward (eyes in the front instead of on the sides of the head are required for binocular vision and good depth perception, without which swinging about in trees would be an extremely hazardous and problematic affair), and primates have, for their sizes, relatively large brains. Unlike most other mammals, primates have color vision. Female primates give birth usually to a single, very helpless, infant.

Monkeys are distributed mainly throughout the globe's tropical areas and many subtropical ones, save for the Australian region. They are divided into four groups: (1) *Prosimians* include several families of primitive primates from the Old World. They look the least like people, are mainly small and nocturnal, and include lemurs, lorises, galago (bushbaby), and tarsiers. (2) *Old World Monkeys* (Family Cercopithecidae) include baboons, mandrills, and various monkeys such as rhesus and proboscis monkeys. (3) *New World Monkeys* (Families Callitrichidae and Cebidae) include many kinds of monkeys, marmosets and tamarins. (4) The *Hominoidea* order contains the gibbons, orangutans, chimpanzees, gorillas and ecotravellers.

New World monkeys, in general, have short muzzles and flat, unfurred faces, short necks, long limbs, and long tails that are prehensile in some of the larger species – used as fifth limbs for climbing about in trees. They are day-active animals that spend most of their time in trees, usually coming to the ground only to cross treeless space that they cannot traverse within the forest canopy. About 75 species of New World Monkeys are distributed from southern Mexico to northern Argentina, and 21 occur in Perú (27 if you follow some authorities who consider several isolated populations to be separate species). The New World monkeys are conveniently divided into two major families: the marmosets and tamarins (Family Callitrichidae) and the typical monkeys (Family Cebidae).

The *marmosets* and *tamarins* are tiny to small in size (70 to 600 g, 2.5 to 21 oz) with long tails that are NOT prehensile. Their feet have claws instead of flattened nails, and they typically give birth to twins. Because they are so small, local hunters seldom waste expensive shells on them, and they can be common even in secondary forests near inhabited areas. Only one species of marmoset and six species of tamarin occur in Perú, including the enigmatic and very rare GOELDI'S MONKEY, which is sometimes placed by itself in its own family, Callimiconidae. The *"typical" monkeys* (Plates 86 and 87) are larger (800 to 1500 g, 1.8 to 3.3 lb) and have long tails that in the largest species are prehensile. Their feet have flattened nails, and they give birth to a single young. They are actively hunted and so are among the first native species to disappear from an area after people settle there.

Natural History
Ecology and Behavior
In the lowlands of Amazonian Perú you can find the New World's smallest primate, the PYGMY MARMOSET (Plate 85). Its tiny size (14 cm, 5.5 in, long without tail) and shyness would make it difficult to see if it weren't for its foraging habits. Besides foraging for insects under bark and leaves in mature lowland Amazonian forests, it gouges out small pits in the trunks of trees with its front teeth, usually low down on the trunk. Sap oozes from these wounds, and the marmosets return again and again to lap up the sap and make new holes, sometimes up to a hundred on a single tree. If you can find a tree with these holes, wait quietly below it, and eventually you will be rewarded with the sight of a single marmoset or small family group jumping to land on the trunk. The home range of a family group is often less than a hectare (2.5 acres), so if you listen carefully near a feeding tree, they can usually be heard somewhere nearby giving their grasshopper-type calls and high-pitched whistles.

The tamarins in Perú are all restricted to the lowlands of the Amazon. All travel in noisy troops giving chirps and twitters that sound more bird-like than primate-like. They feed in mid levels of the forest and dense vine tangles on fruits, insects, flower nectar and occasionally lizards and birds. The very rare GOELDI'S MONKEY is all black and travels very close to or even on the ground. It is seen most often trailing a troop of other species of tamarins.

Titis are small monkeys (1.2 kg, 2.6 lb) with thickly furred, nonprehensile tails that hang straight down. They travel in small family groups and feed on fruits and frequently on leaves, especially bamboo. They have very small home ranges that often center on a dense tree fall or vine tangle, where they spend the night. Although the DUSKY TITI MONKEY (Plate 85) of lowland (below 850 m, 2800 ft) Amazonian Perú is rarely seen, you will almost certainly hear it. The male and female duet early in the morning and at dusk with loud chimpanzee-like whoops that no-one can miss. Because of its small home range, small size and retiring behavior, this is often the only monkey species remaining in extensively cleared parts of the forest. Apparently all it needs to prosper is a small patch of trees and some dense tangle to hide in.

The COMMON SQUIRREL MONKEY (Plate 86) lacks a prehensile tail, and with its white eye mask, black snout and large noisy troop behavior is unmistakable throughout the lowlands of the Peruvian Amazon. Squirrel monkeys feed on fruits, insects and some leaves and are often found associating with a troop of capuchin monkeys. A troop (5 to 40 individuals) usually consists of several adult males and many females and their dependent young, although during non-breeding portions of the year the sexes may separate into uni-sex groups. Squirrel monkeys apparently do not defend exclusive territories: observers have noticed that the home ranges of troops frequently overlap, and they will often tolerate a coalescing of troops into a monstrous supertroop. During a one-month period, a troop may range back and forth over an area (home range) of about 2 sq km (0.8 sq miles). These monkeys are commonly spotted in trees near water – along lake shores, rivers and swamps.

The WHITE-FRONTED CAPUCHIN (Plate 86) is a larger monkey (2.3 kg, 5 lb) that often travels in large and noisy troops. Its white face and light snout as well as its coiled and semi-prehensile tail distinguish it from other monkeys. The BROWN CAPUCHIN MONKEY of the Amazonian lowlands is distinguished by its overall brown color, black cap, tail and legs and a dark vertical line in front of each ear. Capuchins are highly arboreal, but also versatile – they forage over all levels of the forest, from canopy to lower tree trunks, and they also occasionally come to the ground to feed. Their diet is broad, consisting mainly of ripe fruit and insects, but also bird eggs, young birds, baby squirrels, and small lizards. (Although they rarely attack larger animals, one male capuchin was observed to attack a 1.7 m (6 ft) long Green Iguana (Plate 16) and break off and eat the end of its tail.) In one study, a troop was found to consume 20% animal prey (mostly insects), 65% fruit, and 15% green plant material; but insects make up 50% or more of the diet during some periods of the year. Capuchins are very active monkeys, spending 80% or more of daylight hours moving through the forest, foraging in any number of ways, such as looking through leaves and leaf litter, pulling bark off trees, and rolling over sticks and logs. A troop, 2 to 30 strong (often 6 to 10), consisting usually of a single adult male plus females and their young, travels an average of about 2 km (1.2 miles) per day, while remaining within a fairly small home range of a few square km (about a square mile). Troops maintain exclusive territories, aggressively defending their turf whenever they meet other troops of the same species at territorial boundaries.

The COMMON WOOLLY MONKEY (Plate 86) is a large species (males regularly weigh more than 10 kg, 22 lb) with a true prehensile tail. The body color can vary from gray to brown, but the face is almost always darker. Woolly Monkeys feed mostly on fruit and seeds and occasionally on insects and leaves from the canopy of tall forests of the Amazonian lowlands. They move in large, noisy troops giving musical trills, barks and whoops, and each troop needs a minimum of 500 hectares (1200 acres) for a home range. This species is considered in Perú the most desirable monkey for eating, and this hunting pressure, combined with a female being able to give birth only every other year, makes it especially vulnerable to human pressures. Even when protection is provided, populations take a long time to recover.

The WHITE-BELLIED SPIDER MONKEY (Plate 87) is the longest monkey species in Perú, with males reaching up to 1.5 m (5 ft), including the tail. They stay mostly within a forest's upper canopy, rarely descending to the ground, and move quickly through trees using their fully prehensile tail as a fifth limb to climb, swing, and hang. They are known to feed occasionally at night, but they typically feed in the early morning and late afternoon. Spider monkeys eat young leaves and flowers but are especially fond of hard palm fruits. During the day, troops, varying in size from 2 to 25 or more (groups of 100 or more have been reported), range over wide swaths of forest, but stay within a home range of 2.5 to 4.0 sq km (1 or 2 sq miles). Troops usually consist of an adult male and several females and their dependent offspring. Spider monkeys are commonly observed in small groups, often two animals, but frequently they are members of a larger troop; the troop breaks up daily into small foraging parties, then coalesces each evening at a mutual sleeping tree.

Howlers inhabit a variety of forest habitats, but prefer lowland forests. The RED HOWLER MONKEY (Plate 87) is relatively common in the Amazon from 1200 m (4000 ft) down into the lowlands. Howlers are highly arboreal and rarely come to the ground; typically they spend most of their time in the upper reaches of the forest. In contrast to the other monkey species, howlers are relatively slow-moving and more deliberate in their canopy travels. They eat fruit and a lot of leafy material; in fact, in one study, leaves comprised 64% of their diet, fruit and flowers, 31%. Owing to their specialization on a super-abundant food resource – leaves – their home ranges need not be, and are not, very large. Most troops have 10 to 20 individuals, which are made up of females, associated young, and usually one male in Red Howler troops, and multiple males in Mantled Howler troops. Howlers are frequently inconspicuous because they are slow-moving and often quiet, and many people on trails pass directly below howlers without noticing them. They are most assuredly not inconspicuous, however, when the males let loose with their amazing lion-like roaring, which is amplified and modulated by a special bony plate over the throat. Their very loud, deep choruses of roars, at dawn, during late afternoon, and, frequently, during heavy rain, are a characteristic and wonderful part of the rainforest environment. (The initial response of a newcomer to the Neotropics, upon being awakened in the morning by howling howlers, is sure to be "Now what the heck is THAT?") These vocalizations are probably used by the howlers to communicate with other troops, to advertise their locations and to defend them; although troops of these monkeys do not maintain exclusive territories, they do appear to defend current feeding sites. The males' howling can be heard easily at 3 km (1.8 miles) away in a forest or 5 km (3 miles) away across water.

Saki monkeys (Plate 87) are medium sized (up to 2.25 kg, 5 lb) species with long thick hair and nonprehensile tails that are thickly furred. They forage primarily on fruits, seeds and a few leaves, and usually are seen in small family groups of 2 to 4. They wander and feed from the lower canopy down to mid levels of lowland forests in the Amazonian region and are often hard to see because of their shy and retiring behavior. You are most likely to see sakis along streams and lakes as they sit without moving in a low tree, only their long bushy tails hanging straight down telling you they're not just another tangle of dead leaves.

The *night*, or *owl*, *monkeys* are, as their name suggests, active primarily at night. They are relatively small (1 kg, 2.2 lb) with a two-colored tail tipped in black that is nonprehensile. At night, their large eyes reflect light, and they can only be mistaken for an opossum or Kinkajou, neither of which has the striking black and white facial pattern. They feed mostly on fruits in small family groups. The taxonomy of the night monkeys is controversial, with some scientists identifying up to 8 species in Central and South America. In eastern Perú, the NOISY NIGHT MONKEY (Plate 87) occurs in east slope cloud forests as high as 3000 m (9800 ft) and down into the Amazonian lowlands. Your best chance of seeing it is from a canoe at night as you drift along the edge of a forested lake or stream. Look for eye-shine and listen for its low, distinctive three-note hoots that sound like an owl. Occasionally you can see them in the light late in the afternoon as they begin to forage, usually at forest edges.

A variety of animals prey on Perú's monkeys, including Boa Constrictors (Plate 14), birds-of-prey such as eagles (Plate 35), arboreal cats such as Jaguarundi and Margay (Plate 90), and people. Other causes of death are disease, such as yellow fever, and parasite infestations, such as that by *botflies*. Botflies lay their eggs on mosquitos, monkeys being exposed when infected mosquitos land on them to feed. Botfly larvae burrow into a monkey's skin and develop there for ten weeks before emerging as adults. Many howlers, for instance, are observed to have severe botfly infestations of their necks, seen as swollen lumps and the holes created when adult botflies emerge from the monkey's body. In one Panamanian study, each member of a howler population had an average of 2 to 5 botfly parasites; several monkeys in the study died, apparently of high levels of botfly infestation.

Monkeys are especially crucial elements of rainforest ecosystems because they are seed dispersers for many hundreds of plant species, particularly of the larger canopy trees. Mammals transport seeds that stick to their fur from the producing tree to the places where the seeds eventually fall off. Mammals that are *frugivores* (fruit-eaters) also carry fruit away from a tree, then eat the soft parts and drop the seeds, which may later germinate; or they eat the fruit whole and transport the seeds in their digestive tracts. The seeds eventually fall, unharmed, to the ground and germinate (see Close-Up, p. 177). Monkeys, it turns out, are major seed dispersers. For example, in Panamá, a troop of capuchins was estimated to disperse each day more than 300,000 tiny seeds of a single tree species; up to two-thirds of the seeds that passed through the monkeys' digestive systems later germinated (a proportion that was actually higher than seeds that made it to the ground without passing through an animal gut). Monkeys also assist plants in another way: Capuchins eat so many insects that they probably have a significant effect in reducing insect damage to trees. Because some monkeys eat leaves, they also harm trees, but reports are very rare of primates stripping all the leaves from trees, killing them. Also, monkeys at times are seed predators. They extract seeds from fruit and chew them, destroying them, and also eat young fruits and nuts that contain seeds too undeveloped ever to germinate.

Most monkey troops are quite noisy as they forage, moving quickly about in trees and also vocalizing. A variety of other animals take advantage of monkey foraging, apparently attracted by the noise-making: squirrel monkeys and the DOUBLE-TOOTHED KITE (Plate 34) regularly follow capuchins, catching large insects that the capuchins scare up as they move. Various ground-dwellers such as agouti (Plate 92) and peccaries (Plate 91) often congregate under foraging troops, feeding on dropped fruit.

Breeding

Female monkeys in Perú usually produce a single young (tamarins and marmosets two) that is born furred and with its eyes open. The tamarins, marmosets, and most of the small "typical" monkeys, such as titis, night monkeys and sakis, are monogamous, but the SADDLE-BACKED TAMARIN (Plate 85) appears to be occasionally polyandrous – one female mates with two males (a behavior so rare among mammals that scientists are still amazed). The male of these species carries the young until they are large enough to forage on their own. The other monkeys are polygynous, with a male having a harem of 2 to 5 females. The squirrel monkeys, however, are promiscuous, and a male mates with several females in the troop in a sexual scramble. In polygynous and promiscuous species the female carries the young. Squirrel monkeys, which live up to 21 years in captivity, begin reproducing at 3 (females) to 5 (males) years old. The young cling to their mother after birth and are not truly independent until about a year old. Pregnancy is between 160 and 172 days. Mating is during the dry season, with births occurring during the wet season. Female capuchins reach sexual maturity at 3 to 4 years of age, then give birth at 1 to 2 year intervals. Most births occur during the dry season. Young cling to the mother's fur immediately following birth, and are carried by the mothers for 5 to 6 months, until they can travel on their own. Pregnancy is about 180 days. Capuchins live up to 46 years in captivity. Spider monkeys appear to have no regular breeding seasons. Females reach sexual maturity at about 4 years old (males at about 5), then give birth every 2 to 4 years after pregnancies of about 230 days. Young, which weigh about 500 g (a pound) at birth, are carried by the mother for up to 10 months and are nursed for up to a year. Upon reaching sexual maturity, young females leave their troops to find mates in other troops; males remain with their birth troop. Spider monkeys have lived for 33 years in captivity. Female howlers reach sexual maturity at 3 to 4 years of age. They give birth following pregnancies of about 180 days. At 3 months, youngsters begin making brief trips away from their mothers, but until a year old, they continue to spend most of their time on their mother's back; they are nursed until they are 10 to 12 months old. Howlers have survived in the wild for up to 20 years.

Notes

The current range of the RED-BACKED SQUIRREL MONKEY, restricted to fragmented regions on the Pacific coasts of Panama and Costa Rica, is at least 500 km (300 miles) distant from the nearest South American squirrel monkey populations. The discontinuous nature of the distributions is puzzling, and it has led biogeographers to suggest that squirrel monkeys may have arrived in Central America only with the help of people; that is, they may have been introduced there by travellers from South to Central America in Pre-Columbian times.

Owing to their active lifestyles, intelligence, and mischievousness, capuchins are sought after as pets and as "organ-grinder" monkeys; consequently, they are probably the most numerous captive monkeys in North America and Europe. Trade in capuchins for pets, however, is now illegal.

Status

All New World monkeys are listed in CITES Appendix II as species that, although they may not be currently threatened, need to be highly regulated in trade, or they could soon become threatened. The IUCN Red List includes six species of Peruvian primates – GOELDI'S MONKEY, ANDEAN NIGHT MONKEY, BALD UKARI, WHITE-BELLIED SPIDER MONKEY (Plate 87), ANDEAN TITI MONKEY, and YELLOW-TAILED WOOLLY MONKEY (Plate 86). Main menaces to monkeys are deforestation – elimination of their natural habitats – and poaching for trade and meat. The larger monkeys – especially woolly, spiders and howlers – are often hunted for their meat, and therefore are usually rare near human settlements. CENTRAL AMERICAN SPIDER and MANTLED HOWLER MONKEYS are listed as endangered by CITES Appendix I and USA ESA; however, even given their fragmented populations, both are still fairly abundant in protected areas.

Profiles

Dusky Titi Monkey, *Callicebus moloch*, Plate 85a
Emperor Tamarin, *Saguinus imperator*, Plate 85b
Saddle-backed Tamarin, *Saguinus fuscicollis*, Plate 85c

Pygmy Marmoset, *Cebuella pygmaea*, Plate 85d

Common Squirrel Monkey, *Saimiri sciureus*, Plate 86a
White-fronted Capuchin, *Cebus albifrons*, Plate 86b
Common Woolly Monkey, *Lagothrix lagothricha*, Plate 86c
Yellow-tailed Woolly Monkey, *Lagothrix flavicauda*, Plate 86d

Monk Saki Monkey, *Pithecia monachus*, Plate 87a
Noisy Night Monkey, *Aotus vociferans*, Plate 87b
Red Howler Monkey, *Alouatta seniculus*, Plate 87c
White-bellied Spider Monkey, *Ateles belzebuth*, Plate 87d

5. Carnivores

Carnivores are ferocious mammals – including the cat that sleeps on your pillow and the dog that takes table scraps from your hand – that are specialized to kill and eat other vertebrate animals. They all share clawed toes and teeth customized to grasp, rip, and tear flesh – witness their large, cone-shaped canines. Most are meat-eaters, but many are at least somewhat omnivorous, taking fruits and other plant materials. Carnivore populations tend to be sparse and individuals notoriously difficult to see at any time. They range in size from weasels 9 cm (3.5 in) long to bears 3 m (10 ft) long. Five families within the Order Carnivora have Peruvian representatives: *dogs, bears, raccoons, weasels* and *cats*. Of these, only the raccoon family is unique to the New World; the others are widely represented throughout the Old World as well.

The 36 species in the worldwide dog family (Canidae) include wolves, coyotes, foxes and hunting dogs. They are all highly adapted for running; their feet are arranged so that they bear weight on the toes; and they tend to be highly vocal. The bear family (Ursidae) is made up of 8 species of large and robust animals. They have poor eyesight but excellent powers of hearing and smell, and they tend to be highly omnivorous as well as scavengers. The raccoon family (Procyonidae) includes medium-sized species that carry their full weight on the soles of the feet and have long tails, both of which help with maneuverability and balance in their largely arboreal habitats. They are omnivorous and largely nocturnal. The weasel family (Mustelidae) includes weasels, stoats, skunks, minks, wolverines and badgers and is characterized by relatively long bodies, short legs, and walking on the soles of the feet. Most have dense, soft fur and a gland that produces chemicals with powerful odors. Their extremely powerful jaws and sharp teeth can kill large prey quickly. Members of the cat family (Felidae) bear weight on their toes and have retractable claws. They are completely carnivorous and use their extremely sharp and long teeth to dispatch prey with a bite to the back of the head or neck. They tend to have excellent vision, including color vision. They have a short nose and their eyes are set at the front of the head to maximize depth perception.

Natural History
Ecology and Behavior

Dogs. The dogs have 5 representatives in Perú, only two of which you might encounter on your trip, but these encounters will probably be in the form of tracks or *scats* (droppings). The ANDEAN, or CULPEO, FOX (Plate 88) is relatively common in open habitats from the coast up to the puna above 3600 m (12,000 ft). Its long, thin droppings and footprints are common in some areas. It can be quite bold at times and is active day and night. It preys on small mammals and birds, but occasionally scavenges dead animals such as llamas and sheep. The SECHURAN FOX is a small, pale species restricted in Perú to the coastal deserts of the northern and central coasts.

Bears. Only one species of bear occurs in South America, the SPECTACLED BEAR (Plate 88), and it is restricted to cloud forests and puna of the Andes above 1800 m (6000 ft). This large species (200 kg, 440 lb), active both day and night, is solitary and extremely shy. Even some scientists studying it for two or three years have seen nothing of it but tracks, scat, and claw marks on trees. The bears eat mainly tubers, bromeliad buds and other vegetable matter dug out with their powerful claws, but if given the opportunity, they will not turn down a juicy rodent or the chance to scavenge a dead deer or cow. They are usually on the ground but are also amazingly agile tree climbers. Their predilection for corn (maize) sometimes makes them easy to see, as often they will become quite bold around this food source. Unfortunately, local farmers whose corn crops are being raided often shoot bears. These bears live up to 30 years in captivity.

Raccoons. The raccoons make up a New World group of about 15 species (until recently, the Asian Red Panda was thought also to be in this group). Five species occur in Perú, but you are only likely to see a few of them. The most visible ones are *coatis*. Although adult males are usually solitary, female SOUTH AMERICAN COATIS (Plate 88) and juveniles often occur in large groups of up to 30 that move through the undergrowth and mid-levels of trees making barks, whines and other noises. Coatis are immediately recognized by their long tails held vertically as they walk on the ground or along branches. They use their long noses and hand-like fore-paws to investigate every nook and cranny for insects, fruits and small vertebrates. The other frequently seen *procyonid* in Perú is the KINKAJOU (Plate 88), which is limited to moist lowland forests of the Amazon. Kinkajous are nocturnal, solitary and spend most of their time in trees, foraging for fruits and arboreal vertebrates. Alone among the procyonids, their long, thin tail is fully prehensile, permitting them to grasp branches with it and hang upside down. Your best chance for seeing one is by walking out into the forest at night and looking for their eye-shine reflected in the light of your flashlight. They can often be spotted moving about tree branches at night, making squeaking sounds; several often feed together in a single tree. If you are really lucky, you may catch a glimpse of a CRAB-EATING RACCOON (Plate 88) as you quietly float in a canoe at night along a forested stream or lake in the lowlands of Amazonian Perú. This species occurs from Costa Rica to Argentina, but nowhere is it common, and its natural history is poorly known. They are associated with open areas along water and, although omnivores, seem to prefer to eat clams, fish and crabs. They spend the day sleeping in dens, and the best evidence of their presence, short of seeing one, is looking for their small, human-like foot- and hand-prints in wet mud along water.

Weasels. The weasel family is comprised of about 70 species of small and medium-sized, slender-bodied carnivores that are distributed globally except for Australia and Antarctica. In Perú the family is represented by 9 species of weasels, skunks, and otters, but only three are commonly sighted. TAYRA (TIE-rah, Plate 89) are large tree climbers that will often descend to search the ground for a variety of foods – fruit, bird eggs or nestlings, lizards, rodents, rabbits and insects. Although they are often wary animals, they can be quite bold at times and are among the most frequently sighted of the *mustelids*, especially when attracted to fruits in gardens and orchards. STRIPED HOG-NOSED SKUNKS

(Plate 89) are nocturnal and forage solitarily on the ground, where they root about a good deal in the leaf litter and soil, looking for insects, snails, and small vertebrates such as rodents and lizards; occasionally they take fruit. Skunks, with their spray defenses (see below), usually move quite leisurely, apparently knowing that they are well protected from most predators. The LONG-TAILED WEASEL (Plate 89) is one of the most fascinating of the mustelids, largely because the same species occurs from Canada all the way south into Bolivia. In the northern part of its range, it turns white in the winter, but in Central and South America it remains the same color year round. This small mammal (30 cm, 1 ft, long) has to be one of the most ferocious for its size in the world. It runs down narrow burrows and captures rodents and rabbits more than ten times its size, but it also eats birds and lizards in open areas of grassland and bushes above 1000 m (3300 ft). It is active both day and night. Your best chance of seeing one is as it stands up on its hind feet in the puna to survey an area or check on who you are. Weasels are very bold, and if you stand still and squeak like a bird in distress, it is relatively easy to attract them right up to your feet. The GIANT OTTER (Plate 89) once occurred throughout Amazonian South America from Venezuela to northern Argentina, but it is now absent from most of this range. Its huge size (up to 2 m, 6.5 ft, and 34 kg, 75 lb) and noisy vocalizations in family groups of 5 to 8 make it easy to find. Its luxurious pelt makes it a target of intense persecution by people. It remains now only in isolated and highly protected patches of its former range. Otters are active both during the day and at night, hunting in streams, rivers and ponds for fish and crustaceans such as crayfish. Although otters always remain in or near the water, they spend their inactive time in burrows on land. Adapted with webbed feet, flattened tail and a sleek form for moving swiftly and smoothly through water, they move on land awkwardly, with a duck-like waddle. There are only a few places left in Amazonian Perú where you can still hear the haunting whistles, screams and hums of a group of these wondrous animals as they frolic in the water of an isolated stream or lake. If you do experience the sight and sounds of this otter, it will be a memory you will never forget. The smaller MARINE OTTER (Plate 89) is rare along Perú's coastal waters. It is the only marine otter in South America.

Cats. Because all 6 species of cats that occur in Perú are fairly rare, some to the point of being endangered, and because of their mainly nocturnal habits, your chances are slim of seeing even a single wild cat on any brief trip. More than likely, all that you will see of cats are traces; some tracks in the mud near a stream or scratch marks on a tree trunk or log. (Although some communication is vocal, cats also signal each other by making scratch marks on vegetation and by leaving urine and feces to scent-mark areas.)

In Perú, the cat species can be placed into two groups – spotted or unspotted. The 4 spotted species generally are yellowish, tan, or cinnamon on top and white below, with black spots and stripes on their heads, bodies, and legs. The smallest is the ONCILLA, or LITTLE SPOTTED CAT, the size of a small house cat. The largest is the JAGUAR (Plate 90), which is the largest New World cat and the region's largest carnivore, weighing between 60 and 120 kg (130 to 260 lb). The two unspotted cats are the mid-sized JAGUARUNDI (Plate 90), which is black-ish, brown, gray, or reddish, and the PUMA (Plate 90), or MOUNTAIN LION, which is tan or grayish and almost as large as the Jaguar. The Puma, which occurs from the Arctic Circle of North America to Tierra del Fuego in extreme southern South America, has one of the largest geographical ranges of any animal. Female cats of most species are smaller than males, up to a third smaller in the Jaguar. The cats are finely adapted to prey on vertebrate animals, and hunting methods are extremely similar among the various species. They do not run to chase prey for long distances. Rather, cats slowly stalk their prey or wait in ambush, then capture the prey after pouncing on it or after a very brief, fast chase. Biologists are often impressed by the consistency in the manner that cats kill their prey. Almost always it is with a sharp bite to the neck or head, breaking the neck or crushing the skull. Retractile claws, in addition to their use in grabbing and holding prey, give cats good abilities to climb trees, and some of them are partially arboreal animals, foraging and even sleeping in trees.

Aside from some highly social large cats of Africa, most cats are solitary animals, foraging alone, individuals coming together only to mate. Some species are territorial but in others individuals overlap in the areas in which they hunt. Cats, with their big eyes to gather light, are often nocturnal, especially those of rainforests, but some are also active by day. When inactive, they shelter in rock crevices or burrows dug by other animals. Cats are the most carnivorous of the carnivores, that is their diets are more centered on meat than any of the other families. Little is known of the natural history of forest-dwelling Oncillas beyond that they eat birds and small rodents. MARGAYS (Plate 90) are mostly arboreal forest cats that forage in trees for rodents and birds. OCELOTS (Plate 90) eat rodents, snakes, lizards, and birds. They are probably more common than Oncillas and Margays and, although they are quite secretive, they are the most frequently seen of the spotted cats. Active mainly at night, they often spend daylight hours asleep in trees. They also tend to be the most adaptable to human presence, especially if a chicken coop is involved. *El Tigre* (*Otorongo* in the Quechua language), the Jaguar, can be active day or night. These cats inhabit low and middle elevation forests, hunting for large prey such as peccary and deer, but also monkeys, birds, lizards, even caiman. Jaguarundi are both day- and night-active, and are usually seen in forests. They eat small rodents, rabbits and birds. Puma occupy various habitat types from puna to evergreen forest to desert scrub, and they prey on deer and other large mammals.

Breeding

Most dogs are monogamous and although they often dig their own dens for the young, they are not above taking over a hole made by an armadillo or some other burrowing animal, enlarging and modifying it for their own use. The large litter of young is born naked and blind. Pups are fed by both parents even after they emerge from the den. After mating, the fertilized egg of the SPECTACLED BEAR female does not implant in the uterus for several months, a trait apparently held over from its northern cousins, whose semi-hibernation forces them to extend pregnancy so that the young aren't born too early. Spectacled Bears give birth in a den to 1 to 3 naked and helpless young. They are cared for by only the mother for the next 3 years or so until the next litter is born. Mortality among the young is extremely high.

Among all the Peruvian procyonids, females raise young without help from males. Young are born in nests made in trees. Duration of pregnancy varies from about 65 days in raccoons, to about 75 days in coatis, to about 115 days in KINKAJOUS. Raccoons have 3 to 7 young per litter, coatis, 1 to 5 young, and Kinkajous, always only one. Female mustelids give birth in dens under rocks or in crevices, or in burrows under trees. Pregnancy for TAYRA, skunks, and otters usually lasts about 60 to 70 days. Tayra produce an average of two young per litter, skunk, 4 or 5, and otter, 2 or 3. As is true for many of the carnivores, mustelid young are born blind and helpless. Male and female cats of the Neotropics come together only to mate; the female bears and raises her young alone. She gives birth in a den that is a burrow, rock cave, or tree cavity. The young are sheltered in the den while the female forages; she returns periodically to nurse and bring the kittens prey to eat. Most of the cats have one or two young at a time, although PUMA and JAGUAR may have up to four. Pregnancy is about 75 days in the smaller cats, about 100 in the large ones. Juvenile Jaguars remain with their mother for up to 18 months, learning to be efficient hunters, before they go off on their own.

Notes

JAGUAR rarely attack people, who normally are given a wide berth; these cats tend to run away quickly when spotted. Cats in Perú are sometimes seen walking at night along forest trails or roads. General advice if you happen to stumble across a large cat: do not run because that often stimulates a cat to chase. Face the cat, make yourself large by raising your arms, and make as much loud noise as you can.

To the Arakmbut forest people of Amazonian Perú, "*toto*" are harmful spirits that live mainly in the forest. Their predominant activity is cutting down trees; when trees fall mysteriously, locals say that is the toto at work. It is no surprise, therefore, that the Jaguar is considered a major form of toto, invoked often to indicate the dangers that lurk in the forest. For instance, to warn pregnant women of the hazards of walking alone in the forest, the story is told of a woman who knows she might be attacked, but thinks that if she can make it to the river, she will be safe from the big cats. She tries to dash through the forest to the river, but the cats are quicker, and catch her. The Arakmbut people also place chosen small children on a balsa wood platform, wash them carefully, then paint spots on them to enable them to become Jaguar spirits. These children are thought to grow to become powerful warriors who, when the need arises, can transform themselves into real Jaguars to kill the community's enemies.

Mustelids have scent glands on their backsides that produces a secretion called *musk*, which has a strong, characteristic odor. These secretions are used to communicate with other members of the species by marking territories as well as to signal availability for breeding and courtship. In skunks, these glands produce particularly strong, foul-smelling fluids that with startling good aim can be violently squirted in a jet at potential predators. The fluids are not toxic and cannot cause blindness as is sometimes commonly believed, but they can cause temporary, severe irritation of eyes and nose. Most predators that approach a skunk once rarely repeat the exercise.

One facet of mustelid natural history that is particularly helpful to people, though not universally appreciated, is that these carnivores eat a staggering number of rodents. For instance, it has been calculated that weasels each year in New York State eat some 60 million mice and millions of rats. In fact, in the past, TAYRA were kept as pets in parts of South America to protect homes and belongings from rodents.

Status

All of the Neotropical cats are now threatened or actually endangered (MARGAY, ONCILLA, and JAGUAR are listed by CITES Appendix I and USA ESA, as are

Central American populations of PUMA, JAGUARUNDI, and OCELOT. The ANDEAN CAT, a smaller cat that ranges from central Perú to northern Chile and Argentina, is listed as threatened on the IUCN Red List). Their habitats are increasingly cleared for agricultural purposes, they were, and still are to a limited extent, hunted for their skins, and large cats are killed as potential predators on livestock and pets. Jaguar have been eliminated from much of Perú and now are only present in small numbers in protected areas.

Many mustelids in the past were trapped intensively for their fur, which is often soft, dense and glossy, just the ticket, in fact, to create coats of otter or weasel, mink or marten, sable or fisher. The GIANT OTTER is sufficiently rare to be considered endangered (CITES APPENDIX I, USA ESA, and IUCN Red List). The COLOMBIAN WEASEL, the MARINE OTTER, SPECTACLED BEAR, and BUSH DOG are also considered threatened species in Perú, on the IUCN Red List. TAYRA are common animals that usually do well even where people disturb their natural habitats. Another Peruvian mustelid, the GRISON (Plate 89), a grayish and black weasel-like animal, is fairly rare and may be threatened.

Profiles

Kinkajou, *Potos flavus*, Plate 88a
Crab-eating Raccoon, *Procyon cancrivorus*, Plate 88b
Spectacled Bear, *Tremarctos ornatus*, Plate 88c
South American Coati, *Nasua nasua*, Plate 88d
Andean Fox, *Pseudalopex culpaeus*, Plate 88e

Giant Otter, *Pteronura brasiliensis*, Plate 89a
Marine Otter, *Lontra felina*, Plate 89b
Tayra, *Eira barbara*, Plate 89c
Long-tailed Weasel, *Mustela frenata*, Plate 89d
Grison, *Galictis vittata*, Plate 89e
Striped Hog-nosed Skunk, *Conepatus semistriatus*, Plate 89f

Jaguarundi, *Herpailurus yaguaroundi*, Plate 90a
Ocelot, *Leopardus pardalis*, Plate 90b
Margay, *Leopardus wiedii*, Plate 90c
Jaguar, *Panthera onca*, Plate 90d
Puma, *Puma concolor*, Plate 90e

6. Peccaries, Deer, and Llama Relatives

Peccaries, *deer*, and *llamas* (YA-mas) are three Neotropical representatives of the Order Artiodactyla, the globally distributed hoofed mammals (*ungulates*) with even numbers of toes on each foot. Other *artiodactyls* are pigs, hippos, giraffes, antelope, bison, buffalo, cattle, gazelles, goats and sheep. In general, the group is specialized to feed on leaves, grass and fallen fruit.

Three peccary species comprise the Family Tayassuidae. They are confined in their distributions to the Neotropics, although one species pushes northwards into the southwestern USA, where it is often called JAVELINA; two species, the COLLARED PECCARY (Plate 91) and WHITE-LIPPED PECCARY (Plate 91), occur in Amazonian Perú. Peccaries are small to medium-sized hog-like animals covered with coarse, bristly, longish hair, with slender legs, large heads, small ears, and short tails. They have enlarged, sharp and pointed, tusk-like canine teeth. The Collared Peccary is the smaller of the two Peruvian species, adults typically weighing 17 to 30 kg (35 to 75 lb). They come in black or gray as adults, with a band of lighter-colored hair at the neck that furnishes their name; youngsters are reddish-brown or buff-colored. The White-lipped Peccary, named for the white patch of hair on its chin, weighs 25 to 40 kg (55 to 85 lb). Collared Peccaries are more abundant than the White-lipped Peccary, occur in more habitats, and are seen more frequently.

The deer family, Cervidae, has 43 species worldwide, 6 in Perú. Only 2, however, are common enough that you are likely to see them, the WHITE-TAILED DEER (Plate 91) and RED BROCKET DEER (Plate 91). Deer are large mammals with long, thin legs, short tails, and big ears. Males have antlers that they shed each year and regrow. The White-tailed Deer has a remarkably broad distribution from southern Canada to Bolivia. This species does not occur in lowland rainforests, and in Perú it is most common in cleared areas on the Andean slopes at mid-elevations and in river border forests of drier coastal lowlands. South American White-tailed Deer (30 to 50 kg, 65 to 110 lb) are, in general, slightly larger than Red Brocket Deer (24 to 48 kg, 50 to 100 lb), but usually smaller, by a third to a half, than members of their species in the USA and Canada. Very young deer usually have white spots. The Red-brocket Deer, strictly a forest species, is found throughout the lowlands of the Amazon. Both the largest and smallest deer species in South America occur in Perú. The MARSH DEER is the largest (1.1 m, 3.6 ft, at the shoulder), and the NORTHERN PUDU (Plate 91) is the smallest (38 cm, 15 in, at the shoulder).

Llamas and *alpacas* are domestic varieties of the camel family familiar to most travellers. This family (Camelidae) is one of the most primitive of the even-toed ungulates, with only a three-chambered stomach, toes that bear nails rather than hooves, no horns, and (for those of you who really want to impress your fellow travellers) no gall bladder. The llama and alpaca, both found in Perú, were domesticated from wild species several thousand years ago, but the wild species from which they were bred are likely extinct. The two living, wild species of the camel family in South America also both occur in Perú. The smaller VICUÑA (Plate 94) and the larger GUANACO both have the long legs, long slender neck and camel-like heads typical of the group, but their reddish orange backs with whitish under-parts separate them from their domestic cousins.

Natural History
Ecology and Behavior

Peccaries are day-active, highly social animals, rarely encountered singly. COLLARED PECCARIES travel in small groups of 3 to 25 or so, most frequently 6 to 9; WHITE-LIPPED PECCARY herds generally are larger, often 50 to 100 or more (smaller herds occur where they are heavily hunted). They travel single file along narrow forest paths, spreading out when good foraging sites are found. These animals are omnivores, but mainly they dig into the ground with their snouts, *rooting* for vegetation. Peccaries feed on roots, underground stems, and bulbs, but also leaves, fruit (the White-lipped Peccary, with extra-strong jaw muscles, is better adapted for eating hard palm fruits), insects, and even small vertebrates that they stumble across. Because White-lipped Peccaries are larger than Collared Peccaries and travel in larger groups, they need to wander long distances each day to locate enough food. Like pigs, peccaries often wallow in mud and shallow water, and there is usually a customary wallowing spot within their home ranges, the area within which a group lives and forages. During dry seasons, peccaries may gather in large numbers near lakes or streams. Because peccaries are hunted by people, they are usually quiet, wary, and therefore, sometimes hard to notice or approach. Besides their tracks, you can detect that a group has just passed by a cloyingly sweaty smell that lingers after them for a half hour or more in the undergrowth of a forest. Peccaries are preyed upon by large snakes such as boas, and by Puma and Jaguar.

Deer eat leaves and twigs from trees and shrubs that they can reach from the ground (*browsing*), and grass (*grazing*). The RED BROCKET DEER, in particular, also eats fruit and flowers, chiefly those that have already fallen to the ground. WHITE-TAILED DEER inhabit open places and forest edge areas, rarely dense forest, whereas the Red Brocket Deer is a forest species that wanders through terrain with no trails. The large, branched antlers of male White-tails make moving through dense forest a dubious business; male Red Brocket Deer, on the other hand, have short, spike-like, rearwards-curving antlers – plainly better for maneuvering in their dense jungle habitats. Both White-tailed Deer and Red Brocket Deer are active during daylight hours and also often at night, although Red Brocket Deer are most commonly seen during early mornings and at dusk. White-tailed Deer travel either solitarily or in small groups, whereas Red Brocket Deer are almost always solitary. The very rare MARSH DEER is limited to extensive marshy grasslands, and in Perú is found only in the Pampas del Heath Reserve in the extreme southeastern part of the country. The tiny NORTHERN PUDU seldom wanders from the thick undergrowth of highland forests and shrubs. Deer are *cud-chewers*. After foraging and filling a special chamber of their stomach, they find a sheltered area, rest, regurgitate the meal into their mouths and chew it well so that it can be digested. Predators on deer include the big cats – Puma and Jaguar; eagles may take young fawns.

The GUANACO has broad tastes in food and browses on bushes as well as grazes on grass. It can go for long periods without drinking, and because of these adaptations, at one time it occurred from Colombia to the southern tip of Argentina – from the puna highlands to the sea coast. Except for the southern populations, which are still thriving, it is now rare or extinct over most of its former range. The VICUÑA can graze only on grass, and must drink more often. It is limited to highland puna grassland areas above 3500 m (11,550 ft). Unusual among ungulates, its front teeth grow continually throughout life to allow for grinding down from constant grazing. Conservation efforts (p. 5) and large scale management plans have restored Vicuña populations to high levels in several areas of highland Perú.

Breeding

Female peccaries have either one or two young at a time, born 4 to 5 months after mating. The young are *precocial*, meaning that they can walk and follow their mother within a few days of birth. Deer, likewise, give birth to one or two young that, within a week or two, can follow the mother. Until that time, they stay in a sheltered spot while their mother forages, returning at intervals to nurse them. GUANACOS have extremely flexible social structures. In some areas the males are permanently territorial, in other areas only seasonally so, and in yet other areas they are so migratory that territoriality is minimal. They are found in three types of social groups: family herds with a single male, several females and the young offspring; male troops made up mainly of subadults; and solitary males that are sexually mature. VICUÑAS are also polygynous, but they have permanent feeding territories and do not migrate. They have the same three types of social groups seen in Guanacos.

Notes

Both species of peccary enjoy reputations for aggressiveness toward humans, but experts agree that the reputation is exaggerated. There are stories of herds panicking at the approach of people, stampeding, even chasing people. These are large enough beasts, with sufficiently large and sharp canine teeth, to do damage. If you spot peccaries, err on the side of caution; watch them from afar and leave them alone. Be quiet and they might take no notice of you; their vision apparently is poor. If you are charged, a rapid retreat into a tree could be a wise move.

To the Arakmbut forest people of Amazonian Perú, disease symptoms originate with the spirits of the various game animals they take. For instance, armadillos are thought to be responsible for coughs and bronchial disorders. Peccaries are responsible for a broad array of symptoms. COLLARED PECCARY spirits cause severe stomach pain (the spirit jumping on one's abdomen) and WHITE-LIPPED PECCARY spirits cause loose jaw, teeth chattering, headache and fever.

When a WHITE-TAILED DEER detects a predator or person that has not yet spotted the deer, it slinks away with its head and tail down, the white patch under the tail concealed. But when the deer is alarmed – it spots a predator stalking it or hears a sudden noise – it bounds off with its tail raised, its white rump and white tail bottom exposed, almost like a white flag. Animal behaviorists believe that the white is a signal to the deer's party, relatives likely to be among them, that a potential predator has been spotted and that they should flee. Many indigenous people throughout South America, including in Perú, believe that the spirits of their dead relatives reside in deer; many people, therefore, will not hunt or kill deer.

GUANACOS have been hunted widely because of their meat. Vicuñas are even more valued for their high quality wool, which is almost literally worth its weight in gold. In Perú, successful management programs have permitted marketing of this valuable wool to help support continued conservation efforts. The Incas had two species of large domesticated mammals, llamas and alpacas (probably domesticated hybrid forms of Guanaco and Vicuña). It is thought that llamas were domesticated in Perú's highlands between 4550 and 3100 BC. Conquering Spaniards referred to llamas and alpacas, respectively, as *"ovejas de la tierra"* (native sheep) and *"carneros de la tierra"* (native lambs). Thousands of these animals were slaughtered for the "bezoar stones" found in their intestines – actually salt deposits; the stones were thought to have powerful medicinal properties, such as in the treatment of snakebite. In Incan lore, the Southern Cross constellation, known as *"Urcochillay,"* was thought to be a many-colored llama spirit which had control over the health and population growth of llama herds. A perfect white llama, with red cloth coverings and gold earrings, was considered a symbol of royalty.

Status

Peccaries were hunted for food and hides long before the arrival of Europeans to the New World, and such hunting continues. COLLARED PECCARIES, CITES Appendix II listed, are still locally common in protected wilderness and more rural areas. WHITE-LIPPED PECCARIES, also CITES Appendix II listed, are less common, and less is known about their populations; they may soon be threatened. Deer are likewise hunted for meat, skins and sport. Deer range widely in Perú but, owing to hunting pressures, are numerous only in remote areas. RED BROCKET DEER employ excellent anti-hunting tactics, being solitary animals that keep to dense forests. The huge MARSH DEER is so limited to its peculiar habitat, that over-hunting and habitat destruction have caused it to be considered threatened (IUCN Red List). The GUANACO is now extinct in Colombia and Ecuador. In Perú, as recently as the 1950s, it was fairly common in the highlands as well as the lomas and coastal lowlands just north of Lima. Today it occurs only high in the Andes at Calipuy National Park (1000 individuals), and 400 other animals are scattered in isolated populations near Arequipa, Cuzco and Puno. In the 1960s, the VICUÑA population in Perú was estimated at about 5700 animals. Today, with careful management and conservation laws, there are nearly 100,000 in Perú – the most of any country in its range.

Profiles

White-lipped Peccary, *Tayassu pecari*, Plate 91a
Collared Peccary, *Tayassu tajacu*, Plate 91b
Northern Pudu, *Pudu mephistophiles*, Plate 91c
Red Brocket Deer, *Mazama americana*, Plate 91d
White-tailed Deer, *Odocoileus virginianus*, Plate 91e
Vicuña, *Vicugna (Lama) vicugna*, Plate 94b

7. Rodents and Rabbit

Rodents and *rabbits* superficially resemble each other with their large, front incisor teeth. They are, however, only distantly related. Rodents (Order Rodentia) are distributed worldwide from the Arctic to the tropics, and they include *mice, rats, squirrels, chipmunks, marmots, gophers, beavers* and *porcupines*. There are more than 2000 species, representing 44% of the approximately 4630 known mammalian species. More individual rodents are estimated to be alive at any one time than individuals of all other types of mammals combined. Nevertheless, many eco-travellers will discover among rodents a paradox: although by far the most diverse and abundant of the mammals, rodents are, with a few obvious exceptions in any region, relatively inconspicuous and rarely encountered. Rodents' near-invisibility to people, particularly in the Neotropics, can be explained best by the facts that most rodents are very small, secretive or nocturnal, and many of them live in subterranean burrows. Of course, many people do not consider it a hardship that rodents are so rarely encountered.

High rodent abundance and diversity is likely related to their efficient, specialized teeth and associated jaw muscles, as well as to their broad, nearly omnivorous, diets. Rodents are characterized by having four large incisor teeth, one pair front-and-center in the upper jaw, one pair in the lower (other teeth, separated from the incisors, are located farther back in the mouth). With these strong, sharp, chisel-like front teeth, rodents "make their living": gnawing (*rodent* is from the Latin *rodere*, to gnaw), cutting, and slicing vegetation, fruit, and nuts, killing and eating small animals, digging burrows, and even, in the case of beavers, imitating lumberjacks.

The Neotropics contain some of the largest and most interesting of the world's rodents, and more than 90 species occur in Perú. However, only a few representatives of 6 families are commonly spotted by visitors, and we profile 9 species from these families. Squirrels are members of the Family Sciuridae, a worldwide group of 273 species that occurs on all continents except Australia and Antarctica. The family includes *ground*, *tree*, and *flying squirrels*; only 6 species occur in Perú. Family Erethizontidae contains the 12 species of New World porcupines, which are distributed throughout the Americas save for the southern third of South America. Five species of these sharp-spined mammals are native to Perú. The 78 species of *spiny* or *tree rats* are placed in the Family Echimyidae and are almost all restricted to lowland rainforests. About 20 species occur in Perú, but their classification is very poorly known. The six species in Family Chinchillidae are all limited to southern South America and look more like rabbits than any other rodent group. Two of these species occurred in high altitude Peruvian puna, but the namesake of the family, the CHINCHILLA (Plate 93), is probably extinct now in the wild. Three other families that are restricted to tropical America contain a few large rodents that all share an ungulate-type body form with long legs: Family Agoutidae contains the PACA (Plate 92), Family Dasyproctidae includes the *agoutis*, and Family Hydrochaeridae contains a single species, the CAPYBARA (Plate 93), which is the world's largest rodent.

Porcupines generally are fairly large, heavyset rodents (although Perú has some small species that weigh only 0.95 kg, 2 lb) with many sharp spines covering their bodies and often the tail. The spines easily break off to embed themselves in the skin of a predator unfortunate or naive enough to try to bite a porcupine. The most common Peruvian species, the BICOLOR-SPINED PORCUPINE (Plate 93), weighs 3.4 to 4.7 kg (7.5 to 12 lb) and occurs from lowland forests up to 2500 m (8250 ft) altitude in the foothills on both sides of the Andes. Its body is covered with long, black hair that shrouds most of the short, barbed spines. A long prehensile tail, with bare top, is always curled under rather than over a branch for climbing. It has short limbs and small feet with long, curved claws that aid in gripping and climbing trees.

The spiny and tree rats are touted by some experts as the most common terrestrial mammals in the rainforests of Perú. Many of them have long bristles or flat spines on the back, but unlike porcupine spines, these are not barbed and do not readily detach. As common as these rats are, you are likely to encounter only one species, the AMAZON BAMBOO RAT (Plate 92), which has no spines on the back, large eyes and a total length, including the tail, of 65 cm (2 ft). Instead of seeing this large rat, you are much more likely to hear its incessant series of loud quacks given in the middle of the night. You can be forgiven for mistaking these sounds for some loud frog, but they are quite unlike any amphibian in the Amazon: these hollow and ventriloquial sounds are given at increasingly softer levels and more widely spaced intervals until they stop. If you follow the sound, the final approach to the rat itself will be facilitated by its commanding aroma, which has a strong musky component.

BLACK AGOUTI (Plate 92), PACA, and CAPYBARA are large, almost pig-like rodents, usually brownish, with long legs, short hair, and squirrel-like heads. The Black Agouti weighs only 5 kg (11 lb), but is common in secondary and primary forest throughout the Amazonian lowlands of Perú. Paca weigh up to 12 kg (26 lb) and are distinguished by the four rows of white spots along their flanks. Two paca species are found in Perú, one in the Andean cloud forests and the other in the Amazonian lowlands. The huge Capybara (to 65 kg, 140 lb) is most regularly found throughout the lowlands of the Amazon, usually near rivers or marshes.

Rabbits, even though they look like rodents, especially the highland viscachas and chinchillas, are in a separate order, the Lagamorpha. The group is differentiated from rodents by four instead of two front incisor teeth on the upper jaw, large hind legs, and long ears. Only one species occurs in Perú, the BRAZILIAN RABBIT, and it looks for all the world like the cottontail so common throughout North America; it is even in the same genus, *Sylvilagus*. Most ecotravellers to Perú will see this species in clearings just below tree-line (3500 m, 12,000 ft), where it is common on both slopes of the Andes.

Natural History
Ecology and Behavior
Rodents are important ecologically primarily because of their great abundance. They are so common that they make up a large proportion of the diets of many carnivores. For instance, in a recent study of Jaguar, it was discovered that rodents were the third most frequent prey of the large cats, after sloths and iguanas. In addition, rodents, owing to their ubiquitousness and numbers, are themselves important predators on seeds and fruit. That is, they eat seeds and seed-containing fruit, digesting or damaging the seeds, rendering them useless to the plants that produced them for reproduction. Of course, not every seed is damaged (some fall to the ground as rodents eat, others pass unscathed through their digestive tracts), and so rodents, at least occasionally, also act as seed dispersers (see Close-Up, p. 177). Burrowing is another aspect of rodent behavior that has significant ecological implications because of the sheer numbers of individuals that participate. When so many animals move soil around (rats and mice, especially), the effect is that over several years the entire topsoil of an area is turned, keeping soil loose and aerated, and therefore more suitable for plant growth.

The NORTHERN AMAZON RED SQUIRREL (Plate 92) and the AMAZON DWARF SQUIRREL (Plate 92) are both solitary day-active species, generally seen in trees and, occasionally, foraging on the ground. The large red squirrel typically feeds on fruits and large palm nuts. It is usually found low in the forest and often on the ground or in the understory, where it frequently *caches* (hides) food for later meals by burying it in the ground or placing it in tree cavities. In contrast, the dwarf squirrel's diet is largely made up of insects, spiders and other arthropods it searches out on branches, tangles and other vegetation, from high in the canopy to the forest floor. It also apparently eats bark and fungi. This species is quickly and reliably attracted to squeaking noises that mimic a bird or small mammal in distress. This behavior may indicate that dwarf squirrels, like other insectivorous squirrel species, are also partially carnivorous. Although the natural history of these Peruvian species is poorly known, Central American species closely related to the Northern Amazon Red Squirrel are known to have females that defend exclusive living and feeding areas from other females. Males are not territorial; their home ranges, the areas over which they range daily in search of food, overlap those of other males and those of females.

The CHINCHILLA and MONTANE VISCACHA (Plate 93) are colonial animals of rocky slopes interspersed with grassy patches in the highland puna. They feed entirely on grasses, cacti and herbs, and often spend long periods perched on small promontory rocks sunning themselves, or perhaps serving for the group as a look-out for danger. They give high-pitched warning whistles that often make their presence known. The sexes are extremely different in size, with the Chinchilla having larger females and the Montane Viscacha larger males.

BICOLOR-SPINED PORCUPINES are solitary, nocturnal animals, almost always found in trees. They move slowly along branches, using their prehensile tail as a fifth limb. They feed on leaves, green tree shoots, and fruit. During the day they sleep in tree cavities or on branches hidden amid dense vegetation. They are found mostly in higher-elevation forests. The AMAZON BAMBOO RAT is active only at night and spends the daytime resting in thick tangles of vegetation, usually in or near bamboo thickets. They are almost entirely arboreal and feed in family groups mainly on leaves, shoots and stems. Their calls at night are often in duets.

PACA are usually only active at night, foraging individually for fruit, nuts, seeds, and vegetation. They sleep away daylight hours in burrows. Along with the agouti, they can sit up on their hind legs and eat, holding their food with their front paws, much like a squirrel or rat. Several observers have noted that Paca, although usually terrestrial, will, if startled or threatened, dive into nearby water (if available). The smaller agouti are completely terrestrial and naturally day-active, but many populations have become increasingly nocturnal in their habits in areas where they are intensively hunted. They mainly eat seeds and fruit, but also flowers, vegetation, and insects. When threatened or startled, agoutis usually run, giving warning calls or barks as they go, presumably to warn nearby relatives of danger. They make so much noise running through the undergrowth vegetation that it is easy to mistake them for much larger peccaries. In Perú, the immense CAPYBARA is always closely associated with river banks, lake edges and forested swamps, and in the dry season it can be found in groups of up to 20, depending on the availability of water. It is normally diurnal, but under human hunting pressure often becomes more active at night. At the slightest hint of danger it leaps into the water and disappears under the surface to emerge far away. If it is present, its huge and distinctive footprints are common on sandy river beaches and in the mud along lake shores. It feeds largely on aquatic vegetation but also on fruits. Capybara, Paca and agouti, all large and tasty, are preyed on by a variety of mammals and reptiles, including large snakes and such carnivores as Jaguarundi.

Breeding

Relatively little is known of the breeding behavior of most Neotropical tree squirrels and of many other rodents. Tree squirrel nests consist of a bed of leaves placed in a tree cavity or a ball of leaves on a branch or in a tangle of vegetation. One to 3 young are born per litter, although 2 is the norm. Females of species closely related to red squirrels have 2 or 3 litters per year. Actual mating in this species takes place during *sex chases*, during which 4 or more males chase a female for several hours, but with the female apparently choosing which male or males she mates with. Pregnancy is about 45 days; young nurse for 8 to 10 weeks. Breeding tends to be during the dry season, from late December through March.

For rodents, the MONTANE VISCACHA and CHINCHILLA have extremely long gestation periods of 4 to 4.5 months. The viscacha has a litter of two and the Chinchilla normally only one. The young are extremely well developed at birth, but they depend on their mother's milk for up to 6 to 8 weeks.

Porcupines have 1 to 3 young per litter. Pregnancy periods are relatively long, and, as a result, the young are *precocial* – born eyes open and in an advanced state. They are therefore mobile and quickly able to follow the mother.

PACA and agouti appear to live in monogamous pairs on territories, although male and female often tend to forage separately. CAPYBARAS are polygynous with a fluid social system that depends on how much water there is to spread out into.

All three species have precocial young, usually in litters of 1 or 2 for the Paca and agouti and up to 7 for the Capybara. A day after their birth, a mother agouti leads her young to a burrow where they hide, and to which she returns each day to feed them. Pregnancies for agouti and Paca last 115 to 120 days, and for Capybara, 150 days.

Notes

Through the animals' constant gnawing, rodents' chisel-like incisors wear down rapidly. Fortunately for the rodents, their incisors, owing to some ingenious anatomy and physiology, continue to grow throughout their lives, unlike those of most other mammals.

Contrary to folk wisdom, porcupines cannot "throw" their quills, or spines, at people or predators. Rather, the spines detach quite easily when touched, such that a predator snatching a porcupine in its mouth will be impaled with spines and hence, rendered very unhappy. The spines have barbed ends, like fishhooks, which anchor them securely into the offending predator.

PACA, AGOUTI and CAPYBARA meat is considered to be among the most superior of wild meats, because it is tasty, tender, and lacks much of an odor; as such, when it can be purchased in Perú, it is very expensive. All three species are favorite game animals throughout their ranges. In Venezuela, Capybara meat is considered to be the holiday meal for Easter dinner, and Capybaras are widely raised in captivity to meet the demand for this market. In some parts of Perú, local people depend heavily for meat on large tree rats, which they trap at night in the forest. Some attempts are being made to raise these rats in captivity and farm them as a more dependable resource.

The value of CHINCHILLA fur for the coat-making industry is undoubtedly the main contributing factor to its probable extinction in the wild. Skins for coats now come completely from commercially raised Chinchillas in captivity, mostly in North America. Attempts to reintroduce these captive-bred individuals into the puna of Perú have been unsuccessful (they usually die within a few months, without breeding). Apparently, several generations in captivity is enough to lose the adaptations necessary for survival in the wild.

Status

Five of Perú's rodents are listed as threatened by the IUCN Red List, all of them mice except the CHINCHILLA. The Chinchilla is an endangered species, CITES Appendix I and USA ESA listed; although most consider it extinct in the wild, there is always the hope that in some little-disturbed high-elevation valley, some of these rodents still scamper. Habitat destruction and over-hunting have caused local elimination of several of the larger rodent species. One species of porcupine, southeastern Brazil's BRISTLE-SPINED PORCUPINE, is now highly endangered (listed as such by USA ESA).

Profiles

Amazon Bamboo Rat, *Dactylomys dactylinus*, Plate 92a
Northern Amazon Red Squirrel, *Sciurus igniventris*, Plate 92b
Amazon Dwarf Squirrel, *Microsciurus flaviventer*, Plate 92c
Black Agouti, *Dasyprocta fuliginosa*, Plate 92d
Paca, *Agouti paca*, Plate 92e

Bicolor-spined Porcupine, *Coendou bicolor*, Plate 93a
Montane Viscacha, *Lagidium perúanum*, Plate 93b

Chinchilla, *Chinchilla brevicaudata*, Plate 93c
Capybara, *Hydrochaeris hydrochaeris*, Plate 93d

8. Manatee and Tapirs

Along with the *dugongs* of the Indian Ocean, the *manatees*, or *sea cows*, form the tropical Order Sirenia. Despite their similarities to seals and cetaceans (whales and dolphins), they are unrelated to either group and are the only completely aquatic herbivorous mammals in the world. Except for bristles on the snout, they are basically hairless and look like walruses without tusks. They have tiny eyes and back molar teeth that resemble those of elephants. As adaptations for their aquatic life, they have evolved streamlined bodies; their hind feet have developed into a horizontal fluke and their fore-legs into flippers. Only two species of manatees are in the New World tropics. The AMAZONIAN MANATEE (Plate 95), a freshwater species, occurs along the Amazon River and its major tributaries as far west as northeastern Perú, and is only 2.8 m (9 ft) long. Because of its shy and often nocturnal behavior, it is extremely difficult to see as it feeds on aquatic vegetation in a quiet lake, only infrequently rising with its body in a vertical position to put its snout just above the water's surface to breathe. The larger WEST INDIAN MANATEE (up to 4.5 m, 13 ft, long) does not reach Perú and is found in brackish and salt water from Florida to northern Venezuela and coastal Brazil.

Although *tapirs* are only distantly related to either cetaceans or manatees, we include them here because they are almost always associated with swamps, lakes and river edges. They swim well, often with little more than their long snout extending above the water's surface. In fact, if you are going to see one, it will most likely be from a canoe as you come upon a swimming tapir just emerging from the water. There are only four species of tapirs (Family Tapiridae) in the world, three in the New World tropics and one in southeast Asia. Two of the New World species are found in Perú. Although they look like they should be related to pigs or hippopotamus, they are actually related to rhinoceros and horses (in the Order Perissodactyla, made up of hoofed animals (*ungulates*) with odd numbers of toes on some of the feet). Tapirs have three toes on the hind feet and four on the front feet. Their peculiarly elongated snout functions somewhat like an elephant's trunk in grasping vegetation to eat. They have excellent hearing and smelling abilities but relatively poor eyesight. They are the largest terrestrial wild animals in Perú, some males weighing up to 300 kg (660 lb). The BRAZILIAN TAPIR (Plate 94) has the widest range of any tapir species in the world and is found throughout South America east of the Andes and north of Argentina. In Perú, it is the most common species of tapir and is found in isolated areas of forest throughout the lowlands of the Amazon and up to 2000 m (6600 ft) altitude on the east slope of the Andes. This is the tapir species you are most likely to encounter, but that encounter is most likely to consist of distinctive footprints on muddy paths and along sandy river beaches. The most poorly known and smallest tapir species in Perú is the MOUNTAIN TAPIR. It has distinctively white-colored lips and is covered with curly hair, the source of its alternative names of WOOLLY and HAIRY TAPIR. It occurs in cloud forest and puna meadows between 2500 to 4000 m (8000 to 13,000 ft) in Colombia and Ecuador, and it just barely reaches Perú in the extreme north of the country.

Natural History
Ecology and Behavior

The AMAZONIAN MANATEE in Perú feeds mainly at night on aquatic vegetation like floating grasses and water hyacinths. During the dry season when many lakes and small rivers dry up, manatees may retreat to deeper channels in the main rivers where they fast for several weeks or more. Generally this species is extremely difficult to see, but its impressive production of floating dung (like horse apples) is the best sign of its presence. Manatees usually occur alone except during courtship, but they do communicate with each other by sounds they produce underwater. Individuals take about five to six years to reach sexual maturity.

Tapirs are active primarily at night and hide in dense thickets of undergrowth during the day. They browse on leaves and vegetation as well as fruits fallen to the ground. Tapirs follow habitual trails through vegetation, and routinely cross rivers at the same place, thus forming obvious tunnels through the undergrowth and gulleys at river banks, where they are most likely to be seen (and shot if being hunted). Individuals use established wallowing areas in which they apply a layer of mud to their skin to help protect them from horseflies and other biting insects that plague them throughout the year. Although generally solitary, tapirs, by using these habitual trails and wallowing areas together with communal defecation sites, at least loosely associate and communicate with each other. They are shy and retiring, and except for grunts of alarm and high whistles during the mating season, are quiet.

Breeding

Manatees give birth to a single calf after a gestation period of 13 months. The calf is dependent on the mother and accompanies her closely for two or more years. Thus, a female only gives birth every three and a half years or more. Tapirs remain together as mated pairs for only a few weeks of courtship and then separate. Occasionally males will fight to the death over a sexually receptive female. Females are entirely responsible for rearing and caring for the young, which have peculiar horizontal stripes and spots. Usually a single but rarely two calves are born after a gestation period of 13 months. The calf remains with the mother for up to a year. This long gestation period and extended care of the young mean a female can reproduce only every 17 months.

Notes

At least two researchers have noted that tapirs, which can become infested with blood-sucking, disease-carrying ticks, have let other mammals – a coati in one case, a tame peccary in the other – approach them and pick and eat the ticks on their bodies. If this occurs regularly, it is a mutualistic association: tapirs obviously benefit because they are freed temporarily from the harmful ticks, and the tick-eaters receive the nutritional value of the bloodsuckers (yech!).

Manatees, as they floated vertically in the water, were apparently the source of the myth of mermaids. Evidently lonely sailors who had been on board ship way too long imagined these forms to be female humans with fins.

Status

Because they are so heavily hunted, tapirs are very shy and cautious animals. This hunting pressure may be forcing them more and more into nocturnal activity, and, together with low population sizes, may explain why they are so rarely seen. Because they are hunted for meat, and also due to deforestation, all three

Neotropical tapirs are now rare and considered endangered, listed by both CITES Appendix I and USA ESA. Both species of New World manatees have been hunted and killed extensively. Their populations have been severely reduced, and they are considered endangered (CITES Appendix 1, USA ESA, and IUCN Red List).

Profiles

Brazilian Tapir, *Tapirus terrestris*, Plate 94a
Amazonian Manatee, *Trichechus inunguis*, Plate 95b

9. Seals

Seals are familiar marine mammals with hind and fore legs modified as flippers and noses adapted to balance large beach balls. The seals can be divided into three families, the *true* or *earless seals* (Family Phocidae), the *walrus* (Family Odobenidae) and the *eared seals* (Family Otariidae), all contained within the Order Pinnipedia. Most seal species are found in the Arctic and Antarctic areas, but two species, both eared seals, call Perú home. Unlike the true seals, which have ears that are simply holes on each side of the head, and front legs that are held to their sides as the hind flippers propel them through the water, the eared seals have small external ears and powerful front flippers that are used to help with propulsion during swimming. The eared seals are in turn divided into two groups: *fur seals* (8 species worldwide), with dense, soft underfur, and *sea lions* (5 species worldwide), with coarse hair.

The seal you will see most often in Perú is the SOUTH AMERICAN SEA LION (Plate 94). You can tell the males from the females by their much larger size (up to 1.8 m, 6 ft, long) and also by the distinctively raised forehead "bump" and the thick neck, both of which are lacking in the more streamlined females. The much smaller SOUTHERN FUR SEAL (Plate 94) (males are up to 1.4 m, 4.5 ft, long) is easy to confuse with the sea lion, but its smaller size, shorter and more pointed nose, thicker fur and lower, softer voice (not the typical yelping and barking of the sea lion) distinguish it with a little study.

Natural History
Ecology and Behavior

Although considered marine mammals, seals spend a considerable proportion of their lives hauled ashore, usually for breeding and resting. They feed underwater by pursuing fish, squid and other invertebrates. The sea lion feeds largely during the day, but the fur seal feeds mainly at night. Each adult male defends a patch of beach as his territory and mates with females that come to visit him. Male sea lions tend to defend their territory against other males in the shallow water at the edge of the beach, usually sandy areas or gently sloping rocky areas. The fur seal, on the other hand, defends and fights on the beach itself, usually on gently sloping rocky stretches of the coast. Because there are always more males than territories to defend, many males of both species are left as bachelors without a territory and so without females to mate with. These unattached males form *bachelor herds* that spend time together hauled out on more inaccessible beaches and cruising the territorial males' beaches waiting for a lucky break. The dominant males defending territories are constantly challenged by more daring members of the bachelor herd, and this leaves the male with a territory virtually no time to feed or rest. Eventually he becomes worn down to the point of exhaustion, and some lucky bachelor inherits a territory, with its perks and problems, until he in turn is replaced by a fresher bachelor. The older pups gather together in groups, or *crèches* (nurseries), while the mothers go out to feed. Usually one female serves as a baby-sitter for the congregated pups.

Breeding

Male and female seals become sexually mature at about 4 to 5 years old. Females often live to be 15+ but males, because of their stressful lifestyle, rarely live that long. Pregnant females of both species cruise the various male territories, then choose the best territory (and the male that goes along with it) on which to give birth to a single pup. Less than a month after giving birth, the female becomes sexually receptive and mates with the male. Even though her gestation period is nine months, she will not give birth again until a year later. This three-month extension is due to delayed implantation of the fertilized egg onto the lining of her uterus (the same as for bears and some bats). The female suckles each pup for up to 2 or 3 years, and frequently you will see pups of obviously different years and sizes all suckling from the same mother.

Notes

Some scientists consider the *pinnipeds* (seals and walrus) to be specialized aquatic carnivores. At one time they were even placed in the order Carnivora, with the dogs, cats and weasels.

Status

Because of their extremely fine, thick pelts, most species of fur seals were nearly wiped out by hunters in the 19th and early part of the 20th century. Only through a decline in the fur market and draconian conservation efforts were they saved. The Southern Fur Seal is CITES Appendix II listed.

Profiles

Southern Fur Seal, *Arctocephalus australis*, Plate 94c
South American Sea Lion, *Otaria byronia*, Plate 94d

10. Whales and Dolphins

All *dolphins*, *porpoises* and *whales* belong to Order Cetacea, and all but a few freshwater forms are restricted to the *marine* environment (sea water). They never leave the water and generally come to the surface only to breathe. Their hind legs have been lost through evolution and their forelegs modified into paddle-like flippers. Their tails have become broad and flattened into what are called *flukes*. A single or double nostril, called a *blowhole*, is on top of the head. Up to a third of an individual's weight consists of a thick layer of fat (*blubber*) lying under the hairless skin. Although cetacean eyes are relatively small, hearing is well developed. Cetaceans are often divided into two broad categories, *baleen* and *toothed whales*. The baleen group consists of large whale species that have mouths that look like immense radiator grills, filled with long, vertical, brownish strands of baleen, or whalebone. The largest mammal, and probably the largest animal ever, the BLUE WHALE, is a member of this group. It reaches 30+ m (100 ft) in length and 150 tons in weight. It is seen, but rarely, along the Peruvian coast. The other group, which includes a few large whales and all the porpoises and dolphins, have mouths with short, sharp teeth instead of baleen.

In Perú, the baleen whales are represented most frequently by the large HUMPBACK WHALE (14.6 m, 48 ft, long) (Plate 95) and the medium-sized

MINKE, or PIKED, WHALE (8 m, 26 ft, long). The front flippers of the Humpback Whale are huge, white and wing-like. They usually equal a third of the whale's total body length. The dorsal fin is small and often shark-like. It is placed two-thirds of the way back on the body and mounted on a fleshy pedestal, a character that distinguishes it from all other baleen whales. When an individual initiates a deep dive (sounds), its scalloped flukes come well up off the water's surface to expose the underside of the flukes, which are variably mottled white and black (a character so variable and personalized that scientists use it to recognize and track the movements of individuals). The Minke Whale, besides being considerably smaller, is less streamlined than its relatives. It has a sharply pointed nose that is almost triangular. Most distinctive of all, however, is a bright white patch or band across the upper surface of each flipper. The flipper itself is relatively short and is only about 10% of the body length. Minke Whales are often attracted to boats and approach so close that more than one observer bending down over the bow to get a better look has received a cloud of damp, fish-smelling whale breath in the face. When sounding, the Minke rarely shows its flukes.

Among the toothed whales, there are several species that you are likely to see along the coast. The SPERM WHALE is large (up to 20 m, 65 ft, long) and for anyone of the generation that was exposed to whales through reading *Moby Dick*, the species that first comes to mind. The squarish head forms more than one-third of its total weight, and there is a bump on the whale's back but no distinctive dorsal fin. Unlike the other members of this group, which have teeth on both upper and lower jaws, Sperm Whales have teeth only on the lower jaw. The flippers are short and stubby, but the flukes are large and prominent with a central notch. When sounding, the flukes are raised completely out of the water, but unlike in the Humpback, they are entirely dark below and without scalloping. From as great a distance as you can see the blow of water vapor from its blow hole, this species is distinctive. Its blowhole is situated forward and to the left, producing a spout unlike any other whale, as it shoots forward and off to the left. The ORCA, or KILLER, WHALE (Plate 95) is the first whale that comes to mind for anyone in the generation that was first exposed to whales at theme parks and in the movies. It occurs in all oceans of the world, and males average 8 m (27 ft) in length. The distinctive black and white coloring, heavy body, blunt round head and tall dorsal fin (almost 2 m, 6.5 ft, high in males) make them unmistakable. If all else fails, look for the white patch behind the eye, as it is diagnostic.

In the same group as the toothed whales are the smaller dolphins and porpoises. Two marine species, both of which occur worldwide in virtually all tropical and temperate seas, are seen regularly in Perú. The COMMON DOLPHIN (Plate 95) averages 2 m (6.5 ft) in length. You will usually see it in large groups across an expanse of the ocean's surface, leaping and rolling out of the water with breathtaking ease. They readily approach vessels to ride the bow pressure wave and may persist "hitchhiking" like this for 20 minutes or more. If you are close, the yellow patch on the side is obvious. The other commonly seen species here is the BOTTLE-NOSED DOLPHIN (Plate 95), the "Flipper" of TV and the movies. It averages 3 m (10 ft) in length and is uniformly light gray in color. It usually occurs in small groups and has a relatively long and prominent dorsal fin. This species also readily uses the pressure wave of a moving boat to take a free ride.

Along the coast, as you cruise from island to island or scan the ocean from the beach or a cliff, you expect to see dolphins sporting in the ocean shoals, and you undoubtedly will. In the Amazon, however, the last thing many ecotravellers expect is a dolphin, but wonder of wonders, they are here, too. Two species of freshwater dolphins reach the western limits of their ranges in extreme eastern Perú. Here the main channels and tributaries of the Río Ucayali and Río Napo are home to these gentle aquatic mammals. Neither is common in Perú, but the PINK RIVER DOLPHIN (Plate 95), restricted to freshwater in the Amazon and Orinoco River basins, is the one you are most likely to see as it rises from under the water to exhale noisily at the surface. Look for it along the edge of a river or in a quiet, isolated lake. It is large (males reach nearly 3 m, 10 ft, in length), has no distinct fin on the back, and is light gray in color (despite their name they actually show little pink coloring in Perú). The GRAY, or ESTUARINE, DOLPHIN is the second smallest cetacean in the world (1.4 m, 4.5 ft), and it is only rarely seen in Perú, on the Río Marañon, Río Napo and Río Ucayali near the Brazilian border. It is gray-brown to bluish and has a distinctively triangular dorsal fin. It occurs along the Amazon and its major tributaries, out the mouth of the Amazon, and along the coast of northern South America to Panamá.

Natural History
Ecology and Behavior

Both MINKE and HUMPBACK WHALES pass along the coast of Perú when migrating to feed in polar waters and then when returning to equatorial waters to breed. Calves have no blubber and must remain in warmer waters until they have fed sufficiently to put on a layer of the fatty insulation for the cold polar waters. Minkes tend to be alone or in pairs, but Humpbacks are regularly found in family groups of 3 or 4. Baleen whales, which are so large they can only be measured in tons and tens of meters (yards), paradoxically feed mainly on planktonic crustaceans, small shrimp-like animals barely 5 to 10 cm (2 to 4 in) long. These whales swim through the food-rich layers of water, especially in polar regions, with their mouths wide open. Then they close their mouths and use their immense tongues (some weighing 4 tons) to push the water out through their 300-plus baleen plates, straining the small shrimp, which stay in the mouth and are then swallowed in a monumental gulp. In tropical waters, both the Minke and Humpback Whales feed commonly on fish and squid using a similar method of feeding. The Humpback, however, has developed a special and spectacular modification for feeding on fish. Once a school of fish is located, the whale swims under and around the fish, all the while releasing a stream of bubbles. This bubble stream serves as a *bubble net* that frightens and concentrates the fish and forces them to rise as the bubbles rise. The whale then dives and turns to swim vertically up through the bubble net, its wide-open mouth closing only as it reaches the surface to entrap and swallow large numbers of fish. If you are in an area where the humpbacks are using this method, just watch for the air bubbles to break the surface and the whale will soon rise at that very point, mouth first and several meters out of the water. Seabirds quickly learn about this behavior and many will concentrate to wait at the rising bubbles to catch escaping fish.

Humpback Whales also produce some of the most complex and fascinating songs of any animal in the world. Each geographic group has its own song, or *dialect*, that all the individuals there copy and use, but the song changes from year to year. By choosing the right layer of water by depth and temperature, the whale can have these songs travel hundreds of kilometers. Communication and social interactions across such large stretches of ocean give whole new meanings to territoriality, mate attraction and group behavior. Humpbacks also frequently jump completely out of the water, or *breach*, usually in an arching back flip. This behavior may be associated with mate attraction and courtship or it may be to knock off parasitic barnacles growing on the whales' skin.

SPERM WHALES feed on fish, lobsters and sharks, but most of all they feed on squid. An adult can eat up to a ton of squid a day. These whales regularly dive to depths of 1000 m (3300 ft) and individuals have been recorded descending to 2250 m (7400 ft). They use a sonar system at these dark depths to locate prey, and they can stay down for 45 minutes and descend at a speed of 8 kph (5 mph). Many individuals have scars produced by the suckers on the tentacles of giant squid. By measuring the diameter of the sucker marks and extrapolating the body length, researchers have determined that some of these squid may be up to 45 m (150 ft) long (making you wonder if the whale in these interactions is the predator or the prey). Adult male and female Sperm Whales lead such different lives that it's amazing they ever get together. During June to September males leave tropical waters and live at the edge of the pack ice in polar regions, often in large bachelor groups. Females and young seldom get any farther than New Zealand or Hawaii. In November to February all individuals concentrate in tropical waters, and the biggest males (usually those over 25 years old) fight violently to gather harems of up to 25 females. Males at this time can be very aggressive toward ships and people if provoked. Nursing females and their calves also form groups called *nursery schools*. These groups have been seen swimming in a circle to protect calves from predatory ORCA WHALES. Orcas normally travel in extended family groups of 5 to 20 members. When hunting their prey of squid, fish, sharks, seals, sea birds, polar bears, porpoises and other whales, the pod hunts cooperatively, much like a wolf-pack. There is no authenticated record, however, of Orcas attacking humans without provocation. This species produces a low frequency sound unlike any other toothed whale or dolphin, likely used for echolocation.

The COMMON DOLPHIN feeds on lantern fish and squid, at depths of 40 to 280 m (132 to 920 ft) below the surface. It uses echolocation in dark and turbid water to locate prey. It also feeds at the surface on sardines, and occasionally will leap out of the water in pursuit of a flying fish. The large groups in which they travel usually have a hierarchy of leaders that direct movements and activities. The BOTTLE-NOSED DOLPHIN matures at 6 years and lives to be 25 years old. It feeds to depths of 600 m (2000 ft) and eats a broad range of prey, from bottom-dwelling fish, eels, sharks, rays, and hermit crabs to tuna. They have even learned to follow trawlers and shrimp boats to feed on the fish stirred up or discarded from nets. They produce clicks, pops and rasping sounds, sometimes at frequencies of 1000 per second, that function in echolocation of prey. The small groups in which this species travels often hunt cooperatively and defend themselves as a unit against enemies such as large sharks.

In Asia and South America, five similar species of dolphins have evolved unique adaptations to live in freshwater. The most widespread of these species in South America, the PINK RIVER DOLPHIN, feeds chiefly on fish as well as other aquatic organisms such as crabs, which they generally catch in deep shady water near the banks of rivers or at points where smaller tributaries enter larger rivers. They use their excellent eyesight to locate prey in clear water, but in turbid water they emit a series of clicking noises, 30 to 80 per second, which they then use as sonar by listening for them to bounce off potential prey items. They use their ability to flex their necks back and forth to broadcast and scan these clicking sounds over a large area. They also give numerous other sounds, including a screeching alarm call. During the dry season these dolphins are often confined to the main channels of deep rivers, but during the rainy season, they will pursue fish well into flooded forest areas and swamps. This species tends to occur alone or in pairs, and it rarely jumps out of the water. The second species of dolphin found in Amazonian Perú, the GRAY DOLPHIN, is more like typical marine dolphins. They tend to be highly social, sometimes seen in pods of up to 20, but they are shier than the Pink River Dolphin, and often harder to see. The sound of their blow when reaching the surface to breathe after a dive can barely be heard more than 15 m (50 ft) away. It is much softer than the explosive sounds made by surfacing Pink River Dolphins. The smaller Gray Dolphin, however, is more likely to leap out of the water and make its presence known. It feeds primarily on crabs, prawns and catfish, which it locates underwater at close distances with sonar clicks.

Breeding

MINKE WHALES live about 50 years and become sexually mature at 6 years old. The gestation period is 10 months and calves nurse for an additional 6 months. HUMPBACK WHALES reach sexual maturity at 9 to 10 years. Courtship is in shallow waters near the equator and involves a lot of splashing, churning and breaching. If you see a male breaching in courtship, watch for its sexual organ – often more than 2 m (6.5 ft) long and referred to as "Pink Floyd" by tour boat operators. Gestation is about a year and calves nurse for an additional year. A single male SPERM WHALE controls a harem of 20 or so females, but only a few are ready to mate in any one year. Gestation lasts 14 to 16 months, and the young whale suckles the mother's milk for another year or two. A single female may bear a young only once every 4 years. Several females serve as "midwives" and help after birth to nudge the calf to the surface. Little is known of the breeding behavior of ORCAS, but gestation is 12 months. COMMON DOLPHINS mate about 10 m (33 ft) underwater and have a gestation period of 10 months. The young calf usually stays with its mother for about 16 months. BOTTLE-NOSED DOLPHINS mate near the surface, and their courtship involves elaborate stroking, nuzzling and posturing. Gestation lasts 12 months and the birth is often attended by several female "midwives." The calf accompanies its mother for about 2 years.

Dolphins in the Amazon reproduce seasonally, usually giving birth during the flood season. The gestation period is 10.5 months and a single young is produced every two years. The calf is cared for by the mother for almost a year.

Notes

The whales along the Peruvian coast, especially concentrations of SPERM WHALES, attracted whalers in prodigious numbers throughout the 1800s. The American fleet alone in 1830 was made up of 729 ships. Whales were killed by the thousands for the thin, transparent oil they store in a reservoir in the forward part of their heads. This oil was used for lighting lamps. Sperm Whales also produce *ambergris*, a black and terrible-smelling residue found in the intestines, which was used in making expensive perfumes. Some of the famous and immense images etched into the desert sand near Nazca are of ORCA WHALES.

The PINK RIVER DOLPHIN has received considerable attention in the sexual fantasies of local people. In most parts of the Amazon, dolphins are treated with respect and even fear. These people believe that dolphins turn themselves into beautiful women who seduce innocent men and drown them. Alternatively, the dolphins are often blamed for impregnating unwed mothers. Whatever the source of these folk tales, they serve the useful function of protecting the dolphins from being hunted.

Status

As late as 1963, more than 30,000 SPERM WHALES were killed worldwide in a single year. However, this species has been slowly recovering ever since international controls and sanctions were placed on whaling. Populations of other species such as GRAY and MINKE WHALES also seem to have rebounded quickly with protection, but now the large numbers of Minke Whales are being used by whaling countries as an excuse to resume hunting. Part of the Minke's recovery, however, seems to be due to release from competition with BLUE WHALES, which have largely disappeared from much of their former range. Sadly for some species like the Blue Whale, the BOWHEAD WHALE, and the GREAT RIGHT WHALE, over-hunting so reduced their numbers that they may never recover. Only a few countries such as Japan, Norway and Iceland continue to hunt whales, but they also relentlessly pressure others to rescind or get around international laws. Subsistence hunting native peoples in the Arctic and northwestern USA are also allowed permits to hunt whales. All cetaceans are CITES Appendix I or Appendix II listed. The freshwater dolphins of the Amazon are common and widespread, but water contaminants and fishing with explosive charges have evidently reduced populations in some parts of their range. The IUCN Red List includes the PINK RIVER DOLPHIN as threatened in Perú.

Profiles

Pink River Dolphin, *Inia geoffrensis*, Plate 95a
Common Dolphin, *Delphinus delphis*, Plate 95c
Bottle-nosed Dolphin, *Tursiops truncatus*, Plate 95d
Orca Whale, *Orcinus orca*, Plate 95e
Humpback Whale, *Megaptera novaeangliae*, Plate 95f

Environmental Close-up 5
Of Kingfishers and Competition: Big Bills and Little Bills and How They Got That Way

Take a long look at the beautiful birds shown in Plate 50 – Perú's five kingfisher species. The step-wise size differences you see there may not be just a coincidence. Some researchers interpret this pattern of closely related species having such distinctly different sizes as an adaptation against competition. Competition in nature is defined as an interaction in which two or more individuals, populations, or species use the same resource (see also p. 45). As they use this resource, they make it rarer and harder to find, and the result is a "contest" among rivals to get to the remaining resource first. The resource over which the rivalry takes place can be food, nesting sites, water, sunlight or even females to mate with. Whatever this important resource, it is called a *limiting resource* because even though there may be an abundance in the environment of everything else needed successfully to live and have young, the paucity of this one resource serves to limit or restrict the likelihood of having young and surviving. Among kingfishers, studies show that bill size is important for efficiently catching a certain size of fish. The larger the bill, the larger the size of fish that can be taken efficiently. If fish are a limiting resource, then different species of kingfishers can live together on the same stream or lake only because their different bill sizes force them to take different sizes of fish, and competition rivalry is reduced or eliminated. That one kingfisher species seldom, if ever, chases an individual of another species from its territory reinforces this hypothesis of reduced competition by having different body and prey sizes. In other words, Perú's various kingfisher species need not be aggressive toward one another because they do not seek the same food.

Kingfishers are not the only animals to show this pattern of different sizes as a response to competition. Tiger beetles (Plate 97a) eat small insects and spiders on the ground. They use their large, sickle-shaped mandibles to capture, subdue and purée their prey. Generally, the tiger beetle species in any one habitat, such as a sandy river beach, primary forest floor or muddy pond edge, are of different sizes. In some cases, however, even if their bodies are about the same length, their mandibles are very different in size. Studies of these marauding beetles show that the size of food they can most successfully capture and eat is directly related to the length of their mandibles. Thus, just as with the kingfishers, a *community* of tiger beetle species can occupy the same habitat by eating different parts of the available menu, in this case tiny to small insects, because competition for the limiting resource is reduced or eliminated.

Different size bills and mandibles, however, are not the only solutions to overcoming competition. In some areas of Amazonian Perú, you can find 8, 9 or even 10 species of antwrens (Plate 59) in the same forest. They are all similar in body size, and their bills are almost identical in shape and length. These birds all eat the same size and type insects by gleaning them from vegetation. How do these species co-exist without a huge amount of species–species aggression over food? One possibility is that food is not a limiting resource, and there is no competition for food to be overcome. But measurements of the insect abundance strongly suggest that their food is not common and probably is a limiting resource. The answer apparently is that instead of dividing up the food by bill size the antwrens have divided up the forest by *sub-* or *micro-habitats* within it. Rarely do you see two of these antwren species foraging for insects side by side. Some of the antwren species are exclusively canopy dwellers, others stay near the forest floor, and others always appear at mid-levels in the forest. Some specialize on searching dead leaves for insects, some concentrate on vine tangles, and others search undersides of green leaves. Additional differences among the antwren species are found not in the bill or body sizes but in characters such as: leg length, to allow for different leverage on perches in various microhabitats; eye structure, to permit foraging in darker or lighter areas of the forest; and tail and wing length, to allow for better balancing or more flight in higher or lower parts of the forest.

Finally, the effects of competition may be complicated by the result of competitive events in the distant past. In some cases there is no time to evolve different bills, legs, tails or behavior to divide the limiting resource, and direct competition occurs. When such strong competition does occur, one species wins out quickly and drives the losers out of the area or into local extinction (called *competitive exclusion*). Often, the species we see in nature now, and the ways we see species interacting are the results of competition hundreds or thousands of years ago. With no "time machine" to see which species were winners and which were losers, we might only guess at what happened or see no reason to even consider competition as a significant factor in understanding surviving species and their communities. Although competition among species may be largely invisible to us, and much of it that is significant to understanding the form and behavior of current species occurred in the distant past, it is among the most important ecological concepts to comprehend; it is, in fact, considered one of the basic ordering forces of nature.

Chapter 9

INSECTS AND OTHER ARTHROPODS

Introduction

All of the *insects*, together with *spiders*, *scorpions*, *centipedes*, *crabs*, *shrimps* and *barnacles*, are placed together in the megagroup Arthropoda. By some estimates, the *arthropods* make up more than four of every five organisms known and occupy every habitat in the world, including the bottom of the deepest oceans and the ice cap of Antarctica. On the basis of their species numbers, diversity of habitats they inhabit, and the absolute number of individuals, the arthropods must be the most successful group of animals ever to live on Earth.

Among the arthropods, by sheer numbers insects are the dominant group and the one which we emphasize here. They make up more than 75% of all the species of animals in the world (by some estimates that means more than 10 million species), and we guarantee that this is one group of animals that you will see, hear and experience no matter where you go in Perú. With the word "insect," however, your first reaction may be to conjure up images of scurrying cockroaches, clouds of mosquitos, and childhood memories of disgusting small things with buzzy wings and too many legs. But these stereotypes and prejudices are belied by the facts. Insects and their relatives are a beneficial and integral part of virtually all habitats in Perú. Scientists who study insects (*entomologists*) estimate that less than 5% of all insect species are actually harmful to humans, and most of the rest are directly or indirectly beneficial. To name just a few direct benefits: as pollinators of fruit orchards and grain-crop fields, they help supply a large proportion of the food eaten in North America and Europe; as efficient predators, they keep plague species, such as white flies and cotton bole weevils in check (biological control); and as sensitive barometers of pollution, they provide warning of changes in the environment long before we could see them ourselves (acting as *bioindicators*). Even the herbivorous (plant-eating) insects have become essential to the quality and health of our lives. They often force plants to produce defense chemicals, many of which end up, by coincidence, having a physiological effect on humans – so are the source for almost half of the medicines we use today. If we want to be honest about it, we should be thanking insects rather than squashing them.

Because of insects' often restricted ranges and high degree of habitat specialization, some scientists suggest that with habitat destruction and forest clearing, it is almost certain that many species of insects in Perú and other regions are probably becoming extinct every year – most never having been discovered or described by scientists before their demise. In fact, we know so little about the biology and distribution of most insect species in Perú that it is difficult to judge how many are endangered or threatened. A few species, however, such as the WHITE-LINED SPHINX MOTH (Plate 98), have an extensive geographical range. This moth is common throughout North America south through Mexico and Central America, and along the Andes south to Argentina. What causes some species to become restricted to small endemic ranges and permits others to have wide ranges is a focus of many ecological, physiological and biogeographical studies, many of them using insects as test organisms.

The majority of ecotravellers to Perú are most excited about seeing the big hairy and feathered animals. However, the effects of charismatic Jaguars, macaws, and others of their ilk, on the habitats they inhabit, while important, are nowhere as significant as those of the humble arthropods. Without the pollination, seed dispersal, insect control, and decomposing of organic material undertaken largely if not uniquely by insects, the habitats we "ooh" and "ahh" over would be much simpler, less diverse, and much less interesting. Some scientists studying fossil evidence of plant evolution have suggested that a major rise of insects in the Cretaceous period (120 million years ago) is directly linked to the abrupt rise of flowering plants at that time through pollination specialization and codependence of the plants and insects. Thus, the flowering plants are linked inextricably both in their origin and survival with insects.

For the ecotraveller, many arthropods, especially insects, will provide an additional esthetic quality to enhance a trip to Perú. The beautiful butterflies, the dragonflies and beetles, and the bizarre insects to which you can't even begin to put a name, will pique your curiosity and raise your appreciation of Perú's wonderful wildlife. The dreaded insects, such as mosquitos, that you might have anticipated with anxiety, will underwhelm you. In comparison to the clouds of mosquitos people become accustomed to in the summer in many parts of the USA or Europe, you will be pleasantly surprised at how few there are on a path in the middle of the Amazon jungle. Except for a few marshy areas, these pests are insignificant. In the cloud forests and highlands, biting insects are even rarer.

General Characteristics and Classification of Arthropods

All arthropods share the characteristics of having a hard outer skeleton, or exoskeleton (*cuticle*), and multi-jointed legs. These legs are variously modified for walking, swimming, feeding, defense, mating, and for sensing the environment. The *lobsters*, *crayfish* and *shrimp* (Class Crustacea) are found primarily in the ocean (but some are in freshwater and a few are on land). They have two pairs of antennae and ten or more pairs of legs. The *spiders*, *ticks* and *scorpions* (Class Arachnida) are found primarily on land. They have four pairs of walking legs and claw-like mouth parts. Their bodies are divided into a head (*cephalothorax*) and large rear segment (*abdomen*). The *insects* (Class Insecta) are found primarily on land and in freshwater and have two pairs of wings, three pairs of legs (reduced to two in the butterfly subfamily, Nymphalinae) and usually jaw-like mandibles. Their bodies are divided into three distinct parts, a head, *thorax* (which bears the legs and wings), and an abdomen. The class is made up of about 26 orders, such as *beetles*, *flies*, *butterflies*, *wasps*, *true bugs* and *termites*.

Features of Tropical Arthropods

As with most other groups, arthropods, especially insects, are so much more diverse in the tropics than in North America or Europe that it is mind-boggling. What we don't know about these insects is even more overwhelming. On one 5-km (3-mile) path in the Amazon of Perú, specialists in butterflies (*lepidopterists*) found almost 1200 species of butterflies (this doesn't count any of the night-flying moths), many more than are found in all of North America. From a single tree in the Amazon, another biologist found more species of ants than occur in all of England. From the canopy of another tree a researcher collected 1 kg (2.2 lb) of insects and spiders, which contained almost 2000 species, but only about 100 of these species were known before or had scientific names; the rest were completely new to science.

Arthropods in Perú eat a wide variety of food including leaves, nectar, plant juices, other insects, and blood, but few can eat wood. The major component of the tough cell walls that surround plant cells is a sugar-starch called *cellulose*, which is held together by very strong chemical bonds. Every year plants produce 100 billion tons of cellulose worldwide, and it is the most abundant organic compound on Earth. Most herbivorous insects cannot digest these tough cell walls made of cellulose and instead consume the more easily digested ingredients contained inside the plant cells. It turns out that among the few organisms that can actually digest cellulose, especially in its densest form, wood, are termites. In partnership (*mutualism*) with specialized one-celled organisms that occur only in their guts and produce unique enzymes to break down wood, termites have access to an abundant food source with little competition from other organisms. They break otherwise indigestible wood into shorter-chained sugar products that they and other organisms can use and break down further until eventually the chemical chains are so fragmented that they can be taken up through the roots of nearby plants. As a nutrient, these chemicals are then used to make, among other things, cellulose and wood, and the cycle starts all over again. Termites, therefore, help recycle dead wood that otherwise would accumulate and go unused for many years or even centuries as it weathered slowly away.

Reproductive strategies of arthropods are so diverse and remarkable that they often make bird and mammal mating systems seem simple. Some species have *asexual reproduction*, in which only females are present and eggs mature without the influence of sperm. Other species alternate between asexual and sexual reproduction, but many rely fully on sexual reproduction. Mating behavior includes promiscuity, monogamy, and polyandry, but the most common mating system among arthropods, and insects in particular, is polygyny. Among some insects, such as the OWL BUTTERFLY (Plate 98), males form lecs and gather in open areas of the forests to attract females. Like in the birds, mammals and frogs, female arthropods tend to have most of the say in selecting potential mates. Males are often left then with the problem of communicating to a female just how superior their genes are, so a female can choose the best male to father her young. The result is an amazingly diverse array of courtship behaviors, spectacular male colors and ornaments, types of territoriality, and a plethora of other characters – enough to satisfy the programming demands of TV's Discovery Channel for the next thousand years.

Among some insects, the young are like small wingless forms of the adult and are called *nymphs*. They get progressively bigger until they have full wings and reach adult size. In other insect groups, however, the young are completely different from the adults. This young insect is called a *larva*, and it eventually undergoes a sudden transformation (*metamorphosis*) into the adult form. In butterflies, larva are known as *caterpillars*; in flies, *maggots*; in beetles, *grubs*. Most insects spend far more of their lives in these immature stages than as adults, and the change into the adult stage (*emergence*) is often cued for many species simultaneously by the right combination of rain and temperature. For the most part, adults are active during parts of the year that are rainy and warm. Don't worry, however, if your trip to Perú doesn't conform to one of these rainy, warm periods; there will be at least a few arthropods active in any habitat during any month of the year.

Seeing Arthropods in Perú

It may sound ludicrous to provide advice on how to see arthropods, but most species do not seek out humans or come to them uninvited. Many nocturnal species are attracted to lights at night, and it can be rewarding to study the little beasts flapping around the light outside your cabin or at a fluorescent light at a rural petrol station. From a canoe or along a trail at night, shine your flashlight on the vegetation, and you will often see small white reflections that are the eyes of jumping and wolf spiders stalking their insect prey. During the day, look for these night-active spiders on the underside of leaves and the surface of tree trunks, where they spend the day motionless, depending for protection on their abilities to match the background color. Many day-active species concentrate around flowers, rotting fruit and dung. Other species are active only on sandy beaches or rock faces. Some arthropod species such as cicadas make their presence known more by sound than sight, and at dusk the sounds of a forest full of cicadas can make sensitive ears ring. Many other insects, however, make more subtle sounds. Listen for crickets and katydids making their different clicks and churring notes all night long. Because many insects are so small, it is easy to pass them up as uninteresting. But even if you don't have a microscope or magnifying glass, try looking at these interesting, tiny animals. If you have binoculars, reverse them and carefully look through them backwards. As you get within about 2 cm (1 in) from an insect or spider, it will come into focus and be sufficiently enlarged so that you can see lots of detail. You will be amazed at the variety of shapes, forms, and colors you see and at the behaviors you can watch.

Order and Family Profiles

Tens of thousands of species of arthropods occur in Perú. One of Perú's leading entomologists, Gerardo Lamas, estimates that there are more than 4250 species of butterflies alone in Perú. Entire guide books could be written on any of the orders and most of the families of Perú's insects, but there is no room for such detail in a book of this size. Here we focus on 28 species that both represent the range of the common arthropod groups you are likely to see on your trip to Perú and have a fairly well-studied natural history.

1. Dragonflies and Damselflies

Relatively large, often colorful, and actively flying during the day, adult *dragonflies* and *damselflies* (Order Odonata) are easy to recognize. Their four elongate wings are folded back at rest in most damselflies and spread out to the side in dragonflies. The large eyes bulge out from the sides of the head, and are widely separated in the front in damselflies but approach or actually touch each other in the front in dragonflies. The antennae are very small and bristlelike. The abdomen is long and slender with finger-like structures at the end, used by the male to clasp the female in copulation. Present-day *odonates* vary in length from 2 to 18 cm (1 to 7 in), but a species that lived 250 million years ago and known only from fossils had a wing spread of 64 cm (2.5 ft)! Adults catch small insects in the air using their legs like a basket. Unlike all other insects, which have their copulatory organs at the end of their abdomen, male odonates have theirs at the front of the abdomen. The two sexes spend considerable time flying together in "tandem" with the male clasping the female. The female may lay her eggs while in tandem with the male or alone, depending on the species, but she always deposits her eggs in or near water. Some species show considerable territoriality, with the male guarding the female while she deposits eggs in his territory. The nymphs live underwater using gills at the end of the abdomen to breathe. They use modified mouth parts to grab small prey items such as tadpoles, small fish, and larvae of other insects. When they eventually grow large enough, the last nymphal stage crawls out of the water on a blade of grass or detritus. The adult, winged form breaks out of the husk of hard exoskeleton that surrounded the nymph and sits quietly just above the surface of the water. Here its soft brown outer surface slowly hardens and takes on color. During this hardening stage, the young adult is especially vulnerable to predation because it cannot fly well.

You will see many dragonflies and damselflies in virtually every habitat in Perú, and most will look and behave like ones you might have seen in North America or Europe. As a purely Neotropical representative, however, no odonate is more spectacular and different than the huge HELICOPTER DAMSELFLY (Plate 96). There are 19 species of these peculiar damselflies (Family Pseudostigmatidae), and they are all restricted to the tropical lowland forests of South and Central America. On a sunny day in lowland rainforest, especially following a rainy day, these long (15 cm, 6 in), thin damselflies flutter like some small-scale helicopter through the lower and mid levels of vegetation. The four long wings often beat slowly and independently, and their bright yellow or white tips make them obvious and seemingly easy prey for any hungry bird. These damselflies, however, are very maneuverable and almost like magic easily avoid being caught as they rise into the canopy. They search for insects and spiders sitting on leaves, but they also often hover in front of spider webs and pluck out the resident spider when it makes itself obvious. The long abdomen is used to put eggs into hollow bamboo, tree holes, or pineapple-like bromeliads that hold reservoirs of water. Here the nymphs hatch out into the water and feed on mosquito larvae, small frog tadpoles and other odonate nymphs, until they finally emerge from the water as adults. Males of some species defend this larval site for several months, breeding with females that visit them.

Profile
Helicopter Damselfly, *Microstigma rotundatum*, Plate 96a

2. Grasshoppers, Crickets and Cockroaches

Most of the species of this order (Orthoptera) are large, from 2 to 18 cm (0.8 to 7 in) long. They have front wings that are elongated and thickened like leather. At rest, these thickened wings cover the membranous hind wings. The body is elongated and the antennae are very short to relatively long. Young develop gradually into adults. Some of the best songsters in the insect world are found in this order – especially *grasshoppers* and *crickets*. Sounds are produced by *stridulation*: rubbing a scraper over a file-like ridge that is variously located on the legs, wings or other body parts. Each species produces a different song. Along with this sound-producing ability, most species have a large ear (*tympanum*) along the side of the thorax or abdomen. It is used to detect the sounds and distinguish specific rhythms in songs that are used, for instance, for mate attraction or to signal species identity. In some species, many males will sing together in a synchronized chorus. Most species feed on plant material like leaves and seeds, but a few eat other insects and others, such as many cockroaches, are scavengers.

Many of the species of LEAF-MIMICKING KATYDIDS (Plate 96) have wings that so resemble leaves, that you have to look twice to see it is an insect and not part of the plant on which it is resting. These herbivorous insects are night-active and eat leaves mainly from vegetation in the understory of forests. Quite often adults are attracted to lights at night. To make sounds at night, they have little bumps on the insides of their wings that they rub over each other by moving the closed wings back and forth. Usually males make most of these sounds to attract females, and the song of each species is different. The young nymphs also eat leaves. During the day you can find katydids sitting in among the leaves of undergrowth shrubs.

Profile

Leaf-mimicking Katydid, *Cycloptera speculata*, Plate 96b

3. Termites

The small insects in the Order Isoptera, known as *termites*, are the oldest of all social insects and have the most complex societies in the insect world. *Termite* colonies usually have two or three different-sized and shaped types of individuals (*castes*) within a single species, each having different jobs such as workers, soldiers, or reproductives (Plate 96). Within the same colony, there can be individuals with wings (four and held flat) and those without wings. More subtly, there can be further specialization within each caste so that some workers do only one task and other workers a different task. Some colonies have *wild-card nymphs*, which, as they grow, perform a variety of tasks but transform into workers, soldiers or reproductives depending on the colony's needs. Males and females also are different castes.

Most, but not all, termites are light-colored, with soft bodies, long and thread-like antennae and a broad connection between the abdomen and thorax. They look somewhat like white ants, but are quite different. Ants have hard, dark bodies, short and bent antennae and usually a narrow waist connecting the abdomen to the thorax. In ants, the castes are exclusively female except for a few male drones, and the young are white grubs that do not work. In termites, the various body forms, or castes, within a colony are made up of both sexes, and young nymphs are usually workers. Termites must eat the droppings of each other to pass on one-celled organisms that live in their guts and carry the enzymes for breaking down wood (p. 232) – the main food of most termites. Without these helpers, termites would starve. Nests of termites can be completely underground (subterranean), sit on the ground in the form of a hard mud-like cone (termitarium) or be off the ground and attached to the trunk or large branch of a tree (arboreal).

The common arboreal termite nest in the lowlands of Perú is made by the NASUTE TERMITE (Plate 96), named after the soldier caste, which is often called a "nozzle head" for the unique shape of its head. Soldiers and workers may be either males or females, but they are sterile. Fertile queen and king castes carry on reproduction. The soldier of this type of termite squirts a smelly, sticky turpentine-like chemical from the nozzle on its head to cover enemies. This chemical makes it hard for other arthropods, especially enemy ants, to walk or fly and may even be irritating to large predators like anteaters and birds. The workers are more typical in shape and have mandibles. Because the soldiers lack mandibles, the workers must feed them as well as undertake all their other tasks.

The large (1 to 2 m, 3 to 7 ft), round or oval-shaped termite nests are dark brown. They are made from a paste of chewed wood glued together with termite feces. This paste quickly hardens into a stiff exterior that protects the interior, which is filled with tunnels and chambers. Long, thin tunnels, made of the same paste, extend from the nest to feeding sites. These tunnels protect the movements of termites from predators, rainfall and high temperatures. These characteristic tunnels also distinguish termite nests from the often similar-looking nests made by some ants and wasps. Some birds, such as trogons and puffbirds, often hollow out arboreal termite nests and use them as cavity nests for their own young. Spectacular mass flights of dispersing winged termites often follow a heavy rainfall. At this time they are easy pickings for many birds. Evidently, however, the explosion of dispersing termites is so dense and short-lived that the predators in the area are never abundant enough to eat all of them, no matter how easy they are to catch; many survive to start new colonies. These termites frequently live with a wide variety of ants in the same nest. Whether this togetherness is equally beneficial to both species is not yet known for sure.

Profile

Nasute Termite, *Nasutitermes* sp., Plate 96c

4. Cicadas and Relatives

Cicadas and their relatives (Order Homoptera) include minute species such as *aphids* less than 1 mm (0.04 in) long to cicadas more than 5 cm (2 in) long. All are distinguished by mouth parts that have been modified for a piercing-sucking function; in fact they cannot chew. They insert their beak into plants and suck juices from them. The wings at rest are held roof-like over the back.

The EVENING CICADA (Plate 96), as is typical of all cicadas, lives as an adult for only a month or so. Most of its life is spent as a nymph underground sucking plant juices from roots. Nymphs of some species construct large, 25-cm (6-in) high turrets of red clay that cover the moist floor of some Amazonian forests. Nymphs develop gradually into adult forms, and the left-over brownish and hollow skin (*exuviae*) of the last stage before the adult is often left hanging on the side of a tree trunk or some other vertical surface. Because adult cicadas are mainly found in the canopy of the forest, you are most likely to see them only when they are attracted to lights at night. Most likely, however, your encounter with adult cicadas will be auditory. Male cicadas produce sounds, often painfully loud, and each species gives sounds at its own characteristic pitch, intensity and timing. Some species sing in all-male choruses that can become very intense. The sound-producing organs are called *tymbals*, which are thin plates on the side of the abdomen; they are depressed by a pair of large muscles attached to them and then spring back to make a noise. They are depressed and released with extreme rapidity to make the various sounds and pitches. Strangely, these sound producers are located right at the opening of the ears on the side of the abdomen – how can you hear anything with such a noise next to your ear? Most species make their sounds in the late afternoon and early evening.

The PEANUT BUG or LANTERN BUG (Plate 96) is a regular inhabitant of Perú's lowland forests. Throughout Central and South America, local legends assert that it is poisonous, but no scientist has ever been able to substantiate anything more than that it looks dangerous. It is quite large (10 cm, 4 in), but during the day hides camouflaged on the trunks of large trees, sometimes in small groups. If a predator is smart enough to recognize it despite the camouflage, the bug has a whole repertoire of additional anti-predator strategies. It can intimidate would-be predators by flashing open its wings to reveal large eye spots that resemble the eyes of an owl or large bird. If that doesn't work, its snake-like head is marked with apparent eyes, mouth and teeth to alarm the predator – never mind that this entire front part of the "head" is a hollow sham. The bug's real eyes and mouth are hidden back at the base of the wings. Finally, if worse comes to worst, there are reports that it can release a foul-smelling defense chemical. The adults apparently suck plant juices in the canopy, but little is known of the nymph stages.

Profiles

Evening Cicada, *Fidicina mannifera*, Plate 96d
Peanut Bug, *Fulgora laternaria*, Plate 96e

5. Antlions

As adults, all the members of Order Neuroptera have soft bodies, four membranous wings and long antennae. They are relatively weak fliers. Most are predators on other insects, but some species do not feed at all as adults. Larvae of most species live in the ground, but a few live underwater. The representative of this order that you are most likely to see in Perú is the *antlion*. The adults look like dragonflies but have long antennae with knobs on the end (Plate 96). They sometimes come to lights at night. It is the larval form, however, that you will see most commonly. The short, flat larva has enormous mandibles. It excavates a funnel-shaped pit in dry sand and lies in wait at the bottom, often completely buried except for its mandibles. When an insect comes strolling along and accidentally stumbles at the precipitous edge, the antlion flicks sand grains out of the bottom to produce a constant avalanche of sand giving out under the hapless insect. This causes the insect to slide down into the waiting mandibles of the antlion. Crunch!

Profile

Antlion, *Myrmeleon* sp., Plate 96f

6. Beetles

The beetle order (Coleoptera) has more species in it than any other insect order – some estimate more than a million. These species occur in virtually all habitats on land and freshwater, but not in the ocean or in Antarctica. The trait shared by all these species is a front pair of wings hardened into shields (*elytra*) that when the insect is at rest cover the second pair of membranous flight wings and the top of the abdomen. The mandibles of the adults are large and variously used for catching small insect prey, crushing seeds, or chewing wood. The grub larvae often occur in habitats different from those of the adults or have very different behavior.

In the cloud forests and lower puna areas of the eastern slopes of the Andes, several very similar species of the MONTANE TIGER BEETLE (Plate 97) are common residents of road cuts and open clay banks. Even on cloudy or foggy days, you can see a few of these largish (17.5 mm, 0.7 in), deep blue beetles running at the base of road cuts or up their vertical faces. On sunny days they will be everywhere. Although they have wings, they rarely fly. They are predators on other arthropods and search for them using their large eyes. With their long legs, they run the prey down, grab them in their monstrous and sharp mandibles, then purée them. If you catch one, watch out for the mandibles; the bite, together with an enzyme they spit up, can really sting. They lay their eggs on near-vertical clay banks, and when the larvae hatch they immediately burrow horizontally into the bank. Then from this tunnel, the larva waits, its head just perfectly filling the mouth of the tunnel, for an ant or some other arthropod to come within striking distance. The larva, aided by hooks on its back that anchor it in the tunnel, stretches quickly out of the tunnel to grab the prey in its large mandibles. If successful, the larva pulls the prey to the bottom of the tunnel and dismembers it, eventually tossing the inedible parts from the mouth of the tunnel. Almost 100 species of tiger beetles have been found in Perú, most of them at lower altitudes, where the beetles often occur on rocks near streams and on sandy river banks, but also on the forest floor.

The GREEN DUNG BEETLE (Plate 97) is attractive to the eye, but its habits may at first be off-putting to more squeamish ecotravellers. The members of this part of the Family Scarabaeidae (most of which are black) are some of the most intensely studied insects in Perú. They are crucial in passing nutrients and vital chemicals to the rest of the ecosystem by helping decompose dung. They are also unusual among insects because so many of these species have complex behavior when it comes to constructing nests and caring for their young. Some dung beetles, called *dwellers*, merely eat their way through dung and deposit their eggs below a dung pat in a superficial nest. Other species, the *tunnelers*, dig a vertical tunnel below the dung pat and carry, push and drag dung down into the bottom of the tunnel to avoid competitors and predators. The dung is either used as food by the adults or stored as food for young that will emerge from eggs laid here. Finally, a large number of dung beetles are *rollers*. Making a ball of dung, they stand on their fore legs, use their hind legs to push and steer the ball, and transport this resource away from the dung pat area before burying it in a suitable location. The female sometimes helps roll this ball, but more often than not she just rides on top of the ball, walking as the world turns under her. At some distance from the original site of the pat, the pair stops and buries the ball. They mate, and the female lays eggs on the section of dung they buried. When the eggs hatch, the larvae are protected underground from predators and competitors and have a dung banquet upon which they can feed and grow. Males of many species have a prominent horn on the tip of their snout that curves back over the head. The horn is used to battle other males over the dung as well as to impress the females that wait to see who wins the dung fight.

Dung is located mainly by smell, and the beetles' feather-shaped antennae act as super sniffers. Particular types of dung, however, are so prized by some beetle species that they also apparently use their eyes to quickly locate this resource as it falls from the canopy. The beetles use a circling flight with ever tighter loops to home in on the prize. Some species of dung beetles will use almost any type of dung they encounter while others are highly specialized on bird dung, monkey dung, cat dung, and even snail and millipede dung. One highly specialized dung beetle rides around near the anus of sloths (p. 190) and waits for a sloth to climb down from the canopy and defecate. The dung of herbivorous animals tends to be rich in carbohydrates whereas dung of carnivorous animals tends to be rich in nitrogen; and the different needs of various dung beetle species (during larval growth as well as for energy in adult phases) influences their choice of repast.

The spectacular and large (6 cm, 2.4 in) HARLEQUIN LONG-HORNED BEETLE (Plate 97) is a member of the long-horned beetle family (Cerambycidae), which is characterized by extremely long antennae and a propensity to bore into dead or living tree trunks and branches. Some members of this family are unusual in that they directly produce enzymes that break down plant cellulose. Unlike termites and other cellulose-eating insects, they do not rely on one-celled organisms in their gut to provide the proper enzymes. The bright orange, gray and black coloring of the Harlequin Beetle may function to break up its shape visually, so predators do not notice it easily. The front legs of the male are much longer than those of the female and are used both when copulating and for reaching across gaps to walk from branch to branch. The adults are primarily active during the day. After mating, the female chews a gash in the bark of a tree and places her eggs in it. The young hatch out and tunnel deeper into the tree, producing a maze, or *gallery*, of tunnels. Sometimes their damage can be so extensive that they kill the tree. These beetles carry around a mini-ecosystem on their backs: small herbivorous mites graze on the algae and fungi that grow over the body surface of large adults; tiny predaceous pseudoscorpions, in turn, feed on the mites.

Profiles

Montane Tiger Beetle, *Pseudoxycheila sp.*, Plate 97a
Green Dung Beetle, *Oxysternon conspicillatum*, Plate 97b
Harlequin Long-horned Beetle, *Acrocinus longimanus*, Plate 97c

7. Butterflies and Moths

The *butterflies* and *moths* (Order Lepidoptera) are perhaps the world's most easily recognized insects. They have four wings, but the hind- and fore-wing on each side often have a coupling mechanism that makes them look and act like a single large wing. The characteristic shared by all members of this group, however, is the layer of tiny scales covering the wings. They come off easily, and if you handle the wings of a butterfly, look for the scales on your fingers (the scales will look like dust). The adults either do not feed at all (such as in SILK MOTHS, Plate 98, which lack mouth parts) or feed on nectar, defecation or rotting fruit juices. Their mouthparts are shaped into a long thin proboscis that can be rolled up when not extended for feeding. This proboscis can be longer than the insect's body, such as in the SHINX MOTHS (Plate 98), and used to access nectar at the base of long flowers. While partaking of the flower's sweet reward, pollen falls onto the insect's body or head and is passed on to the next flower visited. Males often need extra sodium and other salts for producing sperm, and it is not unusual to see clouds of male butterflies fluttering near and landing on dung, urine, rotting fruit, or even the nose of a basking turtle, to suck up excretions containing these chemicals. Along beaches of Amazonian watercourses, clouds of SULPHUR BUTTERFLIES (Plate 98), GLAUCOUS KITE SWALLOWTAILS (Plate 98), and URANID MOTHS (Plate 97) often assemble where large mammals have recently urinated or defecated. Even salt-ladened human sweat can attract beautiful butterflies, so don't swat all the insects that come flying around you. If you attract butterflies day after day, it may be time to take a shower.

In general, adult butterflies are active during the day and have thread-like antennae with knobs on the end. Butterflies usually rest with their wings folded together, vertically, over their backs. Moths are usually active at night and rest with their wings held horizontally. They have either thread-like antennae without knobs or large feather-shaped antennae. These feather-like antennae are usually found in the males, and they can contain more than 60,000 minute structures called *sensilla*. These structures are used to detect molecules of a perfume (*pheromone*) released by a female ready to mate. Each female moth species releases a different scent, and the pheromone "plume" is carried by the wind. The male follows this plume upwind by zig-zagging back and forth, and moving toward higher concentrations of the molecules until he finds the female. Experiments have shown that males can follow this scent plume for more than 10 km (6 miles).

Larval *lepidopterans* (caterpillars, that is) are almost all plant-eating and use large mandibles to chew holes out of the edges of leaves. Many of the major agricultural pests in the world are larval moths. Some lepidopteran species have their own specific food plant species on which they lay eggs and on which their caterpillars feed when they emerge. The ornate and often colorful chamber in which the larval butterfly metamorphoses into an adult is called a *chrysalis*. The brown silken chamber of the larval moth is called a *cocoon*. The protein (*fibroin*) that is used by many moth species to construct cocoons is the product we weave into silk cloth. However, species of only four moth families are used for commercial production of silk, all of them in Asia. In Perú, one of these families, Saturniidae, has many species that consistently produce elaborate silk cocoons, and species in this family are called *silk moths* (Plate 98), even though there is little commercial use of this silk in the New World.

The intense, almost neon-like blue of the first male MENELAUS' MORPHO BUTTERFLY (Plate 97) you see will be a sight you never forget. There are many species of *morphos* in Perú. Some are duller blue to black, some have females that are very dull, and others, like the one we have illustrated here, have females almost as brilliant as the males. These huge butterflies flap lazily along river edges and forest trails with an up and down movement of the whole body. Apparently entire populations in an area will use the same flight path day after day, so if you see one using a path, just wait and others will eventually fly along the same route. Often you will come across several adults on the ground "puddling" at a muddy area or sucking rotted fruit or feces. With their wings folded, the highly camouflaged undersides make them very difficult to see until suddenly they fly up, flashing the blue uppersides of the wings. Their major enemies are jacamars (p. 146) and other flycatching birds, and the slow flapping of their wings may help them escape these birds. By making themselves alternately obvious and camouflaged as their wings open and close in flight, and randomly changing directions between wingbeats, they apparently confuse pursuing birds trying to anticipate which direction the morphos will be going when next their wings open up. The large larvae (9 cm, 3.5 in) are red and yellow, and the head is covered with specialized hairs that sting like nettles when broken off by a naive predator.

One of the most common butterfly species you will see low on forest paths in Perú is the AURORINA'S CLEAR-WINGED SATYR (Plate 97). Except for the black spots and reddish color at the tail-end of the wings, this butterfly has no scales on its wings, and their wings are thus transparent. At rest, the red rear ends of the wings together with the black spots give the impression of a head, and this confusion is probably a way of diverting a predator's attention from the real head and direction of escape.

Another common forest butterfly in Perú has bold orange and black stripes and is called the *Tiger Butterfly*. In reality this butterfly is not a single species but instead is a jumble of 20 or more confusingly and amazingly similar species of butterflies and moths. This color pattern is common throughout the lowland and lower elevation cloud forests of Perú and represents a "mimicry complex." Within this mimicry complex, MECHANITIS BUTTERFLY (Plate 97) larvae are able to harmlessly absorb and store the nasty chemicals from the specific food plant they eat (deadly Nightshade). When they metamorphose into adults, they keep these chemicals in their body and wings. This species represents a distasteful and poisonous species in the tropical subfamily Ithomiinae that serves as an evolutionary *model*. Its bright color pattern and high population levels ensure that naive predators, such as some birds, will quickly learn and unambiguously remember that bright orange and black stripes mean a terrible taste, causing vomiting or even worse. Another species, the DISMORPHA BUTTERFLY (Plate 97), shares a similar color pattern and size. It, however, is much rarer and in the cabbage butterfly family, Pieridae, most species of which are the familiar white or sulphur-yellow species (such as the ARGENT SULPHUR, Plate 98) we see in our gardens in North America and Europe. This species is not protected by poisons or distastefulness, but instead cheats as a *mimic* of the distasteful species. Because the distasteful model species is more common, the predators have most likely learned to associate any orange-and-black striped butterfly with a very bad gustatory experience, so the rarer but tasty mimic is mistaken for the model species and also avoided. In many cases the males of mimic species are not as similar to the model species as are the females. Perhaps so that females will choose them as mates, the males have to prove their gene superiority by showing they can survive even as imperfect mimics. Alternatively, the males may have different wing patterns because they have to show more clearly just which species they are, so the females don't waste time trying to mate with a confusingly similar male of another species.

Easily mistaken for a swallow-tailed butterfly, the bright metallic green and black LELIUS' URANIA MOTH (Plate 97) is actually a day-flying moth. Besides its spectacular colors, this species is common, often seen puddling along a river's edge in lowland rainforest. It is most famous, however, for its massive migrations, when thousands per day pass over a river or forest site. The explanation for these massive movements of adults may lie in their food plant, a genus of vine (*Omphalea*) related to the rubber plant. As the larvae of these specialized moths munch away at the leaves of this vine, they apparently "induce" the plant to respond by increasing the levels of toxic chemicals in its leaves. After three or four generations of attack from Urania larvae, the levels of plant toxins become so high that the next generation of moths will not be able to handle them, no matter how specialized they are normally at detoxifying them. At this point the adults somehow recognize the futility of laying their eggs on vines in this area, and they all get up and fly hundreds of kilometers to another area that has not had a concentration of Urania moths feeding on these vines for a long time. To save energy, the plants reduce the level of production of toxins when they are not under attack. The eruptive migrations of Urania occur at a low level every year, but about every 4 to 8 years a super movement occurs that lasts only a few weeks. The adults feed on nectar of leguminous trees and are important pollinators.

Profiles

Menelaus' Morpho Butterfly, *Morpho menelaus*, Plate 97d
Aurorina's Clear-winged Satyr, *Cithaerias aurorina*, Plate 97e
Mechanitis Butterfly, *Mechanitis mazaeus*, Plate 97f
Dismorpha Butterfly, *Dismorphia amphiona*, Plate 97g
Lelius' Urania Moth, *Urania lelius*, Plate 97h

White-lined Sphinx Moth, *Hyles lineata*, Plate 98a

Eyed Silk Moth, *Automeris* sp., Plate 98b
Green Long-winged Butterfly, *Philaethria dido*, Plate 98c
"88" Butterfly, *Callicore clymena*, Plate 98d
Owl Butterfly, *Caligo urilochus*, Plate 98e
Glaucous Kite Swallowtail, *Eurytides glaucolaus*, Plate 98f
Argent Sulphur, *Phoebis argante*, Plate 98g

8. Flies

Another very large group of insects is the flies (Order Diptera). Their identifying character is the presence of only a front pair of wings. The rear wings have been reduced to small knobs (*halteres*) used for balance in flight. Most adults are small and soft-bodied, and they include many of the biting insects we stereotype as "bad," such as mosquitos, horseflies, "no-seeums," and black flies; only the females bite. Because of their roles in the spread of disease as well as in agricultural plagues, representatives of this group surely rank high as pests. However, many species of flies are critical for such helpful functions as cleaning up rotted bodies, killing other insects and pollinating flowers. Larvae are grub-like and most live in water, where they feed on dead vegetation, decaying animal matter or other larvae.

One of the largest and most intriguing flies in Perú is the ROBBER FLY (Plate 99). Its long body and big eyes are diagnostic. The many species of robber fly are all predators and hunt flying insects with a spectacular flight from a perch on the ground or low vegetation. Using its long thin wings for quick acceleration and maneuverability, a robber fly pursues and grabs an insect in the air with its long legs. Then, quickly inserting its pointed mouth parts into a body joint of the prey, it injects a venom to quickly dispatch it. The fly then returns to its perch and sucks the body juices from the dead insect. These robber flies are so tough that they often kill wasps and bees larger than themselves. The long, relatively inflexible wings make a lot of noise when they fly, and with a little practice you can hear a robber fly before you see it. Evidently the extreme acceleration needed to move from rest to fast flight requires these long and noisy wings. The high amount of energy these flights need requires fairly warm temperatures, so some species of these flies are active in very hot environments such as around river sand bars. Some species are also active in the forest understory, but only on warm and sunny days; on cloudy days and at night they remain inactive. The grub-like larvae live in the ground or in leaf litter and are predators on the larvae of other insects.

Profile
Robber Fly, *Smeryngo* sp., Plate 99a

9. Ants, Wasps, and Bees

Although this group (Order Hymenoptera) is perhaps best known for its stinging females, it contains some of the most beneficial insect species in the world. *Ants* help turn over and aerate soil as well as disperse seeds. Many species of *wasps* are predators on herbivorous insects and function as a major biological control of numerous pest species. *Bees* are important pollinators of many native and agricultural plants. In Perú, a steadily rising market for honey has made bees even more economically important. The species with wings have four membranous wings, in which the fore- and hind-wing on each side are fastened together with tiny hooks. The mouth parts are either strong mandibles for chewing or modified into a long tongue for sucking up nectar and other liquid food. In most species the abdomen is attached to the thorax by a narrow waist. The larvae are grub-like and usually cared for in hives or nests. Many species are highly colonial. Sex of an egg is determined by whether or not it has been fertilized by male sperm. If it has been fertilized, it develops into a female, but if not, it develops into a male.

The underground nests of LEAF-CUTTER ANTS (Plate 99) are obvious in the lowland forests. The up to 0.2 hectare (half acre) of exposed clay and mud is completely devoid of undergrowth plants. Up to 5 million individuals live in a single colony. All day, columns of ants carrying small pieces of leaves or flowers enter holes in the ground while others exit. The columns of ants extend from the colony via cleared paths to the trees under attack. Their activity usually ceases at nightfall and during extended rainy periods during the day. The leaf pieces are cut with the sharp mandibles of the large worker caste and carried by them like an umbrella back to the nest. Many of these workers are susceptible to attack by flies and wasps trying to lay eggs on them that will later emerge and consume the worker. With her mandibles occupied carrying the leaf load, she cannot protect herself without dropping the leaf. Instead, small caste ants (*minima*) often ride on top of the leaf where they can challenge approaching danger and keep it at bay. In the nest, special galleries are set aside where the leaf bits are received by other workers. These leaves are not food, but instead they are cleaned, scraped and then added to underground gardens. Here a specialized fungus grows on the leaves and produces a spongy layer that is eaten by the entire ant colony and fed to developing larvae. If a queen ant leaves the nest to start a new colony, she must take a mouthful of the fungus to use as a starter for food in the new colony. This farming behavior is important for the forest because it quickly moves immense amounts of nutrients through the system. The ants are very choosy about which plant species they incorporate into their underground gardens. Apparently the chemicals contained in the leaves of some plant species inhibit fungal growth and are thus avoided by the ants.

There are many species of army ants, but the most obvious and well-studied species is BURCHELL'S ARMY ANT (Plate 99). A single colony of this ant can contain more than a million individuals of several castes. Even though they lack eyes, they forage in immense but coordinated raiding columns 3 to 15 m (10 to 50 ft) wide. They swarm across the forest floor, driving escaping animals in front of them, and pouncing on slower insects, spiders and occasionally small lizards; they overpower the prey by sheer numbers and incessant stings. This immense colony is always only temporarily "bivouacked" because they must move on every month or so as their raids reduce the number of prey in the vicinity of the bivouac. The framework of the bivouac nest is actually made up of an immense cluster of ants holding on to each other with their mandibles, usually in the hollow of a tree or base of a buttress root. The eggs, larvae, and single queen are all guarded within this unique structure and carry on their normal functions until the colony moves to its next location. You can tell if the army ant column is raiding or moving by what the workers are carrying. If they are carrying white larvae and not dead insect parts, you know it is a relocation column. Males, with wings and large eyes, are produced in very small numbers, and you are most likely to see them attracted to night lights at the beginning of the rainy season. It is always a good idea to glance down at the trail every once in a while as you walk or stand in the forest, to make sure you are not standing in an army ant column. Otherwise, if you haven't tucked your pants' legs inside your socks, you will soon find out by their stings that the ants are there. Although their stings can be painful, army ants, unlike their Hollywood movie portrayal, do not attack and carry off large vertebrates such as humans. The worst thing you can do, however, is to stomp your feet and crush these ants. They use chemicals rather than sight to coordinate their movements, and crushed ants give off a chemical that elicits defensive behavior by the rest of the column. You don't want that. Just calmly but quickly walk away from the column and brush off your pants' legs and shoes (you have of course already tucked your pants' cuffs into the tops of your socks). One good way to find a raiding column is to listen for the growling calls of antbirds (p. 154) around the ants. A large flock of these noisy and obvious birds usually assembles at the head of the raiding column to catch large flying insects trying to escape the ants, but the birds do not eat the ants.

The large (16 to 22 mm, 0.5 to 1 in), all-black ISULA ANT (Plate 99) is probably the most dangerous animal you will encounter during your trip to lowland rainforests in Perú. If all you do is see it, count yourself lucky, as the sting of this animal is considered one of the most painful in the entire world – it may even cause hallucinations in some people. Its effect varies considerably from person to person, and we have seen big, husky and macho men crying unashamedly in pain from its sting, while some smaller people, male and female, only felt some pain for a minute or so. Never place your hand on a tree while you rest along a trail, because this is the surest way to encounter the Isula Ant. As a warning for potential enemies, these ants make a noise by scraping body parts together, a sound that you should learn and listen for. Because they are so well protected from predators, several other insect species have evolved similar body shapes to mimic these ants. One, an arboreal tiger beetle, not only looks and walks like an Isula Ant but also stridulates using the same sound frequencies as the ant. The nests of this ant are usually in the ground at the base of a tree, and they usually contain fewer than two hundred individuals, one queen and the rest a single caste of workers. They forage, often singly, from the forest floor and undergrowth vegetation all the way up into the canopy. They are active during the daytime in the rainy season and at night during the dry season. Besides hunting live prey, including other insects and occasionally small lizards and birds, they scavenge dead animals and eat nectar from flowers.

As you walk through a rainforest in the lowlands of Perú, you often can hear the low but distinct humming of a large bumblebee-like insect flying lazily through the undergrowth or along the trail. As it gets closer, you will see a large, colorful bee, MERIAN'S ORCHID BEE (Plate 99), investigating nooks and crannies of trees and plants or landing in a wet section of the path to gather mud. If it flies close to you, it is probably only investigating some new smell that has attracted its attention. These bees are docile and do not sting unless severely provoked. They pollinate a wide range of flowers, the males being especially attracted to orchids. Instead of nectar, each orchid species offers a different chemical reward that can smell like wintergreen, vanilla, bubble gum, eucalyptus oil or cinnamon. Evidently the males need this chemical to combine into a particular smell that attracts females. When the male enters the orchid flower to get to the chemical, it has to lean against a part of the interior of the blossom that has a sticky packet of pollen (pollinarium), and, depending on the orchid species, it becomes attached to the bee's chest, back or abdomen. When this bee visits the next blossom of the same species of orchid, an even stickier part of the flower strips the pollinarium off the bee to deposit it on the female part of the flower for pollination. Many smaller species of orchid bees are common in the forest, and they are often bright metallic green or blue. You can identify them as they hover in front of a flower or tree trunk, rubbing their hind legs together.

Profiles

Leaf-cutter Ant, *Atta* sp., Plate 99b
Burchell's Army Ant, *Eciton burchelli*, Plate 99c
Isula Ant, *Paraponera clavata*, Plate 99d
Merian's Orchid Bee, *Eulaema meriana*, Plate 99e

10. Spiders

Probably the most maligned arthropods are the *spiders*. Although almost all the 35,000 species in the world have venom glands that they use together with their fangs to kill prey, only a very few species are dangerous to humans. The benefits spiders provide by controlling populations of insects more than outweigh the problems of a few bites and extra duties for fastidious house-cleaners. Most spiders are on land, but a few hunt underwater. Many spiders build webs to catch flying insects. These webs can be sticky, ornate orbs, flat sheets, funnel-shaped, or combinations thereof. Some spiders even use webbing like nets to throw onto prey. Most spiders catch small- to medium-sized insect prey, but some species are large enough to catch small birds in their webs. Waiting in a retreat at the side of the web, the spider detects a struggling prey by the vibrations transmitted along the strands of webbing. It then rushes out to inject the prey with poison and often wraps it in a cocoon of silk. Several large groups of spiders, however, do not use webs to catch prey but instead rely on ambush, stealth or stalking. All produce *silk*, however, which is a protein produced in the abdomen. It is released from the abdomen through finger-like holes called *spinnerets*. Young spiders often go to a high point in the habitat, spin out a line of silk and then let the wind take them, the silk serving as a balloon or parachute. This method of transportation can disperse spiders over long distances. Eggs are laid in a silk pouch near the web, on the female, or in a crevice. The young hatch out looking like miniature spiders, and they grow gradually.

Because they are all predators and cannibalism is common, most spiders are solitary. Only during courtship and mating do they socialize, and then often to the detriment of the smaller male. Strangely, however, the spider you are most likely to see in the lowlands of Perú is one of 50 species in the world that is colonial or, more accurately, cooperative. The NEOTROPICAL COLONIAL SPIDER (Plate 99) builds communal webs that can be several meters (yards) long, the largest web of any spider in the world. The colony can range in numbers from one female and her offspring to more than 20,000 individuals. The immense webs follow the contour of vegetation along river and forest edges or in the understory of the forest itself. New colonies arise by a number of females moving some distance away from the parent colony and spinning their webs at a fresh site. Because these colonial spiders show no physical caste differences and have no subdivision of labor, their colonies are quite different from the highly organized ant and termite societies. In many ways the colonial spider social organization is more similar to that of communally breeding birds like anis (p. 131). Each male and each female spider builds and maintains its own orb web within the colony. This web is defended from other spiders, and prey captured in a web are not shared (at least voluntarily) with other spiders in the same colony.

One advantage to this colonial existence is that together the webs produce a more efficient trap for insects flying in the area. Each spider captures more prey in the colonial web than it would elsewhere by itself, with only its own small web. Another advantage is that by using the support of other webs, each spider uses less silk to make its orb. Although predators and parasites can more easily locate the immense webs and the spiders living in them, the complex labyrinth of webs often makes it harder for enemies to enter. These immense webs have a disadvantage, however, in that disease, fungi and other microbes can easily be spread throughout the colony. More than 20% of these colonies become extinct every generation because of factors like this that are associated with crowding. Also, the complex arrangement of webs in a colony provides many hiding places for other species of spiders that make their living by stealing prey. They are called *kleptoparasites* and can have drastic effects on the amount of food the owners of the webs actually eat.

Profile

Neotropical Colonial Spider, *Anelosimus eximus*, Plate 99f

11. Crustaceans

The members of this group (Crustacea) include over 40,000 species of *crabs, crayfish, lobsters* and *barnacles*. They include some that are predators, others that are herbivores or parasites, and some that eat dead organisms. Many have the first leg modified into a claw or pincher (*cheliped*). A number of these species, such as the *shrimps*, are important commercially as food. Several shrimp species are "farmed" in the mangrove areas of northern Perú. Human-made shrimp ponds, however, have, in effect, destroyed many of the coastal mangrove habitats in Perú because mangroves are cleared to make way for these ponds. Although most crustaceans are found in oceans, several shrimp species are found in freshwater and a few crabs are common on the floor of moist Amazon forests. The young larval forms of crustaceans are tiny, swimming organisms called *zoea*. They are important because they can disperse great distances on river and ocean currents.

Throughout the world's oceans, one of the most widespread and abundant crabs at the water's edge of sandy beaches is the SAND CRAB (Plate 99). Along the sandy beaches of the Peruvian coast, they gather in immense aggregations. However, they are almost invisible if you don't know how and where to look for them. The largest ones are only 5.5 cm (2 in) long, and their humped back, lack of claws, and grayish or sand-like coloring make them look like ghostly apparitions that your eyes can't fully register as real. Using rhythmic leg movements and tail-flipping, these crabs burrow in the sand of beaches right at the edge of the wave action (in the *swash zone*). While feeding, they position themselves just under the sand's surface and face seaward – with only their eyes and antennae visible. As a wave recedes over them, they strain out small food particles using their second pair of feathery antennae. After each wave breaks, they have to reposition themselves for the next wave, and at that time you can see them scurrying half-buried in the sand and quickly disappearing again. This burrowing action and their scuttling behavior have earned them the alternative name of Mole Crabs. Their numbers are only evident when you see the hundreds of shorebirds and gulls, such as GRAY GULLS (Plate 22), wintering FRANKLIN'S GULLS (Plate 22), and

COMMON TERNS, waiting for each receding wave to expose the crabs and provide a tasty meal. The sensitivity of these crabs to contaminants like oil and DDT, has made them good candidates as *bioindicators* for monitoring the health of Perú's beaches.

The abdomen of most crabs is a flat plate turned under the body between the bases of the legs. In females, this plate is broad and protects the mass of fertilized eggs until the *zoeal* larvae hatch out and swim away in the ocean's currents. The larvae spend several months as *plankton* (floating organisms in the water), filtering tiny plant material from the water to eat and growing until, as small crabs, they return to land. Of course, only a few of a female's thousands of zoea survive their oceanic cruise, as they are often the source of food for many fish and other invertebrates. Sand crab zoea are unusual in that they have an extremely extended planktonic stage in comparison to other crabs. However, when these larvae encounter sand, they are able to settle out of the seawater and immediately begin development towards adulthood in the sand. This long life as a floating larva means that ocean currents can take them great distances, and the behavior of settling out upon contact with sand means they can colonize many areas efficiently. The sand crab that occurs on Perú's beaches, *Emerita analoga*, also occurs along most of the coast of Chile, as well as along the coast of Baja California to Alaska in the north Pacific (but oddly enough not on the intervening tropical sandy beaches of Central America and mainland Mexico). Because this species of crab has the largest sensory nerves of any animal in the world, it has been used extensively in studies of neurobiology.

Profile
Sand Crab (Mole Crab), *Emerita analoga*, Plate 99g

REFERENCES AND ADDITIONAL READING

If, in the course of your travels through Perú, you find yourself becoming more and more interested in the wildlife and plants around you, one of our major goals in writing this book will have been achieved. If you would like to satisfy your heightened natural history interest with additional reading, perhaps to find out about Perú's *other* wildlife (the 80% of it that we had not the space to cover in this book), we list below some of the best and most detailed reference books and articles that would assist you. We used these references ourselves as we wrote this book.

Bates H.W. (1988) *The Naturalist on the River Amazonas*. Penguin Books, Baltimore, MD.

Barrett P. (editor) (1999) *Insight Guide: Perú*. Insight Guides, London, UK.

Campbell J.A. and W.W. Lamar (1989) *The Venomous Reptiles of Latin America*. Cornell University Press/Comstock, Ithaca, NY.

Collins M. (editor) (1990) *The Last Rain Forests*. Oxford University Press, Oxford, UK.

Crump M.L. (1977) The many ways to beget a frog. *Natural History*, vol. 86, pp. 38–45.

D'Abrera B. (1984) *Butterflies of South America*. Hill House, Victoria, Australia.

Eisenberg J.F. and K.H. Redford (1999) *Mammals of the Neotropics: The Central Neotropics, vol. 3*. University of Chicago Press, Chicago, IL.

Emmons L.H. (1997) *Neotropical Rainforest Mammals, 2nd ed*. Chicago University of Chicago Press, Chicago, IL.

Ernst C.H. and R.W. Barbour (1989) *Turtles of the World*. Smithsonian Institution Press, Washington, D.C.

Forsyth A. and K. Miyata (1987) *Tropical Nature*. Charles Scribner's Sons, New York, NY.

Gentry A.H. (1993) *A Field Guide to the Families and Genera of Woody Plants of Northwest South America (Colombia, Ecuador, Perú)*. University of Chicago Press, Chicago, IL.

Gill F.B. (1994) *Ornithology, 2nd ed*. W. H. Freeman, San Francisco, CA.

Hairston N.G. (1994) *Vertebrate Zoology: An Experimental Field Approach*. Cambridge University Press, Cambridge.

Hilty S.L. and W.L. Brown (1986) *A Guide to the Birds of Colombia*. Princeton University Press, Princeton, NJ.

Hogue C.L. (1993) *Latin American Insects and Entomology*. University of California Press, Los Angeles, CA.

IUCN 1996. (1996) *IUCN Red List of threatened animals*. The World Conservation

Union (IUCN), Gland, Switzerland.

Janzen D.H. (1983) *Costa Rican Natural History.* University of Chicago Press, Chicago, IL.

Koepcke M. (1970) *The Birds of the Department of Lima, Perú.* Livingston Publishing Co., Wynnewood, PA.

Kricher J. (1997) *A Neotropical Companion: An Introduction to the Animals, Plants, and Ecosystems of the New World Tropics, 2nd ed.* Princeton University Press, Princeton, NJ.

Lamar W.W. (1997) Checklist and common names of the reptiles of the Peruvian Lower Amazon. *Herpetological Natural History,* vol. 5, pp. 73–76.

Lamar W.W. (2000) *Guide to the Reptiles and Amphibians of the Peruvian Lower Amazon.* In Press.

Pough F.H., R.M. Andrews, J.E. Cadle, M.L. Crump, A.H. Savitzky and K.D. Wells (1998) *Herpetology.* Prentice Hall, Upper Saddle River, NJ.

Rachowiecki R. (2000) *Perú: A Lonely Planet Travel Survival Kit, 4th ed.* Lonely Planet Publications, Victoria, Australia.

Ridgley R.S. (1989) *The Birds of South America, Vol. 1: The Oscine Passerines.* Univ. of Texas, Austin, TX.

Ridgley R.S. (1994) *The Birds of South America, Vol. 2: The Suboscine Passerines.* Univ. of Texas, Austin, TX.

Rodriguez L. and W. Duellman (1994) *Guide to the Frogs of the Iquitos Region, Amazonian Perú.* Natural History Museum, University of Kansas, Lawrence, KS.

Terborgh J. (1992) *Diversity and the Tropical Rain Forest.* Scientific American Library, W. H. Freeman, San Francisco, CA.

Vaughn T.A. (1997) *Mammalogy, 3rd ed.* Saunders, Philadelphia, PA.

Watson L. (1985) *Whales of the World.* Hutchinson, London, UK.

HABITAT PHOTOS

1 Dry sandy cliffs overlooking the Pacific Ocean at the Paracas Peninsula in the southern coastal desert of Perú. © N. Pearson

2 High cliffs of Paracas Peninsula above the crashing waves of the Pacific Ocean in the coastal desert of southern Perú. © N. Pearson

3 Seabird guano island covered with black Guanay Cormorants off Perú's central Pacific coast. © N. Pearson

4 Mountain stream (Río Rimac) rushing through west slope semi-desert at 3500 m (11,550 ft) on the west slope vertiente of central Perú's Andes. © N. Pearson

5 Twenty-meter (66 ft) high Agave (Century) plants in the semi-desert on the west slope vertiente (3500 m, 11,550 ft) of central Perú's Andes. © N. Pearson

6 Marshy stream flowing through moist puna at 5000 m (16,500 ft) in Perú's central Andes. © N. Pearson

7 Quechua Indians crossing Perú's altiplano near Lago Junín in the highland puna of the central Andes. © N. Pearson

8 Village in a dry puna valley (Tarma Valley) in the highlands of central Perú. © N. Pearson

9 Lago Junín in the central Peruvian puna - home to several endemic species including two birds, the Puna Grebe and the Junín Rail. © N. Pearson

10 Steep cliffs leading down to the Río Urubamba and mid-elevation cloud forest on the eastern slope of the southern Peruvian Andes. © N. Pearson

11   Huayna Picchu peak overlooking the ancient Incan ruins of Machu Picchu on the eastern slope of the southern Peruvian Andes. © N. Pearson

12   Mid-elevation cloud forest at the Carpish Pass near the city of Tingo Maria on the eastern slope of the central Peruvian Andes. © N. Pearson

13 El Boqueron Padre Abad, a steep canyon east of Tingo Maria, with a fast-moving stream through mid-elevation cloud forest on the eastern slope of the central Peruvian Andes. © N. Pearson

14 Early successional flood forest (*Cecropia* trees) along a small river in the Amazon lowlands of northern Perú. © N. Pearson

15 Mature flooded forest along the edge of Yarinacocha Lake, an isolated oxbow of the Ucayali River in central eastern Perú. © N. Pearson

16 Looking down from the canopy of primary tierra firme forest in the Amazon lowlands. © N. Pearson

17 A shaded path through tropical dry forest near Pucallpa in central eastern Perú. © N. Pearson

18 Highway tunnel through the spectacular Cañon del Pato in the Cordillera Negra, central Peruvian Andes. © P. Enríquez

19 Uru-uru Indian village and boat made of reeds on a floating island in Lago Titicaca, the highest navigable lake in the world (3812 m, 12, 579 ft). © N. Pearson

20 High stone walls of the ruins of Saqsayhuman near Cuzco—a favorite tourist site but also an excellent place for viewing native plants and animals. © N. Pearson

21 The Cordillera Blanca of the central Peruvian Andes and Huascarán, the highest mountain in Perú at 6768 m (22,334 ft). © P. Enríquez

IDENTIFICATION PLATES

Plates 1–99

Abbreviations on the Identification Plates are as follows:

M;   male
F;   female
IM; immature

The species pictured on any one plate are not necessarily to scale.

Plate 1a
South American Caecilian (also called Ringed Blue Caecilian)
Siphonops annulatus
ID: Mid-sized caecilian resembling a large blue worm; smooth skin with closely spaced lighter blue rings; eye evident as slightly raised, dark spot below surface of skin; to 50 cm (20 in) long, 1.5 cm (0.6 in) wide, but most are smaller.

HABITAT: Found in primary and secondary forest; normally found only underground, but sometimes seen on surface after heavy rain.

REGION: AMA

Plate 1b
Amazonian Salamander
Bolitoglossa altamazonica
ID: Small, slim dark gray to reddish brown salamander; with or without dark blotches or stripe running down length of body; with or without cream bar across snout; underside dark gray, sometimes with white flecks; hands and feet extensively webbed; to 4.9 cm (2 in).

HABITAT: Nocturnal; by day often found in leaf litter on ground; at night on leaves of shrubs; in primary and secondary forest.

REGION: AMA

Plate 1c
Perú Coast Toad
Bufo limensis
ID: Mid-sized; greenish gray, some individuals with dark spots; underside uniform gray; undersides of hands and feet yellow; to 12 cm (4.8 in).

HABITAT: Terrestrial, found along stream and narrow river banks along the coast, also in narrow valleys and along creeks descending to the Pacific from the Andes; nocturnal.

REGION: CDL, WSV

Plate 1d
Marine Toad (also called Giant Toad, Cane Toad)
Bufo marinus
ID: Large, robust, grayish tan to reddish brown toad with rough skin covered with "warts;" with or without darker spots; large, triangular parotoid glands on shoulders behind eyes; extensive webbing between toes; underside cream with grayish brown spots; eyes pale green with fine black lines; to 20 cm (8 in); largest amphibian in South America.

HABITAT: Terrestrial, active by day and night; most commonly found in clearings, along forest edges, near edges of temporary ponds, and around human habitation; rarely observed in forest.

REGION: AMA

Plate 1e
Warty Toad
Bufo spinulosus
ID: Mid-size very warty brown or olive-brown toad with irregular spots; tiny "spines" scattered over body; belly white; parotoid glands small and round; body stout, head broad; to 9.3 cm (3.7 in).

HABITAT: Terrestrial, active by day and night; very resistant to dryness, so they can live in extremely arid environments.

REGION: HAP

Plate 1f
Pebas Stubfoot Toad
Atelopus spumarius
ID: Small, slim-bodied frog with long limbs; skin smooth; greenish yellow to dark brown with black markings and reticulations; underside yellow or orange; undersides of front and back feet red; to 3.9 cm (1.6 in).

HABITAT: Terrestrial, active by day on forest floor; breeds in creeks.

REGION: AMA

Plate I 263

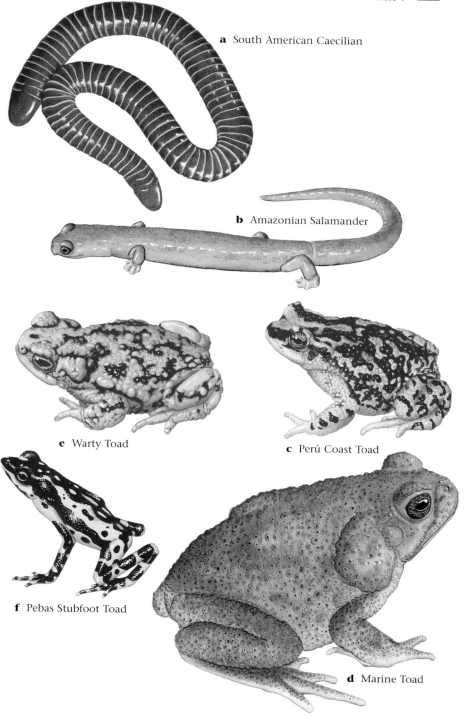

a South American Caecilian

b Amazonian Salamander

e Warty Toad

c Perú Coast Toad

f Pebas Stubfoot Toad

d Marine Toad

Plate 2a
Amazon Horned Frog
Ceratophrys cornuta
ID: Large green or tan frog with robust body and large mouth; dark green or brown markings; upper eyelids with spike-like projections of skin, resembling horns; fingers not webbed, toes half webbed; underside white; to 12 cm (4.8 in).

HABITAT: Terrestrial, nocturnal; often hidden in leaf litter; breed in forest ponds and swamps; juveniles active by day.

REGION: AMA

Plate 2b
Basin White-lipped Frog
Leptodactylus mystaceus
ID: Mid-sized gray or tan frog with robust body and pointed snout; darker gray or brown markings; smooth skin; no webbing between fingers or toes; distinctive dark brown or black face mask, bordered below by wide white stripe; underside white; to 6 cm (2.4 in).

HABITAT: Terrestrial, nocturnal; found in clearings, secondary forest, and primary forest; males call from around small pools or from cavities in ground; juveniles active by day.

REGION: AMA

Plate 2c
Smoky Jungle Frog
Leptodactylus pentadactylus
ID: Large; robust body and limbs; no webbing on hands, slight webbing on feet; prominent fold of skin on each side of upper body; upper body reddish brown with transverse blotches of dark gray, dark brown, or reddish brown; upper lip tan with 4 or 5 black vertical bars; snout wide and rounded; underside cream to gray with bold black markings on belly; to 17 cm (6.8 in).

HABITAT: Terrestrial, in primary forest; nocturnal.

REGION: AMA

Plate 2d
Eyelash Frog
Edalorhina perezi
ID: Small brown frog with flattened body and pointed snout; irregular dark brown markings; fingers and toes not webbed; groin orange with black spot; underside white with distinctive larger black blotches; to 4 cm (1.6 in).

HABITAT: Terrestrial; active by day and night; usually found in primary and secondary forest, often buried in leaf litter; males call from edges of small ephemeral pools of water on ground or in cavities in logs.

REGION: AMA

Plate 2e
Marbled Four-eyed Frog
Pleurodema marmorata
ID: Small cream, green, or brown frog with scattered dark brown spots; skin rough, containing numerous glands; limbs stout; head long; to 3.5 cm (1.4 in).

HABITAT: Terrestrial, nocturnal; found at high elevations, often under rocks in grassy areas above treeline.

REGION: HAP

Plate 2   265

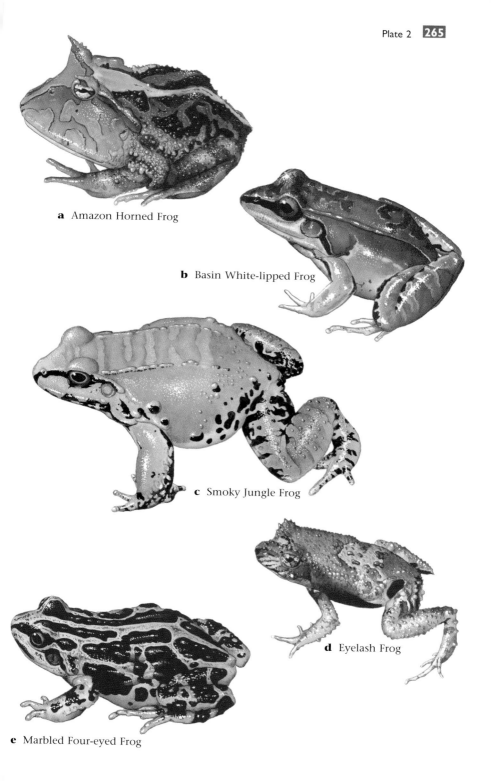

a Amazon Horned Frog

b Basin White-lipped Frog

c Smoky Jungle Frog

d Eyelash Frog

e Marbled Four-eyed Frog

Plate 3a
Río Mamore Robber Frog
Eleutherodactylus fenestratus
ID: Small brown frog with darker markings; posterior surfaces of thighs brown without prominent markings; scattered, enlarged tubercles (tiny "warts") on body; long legs; no toe webbing; to 4.5 cm (1.8 in).

HABITAT: Found both on low bushes and on the ground; nocturnal; found along streams, in clearings and other open areas, and around human habitation.

REGION: AMA

Plate 3b
Perú Robber Frog
Eleutherodactylus peruvianus
ID: Small, reddish tan to brown frog with smooth skin, scattered with tubercles (tiny "warts"); usually with darker brown markings; no webbing between toes; posterior surfaces of thighs dark brown with small red spots; underside cream with brown spots on throat and chest; to 4.6 cm (1.8 in).

HABITAT: Terrestrial, active by day and night; some individuals climb onto low vegetation at night; generally found in primary forest.

REGION: ESA, AMA

Plate 3c
Pachitea Robber Frog
Eleutherodactylus toftae
ID: Small tan to brown frog with narrow snout protruding past upper lip; creamy yellow spot in groin; side of body dark brown; underside cream, dark brown spots on throat; no webbing between fingers or toes; to 2.6 cm (1 in).

HABITAT: Found both in leaf litter on ground and on leaves of shrubs to about 1 m (3 ft) above ground, in primary forest.

REGION: AMA

Plate 3d
Perú Andes Frog
Phrynopus petuvianus
ID: Small gray, tan, or brown frog with dark brown blotches; skin smooth except for scattered warts on sides of body; fingers and toes not webbed; underside dark brown with cream flecks; limbs short, robust; to 2.5 cm (1 in).

HABITAT: Terrestrial, mostly nocturnal; found beneath rocks in seepage areas in ravines in puna habitat.

REGION: HAP

Plate 3e
Marbled Water Frog
Telmatobius marmoratus
ID: Mid-size brown or gray frog with wide, flattened head and round snout; irregular dark spots; underside light yellow; to 7 cm (2.8 in).

HABITAT: Aquatic, nocturnal; found in cold mountain streams and lagoons at high elevations.

REGION: HAP

Plate 3   **267**

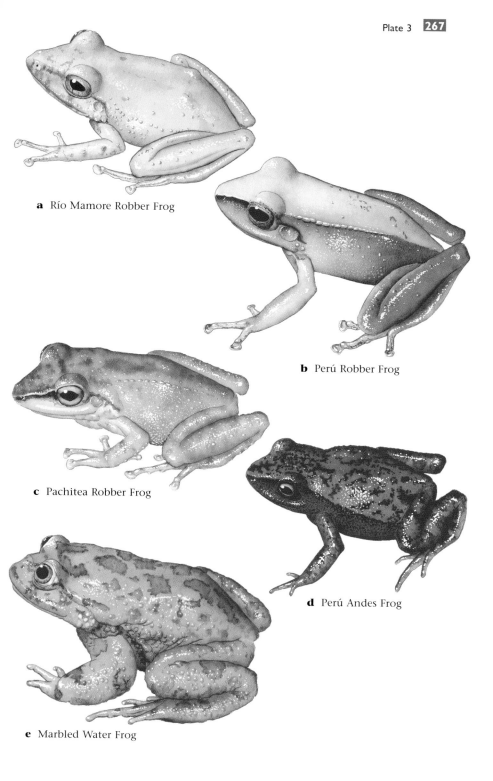

a Río Mamore Robber Frog

b Perú Robber Frog

c Pachitea Robber Frog

d Perú Andes Frog

e Marbled Water Frog

Plate 4a

Casque-headed Treefrog
Hemiphractus scutatus
ID: Mid-sized unusual-looking tan frog with broad, triangular head and large mouth; changes to brown by day; fleshy "horns" on eyelids; underside tan, throat with dark brown bars; to 8 cm (3.2 in).

HABITAT: Terrestrial, nocturnal; found only in undisturbed forest, usually on low bushes at night.

REGION: AMA

Plate 4b

Common Marsupial Frog
Gastrotheca marsupiata
ID: Small green or brown frog, usually with darker green or brown markings (highly variable); underside creamy white with or without grayish brown spots; no webbing between fingers, toes webbed at base; bar between eyes or T-shaped mark that is not connected to dark markings on back; female with pouch opening on back, a little farther forward than vent; to 4.6 cm (1.8 in).

HABITAT: Terrestrial, nocturnal; frequently found under rocks or near streams.

REGION: WSV, HAP

Plate 4c

White-lined Leaf Frog
Phyllomedusa vaillanti
ID: Mid-sized green frog with rough skin; elongated, slightly elevated parotoid glands with distinctive row of white granules running along length of gland; underside grayish brown with two cream spots on throat and one large green spot on chest; to 8.4 cm (3.4 in).

HABITAT: Arboreal, nocturnal; most commonly seen while breeding at forest ponds.

REGION: AMA

Plate 4d

Giant Gladiator Frog
Hyla boans
ID: Large tan or brown frog with long limbs; brown blotches on back; often with irregular white or silver patches on upper part of body; broad head and large eyes; toes and all fingers except first fully webbed; to 11.8 cm (4.7 in).

HABITAT: Arboreal, nocturnal; when not breeding, usually found in trees in forest; during dry season, frogs breed along edges of slow-moving streams; call from trees and the ground by edge of river.

REGION: AMA

Plate 4 **269**

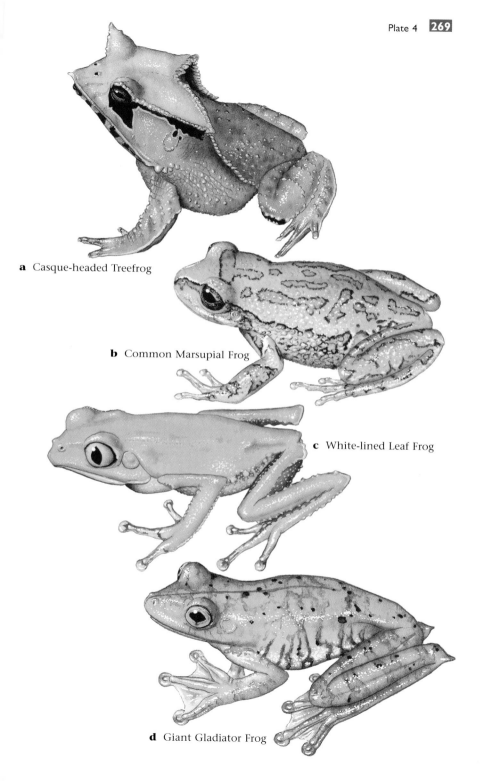

a Casque-headed Treefrog

b Common Marsupial Frog

c White-lined Leaf Frog

d Giant Gladiator Frog

Plate 5a

Quacking Treefrog
Hyla lanciformis
ID: Mid-sized tan frog with long, pointed snout; brown cross-bars on back; some with narrow dark stripe running down center of body; distinctive brown face mask and white stripe on upper lip; long limbs; chest brown with cream spots; to 9.4 cm (3.8 in).

HABITAT: Arboreal, nocturnal; found in open disturbed areas such as pastures and around human habitation.

REGION: ESA, AMA

Plate 5b

Common Laughing Frog
Osteocephalus taurinus
ID: Mid-sized tan to reddish brown frog with dark markings; skin of females smooth, skin of males covered with spiny tubercles (tiny "warts"); side of body tan to creamy white with dark brown spots; dark crossbars on limbs; to 10.3 cm (4.1 in).

HABITAT: Arboreal, nocturnal; found in both primary and secondary forest; in some areas, common in roofs and houses and in palms near human habitation; breeding occurs at temporary ponds in forest.

REGION: AMA

Plate 5c

Blotched Milk Frog
Phrynohyas coriacea
ID: Mid-sized tan, brown, or reddish brown frog with thick, glandular, but smooth skin; often with large rectangular blotch outlined in cream on back; distinctive large purple or bluish black spot above insertion of arm; underside cream; hidden surface of thigh red; to 6.6 cm (2.6 in).

HABITAT: Arboreal, nocturnal; found mostly in primary forest; rarely seen except when breeding after heavy rains, in temporary ponds.

REGION: AMA

Plate 5d

Common Flat Treefrog
Scinax rubra
ID: Small tan or dull green frog with yellow spots rimmed with black on hidden surfaces of thigh and groin; skin smooth; usually with wide cream or tan stripe running down each side of back; to 4.4 cm (1.8 in).

HABITAT: Arboreal, nocturnal; most commonly found in open, disturbed areas such as in clearings and around human habitation; less commonly found in secondary forest.

REGION: ESA, AMA

Plate 5e

Common Clown Treefrog
Hyla leucophyllata
ID: Small creamy yellow frog with dark brown hourglass-shaped mark in center of back; skin smooth; extensive membrane of skin from side of body to posterior edge of upper arm; side of head and flanks brown; hidden surfaces of limbs and webbing between toes orange; some with zebra-like pattern of cream and dark brown; to 4.4 cm (1.8 in).

HABITAT: Arboreal, nocturnal; most commonly found when breeding at night in ponds in forest or disturbed areas, such as water-filled ditches along road and forest edges.

REGION: AMA

Plate 5   **271**

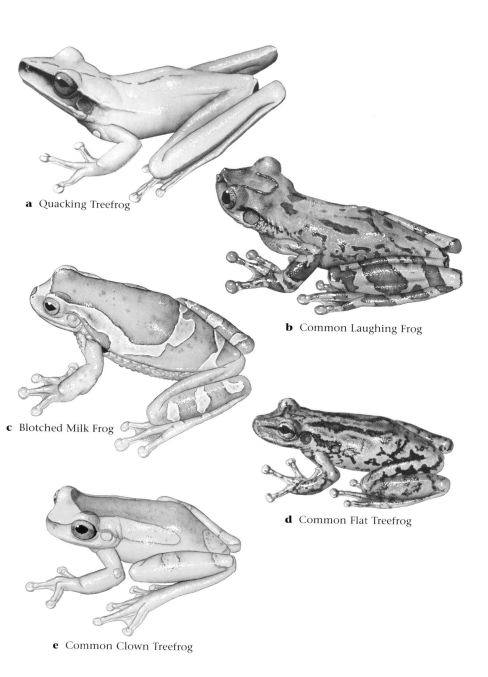

a Quacking Treefrog

b Common Laughing Frog

c Blotched Milk Frog

d Common Flat Treefrog

e Common Clown Treefrog

Plate 6a
Sarayacu Treefrog
Hyla parviceps
ID: Small tan to reddish brown frog with dark brown markings; skin smooth with scattered small tubercles (tiny "warts"); single cream bar extending from beneath eye to upper jaw; thighs black with one or two cream spots on anterior surfaces; underside grayish white with black mottling on belly; bright orange spot on underneath surface of hind limb; to 2.6 cm (1 in).

HABITAT: Arboreal, nocturnal; common in primary and secondary forest; breeds in swamps.

REGION: AMA

Plate 6b
Red-skirted Treefrog
Hyla rhodopepla
ID: Small yellow frog (often white at night) with red flecks; wide red or reddish brown stripe from tip of snout to eyes and continuing behind eyes on each side of body; skin smooth; underside yellow or white; to 3 cm (1.2 in).

HABITAT: Arboreal, nocturnal; found in both primary and secondary forest and along forest edges; congregate at small ponds, pools, and swamps for breeding.

REGION: AMA

Plate 6c
Polkadot Treefrog
Hyla punctata
ID: Small tan or pale green frog with red flecks and spots giving overall reddish appearance at night; stripe (yellow above, red below) running along each side of body; by day red flecks and spots are less distinct; individuals of some populations have brilliant yellow splotches by day; skin smooth; green throat, white belly; iris white with fine black reticulations; to 4.5 cm (1.8 in).

HABITAT: Arboreal, nocturnal; commonly found around permanent, semi-permanent, and temporary ponds in forests and clearings.

REGION: AMA

Plate 6d
Jade Treefrog
Hyla granosa
ID: Mid-sized green frog with finely granular skin; sometimes with tiny red or gold flecks; reddish at night; underside pale green; iris cream, with gold ring around pupil and blue border around rim; to 5.4 cm (2.2 in).

HABITAT: Arboreal, nocturnal; most commonly found near ponds in primary and secondary forest.

REGION: AMA

Plate 6e
Koechlin's Treefrog
Hyla koechlini
ID: Small yellowish tan frog with slightly rough skin; reddish brown by day; usually with dark brown markings; snout short; fingers slightly webbed, toes about three-fourths webbed; side of head dark brown; some with orange spot on thigh; to 2.8 cm (1.1 in).

HABITAT: Arboreal, nocturnal; descends from trees in flooded forest after rains to breed in temporary ponds.

REGION: AMA

Plate 6 **273**

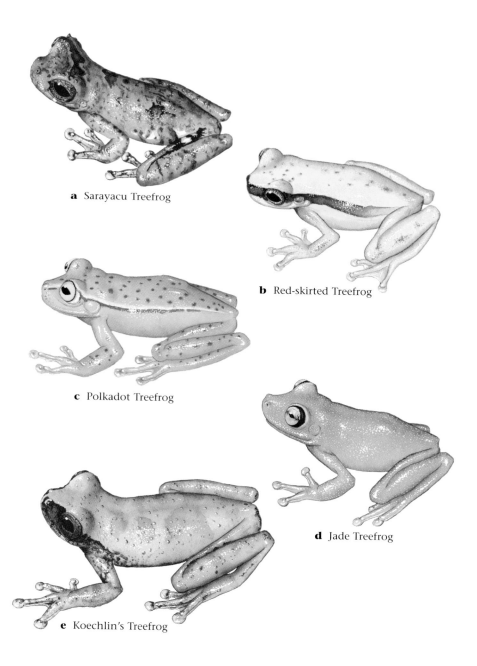

a Sarayacu Treefrog

b Red-skirted Treefrog

c Polkadot Treefrog

d Jade Treefrog

e Koechlin's Treefrog

Plate 7a
Short-legged Treefrog
Hyla leali
ID: Small pinkish tan frog with long body and short legs; most with brown X-shaped mark across shoulders; fingers short; underside cream; white spot on upper lip below eye; to 2.6 cm (1 in).

HABITAT: Arboreal, nocturnal; most commonly found in disturbed, open areas; breed in temporary or semi-permanent ponds at edge of forest.

REGION: ESA, AMA

Plate 7b
Lesser Treefrog
Hyla minuta
ID: Small tan, reddish, or golden brown frog with irregular dark brown markings; skin smooth; snout broadly rounded; thighs orange tan; when frog is sitting, a narrow cream stripe on rump touches cream stripes on heels; underside creamy white; to 2.4 cm (1 in).

HABITAT: Arboreal, nocturnal; most commonly found in primary forest, especially around ponds where it breeds.

REGION: AMA

Plate 7c
Amazon Rocket Frog
Colostethus marchesianus
ID: Small tan to reddish brown frog with small black spots; conspicuous brown stripe, bordered below by white stripe, running down each side of body; belly white, throat light yellow; no webbing on fingers or toes; eyes gold with black flecks; to 1.8 cm (0.7 in).

HABITAT: Terrestrial, active by day; found in primary and secondary forest, in moist areas; male carries tadpoles to small pools of water or slow-moving streams in forest.

REGION: AMA

Plate 7d
Ruby Poison-dart Frog
Epipedobates parvulus
ID: Small frog with dull red granular bumps against a background of dark brown or black; conspicuous bright yellow spot in armpit and groin; flanks and underside blue with black reticulation; to 2.4 cm (1 in).

HABITAT: Terrestrial, active by day; common in undisturbed forest; individuals frequently sleep on leaves of low herbs at night; males carry tadpoles to isolated pools or streams in forest.

REGION: AMA

Plate 7e
Spot-legged Poison-dart Frog
Epipedobates pictus
ID: Small dull greenish gray to dark brown or, more commonly, black frog with distinctive narrow yellow or metallic green stripe across tip of snout, continuing to groin; shorter yellow or metallic green stripe runs along lower jaw from under eye to upper arm; small yellow spot in armpit, a second in groin; underside blue and black; to 2.5 cm (1 in).

HABITAT: Terrestrial, active by day; common in second-growth forests and forest edges; individuals frequently sleep on leaves of low herbs at night; males carry tadpoles to isolated pools or streams.

REGION: AMA

Plate 7 **275**

a Short-legged Treefrog

b Lesser Treefrog

c Amazon Rocket Frog

d Ruby Poison-dart Frog

e Spot-legged Poison-dart Frog

Plate 8a
Amazon River Frog (also called Amazon Bullfrog)
Rana palmipes
ID: Large olive-tan to green frog with smooth skin and robust hind limbs; usually with small brown or black spots; pointed snout; distinct tympanum (external ear disc) almost as large as eye; fingers lack webbing, but toes nearly fully webbed; distinct skin folds along upper sides of body; rear surfaces of legs mottled pale yellow and black; underneath cream to pale yellow with small black spots; to 12.6 cm (5 in).

HABITAT: Terrestrial, active both day and night; commonly found in forest and open areas near ponds, lakes, swamps, and slow-moving streams.

REGION: AMA

Plate 8b
Trueb's Cochran Frog
Cochranella truebae
ID: Small, delicate green frog with greenish black flecks and white spots; eyes large and protuberant, pale gold with fine black reticulations; limbs slender; to 2.5 cm (1 in).

HABITAT: Arboreal, nocturnal; found in cloud forest.

REGION: ESA

Plate 8c
Bolivian Bleating Frog
Hamptophryne boliviana
ID: Small tan to reddish brown frog with moderately robust body and pointed snout; large brown blotch in center of back, with or without faint narrow, white stripe running down middle of back; fingers and toes not webbed; sides of body dark brown; throat dark brown with white flecks, belly white with brown spots; to 4.4 cm (1.8 in).

HABITAT: Terrestrial, nocturnal; found in primary and secondary forest; breed at shallow, temporary ponds in forest.

REGION: AMA

Plate 8d
Surinam Toad
Pipa pipa
ID: Large bizarre-looking tan frog with flattened body and broad, triangular head; usually with darker brown blotches; skin bumpy; snout pointed; eyes tiny; fingers not webbed, toes fully webbed; tips of fingers split into two; dark T-shaped mark on chest; to 17.1 cm (6.8 in).

HABITAT: Fully aquatic; most often found in ponds and swamps in forest.

REGION: AMA

Plate 8   **277**

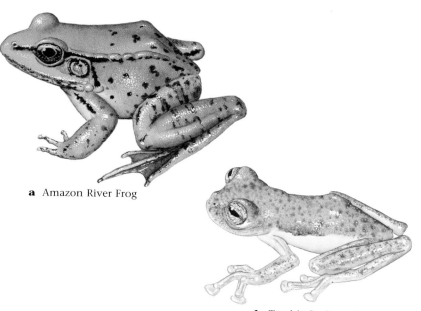

a Amazon River Frog

b Trueb's Cochran Frog

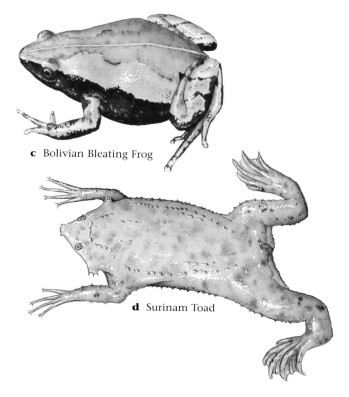

c Bolivian Bleating Frog

d Surinam Toad

Plate 9a

Spectacled Caiman
Caiman crocodilus
ID: Large, brown or olive-brown, often with wide black bars on body and tail; to 2 m (6.5 ft), although most are smaller. *Spectacled* refers to the bony ridges between the eyes; crocodiles lack these.

HABITAT: Forests, in or near streams, swamps, ponds, lakes, and rivers.

REGION: AMA

Note: Regulated for conservation purposes; CITES Appendix II listed.

Plate 9b

Black Caiman
Caiman niger
ID: Large, very dark olive, brown, or, most often, blackish, with white makings or partial bands; snout broad and rounded; to 6 m (19.5 ft) but most less than 4 m (13 ft); juveniles have yellow bands on body and tail.

HABITAT: Large bodies of water, mostly large lakes, in forest; also large rivers and swampy areas near lakes, rivers; nocturnal; much less common than Spectacled Caiman, but recovering rapidly in many places.

REGION: AMA

Note: This species is endangered, CITES Appendix I listed.

Plate 9c

Smooth-fronted Caiman
Paleosuchus trigonatus
ID: Small, with a maximum length of 1.5 m (5 ft); moderately rounded snout; dark olive with darker bands on body and tail; often with lighter blotches on sides of jaws.

HABITAT: Larger streams, small rivers, small ponds, and swamps in forest; nocturnal; also on forest floor, where it forages.

REGION: ESA, AMA

Note: Regulated for conservation purposes; CITES Appendix II listed.

Plate 9d

Yellowfoot Tortoise
Geochelone denticulata
ID: Large, with a moderately domed shell; distinctly textured, raised concentric "growth rings" on each upper shell plate; upper shell dull brown to black, usually with a pale tan to yellow area at the center of each plate; scales on front limbs yellow to orange; rear limbs have stubby, elephant-like feet; to 57 cm (26 in), but most smaller.

HABITAT: Terrestrial in forest; day- and perhaps night-active.

REGION: AMA

Note: Regulated for conservation purposes; CITES Appendix II listed.

Plate 9e

Yellow-spotted River Turtle
Podocnemis unifilis
ID: A large turtle, olive to brown, with a slightly domed, fairly smooth shell; limbs and head uniformly olive to light brown, except for several yellow spots on the head and snout; underside pale yellow; to 68 cm (27 in); males much smaller than females, to only half maximum size.

HABITAT: Ponds, lakes, rivers, and swamps; diurnal; basks on logs in water.

REGION: AMA

Note: Regulated for conservation purposes; CITES Appendix II listed.

Plate 9   **279**

a Spectacled Caiman

b Black Caiman   IM

c Smooth-fronted Caiman

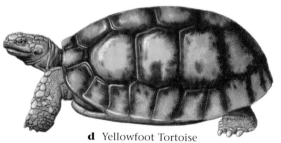

d Yellowfoot Tortoise

e Yellow-spotted River Turtle

Plate 10a
Green Sea Turtle
Chelonia mydas
ID: A medium to large sea turtle; back generally heart-shaped and black, gray, greenish, or brown, often with bold spots or streaks; yellowish white underneath; males' front legs each have one large, curved claw; name refers to greenish body fat; to 150 cm (60 in).

HABITAT: Pacific coast; feeds in shallow ocean water, lays eggs on beaches.

REGION: Ocean

Note: This species is endangered, CITES Appendix I listed.

Plate 10b
Hawksbill Sea Turtle
Eretmochelys imbricata
ID: A small to mid-sized sea turtle; shield-shaped back mainly dark greenish brown; yellow underneath; head scales brown or black; jaws yellowish with dark markings; chin and throat yellow; 2 claws on each front leg; narrow head and tapering hooked "beak" give the species its name; to 90 cm (35 in).

HABITAT: Feeds in clear, shallow ocean water near rocks and reefs, and also in shallow bays, estuaries, and lagoons; lays eggs on beaches.

REGION: Ocean

Note: This species is endangered, CITES Appendix I listed.

Plate 10c
Leatherback Sea Turtle
Dermochelys coriacea
ID: Largest of the world's sea turtles, to lengths of 2 m (6.5 ft) or more and weights of 600+ kg (1300+ lb). Back is black or brown, smooth, covered with a continuous layer of black, often white-spattered, leathery skin (instead of the hardened plates of other sea turtles); 7 ridges along back running front to rear; no claws on limbs; no scales on skin except in juveniles.

HABITAT: An open-ocean turtle, but occasionally feeds in shallow water of bays and estuaries; lays eggs on beaches.

REGION: Ocean

Note: This species is endangered, CITES Appendix I listed.

Plate 10d
Olive Ridley Sea Turtle (also called Pacific Sea Turtle)
Lepidochelys olivacea
ID: A small sea turtle; wide, olive-colored, heart-shaped back a bit flattened, with a ridge down the middle; males have long, thick tails that extend beyond the top shell, and a curved claw on each front limb; skin is olive above, lighter-colored below; to 70 cm (28 in).

HABITAT: Open ocean and coastal areas, in bays, lagoons, near reefs; lays eggs on beaches.

REGION: Ocean

Note: This species is endangered, CITES Appendix I listed.

Plate 10   **281**

a Green Sea Turtle

b Hawksbill Sea Turtle

c Leatherback Sea Turtle

d Olive Ridley Sea Turtle

Plate 11a
Twist-necked Turtle
Platemys platycephala
ID: Flat, with two ridges on upper shell; olive to dark brown upper shell; head bright yellow; to 15 cm (7 in).

HABITAT: Forest streams, swamps, ponds; active by day; somewhat terrestrial.

REGION: AMA

Plate 11b
Matamata
Chelus fimbriatus
ID: Large; broad, upper shell flat with three longitudinal ridges; head broad, with fleshy proboscis on snout; snout and back part of head pale orange-tan; rest of head and limbs dark brown; upper shell dark brown with yellowish tan stripe running longitudinally down center; shell often with thick layer of algae; to 40 cm (16 in).

HABITAT: Rivers, creeks, oxbow lakes.

REGION: AMA

Plate 11c
Ornate Thirst Snake (also called Catesby's Snail-eater)
Dipsas catesbyi
ID: Small, reddish brown, fairly slender; large, paired, darker brown or blackish oval spots, each surrounded by white border, along sides; black head rounded with a white line across blunt snout; white belly with irregular black markings; slightly larger row of scales runs along the backbone; 30 to 70 cm (12 to 28 in).

HABITAT: Forest; on vegetation 1 to 4 m (3 to 13 ft) above ground; nocturnal.

REGION: TDF, AMA

Plate 11d
Blunt-headed Treesnake
Imantodes cenchoa
ID: Long and slender with a bulbous, blunt head with large eyes and elliptical (cat-like) pupils; body noticeably flattened from side-to-side, with a larger row of scales running along the backbone; body with alternating bands of dark chocolate brown and cream or tan; belly tan or cream with brown flecks; to 110 cm (43 in). This and a related species, Amazon Treesnake, *Imantodes lentiferus*, are the most slender colubrid snakes in Perú (and perhaps in the world); they resemble vines.

HABITAT: Both primary and secondary forest; on vegetation 1 to 4 m (3 to 13 ft) above ground, where it is often the most abundant nocturnal tree snake.

REGION: AMA

Plate 11e
Common Cat-eyed Snake
Leptodeira annulata
ID: Small, tan to light brown or reddish brown, with a zig-zag, wavy dark brown stripe running lengthwise along upper body; the dark stripe is usually broken into unconnected blotches on the rear portion of body; creamy white to pinkish tan belly; 40 to 75 cm (16 to 30 in).

HABITAT: Arboreal in secondary and some primary forest; nocturnal.

REGION: AMA

Plate 11 **283**

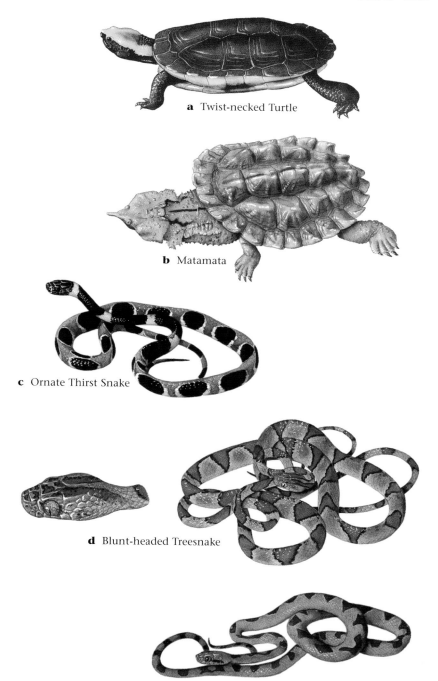

a Twist-necked Turtle

b Matamata

c Ornate Thirst Snake

d Blunt-headed Treesnake

e Common Cat-eyed Snake

Plate 12a

Striped Sharpnose Snake
Xenoxybelis argenteus
ID: Mid-sized, slender, with pointed head and snout; dull green and tan stripes run lengthwise down body; green and white stripes run lengthwise on belly; body rounded (not flattened) in cross-section; long tail, often 70% of body length; they resemble vines; 50 to 100 cm (20 to 40 in).

HABITAT: Arboreal in secondary and primary forest; active during the day, usually in vegetation, but sometimes on ground; sleep on low vegetation at night.

REGION: AMA

Plate 12b

Southern Sharpnose Snake
Xenoxybelis boulengeri
ID: Mid-sized; long slender head and body; long tail; body rounded (not flattened) in cross-section; brown with narrow darker brown stripe and broad white stripe running lengthwise along side of body; underside green; they resemble vines; 75 to 150 cm (30 to 60 in).

HABITAT: Day-active; arboreal in bushes and on tree limbs; sleep at night loosely coiled on or draped over branches.

REGION: AMA

Plate 12c

Black-skinned Parrot Snake (also called Green Parrot Snake)
Leptophis ahaetulla nigromarginatus
ID: Mid-sized, slender, bright green; black edges around the outer margin of each scale on the upper body form a distinctive net-like pattern of black over green; metallic pinkish rust-colored belly; 60 to 100 cm (24 to 40 in).

HABITAT: Arboreal in dense brushy vegetation; occurs in secondary and primary forest; day-active; at night sleeps in vegetation.

REGION: ESA, AMA

Plate 12d

Olive Whipsnake (also called Brown Sipo)
Chironius fuscus
ID: Mid-sized; juveniles tan or gray with brown blotches; adults brown above, yellow below. Small juveniles have white throat and chin; these areas become progressively more yellow with age, and bright yellow in adults; 80 to 100 cm (32 to 40 in).

HABITAT: Mostly in secondary forest, but also in primary forest and forest edge; active by day; sleep on vegetation at night, at heights up to 4 m (13 feet).

REGION: AMA

Plate 12e

Common Mussurana
Clelia clelia
ID: Large, long, with large shiny scales; adults are black with cream-colored belly; juveniles (up to 50 cm, 20 in) are red (with black scale edges) with black snout and white neck-band; to 2+ m (6.5+ ft).

HABITAT: Terrestrial, in forest; day- and night-active.

REGION: AMA

Note: Regulated for conservation purposes; CITES Appendix II listed.

Plate 12 285

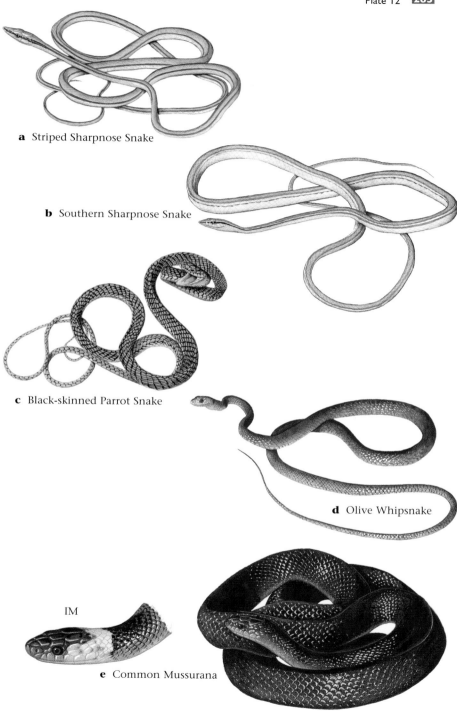

a Striped Sharpnose Snake

b Southern Sharpnose Snake

c Black-skinned Parrot Snake

d Olive Whipsnake

IM

e Common Mussurana

Plate 13a

South American Water Snake
Helicops angulatus

ID: Small but fairly stout-bodied; alternating bands of light brown (or olive) and dark brown on the upper body, the darker bands being slightly wider; pale yellow to pink or orange belly with brown to black markings extending from the bands on the upper surface; small eyes; 40 to 60 cm (16 to 24 in).

HABITAT: Small ponds, streams in forest, rivers; nocturnal.

REGION: AMA

Plate 13b

Giant Earthsnake (also called Brown Ground Snake)
Atractus major

ID: Small; light brown upper body with scattered dark brown spots and blotches; cream to pale yellow belly with scattered brown or black flecks; tongue gray with a white tip; 50 to 70 cm (20 to 28 in).

HABITAT: On ground in leaf litter, but also fossorial (burrowing); primary forest but also secondary forest and clearings; active by day and night.

REGION: AMA

Plate 13c

Common False Viper
Xenodon rabdocephalus

ID: Mid-sized; light brown to dark brown, with brown or black bands; some colors vary, and some forms very closely resemble the venomous Fer-de-Lance; 75 to 90 cm (30 to 36 in).

HABITAT: Active day and night; terrestrial; primary and secondary forest.

REGION: AMA

Plate 13d

Black-headed Calico Snake (also called Tschudi's False Coral Snake)
Oxyrhopus melanogenys

ID: Mid-sized; head black with orange or red ring around neck; broad black rings across body, separated on front part of body by narrow white or pale yellow rings; tricolor pattern on rear half of body: black–yellow–black–red–black–yellow–black; belly pale cream; another form is solid red with black head and a pale neck ring; to 90 cm (36 in).

HABITAT: Day-active, terrestrial; mostly in forest, but sometimes in open areas.

REGION: ESA, AMA

Plate 13 **287**

a South American Water Snake

b Giant Earthsnake

c Common False Viper

d Black-headed Calico Snake

Plate 14a

Red-tailed Boa (also called Boa Constrictor)
Boa constrictor
ID: Large, stout-bodied; tan to light brown upper body with dark brown transverse markings that outline oval-shaped tan markings; triangular head with a wide, dark brown band running from nostril through eye and onto neck; cream-colored belly with scattered brown or black flecks and spots; tiny white bony spurs protrude from body near base of tail; to 4 m (13 ft), but most are much smaller.

HABITAT: Mostly terrestrial, sometimes found in trees; active by day and night in forest.

REGION: MCL, ACL, AMA

Note: Regulated for conservation purposes; CITES Appendix II listed.

Plate 14b

Amazon Tree Boa
Corallus hortulanus
ID: Mid-sized, with body slightly flattened from side-to-side; gray or brown, usually with distinct dark brown circular or oval-shaped markings outlined with cream; some individuals are solid yellow, pink, or red; cream to tan belly with scattered darker markings; scales on upper and lower lips have obvious, deep, heat-sensing pits; to 1.25 m (4 ft).

HABITAT: Arboreal in primary but also secondary forest; often found along shores of creeks, small rivers, and oxbows; nocturnal.

REGION: AMA

Plate 14c

Rainbow Boa
Epicrates cenchria
ID: Mid-sized, with a rounded body (in cross-section); three dark stripes on head; body brown to reddish brown or orange with roughly circular or oval markings that are pale tan, yellow, or orange, outlined in black; under strong light, scales reflect a rainbow of iridescence; creamy white belly; 1 to 2 m (3 to 6.5 ft), but most are smaller.

HABITAT: Mostly terrestrial, somewhat arboreal in forest; mostly active by night, but somewhat by day.

REGION: AMA

Note: Regulated for conservation purposes; CITES Appendix II listed.

Plate 14d

Common Anaconda
Eunectes murinus murinus
ID: Very large, stout-bodied; gray, yellow, or tan, some with green tint, with alternating pairs of large dark brown or black blotches; lighter yellow or tan belly with scattered small dark markings; to 10+ m (33+ ft), but most are much smaller; the Anaconda ties with the Reticulated Python for being the largest snake on Earth; the Anaconda, however, is more massive.

HABITAT: Mostly aquatic in large lakes, rivers, and swamps, but sometimes on land near water.

REGION: AMA

Plate 14 **289**

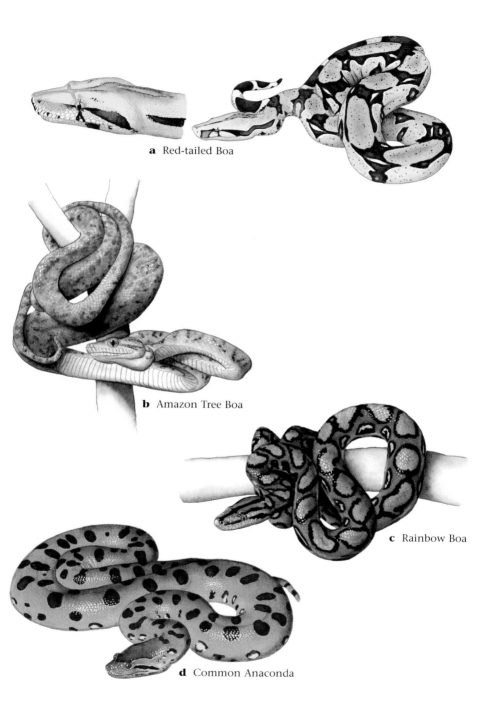

a Red-tailed Boa

b Amazon Tree Boa

c Rainbow Boa

d Common Anaconda

Plate 15a
Langsdorff's Coral Snake
Micrurus langsdorffi
ID: Small; most with alternating rings of dull red, white, and black; red rings (formed by scales that have black pigment in their centers) are the widest, followed by the black (half the width of the red), and narrow white rings (usually no more than one-half scale in width); ring sequence red–white–black–white–red; rings extend onto belly; white chin; to 70 cm (28 in).

HABITAT: Terrestrial; secretive, in leaf litter or under logs and vegetation; active mostly at twilight.

REGION: AMA

Plate 15b
Fer-de-Lance (also called South American Lancehead)
Bothrops atrox
ID: Large, medium-bodied, with rough scales and distinctly lance-shaped head; dull olive, tan, or brown with a pattern of irregular darker and lighter markings, which often form a series of "X" shapes; dark bands extend from behind each eye to the sides of head and neck; cream to yellow belly with irregular darker markings; to 2 m (6.5 ft), but most are much smaller.

HABITAT: Forest, and often near human habitations; terrestrial; mostly active at night, but somewhat by day.

REGION: AMA

Plate 15c
Amazon Bushmaster
Lachesis muta
ID: Large, rough-scaled, with lance-shaped head; light brown, pinkish tan, or golden tan, with diamond-shaped, dark brown or black markings outlined by light tan or cream; top of head brown; black stripe runs from behind eye to angle of jaw; lips tan; distinct raised ridge along backbone; cream-colored belly; to 3.6 m (12 ft); the longest viper on Earth.

HABITAT: Primary forest and forest edges; terrestrial; nocturnal.

REGION: ESA, AMA

Plate 15d
Amazon Streak Lizard (also called Trinidad Gecko)
Gonatodes humeralis
ID: Small; vertical light bar just anterior to front legs; tail banded gray and black; males salt and pepper mixture of yellow and black, with some red scales on neck and head, half circle of cream on neck; females gray with black flecks; to 8 cm (3.2 in).

HABITAT: Arboreal, day-active; primary forest, usually found in shade, on tree trunks; at night sleep on leaves or small branches.

REGION: AMA

Plate 15e
Common House Gecko
Hemidactylus mabouia
ID: Mid-sized, slender; long, fragile tail (breaks easily); large toe pads; large eyes; light to dark tan, with darker tan markings and bands on tail; to 14 cm (5.6 in).

HABITAT: Nocturnal, commonly seen in and on outsides of houses, where they are attracted to insects coming to lights; can watch them foraging at night.

 (human habitation)

REGION: ESA, AMA

Plate 15 **291**

a Langsdorff's Coral Snake

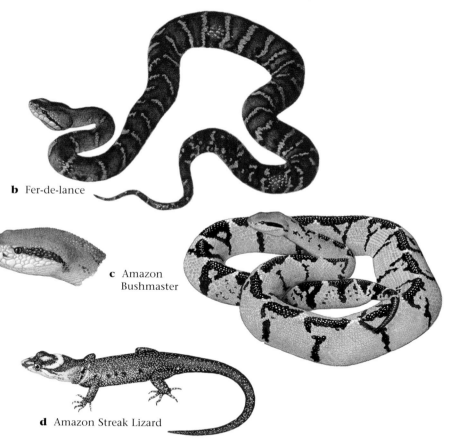

b Fer-de-lance

c Amazon Bushmaster

d Amazon Streak Lizard

e Common House Gecko

Plate 16a
Green Iguana
Iguana iguana
ID: Large, with prominent head crest and throat fan (especially males); bright green to dull olive with irregular darker crossbands; tail banded, extremely long; distinctive, large round scale present just below ear opening; juveniles bright green, becoming darker with age; to 2 m (6.5 ft); largest lizard in Perú.

HABITAT: Forest; mostly arboreal but sometimes on ground; day-active.

REGION: TDF, AMA

Note: Regulated for conservation purposes; CITES Appendix II listed.

Plate 16b
Slender Anole
Norops fuscoauratus
ID: Small, slender, long limbs and tail; gray or tan; females often have pale tan lengthwise stripe running down center of body; chin, throat, belly pale gray with brown flecks; male dewlap (throat fan) large, pale creamy yellow with white scales and white border; 10 to 14 cm (4 to 5.6 in).

HABITAT: Both primary and secondary forest, forest edges, and clearings; often found foraging on ground by day; at night, sleep horizontally or head-down on vegetation usually less than 1 m (3 ft) above ground.

REGION: AMA

Plate 16c
Common Forest Anole (also called Amazon Forest Anole)
Norops trachyderma
ID: Small, slender, with long limbs and tail; upper body brown with darker brown, chevron-shaped markings on back; two distinct white markings on each side of lower jaw; belly cream to yellow with brown flecks; base of tail greatly swollen in males; male dewlap (throat fan) small, orange to red with black scales; 10 to 15 cm (4 to 6 in).

HABITAT: Both primary and secondary forest and forest edges; on ground, but also on low vegetation, tree trunks; prefers shade, shuns clearings; the most common forest anole at many locations; day-active.

REGION: AMA

Plate 16d
Amazon Wood Lizard
Enyalioides laticeps
ID: Large, rough-scaled, long-tailed (tail longer than body); short, chunky head and snout; distinct row of large spiny scales run along the backbone; upper body green to pale brown with irregular black markings along back roughly forming cross-bars; tan or pale orange spots or diagonal bars on back; males have navy blue patch with rust-colored spot in center on throat; belly of males tan, of females pinkish tan; dark band on lower jaw below eye; mouth slightly upturned, resembling a smile; 20 to 32 cm (8 to 13 in).

HABITAT: Primary forest, and to lesser extent secondary forest; arboreal; basks head-up in the sun on trunks of small trees; day-active; retreats to burrow.

REGION: AMA

Plate 16   **293**

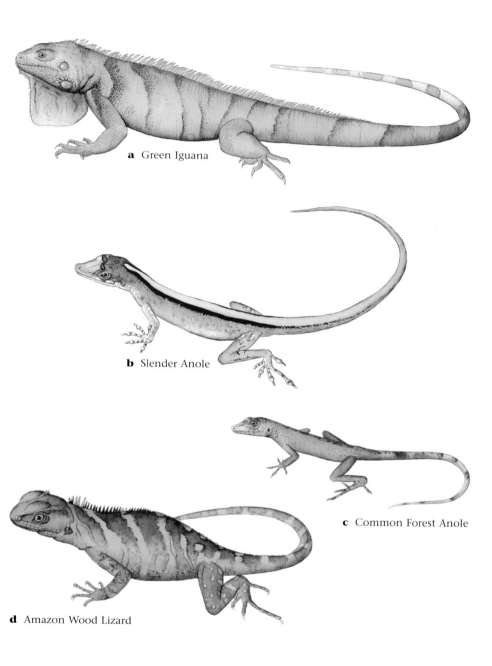

a Green Iguana

b Slender Anole

c Common Forest Anole

d Amazon Wood Lizard

Plate 17a

Pink-bellied Leaf Lizard (also called Rose Whorltail Lizard)
Stenocercus roseiventris
ID: Mid-sized, with small but distinct crest of pointed scales running down center of back; spiny tail; upper part of body tan to reddish brown with darker brown cross bars; cream stripe from lip to anterior part of body; black blotch on side of neck; underside pink; to 21 cm (8.4 in).

HABITAT: Terrestrial, often found near logs or bases of trees in forest; basks in sun; day-active.

REGION: ESA, AMA

Plate 17b

Spiny Whorltail Lizard
Stenocercus crassicaudatus
ID: Mid-sized, with small but distinct crest of pointed scales running down center of back; spiny tail; upper part of body dark gray with black spots; to 23 cm (10.5 in).

HABITAT: Terrestrial, day-active; rock-dwelling.

REGION: ESA

Plate 17c

Perú Pacific Lizard
Microlophus peruvianus
ID: Relatively large, robust; tail 1.5 times length of body; heavy, triangular head; long, strong legs; color variable with elevation and age of individual; juveniles lead-colored with white spots; adults gray, with distinctive black band on neck; some individuals have green and/or blue coloring on back; to 30 cm (12 in).

HABITAT: Terrestrial, day-active; dry coastal areas, in valleys near rivers, riverbanks.

REGION: CDL

Plate 17d

Tschudi's Pacific Lizard
Microlophus thoracicus
ID: Mid-sized; dark gray to dark brown with large black or brown spots and white flecks; to 13 cm (5.2 in).

HABITAT: Sandy areas with thick vegetation cover; day-active, terrestrial.

REGION: CDL

Plate 17　295

a Pink-bellied Leaf Lizard

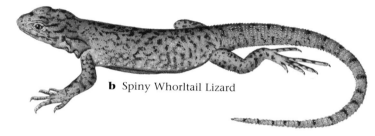

b Spiny Whorltail Lizard

c Perú Pacific Lizard

d Tschudi's Pacific Lizard

Plate 18a
Tiger Pacific Lizard
Microlophus tigris
ID: Mid-sized; dark gray to dark brown, with black or brown markings; males with transverse row of black spots on throat, rest of underside a mixture of orange-red, yellow, black, white, and pale bluish green; females less brightly colored, underside gray, white, or cream; to 16 cm (6.4 in).

HABITAT: Day-active and terrestrial; found in western foothills of Andes where rock and boulders are abundant, but vegetation is sparse; occurs from sea level to about 2800 m (9100 ft).

REGION: CDL

Plate 18b
Blue-lipped Tree Lizard
Tropidurus umbra ochrocollaris
ID: Moderately large; relatively small head and distinctive blue mouth lining; row of large spiny scales (crest) running down center of back; color of males highly variable, from bright green with small black spots to dull olive-green or olive-tan, as in females; narrow black collar; 25 to 30 cm (10 to 12 in).

HABITAT: Primary and secondary forest; day-active, arboreal, on tree trunks; sleep at night on horizontal branches less than 1.5 m (4.5 ft) above ground.

REGION: AMA

Plate 18c
Amazon Thornytail (also called Thornytail Canopy Iguana)
Uracentron flaviceps
ID: Moderately large, stout bodied, with short, wide, thorny-scaled tail; upper body and belly black; in breeding condition, male has pale orange head with black flecks, otherwise gray-tan head; pinkish white collar circles neck; 20 to 25 cm (8 to 10 in).

HABITAT: Primary forest; upper branches of large trees; day-active.

REGION: AMA

Plate 18d
Black-spotted Skink
Mabuya nigropunctata
ID: Mid-sized, rather stocky body; smooth, shiny scales; brown or brown-gray with a bronze sheen; black stripe running along each side of body; 20 to 25 cm (8 to 10 in).

HABITAT: Terrestrial and on logs; often seen sunning; most active during periods of sunshine; day-active.

REGION: AMA

Plate 18 **297**

a Tiger Pacific Lizard

b Blue-lipped Tree Lizard

c Amazon Thornytail

d Black-spotted Skink

Plate 19a

Amazon Racerunner (also called Giant Ameiva)
Ameiva ameiva
ID: Large, slender, with angular pointed head and snout; long tail; powerful jaws; body and sides patterned with bright green; light and dark stripes and spots run lengthwise along body; belly bluish white; 30 to 40 cm (12 to 16 in).

HABITAT: Terrestrial, basks in sun on ground in clearings, riverbanks, and forest edges; day-active.

REGION: AMA

Plate 19b

Forest Whiptail
Kentropyx pelviceps
ID: Moderately large, slender, with angular pointed head and snout, and long tail; wide, bright emerald-green stripe runs from the tip of snout to mid-back, where it becomes reddish brown or tan; dark brown stripes border the green stripe on either side; throat and chest grayish white; belly and undersides of limbs pale orange; 25 to 35 cm (10 to 14 in).

HABITAT: Secondary and primary forest; on ground but also in low vegetation; forest edges, treefall gaps in forest; basks in sun; day-active.

REGION: AMA

Plate 19c

Golden Tegu (also called Black Tegu)
Tupinambis teguixin
ID: Large, fairly stout-bodied, with angular pointed head and snout, and long tail; upper body with shiny scales patterned black and creamy white, forming irregular narrow cross-bands that become wider on tail; to 80+ cm (32+ in).

HABITAT: Basks in sun on ground or on fallen logs; along forest edges, in clearings; day-active.

REGION: AMA

Note: Regulated for conservation purposes; CITES Appendix II listed.

Plate 19d

Puna Lizard
Proctoporus bolivianus
ID: Small, slender, long tail; scales smooth; upper part of body brown with faint tan stripes; belly bluish white, posterior margins of scales black; to 13 cm (6 in).

HABITAT: Terrestrial and day-active; high elevations, 3300 to 4080 m (10,725 to 13,260 ft); often found under rocks.

REGION: HAP

Plate 19 **299**

a Amazon Racerunner

b Forest Whiptail

c Golden Tegu

d Puna Lizard

Plate 20a
White-vented Storm-Petrel
Oceanites gracilis

ID: Small (15 cm, 6 in); dark brown with white rump and white lower belly with black line up middle.

HABITAT: "Walking" on ocean's surface during the day, often within sight of land.

REGION: CDL

Plate 20b
Wedge-rumped Storm-Petrel
Oceanodroma tethys

ID: Small (19 cm, 7.5 in); dark brown with large triangular-shaped white rump patch covering most of tail. The similar Wilson's Storm-Petrel, *Oceanodroma oceanicus*, has a narrow white rump patch, and its feet extend beyond the tail in flight.

HABITAT: Flying with slow wingbeats over the ocean's surface.

REGION: CDL

Plate 20c
Humboldt Penguin
Spheniscus humboldti

ID: Large (70 cm, 2.3 ft); black upperparts, white underparts; prominent white line over eye curving down and forward toward chest obvious both when standing upright onshore or swimming duck-like on the ocean's surface. Immatures all grayish brown.

HABITAT: Beaches and rocks of coastal islands, headlands, or in adjacent waters within sight of land.

REGION: CDL

Plate 20d
Peruvian Diving-Petrel
Pelecanoides garnotii

ID: Medium-sized (23 cm, 9 in), black upperparts, white underparts, short neck and tail, thick bill. Flies short distances with rapid wingbeats; floats on ocean's surface like a cork and swims rapidly under water and through waves using its wings.

HABITAT: Coastal waters, especially around offshore islands and rocky headlands of mainland.

REGION: CDL

Note: This species considered threated, IUCN Red List.

Plate 20e
Peruvian Booby
Sula variegata

ID: Large (74 cm, 2.3 ft); all-white head and underparts; dark back and wings spotted white. The similar Blue-footed Booby, *Sula nebouxii*, is much rarer on the coast of Perú and is distinguished by its streaked head and uniform brown back and wings, and by a white patch at the base of the tail.

HABITAT: Soaring low over ocean's surface and diving into the water from high in the air, this species is often abundant near shore.

REGION: CDL

Plate 20 **301**

a White-vented Storm-Petrel

b Wedge-rumped Storm-Petrel

c Humboldt Penguin

e Peruvian Booby

d Peruvian Diving-Petrel

Plate 21a

Peruvian Pelican
Pelecanus thagus

ID: Very large (1.8 m, 6 ft); brown and white (adult) or grayish (immature) seabird.

HABITAT: Coastal areas and estuaries, where it flies in line or "V" formation low over water's surface or soars high over coastal hills and cliffs; rarely in freshwater lakes near coast.

REGION: CDL

Plate 21b

Neotropic Cormorant
Phalacrocorax brasilianus

ID: Large (69 cm, 2.3 ft); all black; long neck.

HABITAT: Swimming duck-like in water, sitting upright on dead branches in or near the water, or flying in flocks of long lines or "V" formation on or over coastal estuaries, freshwater reservoirs, rivers and cochas.

REGION: CDL, AMA

Plate 21c

Guanay Cormorant
Phalacrocorax bougainvilli

ID: Large (74 cm, 2.4 ft); black with white throat patch, breast and belly.

HABITAT: Large numbers on guano islands offshore and in coastal waters near land.

REGION: CDL

Plate 21d

Red-legged Cormorant
Phalacrocorax gaimardi

ID: Large (74 cm, 2.4 ft); gray spotted white with a large white patch on each side of neck; bill yellow and legs red.

HABITAT: Individuals or small family groups on rocky shore of coast or guano islands offshore.

REGION: CDL

Plate 21e

Anhinga
Anhinga anhinga

ID: Large (84 cm, 2.8 ft); black with long straight bill and very long, slender neck; large silverish patches on upperwings of adults. Female with brownish head and breast; immature brownish overall.

HABITAT: Individuals or pairs on Amazonian lakes or on vegetation along rivers; occasionally soars on broad wings high overhead.

REGION: AMA

Plate 21f

Chilean Flamingo
Phoenicopterus chilensis

ID: Large (1 m, 3.3 ft) with extremely long neck and legs; pink to whitish pink; yellow and black bill; adults with pale-colored legs and contrasting pink "knees." In flight with long neck extended and black flight feathers on trailing half of orange wings. Similar Andean Flamingo, *Phoenicopterus andinus*, has yellow legs, and Puna Flamingo, *Phoenicopterus jamesi*, is small with all red legs. Immatures of all three species are brownish gray.

HABITAT: Nests in saline lakes in highlands of central and southern Perú. Winters in coastal mud flats, mangroves and estuaries along entire coast of Perú. The Andean Flamingo and Puna Flamingo nest in highland saline lakes of extreme southern Perú, and the Andean Flamingo regularly winters on the south coast, especially at Mejía lagoons.

REGION: CDL, HAP

Plate 21 **303**

a Peruvian Pelican

b Neotropic Cormorant

c Guanay Cormorant

d Red-legged Cormorant

F

M

e Anhinga

f Chilean Flamingo

Plate 22a
Gray Gull
Larus modestus
ID: Medium-sized (48 cm, 1.4 ft); only all dark gray gull in Perú, it has black wing- and tail-tips, whitish chin and forehead in the breeding season; head and upper neck brownish in nonbreeding season.

HABITAT: Common on sandy coastal beaches where it feeds on Sand Crabs, *Emerita analoga* (Plate 99), along the edge of retreating waves.

REGION: CDL

Plate 22b
Band-tailed Gull
Larus belcheri
ID: Large (56 cm, 1.8 ft); white body and head with black back and top of wings, and broad, black band at end of tail; in nonbreeding season head turns blackish with a gray neck. The larger (65 cm, 2.1 ft) and less common Kelp Gull, *Larus dominicanus*, is similar but has an all-white tail and maintains a largely white head and neck in the nonbreeding season.

HABITAT: Abundant in all types of sea beaches and coastal lagoons.

REGION: CDL

Plate 22c
Franklin's Gull
Larus pipixcan
ID: Medium-sized (36 cm, 1.2 ft); white with gray back and wings; wing tips black and white; in nonbreeding season with a blackish cap, at beginning of breeding season the entire head becomes black.

HABITAT: Common wintering North American migrant along the coast and agricultural fields near the coast.

REGION: CDL

Plate 22d
Gray-headed Gull
Larus cirrocephalus
ID: Medium-sized (45 cm, 1.5 ft); adults with light gray head, black wing tip with distinct white spots in flight. Similar wintering Laughing Gulls, *Larus atricilla*, with wing tips all black.

HABITAT: Coastal estuaries and river mouths.

REGION: CDL

Plate 22e
Andean Gull
Larus serranus
ID: Medium-sized (46 cm, 1.5 ft); breeding adults with black head, nonbreeding with white head and black spot behind eye. Only gull in the high Andes.

HABITAT: Puna lakes and marshy areas sometimes descending to the coast in winter.

REGION: HAP

Plate 22 **305**

a Gray Gull

non-breeding

b Band-tailed Gull

breeding

breeding

non-breeding

c Franklin's Gull

e Andean Gull

d Gray-headed Gull

Plate 23a

Inca Tern

Larosterna inca

ID: Medium-sized (38 cm, 1.3 ft); unmistakable dark blue-gray head and body with long white moustache on each side of the head; red legs and bill.

HABITAT: Rocky shores of the coast and guano islands offshore.

REGION: CDL

Plate 23b

Large-billed Tern

Phaetusa simplex

ID: Medium-sized (38 cm, 1.3 ft); distinctly patterned black, white and gray wings in flight; large yellow bill.

HABITAT: Larger rivers and occasionally cochas of the Amazonian lowlands.

REGION: AMA

Plate 23c

Yellow-billed Tern

Sterna superciliaris

ID: Medium-sized (25 cm, 10 in); slender white wings with black tips; slender yellow bill.

HABITAT: Larger rivers and occasionally cochas of the Amazonian lowlands, where, in buoyant flight, it hovers and then dives to catch fish.

REGION: AMA

Plate 23d

Black Skimmer

Rynchops niger

ID: Medium-sized (44 cm, 1.4 ft); black on top and white below with an immense red and black bill. Peculiar low flight over water's surface with lower part of bill "skimming" the water.

HABITAT: Coastal estuaries and larger rivers of Amazonian lowlands.

REGION: CDL, AMA

Plate 23e

Sooty Shearwater

Puffinus griseus

ID: Medium-sized (45 cm, 1.5 ft); uniformly sooty brown above and paler brown below with grayish white underwings; long narrow wings flap stiffly with intervals of soaring.

HABITAT: Flying low over the ocean's surface in cold offshore waters; present in some numbers off Perú all year but most common during migration, when long lines of these birds move north to their wintering grounds in the north Pacific or south to their nesting islands in southern Argentina and Chile.

REGION: CDL

Plate 23   307

a Inca Tern

b Large-billed Tern

c Yellow-billed Tern

d Black Skimmer

e Sooty Shearwater

Plate 24 (**See also:** Herons and Egrets, p. 108)

Plate 24a
Boat-billed Heron
Cochlearius cochlearius
ID: Large (49 cm, 1.6 ft); chunky, with monstrously wide bill. Similarly-colored Black-crowned Night-Heron, *Nycticorax nycticorax*, has a long, narrow bill and is common on the coast and uncommon in the Amazon lowlands.

HABITAT: Roosts by day in small group or alone in thick vegetation along water-courses; feeds at night on beaches and vegetated water edges.

REGION: AMA

Plate 24b
Snowy Egret
Egretta thula
ID: Large (61 cm, 2 ft); adults all white with black bill and legs and bright yellow feet.

HABITAT: Coastal estuaries, river mouths, lowland lakes, marshes and rivers, usually solitary.

REGION: CDL, AMA

Plate 24c
Cattle Egret
Bubulcus ibis
ID: Large (51 cm, 1.7 ft); adults all white with orange-yellow bill and greenish yellow legs. During the breeding season the back becomes pinkish orange and the legs and bill reddish.

HABITAT: Marshes, pastures and open areas, often asociated with cattle, and along rivers and lakes from lowlands to 2600 m (8500 ft) elevation, often in flocks.

REGION: TDF, CDL, WSV, ESA, AMA

Plate 24d
Great Egret (also called Common Egret)
Ardea alba
ID: Large (1 m, 3.3 ft); all white with yellow bill and black legs.

HABITAT: Coastal estuaries, river mouths, lowland lakes, marshes and rivers, occasionally in highland marshes; usually solitary.

REGION: CDL, HAP, AMA

Plate 24e
Rufescent Tiger-Heron
Tigrisoma lineatum
ID: Large (70 cm, 2.3 ft); chunky; adults chestnut, black and white; immatures buffy and white with barred back.

HABITAT: Solitary in thick vegetation along lowland watercourses and cochas.

REGION: AMA

Plate 24 **309**

b Snowy Egret

IM

d Great Egret

a Boat-billed Heron

IM

c Cattle Egret

IM

IM

e Rufescent Tiger-
Heron

Plate 25 (**See also:** Herons, p. 108; Marsh and stream birds, p. 110)

Plate 25a

Cocoi Heron
Ardea cocoi
ID: Large (1.2 m, 4 ft); white neck and throat, grayish body, top and sides of head all black.

HABITAT: Solitary in coastal estuaries, mangroves, and lowland river banks, marshes, cochas.

REGION: CDL, AMA

Plate 25b

Striated Heron
(also called Green-backed Heron)
Butorides striatus
ID: Medium-sized (40 cm, 1.3 ft); gray neck, darker back. Gives loud high-pitched squawk when frightened into flight.

HABITAT: Solitary or in pairs low in vegetation near water's surface of mangroves, lowland swamps, small rivers and cochas.

REGION: CDL, AMA

Plate 25c

Capped Heron
Pilherodius pileatus
ID: Large (60 cm, 2ft); white body, cream-colored neck, black cap and bare blue skin on face.

HABITAT: Solitary in vegetation and shallow water along forested lowland streams and lakes; looks hump-shouldered in flight.

REGION: AMA

Plate 25d

Puna Ibis
Plegadis ridgwayi
ID: Large (71 cm, 2.3 ft); dark, with long, reddish, down-curved bill.

HABITAT: Solitary in swampy areas, ponds, streams and moist grasslands in the puna; occasionally descends to coastal marshes in the winter. Replaced in the eastern Amazonian lowlands by the similar but greenish black Green Ibis, *Mesembrinis cayennensis*.

REGION: CDL, HAP

Plate 25e

Gray-necked Wood-rail
Aramides cajanea
ID: Large (37 cm, 2.5 ft); bright red legs, long bill, gray neck contrasting with rusty breast. (Replaced in coastal mangroves by similar Rufous-necked Wood-rail, *Aramides axillaris*.)

HABITAT: Forested swampy areas of lowlands.

REGION: AMA

Plate 25 **311**

b Striated Heron

c Capped Heron

a Cocoi Heron

d Puna Ibis

e Gray-necked Wood-Rail

Plate 26 (**See also:** Marsh and stream birds, p. 110)

Plate 26a
Wattled Jacana
Jacana jacana
ID: Medium-sized (25 cm, 10 in); adults with bright yellow bill, rusty-colored body, yellow-green wings in flight and extremely long toes; immatures with white breast and bold white eyeline.

HABITAT: Grassy edges and lily pads of freshwater swamps and marshes of the lowlands.

REGION: AMA

Plate 26b
Sunbittern
Eurypyga helias
ID: Medium-sized (47 cm, 1.5 ft); slender neck, small head with bold stripes; in flight or during display the spread wings have a distinctive "sunburst" pattern.

HABITAT: Along forested streams and lakes of lowlands.

REGION: AMA

Plate 26c
Sungrebe
Heliornis fulica
ID: Medium-sized (29 cm, 11 in); duck-like with bold white stripes on head and neck.

HABITAT: Swims under overhanging vegetation along lowland lakes and small rivers; escapes by flying low over water, often skittering along the surface with its running feet.

REGION: AMA

Plate 26d
Hoatzin
Opisthocomus hoazin
ID: Large (64 cm, 2.1 ft); rusty colored with buffy breast; crest on head, large wings, long tail.

HABITAT: In small family groups along forested swamps, cochas and small rivers; often sits with wings spread.

REGION: AMA

Plate 26e
Horned Screamer
Anhima cornuta
ID: Very large (91 cm, 3 ft); dark back, white belly; white wing patch in flight obvious; call a deep, throaty, far-carrying gulping.

HABITAT: Swamps, marshes and adjacent tree-tops; individuals or pairs often soar high on broad wings.

REGION: AMA

Plate 26 **313**

IM
a Wattled Jacana

b Sunbittern

c Sungrebe

d Hoatzin

e Horned Screamer

Plate 27a
Muscovy Duck
Cairina moschata
ID: Large (84 cm, 2.8 ft), black; male with red bare face; large white wing patches obvious in flight.

HABITAT: Lowland forested swamps, rivers and cochas.

REGION: AMA

Plate 27b
White-cheeked Pintail
Anas bahamensis
ID: Medium-sized (42 cm, 1.4 ft); all brown with strikingly white cheeks and throat; bill with bright red base.

HABITAT: Coastal estuaries and mangroves and nearby freshwater lakes and marshes.

REGION: CDL

Plate 27c
Yellow-billed Pintail (also called Brown Pintail)
Anas georgica
ID: Large (66 cm, 2.2 ft); uniform pale brown with yellow bill. The other common yellow-billed duck of highland lakes, the Speckled Teal, *Anas flavirostris*, is smaller (43 cm, 1.4 ft), shorter-necked, and darker headed.

HABITAT: Marshes and lakes of puna.

REGION: HAP

Plate 27d
Puna Teal
Anas puna
ID: Medium-sized (43 cm, 1.4 ft); black-capped with contrasting white cheeks and bright blue bill.

HABITAT: Marshes and lakes of puna.

REGION: HAP

Plate 27e
Torrent Duck
Merganetta armata
ID: Medium-sized (40 cm, 1.3 ft); long slender body with red bill; male with black and white head and neck stripes, white breast with dark streaks; female with buffy-orange underparts.

HABITAT: Rushing mountain streams and rivers between 1500 and 3500 m (5000 and 11,500 ft) elevation.

REGION: WSV, ESA

Plate 27   315

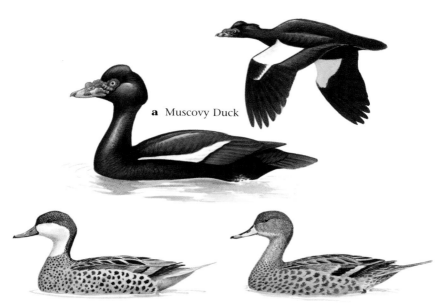

a Muscovy Duck

b White-cheeked Pintail

c Yellow-billed Pintail

d Puna Teal

e Torrent Duck

Plate 28a
Orinoco Goose
Neochen jubata
ID: Large (75 cm, 2.5 ft); buff and rusty-colored; broad white band on inner half of wings obvious in flight.

HABITAT: Sand-bars of remote lowland rivers.

REGION: AMA

Plate 28b
Andean Goose
Chloephaga melanoptera
ID: Large (73 cm, 2.4 ft); all white with black wings and tail; large white wing patch obvious in flight.

HABITAT: High Andean lakes and marshes.

REGION: HAP

Plate 28c
Silvery Grebe
Podiceps occipitalis
ID: Medium-sized (28 cm, 11 in); duck-like with pointed bill; light gray back; white underparts; silvery tufts on sides of head. Very similar to the flightless Puna Grebe, *Podiceps taczanowskii*, which is endemic to the Lago Junín area and has a longer bill that is lighter gray.

HABITAT: Puna lakes above 2800 m (9000 ft) ringed with vegetation.

REGION: HAP

Plate 28d
White-tufted Grebe
Rollandia rolland
ID: Medium-sized (31 cm, 1 ft); duck-like with pointed bill; neck and head black with white ear tuft in breeding plumage; reddish brown body. In winter plumage, neck and head pale and ear tufts absent.

HABITAT: Coastal waters to puna lakes.

REGION: CDL, HAP

Plate 28e
Giant Coot
Fulica gigantea
ID: Large (53 cm, 1.7 ft); goose-sized with pointed, mostly red bill, dark red legs; body all slate-gray. Replaced in marshy puna lakes and rarely on the coast by the similar-colored but much smaller (35 cm, 1.1 ft) Slate-colored Coot, *Fulica ardesiaca*, which has greenish legs and an all white bill.

HABITAT: Isolated ponds and lagoons high in the puna.

REGION: HAP

Plate 28f
Black-necked Stilt
Himantopus mexicanus
ID: Medium-sized (37 cm, 1.2 ft); tall, slender with striking black and white body and pinkish red legs.

HABITAT: Inland ponds, coastal estuaries and mangrove swamps.

REGION: CDL, AMA

Plate 28 **317**

a Orinoco Goose

c Silvery Grebe

d White-tufted Grebe

b Andean Goose

e Giant Coot

f Black-necked Stilt

Plate 29a

Whimbrel
Numenius phaeopus
ID: Medium-sized (44 cm, 1.4 ft); long bill curved downwards; muted black and white stripes on head; brownish body.

HABITAT: Outer sand beaches along the coast.

REGION: CDL

Plate 29b

Pied Lapwing
Vanellus cayanus
ID: Medium-sized (23 cm, 9 in); strikingly black and white-patterned with bright red legs.

HABITAT: Sandy beaches and islands on large rivers of Amazon lowlands.

REGION: AMA

Plate 29c

Andean Lapwing
Vanellus resplendens
ID: Medium-sized (33 cm, 1.1 ft); gray and white with iridescent greenish back; its bold behavior and noisy calls make it obvious.

HABITAT: Resident of wet grassy areas and marsh edges in puna between 2500 and 4000 m (8200 and 13,000 ft) elevation.

REGION: HAP

Plate 29d

Diademed Sandpiper-Plover
Phegornis mitchelli
ID: Small (18 cm, 7 in); subtly beautiful gray-brown and white pattern on head and breast, back chestnut and gray; relatively long bill for a plover.

HABITAT: Andean bogs, streams and lakes of the treeless puna above 4000 m (13,000 ft), from central Perú south.

REGION: HAP

Plate 29e

Killdeer
Charadrius vociferus
ID: Medium-sized (23 cm, 9 in); bold and noisy; two black bands on a white breast; brown upperparts with rusty-orange rump; same species as in North America but breeding in Perú.

HABITAT: Pairs resident along coastal rivers, pastures and moist grassy areas.

REGION: CDL

Plate 29f

American Oystercatcher
Haematopus palliatus
ID: Medium-sized (47 cm, 1.5 ft); black and white with long, straight orange bill. The similar-sized and -shaped Blackish Oystercatcher, *Haematopus ater*, is all blackish with orange bill and legs and occurs only on rocky seashores.

HABITAT: Pairs occur on sandy beaches of islands and estuaries of mainland.

REGION: CDL

Plate 29 **319**

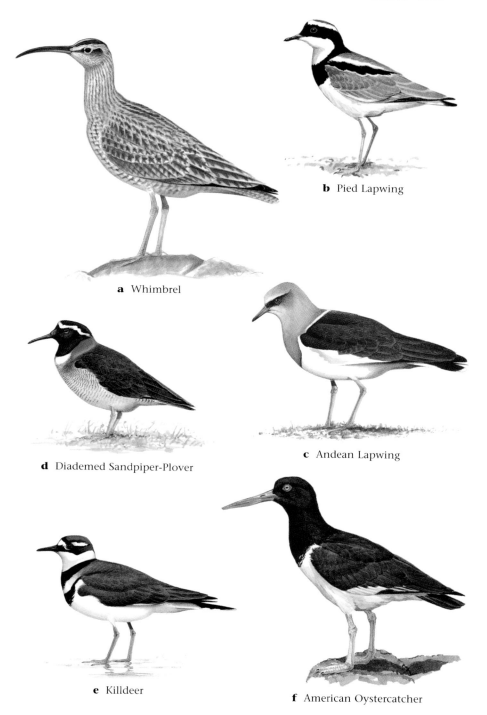

a Whimbrel

b Pied Lapwing

c Andean Lapwing

d Diademed Sandpiper-Plover

e Killdeer

f American Oystercatcher

Plate 30a

Black-bellied Plover
Pluvialis squatarola
ID: Medium-sized (30 cm, 1 ft); light gray nonbreeding plumage with black "wing pits" in flight; in breeding plumage in preparation for migration north (April), sides of face and belly become black.

HABITAT: Solitary on coastal estuaries, mud flats and sandy beaches.

REGION: CDL

Plate 30b

Andean Snipe
Gallinago jamesoni
ID: Medium-sized (30 cm, 1 ft); chunky, short-tailed and long-billed with dark legs, its barred breast and indistinctive eye-stripes are difficult to see as it flies up from underfoot.

HABITAT: Grassy bogs, wet meadows and moist puna above 3200 m (10,500 ft).

REGION: HAP

Plate 30c

Spotted Sandpiper
Actitis macularia
ID: Small (18 cm, 7 in); pale-breasted; bobs up and down while walking or resting; in flight, a long, thin white stripe on upper wing surface; flies with a twittering, stiff-winged beat low over the water's surface; the breast spots only appear on individuals preparing (March to April) to migrate to nesting areas in North America.

HABITAT: Solitary on rocks, branches and sandy beaches primarily along lowland rivers and lakes but also at higher elevations into the puna; some individuals present throughout the year.

REGION: CDL, WSV, HAP, ESA, AMA

Plate 30d

Sanderling
Calidris alba
ID: Medium-sized (20 cm, 8 in); light gray to whitish with short, black legs. Broad white wing stripe in flight. Turns rusty-colored in preparation for migration north in April.

HABITAT: Small groups chase waves back and forth on sandy ocean beaches; winters in Perú (July to April), but a few nonbreeding individuals present all year.

REGION: CDL

Plate 30e

Rufous-bellied Seedsnipe
Attagis gayi
ID: Medium-sized (30 cm, 1 ft); dove- or quail-like with rusty colored belly, dark back.

HABITAT: Dry, open puna vegetation up to snow-line.

REGION: HAP

Plate 30f

Least Seedsnipe
Thinocorus rumicivorus
ID: Small (18 cm, 7 in); dove- or plover-like but legs short; brown and buff upperparts; male with blue-gray head and neck with distinctive black line on throat and breast; female breast and head brown with buff streaks; sharply pointed wings and rapid flight. (Similar Gray-breasted Seedsnipe, *Thinocorus orbignyianus* of high puna is larger.

HABITAT: Dry treeless areas of coast and lomas vegetation.

REGION: CDL, WSV

Plate 30 **321**

a Black-bellied Plover

b Andean Snipe

c Spotted Sandpiper

d Sanderling

e Rufous-bellied Seedsnipe

f Least Seedsnipe

Plate 31 (**See also:** Tinamous and Rhea, p. 117)

Plate 31a

Great Tinamou
Tinamus major
ID: Medium-sized (46 cm, 1.5 ft); short tail; whitish throat and belly; largest tinamou in lowland forests. Gives loud quavering whistles at dawn, in late afternoon, and on moon-lit nights.

HABITAT: Floor of moist lowland forests.

REGION: AMA

Plate 31b

Little Tinamou
Crypturellus soui
ID: Medium-sized (23 cm, 9 in); whitish throat; no barring; smallest tinamou in Perú; gives series of quavering whistles each rising in pitch.

HABITAT: Floor of lowland scrubby secondary forest, gardens and plantations.

REGION: AMA

Plate 31c

Undulated Tinamou
Crypturellus undulatus
ID: Medium-sized (28 cm, 11 in); whitish throat, distinctive barring on sides of belly. Gives low four-note whistle through the day, "ooh, oh-oh, ah," with last note rising.

HABITAT: Floor of lowland, seasonally flooded forest and moist secondary forest.

REGION: AMA

Plate 31d

Andean Tinamou
Nothoprocta pentlandii
ID: Medium-sized (27 cm, 10.5 in); gray breast, brownish black back mixed with cinnamon and boldly streaked buffy white.

HABITAT: Grassy areas amid brush at 3500 m (11,500 ft) down to lomas of central coastal lowlands.

REGION: WSV, HAP

Plate 31e

Lesser Rhea
Pterocnemia pennata
ID: Large (98 cm, 3.2 ft); Ostrich-like with long stout legs and neck; buffy brown with white spots on back; flightless.

HABITAT: Open grassy plains of puna highlands in southern Perú.

REGION: HAP

Note: This species is endangered, CITES Appendix I and USA ESA listed.

Plate 31 **323**

b Little Tinamou

a Great Tinamou

c Undulated Tinamou

e Lesser Rhea

d Andean Tinamou

Plate 32 (**See also:** Guans and Trumpeter, p. 119)

Plate 32a
Speckled Chachalaca
Ortalis guttata
ID: Large (53 cm, 1.7 ft); long tail; pheasant-like with obvious whitish spots on neck and breast. Replaced in the tropical dry forest of extreme northern Perú by the similar-sized Rufous-headed Chachalaca, *Ortalis erythroptera*, which lacks the spots and has a rusty colored head.

HABITAT: Family groups in trees of forest edge and along watercourses; raucous calls between family groups at dawn.

REGION: AMA

Plate 32b
Spix's Guan
Penelope jacquacu
ID: Large (89 cm, 2.9 ft); long neck and tail, bare red skin on face and throat. Gives a wheezing whistle-like call when frightened and flies noisily through mid-levels of forest.

HABITAT: Solitary or in pairs in upper levels of moist lowland forest.

REGION: AMA

Plate 32c
Blue-throated Piping-guan
Pipile cumanensis
ID: Large (69 cm, 2.3 ft); blackish body; white top of head; whitish-blue bare throat and face; large white wing patch in flight. Gives wing-whirring sounds that travel considerable distance.

HABITAT: Tops of lowland forest trees, especially at forest edge or along rivers.

REGION: AMA

Plate 32d
Razor-billed Curassow
Mitu mitu
ID: Large (86 cm, 2.8 ft); blackish; huge red bill; belly chestnut and tail tip white. Low humming sounds given at dawn.

HABITAT: Solitary or in pairs on floor and lower branches of tierra firme forest and along river edges.

REGION: AMA

Plate 32e
Pale-winged Trumpeter
Psophia leucoptera
ID: Large (53 cm, 1.7 ft); blackish with conspicuous white wing patches; long legs; gray back.

HABITAT: Family groups of 5 to 15 on the floor of lowland primary forest; fly to mid-level branches to escape danger and roost at night. Replaced in northeastern Amazonian Perú by the similar Gray-winged Trumpeter, *Psophia crepitans*.

REGION: AMA

Plate 32 **325**

a Speckled Chachalaca

b Spix's Guan

c Blue-throated Piping-Guan

d Razor-billed Curassow

e Pale-winged Trumpeter

Plate 33a
Turkey Vulture
Cathartes aura
ID: Large (75 cm, 2.5 ft); blackish with silverish underwings, long tail, and bright red head; in flight, wings held in a broad "V," or dihedral, with little or no flapping (wingspan 1.8 m, 5.8 ft).

HABITAT: Solitary or in small groups soaring on rising warm air thermals primarily over open country and secondary forest.

REGION: TDF, CDL, WSV, HAP, ESA, AMA

Plate 33b
Black Vulture
Coragyps atratus
ID: Large (62 cm, 2 ft); blackish with white patch on underside of wing, short tail, and all black head; in flight wings held flat and flap frequently (wingspan 1.4 m, 4.6 ft). On the ground, runs like a huge chicken.

HABITAT: Small to large groups soaring on thermals or sitting gathered around garbage or offal; almost always associated with human settlements.

REGION: TDF, CDL, WSV, HAP, ESA, AMA

Plate 33c
Greater Yellow-headed Vulture
Cathartes melambrotus
ID: Large (80 cm, 2.6 ft); similar to Turkey Vulture but with a bright orange-yellow head.

HABITAT: Solitary or in pairs over lowland primary forest in the Amazonian lowlands.

REGION: AMA

Plate 33d
King Vulture
Sarcoramphus papa
ID: Large (80 cm, 2.6 ft); white with short, black tail and black trailing edge of wings; colorful head is difficult to discern at a distance; soars with wings held flat (wingspan 2 m, 6.6 ft).

HABITAT: Solitary or in pairs over lowland forest, usually away from human settlements.

REGION: TDF, AMA

Plate 33e
Andean Condor
Vultur gryphus
ID: Very large (1.3 m, 4.3 ft); black body; top of wings largely whitish; white ruff on neck; dull red head; in flight long, wide wings held almost flat with wingtip feathers spread (wingspan 3 m, 10 ft).

HABITAT: Puna and open areas above 3000 m (10,000 ft), occasionally along the coast near Paracas Peninsula.

REGION: CDL, HAP

Note: This species is endangered, CITES Appendix I and USA ESA listed.

Plate 33 **327**

a Turkey Vulture

b Black Vulture

d King Vulture

c Greater Yellow-headed
Vulture

e Andean
Condor

Plate 34a
American Swallow-tailed Kite
Elanoides forficatus
ID: Large (60 cm, 2 ft), spectacular and beautiful; black and white with pointed wings and deeply forked tail; often soars over rivers and forest canopy in large groups.

HABITAT: Secondary and primary forests of Amazonian lowlands and eastern slopes.

REGION: ESA, AMA

Plate 34b
Double-toothed Kite
Harpagus bidentatus
ID: Medium-sized (35 cm, 1.1 ft); rusty colored breast, light throat with dark center stripe.

HABITAT: Sits on branches in mid-level to canopy of secondary and primary forest in lowlands and foothills; often in association with monkey troop, catching insects scared up by the troop.

REGION: AMA

Plate 34c
Plumbeous Kite
Ictinia plumbea
ID: Medium-sized (36 cm, 1.2 ft); all gray with long pointed wings, which in flight reveal extensive rusty colored wing patches and white tail bands.

HABITAT: Sits at top of tall dead trees; often soars alone or in pairs, especially along large rivers in the Amazonian lowlands.

REGION: AMA

Plate 34d
Black-chested Buzzard-Eagle
Geranoaetus melanoleucus
ID: Large (65 cm, 2.1 ft); extremely wide wings and short, broad tail in flight; in adult underparts whitish except for dark chest and black tail, upperparts blackish with gray wings; immatures variably darker.

HABITAT: Rugged mountain slopes and valleys below 3500 m (11,500 ft) elevation and seasonally down to the coastal lomas, where they feed largely on insects.

REGION: CDL, WSV, ESA, HAP

Plate 34e
Roadside Hawk
Buteo magnirostris
ID: Medium-sized (35 cm, 1.1 ft); rusty-barred breast; in flight, a large rusty colored patch in each wing.

HABITAT: Common sitting alone in bushes and small trees in lowland open areas and secondary forest edge up to 2550 m (8200 ft).

REGION: TDF, ESA, AMA

Plate 34 **329**

a American Swallow-tailed Kite

d Black-chested
Buzzard-Eagle

b Double-toothed Kite

c Plumbeous Kite

e Roadside Hawk

Plate 35a

Harpy Eagle
Harpia harpyja

ID: Very large (1 m, 3.3 ft); crested; adults with black chest band; in flight shows broad, rounded wings and long, banded tail.

HABITAT: Hunts in canopy of remote primary forest in Amazonian lowlands.

REGION: AMA

Plate 35b

Ornate Hawk-Eagle
Spizaetus ornatus

ID: Large (60 cm, 2 ft); adult with rusty colored face and neck; black crest; long banded tail; in flight, soars to great heights and rounded wings are noticeably banded underneath; often calls while soaring, a loud series of whistles with every fifth one slurred up in pitch.

HABITAT: Lowland primary and tall secondary forest to 2000 m (6500 ft).

REGION: ESA, AMA

Plate 35c

Osprey
Pandion haliaetus

ID: Large (60 cm, 2 ft); white underparts, dark upperparts; in flight, long, slender wings held with a peculiar "crook" in the middle and shows black patches at the bend of the wing from underneath.

HABITAT: Always associated with freshwater lakes and rivers or coastal estuaries and river mouths, where it hunts for fish. Nonbreeding in Perú but some individuals present year-round.

REGION: CDL, AMA

Plate 35d

Variable Hawk
Buteo polysoma

ID: Large (60 cm, 2 ft); body color varies from dark to white-breasted, but tail is usually white with a distinct black band near end; in flight, soars with broad wings and broad tail.

HABITAT: Occurs from the coast up to the puna and down to the east slope to the lower foothills.

REGION: TDF, CDL, WSV, HAP, ESA

Plate 35 **331**

a Harpy Eagle

b Ornate Hawk-Eagle

c Osprey

d Variable Hawk

Plate 36a
Black Caracara
Daptrius ater
ID: Medium-sized (45 cm, 1.4 ft); all black with bold white band at base of tail; bare skin of face bright orange; noisy, with a harsh scream given frequently.

HABITAT: Seen in pairs in trees or on beaches of lowland rivers and lakes.

REGION: AMA

Plate 36b
Mountain Caracara
Phalcoboenus megalopterus
ID: Large (51 cm, 1.7 ft); strikingly black and white.

HABITAT: Treeless areas of puna above 3500 m (11,500 ft), where it often sits on the ground and eats small mammals or carrion.

REGION: HAP

Plate 36c
Laughing Falcon
Herpetotheres cachinnans
ID: Large (52 cm, 1.7 ft); chunky body and big-headed; buffy white underparts; black mask; often gives its loud falsetto "laughing" call in morning and afternoon.

HABITAT: Sits solitarily in secondary forest and plantations in the lowlands.

REGION: TDF, AMA

Plate 36d
Collared Forest-Falcon
Micrastur semitorquatus
ID: Large (50 cm, 1.6 ft); white breast; long banded tail; black back and top of head separated by a broad white band, or collar, at the nape of the neck. A dark, mostly black, form of this species also exists, but is rarely seen in Perú.

HABITAT: Sits solitarily in lowland primary and secondary forest.

REGION: TDF, AMA

Plate 36e
Aplomado Falcon
Falco femoralis
ID: Large (50 cm, 1.6 ft); slender-bodied and pointed-winged; light gray above with distinct buffy white line through eye; buffy white throat and breast, black-barred upper belly and rust-colored lower belly. Also present in the highlands above 2500 m (8200 ft) is the smaller but similar-sized and -shaped American Kestrel, *Falco sparverius*. It, however, is lighter-breasted with blue-gray and rusty upperparts (male) or brownish rusty upperparts (female).

HABITAT: Generally in dry treeless habitats above 2000 m (6600 ft) but occasionally on the coast.

REGION: CDL, WSV, HAP

Plate 36f
Bat Falcon
Falco rufigularis
ID: Medium-sized (25 cm, 10 in); dark body with white throat and rusty colored breast; flies with a rapid wingbeat on long, pointed wings; seldom soars.

HABITAT: Solitary or in pairs sitting at the top of tall, exposed trees in Amazonian lowlands and foothills.

REGION: AMA

Plate 36 **333**

a Black Caracara

b Mountain Caracara

d Collared Forest-Falcon

c Laughing Falcon

f Bat Falcon

e Aplomado Falcon

Plate 37 (**See also:** Pigeons and Doves, p. 126)

Plate 37a
Band-tailed Pigeon
Columba fasciata
ID: Medium-sized (36 cm, 1.2 ft); broad fan-shaped tail with gray band at end; white band on nape of neck.

HABITAT: Flocks fly high over mountain ridges and cloud forest treetops between 2000 and 3000 m (6500 and 10,000 ft); low cooing sounds very owl-like.

REGION: WSV, ESA

Plate 37b
Pale-vented Pigeon
Columba cayennensis
ID: Medium-sized (30 cm, 1 ft); rusty back; light gray rump and tail in flight.

HABITAT: Single or in pairs perched on trees or shrubs at edge of lowland swamps, rivers, and cochas or flying over open wet areas.

REGION: AMA

Plate 37c
Ruddy Pigeon
Columba subvinacea
ID: Medium-sized (30 cm, 1 ft); dark brown with cinnamon-colored underwings evident in flight; best identified by its deep whistled and four-noted call, with the third note higher and lengthened. The similar-looking Plumbeous Pigeon, *Columba plumbea*, occurs side by side with it and is best distinguished by its three-note whistle with emphasis on the first and last notes.

HABITAT: Solitary or in pairs in mid-level to canopy of lowland moist primary and tall secondary forest.

REGION: AMA

Plate 37d
White-tipped Dove
Leptotila verreauxi
ID: Medium-sized (28 cm, 11 in); rounded tail with broad white tips; no spots on back or head.

HABITAT: On ground in secondary forests, scrubby vegetation, and forest edge from lowlands to 2000 m (6500 ft) on both sides of the Andes.

REGION: CDL, WSV, AMA

Plate 37e
Ruddy Quail-Dove
Geotrygon montana
ID: Medium-sized (23 cm, 9 in); rusty upperparts, buffy underparts; rusty stripe on cheek; male brighter than female.

HABITAT: Solitary or in pairs on floor of moist secondary and primary forest, from lowlands to 2500 m (8200 ft).

REGION: ESA, AMA

Plate 37 **335**

c Ruddy Pigeon

a Band-tailed Pigeon

b Pale-vented Pigeon

d White-tipped Dove

e Ruddy Quail-Dove

Plate 38a
Croaking Ground-Dove
Columbina cruziana
ID: Medium-sized (18 cm, 7 in); gray-brown with orange-yellow swelling at base of bill. Call a repetitive low growl or croak.

HABITAT: Together in small flocks of 5 to 20 in low desert vegetation, open scrub, and gardens.

REGION: CDL, WSV

Plate 38b
Black-winged Ground-Dove
Metriopelia melanoptera
ID: Medium-sized (23 cm, 9 in); grayish with black wings and tail; white patch on bend of upperwing in flight.

HABITAT: Small flocks on the ground in puna grassy areas with low vegetation above 3000 m (10,000 ft).

REGION: HAP

Plate 38c
Bare-faced Ground-Dove
Metriopelia ceciliae
ID: Medium-sized (19 cm, 7.5 in); brown body and head flecked with white; bare orange skin around eye.

HABITAT: Individuals and pairs in open stony areas from the coast up into the puna.

REGION: WSV, HAP

Plate 38d
Eared Dove
Zenaida auriculata
ID: Medium-sized (25 cm, 10 in); wedge-shaped tail; brown back with black spots; two black lines behind eye.

HABITAT: Solitary, in pairs, or in small flocks on ground in open areas of the coast up into the arid highlands above 1200 m (4000 ft), especially in agricultural areas, city parks and gardens.

REGION: TDF, CDL, WSV, HAP

Plate 38e
Pacific Dove
Zenaida meloda
ID: Medium-sized (28 cm, 11 in); gray with prominent white wing stripes. (Considered by some experts as a subspecies of the North and Central American White-winged Dove, *Zenaida asiatica*).

HABITAT: Solitary, in pairs, or in flocks in coastal lowlands, especially gardens, parks and agricultural areas.

REGION: CDL, WSV

Plate 38f
White-eyed Parakeet
Aratinga leucopthalmus
ID: Medium-sized (36 cm, 1.2 ft); all green with bright red and yellow patches on underwings; long pointed tail. Replaced in drier cloud forest and eastern slope valleys between 2000 and 4000 m, 6600 and 13,200 ft, by the similar Mitred Parakeet, *Aratinga mitrata*, which has all green underwings and a bright red face.

HABITAT: Large flocks of 20 to 100 flying high overhead or in treetops in lowland moist forest and Mauritia Palm swamps.

REGION: AMA

Plate 38 337

a Croaking Ground-Dove

b Black-winged Ground-Dove

c Bare-faced Ground-Dove

d Eared Dove

e Pacific Dove

f White-eyed Parakeet

Plate 39a
Blue-and-yellow Macaw
Ara ararauna
ID: Large (84 cm, 2.8 ft); blue upperparts, yellow underparts, long tail; deep resonating calls.

HABITAT: In pairs or flocks of up to 20 in moist lowland forest, flooded forest, and Mauritia Palm swamps.

REGION: AMA

Plate 39b
Scarlet Macaw
Ara macao
ID: Large (89 cm, 3 ft); bright red with yellow patches on upperwing; long tail; loud, harsh calls.

HABITAT: In pairs or small flocks in moist lowland forest.

REGION: AMA

Plate 39c
Red-and-green Macaw
Ara chloroptera
ID: Large (94 cm, 3.1 ft); deep red with green patches on upperwing; long tail; loud, harsh calls.

HABITAT: The rarest large macaw in most of the Amazonian lowlands.

REGION: AMA

Plate 39d
Chestnut-fronted Macaw
Ara severa
ID: Medium-sized (46 cm, 1.5 ft); green body; red underwings and undertail; whitish bare face patch; harsh voice carries long distances.

HABITAT: In pairs or small flocks in moist lowland forest.

REGION: AMA

Plate 39e
Mealy Parrot
Amazona farinosa
ID: Medium-sized (41 cm, 16 in); all gray-green with broad yellow band on its rounded tail; "twittering" shallow wingbeats in flight reveal small red wing patches.

HABITAT: Pairs seen in treetops or flying low over moist lowland forest.

REGION: AMA

Plate 39f
Red-bellied Macaw
Ara manilata
ID: Medium-sized (51 cm, 20 in); green body; yellow underwings and undertail; yellowish bare face patch; peculiar whining call in flight.

HABITAT: In flocks over moist lowland forest.

REGION: AMA

Plate 39 **339**

a Blue-and-yellow Macaw

b Scarlet Macaw

c Red-and-green Macaw

d Chestnut-fronted Macaw

e Mealy Parrot

f Red-bellied Macaw

Plate 40a
Yellow-headed Parrot
Amazona ochracephala
ID: Medium-sized (36 cm, 1.2 ft); green body and head with yellow crown; bright red patch on upperwing; short tail with indistinct yellow band at end; "twittering" shallow wingbeats in flight.

HABITAT: Pairs and small flocks near swampy forests and cochas.

REGION: AMA

Plate 40b
Colbalt-winged Parakeet
Brotogeris cyanoptera
ID: Medium-sized (20 cm, 8 in); green with short pointed tail.

HABITAT: Flocks of 5 to 50 in primary and secondary lowland moist forest. The loud, shrill chattering of a flock can be heard long before it becomes visible flying high overhead.

REGION: AMA

Plate 40c
Blue-headed Parrot
Pionus menstruus
ID: Medium-sized (25 cm, 10 in); green body with blue head and chest; red under base of short tail; deep wingbeats in flight; high-pitched call.

HABITAT: In small flocks flying high over moist forests, rivers and lakes of Amazonian lowlands and foothills.

REGION: ESA, AMA

Plate 40d
Black-headed Parrot
Pionites melanocephala
ID: Medium-sized (23 cm, 9 in); black crown, yellow cheeks and neck; brilliant green back; creamy-white breast; short tail; high-pitched squealing calls.

HABITAT: In small flocks flying through the canopy of lowland primary forest in northeastern and central Amazonian Perú. Replaced in southeastern Perú by the similar White-bellied Parrot, *Pionites leucogaster*, which has an apricot-colored crown.

REGION: AMA

Plate 40e
Canary-winged Parakeet
Brotogeris versicolurus
ID: Medium-sized (23 cm, 9 in); green with long pointed tail and large white and yellow stripes on upperwings. Small flocks give shrill, metallic notes in flight.

HABITAT: Common in lowlands of northeastern Perú and successfully introduced to the Lima area on the central coast.

REGION: CDL, AMA

Plate 40f
Dusky-headed Parakeet
Aratinga weddellii
ID: Medium-sized (28 cm, 11 in); green and blue body and underwings; gray head; white eye-ring; long pointed tail.

HABITAT: Flocks of 10 to 50 in trees along lowland rivers and swampy forest.

REGION: AMA

Plate 40 **341**

a Yellow-headed Parrot

c Blue-headed Parrot

b Cobalt-winged Parakeet

d Black-headed Parrot

e Canary-winged Parakeet

f Dusky-headed Parakeet

Plate 41a
Striped Cuckoo
Tapera naevia
ID: Medium-sized (29 cm, 11 in); buff and brown-streaked above with pale breast; often difficult to see but easily heard as it gives its monotonous and loud two-noted whistle (second note higher than the first) throughout the day.

HABITAT: Lowland scrubby vegetation, grassy pastures, where it perches on fence posts or low bushes in early morning and skulks on the ground in dense cover the rest of the day.

REGION: AMA

Plate 41b
Squirrel Cuckoo

Piaya cayana
ID: Medium-sized (43 cm, 17 in); chestnut upperparts, gray underparts; extremely long tail with white spots at tip.

HABITAT: Solitary or in pairs; often runs along branches and hops or flies clumsily from tree to tree in mid-level and canopy of secondary and primary forests in lowlands to 2500 m (8200 ft); frequently in mixed-species foraging flocks.

REGION: TDF, ESA, AMA

Plate 41c
Groove-billed Ani
Crotophaga sulcirostris
ID: Medium-sized (29 cm, 11.5 in); all black; dark eye; large thin bill with smooth top; long tail. Loose flight appears uncoordinated.

HABITAT: Family groups in lowland open grassy areas, clearings, pastures and along roads in coastal lowlands, ranging into arid subtropical woodlands on west slope.

REGION: CDL, WSV

Plate 41d
Smooth-billed Ani
Crotophaga ani
ID: Medium-sized (33 cm, 1.1 ft); all black; dark eye; large thin bill with high hump at base; long tail. Loose flight appears uncoordinated.

HABITAT: Family groups in lowland open grassy areas, clearings, pastures and along roads in Amazonian lowlands, ranging up into higher-elevation valleys.

REGION: AMA

Plate 41e
Greater Ani
Crotophaga major
ID: Large (47 cm, 1.6 ft); all glossy black with bluish sheen; white eye; long tail. Loud calls that can sound like a metal factory when an entire flock calls together.

HABITAT: Flocks in low vegetation along lowland streams, lakes and forested swamps.

REGION: AMA

Plate 41   343

a Striped Cuckoo

b Squirrel Cuckoo

c Groove-billed Ani

d Smooth-billed Ani

e Greater Ani

Plate 42a
Tropical Screech-Owl
Otus choliba
ID: Medium-sized (23 cm, 9 in); ear tufts; buffy white breast with dark streaks. Voice at night a rising quavery whistle ending with two quick but distinct, pure notes.

HABITAT: Active at night in secondary forest, forest edge, plantations and gardens from lowlands to 2500 m (8200 ft).

REGION: ESA, AMA

Plate 42b
Spectacled Owl
Pulsatrix perspicillata
ID: Large (48 cm, 1.6 ft); lacks ear tufts; deep-brown back and chest contrasting with white facial markings and white, unstreaked belly. Voice at night a loud, rapid series of resonating hoots resembling someone shaking a large piece of metal sheeting.

HABITAT: Active at night in moist lowland primary and secondary forest.

REGION: AMA

Plate 42c
Ferruginous Pygmy-Owl
Glaucidium brasilianum
ID: Small (16 cm, 6 in); lacks ear tufts; relatively long tail; heavily streaked breast. Voice given commonly during day and night a series of high, whistled "whooks." Replaced by the similar Andean Pygmy-Owl, *Glaucidium jardinii*, above 2200 m (7200 ft), and by the Peruvian (Pacific) Pygmy-Owl, *Glaucidium perúanum*, in tropical dry forests of northern and central Perú in western slope woodlands to 2000 m (7000 ft).

HABITAT: Active during day and at night in lowland secondary forest, forest edge, and gardens.

REGION: AMA

Plate 42d
Burrowing Owl
Speotyto cunicularia
ID: Medium-sized (23 cm, 9 in); soft-brown with white spotting; long legs and short tail.

HABITAT: Stands on the ground "bobbing;" nests in burrows; often active during the day, in open fields and treeless areas from coastal lowlands to puna highlands.

REGION: CDL, WSV, HAP

Plate 42e
Oilbird
Steatornis caripensis
ID: Large (48 cm, 1.6 ft); rusty color with distinct silver spots; long tail; hooked bill.

HABITAT: Active at night around fruiting palms and trees; spends day-time in large breeding caves at isolated sites from lowlands to 3000 m (10,000 ft).

REGION: ESA, AMA

Plate 42 **345**

a Tropical Screech-Owl

b Spectacled Owl

c Ferruginous Pygmy-Owl

d Burrowing Owl

e Oilbird

Plate 43a
Sand-colored Nighthawk
Chordeiles rupestris
ID: Medium-sized (22 cm, 9 in); buffy brown and white; in flight tail white except for black tip; long pointed wings white except for black tips and trailing edge. When disturbed from their roost during the day, they resemble a flock of flying terns.

HABITAT: Roosts during the day in flocks of 10 to 100 on sand-bars of large rivers in lowlands and in isolated trees in open flooded forest; night-active.

REGION: AMA

Plate 43b
Pauraque
Nyctidromus albicollis
ID: Medium-sized (28 cm, 11 in); mottled brown; usually seen in beam of a flashlight when its orangish eyeshine reflects as it sits on the ground or in low vegetation along watercourses. In flight, rounded wings have a bold white (male) or buffy (female) band, and outer tail feathers are white. Voice commonly heard at night is a low, down-slurring whistle-hum.

HABITAT: Solitary on forest edge, pastures, river beaches, open secondary forest and gardens in the lowlands.

REGION: TDF, AMA

Plate 43c
Ladder-tailed Nightjar
Hydropsalis climacocerca
ID: Medium-sized (28 cm, 11 in); buffy brown with white throat; longish tail feathers of male shallowly notched and extensively white.

HABITAT: Roosts during day among sparse grass and cane of sandy river islands and beaches, occasionally on rocky islands.

REGION: AMA

Plate 43d
Common Potoo
Nyctibius griseus
ID: Medium-sized (40 cm, 1.3 ft); gray-brown; long tail. Resembles a broken branch during the day as it sits on exposed trees with its bill pointing up. Most often noticed by its mournful song of low whistles that descend slowly but deliberately in pitch, step-wise ever lower, especially on moon-lit nights.

HABITAT: Forest edge and along forested waterways in lowlands and foothills.

REGION: TDF, AMA

Plate 43e
Great Potoo
Nyctibius grandis
ID: Large (51 cm, 20 in); entirely grayish white.

HABITAT: Perches high in trees during the day, usually at forest edge or along cochas and rivers. On moonlit nights gives a deep, growling call.

REGION: AMA

Plate 43   **347**

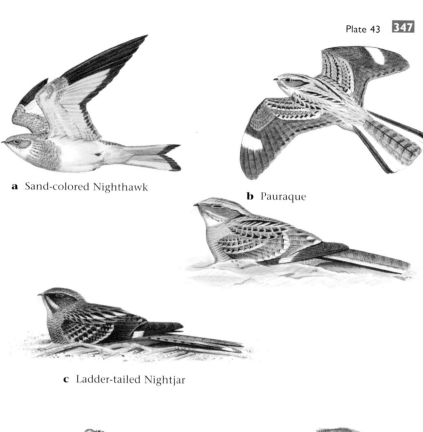

a Sand-colored Nighthawk

b Pauraque

c Ladder-tailed Nightjar

d Common Potoo

e Great potoo

Plate 44a

White-collared Swift
Streptoprocne zonaris
ID: Medium-sized (20 cm, 8 in); black with bold white collar and slightly forked tail.

HABITAT: High overhead in swirling flocks of 10 to 200 individuals. Although they nest at mid-elevations, they often descend to lowlands for a few hours to catch insects.

REGION: TDF, CDL, WSV, ESA, HAP, AMA

Plate 44b

Short-tailed Swift
Chaetura brachyura
ID: Small (10 cm, 4 in); all blackish; pale-gray rump; almost tailless appearance.

HABITAT: In loose flocks overhead in lowland forest and cleared areas; sometimes mixed with other species of swifts.

REGION: TDF, AMA

Plate 44c

Fork-tailed Palm-Swift
Tachornis squamata
ID: Small (13 cm, 5 in); slender, gray-brown with distinctively long, deeply forked tail.

HABITAT: Low over the canopy of lowland open forest or clearings, usually near Mauritia Palm stands, where they roost and nest; usually in small flocks of its own species or mixed with other swift species.

REGION: AMA

Plate 44d

White-winged Swallow
Tachycineta albiventer
ID: Small (14 cm, 6 in); pure white underparts, blue-green upperparts; white patch on upperwing and on rump.

HABITAT: Perches on partially submerged poles and vegetation or flies low over lowland lakes and larger rivers.

REGION: AMA

Plate 44e

White-banded Swallow
Atticora fasciata
ID: Small (15 cm, 6 in); completely bluish black with a bold white breast band; deeply forked tail.

HABITAT: Smaller forested rivers in the eastern lowlands and foothills of the Andes between 300 and 1200 m (1000 and 4000 ft).

REGION: ESA, AMA

Plate 44f

Blue-and-white Swallow
Notiochelidon cyanoleuca
ID: Small (13 cm, 5 in); dark blue upperparts, pure white underparts.

HABITAT: Pastures, clearings, forest edge and over lakes and rivers; often abundant around human settlements, especially on the coast but also regularly up to 2500 m (8250 ft) elevation. An occasional migrant through the Amazon lowlands.

REGION: CDL, WSV, ESA, AMA

Plate 44 **349**

a White-collared Swift

b Short-tailed Swift

c Fork-tailed Palm-Swift

d White-winged Swallow

e White-banded Swallow

f Blue-and-white Swallow

Plate 45a
Rufous-breasted Hermit
Glaucis hirsuta
ID: Small (10 cm, 4 in); green upperparts; buffy brown underparts; bill long and deeply curved down; brownish tail with NO long white central tail feathers as in other hermits.

HABITAT: Common in moist undergrowth of secondary forest and river-associated forests in Amazonian lowlands, especially at cocha edges.

REGION: AMA

Plate 45b
White-necked Jacobin
Florisuga mellivora
ID: Small (10 cm, 4 in); white lower belly, tail and crescent on neck of male contrast with all-blue head and throat; scaly dark throat contrasts with the white lower belly of the female.

HABITAT: Undergrowth of moist lowland secondary forest, forest edge and gardens.

REGION: AMA

Plate 45c
Southern Rough-winged Swallow
Stelgidopteryx ruficollis
ID: Small (13 cm, 5 in); brownish back with pale rump patch; gray-brown breast with contrasting light rusty throat.

HABITAT: Over rivers and nearby cleared areas where it roosts in small groups on exposed branches (lowlands to 2000 m, 6500 ft).

REGION: TDF, WSV, ESA, AMA

Plate 45d
White-bearded Hermit
Phaethornis hispidus
ID: Small (13 cm, 5 in); long bill curved down; grayish green upperparts, gray breast; long dark tail with bold long white tip; white stripes over eye, under eye and in middle of throat.

HABITAT: Moist undergrowth of secondary forest and river-associated forest; often in lecs.

REGION: AMA

Plate 45e
Little Hermit
Phaethornis longuemareus
ID: Tiny (9 cm, 3.5 in); long bill slightly curved down; coppery green upperparts with dirty brown rump; mid-length tail with short white tip; buffy gray underparts; dirty white head stripes but no line down center of throat.

HABITAT: Moist undergrowth of secondary lowland forest up to 1000 m (3300 ft); often in lecs.

REGION: AMA

Plate 45f
Long-tailed Hermit
Phaethornis superciliosus
ID: Small (13 cm, 5 in); long bill strongly curved down; brownish upperparts with contrasting buff rump; long dark tail with long white tip; buffy gray underparts; pale buffy head stripes and line down center of throat.

HABITAT: Moist secondary forest undergrowth of lowlands up to 1600 m (5200 ft) on the lower eastern slopes of the Andes and in tropical dry forest of the northwest; often in lecs.

REGION: TDF, ESA, AMA

Plate 45   **351**

a Rufous-breasted
Hermit

b White-necked Jacobin

M

F

d White-bearded
Hermit

c Southern Rough-
winged Swallow

f Long-tailed
Hermit

e Little Hermit

Plate 46a

Black-throated Mango
Anthracothorax nigricollis

ID: Small (10 cm, 4 in); male green above with black breast and maroon tail; female similar except breast white with black line running down the middle.

HABITAT: Gardens and scrubby forest in Amazonian lowlands below 1000 m (3300 ft).

REGION: AMA

Plate 46b

Fork-tailed Woodnymph
Thalurania furcata

ID: Small (10 cm, 4 in); male with purple breast and green throat; gray-breasted female similar to several other species.

HABITAT: Undergrowth of moist forest and forest edge in Amazonian lowlands and foothills.

REGION: AMA

Plate 46c

Sparkling Violet-ear
Colibri coruscans

ID: Small (13 cm, 5 in); completely glittering green except for violet central breast and eye-mask that extends under bill; commonly heard singing its emphatic series of "sip" notes.

HABITAT: Open forest, clearings, gardens, city parks in the highlands above 2000 m (6500 ft), but winters down to coastal lomas.

REGION: WSV, HAP, ESA

Plate 46d

Amazilia Hummingbird
Amazilia amazilia

ID: Tiny (9 cm, 3.5 in); bronzy green upperparts; throat shiny blue-green; belly, rump and tail rusty. Individuals in coastal northern Perú have white breasts.

HABITAT: Desert scrub and dry, open agricultural areas and gardens.

REGION: CDL, WSV

Plate 46e

Speckled Hummingbird
Adelomyia melanogenys

ID: Tiny (8.5 cm, 3.4 in); brownish upperparts, light brown underparts; dark mask through eyes; buff tail-tips.

HABITAT: Understory of humid forest and forest edge between 1000 and 2500 m (3300 and 8250 ft).

REGION: ESA

Plate 46 **353**

a Black-throated Mango

b Fork-tailed Woodnymph

c Sparkling Violetear

d Amazilia Hummingbird

northwest form

Lima region form

e Speckled Hummingbird

Plate 47a
Tyrian Metaltail
Metallura tyrianthina
ID: Tiny (8 cm, 3.2 in). Male with shiny green upperparts and throat; breast olive-green; tail bright maroon to bronzy; bill very short. Female with orangish throat spotted green.

HABITAT: Humid forest edge, bushes, and small patches of trees in the lower puna above 2000 m (6600 ft); rather than hovering, typically clings to flowers when feeding.

REGION: WSV, ESA

Plate 47b
Giant Hummingbird
Patagona gigas
ID: Medium-sized (19 cm, 7.5 in); largest of all hummingbirds; brown-buff body; white rump.

HABITAT: Open dry highlands between 2000 and 3000 m (6500 and 10,000 ft) with flowering cactus and Century (*Agave*) plants.

REGION: WSV, HAP

Plate 47c
Collared Inca
Coeligena torquata
ID: Small (11 cm, 4.5 in); striking white throat, breast, and large white tail contrast with dark green and black body. In southern Perú, the collar is rusty and not white.

HABITAT: Moist cloud forest undergrowth and flowering bushes between 2000 and 2500 m (6500 and 8200 ft).

REGION: ESA

Plate 47d
Black-breasted Hillstar
Oreotrochilus melanogaster
ID: Small (10 cm, 4 in); male with dark green upperparts, throat and sides of neck; breast velvety black; tail dark blue-green. Female with throat and breast white with green flecks.

HABITAT: Endemic to central Perú, in low bushy areas of the high puna.

REGION: HAP

Plate 47e
Bronze-tailed Comet
Polyonymus caroli
ID: Small (11 cm, 4.5 in); bronzy green upper- and lower-parts; red (orange in female) throat; long and distinctly forked tail coppery.

HABITAT: Shrubby areas and dry forests above 1500 m (5000 ft) on the Pacific slope of the Andes and high inter-Andean valleys.

REGION: WSV, HAP

Plate 47 **355**

a Tyrian Metaltail

b Giant Hummingbird

c Collared Inca

d Black-breasted Hillstar

e Bronze-tailed Comet

Plate 48a

Oasis Hummingbird

Rhodopis vesper

ID: Small (10.7 cm, 4.2 in). Male with shiny green-olive upperparts; throat pink-violet; underparts buffy white; long down-curved bill; long tail deeply forked. Female lacks violet throat and forked tail.

HABITAT: River-associated forest, gardens and forest patches from arid coast up the western slopes of the Andes to 3000 m (10,000 ft).

REGION: CDL, WSV

Plate 48b

Long-tailed Sylph

Aglaiocercus kingi

ID: Medium-sized (18 cm, 7 in); male mostly shiny green with extremely long blue tail feathers (11 cm, 4.3 in); female with distinctively rusty breast and short white-tipped tail.

HABITAT: Forest edge and shrubby areas of mid-elevation forests between 1200 and 2500 m (4000 and 8250 ft).

REGION: ESA

Plate 48c

Black-eared Fairy

Heliothryx aurita

ID: Small (11 cm, 4.5 in); bright shining-green upperparts, black mask through eyes, pure white underparts and tail.

HABITAT: Understory of moist lowland and foothill forest.

REGION: AMA

Plate 48d

Peruvian Sheartail

Thaumastura cora

ID: Small (12.5 cm, 5 in); male with shining green upperparts, pink-violet throat and white breast; long thin, white tail (8 cm, 3.2 in). Tiny female with all whitish underparts and short, white-tipped tail.

HABITAT: Endemic to Perú in coastal oases and shrub-covered, arid slopes up to 3000 m (10,000 ft).

REGION: CDL, WSV

Plate 48e

Sword-billed Hummingbird

Ensifera ensifera

ID: Small (11 cm, 4.5 in); bronze-green; enormous bill, almost as long as body, is held upward when perched.

HABITAT: Forest edge, shrubby slopes and clearings in cloud forest between 2000 and 3000 m (6600 and 10,000 ft); often associated with the long, red and white flower of *Datura*, or "huanto," bushes.

REGION: ESA, HAP

Plate 48 **357**

a Oasis Hummingbird

b Long-tailed Sylph

c Black-eared Fairy

d Peruvian Sheartail

e Sword-billed Hummingbird

Plate 49a
Golden-headed Quetzal
Pharomachrus auriceps
ID: Medium-sized (33 cm, 13 in); brilliant green upperparts; bright red breast; undertail black.

HABITAT: Cloud forest canopy, forest edge, and fruiting trees between 1500 and 2700 m (5000 and 9000 ft).

REGION: ESA

Plate 49b
White-tailed Trogon
Trogon viridis
ID: Medium-sized (28 cm, 11 in); male with metallic greenish back and dark-violet head and chest, bright yellow breast and mainly white undertail; female similar but with grayish head, chest and upperparts, black undertail with white barring, narrow but complete white eye-ring.

HABITAT: Mid-levels of humid primary and secondary lowland forest; often associated with mixed-species foraging flocks.

REGION: AMA

Plate 49c
Collared Trogon
Trogon collaris
ID: Medium-sized (25 cm, 10 in); male with dark metallic green upperparts, head and chest, red breast, black undertail with broad white barring; female with brownish upperparts, head and chest, pinkish breast, grayish undertail, dark bill.

HABITAT: Mid-levels of humid secondary lowland forest.

REGION: AMA

Plate 49d
Violaceous Trogon
Trogon violaceus
ID: Medium-sized (24 cm, 9.5 in); male with metallic green back, blue-violet head and chest, yellow breast, black undertail with fine white barring; female with gray upperparts and chest, yellow breast, black undertail with white barring and small spots, incomplete white eyering.

HABITAT: Open secondary forest and forest edge of lowlands.

REGION: AMA

Plate 49e
Masked Trogon
Trogon personatus
ID: Medium-sized (25 cm, 10 in); male with dark metallic green upperparts, head and chest, red breast, black undertail with fine white barring; female with brownish upperparts, head and chest, pinkish breast, finely white-barred undertail, yellowish bill.

HABITAT: Mid-levels and edge of cloud forest between 1000 and 2000 m (3300 and 6600 ft).

REGION: TDF, ESA

Plate 49 **359**

b White-tailed
Trogon

a Golden-headed
Quetzal

M

F

M

F

c Collared
Trogon

M

F

M

d Violaceous Trogon

M

F

M

F

e Masked Trogon

F

Plate 50 (**See also:** Kingfishers, p. 144)

Plate 50a

Ringed Kingfisher
Ceryle torquata

ID: Medium-sized (38 cm, 1.3 ft); blue-gray upperparts and white neck band; most of breast rusty (male) or blue-gray and rusty (female); crest on top of head.

HABITAT: Open vegetation along large rivers, lakes and mangroves; usually in lowlands but occasionally to 3000 m (10,000 ft).

REGION: CDL, AMA

Plate 50b

Green Kingfisher
Chloroceryle americana

ID: Small (19 cm, 7.5 in); dark green upperparts; small white spots on upperwings; white underparts with single rusty colored breast band (male) or double green (female) breast bands.

HABITAT: Low in vegetation along small to medium-sized lowland streams, lakes, and mangrove estuaries.

REGION: CDL, AMA

Plate 50c

Green-and-rufous Kingfisher
Chloroceryle inda

ID: Medium-sized (22 cm, 9 in); dark green upperparts; small white spots on wings and tail; entirely rusty (male) underparts or with spotted green and white band on chest (female).

HABITAT: Low in dense vegetation along small to medium streams and flooded forest ponds of lowlands.

REGION: AMA

Plate 50d

Amazon Kingfisher
Chloroceryle amazona

ID: Medium-sized (28 cm, 11 in); solid dark green upperparts; white underparts with rusty colored (male) or green (female) breast band.

HABITAT: Along open vegetation of large to medium-sized lowland rivers and lakes in the Amazonian lowlands.

REGION: AMA

Plate 50e

American Pygmy Kingfisher
Chloroceryle aenea

ID: Small (13 cm, 5 in); dark green upperparts; rusty colored chest (male) and white lower belly; narrow dark green chest band (female).

HABITAT: Low in dense vegetation of small streams and forest ponds of lowlands.

REGION: AMA

Plate 50 **361**

a Ringed Kingfisher

F

M

b Green Kingfisher

F

M

c Green-and-rufous Kingfisher

F

M

d Amazon Kingfisher

F

M

e American Pygmy Kingfisher

F

M

Plate 51a
White-eared Jacamar
Galbalcyrhynchus leucotis
ID: Medium-sized (20 cm, 8 in); dark rusty colored with blackish wings, tail and crown; long, narrow red bill and large white spot on cheek. In central and southern Amazonian Perú, some populations lack the white cheek spot.

HABITAT: Solitary or in pairs at top of open *Cecropia* trees along small to medium streams and cochas of lowland forests.

REGION: AMA

Plate 51b
Bluish-fronted Jacamar
Galbula cyanescens
ID: Medium-sized (23 cm, 9 in); metallic blue crown; metallic coppery green upperparts and chest; long bill; belly and undertail rusty colored.

HABITAT: Pairs seen in middle and lower parts of forest edge in foothills and Amazonian lowlands south of the Río Amazonas.

REGION: AMA

Plate 51c
White-necked Puffbird
Notharchus macrorhynchus
ID: Medium-sized (25 cm, 10 in); black upperparts and white underparts except for black breast band; large heavy bill.

HABITAT: Solitary high on exposed branches of tall trees of lowland primary and secondary forest.

REGION: AMA

Plate 51d
Swallow-winged Puffbird
Chelidoptera tenebrosa
ID: Small (15 cm, 6 in); black upperparts, head and throat; rusty colored belly; short tail and white rump obvious only in flight.

HABITAT: Sits in open branches at top of small trees along rivers and lowland forest edge looking like a husky swallow (both when perched or in its short sallying flights that usually return to the same perch).

REGION: AMA

Plate 51e
White-chested Puffbird
Malacoptila fusca
ID: Small (18 cm, 7 in); brown and white streaks, orange bill. Replaced in southeastern lowland Perú by the similar but darker Semi-collared Puffbird, *Malacoptila semicincta*.

HABITAT: Solitary and unobtrusive in thick undergrowth of secondary and primary forest; easily overlooked as it sits quietly for long periods; only its high-pitched "seeeee" call makes it obvious.

REGION: AMA

Plate 51 **363**

a White-eared Jacamar

southern Perú form

b Bluish-fronted Jacamar

M   F

c White-necked Puffbird

d Swallow-winged Puffbird

e White-chested Puffbird

Plate 52a

Black-fronted Nunbird
Monasa nigrifrons
ID: Medium-sized (25 cm, 10 in); dark gray; long bright red-orange bill; dark forehead. Replaced in canopy and edge of lowland primary forest by similar White-fronted Nunbird, *Monasa morphoeus*, which has a white forehead.

HABITAT: Secondary forest canopy and edge of river-associated forest.

REGION: AMA

Plate 52b

Rufous Motmot
Baryphthengus martii
ID: Medium-sized (46 cm, 1.5 ft); bright rusty head, throat and breast; black mask; green upperparts and lower belly; long tail, which it often swings from side to side; bill large but not broad; deep owl-like double-hoots usually before dawn and late afternoon.

HABITAT: Solitary or in pairs; mid-levels of primary and secondary lowland forest.

REGION: AMA

Plate 52c

Broad-billed Motmot
Electron platyrhynchum
ID: Medium-sized (33 cm, 1.1 ft); bright rusty head, throat and upper chest; black mask; green upperparts and lower belly extending fairly high up on the breast; long tail but lacks peculiar racquets at end; bill large and extremely broad; high-pitched nasal call given at dawn and late afternoon.

HABITAT: Dense undergrowth and mid-levels of secondary and moist primary forest in lowlands.

REGION: AMA

Plate 52d

Blue-crowned Motmot
Momotus momota
ID: Medium-sized (39 cm, 15 in); head with blue and black crown, black mask; breast and throat dull rusty colored; upperparts greenish blue; long tail with peculiar racquets at end often swung from side to side; bill large but not broad; voice a low "BOO-boop" usually heard in morning and afternoon.

HABITAT: Solitary or pairs in mid-levels of secondary lowland forest. (The similar-appearing population in cloud forests on the eastern slopes of the Andes is considered by some to be a separate species, the Highland Motmot, *Momotus aequatorialis*.)

REGION: TDF, AMA

Plate 52 **365**

a Black-fronted
Nunbird

b Rufous
Motmot

d Blue-crowned
Motmot

c Broad-billed
Motmot

Plate 53a
Scarlet-crowned Barbet
Capito aurovirens
ID: Medium-sized (20 cm, 8 in); upperparts olive-brown; throat and chest orange; crown bright red (male) or gray-white (female); call commonly heard throughout the day, a series of rolling "brrrrp, brrrrp, brrrrp … "

HABITAT: Thick, low vegetation along lowland streams and lakes, moist secondary forest.

REGION: AMA

Plate 53b
Black-spotted Barbet
Capito niger
ID: Small (18 cm, 7 in); upperparts black with bright yellow spots and stripes; throat and upper breast clear orange-yellow (male) or orange with thick black streaks (female); call resembles deep, owl-like calls of Blue-crowned Motmot, but no hesitation between calls in a series, "BOO-boop, BOO-boop, BOO-boop … ." In southeastern Perú, males have red or orange throats and females have unspotted throats.

HABITAT: Canopy of lowland moist primary and secondary forests, often in mixed-species foraging flocks.

REGION: AMA

Plate 53c
Lemon-throated Barbet
Eubucco richardsoni
ID: Medium-sized (15 cm, 6 in); yellow bill; male with red head, yellow throat, orange breast; female with black mask, gray throat, orange upper breast.

HABITAT: Pairs often in mixed-species foraging flock in canopy and mid-levels of forest from lowlands up to 1200 m (4000 ft).

REGION: AMA, ESA

Plate 53d
Emerald Toucanet
Aulacorhynchus prasinus
ID: Medium-sized (41 cm, 1.3 ft); green body with black throat; large dark bill with varying amount of yellow on upper mandible and no red on rump. In northern Perú, the throat is blue, not black.

HABITAT: Cloud forest and moist forest edge between 1600 and 3000 m (5300 and 10,600 ft).

REGION: ESA

Plate 53e
Golden-collared Toucanet
Selenidera reinwardtii
ID: Medium-sized (33 cm, 1.1 ft); large red bill with black tip; green back, wings and tail; bright yellow cheek; black head and breast (male) or rusty head and breast (female); voice sounds like a loud frog croaking. In central and southern Perú, the red in the bill is replaced by green.

HABITAT: Mid-levels and canopy of lowland tierra firme forest.

REGION: AMA

Plate 53 **367**

b Black-spotted Barbet

M

F

a Scarlet-crowned Barbet

M

F

northern Perú

M

F

c Lemon-throated Barbet

d Emerald Toucanet

e Golden-collared Toucanet

M

F

Plate 54a

Chestnut-eared Aracari
Pteroglossus castanotis
ID: Medium-sized (46 cm, 1.5 ft); underparts yellow with one broad red breast band; head chestnut except for black crown.

HABITAT: Secondary and primary forest canopy of moist lowlands and along rivers.

REGION: AMA

Plate 54b

Curl-crested Aracari
Pteroglossus beauharnaesii
ID: Medium-sized (38 cm, 1.3 ft); underparts yellow with red band across center of breast; cheeks and throat whitish; crown blackish with peculiar curled, plastic-like feathers.

HABITAT: Canopy and edge of lowland primary forest.

REGION: AMA

Plate 54c

Lettered Aracari
Pteroglossus inscriptus
ID: Medium-sized (37 cm, 1.2 ft); underparts yellow with black throat but no breast bands; upper bill mostly yellowish white.

HABITAT: Primary tierra firme forest canopy of lowlands.

REGION: AMA

Plate 54d

Gray-breasted Mountain-Toucan
Andigena hypoglauca
ID: Large (41 cm, 1.3 ft); blue-gray breast; large orange bill with yellow square at base and remainder of lower mandible black.

HABITAT: Cloud forest canopy and forest edge between 2700 and 3400 m (9000 and 11,200 ft).

REGION: ESA

Plate 54e

Cuvier's Toucan
Ramphastos cuvieri
ID: Large (61 cm, 2 ft); black body with white cheeks, throat and upper breast; huge black bill with yellow ridge and base; loud yelping calls distinguish it from the almost identical but smaller Yellow-ridged Toucan, *Ramphastos culminatus*, which gives a low croaking call.

HABITAT: Canopy and tops of isolated trees of primary lowland forest.

REGION: AMA

Plate 54 **369**

b Curl-crested Aracari

a Chestnut-eared Aracari

M

c Lettered Aracari

F

d Gray-breasted Mountain-Toucan

e Cuvier's Toucan

Plate 55 (**See also:** Woodpeckers, p. 150)

Plate 55a

Plain-breasted Piculet

Picumnus castelnau

ID: Small (9 cm, 3.5 in); upperparts olive with pale scalloping; underparts pale yellow; male crown black with reddish dots, female crown all black.

HABITAT: Small branches of mid-level and undergrowth of lowland secondary forests and flooded forest along rivers.

REGION: AMA

Plate 55b

Spot-breasted Woodpecker

Colaptes punctigula

ID: Medium-sized (20 cm, 8 in); yellow-green back with black spots; distinct black spots on buffy breast; sides of head white.

HABITAT: Solitary on isolated trees in lowland clearings and pastures, secondary forest edge, and gardens.

REGION: AMA

Plate 55c

Andean Flicker

Colaptes rupicola

ID: Medium-sized (32 cm, 1.1 ft); back and wings buff barred black; rump yellowish; head and moustache gray; underparts buff barred and spotted black; its calls range from loud three or four-noted whistles to harsh trills.

HABITAT: Common hopping on ground of rolling puna grasslands, gorges and *Polylepis* forest between 2000 and 5000 m (6600 and 16,500 ft); often in social groups of 8 to 10 individuals.

REGION: HAP

Plate 55d

Crimson-mantled Woodpecker

Piculus rivolii

ID: Medium-sized (24 cm, 9.5 in); bright red upperparts; black-barred yellow rump patch; scaled breast.

HABITAT: Solitary or pairs in short trees and bushes of upper cloud forest to lower puna, where it often feeds on the ground (2000 to 3500 m, 6500 to 11,500 ft); sometimes associates with mixed-species foraging flocks.

REGION: HAP

Plate 55e

Cream-colored Woodpecker

Celeus flavus

ID: Medium-sized (25 cm, 10 in); crested; creamy-yellow body, rusty wings and black tail; male with bright red stripe on cheek.

HABITAT: Solitary or pairs in dense undergrowth vegetation of lowland secondary forest; specializes on breaking open arboreal ant and termite nests.

REGION: AMA

Plate 55   **371**

a Plain-breasted
Piculet

b Spot-breasted
Woodpecker

c Andean Flicker

d Crimson-mantled
Woodpecker

e Cream-colored
Woodpecker

Plate 56 (**See also:** Woodpeckers, p. 150)

Plate 56a
Lineated Woodpecker
Dryocopus lineatus
ID: Medium-sized (36 cm, 1.2 ft); crested; upperparts black with white lines on back forming an incomplete "V;" underparts barred brown and black; pairs communicate noisily with a loud churring call.

HABITAT: Solitary or pairs in large trees in secondary forest or forest edge from Amazonian lowlands up to 2000 m (6600 ft).

REGION: ESA, AMA

Plate 56b
Yellow-tufted Woodpecker
Melanerpes cruentatus
ID: Medium-sized (19 cm, 7.5 in); black body with yellow eye-ring and nape of neck; crown red (male) or black (female); belly and lower breast red.

HABITAT: Family groups of 4 to 8 on dead branches high in canopy of lowland primary forest; loud raucous calls obvious.

REGION: AMA

Plate 56c
Crimson-crested Woodpecker
Campephilus melanoleucos
ID: Medium-sized (36 cm, 1.2 ft); crested; upperparts black with white lines on back forming a complete "V," underparts barred brown and black; head of male red except for white and black cheek spot.

HABITAT: Pairs seen on large tree trunks of lowland primary and tall secondary forest to cloud forest at 2000 m (6600 ft); often conspicuous by loud drumming on tree trunks.

REGION: ESA, AMA

Plate 56d
Red-necked Woodpecker
Campephilus rubricollis
ID: Medium-sized (32 cm, 1 ft); upperparts black with no stripes; head, neck and chest red; underparts rusty; female with broad white line below eye.

HABITAT: Pairs seen on large tree trunks of lowland primary forest and tall secondary forest.

REGION: AMA

Plate 56 **373**

a Lineated Woodpecker

M

F

b Yellow-tufted Woodpecker

c Crimson-crested Woodpecker

M

d Red-necked Woodpecker

M

Plate 57a

Olivaceous Woodcreeper
Sittasomus griseicapillus

ID: Small (16 cm, 6 in); no spots or obvious streaks; olive-gray head and underparts; rusty colored back, wings, and tail; straight bill short and thin.

HABITAT: Tree trunks and large branches of mid-levels of Amazonian flooded forest and tall secondary forest in dry forest of northwestern Perú; less common in cloud forest up to 2000 m (6600 ft); often associated with mixed-species foraging flocks.

REGION: TDF, ESA, AMA

Plate 57b

Wedge-billed Woodcreeper
Glyphorynchus spirurus

ID: Small (14 cm, 5.5 in); brown head and underparts with buffy eyeline and breast streaks; rusty back, wings, and tail; bill short and wedge-shaped.

HABITAT: Lower parts of small and medium tree trunks in lowland primary and secondary forest up to 1200 m (4000 ft); usually associated with mixed-species foraging flocks.

REGION: ESA, AMA

Plate 57c

Long-billed Woodcreeper
Nasica longirostris

ID: Medium-sized (36 cm, 14 in); extremely long, thin, straight bill (7 cm, 2.7 in); rusty back, wings and tail; white throat; bold black and white stripes on crown, nape of head, lower breast; loud, low whistles given frequently.

HABITAT: Pairs seen on larger tree trunks in lowland flooded and swamp forest.

REGION: AMA

Plate 57d

Buff-throated Woodcreeper
Xiphorhynchus guttatus

ID: Medium-sized (27 cm, 10.5 in); thick, slightly down-curved bill; dark brown body with thin buffy streaks on upperparts and head; underparts brown with broad buffy white streaks coalescing into entirely buffy throat.

HABITAT: Lower trunks of tierra firme primary forest and tall secondary forest.

REGION: AMA

Plate 57   375

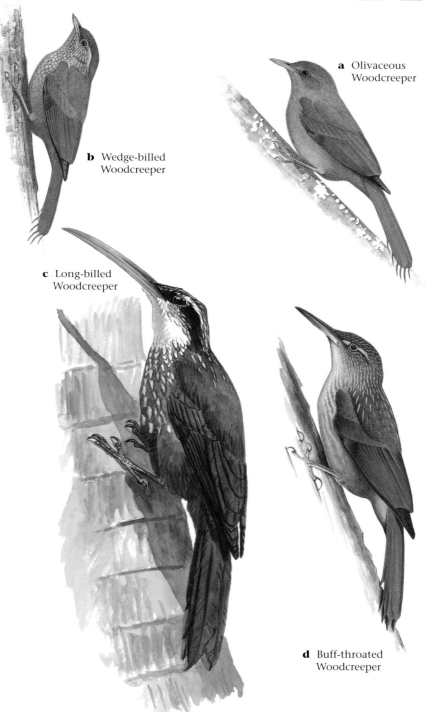

a Olivaceous
Woodcreeper

b Wedge-billed
Woodcreeper

c Long-billed
Woodcreeper

d Buff-throated
Woodcreeper

Plate 58 (**See also:** Ovenbirds, p. 153)

Plate 58a
Coastal Miner
Geositta peruviana
ID: Small (14 cm, 5.5 in); pale brown upperparts with whitish eyeline; underparts whitish.

HABITAT: Runs rapidly across barren desert floor below 400 m (1300 ft); sometimes around isolated buildings and sparse, low bushes of coastal desert.

REGION: CDL

Plate 58b
Bar-winged Cinclodes
Cinclodes fuscus
ID: Small (18 cm, 7 in); brown with white eyestripe; whitish throat; rusty wing-stripe and rusty tail feathers obvious in flight.

HABITAT: Runs on ground in open puna above 3500 m (11,500 ft), usually near clay banks and water.

REGION: HAP

Plate 58c
Pale-legged Hornero
Furnarius leucopus
ID: Small (17 cm, 6.5 in); bright buffy color with gray crown and white eyeline; black wings with bright rusty colored patch obvious in flight; short tail and light colored legs; loud ringing trills given throughout the day.

HABITAT: Common on the ground in open areas, secondary forest floor, city parks and along roads in pasturelands.

REGION: TDF, AMA

Plate 58d
Pearled Treerunner
Margarornis squamiger
ID: Small (15 cm, 6 in); brown body; bold white eyeline; white throat and white tear-drop spots on breast and side of neck; rusty back and tail.

HABITAT: Climbs like a woodcreeper along the tops and bottoms of large branches, usually in thick epiphyte cover of high-elevation cloud forest trees and *Polylepis* stands (between 1800 and 3800 m, 6900 and 12,500 ft); almost always in large mixed-species foraging flocks.

REGION: HAP, ESA

Plate 58e
Andean Tit-Spinetail
Leptasthenura andicola
ID: Small (16 cm, 6 in); dark brown with white streaks on body and head; long dark tail with two distinctly longer feathers.

HABITAT: Low bushes and tall grass of puna and *Polylepis* forest edge in central and southern Perú; in pairs or with mixed-species foraging flocks.

REGION: HAP

Plate 58f
Peruvian Seaside Cinclodes
Cinclodes taczanowskii
ID: Small (22 cm, 8.5 in); dark brown upperparts; light streaks on underparts.

HABITAT: Restricted to rocky intertidal areas of coast, where it feeds on invertebrates in tidal pools.

REGION: CDL

Plate 58   **377**

b Bar-winged Cinclodes

a Coastal Miner

c Pale-legged Hornero

d Pearled Treerunner

e Andean Tit-Spinetail

f Peruvian Seaside Cinclodes

Plate 59 (**See also:** Antbirds, p. 154)

Plate 59a
Great Antshrike
Taraba major
ID: Medium-sized (20 cm, 8 in); pure white underparts; black (male) or rusty colored (female) upperparts; red eye; voice commonly heard is an accelerating series of short whistled notes (bouncing ball) ending in a low growl.

HABITAT: Dense undergrowth and bushy secondary forest in lowlands.

REGION: TDF, AMA

Plate 59b
Barred Antshrike
Thamnophilus doliatus
ID: Small (15 cm, 6 in); male black and white barred upperparts and underparts; female rusty colored upperparts and buffy underparts.

HABITAT: Thickets and secondary forest undergrowth of Amazonian lowlands.

REGION: AMA

Plate 59c
Black-spotted Bare-eye
Phlegopsis nigromaculata
ID: Small (18 cm, 7 in); bright red bare skin around eye; upperparts olive-brown with tear-shaped black spots on back; underparts black.

HABITAT: Near army ant columns in undergrowth of moist primary lowland forest.

REGION: AMA

Plate 59d
White-flanked Antwren
Myrmotherula axillaris
ID: Small (10 cm, 4 in); male blackish with white dots on upperwings and long white plumes on side of breast; female gray-brown with rusty colored dots on upperwings and long white plumes on side of breast; wings flicked often to expose the white feathers on side of breast.

HABITAT: Undergrowth and lower levels of moist lowland primary and tall secondary forest; almost always in large mixed-species foraging flocks.

REGION: AMA

Plate 59e
Black-faced Antthrush
Formicarius analis
ID: Small (18 cm, 7 in); dark brown upperparts; black throat; gray breast; rusty colored lower belly; walks on forest floor with black tail cocked up; voice commonly heard is a descending series of loud short whistles.

HABITAT: Solitary on floor of lowland moist primary and tall secondary forest.

REGION: AMA

Plate 59f
Rufous Antpitta
Grallaria rufula
ID: Small (15 cm, 6 in); completely rusty to ochraceous brown; indistinct pale eyeline; long legs; very short tail.

HABITAT: Runs or hops on ground among scattered bushes and sings from tops of open shrubs and fence posts in bamboo areas between 2300 and 3600 m (7550 and 11,800 ft).

REGION: ESA

Plate 59 **379**

a Great Antshrike

b Barred Antshrike

c Black-spotted Bare-eye

d White-flanked Antwren

e Black-faced Antthrush

f Rufous Antpitta

Plate 60a
Blue-crowned Manakin
Pipra coronata
ID: Small (9 cm, 3.5 in); males in northeastern Perú all black with bright blue crown; in central and southeastern Perú bright greenish yellow with a light blue crown; female with bright green upperparts and grayish yellow underparts.

HABITAT: Undergrowth and lower levels of moist primary and tall secondary forest in the lowlands; fruiting trees.

REGION: AMA

Plate 60b
Band-tailed Manakin
Pipra fasciicauda
ID: Small (11 cm, 4 in); male with bright red and yellow underparts, black back, wings, and tail with white base and black tip, bright red crown; female with olive upperparts, greenish yellow underparts. Replaced in northeastern Perú by similar Wire-tailed Manakin, *Pipra filicauda*, which differs by wire-like tail feather extensions in both male and female.

HABITAT: Undergrowth of dense lowland flooded forest and moist secondary forest, fruiting trees in central and southeastern Perú.

REGION: AMA

Plate 60c
White-crowned Manakin
Pipra pipra
ID: Small (9 cm, 3.5 in); red eye; male black except for white crown and neck; female with olive-green upperparts, gray crown and sides of head, grayish olive underparts.

HABITAT: Undergrowth of moist lowland forest in northeastern and central Perú.

REGION: AMA

Plate 60d
Round-tailed Manakin
Pipra chloromeros
ID: Small (11 cm, 4 in); male all black with bright red head and yellow thighs; female with olive upperparts, grayish olive underparts; males on lecs give high-pitched buzzing and mewing calls.

HABITAT: Undergrowth of moist forest of central and southeastern Perú below 1400 m (4600 ft).

REGION: ESA, AMA

Plate 60e
Thrush-like Manakin
Schiffornis turdinus
ID: Small (17 cm, 7 in); olive-brown with dark eyes, bill, and legs; most commonly noticed by its clear four-note whistle; considered a flycatcher or cotinga by some experts.

HABITAT: Undergrowth of moist lowland secondary and edge of primary forest; often perches low on thin trunks of saplings.

REGION: AMA

Plate 60   **381**

a Blue-crowned Manakin

F

M

M

F

M

b Band-tailed Manakin

F

c White-crowned Manakin

M

d Round-tailed Manakin

M

e Thrush-like Manakin

Plate 61a
Black-necked Red-Cotinga
Phoenicircus nigricollis
ID: Medium-sized (24 cm, 9.5 in); male brilliant red except for black face, back, wings and tail tip; female upperparts maroon to olive-brown, underparts pink.

HABITAT: Mid-level to canopy of tierra firme primary forest of northeastern Perú; males in noisy lecs of 3 to 5.

REGION: AMA

Plate 61b
Plum-throated Cotinga
Cotinga maynana
ID: Medium-sized (20 cm, 8 in); male strikingly turquoise blue with purple throat and yellow eye; female with gray upperparts and buffy underparts spotted gray. (Similar Spangled Cotinga, *Cotinga cayana*, is paler blue with extensive black spotting and a dark eye; females difficult to distinguish.)

HABITAT: Canopy of moist lowland primary and tall secondary forest; fruiting trees.

REGION: AMA

Plate 61c
Red-crested Cotinga
Ampelion rubrocristatus
ID: Medium-sized (21 cm, 8 in); dark gray with light-colored bill; white tail spots obvious in flight; dark-red crest is obvious only when displayed.

HABITAT: Solitary perched on tall dead tree in cloud forest above 2500 m (8200 ft).

REGION: ESA

Plate 61d
Green-and-black Fruiteater
Pipreola riefferii
ID: Medium-sized (20 cm, 8 in); orange bill and legs; dark eye; green upperparts; yellowish breast; head black (male) or green (female).

HABITAT: Pairs or small family groups in cloud forest canopy, forest edge and fruiting trees between 1500 and 2500 m (5000 and 8200 ft).

REGION: ESA

Plate 61e
Screaming Piha
Lipaugus vociferans
ID: Medium-sized (28 cm, 11 in); all gray; most often noticed by the ear-splitting whistle-screams of lecking males.

HABITAT: Mid-level to canopy of primary tierra firme and flooded forest of the lowlands.

REGION: AMA

Plate 61 **383**

b Plum-throated Cotinga

a Black-necked Red-Cotinga

M

F

F

M

c Red-crested Cotinga

M

F

e Screaming Piha

d Green-and-black Fruiteater

Plate 62a

Amazonian Umbrellabird
Cephalopterus ornatus
ID: Large (51 cm, 1.6 ft); black with permanent crest and hanging wattle on throat; flies in an undulating up-and-down pattern reminiscent of a large, crested woodpecker; males at lecs give low mooing sounds.

HABITAT: Flooded forest edge and large river islands of the lowlands, usually associated with *Cecropia* trees.

REGION: AMA

Plate 62b

Purple-throated Fruitcrow
Querula purpurata
ID: Medium-sized (30 cm, 1 ft); all black; male with an indistinct purple throat; most readily noticed by its noisy slurred whistles.

HABITAT: Family groups of 4 to 6 in the canopy of moist lowland primary and tall secondary forest.

REGION: AMA

Plate 62c

Bare-necked Fruitcrow
Gymnoderus foetidus
ID: Medium-sized (34 cm, 1.2 ft); black and gray; small featherless head; in flight, the wide wings of the male flash black and silver.

HABITAT: Canopy of lowland primary and secondary forest, fruiting trees; flying high overhead along rivers.

REGION: AMA

Plate 62d

Masked Tityra
Tityra semifasciata
ID: Medium-sized (20 cm, 8 in); bright red bill and bare area around eye; body white except for black wings and tail; male with black face; female with brown back, face and crown. (The similar Black-tailed Tityra, *Tityra cayana*, has an all-black crown, and the Black-crowned Tityra, *Tityra inquisitor*, has an all-black bill and no red around the eye.)

HABITAT: Tops of trees on forest edge, secondary and primary forest. Often noticed by its frog-like croaks and nasal grumbling.

REGION: AMA

Plate 62e

Andean Cock-of-the-rock
Rupicola peruviana
ID: Medium-sized (32 cm, 1 ft); male bright red with crest, gray and black wings; female rusty orange with small crest and brownish wings and tail.

HABITAT: Middle and low levels of cloud forest vegetation, especially near rocky streams.

REGION: ESA

Plate 62   **385**

a Amazonian Umbrellabird

b Purple-throated Fruitcrow

M

F

d Masked Tityra

M

F

M

F

c Bare-necked Fruitcrow

e Andean Cock-of-the-rock

Plate 63a
Black-billed Shrike-Tyrant
Agriornis montana
ID: Medium-sized (24 cm, 9.5 in); grayish brown with brown-streaked throat and large white tail obvious in flight.

HABITAT: Runs on ground and perches on low bushes and fences in the highlands, 2500 to 4500 m (8250 to 14,850 ft); often easy to approach.

REGION: HAP

Plate 63b
Vermilion Flycatcher
Pyrocephalus rubinus
ID: Small (14 cm, 5.5 in), flat black bill; male upperparts and eye mask black, crown and underparts bright red; female upperparts pale brown and underparts whitish streaked pink on the sides; from Lima south on the coast, about half of the males and females are sooty gray-brown.

HABITAT: Pairs on exposed branches in open areas in lowlands; resident throughout drier shrubby areas of coastal mainland; in Amazonian lowlands present only as Austral migrants wintering in canopy and clearings (June to September).

REGION: TDF, CDL, WSV, AMA

Plate 63c
Common Tody-Flycatcher
Todirostrum cinereum
ID: Small (9 cm, 3.5 in); long flat bill; white eye; gray crown, cheeks; olive-gray back; bright yellow underparts; thin tail often held angled up over the back. Largely replaced in taller moist forests by Yellow-browed Todirostrum, *Todirostrum chrysocotaphum*, which is similar but has black crown and cheeks, yellow eyeline, white throat with bold black spots on the breast.

HABITAT: Sits on open branches in undergrowth and mid-levels of lowland secondary forest.

REGION: TDF, AMA

Plate 63d
Torrent Tyrannulet
Serpophaga cinerea
ID: Small (11 cm, 4 in); black head, tail and wings; rest of body light gray to white.

HABITAT: Pairs obvious on boulders along rushing mountain streams, where they flick tails and give loud "chip" notes that can be heard over the roar of the stream.

REGION: WSV, ESA

Plate 63e
Plain-capped Ground-Tyrant
Muscisaxicola alpina
ID: Medium-sized (19 cm, 7.5 in); robin-like; all-black bill; gray-brown upperparts, whitish underparts, black tail; distinct white eyeline.

HABITAT: Pairs or small flocks run on the ground or perch on fence wires in puna above 3300 m (10,800 ft).

REGION: HAP

Plate 63f
Black Phoebe
Sayornis nigricans
ID: Medium-sized (19 cm, 7.5 in); all blackish except for white lower belly and white flashes in opened wings.

HABITAT: Pairs perch on boulders, electric wires and buildings near mountain streams between 500 and 2500 m (1650 and 8250 ft).

REGION: TDF, ESA

Plate 63 **387**

a Black-billed Shrike-Tyrant

M

b Vermilion Flycatcher

F

c Common Tody-Flycatcher

d Torrent Tyrannulet

sooty form

e Plain-capped Ground-Tyrant

f Black Phoebe

Plate 64a
Tropical Kingbird
Tyrannus melancholicus
ID: Medium-sized (22 cm, 8.5 in); gray head; olive back; brown tail with distinct notch; gray throat; olive-yellow upper breast, bright yellow lower breast.

HABITAT: Most common and easily seen flycatcher in open areas; perches alone on exposed branches and dead treetops in pastures, secondary forest edges and along rivers and lakes throughout lowlands and up to 2500 m (8200 ft).

REGION: TDF, CDL, WSV, ESA, AMA

Plate 64b
Great Kiskadee
Pitangus sulphuratus
ID: Medium-sized (22 cm, 8.5 in); chunky shape; black crown with bold white head band; brown back; rusty edges to wing feathers; bright yellow underparts; calls out its name in a loud voice throughout the day, "kis-ka-DEE."

HABITAT: High in secondary forest, forest edge, lake and river edges, gardens, city parks throughout Amazonian lowlands.

REGION: AMA

Plate 64c
Lesser Kiskadee
Pitangus lictor
ID: Small (18 cm, 7 in); smaller replica of the Great Kiskadee, but more slender, less rusty in the wings; a nasal, wheezing voice completely unlike that of the Great Kiskadee.

HABITAT: Pairs seen on low, exposed vegetation along the water's edge of cochas and small, slow streams of Amazonian lowlands.

REGION: AMA

Plate 64d
Social Flycatcher
Myiozetetes similis
ID: Small (17 cm, 6.5 in); olive-gray back, tail and wings, with no rust in wings; small black bill; yellow breast and contrasting white throat; harsh staccato calls.

HABITAT: Pairs or small family groups perch together in mid to high levels of secondary forest, pasture edge and vegetation along watercourses.

REGION: TDF, AMA

Plate 64e
Piratic Flycatcher
Legatus leucophaius
ID: Small (15 cm, 6 in); short bill; dark brown upperparts; bold white eyeline, cheek patch and throat; yellowish underparts with faint dark streaking; no rusty color in wings or tail.

HABITAT: Alone perched high on exposed treetop or dead branch of secondary forest, forest edge and clearings with scattered tall trees in moist lowlands.

REGION: AMA

Plate 64 **389**

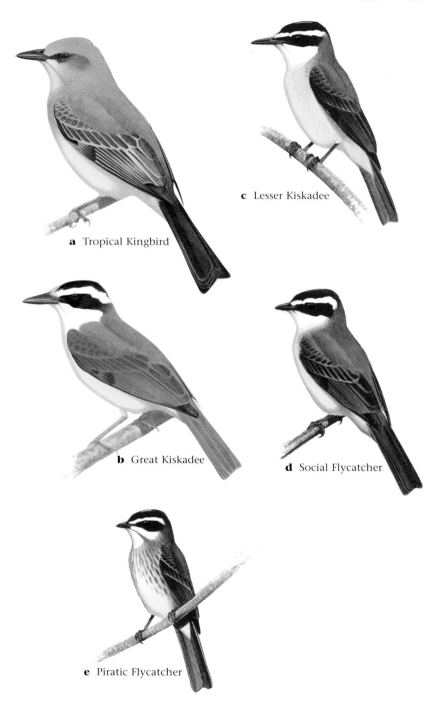

a Tropical Kingbird

c Lesser Kiskadee

b Great Kiskadee

d Social Flycatcher

e Piratic Flycatcher

Plate 65a
Long-tailed Tyrant
Colonia colonus
ID: Medium-sized (24 cm, 9.5 in); all black with white crown and long central tail feathers (12 cm, 5 in) that makes up over half the bird's total length.

HABITAT: Perches in dead trees of canopy or edge of lowland secondary forests and conspicuously sallies out after insects to capture them in the air.

REGION: AMA

Plate 65b
White-browed Chat-Tyrant
Ochthoeca leucophrys
ID: Small (15 cm, 6 in); grayish brown upperparts with white eyeline; grayish-white underparts.

HABITAT: Pairs perched prominently on top of fence posts, bushes and shrubbery of west slope arid areas and highlands up to 3500 m (11,500 ft); occasionally near the coast in southern Perú.

REGION: CDL, WSV, HAP

Plate 65c
Short-tailed Field-Tyrant
Muscigralla brevicauda
ID: Small (11 cm, 4 in); brownish gray upperparts with rusty patch on rump and upper tail; extremely short tail and long legs.

HABITAT: Runs on the ground in barren coastal desert areas up to 1300 m (4300 ft).

REGION: CDL, WSV

Plate 65d
Many-colored Rush-Tyrant
Tachuris rubrigastra
ID: Small (11 cm, 4 in); golden underparts and thin eyeline; black crown and mask; upperparts dark green with conspicuous white stripe on wing.

HABITAT: Wren-like flycatcher found only in freshwater reed swamps along the coast and in the puna highlands of central and southern Perú; it flies actively among the reeds and often hangs acrobatically to glean insects from the underside of vegetation.

REGION: CDL, WSV, HAP

Plate 65e
Andean Negrito
Lessonia oreas
ID: Small (12 cm, 5 in); male all black with rusty patch on back; female similar but lower parts browner.

HABITAT: Runs on ground usually near highland ponds and marshy areas of central and southern Perú.

REGION: HAP

Plate 65 **391**

a Long-tailed Tyrant

b White-browed Chat-Tyrant

c Short-tailed Field-Tyrant

d Many-colored Rush-Tyrant

M

e Andean Negrito

F

Plate 66a
White-tailed Jay
Cyanocorax mystacalis
ID: Medium-sized (33 cm, 1.1 ft); blue back; pure white underparts, neck, cheek and outer tail feathers; black face and throat.

HABITAT: Small family groups in arid scrub, dry forest and open areas; a Tumbesian endemic and the only jay in its area.

REGION: TDF

Plate 66b
Violaceous Jay
Cyanocorax violaceus
ID: Medium-sized (37 cm, 1.2 ft); pale blue-gray with black crown, face and upper breast; harsh, high-pitched calls.

HABITAT: Small family groups in moist lowland forest edge, flooded forests and small clearings throughout the Amazonian lowlands.

REGION: AMA

Plate 66c
Green Jay
Cyanocorax yncas
ID: Medium-sized (30 cm, 1 ft); green above and yellow below; bold yellow patches in tail obvious in flight.

HABITAT: Small family groups in cloud forest undergrowth, clearings and pasture edges between 1400 and 2600 m (4500 and 8500 ft); usually first noticed by their nasal sounds and clicking calls.

REGION: ESA

Plate 66d
White-collared Jay
Cyanolyca viridicyana
ID: Medium-sized (34 cm, 1.1 ft); greenish blue with black forehead and mask; narrow white breast band and whitish forecrown; often shy and quiet but at other times bold and noisy.

HABITAT: Small family groups low in cloud forest undergrowth and alder forest edges between 2000 and 3000 m (6600 and 10,000 ft).

REGION: ESA

Plate 66e
White-capped Dipper
Cinclus leucocephalus
ID: Small (16 cm, 6 in); dark gray with strikingly white crown and throat; population in northern Perú (subspecies *leuconotus*) has a white back and more extensive white breast.

HABITAT: Solitary or in pairs on rocks of mountain streams above 1000 m (3300 ft), where they bob up and down on their legs and run or fly into the water.

REGION: WSV, ESA

Plate 66 **393**

b Violaceous Jay

a White-tailed Jay

c Green Jay

d White-collared Jay

northern Perú

central and southern Perú

e White-capped Dipper

Plate 67a
Inca Wren
Thryothorus eisenmanni
ID: Small (16 cm, 6 in); upperparts bright reddish brown; gray head with bold white eye-line; breast and throat white with distinct black spots; no barring on wings, tail, or belly.

HABITAT: Endemic to three valleys in southern Perú; solitary or pairs in brushy areas and montane forest edge between 1800 and 3500 m (6000 and 11,500 ft); common around the Machu Picchu ruins.

REGION: ESA, HAP

Plate 67b
Thrush-like Wren
Campylorhynchus turdinus
ID: Medium-sized (21 cm, 8 in); brown upperparts; white underparts densely spotted; long tail.

HABITAT: Family groups in vine tangles, palm fronds and upperparts of forest edge and tall secondary forest of Amazonian lowlands up to 1100 m (3600 ft) at the base of the Andes; explosive and rollicking songs obvious.

REGION: ESA, AMA

Plate 67c
Southern Nightingale-Wren
Microcerculus marginatus
ID: Small (11 cm, 4 in); upperparts brown, underparts white; short tail.

HABITAT: Walks stealthily on the ground but usually in thick vegetation and vine tangles; difficult to see, but its single flute-like notes, each subsequent one lower in tone and with a longer interval of silence than the previous one, are a common sound of Amazonian forests.

REGION: AMA

Plate 67d
Gray-breasted Wood-wren
Henicorhina leucophrys
ID: Small (10 cm, 4 in); short tail usually held up; dark rust upperparts; crown black; bold white eyestripe; gray underparts. Replaced in Amazonian lowlands of northeastern Perú by White-breasted Wood-wren, *Henicorhina leucosticta*, which is similar except for its white breast.

HABITAT: Undergrowth and ground of cloud forest between 1500 and 3000 m (5000 and 10,000 ft).

REGION: ESA

Plate 67e
House Wren
Troglodytes aedon
ID: Small (11 cm, 4.5 in); brown upperparts, buffy underparts; buffy eyestripe; faint black barring on wings, tail.

HABITAT: Low vegetation and ground in clearings and dry open areas from lowlands to puna.

REGION: TDF, CDL, WSV, HAP, ESA, AMA

Plate 67f
Musician Wren
Cyphorhinus aradus
ID: Small (13 cm, 5 in); olive-brown upperparts; bright rusty underparts and eyeline; bright blue bare patch of skin around eye; often noticed by its flute-like whistled song, so uncoordinated it sounds like a young boy learning to whistle.

HABITAT: Floor and dense undergrowth of humid tierra firme forest in Amazonian lowlands.

REGION: AMA

Plate 67 **395**

a Inca Wren

b Thrush-like Wren

c Southern Nightingale-Wren

d Gray-breasted Wood-wren

e House Wren

f Musician Wren

Plate 68 (**See also:** Thrushes and Mockingbirds, p. 166; Wrens, p. 163)

Plate 68a
Long-tailed Mockingbird
Mimus longicaudatus
ID: Medium-sized (30 cm, 1 ft); brownish gray upperparts, light gray underparts; long tail with large white tips obvious in flight.

HABITAT: Solitary or in pairs on low shrubs in open areas, pastures, and arid secondary forest edge of coast up to 2000 m (6600 ft).

REGION: TDF, CDL, WSV

Plate 68b
Donacobius (also called Black-capped Donacobius)
Donacobius atricapillus
ID: Medium-sized (22 cm, 9 in); brown back and wings; black tail, crown and cheeks; bright buffy underparts; long bill.

HABITAT: Family groups at the top of tall aquatic grass and low marsh vegetation of Amazonian lowlands; loud voices are obvious.

REGION: AMA

Plate 68c
Great Thrush
Turdus fuscater
ID: Medium-sized (33 cm, 1.1 ft); gray-brown with bright orange legs and bill; populations in southern Perú (subspecies *ockendoni*) blackish.

HABITAT: Common in moist areas such as pastures, city parks, gardens and *Eucalyptus* groves throughout the highlands above 2000 m (6500 ft). Replaced on the coast, western slopes, and drier parts of highland Andes by the smaller and lighter brown Chiguanco Thrush, *Turdus chiguanco*.

REGION: HAP

Plate 68d
Lawrence's Thrush
Turdus lawrencii
ID: Medium-sized (23 cm, 9 in); gray-brown upperparts, olive underparts except for white lower belly and white throat with fine black streaks; bright yellow bill, eyering.

HABITAT: Feeds on ground and undergrowth of moist lowland primary forest, but sings its flute-like songs that mimic other bird species from high in the canopy.

REGION: AMA

Plate 68e
Black-billed Thrush
Turdus ignobilis
ID: Medium-sized (24 cm, 9.5 in); brown upperparts; olive underparts with white lower belly; black bill.

HABITAT: Thick scrub and low secondary vegetation of Amazonian lowlands, often around human habitation.

REGION: AMA

Plate 68   **397**

a Long-tailed Mockingbird

b Donacobius

c Great Thrush   southern Perú form

e Black-billed Thrush

d Lawrence's Thrush

Plate 69a
Slate-throated Redstart
Myioborus miniatus
ID: Small (13 cm, 5 in); upperparts including head, throat and chest slate gray; underparts bright yellow; conspicuous white outer tail feathers often spread during foraging.

HABITAT: Very active in undergrowth and cloud forest edge between 700 and 2500 m (2300 and 8200 ft); usually associated with mixed-species foraging flocks.

REGION: ESA

Plate 69b
Spectacled Redstart
Myioborus melanocephalus
ID: Small (15 cm, 6 in); slate gray upperparts, bright yellow underparts; short yellow eyeline and eyering forming "spectacles;" conspicuous white outer tail feathers often spread during foraging.

HABITAT: Undergrowth of cloud forest and low, thick bushes from 2000 m (6500 ft) to tree-line; often in mixed-species foraging flocks.

REGION: ESA

Plate 69c
Blackburnian Warbler
Dendroica fusca
ID: Small (13 cm, 5 in); unmistakable in March to April, just before migrating north to North American breeding grounds, with male's brilliant orange and black head; nonbreeding and female plumage recognized by yellow eyestripe, yellow throat and streaks on side of breast.

HABITAT: Common during northern winter in mixed-species foraging flocks in mid-levels and canopy of open cloud forest between 1000 and 2500 m (3300 and 8200 ft).

REGION: ESA

Plate 69d
Canada Warbler
Wilsonia canadensis
ID: Small (13 cm, 5 in); gray upperparts; bright yellow underparts with "necklace" of short black stripes on chest; female and nonbreeding male with fainter necklace.

HABITAT: Winter resident in undergrowth of open cloud forest; during migration, in undergrowth of primary and secondary lowland forest.

REGION: ESA, AMA

Plate 69e
Three-striped Warbler
Basileuterus tristriatus
ID: Small (13 cm, 5 in); black head with three buffy stripes; olive upperparts, pale yellow-olive underparts.

HABITAT: Pairs forage in undergrowth of secondary cloud forest (1000 to 2000 m, 3300 to 6500 ft), often in mixed-species foraging flocks.

REGION: ESA

Plate 69f
Buff-rumped Warbler
Basileuterus fulvicauda
ID: Small (14 cm, 5.5 in); olive-brown upperparts, buffy white underparts; bright buffy tail and rump conspicuous in flight; loud series of musical "chew" notes often reveals its presence.

HABITAT: On ground or low vegetation in Amazonian lowlands along small forested streams; fans its bright tail frequently.

REGION: AMA

Plate 69 **399**

a Slate-throated Redstart

b Spectacled Redstart

F

M

c Blackburnian Warbler

M

F

d Canada Warbler

f Buff-rumped Warbler

e Three-striped Warbler

Plate 70a
Cinereous Conebill
Conirostrum cinereum
ID: Small (12 cm, 5 in); dark gray upperparts, light gray underparts; cinnamon-colored patch under base of tail; bold white eyeline; white wing patch; sharp pointed bill.

HABITAT: Open forests, shrubby areas, gardens and city parks between 3000 and 3600 m (9800 and 11,800 ft) but also a seasonal migrant to coastal desert.

REGION: CDL, WSV, HAP, ESA

Plate 70b
Giant Conebill
Oreomanes fraseri
ID: Small (17 cm, 7 in); gray upperparts, rusty colored underparts; whitish cheek patches and forehead; long pointed bill.

HABITAT: Almost exclusively restricted to groves of *Polylepis* forest between 3300 and 4500 m (10,800 and 14,800 ft), where it climbs up and down trunks and large branches.

REGION: HAP

Plate 70c
Black-throated Flower-piercer
Diglossa brunneiventris
ID: Small (14 cm, 6 in); upperparts black with gray rump and shoulder patches; underparts bright rusty with a black throat; peculiarly curved and hooked bill.

HABITAT: Low bushes and lone trees near tree-line (2500 to 4000 m, 8250 to 13,200 ft).

REGION: HAP

Plate 70d
Masked Flower-piercer
Diglossopis cyanea
ID: Small (15 cm, 6 in); dark blue; black mask; red eye; peculiarly curved and hooked bill.

HABITAT: Solitary or in mixed-species foraging flocks around large flowers in the canopy of cloud forest between 2200 and 3000 m (7200 and 9800 ft).

REGION: ESA

Plate 70e
Bananaquit
Coereba flaveola
ID: Small (11 cm, 4.5 in); black crown and cheek; white eyeline; gray throat; underparts and rump bright yellow; gray back; wing with a small white patch; short bill thin and curved down.

HABITAT: Active in pairs around flowering and fruiting trees, bushes and shrubs in open secondary forest, gardens and city parks of the lowlands; usually absent from primary forest areas.

REGION: TDF, AMA

Plate 70f
Tropical Parula
Parula pitiayumi
ID: Small (11 cm, 4 in); dull blue upperparts, black mask, bright yellow-orange underparts.

HABITAT: Forest edge and secondary forest of tropical dry forest and lower cloud forest (below 2500 m, 8250 ft); often in mixed-species foraging flocks of tanagers.

REGION: TDF, ESA

Plate 70 **401**

b Giant Conebill

a Cinereous Conebill

c Black-throated Flower-piercer

d Masked Flower-piercer

e Bananaquit

f Tropical Parula

Plate 71a
Golden Tanager
Tangara arthus
ID: Small (14 cm, 5.5 in); bright golden head, rump and underparts; blackish back, wings and tail; small black "ear" patch; rusty color confined to throat in northern populations but extends to chest in southern populations.

HABITAT: Cloud forest canopy, forest edge, and fruiting trees between 1000 and 2500 m (3300 and 8200 ft); usually in mixed-species foraging flocks.

REGION: ESA

Plate 71b
Yellow-bellied Dacnis
Dacnis flaviventer
ID: Small (13 cm, 5 in); male with bright yellow underparts with black throat, mask, back, wings and tail; crown gray-green; female with pale brown-olive upperparts, buffy yellow underparts.

HABITAT: Pairs seen in mid-levels to canopy of lowland tierra firme and flooded forest to moist tall secondary forest.

REGION: AMA

Plate 71c
Purple Honeycreeper
Cyanerpes caeruleus
ID: Small (11 cm, 4 in); long slender bill curved down; short tail; male glistening purple with black throat, wings and tail, bright yellow legs; female with green upperparts, green to yellow underparts streaked white; legs dull yellow. (The similar Red-legged Honeycreeper, *Cyanerpes cyaneus*, occurs in the same areas and is distinguished by red legs in both sexes and a black back and blue crown in males.)

HABITAT: Canopy and upper levels of moist lowland primary and tall secondary forest up to 1300 m (4300 ft), often in mixed-species foraging flocks.

REGION: AMA

Plate 71d
Blue-and-black Tanager
Tangara vassorii
ID: Small (13 cm, 5 in); in northern Perú shiny dark blue except for black wings and tail; dark eye; short straight bill; in central and southern Perú (the form illustrated) the subspecies, *atrocaerulea*, has an all-black back, black spots on breast and a buffy white neck.

HABITAT: High elevation cloud forest to tree-line (2000 to 3400 m, 6600 to 11,000 ft); usually in flocks of its own species or with mountain-tanager flocks.

REGION: HAP, ESA

Plate 71e
Blue Dacnis
Dacnis cayana
ID: Small (13 cm, 5 in); male bright turquoise blue with small black throat patch, mainly black tail, wings; female green with blue-gray head.

HABITAT: Humid lowland secondary forest and shrubby clearings, flowering and fruiting trees; often in mixed-species foraging flocks.

REGION: AMA

Plate 71f
Green Honeycreeper
Chlorophanes spiza
ID: Small (14 cm, 5.5 in); male shiny green with black face and crown, red eye, and bright yellow bill; female yellow-green with dark eye.

HABITAT: Pairs forage in mid-level to canopy of moist lowland primary and tall secondary forest; often in large mixed-species foraging flocks.

REGION: TDF, AMA

Plate 71 403

a Golden Tanager

F

b Yellow-bellied Dacnis

M

F

c Purple Honeycreeper

d Blue-and-black Tanager

M

M

F

e Blue Dacnis

M

f Green Honeycreeper

F

Plate 72a
Green-and-gold Tanager
Tangara schrankii
ID: Small (14 cm, 5.5 in); golden yellow crown, rump and center of breast shading into bright green on underparts; black forehead and side of face; back streaked black.

HABITAT: Canopy of humid lowland primary and tall secondary forest; usually in mixed-species foraging flocks.

REGION: AMA

Plate 72b
Paradise Tanager
Tangara chilensis
ID: Small (14 cm, 5.5 in); bright yellow-green head; bright red rump (red and yellow in central Perú); blue-green underparts; black tail, wings, back, and lower belly.

HABITAT: Canopy of humid primary and tall secondary forest of Amazonian lowlands and eastern Andean slopes up to 1500 m (5000 ft); usually in mixed-species foraging flocks.

REGION: ESA, AMA

Plate 72c
Turquoise Tanager
Tangara mexicana
ID: Small (14 cm, 5.5 in); upperparts black with dark blue rump, forehead, face and shoulders; underparts dark blue with bright yellow belly.

HABITAT: In mixed-species foraging flocks in secondary forest and forest edge of Amazonian lowlands.

REGION: AMA

Plate 72d
Beryl-spangled Tanager
Tangara nigroviridis
ID: Small (14 cm, 5.5 in); breast flecked greenish blue and black; crown, neck and rump shiny pale green; face mask, back, wings and tail blackish.

HABITAT: Cloud forest edge, isolated treetops in pastures, and secondary forest at fruiting trees between 1500 and 2500 m (5000 and 8200 ft); usually in mixed-species foraging flocks.

REGION: ESA

Plate 72e
Bay-headed Tanager
Tangara gyrola
ID: Small (14 cm, 5.5 in); bright rusty head; blue-green underparts and rump; bright green back, wings, tail.

HABITAT: Canopy and mid-levels of primary and tall secondary forest of Amazonian lowlands and eastern Andean slopes up to 1500 m (5000 ft); usually in mixed-species foraging flocks.

REGION: ESA, AMA

Plate 72f
Orange-eared Tanager
Chlorochrysa calliparaea
ID: Small (13 cm, 5 in); bright green upperparts, blue-green underparts; orange crown, "ear" and rump; black throat.

HABITAT: Cloud forest canopy, forest edge, and fruiting trees between 1100 and 1700 m (3600 and 5600 ft); usually in mixed-species foraging flocks.

REGION: ESA

Plate 72 **405**

a Green-and-gold Tanager

b Paradise Tanager

c Turquoise Tanager

d Beryl-spangled Tanager

e Bay-headed Tanager

f Orange-eared Tanager

Plate 73a
Grass-green Tanager
Chlorornis riefferii
ID: Medium-sized (21 cm, 8 in); bright green with rusty face and lower belly; bright orange legs and bill.

HABITAT: Small groups of 3 to 6 in canopy of cloud forest and forest edge between 2200 and 2800 m (7200 and 9000 ft); often in mixed-species foraging flocks.

REGION: ESA

Plate 73b
Thick-billed Euphonia
Euphonia laniirostris
ID: Small (11 cm, 4 in); male with bright yellow underparts (including throat) and crown, dark blue upperparts; female olive-green upperparts and gray-yellow underparts.

HABITAT: Open lowland forest, dry secondary scrub, gardens, city parks; often in mixed-species foraging flocks.

REGION: TDF, AMA

Plate 73c
White-vented Euphonia
Euphonia minuta
ID: Small (10 cm, 4 in); male with bright yellow breast and crown, dark blue upperparts and throat, white lower belly and undertail; female olive upperparts, gray throat, olive-yellow breast and white lower belly. (The similar and equally widespread Orange-bellied Euphonia, *Euphonia xanthogaster,* has all yellow underparts including the underbelly and in southeastern Perú, a rusty crown.)

HABITAT: Canopy of tall moist primary forest in lowlands.

REGION: AMA

Plate 73d
Opal-rumped Tanager
Tangara velia
ID: Small (14 cm, 5.5 in); crown and back black, rump and forehead whitish, tail and wings blue; underparts purplish-blue with bright rusty lower belly. (Similar Opal-crowned Tanager, *Tangara callophrys,* distinguished by white of forehead extending along side of head and black lower belly.)

HABITAT: Canopy of humid lowland primary and tall secondary forest; usually in mixed-species foraging flocks.

REGION: AMA

Plate 73e
Common Bush-Tanager
Chlorospingus opthalmicus
ID: Small (14 cm, 5.5 in); gray to brownish head; white eye; yellow-olive upperparts; buffy gray underparts.

HABITAT: Noisy flocks of 5 to 10 in dense undergrowth and lower levels of cloud forest (800 to 2600 m, 2600 to 8500 ft) around which large mixed-species foraging flocks form.

REGION: ESA

Plate 73f
Swallow Tanager
Tersina viridis
ID: Small (15 cm, 6 in); male shiny turquoise with black mask, faint barring on sides of breast, white lower belly; female all grass-green with barring on sides of breast.

HABITAT: Small flocks or pairs perch high on exposed branches in lowland moist forest to lower reaches of cloud forest at 2000 m (6600 ft) elevation.

REGION: ESA, AMA

Plate 73 **407**

a Grass-green Tanager

M

F

b Thick-billed Euphonia

M

c White-vented Euphonia

F

d Opal-rumped Tanager

e Common Bush-Tanager

f Swallow Tanager

M

F

Plate 74a
Scarlet-bellied Mountain-Tanager
Anisognathus igniventris
ID: Small (19 cm, 7.5 in); black upperparts with bright blue shoulders and rump; scarlet "ear" patch; underparts scarlet with black upper breast, throat.

HABITAT: Small groups in open cloud forest, scrubby bushes and scattered trees at high elevations (2500 to 3500 m, 8200 to 11,500 ft).

REGION: HAP, ESA

Plate 74b
Blue-winged Mountain-Tanager
Anisognathus somptuosus
ID: Small (18 cm, 7 in); black upperparts; bright yellow crown; pale blue in wings and tail; underparts bright yellow.

HABITAT: Small groups of 2 to 8 in cloud forest edges, isolated trees in pastures, and secondary forest between 1500 and 2500 m (5000 and 8200 ft); often in mixed-species foraging flocks.

REGION: ESA

Plate 74c
Hooded Mountain-Tanager
Buthraupis montana
ID: Medium-sized (23 cm, 9 in); brilliant blue upperparts; black head; red eye; bright yellow underparts.

HABITAT: Groups of 2 to 6 in primary cloud forest canopy between 2000 and 3200 m (6600 and 10,500 ft); occasionally in mixed-species foraging flocks.

REGION: ESA

Plate 74d
Palm Tanager
Thraupis palmarum
ID: Small (18 cm, 7 in); olive-gray; blackish tail; wings in flight show contrasting black and bright olive pattern.

HABITAT: Pairs seen in isolated trees in open scrub and agricultural areas, secondary forest, parks, gardens; often near or in palms.

REGION: AMA

Plate 74e
Blue-gray Tanager
Thraupis episcopus
ID: Small (17 cm, 7 in); pale blue-gray with blue (coastal) or white (Amazonian) shoulders.

HABITAT: Pairs seen in open woodland, scrubby forest, secondary forest, gardens, and city parks.

REGION: TDF, AMA

Plate 74f
Blue-and-yellow Tanager
Thraupis bonariensis
ID: Small (17 cm, 7 in); male with bright blue head, wings and tail; dark olive-green back with bright orange-yellow rump; bright yellow underparts; female with dingy buff and gray body, bluish head.

HABITAT: Semi-open bushes and low trees of arid mountain slopes (to 3300 m, 11,000 ft) down to gardens and agricultural areas of north and central coast.

REGION: CDL, WSV, HAP

Plate 74 **409**

a Scarlet-bellied Mountain-Tanager

b Blue-winged Mountain-Tanager

c Hooded Mountain-Tanager

d Palm Tanager

Amazonian form

Coastal form

e Blue-gray Tanager

F

M

f Blue-and-yellow Tanager

Plate 75 (**See also:** Tanagers, p. 170)

Plate 75a
White-shouldered Tanager
Tachyphonus luctuosus
ID: Small (13 cm, 5 in); male glossy black with large white shoulder patches; female with gray head, olive-green upperparts and bright yellow underparts.

HABITAT: Mid-levels and canopy of moist lowland primary and secondary forest; frequently in mixed-species foraging flocks.

REGION: AMA

Plate 75b
Magpie Tanager
Cissopis leveriana
ID: Medium-sized (28 cm, 11 in); conspicuous with its long tail and striking black and white pattern.

HABITAT: Pairs seen in secondary lowland forest edge, shrubby areas, and vegetation along rivers and lakes.

REGION: AMA

Plate 75c
Masked Crimson Tanager
Ramphocelus nigrogularis
ID: Small (19 cm, 7.5 in); bright crimson head, upper breast; black mask, back, wings, tail and center of lower belly; silvery white lower part of bill.

HABITAT: Small groups in low vegetation and short trees along small rivers, cochas, and lakes of Amazonian lowlands.

REGION: AMA

Plate 75d
Blue-capped Tanager
Thraupis cyanocephala
ID: Small (18 cm, 7 in); head shiny blue; upperparts yellow-green; underparts pale blue with bright yellow lower belly and base of tail.

HABITAT: Scrubby woodlands, shrubs and secondary forest edge at 1800 to 3000 m (6000 to 10,000 ft) in tropical dry forest and lower cloud forest.

REGION: TDF, ESA

Plate 75e
Silver-beaked Tanager
Ramphocelus carbo
ID: Small (18 cm, 7 in); male velvet black with deep red overtones, especially on head and upper breast; silvery white lower part of bill; female dark red-brown.

HABITAT: Noisy groups of 4 to 8 in lowland scrubby areas, forest edge, and river edges.

REGION: AMA

Plate 75　**411**

a White-shouldered Tanager

M

F

b Magpie Tanager

c Masked Crimson Tanager

M

F

d Blue-capped Tanager

M

F

e Silver-beaked Tanager

Plate 76 (**See also:** Orioles and Blackbirds, p. 173)

Plate 76a
Peruvian Meadowlark
Sturnella bellicosa
ID: Medium-sized (21 cm, 8 in); upperparts black streaked with brown; thin white line over eye; throat and upper breast bright red; lower belly black; long, thin, pointed bill.

HABITAT: Sitting on the ground, low bushes or on telephone wires of open pastures, grassy fields and irrigated areas from near the coast up to 2500 m (8200 ft).

REGION: CDL, WSV

Plate 76b
Scrub Blackbird
Dives warszewiczi
ID: Medium-sized (27 cm, 11 in); all glossy black; dark eye.

HABITAT: In groups on the ground or low vegetation of open farmland, city parks, and patches of secondary vegetation and cactus from north and central coast up to 3000 m (10,000 ft); loud ringing songs are obvious.

REGION: CDL, WSV

Plate 76c
Giant Cowbird
Scaphidura oryzivora
ID: Medium-sized (37 cm, 1.2 ft); male glossy black with conspicuous ruff on neck; female smaller, duller black, and little or no ruff on neck.

HABITAT: In pairs or small groups in open lowlands (rarely to 2000 m, 6600 ft); often along river sand-bars; usually near oropendola nests (the cowbirds lay their eggs in oropendola nests).

REGION: TDF, ESA, AMA

Plate 76d
Yellow-hooded Blackbird
Agelaius icterocephalus
ID: Medium-sized (17 cm, 7 in); male all black with yellow head and yellow extending to chest; female dull olive with yellowish face.

HABITAT: Marshes, river islands and wet grasslands of Amazonian lowlands in northeastern Perú.

REGION: AMA

Plate 76e
Oriole Blackbird
Gymnomystax mexicanus
ID: Medium-sized (28 cm, 11 in); black back, wings and tail contrasting with bright yellow head and underparts.

HABITAT: Pairs seen in top of small bushes in marshes and low, open vegetation along rivers and cochas in the Amazonian lowlands of northeastern Perú.

REGION: AMA

Plate 76   413

a Peruvian Meadowlark

b Scrub Blackbird

c Giant Cowbird

d Yellow-hooded Blackbird

M

F

e Oriole Blackbird

Plate 77 (**See also:** Orioles and Blackbirds, p. 173)

Plate 77a

Olive Oropendola
Psaracolius bifasciatus

ID: Large (50 cm, 20 in); olive-green head, neck, and chest; rest of body chestnut except for yellow tail; black bill tipped orange, bare pink patch on face.

HABITAT: High in canopy of tierra firme forest.

REGION: AMA

Plate 77b

Crested Oropendola
Psarocolius decumanus

ID: Medium-sized (47 cm, 1.5 ft); males are distinctly larger than females (37 cm, 1.2 ft) but both are glossy black with rusty rump and lower belly, bright yellow tail, and long, straight, whitish bill.

HABITAT: Large flocks in tall humid forest edges of lowlands up to 1200 m (4000 ft) on the lower slopes of the Andes; in the morning and late afternoon often seen flying high across open rivers and marshes from and to their night-time roosts.

REGION: AMA

Plate 77c

Russet-backed Oropendola
Psarocolius angustifrons

ID: Males are larger (49 cm, 1.6 ft) than females (35 cm, 1.2 ft), but both are rusty olive with bright outer tail feathers obvious in flight and an all-dark bill.

HABITAT: Large flocks in open secondary forest, isolated trees in pastures, and tall vegetation along rivers and lakes, from Amazonian lowlands up to 2000 m (6600 ft).

REGION: ESA, AMA

Plate 77d

Yellow-rumped Cacique
Cacicus cela

ID: Medium-sized (30 cm, 1 ft); males are noticeably larger than females (23 cm, 9 in) but identical in their color pattern; black with yellow wing patch, rump, and base of tail.

HABITAT: Usually in flocks of 5 to 25 in tall vegetation along lowland river and lake edges, open areas, and frequently near human habitation; also at fruiting trees in primary forest canopy.

REGION: AMA

Plate 77e

Troupial
Icterus icterus

ID: Medium-sized (23 cm, 9 in); bright orange with black "bib" and face; black tail; black wings with small white patch; orange shoulder; its cheery song is a series of two- and three-noted loud piping whistles.

HABITAT: Moist forest edge and secondary vegetation along forested marshes and rivers in Amazonian lowlands.

REGION: AMA

Plate 77 **415**

a Olive Oropendola

b Crested Oropendola

c Russet-backed Oropendola

d Yellow-rumped Cacique

e Troupial

Plate 78a
Streaked Saltator
Saltator albicollis
ID: Medium-sized (20 cm, 8 in); upperparts light brown with conspicuous white eyeline; breast with light streaks.

HABITAT: Pairs seen in parks, gardens and river-associated forest from coast up to 2500 m (8200 ft).

REGION: TDF, CDL, WSV

Plate 78b
Red-capped Cardinal
Paroaria gularis
ID: Small (17 cm, 7 in); bright red head; black upperparts and throat patch; white underparts; immature with brown head.

HABITAT: Low in vegetation bordering cochas, lakes and small rivers in the Amazonian lowlands.

REGION: AMA

Plate 78c
Blue-black Grassquit
Volatinia jacarina
ID: Small (11 cm, 4 in); male all blue-black except for white underwings; female brown upperparts, buffy white underparts streaked brown.

HABITAT: Open fields, agricultural areas, and low shrubby patches throughout the coastal and Amazonian lowlands.

REGION: TDF, CDL, WSV, AMA

Plate 78d
Chestnut-bellied Seed-Finch
Oryzoborus angolensis
ID: Small (13 cm, 5 in); thick dark bill; male with black head and upperparts; underparts dark-rusty; underwings and small patch in upperwing white, obvious in flight; female all brown.

HABITAT: Pairs seen in moist grassy areas and shrubby forest edge in the lowlands.

REGION: AMA

Plate 78e
Buff-throated Saltator
Saltator maximus
ID: Medium-sized (21 cm, 8 in); green-olive back, wings and tail; gray head with short white line over eye; small white throat patch with black border; underparts buffy gray. (Occurs together in the Amazonian lowlands with Grayish Saltator, *Saltator coerulescens*, which has all-gray upperparts.)

HABITAT: Shrubby undergrowth, forest edge, and low secondary forest of lowlands.

REGION: AMA

Plate 78f
Golden-billed Saltator
Saltator aurantiirostris
ID: Medium-sized (20 cm, 8 in); gray upperparts with black face and breast band, white eyeline and throat; bill bright orange; underparts buffy gray.

HABITAT: Dry shrubby forests from 1500 to 3000 m (5000 to 10,000 ft).

REGION: WSV, HAP, ESA

Plate 78 417

a Streaked Saltator

IM

b Red-capped Cardinal

F

M

c Blue-black Grassquit

M

F

d Chestnut-bellied Seed-Finch

e Buff-throated Saltator

f Golden-billed Saltator

Plate 79 (**See also:** Sparrows and Finches, p. 175)

Plate 79a
Chestnut-bellied Seedeater
Sporophila castaneiventris
ID: Small (10 cm, 4 in); male all blue-gray except for deep rusty colored center of throat, breast and lower belly; female olive-brown upperparts, buffy underparts.

HABITAT: Open fields, grassy areas, floating vegetation along edges of cochas and small rivers in the lowlands.

REGION: AMA

Plate 79b
Yellow-bellied Seedeater
Sporophila nigricollis
ID: Small (11 cm, 4 in); male olive-brown upperparts; black head and throat; pale yellow underparts; female olive-brown upperparts, yellowish brown underparts.

HABITAT: Open fields, grassy areas and roadsides in lowlands.

REGION: TDF, AMA

Plate 79c
Black-and-white Seedeater
Sporophila luctuosa
ID: Small (11 cm, 4 in); male black above with black throat and chest; white underparts and white spot in wing; female olive-brown.

HABITAT: Open fields, grassy areas and roadsides in lower Andean slopes and lowlands.

REGION: ESA, AMA

Plate 79d
Plumbeous Sierra-Finch
Phrygilus unicolor
ID: Small (15 cm, 6 in); male gray with dark bill; female with brown upperparts streaked dark brown, and underparts whitish streaked brown.

HABITAT: Low bushes and on ground in open puna between 3000 and 4500 m (10,000 and 14,800 ft).

REGION: HAP

Plate 79e
Peruvian Sierra-Finch
Phrygilus punensis
ID: Small (16 cm, 6 in); head gray, back yellow-olive, breast yellow-orange. Similar Blue-and-yellow Tanager (Plate 74f) has a bright yellow rump lacking in the Peruvian Sierra-Finch.

HABITAT: Rocky high altitude areas with small shrubs and short trees between 2000 to 4000 m (6600 and 13,200 ft) elevation, often on the ground in small flocks.

REGION: WSV, HAP

Plate 79f
White-winged Diuca-Finch
Diuca speculifera
ID: Medium-sized (19 cm, 7.5 in); upperparts gray with white spot below eye; wings black with large white patch obvious in flight; underparts gray and white.

HABITAT: High puna grasslands (4000 to 5500 m, 13,100 to 18,000 ft) of central and southern Perú.

REGION: HAP

Plate 79 **419**

a Chestnut-bellied Seedeater

M

F

b Yellow-bellied Seedeater

c Black-and-white Seedeater

F

M

d Plumbeous Sierra-Finch

M

F

e Peruvian Sierra-Finch

f White-winged Diuca-Finch

Plate 80a
Band-tailed Seedeater
Catamenia analis
ID: Small (12 cm, 5 in); male gray with bright yellow bill, rusty colored lower belly, and blackish tail with conspicuous white band across center visible in flight.

HABITAT: Pastures, shrubby areas, and grasslands of western slopes (1000 to 3000 m, 3300 to 10,000 ft).

REGION: WSV, HAP

Plate 80b
Collared Warbling-Finch
Poospiza hispaniolensis
ID: Small (14 cm, 5.5 in); tail black with large white patches obvious in flight; male upperparts gray, eyeline white, cheek black, underparts white with black breast band; female upperparts grayish brown with brown streaks, underparts whitish with buffy streaks.

HABITAT: Coastal desert scrub, low bushes on the dry western slopes up to 2500 m (8200 ft).

REGION: CDL, WSV

Plate 80c
Rufous-collared Sparrow
Zonotrichia capensis
ID: Small (15 cm, 6 in); upperparts brown with black streaks on back; rusty neck; gray head with prominent black lines; underparts whitish with black and rusty patch on side of upper breast.

HABITAT: Open areas from coast to highlands including pastures, low shrubby areas, gardens and city parks (1000 to 3700 m, 3300 to 12,000 ft).

REGION: TDF, CDL, WSV, HAP, ESA

Plate 80d
Hooded Siskin
Carduelis magellanica
ID: Small (12 cm, 5 in); olive back; yellow rump patch; black tail; wings black with bold yellow stripes obvious in flight; breast bright yellow; head black (male) or olive-yellow (female).

HABITAT: Small flocks in open secondary forest, shrubby areas, agricultural fields, gardens and city parks from the coast to 3000 m (10,000 ft).

REGION: CDL, WSV, HAP

Plate 80e
Southern Yellow Grosbeak
Pheucticus chrysogaster
ID: Medium-sized (22 cm, 9 in); thick bill; bright yellow with black streaks on back; black wings with white patches obvious in flight; black tail with white tips; female similar but not as bright yellow.

HABITAT: Secondary forest, open scrubby areas, forest edge, gardens, and city parks from the coastal lowlands up west slope to 3000 m (10,000 ft).

REGION: CDL, WSV, HAP

Plate 80f
Greenish Yellow-Finch
Sicalis olivascens
ID: Small (14 cm, 5.5 in); male upperparts dull olive, underparts yellow; female duller.

HABITAT: Semi-open areas, rocky ravines, scrubby slopes, fields, and towns at 2500 to 3800 m (8200 to 12,500 ft), sometimes in large flocks.

REGION: WSV, HAP

Plate 80 **421**

a Band-tailed Seedeater

b Collared Warbling-Finch

c Rufous-collared Sparrow

d Hooded Siskin

e Southern Yellow Grosbeak

f Greenish Yellow-Finch

Plate 81 (**See also:** Opossums, p. 187; Anteaters, p. 189)

Plate 81a

Silky Anteater (also called Pygmy Anteater)
Cyclopes didactylus
ID: Small (body length 18 cm, 7 in) with gray, brownish or yellowish dense, silky fur; darker on top; long (19 cm, 7.5 in) prehensile tail.

HABITAT: Low and middle levels of lowland wet forests of eastern Perú; arboreal, especially among vines and thin tree branches; nocturnal.

REGION: AMA

Plate 81b

Brown Four-eyed Opossum
Metachirus nudicaudatus
ID: Like a large brown rat (body length 27 cm, 10.5 in); distinctive buff spot above each eye; tail long (30 cm, 1 ft) and completely hairless.

HABITAT: Mature lowland forests and tall secondary forests with undergrowth; forages both in the trees and on the ground; active at night and shy.

REGION: AMA

Plate 81c

Common Opossum
Didelphis marsupialis
ID: Large (body length 40 cm, 15 in); black or gray; naked black ears and long, naked, black tail (40 cm, 15 in) with a white tip.

HABITAT: Common below 2000 m (6560 ft) along the coast of northern Perú and throughout the Amazon; found around villages, in secondary forests and river edge vegetation, on the ground or in trees; night-active. (Replaced at higher elevations on the eastern slopes up to 4000 m, 13,200 ft, by the similar White-eared Opossum, *Didelphis albiventris*, which has a white face and ears and contrasting black mask through the eyes.)

REGION: TDF, CDL, WSV, ESA, AMA

Plate 81d

Long-furred Woolly Mouse Opossum
Micoureus demerarae
ID: Small (body length 18 cm, 7 in); grayish brown; resembles more a rodent than a marsupial; long body fur; bicolored tail, black at the base, whitish at the end. (Occurs together on the eastern slopes of the Andes with the similar Short-furred Woolly Mouse Opossum, *Micoureus regina*, which is reddish brown with tail uniformly colored brown.)

HABITAT: Primarily high above the ground in branches of trees in secondary and primary forests as well as in plantations and gardens in the eastern lowlands; occasionally forages on the ground; hisses actively if approached too closely; night-active.

REGION: AMA

Plate 81e

Water Opossum
Chironectes minimus
ID: Only medium-sized (body length 28 cm, 11 in) mammal with mottled black and light gray color pattern and webbed hind toes in lowland Perú.

HABITAT: Active at night, swimming in water of lowland lakes and rivers and on the eastern Andean slopes up to 1800 m (6000 ft); does not climb vegetation.

REGION: ESA, AMA

Plate 81 **423**

a Silky Anteater

b Brown Four-eyed Opossum

c Common Opossum

d Long-furred Woolly Mouse Opossum

e Water Opossum

Plate 82 (**See also:** Anteaters, Sloths, and Armadillos, p. 189)

Plate 82a
Southern Two-toed Sloth
Choloepus didactylus
ID: Medium-sized (body length 65 cm, 26 in); buffy-colored on throat, chest and back; long protruding snout; active mainly at night. (Replaced on the eastern Andean slopes up to 1800 m, 6000 ft, by the similar Hoffmann's Two-toed Sloth, *Chloepus hoffmanni*, which has a light throat contrasting with the rest of its light-brown body; but both species apparently occur together in the northern and central lowlands of Perú.)

HABITAT: Restricted mainly to moist lowland primary forest high in the canopy; uses its two sharp toes on front feet as effective weapons and can be quite aggressive when cornered.

REGION: AMA

Plate 82b
Brown-throated Three-toed Sloth
Bradypus variegatus
ID: Medium-sized (body length 60 cm, 24 in); pale brown and gray but takes on distinctive green tinge during the rainy season, when algae and fungi grow on its hair; flat, black and white masked face and hooked claws.

HABITAT: Restricted to moist lowland forests or moist riverine forest in drier areas. Most easily seen in open *Cecropia* forests along rivers; a docile and non-aggressive species active during the day.

REGION: TDF, AMA

Plate 82c
Nine-banded Armadillo
Dasypus novemcinctus
ID: Medium-sized (body length 40 cm, 16 in); long pointed tail (30 cm, 12 in); long nose; body armor plating covers the entire sides; 6 to 11 movable expansion bands across the back, most individuals with 9.

HABITAT: Active day and night in lowland forests, savanna, and open areas.

REGION: CDL, ESA, AMA

Plate 82d
Giant Armadillo
Priodontes maximus
ID: Large (body length 90 cm, 35 in) with long scaled tail (52 cm, 20 in); incomplete armor plating; huge, curved central claw on front feet.

HABITAT: Active at night in lowland primary forest; spends the daytime resting in large burrows dug into the forest floor.

REGION: AMA

Note: This species is endangered, CITES Appendix I and USA ESA listed.

Plate 82e
Giant Anteater
Myrmecophaga tridactyla
ID: Large (body length 1.6 m, 5 ft); striking and bold black, gray and white coloring; long, thin head and muzzle; long (75 cm, 30 in), feather-like tail.

HABITAT: Active day or night; rare everywhere but most regularly found in primary lowland forest and grassy savannah; found only on the ground; long claws on its front feet and a very aggressive nature when cornered can make it extremely dangerous.

REGION: AMA

Note: This species is threatened, CITES Appendix II listed.

Plate 82f
Southern Tamandua
Tamandua tetradactyla
ID: Medium-sized (body length 70 cm, 28 in); distinct yellowish and black pattern; long (50 cm, 20 in) furry tail is prehensile and used for climbing. An all-blonde form occasionally occurs. (Replaced in tropical dry forest of northwestern Perú by the similar but smaller Northern Tamandua, *Tamandua mexicana*.)

HABITAT: Active day and night either in trees or on ground of secondary and primary lowland forest.

REGION: AMA

Plate 82 **425**

a Southern
Two-toed
Sloth

b Brown-throated
Three-toed Sloth

c Nine-banded
Armadillo

d Giant
Armadillo

e Giant
Anteater

f Southern Tamandua

Plate 83 (**See also:** Bats, p. 193)

Plate 83a

Greater Fishing Bat (also called Bulldog Bat)
Noctilio leporinus
ID: Large (body length 9.7 cm, 4 in); brown to reddish brown with 60 cm (2 ft) wingspan; squared snout with no noseleaf.

HABITAT: Lowland lakes, estuaries, rivers, pastures and cleared areas; usually seen flying over water at night hunting for fish.

REGION: AMA

Plate 83b

Jamaican Fruit-eating Bat
Artibeus jamaicensis
ID: Large (body length 9 cm, 3.5 in; wingspan 40 cm, 16 in); brown to gray coloring; lack of a tail, prominent noseleaf and no white lines on the back are distinctive.

HABITAT: Low and middle elevation wet and dry forests; feeds at night mainly on fruit, especially figs.

REGION: TDF, ESA, AMA

Plate 83c

Common Vampire Bat
Desmodus rotundus
ID: Medium-sized (body length 7.5 cm, 3 in); triangular-shaped ears; razor-sharp front teeth; "thumb" on the wing twice as long as that of any other species of bat.

HABITAT: Nocturnal in lowland to mid-elevation (1800 m, 6000 ft) forests and clearings; most common in pastures and agricultural areas where there are large domestic animals to supply its blood meals.

REGION: TDF, CDL, WSV, ESA, AMA

Plate 83d

White-lined Sac-winged Bat
Saccopteryx bilineata
ID: Small (body length 5 cm, 2 in); dark brown with two bold white lines running the length of the back; sharp-pointed nose lacking a noseleaf.

HABITAT: Nocturnal in lowland forest clearings and along forest paths, where they pursue insects.

REGION: AMA

Plate 83e

False Vampire Bat
Vampyrum spectrum
ID: Largest bat in the New World (body length 15 cm, 6 in), with a huge wingspan (85 cm, 33 in); long snout with noseleaf and large rounded ears.

HABITAT: Nocturnal in lowland and mid-elevation forests (1650 m, 5500 ft) and clearings; preys on small to medium-sized birds such as anis and trogons and also other bats, rodents and occasionally fruit.

REGION: ESA, AMA

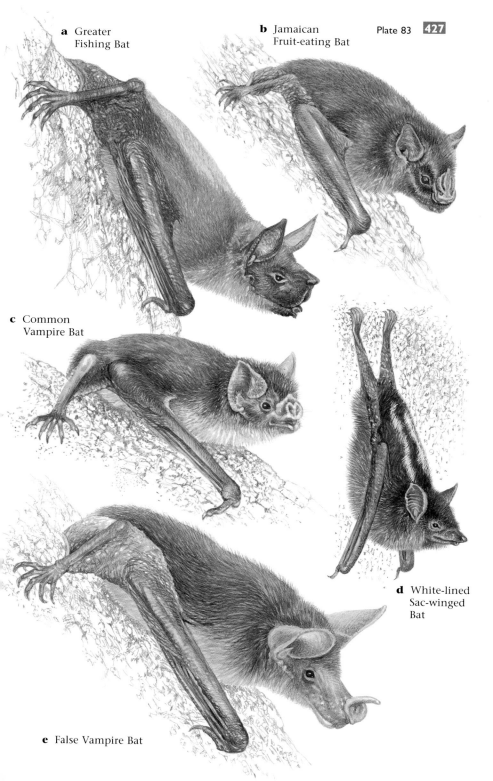

a Greater Fishing Bat

b Jamaican Fruit-eating Bat

Plate 83 **427**

c Common Vampire Bat

d White-lined Sac-winged Bat

e False Vampire Bat

Plate 84 (**See also:** Bats, p. 193)

Plate 84a

Short-tailed Fruit Bat
Carollia perspicillata
ID: Small (body length 5.5 cm, 2 in); light brown; large noseleaf.

HABITAT: Moist lowlands up to 1200 m (4000 ft) elevation; feed on the forest undergrowth fruits of piper plants.

REGION: ESA, AMA

Plate 84b

Sucker-footed Bat
Thyroptera tricolor
ID: Small (body length 4 cm, 1.5 in); short muzzle lacking a noseleaf; silver-white breast contrasting with dark brown upperparts.

HABITAT: Moist lowland forests, gardens and banana plantations; feed nocturnally on insects along forested rivers and clearings. Unique suction cups on ankles and thumbs attach to leaf surfaces while roosting during the day, especially inside young *Heliconia* and banana leaves that are still rolled into tubes before opening as mature leaves.

REGION: AMA

Plate 84c

Common Long-tongued Bat
Glossophaga soricina
ID: Medium-sized (body length 5.5 cm, 2 in); long snout with spear-shaped noseleaf.

HABITAT: Restricted to moist lowland forests; hovers while using its long tongue to reach flower nectar; also catches insects resting on plant leaves.

REGION: AMA

Plate 84d

Long-nosed Bat
Rhynchonycteris naso
ID: Small (body length 4 cm, 1.5 in); grizzly-white; distinctively long pointed snout lacking noseleaf.

HABITAT: Always in moist areas near lowland primary forest; hunts insects at night low over nearby water surfaces; several individuals roost together during the day on shaded logs along rivers and fly low over the water as a flock when frightened.

REGION: AMA

Plate 84e

Black Myotis
Myotis nigricans
ID: Small (body length 4 cm, 1.5 in); dark brown with a short nose and no noseleaf.

HABITAT: Common at night hawking for insects in the air over open areas of dry to moist forest from sea level to over 1200 m (4000 ft); also common around human habitation.

REGION: TDF, ESA, AMA

Plate 84 **429**

a Short-tailed Fruit Bat

b Sucker-footed Bat

c Common Long-tongued Bat

e Black Myotis

d Long-nosed Bat

Plate 85a

Dusky Titi Monkey
Callicebus moloch

ID: Small (body length 30 cm, 12 in); long (40 cm, 16 in) bushy tail; white forehead and rusty chest contrast with gray upperparts; often noticed by its whooping calls in early morning; moves little and is difficult to see when disturbed. In extreme southeastern Perú, the form *brunneus* occurs, which is much darker brown on the back, legs and head.

HABITAT: Active only during the day in dense vegetation and vine tangles of lowland secondary and primary forest.

REGION: AMA

Plate 85b

Emperor Tamarin
Saguinus imperator

ID: Small (body length 25 cm, 10 in; tail 40 cm, 16 in); gray-buff body, contrasting orange tail and long, drooping, white moustache are unmistakable.

HABITAT: Active only during the day; often associated in mixed troops with Saddle-backed Tamarins in the mid levels of lowland tierra firme forest of southeastern Perú.

REGION: AMA

Plate 85c

Saddle-backed Tamarin
Saguinus fuscicollis

ID: Small (body length 24 cm, 9 in; tail 33 cm, 13 in); black head and feet; mostly chestnut body. The high chirping notes of the small family groups can easily be confused with sounds of a bird flock. Common throughout lowlands of Amazonian Perú. In extreme northeastern Perú, it can be confused only with the rarer Black-mantled Tamarin, *Saguinus nigricollis*, which has all-black foreparts, lacks the light speckling on the back, and often occurs in large troops of 40 or more.

HABITAT: Active during the day in mid levels of secondary and primary tierra firme forest with dense tangles of vines and branches.

REGION: AMA

Plate 85d

Pygmy Marmoset
Cebuella pygmaea

ID: Smallest primate in Perú (body length 14 cm, 5.5 in; tail 20 cm, 8 in); buffy gray; easily seen only at its sap-sucking sites low on tree trunks.

HABITAT: Primary tierra firme forest during the day.

REGION: AMA

Plate 85   **431**

a Dusky Titi Monkey

b Emperor Tamarin

c Saddle-backed Tamarin

d Pygmy Marmoset

Plate 86a
Common Squirrel Monkey
Saimiri sciureus

ID: Medium-sized (body length 30 cm, 12 in); long nonprehensile tail (40 cm, 16 in); combination of black snout and white face and ears is unique. (The populations of central and southern Amazonian Perú are considered a separate species, *Saimiri boliviensis*, by some experts.

HABITAT: Active during the day when its large, noisy troops move at mid to upper levels of primary and secondary lowland forests.

REGION: AMA

Plate 86b
White-fronted Capuchin Monkey
Cebus albifrons

ID: Medium-sized (body length 40 cm, 16 in); long (45 cm, 18 in) prehensile tail usually carried coiled; combination of a dark cap and light-colored body and feet unique in Perú. Similar sized and shaped Brown Capuchin, *Cebus apella*, occasionally occurs in the same troops with the White-fronted Capuchin throughout Amazonian Perú, but the Brown Capuchin has dark legs and feet and darker brown body.

HABITAT: Active during the day; large, noisy troops move at all levels, from the ground to canopy, of primary and secondary forest.

REGION: ESA, AMA

Plate 86c
Common Woolly Monkey
Lagothrix lagothricha

ID: Medium-sized (body length 40 cm, 16 in); uniformly colored gray to black; long prehensile tail (70 cm, 28 in) carried coiled.

HABITAT: Travels during the day in noisy and often large troops through mid levels to canopy of lowland tierra firme forest.

REGION: AMA

Plate 86d
Yellow-tailed Woolly Monkey
Lagothrix flavicauda

ID: Medium-sized (body length 52 cm, 21 in); uniformly colored dark reddish brown except for pale muzzle; long prehensile tail (60 cm, 24 in) dark brown on top but yellowish below.

HABITAT: Travels during the day in small troops through mid levels to canopy of mid-elevation (1800 to 2500 m, 6000 to 8250 ft) cloud forest.

REGION: ESA

Note: This species is endangered, CITES Appendix I and USA ESA listed.

Plate 86   **433**

a Common Squirrel Monkey

b White-fronted Capuchin Monkey

c Common Woolly Monkey

d Yellow-tailed Woolly Monkey

Plate 87a
Monk Saki Monkey
Pithecia monachus

ID: Large (body length 40 cm, 16 in); shaggy gray and black body hair, naked face and long shaggy tail (45 cm, 18 in). In the lowlands along the Brazil border south of the Río Amazonas, another shaggy species, the Bald Uakari Monkey, *Cacajao calvus*, occurs. Its short and shaggy tail together with bright rusty fur and an all red bare head are distinctive.

HABITAT: Both sakis and uakaris are active during the day and occur in the upper levels of primary forest, the sakis in small family groups and the uakaris in large troops.

REGION: AMA

Plate 87b
Noisy Night Monkey
Aotus vociferans

ID: Medium-sized (body length 33 cm, 13 in); black and white face pattern, dark ears; long nonprehensile tail (30 cm, 12 in) hang straight down; often gives low owl-like hoots at night.

HABITAT: Small family groups rest during the day in dense vine tangles and forage at night in the upper canopy; occurs in Amazonian tierra firme and flooded forest. Several other very similar night monkey species replace it in central and southern Perú, where they occur from lowlands up to cloud forest, regularly reaching elevations higher than any other monkey in Perú (3500 m, 11,500 ft).

REGION: ESA, AMA

Plate 87c
Red Howler Monkey
Alouatta seniculus

ID: Large (body length 55 cm, 22 in); bright rusty color, long prehensile tail (60 cm, 24 in), and lion-like roars. (Replaced in tropical dry forest of extreme northwestern Perú by the all-black Mantled Howler Monkey, *Alouatta palliata*.)

HABITAT: Small family groups sit quietly or move slowly during the day through the upper levels of primary forest of the Amazon; easiest to see along forested rivers.

REGION: AMA

Plate 87d
White-bellied Spider Monkey
Ateles belzebuth

ID: Large (body length 50 cm, 20 in); all-dark except for a light chest; long arms, legs and prehensile tail (78 cm, 31 in); distinctive screaming calls.

HABITAT: Active day and night; small to large troops forage mainly in the canopy of primary lowland forest of northeastern Perú north of the Río Marañon and Amazonas. (Throughout the rest of central and southern Amazonian Perú replaced by the Black Spider Monkey, *Ateles chamek*, which is all black with a black face.)

REGION: AMA

Plate 87 **435**

a Monk Saki Monkey

b Noisy Night Monkey

c Red Howler
Monkey

d White-
bellied
Spider
Monkey

Plate 88a
Kinkajou
Potos flavus
ID: Medium-sized (body length 52 cm, 20 in); large eyes, small ears, short hair and long, prehensile tail (48 cm, 29 in); active only at night; bright eye-shine reflected from a flashlight is the best way to find it.

HABITAT: Moist lowland forest, where it moves noisily through the upper levels of primary and secondary forest and even into plantations and gardens.

REGION: AMA

Plate 88b
Crab-eating Raccoon
Procyon cancrivorus
ID: Medium-sized (body length 60 cm, 24 in); black mask and prominently ringed tail (35 cm, 14 in) carried low to the ground.

HABITAT: Active only at night on the shores of streams, lakes and marshes of Amazon lowlands.

REGION: AMA

Plate 88c
Spectacled Bear
Tremarctos ornatus
ID: Only bear in South America; huge size (body length 2 m, 6.5 ft) and black body.

HABITAT: Associated with the Andes Mountains primarily in cloud forest between 1500 and 3000 m (5000 to 10,000 ft), but occasionally higher into puna or lower into upper Amazonian forest; active day and night.

REGION: HAP, ESA

Note: This species is endangered, CITES Appendix I listed.

Plate 88d
South American Coati
Nasua nasua
ID: Medium-sized (body length 50 cm, 20 in); long, tapered snout and long tail (48 cm, 19 in) held up in the air.

HABITAT: Day-active; females travel in large groups on the ground and into the mid-levels of primary and secondary lowland forest; males travel solitarily.

REGION: AMA

Plate 88e
Andean Fox (also called Culpeo Fox)
Pseudalopex culpaeus
ID: Medium-sized (body length 71 cm, 28 in); orangish cast to a gray-brown coat and a dark back; long bushy tail (40 cm, 16 in) usually black but can be gray to orangish. (Replaced in coastal deserts of northern and central Perú by the much smaller and paler Desert Fox, *Pseudalopex sechurae*.)

HABITAT: Active mainly at night in the coastal lowlands, vertiente, and drier parts of puna and highland Perú up to 4500 m (14,750 ft).

REGION: CDL, WSV, HAP

Plate 88 437

a Kinkajou

b Crab-eating Raccoon

d South American Coati

c Spectacled Bear

e Andean Fox

Plate 89a
Giant Otter
Pteronura brasiliensis
ID: Large size (body and tail together 1.5 m, 5 ft); dark fur with spotted throat and noisy calls. The smaller Neotropical Otter, *Lontra longicaudis*, also in Amazonian waterways, has an all-white breast.

HABITAT: Remote rivers and cochas of the Amazonian lowlands.

REGION: AMA

Note: This species is endangered, CITES Appendix I and USA ESA listed.

Plate 89b
Marine Otter
Lontra felina
ID: Medium-sized (body and tail together 90 cm, 3 ft); dark fur with a paler chest on some individuals.

HABITAT: This species is confined to ocean areas in which rocky headlands produce strong surf and winds blow regularly. Remote parts of the Paracas Peninsula are the best place to look for it.

REGION: CDL

Note: This species is endangered, CITES Appendix I and USA ESA listed.

Plate 89c
Tayra
Eira barbara
ID: Large (body and tail 1 m, 3.3 ft); dark and short-legged; buffy throat and often an all-buffy head.

HABITAT: Active running on the ground or along branches of large trees, mainly during the day in moist and dry lowland forests up to cloud forests at 3000 m (10,000 ft).

REGION: TDF, ESA, AMA

Plate 89d
Long-tailed Weasel
Mustela frenata
ID: Small (body and tail 30 cm, 12 in), long and slender, this bold species is often easy to see and approach.

HABITAT: Active during the day near tree-line and up to low puna, as well as in open lowlands of coastal Perú.

REGION: TDF, WSV, HAP

Plate 89e
Grison
Galictis vittata
ID: Medium-sized (body and tail 55 cm, 22 in); distinctive black, gray and white color pattern different than any other species in Amazonian Perú.

HABITAT: Active at night, often in family groups, on the floor of lowland primary and secondary forests.

REGION: AMA

Plate 89f
Striped Hog-nosed Skunk
Conepatus semistriatus
ID: Medium-sized (body length 40 cm, 16 in); black and white stripes, all-white bushy tail (19 cm, 7 in), and distinctive smell. Do not try to pet this mammal. (Replaced on the coast, vertiente, and highlands of central and southern Perú by the similar Andean Hog-nosed Skunk, *Conepatus chinga*.)

HABITAT: Active at night; often bold in open areas at higher altitudes of the Andes but also down to the coast and tropical dry forest of northwestern Perú.

REGION: TDF, CDL, WSV, HAP

Plate 89   **439**

a Giant Otter

b Marine Otter

c Tayra

d Long-tailed
Weasel

e Grison

f Striped
Hog-nosed Skunk

Plate 90a

Jaguarundi
Herpailurus yaguaroundi
ID: Small (body length 60 cm, 24 in); uniformly gray or reddish brown; proportionately short legs; long tail (50 cm, 20 in).

HABITAT: Active mostly during the day, it is most often seen on the floor or clearings of primary and secondary forest from lowlands up to 2200 m (7250 ft), sometimes near human habitations.

REGION: AMA

Note: This species is considered endangered in Central America (USA ESA listed) and near-threatened in South America (CITES Appendix II listed).

Plate 90b

Ocelot
Leopardus pardalis
ID: Medium-sized (body length 80 cm, 32 in); distinctive spotting and proportionately short tail (36 cm, 14 in); most frequently noticed by its tracks. The similar sized Andean Cat, *Felis jacobita*, is gray with black spots and restricted to treeless dry puna above 3000 m (10,000 ft).

HABITAT: Active day and night; occurs mainly on the ground in moist and dry forests from lowlands up to 1800 m (6000 ft); often spends the day sleeping in trees.

REGION: ESA, AMA

Note: This species is endangered, CITES Appendix I and USA ESA listed.

Plate 90c

Margay
Leopardus wiedii
ID: Smaller (body length 60 cm, 24 in) than the similarly spotted Ocelot, but a longer tail (45 cm, 18 in); very shy, it is most likely to be noticed by its tracks.

HABITAT: Primarily nocturnal, it spends most of its time in trees of secondary and primary moist lowland forest.

REGION: AMA

Note: This species is endangered, CITES Appendix I and USA ESA listed.

Plate 90d

Jaguar
Panthera onca
ID: Largest (body length 1.5 m, 5 ft; tail 60 cm, 24 in) spotted cat in the New World. Its presence is most likely to be noted by its huge tracks along river beaches or lake banks.

HABITAT: Active day and night in moist and dry forests from lowlands up to 2000 m (6600 ft); usually stays on the ground except to flee danger, when it will climb trees.

REGION: ESA, AMA

Note: This species is endangered, CITES Appendix I and USA ESA listed.

Plate 90e

Puma
Puma concolor
ID: Large (body length 1 m, 3.3 ft); uniformly colored with a long black-tipped tail (80 cm, 32 in); footprints smaller and different shape than Jaguar's.

HABITAT: Primarily on the ground in a wide range of habitats, from coastal scrub and dry forest to moist lowland and mid-altitude cloud forest; occasionally into high-elevation puna (to 5800 m, 19,000 ft).

REGION: HAP, ESA, AMA

Plate 90 **441**

brown form

red form

a Jaguarundi

LF

LH

c Margay

LF

LH

b Ocelot

LF

LH

d Jaguar

LF

LH

LF

LH

e Puma

Plate 91a
White-lipped Peccary
Tayassu pecari
ID: Larger (body length 1 m, 3.3 ft), darker, and lacks the collar of the Collared Peccary; often forages in herds of up to 100 or more individuals.

HABITAT: Active during the day in moist lowland forests.

REGION: AMA

Plate 91b
Collared Peccary
Tayassu tajacu
ID: Smaller (body length 90 cm, 35 in) than the White-lipped Peccary; brown with a grizzled collar; occurs mainly in small family groups.

HABITAT: Active during the day in lowland moist and dry forests.

REGION: AMA

Plate 91c
Northern Pudu
Pudu mephistophiles
ID: The smallest deer in South America, it has short legs and stands only 38 cm (15 in) at the shoulder. Adults and fawns uniformly dark brown except for a blackish face. Males with short spike antlers during breeding season.

HABITAT: Confined to high elevation forests and dense shrubby areas in northern and central Perú between 1700 and 4000 m (5600 and 13,200 ft).

REGION: HAP

Note: This species is vulnerable, CITES Appendix II listed.

Plate 91d
Red Brocket Deer
Mazama americana
ID: Medium-sized (body length 1.2 m); rusty color distinguishes it from the slightly smaller and darker Gray Brocket Deer, *Mazama gouazoubira*, which occurs in drier, more open areas of the Amazonian lowlands.

HABITAT: Active night and day in moist and dry lowland forests, swampy areas, secondary forests and plantations.

REGION: AMA

Plate 91e
White-tailed Deer
Odocoileus virginianus
ID: Large (body length 2 m, 6.5 ft); males with branching antlers; large white tail held up when running from danger.

HABITAT: Most common near tree-line and open areas above 3000 m (10,000 ft) in the Andes but also in open dry forests of the lowland coast.

REGION: TDF, WSV, HAP

Plate 91 **443**

a White-lipped Peccaary

LF

LH

b Collared
Peccary

LF

LH

c Northern Pudu

d Red Brocket
Deer

e White-tailed
Deer

Plate 92a
Amazon Bamboo Rat
Dactylomys dactylinus
ID: Large (body length 30 cm, 12 in); squared snout and long, naked tail (40 cm, 16 in); loud staccato calls at night are the easiest way to notice it.

HABITAT: Active at night; usually associated with bamboo stands, thick river-edge vegetation, or the canopy of lowland moist forest.

REGION: AMA

Plate 92b
Northern Amazon Red Squirrel
Sciurus igniventris
ID: Medium-sized (body length 27 cm, 11 in), noisy, brightly colored squirrel; large bushy tail longer (30 cm, 12 in) than its body.

HABITAT: Active during the day on the ground and lower branches of lowland primary and secondary forest of the Amazon lowlands. Overlaps with the similar Southern Amazon Red Squirrel, *Sciurus spadiceus*, throughout the Amazonian lowlands except in extreme southeastern Perú, where *spadiceus* replaces *igniventris*.

REGION: AMA

Plate 92c
Amazon Dwarf Squirrel
Microsciurus flaviventer
ID: Small (body length 14 cm, 6 in), reddish brown with short ears and a short (10 cm, 4 in), bushy tail.

HABITAT: Day-active from the ground to canopy of moist Amazonian lowland forests.

REGION: AMA

Plate 92d
Black Agouti
Dasyprocta fuliginosa
ID: Medium-sized (body length 60 cm, 24 in); all dark and virtually tailless; resembles a small peccary.

HABITAT: Most often seen during the day foraging or running noisily through the forest undergrowth in northern Amazonian lowlands. (Replaced in the southeastern lowlands by the brownish orange Brown Agouti, *Dasyprocta variegata*.)

REGION: AMA

Plate 92e
Paca
Agouti paca
ID: Medium-sized (body length 70 cm, 28 in); chestnut color with several rows of white spots on its sides and virtually tailless.

HABITAT: Active at night along the banks of rivers and lakes or the undergrowth of lowland forests; they often retreat to the water to escape danger. (Replaced between 2000 and 3000 m, 6500 to 10,000 ft, elevation, by similar but longer-haired Mountain Paca, *Agouti taczanowskii*.)

REGION: AMA

Plate 92 **445**

a Amazon Bamboo Rat

b Northern Amazon
Red Squirrel

c Amazon
Dwarf Squirrel

d Black Agouti

e Paca

Plate 93a

Bicolor-spined Porcupine
Coendou bicolor

ID: Medium-sized (body length 42 cm, 17 in); all dark with distinctive prehensile tail as long or longer than body.

HABITAT: Night-active in mid levels of lowland and mid-elevation primary and secondary forests. (Overlaps in the extreme southeastern lowlands of Perú with the larger and lighter colored Brazilian Porcupine, *Coendou prehensilis*.)

REGION: ESA, AMA

Plate 93b

Montane Viscacha
Lagidium perúanum

ID: Looking like a cross between a squirrel and a rabbit, this medium-sized (body length 37 cm, 15 in) rodent has long ears and a long curved tail (27 cm, 11 in). Related to Chinchillas, the fur is short and dense, grayish brown to yellow-brown on the back and sides, whitish on the belly.

HABITAT: Active during the day, colonies of these animals occupy tallus slopes and rocky crevices, often sitting conspicuously on top of large boulders. They are fairly common between 3000 and 5000 m (9900 and 16,500 ft) elevation in central and southern Perú.

REGION: HAP

Plate 93c

Chinchilla
Chinchilla brevicaudata

ID: Looking like a short-eared rabbit, this medium-sized (body length 36 cm, 14 in) rodent has a long tail (14 cm, 5.5 in). It is famous for its dense gray-brown fur, popular for making fur coats. It is now very rare throughout its former range in southern Perú, northern Chile and Argentina. Some experts think it is extinct in the wild.

HABITAT: Occupying grassy areas of the high altitude puna above 4500 m (14,750 ft), it lived in colonies in shrub and grassy areas with rocks and tallus.

REGION: HAP

Note: This species is endangered, CITES Appendix I and USA ESA listed.

Plate 93d

Capybara
Hydrochaeris hydrochaeris

ID: Large (body length 1.2 m, 4 ft) brown rodent most likely to be confused with a pig.

HABITAT: Active during the day and almost always along Amazonian lowland lakes and rivers, into which they dive to escape danger.

REGION: AMA

Plate 93   447

a Bicolor-spined Porcupine

b Montane Viscacha

c Chinchilla

d Capybara

LF

LH

Plate 94a

Brazilian Tapir
Tapirus terrestris
ID: Large (body length 2 m, 6.5 ft); dark; long snout is diagnostic; its huge tracks in muddy areas are also readily identified. (Replaced in cloud forests of extreme northern Perú, between 2000 and 4000 m, 6500 to 13,200 ft, by the smaller Mountain Tapir, *Tapirus pinchaque*, which has long, brown hair and white lips.)

HABITAT: Primarily active at night, it is almost always associated with swampy and moist areas in lowland Amazonian forests.

REGION: ESA, AMA

Note: This species is considered endangered (USA ESA listed) or threatened (CITES Appendix II listed).

Plate 94b

Vicuña
Vicugna vicugna (Lama vicugna)
ID: This small (80 cm, 2.6 ft, tall at the shoulder), wild relative of the domesticated llama, with its reddish-orange body and contrasting white underparts, is readily distinguished from all other wild camelids except its rare cousin, the Guanaco, *Lama guanicoe*, which is larger (1.1 m, 3.6 ft) and has a grayish head.

HABITAT: Found only in puna grasslands, this species was almost exterminated in Perú. Reserves and management have restored its populations in several areas of highland central and southern Perú. The Guanaco, however, is now very rare in highland Perú and extinct on the coast and vertiente.

REGION: HAP

Note: This species is considered endangered (USA ESA listed) or threatened (CITES Appendix II listed for Perú).

Plate 94c

Southern Fur Seal
Arctocephalus australis
ID: Body length of male 2.5 m (8 ft), weight 155 kg (340 lb); body length of female 1.5 m (5 ft), weight 130 kg (286 lb). Its pointed snout, fine, dense, white-frosted fur (especially on the neck of males) and hoarse calls distinguish it from the otherwise similar sea lion.

HABITAT: Feeds on fish and squid in the ocean. Seasonally inhabits breeding and calving areas along steep, often inaccessible rocky areas of the southern coast of Perú north to Lima.

REGION: CDL

Plate 94d

South American Sea Lion
Otaria byronia
ID: Body length of male 3 m (10 ft), weight 320 kg (700 lb); body length of female 2.2 m (7 ft), weight 130 kg (286 lb). Its broad snout, coarse fur and barking calls distinguish it from the otherwise similar fur seal.

HABITAT: Feeds on fish and squid in the ocean. Seasonally inhabits breeding and calving areas along rocky or gravel beaches and caves.

REGION: CDL

Plate 94   **449**

a Brazilian Tapir

LF

LH

b Vicuña

d South American Sea Lion

c Southern Fur Seal

Plate 95a
Pink River Dolphin
Inia geoffrensis
ID: Medium-sized (body length 2.3 m, 7.5 ft); long snout and little or no dorsal fin. The smaller Gray River Dolphin, *Sotalia fluviatilis*, has a distinctive triangular dorsal fin.

HABITAT: Both freshwater dolphins in Perú are restricted to rivers and cochas of the Amazonian lowlands, but the Pink River Dolphin occurs only in the extreme northeast.

REGION: AMA

Plate 95b
Amazonian Manatee
Trichechus inunguis
ID: Large (body length 2.5 m, 8 ft) and seal-like; grayish black; found only in freshwater, where they come to the surface to breath. Look for their round droppings floating on the water's surface.

HABITAT: Rivers and cochas of extreme northeastern and southeastern Amazonian lowlands.

REGION: AMA

Note: This species is endangered, CITES Appendix I and USA ESA listed.

Plate 95c
Common Dolphin
Delphinus delphis
ID: Medium-sized (body length 2 m, 6.5 ft), distinctive color patches on its sides.

HABITAT: Large pods in open ocean along the coast of Perú.

REGION: CDL

Plate 95d
Bottle-nosed Dolphin
Tursiops truncatus
ID: Large (body length 3 m, 10 ft); uniform gray color.

HABITAT: Open ocean along the coast; in small groups.

REGION: CDL

Plate 95e
Orca Whale (also called Killer Whale)
Orcinus orca
ID: Medium-sized (8 m, 27 ft); bold black and white pattern; white patch behind each eye is distinctive; tall (2 m, 6.5 ft) dorsal fin of males can be seen at great distances.

HABITAT: Open ocean along the coast.

REGION: CDL

Plate 95f
Humpback Whale
Megaptera novaeangliae
ID: Large (body length 14.6 m, 48 ft); huge, white front flippers. When sounding, it raises its flukes out of the water, the undersides of which are mottled white.

HABITAT: Open ocean along the coast.

REGION: CDL

Note: This species is endangered, CITES Appendix I and USA ESA listed.

Plate 95 **451**

a Pink River Dolphin

b Amazonian Manatee

c Common Dolphin

d Bottle-nosed Dolphin

e Orca Whale

f Humpback Whale

Plate 96a
Helicopter Damselfly
Microstigma rotundatum
ID: Long (15 cm, 6 in), thin body; large wings flap slowly through the middle and upper levels of moist primary lowland forests on sunny days. Look for large white or yellow wing tips.

REGION: AMA

Plate 96b
Leaf-mimicking Katydid
Cycloptera speculata
ID: Green or brown body and wings look like a live or dead leaf; during the day sits on vegetation that matches its coloration; active at night, when it is often attracted to lights.

REGION: AMA

Plate 96c
Nasute Termite
Nasutitermes sp.
ID: Body mainly white; worker with mandibles; soldier with "nozzle head" for spraying enemies; forest undergrowth of lowlands; active during the day.

REGION: AMA

Plate 96d
Evening Cicada
Fidicina mannifera
ID: Delicate colors; wings held over back tent-like; usually seen during the day resting on vertical trunks of moist lowland forest; active at night feeding and calling.

REGION: AMA

Plate 96e
Peanut Bug (also called Lantern Bug)
Fulgora laternaria
ID: Large (10 cm, 4 in), well-camouflaged; spends the day often in small groups roosting on vertical tree trunks in moist primary and tall secondary lowland forest; active at night. Large "eye" spots on wings revealed in flight.

REGION: AMA

Plate 96f
Antlion
Myrmeleon sp.
ID: Larvae at the bottom of inverted cones in dry sand in open lowland areas; also in shade of vegetation or buildings; dragonfly-like adult with long antennae with clubs at ends, attracted to lights at night.

REGION: TDF, CDL, WSV, ESA, AMA

Plate 96 453

a Helicopter Damselfly

b Leaf-mimicking Katydid

e Peanut Bug

c Nasute Termite

d Evening Cicada

Antlion sand pits

Antlion larva

f Antlion

Antlion adult

Plate 97a
Montane Tiger Beetle
Pseudoxycheila sp.
ID: Velvet greenish blue with two bright yellow-orange spots on the back; active on sunny days above 2000 m (6600 ft) elevation, where it runs along near-vertical clay banks.

REGION: ESA

Plate 97b
Green Dung Beetle
Oxysternon conspicillatum
ID: Dark metallic green; male with a prominent horn; commonly attracted to fresh dung in moist lowland primary and tall secondary forest; active during the day.

REGION: AMA

Plate 97c
Harlequin Long-horned Beetle
Acrocinus longimanus
ID: Large (6 cm, 2.4 in) and colorful, most often seen when attracted to lights at night in moist primary lowland forest; male's front legs (7 cm, 2.8 in) are half again as long as those of the female.

REGION: AMA

Plate 97d
Menelaus' Morpho Butterfly
Morpho menelaus
ID: Huge bright blue male (wingspan 10 cm, 4 in) is unmistakable; female is somewhat less garishly blue; flaps lazily along open corridors through forest or along river edges of lowland forest during sunny days. At rest, the camouflaged underwings hide the butterfly.

REGION: AMA

Plate 97e
Aurorina's Clear-winged Satyr
Cithaerias aurorina
ID: Brownish with clear forewings and reddish patches on hindwings (wingspan 5 cm, 2 in); common during the day on forest floor and along shaded trails of moist lowland forest.

REGION: AMA

Plate 97f
Mechanitis Butterfly
Mechanitis mazaeus
ID: Bright orange, black, and yellow "tiger" pattern (wingspan 6.5 cm, 2.5 in); poisonous and distasteful, it serves as a "model" to be mimicked by other, less dangerous, butterfly species; mid-levels of moist primary and tall secondary forest; active on sunny days.

REGION: AMA

Plate 97g
Dismorpha Butterfly
Dismorphia amphiona
ID: Bright orange, black, and yellow "tiger" pattern (wingspan 6 cm, 2.4 in); lacks toxins and is cheating by mimicking the distasteful and similar-appearing model species, such as 97f; mid-levels of moist primary and tall secondary forest; active on sunny days.

REGION: AMA

Plate 97h
Lelius' Urania Moth
Urania lelius
ID: Brilliant green and black color (wingspan 7 cm, 6.5 in); common on moist river beaches, where males "puddle" to suck sodium and other essential chemicals from the sand; also often in large numbers migrating over the canopy of moist lowland forest; active on sunny days.

REGION: AMA

Plate 97 **455**

a Montane Tiger Beetle

c Harlequin Long-horned Beetle

b Green Dung Beetle

d Menelaus' Morpho Butterfly

e Aurorina's Clear-winged Satyr

g Dismorpha Butterfly (mimic)

f Mechanitis Butterfly (model)

h Lelius' Urania Moth

Plate 98a
White-lined Sphinx Moth
Hyles lineata
ID: Long narrow wings, forewings with bold buffy streak, and hind wings mainly red (wingspan 6 cm, 2.4 in). The folded wings at rest are streamlined and triangular in shape – typical of sphinx moths. In the early evening and at night they can be seen hovering at low flowers, resembling small hummingbirds; commonly attracted to lights at night.

REGION: WSV, HAP, ESA

Plate 98b
Eyed Silk Moth
Automeris sp.
ID: Camouflaged forewings leaf-like (wingspan 6 cm, 2.4 in); hind wings, when exposed, each with a large, black "eye" spot; often attracted to lights at night.

REGION: TDF, AMA

Plate 98c
Green Long-winged Butterfly
Philaethria dido
ID: Large (wingspan 8 cm, 3 in), pale green wings with dark brown margins diagnostic; active in and above the canopy of lowland forests but descends at midday to fly low along the edge of light gaps.

REGION: AMA

Plate 98d
"88" Butterfly
Callicore clymena
ID: Fast-flying with bright red fore wings and blue hind wings (wingspan 5 cm, 2 in); distinctively spotted under wings often bear the shape of a two-digit number "88," "69," or other such combinations. Most frequently seen on the ground or on low bushes of lowland forest. Often attracted to defecation, rotting fruits, or dead animals on forest floor.

REGION: AMA

Plate 98e
Owl Butterfly
Caligo urilochus
ID: Very large (wingspan 13 cm, 5 in), blue-gray above. Underside of hind wings with two large "owl eyes." Perches on tree trunks in dense shade through most of the day, flying late in afternoon and early morning.

REGION: AMA

Plate 98f
Glaucous Kite Swallowtail
Eurytides glaucolaus
ID: Large (wingspan 8 cm, 3 in) and showy, whitish swallowtail is common along river beaches and sand-bars, where males often gather in large concentrations to puddle.

REGION: AMA

Plate 98g
Argent Sulphur
Phoebis argante
ID: Males yellowish orange above and below (wingspan 3.5 cm, 1.4 in); females with black edges on yellowish wings, but some individuals are whitish. Males commonly puddle in large concentrations along lowland watercourses.

REGION: AMA

Plate 98   **457**

a White-lined Sphinx Moth

b Eyed Silk Moth

c Green Long-winged Butterfly

d "88" Butterfly

e Owl Butterfly

f Glaucous Kite Swallowtail

g Argent Sulphur

Plate 99 (**See also:** Arthropods, pp. 243–248)

Plate 99a

Robber Fly
Smeryngo sp.

ID: Brownish yellow color; sits on ground or low vegetation in moist lowland forest waiting to pounce on small insects flying by on sunny days; wings produce loud buzzing in flight.

REGION: AMA

Plate 99b

Leaf-cutter Ant
Atta sp.

ID: Tan and brown; travel in long narrow columns carrying leaf or flower bits like open umbrellas; often create obvious well-worn paths through leaf litter on the ground of lowland moist forest; several size castes in a colony; small caste ants often ride on top of leaf pieces (as shown) to ward off danger.

REGION: AMA

Plate 99c

Burchell's Army Ant
Eciton burchelli

ID: Tan and brown; travel in massive attack columns through moist lowland forest floor and lower vegetation searching for insect prey; several castes in a colony (two castes shown); soldiers have very impressive mandibles.

REGION: AMA

Plate 99d

Isula Ant
Paraponera clavata

ID: Medium-sized (2 cm, 0.75 in), all blackish brown; usually alone or in small groups; listen for their warning sounds and avoid at all costs being stung – an experience in pain you will not soon forget; lowland moist forests, canopy to forest floor.

REGION: AMA

Plate 99e

Merian's Orchid Bee
Eulaema meriana

ID: Bumblebee-like; black body with bright yellow and orange rings on the rear; listen for its deep humming during the day; a non-aggressive resident of moist lowland forest.

REGION: AMA

Plate 99f

Neotropical Colonial Spider
Anelosimus eximus

ID: Most easily recognized by the huge gossamer webs that stretch for meters (yards) along riverside vegetation and forest borders. Hundreds of spiders can live together, each with its own small web united with those of its neighbors.

REGION: AMA

Plate 99g

Sand Crab (also called Mole Crab)
Emerita analoga

ID: Long (5.5 cm, 2 in) narrow body, feathery antennae; scuttles half-buried in the wet beach sand that is exposed as an ocean wave recedes.

REGION: CDL

Plate 99 **459**

a Robber Fly

b Leaf-cutter Ant

soldier

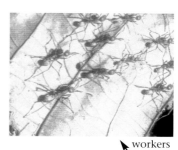

workers

c Burchell's Army Ant

d Isula Ant (PAINFUL STING!)

e Merian's Orchid Bee

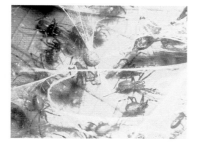

f Neotropical Colonial Spider

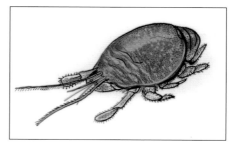

g Sand Crab

SPECIES INDEX

Note: plate numbers refer to identification plates, page numbers in *italics* refer to illustrations

GENERAL INDEX